THE DYNAMICS OF CONSUMER BEHAVIOR

THE DYNAMICS OF CONSUMER BEHAVIOR

Winston H. Mahatoo

Professor of Marketing
Faculty of Business
McMaster University
Hamilton, Ontario

John Wiley & Sons
Toronto   New York   Chichester   Brisbane   Singapore

*To my wife, Astrid, and to our children,
Elida, Karinelle, and Karl.*

CANADIAN CATALOGUING IN PUBLICATION DATA

Mahatoo, Winston H. (Winston Harnarayan), 1927–
   The dynamics of consumer behavior

Includes bibliographical references and indexes.
ISBN 0-471-79759-6

1. Consumers.   2. Marketing research.   I. Title.

HF5415.3.M34 1984   658.8'342   C84-098463-4

DESIGN: Brant Cowie/Artplus Ltd.

Printed and bound in Canada by
T. H. Best Printing Company Limited

10 9 8 7 6 5 4 3 2 1

Table of Contents

List of Case Studies

Acknowledgements

No book is the result of one person's work. Many people with whom I have worked, played, and talked (from near or far) have made contributions, direct or indirect, to this volume.

First, I should like to thank all my students over nearly two decades for the part that they played in stimulating, developing, and refining my ideas on many facets of consumer behavior.

I appreciate the role played by my colleagues in the Faculty of Business at McMaster University, particularly those in the Marketing Area, for their help and encouragement, sometimes in structured discussions, sometimes in casual, less formal conversations. I would particularly like to thank Professors Peter Banting, Randolph Ross, the late Bent Stidsen, and Richard Whiteley.

I am grateful to the many typists who labored for long hours over the manuscript, and to the Faculty of Business for allowing the manuscript to consume so much of the word processor's time. Special thanks are due to Amy Cesarini and Patti Wiebe.

Most of all, I am deeply indebted to my family for their many sacrifices and for their patience and tolerance. Many were the times when my preoccupation with the task at hand made life quite trying.

W.H.M.

Preface

There are large numbers of texts on consumer behavior and most of them are, for the most part, quite good. So why another one? The honest answer is twofold. First, after teaching a course in consumer behavior to both undergraduates and graduates for about fifteen years, I have remained dissatisfied with the treatment of the psychological and other behavioral science concepts in consumer behavior. One of the primary purposes for writing this book, therefore, is to clarify and elucidate where, for so long, there has been considerable ambiguity, inconsistency, and even confusion. In the words of a colleague, "the concepts and definitions in consumer behavior were probably written either by psychologists and behavioral scientists who knew little about marketing or by marketing specialists who knew little about psychology and behavioral science." As a psychologist with over twenty-five years of marketing experience, including almost twenty years of university teaching, I believe I can be excused for thinking that I may be able to correct that situation.

The second reason, also deriving from my years of teaching, is my strong belief that the overall presentation of the material in consumer behavior has tended to turn off the majority of students because of undue verbosity or because the material is presented in too much or too little detail. So often authors have failed to keep in sight the original purpose of the exercise.

The overriding aim of this book is to show the relevance and applicability of the subject under discussion to marketing decisions in such a way that the book will appeal to students as well as practitioners. Instructors will be able to take undergraduates as far as is appropriate, in their judgement, and to direct graduates into more advanced channels of discussion and research based on the references provided. Practitioners will be able to cull useful insights from the comments about the marketing significance of concepts, techniques, and methods throughout the text.

The last twenty years, and the last decade in particular, have witnessed a phenomenal explosion in research into consumer behavior. The ever-present danger for authors is that they will fail to see the forest for the trees. I have sought deliberately to avoid this pitfall by attempting to be comprehensive without being exhaustive (and thus perhaps exhausting). Throughout, I have endeavored to crystallize and paraphrase in order to present the basic ideas in a clear and simple fashion. At the same time, care has been taken to provide significant references that will permit further exploration of each topic.

The inclusion of the word "dynamics" in the title is significant because the book looks behind the behavior of consumers in order to try to understand why they act as they do. In fact, since marketing deals with people and since consumer behavior is part of human behavior, this book will be of interest to anyone seeking to gain insights into their own or others' behavior.

No attempt is made to provide distributive or market data, such as buying statistics or quantitative market descriptions. Data on market demographics and expenditure patterns are easily available from general marketing texts.

This book shows how the systematic study of consumer behavior provides insights of fundamental value to the development of marketing strategies. Each subject area is discussed in detail in terms of its usefulness to the marketer — what information it provides, how the information can be used, and how it relates to other areas of information.

Although knowing what causes consumers to behave as they do is undoubtedly necessary to marketers, it is not enough. Marketers may be able, for example, to make the right products but they also must ensure that their markets are aware of them. In other words, it is crucial to *communicate* with the market, and in the right way. Based on thorough, reliable data about consumers' needs, preferences, motives, and attitudes, marketers may develop the "right" products, but it is to no avail if the market does not perceive the products as they are. The implications and fundamentals of effective marketing communication will be treated in terms of how each aspect of information affects and is affected by the communication process.

Rather than moving directly into a discussion of concepts and principles, each chapter of the book begins with a number of marketing examples that are used as both the launching point and the integrative frame of reference for the discussion of the particular topic. Principles and concepts are presented not *in vacuo* but in a context that facilitates an understanding of their meanings and interrelationships. Each topic is terminated with a case situation intended to bring out the main concepts, principles, and applications discussed in the chapter or chapters.

As a result of my experience with teaching consumer behavior, I have settled upon a sequence of topics in the book that I think most effectively unfolds the material, while optimizing student interest and understanding. The subject will be treated in five parts:

- an introduction;
- the consumer decision;
- within-the-individual (internal) influences;
- external cultural and social influences; and
- external business influences.

After the Introduction (Part I), Part II considers the consumer decision process, in particular differentiating between high-involvement and low-involvement decisions. Part III deals with those factors that influence how the individual takes in, interprets, and assimilates the outside world — such topics as perception, learning, motivation, attitude, and personality.

Part IV, dealing with environmental influences, covers such topics as culture, subculture, society, reference groups, social class, and the family.

Part V takes a look at current formulations of the process of communication as part of the commercial influences that bear upon the consumer. In particular, retail influences and the effects of promotional activities (advertising, sales promotion, personal selling) are reviewed.

The concluding chapter attempts to "tie things together" with a review of some integrative models of consumer behavior and a look at current and future developments in the field.

One final word — this book assumes a knowledge of at least basic marketing principles. It does not define common concepts or outline basic principles that are covered in any first course in marketing. Nor does this book try to be a self-contained unit. For example, it recognizes the relevance of marketing research and the importance of research techniques and methods in securing data about the consumer but it stays clear of the treatment of any such material, assuming that the individual interested in consumer behavior will necessarily see fit to take a course in marketing research. Indeed, it is my opinion that it would be highly advantageous and desirable, though not absolutely necessary, to take a course in marketing research before undertaking this course in consumer behavior.

W.H.M.
November 1984

I

Introduction and Overview

This section of the book contains two chapters. Chapter 1 opens with a description of the nature and benefits of the study of consumer behavior and then goes on to review the disciplines from which consumer behavior developed.

Chapter 2 describes the basic model on which the structure of the book is based. The central concept of the consumer decision process is considered and the internal and external factors that influence the decision are briefly outlined.

1

Introduction to Consumer Behavior

EXAMPLES

Consumer situations are complex and varied. Often they are difficult to understand but (whether in the consumer or the industrial market) they always need to be understood by the marketer. Here are a few examples of consumer situations.

1. "For decades, the Steel Company of Canada shipped trainfuls of Stelco common nails from its plant to all parts of the nation . . . Stelco didn't know who was using those mountains of nails or for what purposes, nor was it of any real concern to Stelco management. Nails were being bought. That was all that mattered . . . . until Stelco developed a brand new kind of nail with a spiral thread.

   The new nail was a revolutionary, fundamental innovation after sixty years of absolutely no significant changes in the common nail. Stelco executives . . . were certain that their new Ardox nail would almost completely replace the common nail. And why not? It was stronger. It could be driven straight and true, guided smoothly into the wood by those spiral grooves. It provided less chance of splitting the wood . . . it held more tightly . . . and the Ardox nail was inexpensive.

   Yet after almost two decades on the market, Ardox nails still haven't reached their expected sales volumes . . . Although a number of reasons could be given, the main one is that Stelco didn't know who was buying and using their nails. Of course, the company knew to whom they were selling nails . . . to hardware and industrial distributors . . . but . . . who actually bought and used nails?

   . . . the main problem was, and still remains, inadequate knowledge of end-users' behavior, perceptions, and purchase motivations."[1]

2. (a) 'C'-plus Orange, introduced by Canada Dry in 1972, has a 2% to 3% market share in a section of the industry* where 1% is considered good. It is described as the most successful new product (in soft drinks) in Canada since 7-UP was introduced about the time of World War II.[2]

(b) Canadian demand for bottled water is only 5% of the demand in the U.S. Almost 85% of what is sold in Canada is consumed in Quebec, reflecting the "typical French-Canadian preoccupation with the liver." Some of this 85%, however — and most of the other 15% — is sold to European immigrants, to whom drinking bottled water is a natural part of keeping healthy. The rest of Canada seems content to drink from the tap.[3]

3. *Ready-to-eat cereals*: In a study of the nutritional value of a number of popular cereals, the ranks obtained by certain brands did not correspond to their ranks in actual sales:

	Rank in Nutritional Value (1970)	Rank in Actual Sales (1971)
General Mills' Cheerios	25	2
Kellogg's Corn Flakes	38	1
Kellogg's Rice Krispies	39	3
Kellogg's Sugar Frosted Flakes	58	4

Contrary to what might have been expected, nutritional content is not the principal reason that most people purchase ready-to-eat cereals. Some of the other reasons will be discussed in later chapters.

4. A study of brand loyalty [4] found that:
(a) consumers develop loyalty to particular brands even when competing brands are identical; that is, even where there are no discernible product differences . . . this is apparently true even in the complete absence of advertising of any kind.

(b) Consumers may pay as much as seven cents more for a loaf of bread that is a preferred brand, even though the rejected brands come from the same bakery batch and are, effectively, identical to the preferred brand.

---

* The soft drink industry reached $2 billion in sales in 1983, with Coca-Cola the leader (39.4%), followed by Pepsi (25.4%). *The Globe and Mail* (25 April 1984), p. B8.

What is clear from the examples is that the reasons for consumer behavior are often complex and hard to identify and understand. What appears to be the reason for purchase could easily turn out to be wrong in one case and entirely true in another.

Situations cover the gamut of consumer and industrial products, and involve any of the functions of marketing — product attributes, packaging, labelling, naming, advertising, retailing — and the study of consumer behavior is extremely broad and very diverse.

THE FIELD OF CONSUMER BEHAVIOR

The field of consumer behavior is concerned with the study of the factors that influence people's behavior in a buying situation. It therefore deals with but one facet of the total life of the individual. In the course of their lives, human beings play a large variety of roles[5] — mother, wife, sister, daughter, club president, shopper, etc. — each of which brings into play different sets of activities, needs, attitudes, and preferences. The consumer role is that aspect of the individual's life involved in the acquisition, management, and use of economic goods and services.[6] Consumers are constantly choosing from among products, among varieties or brands, among stores, among television or radio stations and programs, or among magazines or newspapers.

The consumer is continually making choices and that is the perspective from which we view the consumer in this book. The book focusses on the needs that have to be satisfied, how they were formed, how they express themselves, how they can be fulfilled, and how they can be influenced by marketing activity.

WHAT IS CONSUMER BEHAVIOR?

Understanding consumer behavior means and implies a lot more than is suggested at first. Unfortunately, the terms "consumer" and "behavior" are both quite restrictive in their connotations. They have more significance for us than their literal meanings suggest.

For example, while the word consumer means "the person who uses up or consumes" a product,[7] we are interested in more than just the consumer or the user. Often in the purchase of a product the user may have little to do with the product choice and sometimes the buyer may be a different person from the chooser òr the user. Sometimes, too, there can be influencers, so that there can be four possible types of agents in a purchase decision — choosers, buyers, users, and influencers. In many cases, of course, at least three functions may be served by the same individual. To understand a product purchase decision, the marketer should really be interested in all of those individuals who have some influence on the acquisition of products.

A few examples will illustrate the basic importance of this distinction. Although worn by men, ties are generally bought by women (mothers, wives, or girlfriends). Manufacturers should be very concerned with women's attitudes and preferences when they design, distribute, and price their ties. In the purchase of a house, all or several members of a family (and some individuals outside of the family) will have some input into the decision to buy. In other cases, such as breakfast cereals, the mother may decide about the particular type or brand to buy for her children or what the children prefer may be bought for the whole household. For razor blades, the wife may simply serve as a buying agent for her husband, who specifies the brand and type he wants. Alternatively, the mother may decide that her children should use Brand X toothpaste, despite the fact that they prefer Brand Y, and father actually makes the purchase.

It is important for the marketer to understand these distinctions, and not assume that the target is necessarily the user or the buyer of the product.

Behavior covers the *what, when, where, how, how often,* and *how much* of purchasing activity. These are necessary data for describing and assessing a market; but we are interested in more than such distributive information.[8] If we are to understand those activities, we have to study the reasons that underlie them; we are, therefore, interested in mental or psychological activity. Behavior denotes both physical and psychological activity, both the *overt* and *covert* acts of the individual. Overt acts are observable expressions and covert acts are the changes in perception, learning, motivation, attitudes, and other aspects of the individual's psyche.

Consumer behavior is exhibited by decision makers in industrial organizations as well as by the ultimate consumer. While there clearly are differences between these two groups, many of the same constructs can be used to understand their behaviors. For example, they both operate within certain cultures, characterized by certain values, mores, customs, and laws. Both are subject to individual as well as group influences; are exposed to commercial communications; and seek and obtain information about product choices before a purchase is made. It is often asserted that organizational buyers are more objective and rational in their purchases than individual buyers, but a closer look reveals that both groups are influenced by such criteria as price, durability, service, and credit. The organizational buyer is also swayed by subjective considerations, such as personal rapport with a representative, or the effect of the purchase on his or her own status (based on the perceptions of others) and on the possibility of a promotion or a salary increase.

WHY STUDY CONSUMER BEHAVIOR?

Consumer behavior analysis grew as a specialized field of systematic study out of the development of the marketing concept[9] after World War II. A sense of relief and freedom, fueled by increasing buyer affluence, brought about a gigantic expansion in the number of competitive products and brands. This was made possible by a massive productive capacity that was suddenly freed from the manufacture of the goods of war. The growing economic means of the buyers and widening scope of product choice led to a state of extreme competition for the consumer dollar, so that (as in any buyers' market) the consumer was in command and corporate success depended on the ability of companies to offer what consumers sought.

Benefits to Management

The more one understood the consumer, the greater would be the likelihood of corporate survival. Consumer behavior data, therefore, assumed considerable importance and formed the very base of marketing strategy. The more a company knew about its market (its habits, preferences, attitudes, needs), the more effective its strategy was likely to be, because decisions about the market and the product/promotion/price/place mix would then be more likely to be on target. Put another way, it was hoped that the study of consumer behavior would make possible the prediction of what and under what circumstances the consumer would buy.

Studying consumer behavior benefits management in three ways. First and foremost, proper consumer data can lead to **market segmentation:** the identification of the most advantageous and profitable target markets to which to direct one's strategies. It is only from a thorough knowledge of the consumers in a population that meaningful, useful segmentation is possible. The more reliable and complete the information about the market, the sounder the decision the marketer can make regarding the groups for which the marketer's offering is most suitable. Segmentation is a basic strategy for most marketers.[10] It is so important that the subject will be covered in greater detail in a later chapter (Chapter 12).

Second, good consumer behavior data result in improvements in marketing strategy, for the manufacturer as well as for the retailer, by marketing the right product, in the right place, at the right price, with the right promotion. Such strategies are more likely to lead to greater sales, greater profits, increased consumer satisfaction, and fewer product failures.

Third, by uncovering the nature and extent of unmet consumer needs, consumer behavior studies can result in the identification of new market opportunities. Such discoveries can lead to innovations in goods and services that make for greater corporate success and increased consumer satisfaction. What is most important for the marketer to recognize is that such "new" needs have not necessarily been dormant all along, waiting to be uncovered. The dynamism of the market itself creates changes in market demand, which the marketer needs to recognize. The large number of changes — technological, psychological, sociological, ecological — taking place around us and the rapidity with which they are occurring[11] make it imperative that the marketer acquire reliable, up-to-date information about consumers to compete successfully.

The concept of **mobility** well incorporates these phenomena. Increased willingness and capability to move over long distances have led to a great deal of **geographical mobility** — from city centres to suburbs, from rural areas to urban, and from one region to another. The result in such areas can be significant changes in market composition over relatively short periods of time. Market composition means not just the demographic make-up of the market, but its combinations of needs, preferences, attitudes, and values. The marketer needs to stay abreast of the population shifts resulting from such geographical mobility because of the accompanying changes in needs and preferences. The shift to the suburbs, for example, was directly responsible for the increased purchase of automobiles, the increased demand for single-dwelling housing, the growth in the home-maintenance and home-repair market, and the greater demand for moving companies and rented trucks.

Some have noted a recent shift back from suburbs to the city — a development that is of some concern to marketers in the home construction industry. It could result not only in fewer home building starts but also in a shift away from do-it-yourself home improvements as people move back into apartments.

The possibility has also been raised that, by the turn of the century, advances in communications technology could reverse the rural-to-urban trend.[12] Workplaces will be decentralized, office personnel will work at home, commuting will be considerably reduced, and the entire pattern of social life drastically altered — with radical consequences for consumer behavior and marketing.

Similarly, changes in social habits and behavior need to be closely watched and, for best advantage, anticipated by the marketer. For example, the increasing number of women in the job market has brought about numerous needs and created shifts in emphasis. In an age as fluid as ours, the marketer needs to monitor carefully the effects of **social mobility.**

Finally, changes in values and attitudes result in new behaviors. The changing attitudes of men toward clothing and personal hygiene have opened up new vistas for marketers — colored shirts, jeans, and hair spray and hair dryers. Marketers need to remain alert to the marketing implications of changes in behavior brought about by such **psychic mobility.**

Benefits to the Consumer

Understanding consumer behavior can also yield certain kinds of benefits to the individual consumer:

- increased understanding of one's own behavior as a consumer leads to wiser product and brand choices;
- better knowledge improves the consumer's ability to evaluate products and their claims; and
- knowledge of marketing communications methods brings insight into what lies behind the way in which commercial messages are presented. An understanding of the appeals and motivations behind the advertisement may assist the consumer in identifying the advertiser's intentions and make for a more objective evaluation of the advertisement.

Such insights can only help to provide better protection for the consumer.

Metamarketing

The usefulness of consumer behavioral data is not restricted to profit-making business organizations. Such non-profit organizations as governments, political parties, universities, charities, churches, and school systems take advantage of the insight provided by consumer studies into the needs, attitudes, interests, and opinions of their respective target groups. **Metamarketing** is the application of marketing principles and methods to the solution of the various problems confronting non-profit organizations as they seek to satisfy the needs of their particular communities.

The application of consumer behavior data and analytical techniques can also be very useful in the area of public policy, where a knowledge of the behavior, preferences, and attitudes of citizens can lead to more efficient and satisfactory service from entities such as power utilities and public transportation systems.

Societal Marketing

Another aspect of marketing that is becoming increasingly important in influencing consumer choice behavior is the societal dimension. Resource shortages, population growth, environmental pollution, inflation, and third world conditions are all tending to inculcate in the minds of increasing numbers of consumers a broader, more global approach to the economic problems of our society. More and more individuals are considering the eventual impact of a product's use on society, on the environment, and on social values. A detergent may be evaluated on the basis of its phosphate content and the effect on the country's lakes and rivers; a company may be judged on its concern for how its manufacturing activities affect the environment; an advertising program may be evaluated on the extent to which it reflects what are perceived to be current social values or relationships.

Any study of consumer behavior must take into consideration factors that go beyond product performance, product attributes, and satisfaction of personal needs. Because of this, questions are being raised about the relevance of the marketing concept. Not only are doubts expressed about whether the marketing concept is truly being practised by marketers,[13] but some have raised the very disturbing question of whether it is still a valid corporate objective. To what extent should a company apply the marketing concept and at what point does the long-run societal interest take over?[14]

De-Marketing

Change has been rapid in our society. The 1970s and 1980s have brought a number of serious problems — pollution, overpopulation, recession, inflation, and shortages of heating oil, gasoline, and even such staples as sugar and coffee — and they appear each day to be increasing in both number and seriousness. Marketing has responded with strategies designed to discourage, rather than stimulate, demand for many products and services. Hospitals and medical services, for example, are emphasizing in-home and out-patient care in order to bring down the sky-rocketing costs to society of in-hospital care. Utility companies are using advertisements to persuade taxpayers to use less energy (see Figure 1.1) and politicians are exhorting citizens to exercise greater control and "live within their means." It is a far cry from the consumption-oriented society of a few years ago. In many areas of our lives, **de-marketing** efforts are trying to reduce demand and to conserve.

Ontario Hydro
T.V. 30 Seconds
"NIGHT PATROL"

Me and my sidekick Sam were on a night job ... looking for guys that waste electricity.

Now that ain't smart, a lit window at 2 a.m. Give it an off, Sam!

OFF!

... and who's around to read that? Let 'em have it, kid.

OFF!

Why this parking lot looks ready for night football.
OFF!

OFF it again Sam.

OFF OFF!

Well kid, they got the message. When you're through with the lights switch 'em ... OFF!

your hydro

Goodnight sweetheart.

CHARACTERS SHOWN AS DRAWINGS ABOVE APPEAR AS ACTUAL PUPPETS IN COMPLETED COMMERCIAL

FIGURE 1.1: Ontario Hydro 30-Second TV Advertisement "Night Patrol" *Courtesy* Ontario Hydro

More business will be conducted via telephone, more products [even solids] will move through pipelines, and cheaper forms of transportation, such as trains, will be more popular . . . to cope with the [energy] crisis [society will] need to conserve [insulate, drive lighter cars, etc.] and use alternative fuels, particularly coal, but also solar and nuclear energy.[15]

Such efforts will be far more likely to succeed if they are based on a proper understanding of the behavior of the consumer. By knowing consumption patterns and consumer attitudes and preferences, governments, industries, or companies will be in a better position to develop workable plans.

The kinds of data that the study of consumer behavior employs in the pursuit of that understanding are drawn from a number of fields of knowledge devoted to the study of human activities — specifically, the social and behavioral sciences.

SOURCES OF CONSUMER BEHAVIOR INFORMATION

Consumer behavior is an eclectic discipline having its roots in a number of more basic fields of study. Just as medicine relies on biochemistry, physiology, and anatomy, so consumer behavior brings together knowledge from such areas as psychology, sociology, anthropology, and economics.

This book does not attempt a lengthy coverage of this topic; rather, it points out the nature and extent of the contributions of each field of study to consumer behavior. I hope to delineate clearly the particular viewpoint that each of the disciplines brings to the understanding of the dynamics of consumer behavior.

Psychology

Generally speaking, psychology deals with the individual. Several subfields may be identified:

General psychology provides us with information about perception, learning, motivation, attitudes, and personality.

Perception deals with how the individual "takes in" and interprets the outside world and provides the student of consumer behavior with valuable insights into what marketing stimuli (advertising, appeals, packaging) are attended to and how they are received by the individual. An important fact, for example, is that the same stimuli are perceived differently by different individuals. Since all individuals behave and react in accordance with their perceptions, the importance of perceptual psychology to consumer behavior can hardly be overemphasized.

Learning has been defined as "all changes in behavior that result from previous behavior in similar situations."[16] Learning psychology has contributed such concepts as drive, cue, reinforcement, and incentive (see Chapter 8), all of which are strongly relevant to marketing behavior, especially for such phenomena as brand loyalty, advertising effectiveness, new product acceptance, and communications influence. The basic principles of learning are of extreme significance since all marketers can be said to be engaged in the process of getting consumers to learn as much as possible about what sellers have to offer as potential sources of satisfaction or reward.

Motivation deals with the why of individual behavior, so the concepts of need, drive, and motive (Chapter 10) contribute significantly to the marketer's understanding of consumer behavior. Such understanding is very helpful in developing advertising appeals, arousing interest, stimulating action, and directing choice.

Attitude studies have pointed out how individual predispositions or orientations arise, develop, and change. Attitude change is central to the marketer, since very often success with the consumer is dependent upon the ability to influence and change existing attitudes.

Psychological theories of **personality** can also shed light on why and how consumers behave as they do, particularly in terms of consumer typology; that is, by grouping consumers according to personality types. Different individuals reveal characteristic ways of behaving and reacting so that specific formulations of individual types can be very helpful in understanding the behavior of a market.

Social psychology deals with the behavior of individuals in groups; that is, the influence on an individual of others with whom he or she is in contact. Others may inhibit or facilitate behavior by playing a restricting or supportive role.

Psychoanalysis has also offered many insights into the dynamics of behavior. For example, Freud's formulation of the role of the unconscious[17] in determining behavior adds a unique, if controversial, dimension to the understanding of consumer behavior. Other notions, such as the primary influence of the formative years of an individual upon his or her personality and the dynamic relationship of the id, ego, and superego, provide a useful basis for analyzing behavior.[18] For example, Lasswell's suggestion of the "triple appeal" proposes that advertising should seek to satisfy the demands of the id, the ego, and the superego through the appropriate combination of message elements.[19] We should also recognize the contributions of other psychoanalysts with different approaches from that of Freud, such as Adler, Jung, Horney, and Fromm, to whom we shall return later.

Sociology

While social psychology is concerned with groups from the individual's point of view, sociology deals with the behavior of groups and studies group phenomena. The contributions that sociology has made to consumer behavior relate to the application of such concepts as role, socialization, social class, life style, reference group, peer group, the family, the working wife, and other such groups within society. Strictly speaking, sociology confines itself to group behavior within a society or to comparative studies of parallel groups in different societies. Because marketers are interested in selling their products to large segments of a society, the level of aggregation at which sociology functions has a great deal in common with the marketers' view of the world.

Anthropology

The anthropologist studies the ways in which cultures have come to solve their problems. For instance, such phenomena as marriage institutions, child rearing, religion, and communication are areas of interest for the anthropologist.[20] Since the findings are general, they are likely to be more useful in distinguishing among products than among brands. The anthropological approach will assist us in understanding such relevant subcultures as French-Canadians, German-Canadians, and black Americans. We shall also see how the concepts of laws, mores, customs, and folkways employed by anthropologists in their study of institutions can be of direct usefulness to the marketer.

Economics

As the science that deals with the allocation of resources for the satisfaction of human needs, economics is devoted to the study of the use of goods and services.

Macroeconomics is concerned with the system as a whole — as it seeks to fulfill the needs of society. Ours is but one of several macroeconomic systems. The two major advanced economic systems are based on political ideology. On the one hand, the *controlled* system, typical of communist countries, is built upon pre-set goals. A central planning group identifies the goals of the society, determines the needs, and allocates the resources accordingly. Unfortunately, none of these stages is simple or easy and the system suffers from a considerable degree of inefficiency. Some of the problems caused by the inefficiency of the

Soviet Union's central planning are outlined in an article in *Time* Magazine:

> The shopping lines almost define the society. The stores are always out of something, low on something else, sometimes rationing flour, meat, or butter....
>
> The Soviet Union has one of the industrialized world's worst distribution and retail trade systems. Thus this spring there are no sheets, underwear or children's shirts.... Those who can make their own clothes find material scarce and expensive. For example, four yards of polyester fabric costs the equivalent of $30; the same in an American store costs $2.50. Needles, thread, thimbles and buttons are also 'impossible to find'.... Household appliances burn out. Furniture splinters and loses its veneer....[21]

On the other hand, the *free enterprise* system is not subject to a central committee for the determination of society's needs or the allocation of resources. Planning takes place at the level of the firm. To the extent, however, that the system is subject to government constraints, to marketing boards or to multi-divisional, multinational giants, perfect competition cannot be said to be at play, although the essential assumptions underlying the capitalist system remain valid.

Microeconomics deals with the same phenomena but from the point of view of individual firms. Where it considers the consumer, it focusses on the *average* consumer. Economists have made certain general assumptions about the behavior of consumers in an attempt to explain the allocation of resources, but their interest does not lie in the individual consumer. Economics was the first discipline to systematize overall consumer behavior and, in so doing, partially to account for certain general patterns. The assumptions of the rational person with complete knowledge, the use of marginal analysis, and income, demand, and price analysis have contributed significantly to an understanding of how consumers behave.

With such knowledge as a starting point, it was left for a separate discipline of consumer behavior to explore the dynamics of consumer behavior and to seek to explain why consumers behave the way they do.

SUMMARY

The study of consumer behavior covers every aspect of marketing involving any kind of consumer choice. Its aim is to describe and understand. Often the reasons are complex and hard to identify. We are interested in not just those who buy and / or use but in all of those individuals who have some impact on both consumer and industrial decisions.

The study of consumer behavior yields a number of benefits to business, to consumers, and to non-profit organizations, as well as to public policy and consumer protection. Its richness and diversity derive from a host of social science and other disciplines such as psychology, psychoanalysis, sociology, economics, and anthropology, all of which help us to understand the behavior of the consumer.

QUESTIONS

1. If, as found in Example 3 at the beginning of the chapter, the sales of cold cereals show a very low correlation with nutritional content, what would you say are some of the reasons for cold cereal usage?

2. "Our study of consumer behavior will deal with understanding consumer *choice* behavior." Explain.

3. Show how the concepts used in analyzing

the final consumer are to a large degree also applicable to the industrial consumer.

4. In what ways does the study of consumer behavior benefit (a) management, (b) the consumer, (c) public policy?

5. How could the approaches and techniques used in the study of consumer behavior be applied to non-profit organizations, such as universities, hospitals, public charities, and political parties?

6. Explain the concept of "mobility" and discuss its importance to the marketer.

7. If you were asked to identify *two* behavioral science disciplines from which consumer behavior has benefitted the most, which would you choose? Why?

8. "The study of consumer behavior is relevant and necessary in a free enterprise system such as ours, but not in a controlled system, such as that of the Soviet Union." Do you agree or disagree? Why?

NOTES TO CHAPTER 1

[1]Peter M. Banting, "Unsuccessful Innovation in the Industrial Market," *Journal of Marketing*, 42:1 (January 1978), p. 100. Reprinted with permission of the American Marketing Association.

[2]Douglas Fetherling, "The Drugstore That Made Canada Famous," *Canadian Business* (June 1978), p. 69.

[3]Ibid., p. 104.

[4]W.T. Tucker, "The Development of Brand Loyalty," *Journal of Marketing Research*, 1 (August 1964), pp. 32-5.

[5]T. Shibutani, *Society and Personality* (Englewood Cliffs, New Jersey, Prentice-Hall, 1961), p. 46.

[6]A good, concise description of the concept of role and its application to consumer behavior is given in James U. McNeal (ed.), *Dimensions of Consumer Behavior*, 2nd ed. (New York: Appleton-Century-Crofts, 1969), pp. 9-17.

[7]*The Oxford Universal Dictionary*, 3rd ed. (London: Oxford University Press, 1955), p. 379.

[8]Robert A. Dahl, Mason Haire, and Paul F. Lazarsfeld, *Social Science Research on Business: Product and Potential* (New York: Columbia University Press, 1959), pp. 103-4.

[9]"The marketing concept . . . holds that the key task of the organization is to determine the needs and wants of target markets . . . ": Philip Kotler and Ronald E. Turner, *Marketing Management*, 4th Canadian ed. (Scarborough, Ontario: Prentice-Hall, 1981), pp. 30-3.

[10]Larry J. Rosenberg, *Marketing* (Englewood Cliffs, New Jersey: Prentice-Hall, 1977), pp. 150-3; 161-6.

[11]Alvin Toffler, *Future Shock* (New York: Bantam, 1971).

[12]James Martin, *The Wired Society* (Englewood Cliffs, New Jersey: Prentice-Hall, 1978), p. 182.

[13]Edward McKay, *The Marketing Mystique* (New York: American Management Association, 1972), pp. 22-30; Peter F. Drucker, *Management: Tasks, Responsibilities, Practices* (New York: Harper and Row, 1973), p. 64.

[14]Martin L. Bell and C. William Emery, "The Faltering Marketing Concept," *Journal of Marketing*, 35:4 (October 1971), pp. 37-42; Laurence P. Feldman, "Societal Adaptation: A New Challenge for Marketing," *Journal of Marketing*, 35:3 (July 1971), pp. 54-60; Leslie M. Dawson, "The Human Concept: New Philosophy for Business," *Business Horizons* (December 1969), pp. 29-38; George Fisk, "Criteria for a Theory of Responsible Consumption," *Journal of Marketing*, 37:2 (April 1973), pp. 24-31.

[15]John Sheldon, "Energy Crisis to Spurt Use of Phones, Trains, Pipelines," *Marketing News*, 13:19 (21 March 1980), p. 9.

[16]Bernard Berelson and Gary A. Steiner, *Human Behavior* (New York: Harcourt, Brace, and World, 1964), p. 135.

[17]Robert S. Woodworth, *Contemporary Schools of Psychology* (New York: Ronald Press, 1948), p. 170.

[18]See Calvin S. Hall and Gardner Lindzey, *Theories of Personality*, 3rd ed. (New York: John Wiley & Sons, 1978).

[19]James H. Myers and William H. Reynolds, *Consumer Behavior and Marketing Management* (Boston: Houghton Mifflin, 1967), pp. 91-2.

[20]Ruth Benedict, *Patterns of Culture* (Boston: Houghton Mifflin, 1934), pp. 1-2.

[21]"A Fortress State in Transition," *Time* Magazine (23 June 1980), p. 21.

CHAPTER

2

An Overview of the Organization of the Book

Chapter 1 provided a general introduction to the study of consumer behavior — its nature, its benefits, and its origins. It prepared us to begin our examination of the determinants of consumer behavior and to show how each, individually and in combination with others, can provide the kinds of information upon which effective marketing strategies must be based.

Before we continue, some idea of the basic structure or organization of the book is necessary. This will not only provide a global view of the contents of the book but will enable the reader to understand better the basic consumer decision model that explains the sequence of topics and the interrelationships among them.

Figure 2.1 presents the basic model of consumer behavior after which the structure of the book is patterned. At the center of the model is the **consumer purchase decision** — that is, the eventual consumer choice decision. This should be looked upon as a process rather than a single act, since it involves a number of steps (problem recognition, information search and evaluation, alternative evaluation, and the final decision) by which the consumer arrives at the decision to buy or not buy.

The process and the behavior are the results of many influences. In any situation, an individual is subjected to a number of forces, from within and from outside, which constitute his or her psychological field or life space.[1]

All behavior — consuming, purchasing, thinking, crying — is a function of the life space, which in turn consists of the total manifold of "facts" which psychologically exist, all of the influences for an individual at a given moment in time. The life space is the totality of the individual's world as [the individual] perceives it; it is the individual's perception of "reality..."[2]

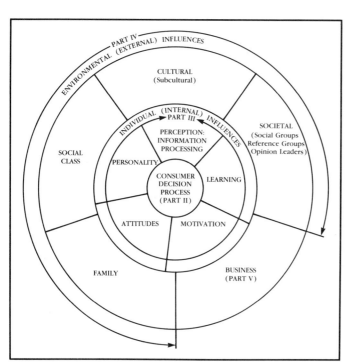

FIGURE 2.1: A Simple Model of the Influences on Consumer Behavior (and the Organization of the Book)

As shown in Figure 2.1, the consumer's decision is the result of two sets of influences:

- internal or individual influences
- external or environmental influences

The internal or individual influences include the consumer's perceptions, knowledge (learning), needs and motives (motivation), attitudes, and personality. External or environmental influences include the particular culture or subculture, groups within the society, social class, families, and business organizations.

It is essential to recognize that behavior is the result of the interaction among these various influences. For example, the way an individual reacts to an advertisement will depend not only on what the ad contains but on the individual's perceptions, needs, attitudes, and personality; and on the cultural norms and values, and the reference group and family influences, as they have affected and currently influence the individual.

Figure 2.1 does not indicate any directions of influence; these are provided in subsequent

flow diagrams in this chapter. It does, however, illustrate the pervasive influence of environmental factors on the internal factors and the combined influence of both sets on the consumer. A flow-chart model would also have included *post*-decisional phenomena, as can be seen in the more detailed models discussed in a later chapter. In the main, what this involves is feedback to the individual (affecting one or more of the internal factors) representing what the consumer has learned from the experience. Such information will be learned and could affect the consumer's decision the next time a similar problem arises.

Each of the components in Figure 2.1 will be covered in detail. Part II starts with an examination of the Consumer Decision Process (Part I is devoted to this Overview and the Introduction). It is important to understand the different kinds of decisions in which consumers can be involved in order to appreciate which factors influence those decisions and in what ways. Part III considers in detail each of the internal (individual) factors, Part IV the broad cultural and social factors. Part V reviews the role of business influences. The final section — Part VI — attempts a synthesis by presenting the most significant integrative models that have so far evolved in the field. It concludes with an evaluation of the current "state of the art" of consumer behavior and a brief discussion of the nature and implications of its future developments.

PART II: THE CONSUMER DECISION PROCESS

There are different kinds of consumer decisions. Purchasing an automobile is quite a different decision from purchasing a ball-point pen. In other words, some decisions take longer to reach, involve products that are more important to the individual, and may mean greater risk. Others are far less complex, are made quickly, and involve little thought or risk. Because the decisions of the first type are more involving than the second, they have been labelled **high-involvement** decisions and the latter have been labelled **low-involvement** decisions. In studying the consumer purchase decision, a basic distinction must be made between these two types of decisions.

High-involvement decisions mean more to the individual, and are more important to the self-image. Thus they are more involving. They also are more likely to involve greater risk — greater financial risk (higher price), social risk (more important in the eyes of the reference group), and psychological risk (more likely to cause anxiety and loss of self-esteem). Such purchases are more carefully considered, more time and energy are spent on them, and more alternatives are evaluated. In general, the entire process through which a decision is made is quite complex.

Low-involvement decisions, on the other hand, occur with purchases that involve far less financial, social, or psychological risk. Such purchases are not important to the self-image of the individual and are made quickly. As a result, the process by which low-involvement purchases are made is much more simple.

The differences in the underlying processes involved are important because they entail quite different marketing strategies.

PART III: INDIVIDUAL (INTERNAL) INFLUENCES

The many aspects or characteristics of an individual that influence behavior are illustrated in Figure 2.2. Generally speaking, behavior starts with a *stimulus* — some kind of informational input, which may emanate from within the individual (e.g., hunger pangs) or from outside. The latter include marketing stimuli (e.g., an advertisement), social stimuli (e.g., the presence of friends), or environmental stimuli (e.g., temperature). Individuals will perceive and process such stimulus inputs on the basis of their existing psychological state (made up of current knowledge and past experiences), their needs and motives (motivation), their attitudes (brand-specific and general attitudes), and their personalities and life-styles. Each of these is affected by the others, as illustrated in Figure 2.2. For example, what we learn is the result of what and how we perceive, our motivational state and attitudes, and the influence of our personalities and life-styles. The same relationships can be described for motivation, for attitudes, and for personality and life-style.

Perception

Perception is, in essence, information processing that begins with exposure to the stimulus, is followed by attention, and then comprehension. However, such information, although comprehended, may not be retained unless it is first accepted as fitting in with the existing cognitions of the individual. As shown in Figure 2.3, what and how the individual perceives is the end result of three main sets of factors: the source of the stimulus (e.g., opinion leader, TV advertisement),

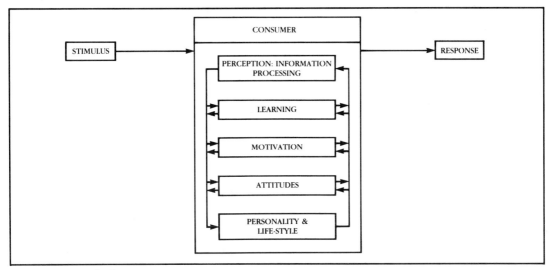

FIGURE 2.2: Internal Influences on Consumer Decision Process

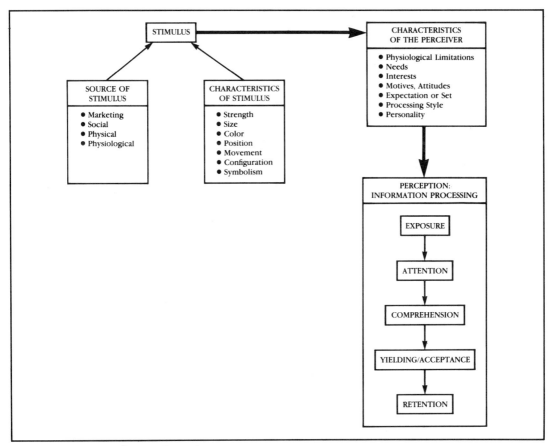

FIGURE 2.3: Consumer Information Processing

the characteristics of the stimulus (e.g., size, complexity, symbolism), and the characteristics of the individual, as described earlier.

A number of consumer perceptual phenomena of practical significance to marketers — the price-quality relationship, risk, attribution, brand image, corporate image, symbolism — will be discussed in two subsequent chapters.

Learning

Why and how are certain things remembered when others are not? What consumers learn depends on what they perceive; how much and how well they learn and how they respond are influenced by their motivation and attitudes. Thus, for example, the greater a consumer's need, the greater will be his or her interest; the more positive a consumer's attitudes, the greater the likelihood of making and learning the response desired (e.g., purchase of the brand).

Retaining a message (stimulus), which is the ultimate result of perception, is one form of learning. It is affected by the source and nature of the stimulus itself (e.g., fear appeal, frequency of exposure) and by the characteristics of the perceiver (e.g., needs, motives, interests.) As well as being stored in the consumer's memory, new information can cause other changes (learning) in the consumer's beliefs, attitudes, or personality.

Psychologists consider learning to be "the fundamental process in the understanding of human behavior."[3] Understanding the learning process will facilitate understanding the other influences examined in the book (such as perception, attitudes) since learning is a necessary part of all of them. In the broadest sense, what and how one learns determines one's ability to adapt to the environment.

For marketers, understanding learning involves understanding a large number of behavioral phenomena, such as how buying patterns become established, how brand concepts are formed, how advertising messages are retained and how consumer needs can be influenced.

Chapter 9 is devoted to important learning phenomena in consumer behavior, such as loyalty, adoption, diffusion, brand awareness, and fashion acceptance.

Motivation

Motivation probably represents the true origin of the behavioral chain because the individual is not likely to act without a reason. The motivational state of the individual is part of his or her existing psychological state (needs, motives, attitudes, personality), which can change with learning through the input of new information. In other words, motivation is interrelated with the other individual processes (Figure 2.2), both influencing and being influenced by what we perceive and learn and the attitudes we hold. An individual's motivational make-up is a significant part of his or her personality.

Determining the consumer's motivations is at the heart of consumer behavior research because it means understanding the reasons behind the behavior of the consumer.

Attitudes

An individual's general inclination for or against any person, object, or idea is referred to as an attitude. As shown in Figure 2.1, attitudes can be an important internal influence on behavior. How people feel about a brand, for example, will determine, for the most part, whether or not they choose that brand. Attitudes consist of three components. They are based on the beliefs the individual has about the object (the cognitive component), on how the individual feels about it (the affective component), and on whether the individual will act on these feelings (the action component).

As indicated in Figure 2.2, attitudes can be influenced or changed by an individual's perceptions, needs, or motives, just as attitudes may influence what the individual perceives and what kinds of satisfactions are sought.

Creating or changing attitudes is of central importance to the marketer; the chapters on attitudes will emphasize the role of attitudes in influencing behavior and whether (and how) they can be changed.

Personality and Life-Style

Personality does not deal with a separate individual process, as in the cases of perception, learning, motivation, and attitude, but with what might be called a higher-order concept, which serves to summarize or integrate the others. The concept of **personality** thus permits the characterization of individuals.

> Personality [is] the unique organization of factors [that] characterizes an individual and determines his [her] pattern of interaction with the environment. More colloquially, personality is an individual's total make-up — the type of person that he [she] is.[4]

I will review the different ways of determining personality types, the evolution of such typologies, their applications to consumer behavior, and their relationships with purchasing motivations.

Life-style is another integrative concept that reflects what the individual is or does. Both personality and life-style are expressive of all the individual determinants combined and they will, therefore, be treated together.

PART IV: ENVIRONMENTAL (EXTERNAL) INFLUENCES

Figure 2.1 shows that a number of external variables affect the behavior of the consumer. Part IV reviews non-business influences, such as culture, subculture, reference groups, social class, and the family. It is important to recognize that Figure 2.1 implies that the internal factors are affected by these external forces. For example, the *attitude* toward owning a Cadillac varies from one culture to another or even among social classes in the same culture.

Culture

Culture (of which subculture is a part) provides the broadest influence. The values and norms of a culture are applied to specific brand or other choices by smaller-scale groups called **reference groups**. Such groups include work/peer groups, and the family (Figure 2.4).

Consumer behavior is influenced by the society's values, attitudes, needs, and orientations. For example, a society with certain religious values will have particular needs and preferences, and the marketer, particularly the international marketer, will need to understand these and prepare strategies accordingly.

Subcultures

Sometimes subgroups within a society display sufficient differences in their values and attitudes to warrant a **segmentation** strategy by the marketer — for example, the French-Canadian and the Italo-Canadian subcultures in Canada or the Negro-American and the Hispanic-American subcultures in the United States.

Chapter 14, Culture and Subculture, demonstrates how cultural and subcultural characteristics play an important role in the formation of separate strategies for the different groups.

Social Class

Social class is the stratification of a society into broad groups that share certain attitudes, values, or life-styles. Strictly speaking, social class does serve as a reference group for certain norms (e.g., product preferences, media behavior) but it is not generally considered a reference group because its influence is not personalized or direct. However, its influence is so pervasive that social class will be considered as a separate topic.

Family

Another social group that is of central importance — **the family** — is considered in Chap-

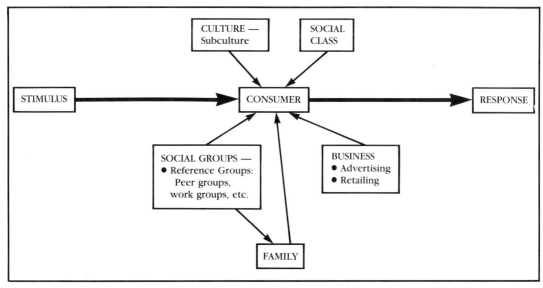

FIGURE 2.4: Environmental (External) Influences on the Consumer Decision Process

ter 16. The family has a tremendous impact on the formation of personality, values, attitudes, preferences, and habits. Different types of families can be identified and the roles played by different family members assessed. The chapter pays direct attention to the influence of children on household decision making.

PART V: ENVIRONMENTAL (EXTERNAL) BUSINESS INFLUENCES

The consumer is also influenced by a number of external forces that are generated by business organizations, such as marketing communications, salespeople, and retail store strategies.

Communications

Figure 2.5 shows the main aspects of marketing communications. They will be considered primarily from the point of view of their impact on consumer behavior. Both mass communications and personal selling are covered.

Part V reviews a number of the different kinds of communications approaches made by business to the consumer and discusses the pros and cons of some of the controversial aspects of those approaches.

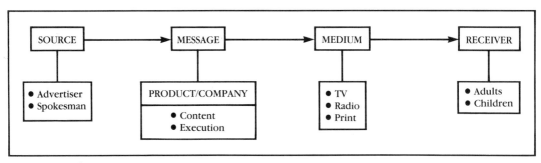

FIGURE 2.5: Marketing Communications

Retail Store Strategies

Chapter 18 considers the factors that affect store choice and the various retailing tactics (such as special displays, shelf space, pricing) that influence the consumer's in-store behavior.

PART VI: SYNTHESIS, POSTSCRIPT, AND PROGNOSIS

The last section of the book essentially provides an overall evaluation of the field of consumer behavior. It describes and assesses the contributions of the most significant attempts to integrate what is known about consumer dynamics. Of the many such models that have been proposed the two most complete ones are reviewed.

The final chapter comments on the "state of the art," elaborates on its limitations and shortcomings, and assesses the general usefulness of consumer data. It concludes with a discussion of future developments in the field and what their impact is likely to be.

SUMMARY

Figure 2.6 summarizes the relationships discussed in the chapter. Consumers respond to stimuli from marketing, social, physical, or physiological sources. The consumer response

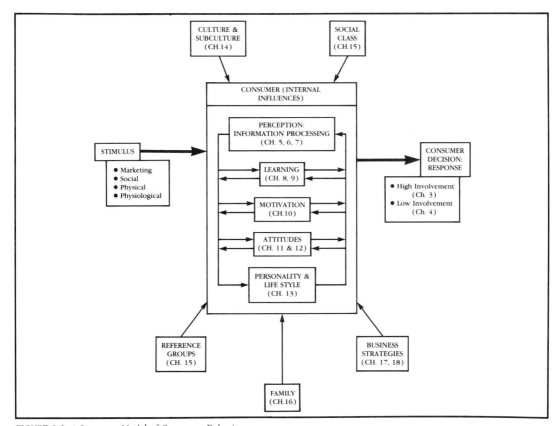

FIGURE 2.6: A Summary Model of Consumer Behavior

is determined by two sets of influences: internal, psychological influences and external influences.

The internal influences include how incoming information is received and interpreted (perception), how it is stored in memory (learning), the needs and motives that direct the response (motivation), the attitudes or predispositions to the choices confronting the consumer, and the individual's style or behavioral tendencies (personality).

The external influences, which have a direct bearing on the internal influences, include the cultural, social, and business environments. The influence of the social environment will be examined in terms of reference groups, social class, and the family.

The response that results from the interaction of these influences with a particular stimulus can be of two primary kinds — a decision that is carefully considered and takes some time (high involvement) or one that is fairly routine and quickly made (low involvement).

Figure 2.6 also indicates the chapters in which all of these topics are discussed.

QUESTIONS

1. Explain the following terms: (a) decision process, (b) life space, (c) internal factors.

2. Give an example of how perception, learning, motivation, attitudes, and personality are interrelated and interact with each other.

3. Give an example to illustrate how the environmental factors influence the internal factors and, through them, the decision process.

4. Define "involvement" and distinguish between high-involvement and low-involvement decisions.

5. Explain the significance of the acceptance stage in information processing.

6. List as many ways as you can think of in which understanding the learning process is of practical importance to marketers.

7. With the help of Statistics Canada data, determine the size and other demographic characteristics of the major subcultures in Canadian society.

8. Why is the family of central importance in the study of consumer behavioral phenomena?

NOTES TO CHAPTER 2

[1]Kurt Lewin, *A Dynamic Theory of Personality* (New York: McGraw-Hill, 1935).

[2]Harold H. Kassarjian, "Consumer Behavior: a Field Theoretical Approach," in Harold H. Kassarjian and Thomas S. Robertson (eds.), *Perspectives in Consumer Behavior*, rev. ed. (Glenview, Illinois: Scott, Foresman, and Company, 1973), p. 108.

[3]Bernard Berelson and Gary A. Steiner, *Human Behavior: An Inventory of Scientific Findings* (New York: Harcourt, Brace and World, 1964), p. 133.

[4]Benjamin Kleinmuntz, *Personality Measurement* (Homewood, Illinois: Dorsey, 1967), p. 9.

The Consumer Decision Process

To understand the external and internal influences on consumer decisions, it will first be necessary to discuss in detail the nature and complexities of the decision process.

Chapter 3 begins with a description of the kinds of consumer decision-making behavior — specifically, two types of high-involvement and two types of low-involvement decisions. It then presents a detailed review of high-involvement decisions using complex decision making, its main manifestation, as the basic model of decision making. Low-involvement decisions are discussed in Chapter 4.

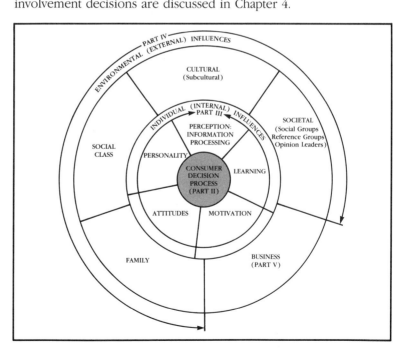

3

Complex Decision Making

Consumer decision making is more than just a single act. It is not simply a decision to buy or not buy. Rather, it is a process consisting of a number of steps that begin before the purchase and reach beyond the buying act. The nature of the decision process varies, depending upon the product and the consumer. To understand the behavior of the consumer, the marketer needs to determine the kind of decision-making behavior that is involved with the particular product.

KINDS OF DECISION MAKING

De Bruicker has suggested that decision-making behavior may be classified on the basis of:

- involvement with the product, topic, or issue; and
- the degree of the individual's perceived differentiation among options (e.g., brands).[1]

Involvement is the importance of the stimulus to the individual, and to the individual's self-image.[2] It has also been seen as commitment to a specific issue or situation: for example, a social issue such as abortion.[3] Thus the low-involved consumer not only thinks of a product as trivial but may also show little bond with any brand.[4]

Because of its subjective nature, involvement is not easy to measure. Some researchers have turned to observable, external criteria such as price (the higher the price, the greater the involvement), purchase cycle (less frequently purchased products are more involving), and perceived risk (the greater the perceived risk, the greater the involvement) but these are quite broad and the relationships do not always hold. A more acceptable measure is based on social judgement theory, which takes into account the number of attributes and the latitude of acceptance.[5] A long, narrow range of acceptance (long = many attributes; narrow = little latitude) is indicative of high involvement. There are several advantages to this measure: it yields a single numerical score, it can indicate relative involvement level, and it identifies the key attributes used by consumers, and their acceptable value ranges.

The second criterion, **perceived brand differentiation,** is not as difficult to measure. It is based on determining the number of brands considered by the consumer and the extent to which these brands are seen to be different from one another.

Taking the two dimensions of involvement and perceived brand differences, and allowing for a high and a low category in each, De Bruicker identified four types of decision-making behavior, as shown in Figure 3.1.

This classification identifies two types of high-involvement and two types of low-involvement decision-making behavior.

High-Involvement Decision Making

This involves products that are important to the individual. They have high personal relevance, being closely related to the individual's self image, and involve greater risk — social risk (loss of esteem in the eyes of relevant others), financial risk (products higher in price), and psychological risk (a bad choice may be injurious to one's ego). In high-involvement decisions the range of acceptable brands will be narrow, the number of criteria on which brands are judged will be large, and the degree of flexibility surrounding each criterion will be quite small.[6]

Much of the thinking behind the range of brands and criteria in high-involvement decisions comes from **social judgement theory.** Many years ago Sherif postulated that degree of commitment would influence an individual's position on an issue (in this case, a social issue).[7] On any issue having a range of positions, an individual would have an ideal position, a range of acceptable positions around it, a range of unacceptable positions, and a range of non-commitment. Sherif labelled these three ranges the latitude of acceptance, the latitude of rejection, and the latitude of non-commitment, and suggested that high commitment or involvement would mean a narrow latitude of acceptance and a broad latitude of rejection.

Because the latitude of acceptance in a high-involvement situation is narrow, a message that is agreed with will, by definition, be close to the ideal and, the theory suggests, such a message will be interpreted more positively than it actually is (**assimilation effect**). Conversely, a message that is disagreed with will fall in the latitude of rejection and be perceived more negatively than it is (**contrast effect**). In other words, the highly involved consumer is more selective and more likely to reject discrepant messages.

BRAND DIFFERENTIATION	INVOLVEMENT	
	HIGH	LOW
HIGH (significant perceived differences among brands)	Beliefs → Evaluation → Behavior Complex decision making True loyalty	Beliefs → Behavior → Evaluation Variety seeking
LOW (Small or no perceived differences among brands)	Behavior → Evaluation → Beliefs Dissonance reduction	Beliefs → Behavior Inertia Spurious loyalty

FIGURE 3.1: Four Types of Decision-Making Behavior

SOURCE: F. Stewart De Bruicker, "An Appraisal of Low-Involvement Consumer Information Processing," in John C. Maloney and Bernard Silverman (eds.), *Attitude Research Plays for High Stakes* (Chicago.: American Marketing Association, 1979), p. 124. Reprinted with permission of the American Marketing Association.

It has also been suggested that in high-involvement decisions, the consumer weighs the large number of attributes in a **compensatory** manner (that is, the strengths in certain attributes help to make up for weaknesses in others); in low-involvement decisions, the smaller number of attributes are evaluated in a **non-compensatory** manner (that is, low performance on one attribute will lead to rejection of the brand).[8]

As shown in Figure 3.1, the two kinds of high-involvement decision making differ in one significant respect. *The upper left quadrant* represents a process that starts with certain beliefs, proceeds to the development of attitudes through a considerable amount of information search and evaluation, and ends with the behaviorial decision. High involvement and significant perceived differences among brands make for complex decision making. Examples of products that involve complex decision making are automobiles, houses, furniture, major clothing, jewelry, stereos, and television.

When a brand satisfies the consumer's need, the purchase response is strengthened and the likelihood of repurchase is increased. What starts out as complex decision making later omits the search and evaluation stages and need arousal leads directly to purchase. Because such repurchase is based on brand preference, it is considered true **brand loyalty**.

Habitual purchasing can revert to complex decision making if, for example, the product fails to meet expectations and causes dissatisfaction. Cigarette smokers who suddenly find that their favorite brand tastes bitter engage in search and evaluation of other brands in order to make new choices.

Other factors can cause the brand-loyal consumer to revert to complex decision making:

- the introduction of a new brand (which may lead to new search and brand evaluation);

- a change in needs (such as information about the ill effects of smoking); or

- boredom.

In brand loyalty, satisfaction has reinforced the link between product usage and product benefits and the consumer has learned to expect certain rewards from the purchase behavior.

Examples of high-involvement products that become habitual purchases (brand loyalty) are characterized by frequent purchasing: cigarettes, beer, personal products.

Brand loyalty will be discussed in greater detail as a learning phenomenon in Chapter 9.

It should be emphasized that a given product is not regarded in the same way by all consumers. A product that for some consumers is highly involving may not be for others. For example, laundry detergent may be highly involving to a consumer for whom household duties are very important and low-involving to a career-oriented consumer. Their perceptions of the brands and their decision-making behavior will be quite different.

The lower left quadrant of Figure 3.1 includes those high-involvement decisions in which consumers perceive few brand differences. In those instances, decision making is not complex. Purchase is made with little or no information search and evaluation. Consumers know little about how to judge different brands and see few differences among them. Brands may be grouped on the basis of one attribute (e.g., price) but the brands in a group are thought to be homogeneous. Purchase may, therefore, be guided by sales personnel, friends, or relatives.

Because the decision is highly involving and because the brands are seen as similar, postpurchase dissonance is very likely to occur, regardless of which brand is chosen. Information search and evaluation will take place after the purchase. It is restricted and selective, the main purpose being to support the original choice by reducing the dissonance between what was expected of the brand and how it actually performed. Thus this type of decision behavior is referred to as **dissonance reduction.** Carpets are a good example of such a product. For the many consumers for whom carpets are highly involving, brand choice is made without much information about the brands. To reduce post-purchase dissonance, attempts are made to seek out information that supports the choice. Non-supportive information tends to be ignored.

Not many products fall into this category.

Low-Involvement Decision Making

Figure 3.1 outlines two types of low-involvement behavior.

The lower right quadrant is characterized by low involvement and few or no perceived brand differences. In such conditions, little or no information processing occurs before purchase. Based on scanty information (sometimes only awareness), purchase is made and repeated with little or no evaluation.

This passive decision process is labelled **inertia.** A brand is repurchased without any decision process, resulting in a kind of **spurious brand loyalty.**

Most consumer decisions probably fall in this category — examples include such products as canned goods, salt, facial tissue, and soap.

The upper right quadrant represents the kind of decision making that occurs when involvement is low but brand differences are high. Because involvement is low, brand evaluation is limited and does not precede behavior. Because of the product's low importance and low risk, consumers are often not reluctant to switch brands especially since there are clear differences among the acceptable brands. This behavior is described as **variety seeking.** Consumers are not likely to be seriously dissatisfied with their current brand and they switch out of a desire for change or novelty.

Salad dressing is a good example of this type of decision behavior. A brand is purchased a few times and then the consumer switches to another brand, even though the first brand is still rated favorably.

In Chapter 4, low-involvement decision making, including appropriate marketing strategies, will be treated in greater detail. The rest of this chapter is devoted to complex decision making.

COMPLEX DECISION MAKING

The most elaborate form of consumer decision-making behavior, complex decision making, will be treated at some length in order to serve as the basic process against which the three other kinds of decision behavior will be presented and suggestions for appropriate marketing strategies made.

A consumer decision starts with a need felt by the individual who, faced with a problem, sets out to do something about it. Thus, consumer decision making is essentially problem solving. How a consumer recognizes a need and acts on it closely follows the classic schema for problem solving proposed many years ago by the educational psychologist, John Dewey. Dewey identified six stages:[9]

- problem recognition;
- internal search for information;
- external search for information;
- evaluation of alternatives;
- decision; and
- post-decision outcome.

Translated into consumer decision-making terms, these steps may be cast as follows:

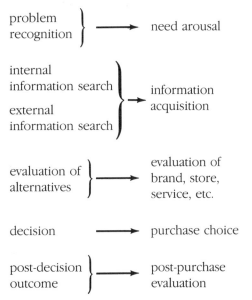

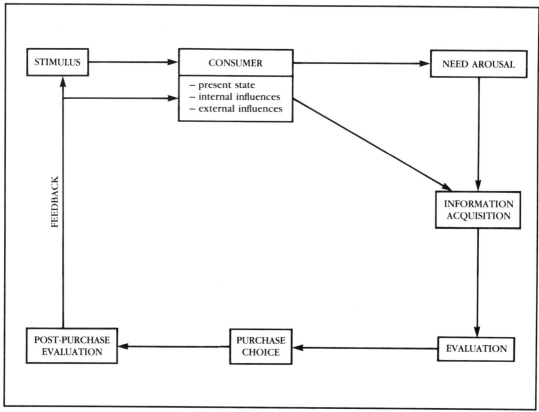

FIGURE 3.2: Basic Stages in Complex Decision Making

Figure 3.2 presents a basic model of complex decision making, showing the relationships among these steps. Each of the stages of this model is discussed in the following pages.

Need Arousal or Problem Recognition

When the consumer becomes aware of a discrepancy between the existing state and a desired state, need is aroused.

Decision making will begin if that discrepancy goes beyond a certain level, depending upon the individual and the circumstances. For example, an individual whose automobile has been slightly unreliable for a number of months may not think the problem is serious and does nothing about it. However, when the car refuses

to start on two consecutive mornings, the consumer starts thinking about replacing it. Arousal of need has occurred.

The **existing state** is the total situation of the consumer: the current needs, attitudes, and motives; the **desired state** is the situation after the kinds of changes the consumer wishes.

The existing state and the desired state are functions of the consumer's motivations, personality, and past experience, of cultural and social influences, and of past marketing stimuli. Once the need is aroused and the decision-making process initiated, the existing state will change as new information is processed. There are three ways in which the existing state may change and therefore fall short of the desired state:

● *Depletion of Supplies* — usually leading to the purchase of fresh quantities or a replacement, if the last "solution" proved to be unsatisfactory.

- *Changed Needs* — for example, a new baby, a growing family, a change of jobs, increased money supply, and purchasing a new house all have attendant needs.
- *Marketing Activity* — when companies introduce a new or improved product or suggest new uses for their product, they are really attempting to generate dissatisfaction with the existing state and thus need arousal.

Recognition of a need is not always as simple as it may seem. A consumer may not have a clear idea of what the problem is or there may be a conflict among needs (e.g., as to which need should be satisfied) that must be resolved before action can be taken.

Need arousal can also occur if the desired state changes. Changes in the desired state can be brought about by arousing motives and by direct social or marketing influences.

A motive is something that causes a person to act. Thus certain states that an individual considers worthy of attainment can lead to the desire for products that are seen as conducive to reaching those states. The desired state can be changed by stimulating motives that did not previously play a role in the consumer's life. For example, impressing upon a consumer the importance of economy in gas consumption could alter the consumer's perception of the kind of car that would be desirable.

Motives can be aroused in two different ways:

- through **internal drive activation** — for example, where hunger leads to the arousal of status, conformity, economy, or other motives that direct the behavior undertaken to reduce the hunger;
- through **external drive activation**, such as when an advertisement arouses a status or conformity motive.

The norms and expectations of social groups (peer groups, family, social class) can also have a strong influence on the desired state. Real-izing a neighbor has bought a new car, acquiring a new reference group (such as when a recent graduate joins a law firm), or changing social or cultural patterns (e.g., a new style of clothing) can result in changes in the desired state and thus need arousal.

A controversial question has been whether marketing activities can significantly change the desired state in such a way that consumers are led to seek to satisfy needs that would otherwise have been ignored.

Marketers claim, with considerable truth, that they only stimulate already existing needs and that all they are doing is identifying problems and suggesting new ways in which motives may be satisfied.

However, it is difficult to see how the marketer can avoid accentuating certain ends (values) through promotional activities. For example, it is very difficult to deny that "life-style" ads (beer being consumed at pool side by young, athletic, sexy, good-looking males and females who are obviously successful) are likely to have an effect on the goals and behavior of young people. To the extent that the desired state is affected, the marketer can be said to be "creating a need" by expanding its scope and increasing demand. It is to be noted that the marketer's ability to influence such desired states may be more limited than generally thought.

Information Acquisition

Information can be acquired through internal search or through external sources.

Internal search occurs when the individual draws upon information already stored in long-term memory as a result of prior experience and information processing (see Chapter 8).[10] Depending on what the consumer already knows, the internal search may be sufficient to make the decision. Most times, however, it is necessary in complex decision making to turn to **external sources**, such as mass media, friends, relatives, opinion leaders, showrooms, brochures, and sales personnel.

Because of its introspective, subjective nature, internal search is difficult to identify and analyze. One technique that attempts to do this is **protocol analysis**, in which a systematic analysis is made of reports given by individuals, as they think aloud, about a particular decision. The assumption is that the individual makes use of information stored in memory and that those items can be identified verbally. As one study points out, there are numerous problems with the technique.[11]

External Search

It appears that external search probably occurs in a *minority* of consumer decisions.[12] However, in high-involvement decisions that are urgent, important, highly risk-involved, and in which preferences have not already been established, there is likely to be extended search activity, providing excellent opportunities for the marketer to reach consumers.

The amount of the consumer's search activity depends on several factors:

- the perceived value of the search (that is, how much useful information is likely to be added to what is already known);
- the personality of the consumer (for example, someone who enjoys shopping is more likely to engage in search activity; confidence in the ability to judge different brands and make decisions leads to more search; the inability to tolerate delay sometimes curtails external search); and
- the *costs* of obtaining that information (in terms of time, energy, money, physical and psychological discomfort, and opportunity).[13]

There are a large number of possible sources of information, so great care needs to be exercised in the selection of the channels to be used to reach a market. For example, a television manufacturer who finds that most consumers visit showrooms and seek information from salespeople should focus on this source

of information, utilizing brochures, displays, perfectly tuned sets, and knowledgeable sales staff.

The various communications media and techniques will be discussed in Chapter 17.

In general, there are three types of information sources:

- commercial or marketer-controlled (advertising, point-of-purchase displays, product labels, packages, salespeople, sampling, demonstrations);
- personal (friends, relatives, opinion leaders); and
- "neutral" (government tests, private test sources such as *Good Housekeeping* and *Consumer Reports*).

The relative importance of information sources varies with the individual and with the product. However, consumers tend to use more than one source, so that the search process is really cumulative.[14]

Mass media appear to play an informative role, while personal sources and non-marketer-dominated sources generally perform an evaluative function. Friends and relatives tend to be consulted for information about quality and performance but rarely for price.[15] Advertising is used as a source of information by an average of about 20% of consumers, although this varies for different products: food (26%),[16] shoes (9%), and furniture (52%).[17]

Personal sources have been found to be very influential in consumer purchase decisions. Opinion leaders and other personal sources play a very important role — much more so than at first supposed. For example, more than 58% of durable goods buyers turned for advice to acquaintances.[18]

Shopping is another important source of information. Studies conducted around two decades ago found that durables generate the largest amount of shopping activity. This is not surprising in view of the larger risks involved. One study found significant variations in the amount of shopping activity for different durables.[19]

With "soft" goods, such as clothing and food, shopping activity varies for different products. An early study indicated that 54% of food shoppers visited only one store, 37% two or more stores, and the remaining 9% had no identifiable pattern.[20]

No recent studies on shopping activity have been reported. It should be noted that shopping patterns change over time as economic and social conditions change, so that too much reliance should not be placed on any of the patterns cited. They are purely illustrative.

In general, it seems that the extent to which consumers look to different sources for information depends upon the characteristics of the consumers themselves (amount of information already available, self-confidence), the type of information (personal source for evaluative information), the perceived risks (personal sources and shopping activity), and the stage in the product life cycle.* Mass media sources are more important in the introductory stage of the product life cycle, when the main emphasis is on building awareness, and personal sources are more important in the growth and maturity stages because they provide evaluative input.[21]

Consumers may also seek information about how to judge a product. For example, a consumer deciding about a high-involvement product that is unfamiliar may first attempt to determine which attributes are important in evaluating it and then compare brands against these evaluative criteria.

Information overload can result from exposure to too much information. It becomes a crucial factor in effective decision making, especially if such overload is counter-productive and results in poorer decisions. More will be said about this in Chapter 5 in the discussion of consumer information processing.

---

*The product life-cycle has been defined as "the path of a product from introduction to decline. The stages of the product life-cycle include introduction, growth, maturity, and decline." M. Dale Beckman, David L. Kurtz, and Louis E. Boone, *Foundations of Marketing*, 2nd ed. (Toronto: Holt, Rinehart and Winston, 1982), p. 790.

Brand Evaluation

Evaluation usually takes place as the information is obtained. The objective of such information evaluation is to make a choice — among brands, products, or stores — on the basis of the information acquired. Information processing itself affects what is processed, how it is understood or interpreted, and what is retained. Information processing is subjected to selective perception (see Chapter 5) and is thus strongly influenced by psychological and social factors.

In order to decide on a product and/or a brand, the consumer, with the information that has filtered through, is now in a position to evaluate the options available in terms of those attributes that the consumer considers important: the evaluative criteria. These **evaluative criteria** are the result of the individual's experience, values, motives, and attitudes, as well as social influences. Different individuals place different weights on the various criteria. Evaluative criteria may include not only physical characteristics (such as color, size, design, or performance) but psychological and social characteristics as well (status, masculinity, reputation). As described in the preceding section, the evaluative criteria themselves are sometimes a product of an information search. Through a comparison of the options, a choice is eventually made. For example, the consumer who wants fuel economy, good winter performance, and low maintenance costs in a car will evaluate information about the different makes and come up with a choice.

Brand evaluation seems to occur in two ways: choice by processing brands (CPB) and choice by processing attributes (CPA).[22] In CPB one brand is evaluated on all of the criteria before another brand is processed.[23] In CPA all brands considered are evaluated on one attribute, and then on the next attribute, and so on.[24]

CPB appears to be the more frequently used processing approach. One study suggests that CPA is more likely to occur in early stages of the decision process and CPB as one gets closer to the final choice.[25]

Whichever method is used, brand evaluation leads to beliefs about the brands. For example, new information may result in either a new belief or a change in belief that a certain make of automobile gives excellent fuel economy. The total set of beliefs stemming from the evaluation constitute the individual's *attitude* to the brand, which will play a large part in influencing the intention to purchase and the actual purchase. How beliefs are combined to form attitudes and the relationships between attitudes, intention, and behavior will be discussed in Chapter 11.

Figure 3.3 presents this stage in complex decision making. Note that the criteria used in brand evaluation may come from the information acquired or, in some instances, they may guide the information search. Evaluative crite-

ria are also influenced by the norms and values of the culture, reference groups, the family, previous experience, and by the motives and attitudes of the individual.

The choice criteria consist of **qualifying** criteria and **determining** criteria.[26] The former are necessary if the consumer is going to purchase the product at all, and the latter are critical for brand selection. The most important attributes are not necessarily the determining ones. For example, while style and fabric may be the two most important criteria for men's suits, they may be equally shared by all brands considered and a third or fourth-rank attribute (e.g., color) may determine brand choice.

I referred above to "all brands considered," intentionally meaning to differentiate this set from the total set of brands of which the consumer is aware (see Chapter 9). Howard and Sheth first introduced the concept of the "evoked

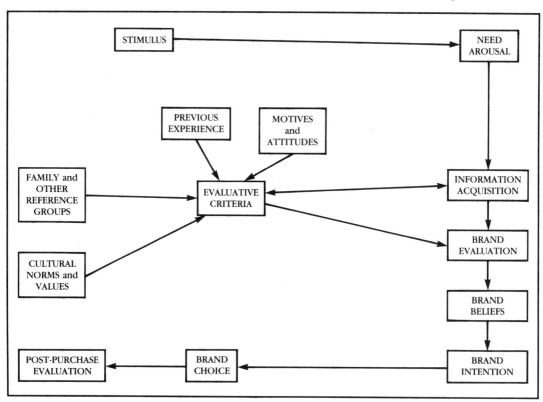

FIGURE 3.3: Brand Evaluation in Complex Decision Making

set" to refer to those brands that a consumer actively considers from among all the brands in the awareness set. It is important for marketers to ascertain whether their brands are in the consumer's evoked set and not just whether the consumer is aware or unaware of them.

The Purchase Act

The outcome of the first four stages can be a decision to buy or not to buy, or to delay a decision until further information is secured or perhaps until circumstances change.

The functions at any of the stages in the decision process may be performed by different family members. The problem may be recognized by one or more members, search and evaluation also by the same or other members (see Chapter 16), and the purchaser may or may not have participated in any of the earlier stages. Several points need to be underlined:

- the buyer is not necessarily a decision maker, and the marketer is interested in the decision maker(s);
- different family members can play different roles at the various stages in the decision process;
- marketers need to decide which stage(s) should be focussed on and who are the crucial decision makers at each stage — for example, external search by the husband may be the primary focus in television purchasing;
- strategies involving different stages may be developed and targeted to different individuals, or they may need to be applied at different times of the year.

The purchase act itself is made up of a number of sub-decisions, each of which can be made by different individuals. For example, the purchase of an automobile can involve the following sub-decisions:

- how much to spend;
- when to buy;
- where to buy;
- what make to buy;

- what model to buy; and
- what color to buy.

It would be important, then, for the marketer to determine the sub-decisions involved with the particular product in order to understand fully who makes the purchase decision and how it is made.

Post-Purchase Evaluation

A very important stage of the consumer decision process is the impact of current decisions on future purchasing behavior. Actual use of a product will either confirm or disconfirm prior expectations resulting from brand evaluation. Three general outcomes are possible:

- Satisfaction;
- Dissatisfaction; and
- Cognitive dissonance.

Satisfaction occurs when a product performs according to expectations.[27] In other words, the brand chosen has served to fulfill the consumer's need and thus reinforce the response of purchasing that brand. The reinforcement of such a response means that beliefs and attitudes about the brand are positively influenced and the likelihood of repurchase is increased.

Dissatisfaction occurs, of course, in the opposite kind of situation, when product performance disconfirms prior expectations. It leads to negative beliefs and attitudes about the brand and repurchase is not likely to occur. A disappointed consumer is not likely to recommend such a product to others.[28]

The results of satisfaction and dissatisfaction are recorded in long-term memory and become inputs to the internal search stage in later decisions.[29]

The marketer should make every effort to ensure that all of the communications under his or her control are well integrated and coordinated so that they are not likely to contribute to dissatisfaction by creating false expectations.[30] Claims should be made and beliefs generated that will be confirmed through product performance. There should be as close a match as possible between consumer needs, desires, and life-style on the one hand, and product design, performance, and information on the other.

The third possible outcome of the purchase decision is cognitive dissonance, where the consumer experiences feelings of doubt or psychological discomfort about the choice made. Such a state of tension occurs when two things that the consumer knows about a situation are inconsistent with each other.[31] It is often felt right after the purchase, when the consumer may begin to have second thoughts about the product chosen.

For example, feelings of insecurity and uneasiness may follow the purchase of one make of car because the consumer is now committed to the purchase even as the attributes of the unchosen makes look more attractive.

Dissonance is more likely to occur in complex decision making; that is, with high-involvement purchases. Dissatisfaction is more likely in low-involvement situations.

Dissonance-causing information can come from a personal source, from advertising, or from experience with the product.

Cognitive dissonance gives rise "to activity oriented toward reducing or eliminating the dissonance"[32] — toward achieving cognitive consistency. To do this the individual may re-evaluate the options or search out information that will support the decision.

Re-evaluation may mean regarding the chosen option as more attractive, lowering the attractiveness of the other options, or viewing all options as equally desirable.[33]

Other ways of handling cognitive dissonance, including where a consumer admits a mistake, will be discussed in Chapter 12. The significant role that dissonance plays in attitude change will be examined in greater detail there.

Post-purchase evaluation feeds back into every step of the decision process (Figure 3.2). Experience with the product will affect the perception of a similar stimulus on a subsequent occasion, the consumer's evaluative criteria, the extent of internal and external search, and brand evaluation.

CHARACTERISTICS OF THE COMPLEX DECISION-MAKING PROCESS

The decision-making process will be more comprehensible with what we now know about the characteristics of the process:

- the process occurs unconsciously, without any awareness of steps or stages on the part of the consumer;
- all six steps are not involved in every decision — three variations have been identified: routinized decisions or habit, limited decisions in those cases where there is some previous experience with the product, and extended or complex decisions;[34]
- there can be *role differentiation* among family members at each stage of the process and even within stages, such as the sub-decisions that make up the purchase act (the specific decision makers involved at each stage will determine the strategies to be developed by the marketer);
- excessively high involvement or arousal can lead to cognitive strain because of exaggerated effort, and can result in poor decision making (when involvement is not excessive, the individual behaves adaptively, and arrives at a decision after highly selective attention and search);
- in complex decision making, the amount of information the consumer already has is a strong determinant of the amount of search — the amount and kind of search in turn strongly influence the communication strategy pursued by the marketer.

SUMMARY

Consumer decisions can be classified into two main groups — high-involvement and low-involvement decisions. Each of these may be subdivided into two types: high or low perceived brand differences.

High-involvement and high-brand differentiation make for complex decision making, with its variant, true brand loyalty. High involvement and few perceived brand differences result in dissonance-reduction behavior. The two types of low-involvement decisions are variety seeking and inertia.

Complex decision making consists of five* basic stages. It starts with need arousal, which results from the interaction of internal or external stimuli with the individual so that there is a discrepancy between the individual's actual state and the desired state. Need arousal leads to the acquisition of information. The next stage, brand evaluation, matches what is learned about the brands with the consumer's evaluative criteria in order to arrive at a brand choice. The last stage, post-purchase evaluation, can lead to satisfaction, dissatisfaction or cognitive dissonance, any of which can affect subsequent decision making.

Brand loyalty is a variant of complex decision making. The reinforcement of a positive link between purchase and product rewards leads to repeat purchase behavior based on a preference for the brand. Search and brand evaluation are now omitted.

The second type of high-involvement decision starts with the purchase behavior, which is followed by evaluation based on product performance, and then the development of attitudes to the brand. The consumer in this kind of situation is engaged in seeking out information that will support the purchase decision and reduce dissonance.

---

*That is, when internal and external search are combined as information acquisition.

QUESTIONS

1. Explain why it is important for the marketer to recognize that the consumer purchase decision consists of a number of steps or stages.

2. Using the model of complex decision making, develop a marketing strategy for a camera manufacturer such as Canon.

3. Define involvement. Make a list of ten high-involvement and ten low-involvement products. What criteria did you use to distinguish between the two?

4. Discuss the kinds of changes in a person's actual state that can lead to need arousal.

5. Explain the relationship between motive arousal and need arousal. Illustrate with an example of a social motive.

6. What are the main factors that affect the amount of external search in which a consumer is likely to engage?

7. How do beliefs, attitudes, and intentions arise? Describe their interrelationships.

8. Why is the purchase act itself not as simple as it looks?

9. Distinguish between dissatisfaction and cognitive dissonance. How does the individual attempt to reduce dissonance and why?

10. Explain brand loyalty in the context of complex decision making.

NOTES TO CHAPTER 3 ▬▬▬▬

[1]F. Stewart De Bruicker, "An Appraisal of Low-Involvement Consumer Information Processing," in John C. Maloney and Bernard Silverman (eds.), *Attitude Research Plays for High Stakes* (Chicago: American Marketing Association, 1979), p. 124.

[2]H.E. Krugman, "Measurement of Advertising Involvement," *Public Opinion Quarterly*, 30 (Winter 1966-67), pp. 583-96; J.A. Howard and J.N. Sheth, *The Theory of Buyer Behavior* (New York: John Wiley and Sons, 1969), p. 419.

[3]C.W. Sherif, M. Sherif, and R.E. Nebergall, *Attitude and Attitude Change: The Social Judgement Involvement Approach* (New Haven: Yale University Press, 1965), p. 65.

[4]John L. Lastovicka and David M. Gardner, "Components of Involvement," in Maloney and Silverman, op. cit., p. 68.

[5]Michael L. Rothschild and Michael J. Houston, "The Consumer Involvement Matrix: Some Preliminary Findings," in Barnett A. Greenberg and Danny N. Bellenger, *Proceedings of the American Marketing Association Educators' Conference*, Series #41 (1977), pp. 95-8.

[6]Michael L. Rothschild, "Advertising Strategies for High and Low Involvement Situations," in Maloney and Silverman, op. cit., p. 80.

[7]C.W. Sherif, M. Sherif, and R.W. Nebergall, *Attitude and Attitude Change* (Philadelphia: Saunders, 1965).

[8]Michael L. Rothschild, "Advertising Strategies for High and Low Involvement Situations," in Maloney and Silverman, op. cit., p. 79.

[9]John Dewey, *How We Think* (New York: D.C. Heath, 1910).

[10]A good discussion of internal search can be found in James R. Bettman, *An Information Processing Theory of Consumer Choice* (Reading, Massachusetts: Addison-Wesley, 1979), pp. 107-11.

[11]James R. Bettman and C.W. Park, "Effects of Prior Knowledge and Experience and Phase of the Choice Process on Consumer Decision Processes: A Protocol Analysis," *Journal of Consumer Research*, 7: 3 (December 1980), pp. 234-48.

[12]Jacob Jacoby et al., "Pre-purchase Information Acquisition," in Beverlee B. Anderson (ed.), *Advances in Consumer Research*, 3 (Atlanta: Association for Consumer Research, 1975), pp. 306-14.

[13]Wesley C. Bender, "Consumer Purchase Costs — Do Retailers Recognize Them?" *Journal of Retailing* (Spring 1964), pp. 1-8; Brian T. Ratchford, "The Value of Information for Selected Appliances," *Journal of Marketing Research*, 17 (February 1980), pp. 14-25.

[14]G. Katona and Eva Mueller, "A Study of Purchase Decisions," in Lincoln H. Clark (ed.), *Consumer Behavior: The Dynamics of Consumer Reaction* (New York: New York University Press, 1955), pp. 30-87.

[15]Bruce Legrand and John Udell, "Consumer Behavior in the Market Place," *Journal of Retailing*, 40 (Fall 1964), pp. 32-40.

[16]George Fisk, "Media Influence Reconsidered," *Public Opinion Quarterly*, 23 (1959), pp. 83-91.

[17]L.P. Bucklin, "The Information Role of Advertising," *Journal of Advertising Research*, 5 (September 1965), pp. 11-5.

[18]Katona and Mueller, op. cit., p. 45.

[19]Legrand and Udell, op. cit., pp. 32-40.

[20]Bryan Thompson, "An Analysis of Supermarket Shopping Habits in Worcester, Massachusetts," *Journal of Retailing*, 43 (Fall 1967), pp. 17-29.

[21]Legrand and Udell, op. cit.; Michael Berry and B. Curtis Hamm, "Canonical Analysis of Relations Between Socioeconomic Risk and Personal Influence in Purchase Decisions," *Journal of Marketing Research*, 6 (August 1969), pp. 351-4; Everett M. Rogers and George M. Beal, "The Importance of Personal Influence in the Adoption of Technological Changes," *Social Forces*, 36 (1958), pp. 329-35.

[22]Bettman (1979), op. cit., pp. 132-3.

[23]James R. Bettman and Pradeep Kakkar, "Effects of Information Presentation Format on Consumer Information Acquisition Strategies," *Journal of Consumer Research*, 3 (March 1977), pp. 233-40.

[24]David A. Sheluga, James Jaccard, and Jacob Jacoby, "Preference, Search, and Choice: An Integrative Approach," *Journal of Consumer Research*, 6 (September 1979), pp. 166-76.

[25]James R. Bettman and C. Whan Park, "Effects of Prior Knowledge and Experience and Phase of the Choice Process on Consumer Decision Processes: A Protocol Analysis," *Journal of Consumer Research*, 7:3 (December 1980), pp. 234-48.

[26]E. Jerome McCarthy and Stanley J. Shapiro, *Basic Marketing* (Georgetown, Ontario: Irwin-Dorsey, 1979), pp. 233-4.

[27]John E. Swain and Linda J. Combs, "Product Performance and Consumer Satisfaction: A New Concept," *Journal of Marketing*, 40 (April 1976), pp. 25-33.

[28]Ralph E. Anderson, "Consumer Dissatisfaction: The Effect of Disconfirmed Expectancy on Perceived Product Performance," *Journal of Marketing Research*, 10 (February 1973), pp. 38-44.

[29]Richard I. Oliver and Gerald Linda, "Effect of Satisfaction and Its Antecedents on Consumer Preference and Intention," in Kent B. Monroe (ed.), *Advances in Consumer Research*, 8 (Ann Arbor, Michigan: Association for Consumer Research, 1981), pp. 88-93.

[30]Bruce G. Vanden Bergh and Leonard N. Reid, "Effects of Product Puffery on Response to Print Advertisements," in James H. Leigh and Claude R. Martin, Jr. (eds.), *Current Issues and Research in Advertising 1980* (Ann Arbor, Michigan: Graduate School of Business, University of Michigan, 1980).

[31]Jack W. Brehm, "Motivational Effects of Cognitive Dissonance," in Marshall R. Jones (ed.), *Nebraska Symposium on Motivation* (Lincoln: University of Nebraska Press, 1962), p. 52.

[32]Leon Festinger, *A Theory of Cognitive Dissonance* (Evanston, Illinois: Row Peterson, 1957); Leon Festinger, "The Motivating Effect of Cognitive Dissonance," in Gardner Lindzey (ed.), *Assessment of Human Motives* (New York: Grove Press, 1958), p. 70; John Cohen and M.E. Goldberg, "The Dissonance Model in Post-Decision Product Evaluation," *Journal of Marketing Research,* 7 (1970), pp. 315-21.

[33]L.A. LoScioto and R. Perloff, "Influence of Brand Preference on Dissonance Reduction," *Journal of Marketing Research*, 4 (1967), pp. 286-90.

[34]John A. Howard, *Consumer Behavior: Application of Theory* (New York: McGraw-Hill, 1977), p. 9.

4

The Low-Involvement Decision

Low-involvement decisions deal with products that are of little importance to the consumer. They have little or no personal relevance and carry very low financial, psychological, and social risks.[1] It has been suggested that *most* consumer decisions are of this kind — unimportant, uninvolved, insignificant, and minor — and that explaining them does not need a grand theory of behavior.[2]

A study conducted by Hupfer and Gardner asked college students to rate the importance, on a seven-point scale, of a number of issues and products.[3] The researchers found that, *for the sample studied*, most of the products were rated as relatively unimportant. Examples were facial tissues, colas, toothpaste, and even bicycles.

This implies that for many consumer purchases, a decision process may never occur, perhaps not even on the first purchase and that perhaps "much theorizing on consumer decision-making is less broadly applicable than has been assumed."[4]

It also implies that the entire assumption that advertising must provide information in order to generate beliefs and attitudes (as was described for complex decision making in the last chapter) may be invalid in a large number of instances. In fact, choice may be completely absent in such cases. Olshavsky and Granbois suggest a number of ways in which this may occur:

> Purchases can occur out of necessity, they can be derived from culturally-mandated life-styles or from interlocked purchases; they can reflect preferences acquired in early childhood; they can result from simple conformity to group norms or from imitation of others; purchases can be made exclusively on recommendations from personal or nonpersonal sources; they can be made on the basis of surrogates of various types; or they can even occur on a random or superficial basis.[5]

Thus purchase behavior can occur without any conscious information search or brand evaluation. In low-involvement decisions, the consumer moves from need arousal directly to behavior — search and evaluation may occur after. Whatever information is retained by the consumer is the result of a passive process, what Lastovicka calls "information catching."[6] Little active attention is paid to product messages.

> What seems to happen is that we store a picture memory, an image without words. There is no recall because recall is the word form of the picture.... the nature of effective impact of communication or advertising on low-involvement topics, objects, or products, consists of building or strengthening the picture-image memory potential. Such potential is properly measured by recognition and not by recall.[7]

The "picture-image" constitutes a kind of belief about the existence of the brand; it is called into play when the need arises. There is no development of a positive or negative attitude to the brand at this stage.

Because it is a low-involvement product, weak attitudes toward the brand may develop after the purchase as a result of, for example, changes in product features or product performance.

The basic difference between high- and low-involvement purchases is that in high-involvement purchases search and evaluation precede the purchase; in low-involvement purchases there is usually no search and evaluation; if it occurs, it takes place after the purchase.

Based on social judgement theory, referred to in Chapter 3, Rothschild suggests that low-involvement decisions show two other characteristics: a wide range of acceptable brands and few evaluative criteria (with wide latitudes of acceptance).[8]

In summary, low-involvement decisions are characterized by:

- products of low personal relevance or importance;
- little or no risk;
- passive exposure to information;
- no pre-purchase search or evaluation;
- post-purchase evaluation that does not occur or is restricted to only a few criteria;
- wide latitudes of acceptance for the criteria; and
- wide range of acceptable brands.

TYPES OF LOW-INVOLVEMENT DECISIONS

It was noted in Chapter 3 (Figure 3.1) that high-involvement and low-involvement decisions are each divided into two subgroups on the basis of high versus low perceived differences among brands. Figure 4.1 shows these two types of low-involvement decisions.

Variety seeking describes the behavior when there is high perceived brand differentiation. Since involvement is low, there is little risk in switching brands and switching is encouraged

		LOW INVOLVEMENT
		Variety Seeking
	HIGH	Beliefs → Behavior → Evaluation
PERCEIVED BRAND DIFFERENTIATION		Inertia Spurious Loyalty
	LOW	Beliefs → Behavior

FIGURE 4.1: Types of Low-Involvement Decisions

by the strong perceived differences among brands. The consumer will therefore be inclined to try a number of brands, mainly out of a desire for change.

The consumer's beliefs, in the form of a picture image or a general awareness, lead directly to behavior. Whatever evaluation there is takes place after the purchase. Because brand differences are high, some evaluation does take place and even though consumers may not be seriously dissatisfied with their current brand, they switch to another just for a change.

Not many products fall in this category. Some examples are cereals, candy, chocolate bars, and salad dressing.

Low brand differentiation and low involvement lead to random choice behavior and repeat purchasing of that brand. Such repeat purchasing is not based on a preference for the brand and because it appears to be loyal behavior it is referred to as **spurious brand loyalty**.

The general awareness that results from a passive kind of information processing leads to the purchase of any brand. Since brand differences are low, the same brand continues to be purchased, with little or no brand evaluation.

Because of what appears to be a lack of any active cognitive choice, this type of behavior has been referred to as **inertia**. Most everyday consumer products are thought to belong to this category.

THEORETICAL BASIS OF LOW-INVOLVEMENT DECISIONS

A paper written by Krugman about twenty years ago was the seminal work that drew attention to the dominant role of low involvement in consumer behavior.[9] Krugman described television as an uninvolving medium whose messages were processed passively (while other things were being attended to) and achieved awareness and familiarity but little or no change in attitude. There was no significant information processing. What occurs is some form of brand registration as a result of repetition. For Krugman, mere exposure through a commercial is enough to lead to purchase.

Zajonc has found that exposure to an object tends to develop a preference for it in a subsequent choice situation, even if there is no recollection of the earlier exposure.[10] A recent study, however, suggests that exposure *per se* may not be enough. While the process may be passive, exposure must be accompanied by some background feature (such as music, colors, or humor) so that, through classical conditioning (See Chapter 8), the advertised product is recognized and preferred.[11]

Television is an uninvolving medium because the viewer pays little attention to its messages; whatever learning takes place is passive. Furthermore, the pace of viewing and the possibility of "making connections" are out of the viewer's control.[12] Print media are the opposite. Time spent on messages in these media is controlled by the reader and processing is more active. Because of the active versus passive audience involvement, McLuhan labelled television a cool medium, and print a hot medium.[13]

Krugman argues that the nature of the processing of information from television makes that medium suitable for low-involvement decisions and the active participation that the print media require makes them more appropriate for high-involvement decisions.

Recent developments in the study of brain hemispheral lateralization and the specificity of function attributed to the left and to the right brain suggest that high-involvement decisions are predominantly a left-brain activity and low-involvement decisions involve right-brain activity.[14] Specifically, the functions served by each hemisphere match very closely the kinds of processing that occur in high and low involvement.

> . . . the left hemisphere is primarily responsible for traditional, cognitive activities relying on verbal information, symbolic representation, sequential

analysis, and the ability to be conscious and report what is going on . . . . the right brain — without the individual being able to report verbally about it — is more concerned with pictorial, geometric, timeless and non-verbal information.[15]

Krugman further suggests that "it is the right brain's picture-taking ability that permits the rapid screening of the environment — to select what it is the left brain should focus on."[16]

This area of research may be important to the study of consumer behavior for two reasons. First, it suggests that advertising may have effects that cannot be measured by current research methods.[17] For example, it is possible that much of the advertising that currently appears to have no effect may yet have a strong influence on attitudes and behavior. Second, measurement of the location of brain activity could help marketers determine the level of involvement surrounding a product and therefore the kind of advertising that is appropriate.[18]

STRATEGY

Strategy directed at low-involved consumers should take into account their characteristics:

- mostly inertial or random brand-choice behavior;
- occasional variety-seeking behavior;
- passive exposure to information, resulting in a general awareness or picture-image of the brand;
- no pre-purchase search or brand evaluation; and
- subject more to broadcast media than print media or word of mouth.

Because inertial consumers perceive little difference among brands, Tyebjee suggests that they:

- may view the product class as relatively homogeneous; and
- may require communication differentiation rather than product differentiation.[19]

Change Strategies

The aim of the marketer of a low-involvement product will be to expand competitive potential by shifting consumers from behavior characterized by inertia or variety seeking to brand loyalty. Two strategies are possible:

- increasing the level of involvement with the product from low to high; and
- changing inertia buying to variety-seeking behavior.

Increasing the Level of Involvement

A number of methods have been suggested for raising the consumer's involvement towards a product or brand.[20] The principal objective is to generate interest and brand evaluation in order to establish brand preference.

One successful strategy is linking the product with a highly involving issue in the way that Crest toothpaste was linked with cavity prevention. This serves to widen the latitude of rejection of competitive brands. Decaffeinated colas, for example, could be linked with the important current issue of good health. A similar approach is introducing into the product an attribute that is new or that had not been considered important, such as minerals in cereals or additives in gasoline. Another strategy is linking the product with an involving advertising theme, one that is ego-involving rather than utilitarian. Value-expressive ads could depict youth, progress, or achievement so that if the product were shown in scenarios reflecting these values, it would be identified with these values. The product can also be linked with situations or activities that are involving for the consumer. For example, soft drink consumers could be shown consuming the brand at special times (parties, festive occasions) and in special places (while travelling, at an important event) or as a reward for a job well done (finishing a race, finishing painting the house).

The advertiser can also attempt to alter the importance of specific product attributes so that interest in the product increases. If one of the attributes of pop is less carbonation and the consumer does not consider this important, the marketer must convince the consumer of the benefits of that attribute. A fear appeal ad may be useful in such a situation. For example, an ad pointing out that the consumer may run the risk of yellow teeth and social ridicule by not using a particular brand of toothpaste could convince the consumer of the importance of having white teeth.

Encouraging Variety Seeking

A second strategy for achieving at least some brand differentiation involves shifting the consumer from inertia buying to variety-seeking behavior. Even if the product remains subject to low-involvement decision making, attempts can be made to generate greater brand activity and brand switching.

Whether this is a desirable approach depends on the current status of the brand. If the brand is well established and enjoys a significant share of the market, it may be unwise to stimulate variety-seeking behavior, since the brand may end up losing some of its customers to other brands, through the very act of generating brand comparisons. It would be better to concentrate on using reminder advertising and other promotional tactics (such as shelf displays or mnemonic devices) to maintain the brand's level of familiarity and to keep it in front of the consumer.

On the other hand, a minor brand would probably benefit from encouraging variety-seeking behavior, since by inducing consumers to switch brands it is likely to gain in the shuffle. Employing such tactics as premiums, deals, lower prices, free samples, coupons, and contests could be quite effective.

No-Change Strategies

Since high-involvement decisions are characterized by pre-purchase search and evaluation (except for the few products for which consumers perceive little or no brand difference), marketers are able to make effective use of a wide range of message designs and presentations. The characteristics of low-involvement decisions, on the other hand, impose greater restrictions on marketing activities.

Some suggestions have been made about using adaptive advertising (rather than advertising aimed at bringing about changes) for the uninvolved consumer.

Since the consumer is likely to be easily satisfied and since there is little interest and attention, there is little information processing. Thus **short messages** with few points are likely to be most effective.[21] They serve mainly as reminders.

High repetition is advisable. Because of low interest, repeated exposure is more likely to bring about passive learning of limited content. Repetition leads to brand familiarity and to purchase intention without any intervening attitude change. Further research is needed to indicate which is more effective — repetition of a brand name or concept within a commercial or repetition by several airings of the same commercial. Should a commercial only repeat the brand name and not be concerned about accompanying material?

Positioning of TV commercials is important. Rothschild reports a study that found that advertising for low-involvement products should avoid late positions in a stream of messages because attention and recall are negatively affected.[22] Clutter also seems to detract strongly from effectiveness. Because of the limited amount of information processing, positioning is a very important factor.

Television is the most appropriate medium. In general, **broadcast media** are preferable to print media because they are best suited to a passive audience that pays little interest or attention and processes little or no information. **Visual content** is important to the mental picture of the brand that consumers acquire. **Visual aids**, such as TV advertising and point-of-purchase displays, packaging, symbols, carton and scenic images, and mnemonic devices are very effective, particularly since decisions are made in the store.

Consumers will accept a broad range of messages because of the wide latitude of acceptance in low-involvement situations. Because consumers will be more amenable to messages from competing brands than in high-involvement situations, brand registration is very important.

Advertising has been emphasized here because the majority of low-involvement decisions (the inertia type) are characterized by low perceived brand differences and, in order to achieve some differentiation, reliance is placed on advertising and other communications.

SUMMARY

Low-involvement decisions deal with products of little importance or personal relevance to the consumer. They involve little risk and no pre-purchase search or evaluation. There are two types of low-involvement decisions: random choice behavior or inertia, which make up most consumer decisions, and variety-seeking behavior. Inertia-type behavior occurs when brand differentiation is low and variety-seeking when perceived brand differences are high.

Other characteristics include passive information processing, such as occurs with TV messages, brand registration in the form of a general mental picture, wide latitude of acceptance, and few evaluative criteria.

Recent studies of brain hemispheral lateralization suggest that the kinds of processing associated with low-involvement decisions occur in the right hemisphere and high-involvement processing occurs in the left hemisphere. These findings open up the possibility of more sensitive, objective measurement of the nature of involvement with different products.

Although most consumer decisions are of the low-involvement kind, marketers still appear to think and plan in terms of high-involvement decisions, employing for low-involvement products strategies that are appropriate for complex decision making.

Three kinds of strategies considered appropriate for low-involvement products were described:

- Two change strategies:

  – increasing the level of involvement from low to high; and

  – bringing about variety-seeking for products characterized by inertia type buying; and

- a no-change strategy.

Several techniques were suggested for improving the effectiveness of advertising and other promotional tools in low-involvement situations.

QUESTIONS

1. Distinguish between high-involvement and low-involvement decisions.

2. How would you differentiate between brand loyalty in high-involvement and low-involvement situations?

3. Describe the differences between the two types of low-involvement behavior.

4. Krugman has stated that "high involvement is more a left brain and low involvement a right brain activity." Discuss the significance of this statement for the marketer.

5. What contributions has social judgement theory made to our understanding of low-involvement decision making?

6. Evaluate the measures currently used for determining degree of involvement.

7. Pick a low-involvement product and show how, with advertising, you would attempt to shift it from low to high involvement.

8. Discuss the components suggested for adaptive advertising directed at the uninvolved consumer.

NOTES TO CHAPTER 4

[1]Richard Vaughn, "The Consumer Mind: How to Tailor Ad Strategies," *Advertising Age* (9 June 1980), pp. 45-6.

[2]H.H. Kassarjian, "Presidential Address, 1977: Anthropomorphism and Parsimony," in H.K. Hunt (ed.), *Advances in Consumer Research*, 7 (Ann Arbor, Michigan: Association for Consumer Research, 1978); H.H. Kassarjian and Waltraub M. Kassarjian, "Attitudes Under Low Commitment Conditions," in John C. Maloney and Bernard Silverman (eds), *Attitude Research Plays for High Stakes* (Chicago: American Marketing Association, 1979), p. 8.

[3]Nancy T. Hupfer and David M. Gardner, "Differential Involvement With Products and Issues: An Exploratory Study," in David M. Gardner (ed.), *Proceedings of the 2nd Annual Conference of the Association for Consumer Research* (College Park, Maryland: Association for Consumer Research, 1971), pp. 262-9.

[4]Richard W. Olshavsky and Donald H. Granbois, "Consumer Decision Making — Fact or Fiction?" *Journal of Consumer Research*, 6 (September 1979), pp. 93-100.

[5]Ibid., p. 98.

[6]John L. Lastovicka, "Questioning the Concept of Involvement-Defined Product Classes," in William L. Wilkie (ed.), *Advances in Consumer Research*, 6 (Ann Arbor, Michigan: Association for Consumer Research, 1979), pp. 174-9.

[7]Herbert E. Krugman, "Low-Involvement Theory in the Light of New Brain Research," in Maloney and Silverman, op. cit., pp. 19, 20.

[8]Michael L. Rothschild, "Advertising Strategies for High- and Low-Involvement Situations," in Maloney and Silverman, op. cit., p. 80.

[9]H.E. Krugman, "The Impact of Television Advertising: Learning Without Involvement," *Public Opinion Quarterly*, 29 (Fall 1965), pp. 349-56.

[10]R.B. Zajonc, "Feeling and Thinking: Preferences Need No Inferences," *American Psychologist*, 35:2 (1980), pp. 151-75.

[11]Gerald J. Gorn, "The Effects of Music in Advertising on Choice Behavior: A Classical Conditioning Approach," *Journal of Marketing*, 46 (Winter 1982), pp. 94-101.

[12]H.E. Krugman, "The Measurement of Advertising Involvement," *Public Opinion Quarterly*, 30 (Winter 1966), pp. 584-5.

[13]Marshall McLuhan, *The Medium is the Message* (New York: Random House, 1967).

[14]R.W. Sperry, "Lateral Specialization of Cerebral Function in the Surgically Separated Hemispheres," in F.J. McGuigan and R.A. Schoonover (eds.), *The Psychophysiology of Thinking* (New York: Academic Press, 1973), pp. 209-29.

[15]Fleming Hansen, "Hemispheral Lateralization: Implications for Understanding Consumer Behavior," *Journal of Consumer Research*, 8 (June 1981), p. 23.

[16]H.E. Krugman, "Sustained Viewing of Television," *Journal of Advertising Research*, 20 (June 1980), p. 65.

[17]S. Weinstein, V. Appel, and C. Weinstein, "Brain-Activity Responses to Magazine and Television Advertising," *Journal of Advertising Research*, 20 (June 1980), pp. 57-63; J.R. Rossiter, "Brain Hemisphere Activity," *Journal of Advertising Research*, 20 (October 1980), pp. 75-6.

[18]Gerald J. Gorn, op. cit., p. 100.

[19]Tyzoon T. Tyebjee, "Refinement of the Involvement Concept: An Advertising Planning Point of View," in Maloney and Silverman, op. cit., p. 108.

[20]Michael L. Rothschild, op. cit., pp. 74-93.

[21]Ibid.

[22]Ibid.

PAUL FINNEY TAKES UP TENNIS*

Over the last few years, Paul Finney had been so busy with his studies that he had had little free time and had done almost nothing in the way of sports activities. However, in his new job teaching Economics at Fanshawe College of Applied Arts and Technology, he was determined to resume active participation in sports.

In the fall and winter he took up badminton. Quite a few of the faculty at Fanshawe played badminton at noon in the gym and he was always able to find a partner for a game. Around February, Paul began to think about the coming summer months. He suspected that most of his associates at the College gave up badminton over the summer in favor of outdoor activities. Most of them seemed to be looking forward to playing either golf or tennis.

Paul had played golf before but not regularly. Four years ago, he and several classmates had taken summer jobs in Ottawa. Using borrowed or rented clubs, they had probably played about a dozen times at the Chaudiere Club in nearby Hull. Both his parents were avid golfers and had encouraged him to take up the game so frequently and forcefully that Paul sometimes wondered if he hadn't rebelled against the whole idea.

Paul had never played tennis, but he had watched Davis Cup matches on television. There were several courts right on the campus and quite a few of his associates at the College seemed to be tennis players. Given his experience with badminton, Paul began to think seriously about taking up tennis in the coming summer.

One day in March, he received a sale catalogue from Eaton's mail-order department. He enjoyed browsing through mail-order catalogues — particularly those advertising a sale — even if he had no specific purchase in mind. Just a couple of pages from the back, he

---

Adapted from Blair Little, John R. Kennedy, Donald H. Thain, and Robert E.M. Nourse, *Canadian Problems in Marketing*, 4th ed., pp. 8-15. Adapted with permission of the University of Western Ontario.

noticed a tennis racquet. It seemed to be a pretty good bargain — a Dunlop, regularly $17.94, on sale for $10.95. He decided to keep it in mind.

A few weeks later, while visiting the home of a fellow teacher, Dave Babcock, who was an active tennis player, Paul sought Dave's opinion about what kind of racquet he should get. "I saw one on sale the other day in the Eaton's catalogue," he said, "but I haven't any basis for evaluating whether the thing's any good or not. Have you any suggestion as to what I should be looking for in a racquet?"

"It's really been some time since I bought a racquet," Dave replied. "I don't really know what to tell you. The man you'd be best to ask is Bill Englander in the Math Department. He's played a lot of tennis and is very good."

Arriving early for a faculty meeting the next day, Paul noticed Bill Englander. He had met Bill before and had spoken with him on numerous occasions so it wasn't difficult to broach the tennis racquet question.

Bill was not too keen on Dunlop racquets, except for their Max-Ply, which, he felt, was a first-class racquet. He doubted that the one Paul had seen advertised in the Eaton catalogue was a Max-Ply because "they run somewhat more expensive than $17.95 and aren't the kind of racquet that's likely to go on sale."

"A lot of people I know use Slazengers," Bill observed, "but I personally don't like them too well." He proceeded to explain why, but Paul's thoughts began to wander. While Paul sensed a definite tone of authority and expertise in Bill's remarks, he wasn't sure if Bill wasn't thinking more in reference to himself than to a beginner, as Paul was. There was little doubt that the fellow could be trusted to recommend a good racquet — the only problem was that it might be *too* good.

As if he could read Paul's thoughts, Bill continued, "But my choice for somebody starting would be a Spalding. After they started making their racquets in Belgium two years ago, they really lowered their prices." When Paul asked what would be a reasonable price to pay for it, Bill's answer was, "Well, I would think that somewhere between $12 and $15 would buy you a decent racquet. Of course, you'd also have to pay to have it strung. That would cost anywhere from $5 to $15, depending on what kind of stringing you get."

Since Paul knew nothing about having a racquet strung he asked Bill for his advice and, after some discussion about the merits of different kinds of stringing, Bill thought Paul should probably get braided nylon.

When he got home that night, Paul checked the Eaton's sale catalogue again. Bill was right — the advertised racquet was not a Max-Ply.

In the next three or four weeks, Paul made no further move to buy a tennis racquet, but he did think about it a lot. He mentioned his plan to take up tennis to Bob Foulkes, a frequent badminton partner, and that he was in the market for a racquet. At this time, too, the Davis Cup matches between Canada and Mexico were being played and Paul followed the reports in the newspapers closely.

In a casual conversation with a neighbor, Tom Norton, Paul discovered that Tom was also a tennis player and that he had bought a new Dunlop Max-Ply the previous summer. Tom offered to sell Paul his old racquet (which was not a Max-Ply) at a good price but Paul did not take him up on it. Paul frequently met Bill Englander at the College and Bill never failed to ask if Paul had bought a racquet yet. Each time Paul would explain that he hadn't yet but that he definitely would be.

Soon after, Paul decided to visit Tom Munro Sports on his way to work. Of the two sporting goods stores in the city, Munro's seemed to be the one that most of Paul's friends talked about patronizing. As he was walking toward the tennis section, Paul was approached by a youthful-looking sales clerk. Paul indicated his interest in a tennis racquet and specified the Spalding, whereupon the clerk explained that they did not carry Spaldings any longer. He said that he was surprised that Paul had asked specifically for a Spalding (he, in fact, asked if Paul was new to the city) because he didn't recall ever having anyone ask him for a Spalding before. They just weren't that popular with tennis players in the area. He went on to recommend a Dunlop Max-Ply, which, he said, "all the good tennis players (in the city) use . . . It's truly an excellent racquet." The price was $26.95. Paul said he would think about it for a while. He purchased a pair of white shorts and left.

About a week later Paul visited College Sports, the other main sporting goods store. He noticed that they carried Slazenger, Wilson, and Dunlop but no Spaldings. Without examining any of the racquets, he left the store.

A few weeks later while in the Simpson's department store, Paul decided to walk by their sporting goods department. He was surprised at the number of racquets on display but all of a single brand, Jelinek, ranging in price from $3.95 to $10.95. He also noticed the Jelinek brand was made in Japan.

As he moved to the other side of the display, Paul found some more racquets — most of them Spaldings and a few Max-Ply Dunlops. All were prestrung, except for the Max-Ply. Of the four Spalding racquets on display, three were strung with twisted nylon and the fourth was a Fred Stolle model, strung with braided nylon. A clerk standing nearby could not explain the difference between twisted nylon and braided nylon. When the clerk remarked that he didn't know very much about tennis racquets, Paul replied, "That's all right. I'm pretty sure this is what I'm looking for anyhow," handing the clerk the Fred Stolle racquet. Paul had decided to purchase the Fred Stolle Spalding with braided nylon strings.

He also thought he would get a cover for his racquet. No one had specifically suggested that, but he recalled having seen players walking to and from tennis courts at various times in the past. Most of them had a wooden press or cloth protecting the racquet when it was not in use. Paul ended up buying a cheap nylon cover with nothing written on it.

He played his first game a few days later with Jack Bailey, a fellow faculty member. He noticed that Jack also had a Spalding racquet, although not a Fred Stolle model. Paul found that during the weeks that followed he came to think and talk about tennis quite a bit. For example, he told John Lowery, another teacher, of his experience at Munro Sports, and described to a former classmate how carefully he'd considered the matter of a tennis racquet purchase.

Paul also told his neighbour, Tom Norton, about the difficulty he had encountered in finding a Spalding racquet. Tom replied that he wished he had known that, because Sayvette, a local discount house, carried them. Paul didn't say anything but the next time he was near Sayvette he checked the tennis racquets. He noted the two models they carried were cheaper racquets priced at $3.95 and $5.95.

Paul showed his racquet to Bob Foulkes, his most frequent badminton partner, who noticing that it was a Spalding asked if his badminton racquet was also a Spalding. Paul didn't really know. "I don't remember ever looking to see who the manufacturer was. I've had the racquet for about six years now." Later that day he checked at home. The model name was "Varsity," not "Viceroy" as he had thought, and the manufacturer was Spalding.

QUESTIONS

1. Analyze the role of reference group influence in Paul Finney's decision to buy a tennis racquet. Indicate the relevant concepts involved.

2. What other significant purchase-decision phenomena can you identify?

3. What would you say were the principal evaluative criteria in Paul's choice of a tennis racquet?

PART

III

Internal
Influences

This section deals with the internal influences that affect the behavior of the consumer. Behavior begins with a stimulus that the individual takes in and interprets and then responds to. It seems reasonable to begin with the element that triggers the whole behavioral response. Subsequent chapters in this section deal with learning, motivation, attitudes, and personality.

It bears repeating that, as emphasized in Chapter 1, all of these elements interact with each other and each has an influence on the others.

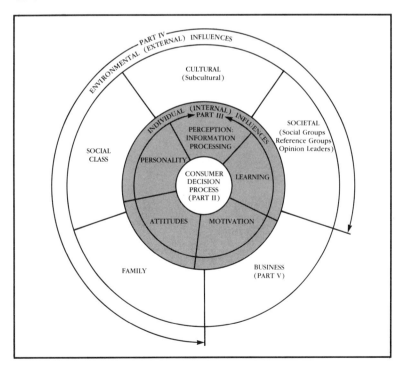

CHAPTER

5

Perception

EXAMPLES

1. Brand Image

In Ontario there are well over thirty brands of beer available, covering both ale and lager. According to objective laboratory tests, these brands vary quite considerably in heaviness or "body." If they were placed on a continuum ranging from light (not much body) to heavy (lots of body), they would, theoretically, be distributed over the entire range, as illustrated below:*

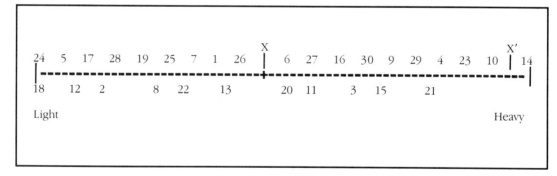

A few years ago, one of the brewing companies conducted a "brand image" study to determine how consumers (in this case, target beer drinkers) perceived one of their brands (which we shall call X). They knew from laboratory tests that this brand fell just about mid-way on the light-heavy continuuim (see diagram above). There had been a deliberate decision to manufacture this brand as a "medium" brand. However, to their surprise, the study revealed that among most people who didn't drink the brand, it was rated as "heavy" (X' above), indeed among the heaviest available.

---

*The numbers range from 1 to 30 and represent thirty theoretically different brands.

Even though this brand was *in fact* a "medium" brand, for some reason those beer drinkers tended to regard it as very heavy. Further studies were carried out to ascertain the cause of this perception (and many were discovered) and appropriate corrective action was taken. For example, it was found that the solid background color of the label was partly responsible for that perception.

The significant point here is that how consumers perceived the brand was considerably at variance with how it actually was. And, of course, consumers' attitudes to the brand were based on their perceptions. In other words, consumer attitudes and behavior were based not on the objective reality (i.e., the laboratory specifications of the brand) but on the perceived reality. Marketers should always keep this in mind and never assume that consumers perceive a product in the same way as they — the marketers — know it to be.

In this case some of the causes of this perception were identifiable and changes were made in the label and in advertising to reduce, as later studies demonstrated, the discrepancy between the perceptions and reality. A cardinal rule for the marketer is to keep the discrepancy between the perceived reality and the objective reality as small as possible or, ideally, non-existent. There is no greater ideal for the marketer than to hope that the consumer will perceive a brand exactly as it is, assuming of course that the product's quality is very high.

The observation may be made that the company could have pursued its course and continued to sell its brand to those who were already buying it, some because they perceived it as a medium brand and others because they considered it a heavy brand. But if this user group were relatively small and if the non-buyers with the "heavy" brand image were a significantly larger group, the company would be well advised to attempt to modify that image in line with both what they knew that target wanted and what they knew their brand to be. This way, they could expand their market if they were confident (on the basis of research) that changes made would not turn off their current customers. In addition, those that drank it because of its "heavy image" would, as a result of the new image, not be lost to the company, since there was a good chance that many of them would turn to another of the company's brands in the upper reaches of the heaviness continuum. Thus this internecine rivalry would be reduced and the market potential for brand X enhanced.

2. Product Identification

A Canadian apple juice manufacturer was dissatisfied with its brand's growth in sales and market share, particularly in Ontario. He was puzzled because the brand obtained excellent results in blind product comparison tests against the leading brands; it was clear that the brand's low performance was attributable not to the product itself but to some other factor or factors. Based on the level of expenditures and on consumer response data, advertising was ruled out as a likely cause. It was decided to test the effectiveness of the package. Laboratory tests were conducted for color visibility, brand recognition, product name recognition, symbol identification, copy legibility, and identification of illustration.

All of the measures taken were satisfactory, except for illustration identification. It was found that very few consumers could identify correctly (on brief exposure) the apple illustration on the label. Its color, shape, and location on the label all seemed to cause consumers to perceive it as a *tomato*.

If this were true, consumers were probably mistaking the product for tomato juice as they quickly scanned the shelves on their way along the aisle. A redesigned label showing a more clearly identifiable apple yielded vastly improved performance on the test and was later responsible for an upward swing in the brand's performance in the marketplace.

Because the brand name was not well known in Ontario, the product illustration became an important element in correct product perception and identification. The perception of a tomato led to incorrect categorization of the package and the product.

3. Advertising

Sometimes it is difficult to tell, without research, how the consumer is likely to interpret a slogan or an advertising message. More precisely, it is difficult to tell whether the consumer will understand the message in the way the advertiser intends. Some years ago another Canadian beer company initiated a new advertising campaign using the slogan, "Big Ale in the Big Land." No doubt the advertiser had a specific message in mind, say, "The best quality ale in this big country of ours." But it is not hard to see that "Big Ale" may also have been perceived by various groups to mean "the strongest, heaviest ale," "the highest status brand," or "the brand with the largest share." The implications of these other interpretations are not all positive. For example, it may not be good, depending on your target market, for a brand of beer to be considered strong or heavy, and to be seen as "highest status" may be very positive but also very restricting.

Coincidentally, the interpretation of "Big Land" would depend greatly on the individual's subjective frame of reference. A consumer in Canada could conceivably have understood it to mean the United States, just as a consumer in Ohio might have taken "Big Land" to refer to the state of Texas.

Human perceptions are so strongly influenced by subjective frames of reference that it is important for the advertiser to ascertain in pretests exactly what a message means to the particular market involved and whether it is communicating what is intended. Most importantly, such pre-testing will also indicate how to enhance the clarity, unambiguity, and effectiveness of the message.

4. Packaging

Based on the observation that bags of corn chips, potato chips, pretzels, and similar polyvinyl food packages were extremely difficult to open, necessitating the use of scissors, and often resulting in the destruction or the tearing of the package and sometimes in spillage, two researchers decided to examine how this packaging attribute affected consumer perceptions of the total product.[1]

Two sets of potato chips were tested in wax-coated paper bags and in polyvinyl bags. The chips were from the same batch and there was no difference in freshness between those in the wax-coated bags and those in the polyvinyl bags. It was found that "93% of the respondents preferred the chips from the difficult-to-open packages (polyvinyl) over the easy-opening packages (wax-coated)." It was concluded that the difference was psychological: products packaged in polyvinyl bags were perceived to be of higher quality.

"Even though the polyvinyl bags create consumer frustration, this is more than offset by the enhancement of the product image. The tightly-sealed package is perceived as the mechanism for maintaining product quality."

5. Sensory Perception

Several studies have demonstrated the inaccuracy of sensory discrimination among consumers, particularly where the products are quite similar. Despite the claims of clear product or brand differences by marketers, there are numerous instances of the consumer's inability to distinguish among brands on the basis of sensory perception in the absence of any identification. Studies done as early as the 1930s and 1940s showed an inability to discriminate among unidentified brands of cigarettes[2] or brands of cola beverages[3] or beer.[4]

Another illustration of this phenomenon was an ice-cream study in which it was found that, when given a cream-colored sample and a white sample of ice cream, consumers preferred the cream-colored product for its taste, even though it contained less butterfat and was therefore less rich in taste. Consumers were obviously reacting to the color and did not know it.

It should be recognized, of course, that some of the problems with sensory discrimination may be caused by the relative similarity of certain products. Where the brands are quite homogeneous, as with cola beverages, cigarettes, or beer, the problems may be understandable. Where brands are somewhat more divergent, as, for example, menthol versus regular cigarettes or ale versus lager beer,[5] our taste sense may be more reliable.

It is worth remembering that of all our senses taste is by far the least sensitive. The physiological psychologist Weber found many years ago that vision is capable of noticing a change of 1/62 in the strength of a stimulus while the sense of taste requires a change of one-fifth.[6]

The above examples illustrate some of the ways in which perception operates with regard to different kinds of marketing stimuli. It is clear that many factors come between the objective stimulus and how it is perceived.

This chapter starts by defining perception, goes on to review the process itself and the factors that influence it, and then discusses its principal manifestations in marketing.

DEFINITION

Perception has to do with how the individual takes in the world, and the interpretation or the meaning he or she gives to sensual *input* (vision, hearing, smell, taste, touch, balance, muscular tension). By "input" I mean "information," in the sense in which Howard uses the term:

> External events with which the consumer's sense organs have come into contact. Descriptively, they are typically symbols that represent the brand; they may be linguistic (spoken word), orthographic (printed word), or pictorial (picture or cartoon). They may also be the physical brand itself. Analytically, they have content and form characteristics: "content" refers to the elements that convey the nature of the concept, and "form" refers to the manner in which the concept is conveyed.[7]

Perception, therefore, is much more than the sensation of the "external events" impinging upon the senses. *It's what the individual makes of them*. The process by which the individual arrives at these interpretations is more popularly known today as **information processing**. Because of their different psychological make-ups, individuals perceive the same input differently. The sensation (or physical stimulation) of the object "Rolls Royce" comes, with learning, to acquire additional meanings of prestige, status, and wealth. Perception thus can be said to be, for the individual, a combination of the physical and the socio-psychological. As Berelson and Steiner put it, perception is the process "by which people select, organize, and interpret sensory stimulation into a meaningful and coherent picture of the world."[8]

This is why, for example, the brand of beer, the potato chips, and the ice cream were perceived in ways not entirely consistent with their known attributes. Consumers added to them meanings and associations from other cues without being aware of the influence of those cues. A **cue** may be defined as a part or aspect of a larger stimulus that possesses a particular association or meaning (e.g., the cream color of the ice cream in our example).

The advantages to the marketer of employing such cues in communications with the market are evident. Knowledge of their significance will dictate making good use of them, if they have positive associations, and avoiding them, if negative.

INFORMATION PROCESSING

Information processing has been defined as "the means by which a sensory input is transformed, reduced, elaborated, stored, recovered, and used by a consumer."[9] It consists of five stages:

- exposure;
- attention;
- comprehension;
- yielding/acceptance; and
- retention.

Selectivity occurs throughout information processing so that at each stage a selection-reduction operation is at play. Also, as explained in Chapters 3 and 4, processing differs in accordance with the degree of involvement with the decision. Figure 5.1 illustrates the differences in processing in high- and low-involvement purchases.

Under high-involvement conditions, the consumer engages in deliberate search and processing, including information evaluation (yielding/acceptance) that could result in message retention. With low involvement, there is

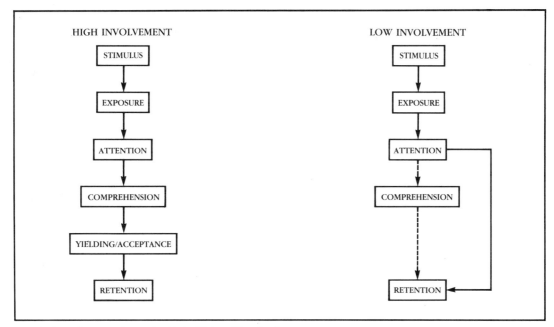

FIGURE 5.1: Information Processing Under High and Low Involvement

little or no search for information. Exposure and attention are involuntary or passive[10] so that whatever is retained could be a general awareness of pictorial, imaginal elements for which no comprehension necessarily takes place. Yielding/acceptance is generally absent.

Let us examine these stages in some detail.

Exposure

Exposure means the opportunity for a stimulus to activate an individual's senses. Mainly because of physiological limitations (that is, the human nervous system cannot handle an unlimited amount of information), the perceiving organism will not necessarily be exposed to all the stimuli sent its way. In that sense, in the first stage of information-processing there is selective exposure. Of course, physical proximity also plays its part. That is, if a message is placed where the target audience is known to be, then at least there is likely to be audience exposure to it. This notion underlies the careful planning that goes into the marketer's choice of media, program, and time, in order to optimize the chances of getting exposure of the message to the target audience.

Attention

Attention is that stage of the process at which certain stimuli, from among those to which there was selective exposure, engage the individual and begin to be differentiated and categorized in the course of being identified. Note then that here too there is **selectivity.** Individuals attend to only a few of the stimuli to which they are exposed.

Comprehension

By differentiating an incoming stimulus and then categorizing it, the individual gives the stimulus meaning, on the basis of past experience. Thus a marketing stimulus (product, advertising, package) should permit the consumer to make a ready identification of the use to which it is to be put. The greater the extent to which the marketer can bring about the proper **categorization** of the product, the greater will be its differentiation from other products.

FIGURE 5.2a: An Example of Product Categorization (Differentiation)

Advertisement prepared by Grey Advertising, Inc. for Swift & Company, a subsidiary of Esmark, Inc.

For example, in Figure 5.2a it would be important for the advertiser to ensure that Sizzlean is categorized as a bacon-type product and that how it is different from bacon is clearly communicated. In Figure 5.2b the objective is generalization in order to have Sani-Drain perceived in the same category as Drano.

A fabric softener, Starch-Eze, introduced by the Monsanto Chemical Company, was a failure because of incorrect perceptual categorization. Because of its name, the product was perceived as an inexpensive, easy-to-use starch, when in fact it had quite different properties. It had to be applied every ten or twelve washings (not every washing, as with traditional starch), it was quite expensive, had to be diluted, and it was more than a fabric stiffener (it protected the fibers). This improper categorization led to considerable consumer confusion and dissatisfaction.[11]

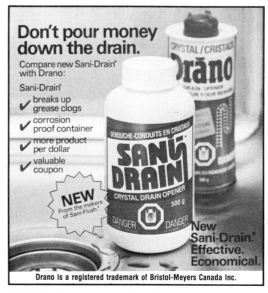

FIGURE 5.2b: An Example of Categorization through Generalization

Courtesy Boyle-Midway Canada Ltd./Ltée

The meaning that the individual derives from the stimulus is strongly dependent on the perceiver's needs, motivations, values, attitudes, and is also subject to selectivity (**selective comprehension**).[12]

There may also be **selective distortion** because the objective stimulus may be quite different from how it is perceived. The examples at the beginning of the chapter illustrate this well. Consumers are unable to distinguish among brands of beer or cola beverages or cigarettes in the absence of brand identification. They rely strongly on communication from the marketer and interpret it in accordance with their own preferences. Consumers, in other words, will distort information, unconsciously, in order to keep it more consistent with, and therefore less threatening to, their attitudes and values. Heavy cigarette smokers are likely to distort messages from the Canadian Cancer Society to minimize or cast doubt on claims about the harmful effects of smoking.[13]

A recent study suggests that advertising miscomprehension (and that of other material as well) is extremely high. It found that "only 16.8% 'fully comprehended' (i.e., were able to answer correctly all six quiz items for) either the first or second commercial that they viewed."[14] The study reported that only 3.5% of subjects fully comprehended the two communications to which they were exposed; that "the percentage of viewers miscomprehending at least some portion of the communications that they viewed was 84.5% for program excerpts, 81.3% for commercial advertisements, and 82.7% for non-commercial ads;" that every test communication was miscomprehended to some degree; and that, on the average, approximately 30% of the relevant informational content in the 60 communications tested was miscomprehended.[15]

The authors themselves acknowledged a number of limitations but a few fundamental criticisms seriously call their findings into question. For example, Ford and Yalch have pointed out the lack of consideration of the appropriate target audiences.[16] Persons were used for whom some messages may have had little relevance or interest, thus pushing the miscomprehension rates upward. Furthermore, miscomprehension rates should be based on typical levels of exposure, not forced, single exposure. Finally, "it is not clear whether the construct being measured is recall or comprehension." This is important because, in essence, the test should not measure comprehension of what is not recalled. Ford and Yalch also take issue with the design, content, and level of difficulty of the quiz statements.

One of Jacoby and Hoyer's objectives was "to determine whether there is a 'normative range' of miscomprehension associated with television communications." The researchers' claim that their data allowed them to make the estimate that "anywhere from one-fourth to one-third of the material information content of communications" is miscomprehended has been described as "not only simplistic but misleading as well."[17] Mizerski questions the measure of comprehension (recall) used and suggests that

different measures need to be used because "the level of comprehension is defined by the measure used."

Whether the findings are valid or not, there is no denying the significance of selective comprehension. Jacoby and Hoyer observe:

> language is an imprecise means of communicating; . . . every human being brings a unique set of values and expectations to the situation in terms of these subjective factors; . . . the limitations imposed by televised communications [which] are essentially instances of one-way communication; . . ., [and] the various processes involved in comprehending and storing information usually require a span of time (e.g., five to eight seconds) for each new item of information. Thus the rate at which information is conveyed in televised communication may be such that it is too fast for the individual to comprehend *all* of what is going on, at least for messages of more than a few seconds' duration.[18]

Yielding/Acceptance

This involves the reaction of the individual to the message. The message may lead to the strengthening of existing beliefs and attitudes, or their modification. The message can also have no effect on current cognitions. The responses of the individual assessing the message will determine the kind of impact the message has. If little time is devoted to it, it is not likely to move to the next stage of retention; if, on the other hand, much time is spent in **rehearsing** the message, it is more likely to have an impact on the individual's cognitive structure.

Wright identifies three types of responses as being the primary mediators of message acceptance:[19]

- Counterarguments, which tend to neutralize or counter message evidence;
- source derogation, where the source of the message is viewed negatively (e.g., as biased);
- support arguments, which indicate agree-

ment with the message. This type of response leads to message acceptance.

Yielding/acceptance can be measured by:

- determining attitude change after exposure to the message. We shall have more to say about this when we discuss attitudes; and
- thought sampling after exposure, wherein verbal reports on mental events are obtained from subjects upon exposure to a stimulus. The notion of "sampling" recognizes the possibility that "all such verbalizations are partially incomplete because basic mental processes to which a subject has no access cannot be verbalized" as well as the influence of editing, memory loss, and distortion.[20]

Retention

The final stage in information processing that marks a successful message is when it is stored in memory for later recall. It has reached the level of retention. Here again, not all the stimuli comprehended by the individual will be placed in "long-term memory" — some will be dropped and some retained, through a process of **selective retention**. Howard summarizes the factors that affect such retention:

Although **meaningfulness** is the most important characteristic of content affecting the ease of transfer to long-term memory, it is not the only characteristic. Other nonlinguistic factors are **familiarity** and **similarity**. If the content is familiar, it is more likely to be transferred and stored. If elements of the stimulus are similar to what was previously retained, it is also more likely to be stored.

Another characteristic of a message ... is **relevance** ... Relevance refers to the degree to which information relates to a concept the buyer values highly. Specifically, it is information that will serve a buyer's motives in making a choice.[21]

We have seen how the individual consumer processes information, from exposure to retention, how processing varies with the level of involvement, and how at all stages there is con-

tinuous selectivity. Now, I will examine the factors that affect the process.

FACTORS AFFECTING PERCEPTION

The factors affecting perception are many and complex. There is a great deal to be learned about the exact ways in which they exert their influence and how they interact with each other. I will try to show how these factors are related to the different stages of information processing just discussed.

Basically, there are two types of factors: characteristics of the stimulus and characteristics of the perceiver.

Stimulus Characteristics
Physical Attributes

An individual's perceptual response to a stimulus is affected by such characteristics as its size, color, position, intensity, contrast, novelty, and movement. All of these tend mostly to give attention-getting value to the stimulus.

The larger the stimulus, the greater is its ability to capture attention. This is true of a display in a supermarket or a package or a print ad. Unfortunately, apart from this common-sense relationship, not much is known about the ratio of change of response to a change in stimulus size. For example, whether doubling the size of an ad will double its attention value is a moot point.

Starch, in studies of print ads, concluded that, while the number of readers increases as the size of the ad increases, doubling the size does not necessarily double the number of readers. He found, for example, that the contribution of ad size to readership decreased in the order of double page, single page, horizontal half-page, and vertical half-page.[22]

In 1962, Ulin conducted an interesting study of the effectiveness of similar ads in magazines of different size and concluded:

While there may be exceptions, under normal circumstances, magazine page size does not appear to influence advertising effectiveness. All other things being equal, a page in a magazine of one size appears to have about the same degree of effectiveness as a page in a magazine of another size, within the range included in the study.[23]

The effectiveness of an ad is related not so much to its actual size *per se* but more to its relative size in the context in which it appears. Color in a black-and-white context will certainly produce more attention than in a multi-colored context (see Plate I in the color-plate section). The effectiveness of color in capturing attention is dependent upon where it is used. It will also be more effective when it enhances the realism and the appeal of a communication such as the use of colors in advertising fruits and vegetables or meat.

We also know that different colors have symbolic meanings so that a specific color *per se* will have certain connotations. As an example, blue is generally used with detergents or red with hot sauces. Color can increase attention value, depending upon the context, and it also can affect our total perception; that is, our comprehension and retention. Example 1 illustrated this very well. The color of the beer label contributed significantly to its perception as a heavy brand. I will discuss the symbolism surrounding colors in Chapter 7.

The placing of a stimulus will determine whether or not, in the first place, there will be exposure. An ad or a commercial placed in the wrong medium or at the wrong time of day or in a context of considerable commercial clutter will fail to achieve adequate attention.

A women's department store, seeking to upgrade its image and to communicate the quality of its merchandise, thought it natural to advertise in the city newspaper that was regarded as reaching the upper half of the socio-economic scale. The problem was that the particular women it was trying to reach did not read that newspaper.

Certain positions in newspapers and magazines are more likely to get exposure and attention. Myers and Reynolds claimed that "the upper half of a printed page produces more attention than the lower half, and the left-hand side more than the right-hand side," except for cultural variations.[24] However, other evidence suggests that there is no difference between right-hand or left-hand pages.[25]

In newspapers the last page or the last page of a section is a preferred position, just as the inside of the front cover or the inside and back of the back cover of magazines are highly desirable locations for advertisements. Note, for example, the advertisers that dominate these positions in *Time* Magazine. Such positions are, of course, also more expensive than inside locations.

In television, the reach of a program considered appropriate to the target market will markedly affect the cost of advertising time. The "Johnny Carson Show" can command $25,000 for a minute of commercial time and the Olympics can demand $80,000 per minute or even more.

The **intensity** of a stimulus refers to the strength of its physical impact: the loudness of sound, the brightness of color, or the sharpness of taste. The greater the intensity, the greater the attention value of the stimulus. Intensity derives its major impact from its **contrast** effect with antecedent or surrounding conditions. The sudden increase in volume of a TV commercial late at night or the dark red figure on a light-colored background will ensure attention. This "differential intensity" can be quite effective:

A cannon shot on a quiet street or sudden silence in the midst of a din gets attention whether or not anyone expects it or wants to hear it. Thus contrast, as illustrated by THIS word is one of the most attention-compelling attributes of a stimulus.[26]

Related to contrast are two other characteristics of stimuli — **novelty** and **isolation**. The new package or the new poster on a billboard (novelty), or the black dot in the middle of a blank page (isolation), attract the eye more quickly.

Movement, or apparent movement, tends to increase the attention value of a stimulus. Rotating signs, neon lights, or alternating billboard advertisements are good examples. "Apparent movement" is the perception of movement when no movement actually occurs. This is known as the **phi phenomenon**. For example, two lights at the right distance from each other and "turned on and off at the appropriate rate are seen as one light moving back and forth between these points . . . Note that phi is not due to movement of the eye — it can occur simultaneously in many directions, as in a motion picture."[27]

It is interesting that certain designs and shapes such as a jagged line or a wavy line or a streamlined jet aircraft can evoke an experience of movement.

The story is told of an advertising agency that produced for its Canadian airline account an advertisement showing the tail-end of one of its client's aircraft, the purpose being to reinforce company identification. Unfortunately the tail-section was drawn in such a way that, in a pre-test, consumers said that the plane seemed to be "going down" — a notion to be avoided at all costs, by an airline! Needless to say, the advertisement was changed appropriately.

What is noteworthy is that a slight downward slope suggested by the angle of the tail-section was enough to generate a perception of movement that was, in this case, highly undesirable. This is probably why you will never find an airline advertisement with a picture of a plane sloping downward.

Stimulus Configuration or Organization

Apart from the individual, physical attributes discussed above, it has also been shown that the human perceptual mechanism tends to respond to the whole stimulus, to the interrelationships among its parts, and to the organization or configuration of its parts. This notion was first introduced by Gestalt psychologists (*gestalt* is German for shape), who emphasized that the whole is greater than the sum of its parts, and possesses a quality (that is, a "gestalt") all its own.

> For example, take the notes of the musical scale: arrange them in one order and rhythm and you have one tune; give them another order and you have another tune . . . When you recognize a tune, it is not the notes that you recognize but the tune itself. . . . The tune has a quality of its own, a form quality.[28]

Gestalt theorists have provided us with a number of dynamic principles that are useful to marketers. Deriving from the basic idea of the importance of the overall impression that results from the many component elements are several configurational effects or "principles of organization."[29]

In any image, some elements are the main objects of focus (figure) and the rest are background (ground), so that the image resolves itself as a figure on a ground. "The figure appears well defined, at a definite location, solid and in front of the ground. In contrast, the ground appears amorphous, indefinite, and continuous behind the figure. The common contour of figure and ground appears to belong to the figure rather than to the ground."[30]

The possibility of ambiguity (or reversal of figure and ground) must be recognized, because it must be carefully avoided by marketers. (See Figure 5.3). Some stimuli are inherently ambiguous[31] but, frequently, the perception of what is figure and what is ground can be learned and may depend on the individual's physical or psychological state.[32]

Advertisers have to make sure that what they intend to be the figure is unqualifiedly the focus of the advertisement. For example, the musical background of a commercial should not detract from the central message. It should rather be as unobtrusive as possible, serving to support and enhance the central element. Or, with some commercials in which sexy-looking females are shown "decorating" the product (car, boat, lathe), the ground (in this case the female) may cap-

The Peter-Paul goblet

What do you see, the goblet or the famous twins? Which-ever you see, try to find the other. Then, when you have found the other, try to turn the perception back to what it was at first.

A reversible cross

Keep your eyes fixed near the center of the figure, and note whether you see an × or a +. Maintain your fixation and see how long the cross at which you are looking lasts.

FIGURE 5.3: Reversible Figure-Ground Patterns

SOURCE: Edwin B. Newman, "Perception," in Edwin G. Boring, Berbert S. Langfeld, and Harry P. Weld (eds).), *Foundations of Psychology* (New York: John Wiley & Sons, 1948), pp. 215-49

ture attention to such an extent that the message of the ad (the figure) may have only a slight impact on the consumer.

In a sense, the way in which a company is thought of by consumers (corporate image) can function as the ground against which messages or products (figure) are evaluated. It is obvious that a company should, through public relations, advertising, and community activities, create the kind of corporate image that enhances the acceptability of its messages and products, in terms of such elements as credibility, quality, and reliability.

Generally speaking, familiar objects (e.g., preferred brand, familiar face) or objects that are physically near or of similar size and type tend to be perceived as the figure.

Closure refers to the tendency of the human organism to perceive a complete picture by filling in the missing elements in an incomplete stimulus. For example, in Figure 5.4, an individual will see a complete star by overlooking the gaps. Apparently such irregularities create **tension**, which the organism must remove.

The tendency to close a gap is regarded as revealing a fundamental principle of brain dynamics, a tend-ency of the brain activity to bridge a gap, like the tendency of an electric current to jump a small gap in the circuit... With the gap present there is a state of unbalanced tensions, but closure brings equilibrium. The sensory brain activity tends toward equilibrium or minimum tension.[33]

FIGURE 5.4: Closure

SOURCE: Robert S. Woodworth, *Contemporary Schools of Psychology* (New York: Ronald Press, 1948), p. 125.

Closure has been used in many interesting ways in advertising — letters left out of names, brand names written with incomplete letters, slogans or jingles with parts left out, and signs on billboards slowly evolving as parts are added over a period of several weeks.

Because of closure the drawing in Figure 5.5 is seen as a dog, and not twenty discrete blotches.

FIGURE 5.5: Closure

SOURCE: Roy F. Street, *A Gestalt Completion Test: A Study of a Cross Section of Intellect* (New York: Teachers College Press, Columbia University, 1931), p. 41.

Figure 5.6 presents an interesting example of another kind of closure. In the top half of the figure the seven lines fall naturally into three pairs and one isolate, by virtue of their proximity relations. However, when short horizontal lines are inserted as shown in the lower half of the figure, the same lines are seen through closure as three squares, overriding the influence of proximity.

Advertisers often use questions in headlines, leaving the reader to formulate the obvious answer or to seek the answer that is buried in the copy.

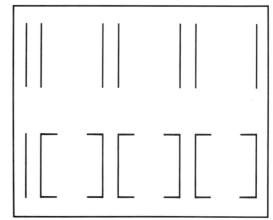

FIGURE 5.6: Closure Overcomes Proximity

SOURCE: David Krech and Richard S. Crutchfield, *Elements of Psychology* (New York: Knopf, 1958), p. 93.

Perhaps the best-known example of closure is the old jingle used by Salem cigarettes. In the beginning the commercial presents the full jingle, "You can take Salem out of the country but you can't take the country out of Salem," and as the end is reached the viewer hears only "You can take Salem out of the country, but . . . " and cannot help at least mentally completing it.

Another classic example was the Clairol ad that asked the question, "Does she . . . or doesn't she?" The ad shown in Figure 5.7 makes use of the principle of closure. It expects the consumer to complete the headline copy, "Me and the boys and our . . . " with " . . . 50. Me and the boys and our beer." What is even more interesting is that it expects this to be done, not from prior information in the ad but from learning resulting from earlier exposures to radio and television advertising.

Such incomplete stimuli have several advantages:
- they attract attention;
- they create tension and, until it is eliminated or reduced, they increase involvement; and
- because of the tension and involvement, and the tension reduction that follows closure, they end up being better remembered.

FIGURE 5.7: An Example of Closure in Advertising

Courtesy Labatt Brewing Company Limited

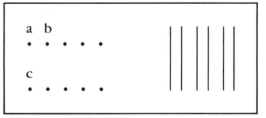

FIGURE 5.8: Proximity

SOURCE: David Krech, Richard S. Crutchfield, and Egerton A. Ball-achey, *Individual in Society* (New York: McGraw-Hill, 1962), p. 25.

FIGURE 5.9: Similarity

SOURCE: Michael Wertheimer, "Principles of Perceptual Organiza-tion." in David C. Beardsley and Michael Wertheimer (eds.), *Readings in Perception* (New York: Van Nostrand, 1958), pp. 128-9.

Closure would appear to be a useful device for marketers to use in their promotion but there are some risks. The missing elements or solution may not always be evident to all consumers, so that the result may be frustration among those who fail to make closure or a false perception among those who fill in the wrong "solution." Closure is a device, therefore, that ought to be used with care.

Individuals tend to *group* elements into wholes on the basis of *proximity* and *similarity*. In other words, things that are closer to each other or that are more like each other tend to be perceived as going together.

In Figure 5.8, dot a is perceived as belonging with b rather than with c because a is closer to b.

In Figure 5.9, the elements are perceived, on the basis of their similarity, as forming horizontal rather than vertical series.

Even though the @'s and the *'s are closer together, we tend to perceive horizontal lines of @'s and *'s rather than columns of @'s and *'s. Horizontal similarity tends to overcome greater vertical proximity.

This phenomenon of grouping applies not only to spatial proximity. *Proximity in time* works in much the same way. The birth of a two-headed calf occurring at the same time as a calamitous flood can be organized together as an indicator of the work of the Devil.[34] Marketers should seek to avoid negative groupings while taking advantage of positive ones. A brand displayed with inferior brands is likely to be grouped with the inferior majority in the minds of consumers. On the other hand, showing a brand in proximity to highly desirable or appealing figures or events will enhance the positiveness of its image.

Examples of advertising that has made use of such grouping are: Coca-Cola and beach par-

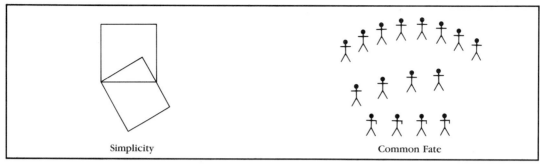

Simplicity   Common Fate

FIGURE 5.10: Simplicity and Common Fate Principles of Organization
Adapted from Philip G. Limbardo, *Psychology and Life*, 10th ed. (Glenview, Illinois: Scott, Foresman, and Company, 1979), p. 355.

ties, and Molson Golden and poolside parties.

From among a number of stimulus patterns, an individual will perceive the *simplest* or the *best*. "Best" is defined in terms of similarity, continuity, proximity closure, and symmetry.[35]

In Figure 5.10 the best form perception appears to be two overlapping squares instead of a triangle and two irregular forms, equally possible from the sensory input.

Common fate is the case where elements that move in the same direction are seen as a unit.

The principle of **simplicity** would suggest to the marketer that in advertising and packaging, the most successful designs or graphic patterns are the simple ones, in the sense of communicating a coherent, unified message that will be retained.

Beyond their physical attributes and their configurational properties, stimuli come to acquire certain associations of social and psychological significance. Objects become symbols.

A symbol is a general term for all instances where experience is mediated rather than direct; where an object, action, work, picture or complex behavior is understood to mean not only itself but also some other ideas or feelings.[36]

These meanings derive from the individual's experiences with the object so that, in the course of his or her psychological development, the individual learns to associate connotations of personal, social, or cultural significance with different aspects of the stimulus.

The color or shape or sound, for example, will come to be interpreted in specific ways. Because these meanings can be said to be not strictly personal (or individual) but characteristic of groups, they can be important to the marketer in communicating with the target.

I will deal in detail with symbolism in marketing in the next chapter.

Characteristics of the Perceiver

The mere volume of incoming stimuli necessitates a selective process that will make the sensory input manageable. This selection results basically from two characteristics of the perceiver: physiological limitations and psychological make-up.

Physiological Limitations

Human perception is marked by certain limits regarding the kinds of stimuli that a person is capable of perceiving. Even within these limits there are individual differences. Fortunately, humans have enough in common to permit group generalizations. The main characteristics that we regard as relevant to our purposes include sensory threshold, adaptation, differential threshold, and span of attention.

The **sensory threshold** is the lowest level of intensity at which an individual becomes aware of a stimulus. The term "absolute threshold" has been applied to this value but its validity has been questioned because of the technical difficulties in determining such a point. Instead, the threshold has become the average value over a large number of trials.

It should be noted too that the threshold varies among individuals and, even with the same individual, it depends upon the physical or psychological state. For example, "sensitivity, or the ability to detect stimuli, increases with disuse or rest. The longer in total darkness the more sensitive vision becomes ('sensory adaptation')."[37]

Sensory adaptation refers to changes in threshold that occur with use or disuse of the sense. Following heavy stimulation, the threshold will rise; a stimulus of greater intensity will be necessary than if the organism had been at rest.

This leads one to wonder about the effectiveness of individual commercials in the clutter that we experience nowadays on television.

Advertisers have sought to compensate for such adaptation by increasing the volume of their commercials (compared to the volume of the sound in the program) and even by changing advertising campaigns, slogans, and packages. In this way, consumers will not get so used to these stimuli that they will come to "see" less and less of them.

While the lower threshold is more relevant, the existence of an **upper threshold** should be recognized. For example, humans are incapable of hearing certain sound frequencies within the normal hearing range of dogs.

The phenomenon of subliminal perception (that is, the perception of and response to stimuli of intensities below the threshold level) has been of considerable controversy for many years. Ethical questions have arisen around the concern that if consumers can be subjected to stimuli and not be aware of them, they could be influenced to buy and act against their will.

I will review this problem in the next chapter. There are also limits to the differences in stimulus intensity that humans can detect. The minimum change necessary is called the **differential threshold** or the **just noticeable difference** (jnd). The jnd varies with

- the particular sense;
- the particular stimulus (advertisement, package, price);
- the product;
- the intensity of the stimulus before the change was made.

On the last point, German physiologist Ernst Weber formulated a relationship now known as **Weber's Law**.[38] He found the jnd was not an absolute amount but was proportional to the initial stimulus intensity; that, in any particular case, the jnd bore a constant relationship to the initial stimulus.

For example,

$$\frac{\text{change in price}}{\text{initial price}} = k \text{ (constant) or } \frac{\Delta I}{I} = k$$

Let us say that it has been found that for coffee $k = .05$. This means that a change in the price of coffee must be increased by 5% before the majority of consumers will notice it. If the initial price is $4.00 a pound, the change in price (jnd) that would be noticed would be

$$jnd = \$4.00 \times .05$$
$$= \$0.20$$

and the smallest increased price that could be noticed would be $4.20. If the original price were $1.00, the jnd new price would be $1.05, not $1.20.

Of course, for the marketer, the jnd in the case of a price increase would serve as the upper limit; increases should be *within* that limit to ensure that consumers do not notice the change.

By the same token, price reductions should be the exact opposite and should be of *at least* the magnitude of the jnd if the consumer is to be aware of them.

Other areas of application in marketing would include:

- package size;
- ad copy where corrective advertising or disclaimers have to be presented in a certain size in accordance with the size of other copy in the ad;[39]
- label size and color;[40] and
- product changes.[41]

The k values in each particular case will need to be determined by the marketer before Weber's Law may be applied.

In the examples of sensory perception given at the beginning of the chapter, it would appear that the product differences among the brands of beer or colas or cigarettes were too small (below the jnd) to be detected by consumers. If the manufacturer's purpose had been to establish product differences, clearly their efforts were wasted. They might as well have relied solely on marketing differences in the first place.

The number of objects or units that the human being can apprehend is quite limited. Krech asserts that "the range in span of apprehension is found to be from 6 to 11. Furthermore, the span varies in the same person from moment to moment. It is partly because of individual differences in span of apprehension that two witnesses of the same set of events may give conflicting testimony."[42] This limitation no doubt lies at the base of the selectivity of our perceptual process.

A related concept to the span of attention is its fluctuation; that is, the tendency to shift attention from one object to another. It is estimated that such fluctuations can occur as often as every five seconds. In messages directed at the consumer, the marketer should limit the content of ads to conform to these characteristics of human attention. Shifting to different voices in the same commercial, increasing sound volume, quick picture changes in TV commercials, or switches from audio to video are attempts in this direction.

In Chapter 3 reference was made to the influence of brain hemispheral lateralization on information processing and its potential for measuring involvement. Hansen has pointed out the major differences between the left- and right-brain processes.[43] The specialized functions of the left brain include speech, arithmetic, and symbolic information processing; those of the right brain are vision, audition, and musical impressions.

Some individuals are left-brain dominated and others right-brain dominated and so their information processing tends to rely more heavily on the appropriate specialized functions.

It has also been suggested that hemispheral specialization is related to the basic asymmetry of the human face.[44] The right side is our public face and is usually the happier side. The left side is our private face and is usually the more serious. Thus since the right brain controls the left side of the face, it is the sad hemisphere and the left brain is the happy hemisphere.

Psychological Factors

Every individual brings into a situation a unique psychological make-up; his or her perceptions are the result of not only the characteristics of the stimulus and the person's physiological idiosyncracies and limitations but also motivations, experiences, and personality.

In general, personal factors, such as interests, needs, attitudes, and values, can either sensitize the individual and lower his or her threshold for attending to stimulus objects (a kind of perceptual vigilance) or attempt to shut out and raise the threshold for other stimuli (a kind of perceptual defence).[45]

Perceptual vigilance accounts for many consumer behavioral phenomena. It is a form of selective attention that leads consumers to disregard unnecessary information and guide them to relevant information, such as promotion for preferred brands. Information that is consistent with existing needs, beliefs, attitudes, and values tends to be attended to and processed more quickly.

Perceptual defence, on the other hand, is activated in response to threatening stimuli that are not consistent with existing attitudes and values. Perceptual defence acts to avoid or distort such inconsistent information.

People have a perceptual readiness for things in which they are interested. Certain stimuli will be more likely to be attended to by women and others by men. Similarly, a Chevrolet owner will be more likely to notice a Chevrolet ad than a Ford ad. On the other hand, there are qualifications. A consumer who is thinking of "moving" from a Chevrolet to a Volkswagen may become very aware of VW advertising.

This concept of **interest** is important for the marketer. It confirms the necessity for reminder advertising. Because of their interest, brand users attend to that brand's advertising; in this way, their choice is reinforced.

On the other hand, the marketer can guard against the effects of perceptual defence by making the advertisement somewhat ambiguous. If the consumer is likely to shut out the ad because a direct message may arouse feel-

ings of anxiety, an ambiguous message will not run the risk of avoidance or distortion and will allow the consumer to project his or her own needs onto the situation.

It has also been found that the motivational state of the individual will affect his or her perceptions. This could be a conscious process, such as when a consumer has decided to buy a color TV and carefully scrutinizes every advertisement for color TVs during the search period. Needs and motives can also operate unconsciously to influence one's perception.

The influence of need is illustrated by the classic study of Bruner and Goodman, who found that poor children tended to overestimate the sizes of coins, when compared with discs of the same size, more than did wealthy children, suggesting that because the coins had more value for the poor children, they were perceived as larger (see Figure 5.11).[46]

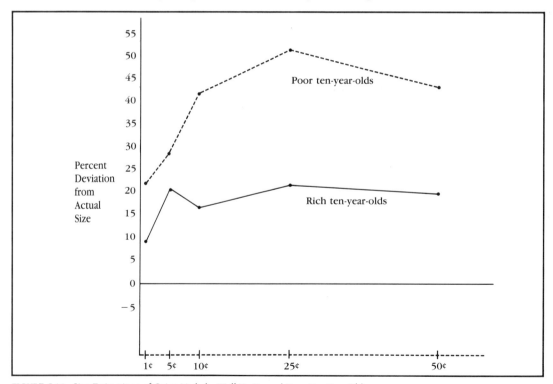

FIGURE 5.11: Size Estimations of Coins Made by Well-To-Do and Poor Ten-Year-Olds

SOURCE: Jerome S. Bruner and Cecile C. Goodman, "Value and Need as Organizing Factors in Perception," *Journal of Abnormal and Social Psychology*, 42 (1947), p. 33-4.

Our expectations are influenced by our previous experience, our knowledge, and our memory. And what we perceive is often what we expect to see or what we are looking for. This **mental set** functions at the unconscious level to delimit our capability to perceive.

In other words, we tend to perceive the world from our own vantage points and with our unique backgrounds.

> A popular singer and a fire inspector view the auditorium from behind the asbestos curtain . . . the singer notes the large number of teenage girls in the audience; the fire inspector . . . that there are only three exit doors.[47]

This is a particularly important phenomenon for the marketer. In order to ensure that the intended audience will attend to the message, comprehend it correctly and retain it, the marketer must understand their background and thus the expectations aroused by certain cues.

These expectations can predispose individuals to certain perceptions, some of which may sometimes be inaccurate or distorted. We tend to generalize from one or a few characteristics to form a total picture. Example 4 demonstrated how a single cue (the polyvinyl package) influenced the perception of potato chips as crisp and fresh. Similar results have been found with bread.

Different kinds of individuals may have certain characteristics associated with their appearance, so that someone with a similar appearance may also be attributed with those characteristics. Marketers use such figures to advantage in their advertising — the race car driver for virility, the young executive as a swinger, or the well-dressed, handsome, grey-haired father figure as trustworthy and believable.

Such **stereotyping** can extend to situations or events as well where we react to one **cue** and build upon it a total perception. Thus by simply showing a consumer looking in a certain way at a product, one can generate an entire chain of impressions. To employ such devices

effectively, the advertiser must create the intended situation, expression, or physical appearance and, more importantly, ensure that the expected stereotyping is what actually occurs.

How information is acquired, organized, and interpreted also depends upon the individual's processing style. According to Bettman, there are two major possibilities: Choice by Processing Brands (CPB), and Choice by Processing Attributes (CPA).[48] In other words, consumers can search for and evaluate the attributes of one brand before assessing other brands or they can evaluate a number of brands first on one attribute and then on another, and so on.

Bettman and Kakkar found that "the strategies used to acquire information are strongly affected by the structure of the information presented . . . Acquisition strategies are totally adapted to the task environment."[49] A marketer can induce the processing style to which the information presentation context best lends itself. For example, since supermarket shelves are organized by brand, it would be advantageous to encourage CPB. If, however, a marketer thinks a product has an advantage on a particular attribute, comparative advertising or package information can be used to encourage CPA.

Although CPB may be the more generally used strategy, there is some evidence to suggest that processing may vary with the stage in the decision process. It seems that consumers may employ CPA in the early stages and turn to CPB as the choice process unfolds.[50] Consumers with prior knowledge and experience also tend to process information by brand. Russo and Johnson attribute this to the fact that, since experience is largely brand-based (advertising, point-of-purchase displays, usage), the memory structure "tends to be more organized around brands."[51]

Consumers' processing style can also be characterized by their attitude to new information, that is, their ability to tolerate the tension such information creates. Two types have been identified:

- sharpeners — those who can tolerate the new information and the discomfort it may cause; and
- levelers — those who prefer simpler information and are more likely to overlook differences.

Another view suggests that consumers who are more receptive to new information may be more capable of differentiating among product messages. They are most likely innovators, who tend to try new products and to be exposed to a wide range of information sources.[52]

Consumers appear to have finite limits to the information they can absorb and process during any unit of time; more is not necessarily better and too much information can lead to poorer decision making and dysfunctional performance.[53]

We referred earlier to the limitations of the human perceptual process and the resulting selectivity that takes place. Individuals differ in their ability to assimilate, retain, and integrate information in order to form complex judgements.[54] The use made of available attributes describing a stimulus, the degree of differentiation among stimuli along the attributes, and how perceived information is organized or interrelated will show considerable individual differences. For example, it seems that medium/high socio-economic status groups are more accomplished information processors than low SES groups.[55] Thus it would appear reasonable that there can be **information overload**. However, the studies done to demonstrate its effects have led to considerable controversy.

Studies by Jacoby et al[56] and Scammon[57] have been criticized for their definitions, methodology, and analysis.

Reanalysis of their data by Malhotra et al. did not support the information overload hypothesis but did not unequivocally reject it either. The small sample sizes and complex statistical manipulation underline the need for more definitive studies that take into account the importance of the information provided (high versus low involvement), the relative importance of the choice alternatives, and the presentation format.

SUMMARY

The acquisition, interpretation, and organization of incoming information is a selective, subjective process that spans a number of steps from exposure, attention, and comprehension to retention (see Figure 5.12). These stages are affected by two main kinds of factors:

- the characteristics of the incoming stimuli or information; and
- the characteristics of the perceiver.

Stages	Stimulus Characteristics	Perceiver Characteristics
Exposure	Position (media)	Threshold
Attention	Size; color; intensity; movement.	Span of attention; perceptual vigilance; defence; interests; needs; values.
Comprehension	Color; configuration (figure-ground, closure, grouping, simplicity); format; amount.	Interests; needs; values; expectation (set); symbolic meaning.
Yielding/Acceptance	Content; amount.	Beliefs; attitudes; values.
Retention	Meaningfulness; Familiarity; Relevance.	Rehearsal; motivation.

FIGURE 5.12: The Influence of Stimulus and Perceiver Characteristics on Information Processing

It should be noted that in low-involvement decisions there is limited comprehension and no yielding/acceptance. Retention is limited and evaluation takes place after the purchase.

QUESTIONS

1. If sensory discrimination among colas is so difficult, discuss the significance of "the Coke-Pepsi Taste Test War."

2. Discuss, with examples, the importance of *cues* in marketing communications.

3. How does information processing differ in high-involvement and in low-involvement situations?

4. Define and comment on the marketing significance of: (a) figure-ground, (b) closure, (c) grouping.

5. Comment on the concept of sensory adaptation and its relevance to television advertising.

6. Discuss the meaning of the jnd and how it may be applied to (a) price, (b) product, (c) package, (d) corrective advertising.

7. What theory of behavior underlies perceptual vigilance and perceptual defence? Distinguish between these two perceptual phenomena.

8. Explain the relationship between expectations and cues. How are they related to generalization and stereotyping?

9. How does processing style affect consumer information processing?

NOTES TO CHAPTER 5

[1] Carl McDaniel and R.C. Baker, "Convenience Food Packaging and the Perception of Product Quality," *Journal of Marketing*, 41:4 (October 1977), pp. 57-8.

[2] R.W. Husband and J. Godfrey, "An Experimental Study of Cigarette Identification," *Journal of Applied Psychology*, 18 (1934), pp. 220-51.

[3] N.H. Pronko and J.W. Bowles, Jr., "Identification of Cola Beverages: I. First Study," *Journal of Applied Psychology*, 32 (1948), pp. 304-12; "Identification of Cola Beverages: II. A Further Study," *Journal of Applied Psychology*, 32 (1948), pp. 559-64; "Identification of Cola Beverages: III. A Final Study," *Journal of Applied Psychology*, 33 (1949), pp. 605-8; "Identification of Cola Beverages: IV. Postscript," *Journal of Applied Psychology*, 34 (1950), pp. 68-9; F.J. Thumin, "Identification of Cola Beverages," *Journal of Applied Psychology*, 46 (1962), pp. 358-60.

[4] Ralph L. Allison and Kenneth P. Uhl, "Influence of Beer Brand Identification on Taste Perception," *Journal of Marketing Research*, 1:3 (August 1964), pp. 36-9.

[5] G.A. Mauser, "Allison and Uhl Revisited: The Effects of Taste and Brand Name on Perceptions and Preferences," in William L. Wilkie (ed.), *Advances in Consumer Research*, 6 (Ann Arbor, Michigan: Association for Consumer Research, 1979), pp. 161-5.

[6] Bernard Berelson and Gary A. Steiner, *Human Behavior: An Inventory of Scientific Findings* (New York: Harcourt, Brace and World, 1964), p. 96.

[7] John A. Howard, *Consumer Behavior: Application of Theory* (New York: McGraw-Hill, 1977), p. 306.

[8] Berelson and Steiner, op. cit., p. 88.

[9] Carl E. Block and Kenneth J. Roering, *Essentials of Consumer Behavior* (Hinsdale, Illinois: Dryden Press, 1979), p. 402.

[10] H.E. Krugman, "The Measurement of Advertising Involvement," *Public Opinion Quarterly*, 30 (Winter 1966), pp. 584-5; "Memory Without Recall, Exposure Without Per-

ception," *Journal of Advertising Research*, 17 (August 1977), pp. 7-12.

[11]Kenneth E. Runyon, *Consumer Behavior and the Practice of Marketing*, 2nd ed. (Columbus, Ohio: Charles E. Merrill, 1980), pp. 322-3.

[12]Robert P. Abelson, "Psychological Status of the Script Concept," *American Psychologist*, 36 (1981), pp. 715-29; Arno J. Rethans and Jack L. Taylor, "A Script Theoretic Analysis of Consumer Decision Making," in Bruce J. Walker (ed.), *Proceedings of the American Marketing Association Educators' Conference Series* (Chicago, Illinois: American Marketing Association, 1982), #48.

[13]C. Connell and J.C. MacDonald, "The Impact of Health News on Attitudes and Behavior," *Journalism Quarterly*, 33 (Summer 1956), pp. 315-23.

[14]Jacob Jacoby and Wayne D. Hoyer, "Viewer Miscomprehension of Televised Communication: Selected Findings," *Journal of Marketing*, 46 (Fall 1982), pp. 12-26. Reprinted with permission of the American Marketing Association.

[15]Ibid., pp. 18-20.

[16]Gary T. Ford and Richard Yalch, "Viewer Miscomprehension of Televised Communication: A Comment," *Journal of Marketing*, 46 (Fall 1982), pp. 27-31.

[17]Richard W. Mizerski, "Viewer Miscomprehension Findings Are Measurement Bound," *Journal of Marketing*, 46 (Fall 1982), pp. 32-4.

[18]Jacoby and Hoyer, op. cit., p. 25.

[19]Peter Wright, "The Cognitive Processes Mediating Acceptance of Advertising," *Journal of Marketing Research*, 10 (February 1973), pp. 53-62.

[20]Peter Wright, "Message-Evoked Thoughts: Persuasion Research Using Thought Verbalizations," *Journal of Consumer Research*, 7 (September 1980), pp. 151-75.

[21]John A. Howard, op. cit., pp. 75-6.

[22]D. Starch, "What 198 Readership Studies of Newspaper Ads Revealed," *Tested Copy*, no. 80 (Mamoroneck, New York, January, 1957); "An Analysis of 12 Million Inquiries," *Media/Scope*, 3 (January 1959), pp. 23-7; "What Stirs the Newspaper Reader?" *Printer's Ink*, 21 (June 1963), pp. 45-9.

[23]Lawrence G. Ulin, "Does Page Size Influence Advertising Effectiveness?" *Media/Scope*, 16: 7 (July 1962), p. 50.

[24]James H. Myers and William H. Reynolds, *Consumer Behavior and Marketing Management* (New York: Houghton Mifflin, 1967), p. 7.

[25]*Media/Scope*, "How Important is Position in Consumer Magazine Advertising?" (June 1964), pp. 52-7.

[26]Berelson and Steiner, op. cit., p. 100.

[27]Ibid., p. 99.

[28]Robert S. Woodworth, *Contemporary Schools of Psychology* (New York: Ronald Press, 1948), p. 125.

[29]Ibid., p. 128.

[30]Ibid., pp. 104-5.

[31]D.O. Hebb, *The Organization of Behavior* (New York: John Wiley & Sons, 1949), p. 19.

[32]R. Schafer and G. Murphy, "The Role of Autism in Figure-Ground Relationship," *Journal of Experimental Psychology*, 32 (1943), pp. 335-43.

[33]R.S. Woodworth, op. cit., p. 130.

[34]David Krech, Richard S. Crutchfield, and Egerton L. Ballachey, *Individual in Society* (New York: McGraw-Hill, 1962), p. 26.

[35]Berelson and Steiner, op. cit., p. 108.

[36]Sidney J. Levy, "Symbols for Sale," *Harvard Business Review*, July 1959, p. 119.

[37]Berelson and Steiner, op. cit., p. 92.

[38]Ibid., p. 95.

[39]John Revett, "FTC Threatens Big Fines for Undersized Cigarette Warnings," *Advertising Age* (17 March 1975,) pp. 1, 74.

[40]Walter P. Margulies, "Design Changes Reflect Switches in Consumer Retail Graphics," *Advertising Age* (4 February 1972), p. 41.

[41]S.H. Britt and V.M. Nelson, "The Marketing Importance of the 'Just Noticeable Difference'," *Business Horizons*, 14 (August 1976), pp. 38-40.

[42]Krech, Crutchfield, and Ballachey, op. cit., p. 21.

[43]Flemming Hansen, "Hemispheral Lateralization Implications for Understanding Consumer Behavior," *Journal of Consumer Research*, 8 (June 1981), pp. 23-37.

[44]Marcel Kinsbourne, "Sad Hemisphere, Happy Hemisphere," *Psychology Today* (May 1981), p. 92.

[45]Krech, Crutchfield, and Ballachey, op. cit., p. 21.

[46]Jerome S. Bruner and Cecile C. Goodman, "Value and Need as Organizing Factors in Perception," *Journal of Abnormal and Social Psychology*, 42 (1947), pp. 33-4.

[47]Krech, Crutchfield and Ballachey, op. cit., p. 21.

[48]James R. Bettman, *An Information Processing Theory of Consumer Choice* (Reading, Massachusetts: Addison-Wesley, 1979), pp. 132-3.

[49]James R. Bettman and Pradeep Kakkar, "Effects of Information Presentation Format on Consumer Information Acquisition Strategies," *Journal of Consumer Research*, 3 (March 1977), p. 239.

[50]James R. Bettman and C. Whan Park, "Effects of Prior Knowledge and Experience and Phase of the Choice Process on Consumer Decision Processes: A Protocol Analysis," *Journal of Consumer Research*, 7 (December 1980), pp. 234-48.

[51]J. Edward Russo and Eric J. Johnson, "What Do Consumers Know About Familiar Products?" in Jerry C. Olson (ed.), *Advances in Consumer Research*, 7 (San Francisco: Association for Consumer Research, 1980), pp. 417-22.

[52]Elizabeth C. Hirschman, "Cognitive Complexity, Intelligence, and Creativity: A Conceptual Overview with Implications for Consumer Research," *Research in Marketing*, 5 (1981), pp. 59-69.

[53]N.K. Malhotra, A.K. Jain, and S.W. Lagakos, "The Information Overload Controversy: An Alternative Viewpoint," *Journal of Marketing*, 46 (Spring 1982), pp. 27-37.

[54]W.A. Henry, "The Effect of Information Processing Ability on Processing Accuracy," *Journal of Consumer Research*, 7 (March 1980), pp. 42-8.

[55]N. Capon and M. Burke, "Product Class and Task-Related Factors in Consumer Information Processing," *Journal of Consumer Research*, 7 (December 1980), pp. 314-26.

[56]J. Jacoby, D. Speller, and C. Kohn, "Brand Choice Behavior as a Function of Information Load," *Journal of Marketing Research*, 11 (February 1974), pp. 63-9; *Journal of Consumer Research*, 1 (June 1974), pp. 33-42.

[57]D. Scammon, "Information Load and Consumers," *Journal of Consumer Research*, 4 (September 1977), pp. 148-55.

6

Perceptual Phenomena In Consumer Behavior

The perception is the reality, and consumers do not necessarily react to the product *per se* but to their perception of it. This is true of a product, of its separate attributes, of a company, of an advertisement, or of another individual. How the characteristics of a stimulus interact with the characteristics of the individual (Chapter 5) to determine behavior is well reflected in a number of specific levels and areas of consumer activity:

- subliminal perception;
- price-quality perception;
- perceived risk;
- perception of causality (attribution); and
- perceived image.

Each of these is discussed in this chapter.

SUBLIMINAL PERCEPTION

In the discussion of the physiological limitations of human perception, I referred to the problem of subliminal perception and indicated that I would return to it later — to review its nature and its implications.

On the surface, the term appears to be self-contradictory. If a stimulus is below the threshold (*sub* = below; *limen* = threshold), it cannot be perceived. Part of the reason for the perception of stimuli at below-threshold intensity may be related to the manner in which a threshold is determined. An individual's perceptual threshold is that stimulus value that is correctly detected half of the time. The defined threshold is the average of the values obtained from a sample of subjects. The threshold is a statistical abstraction, so some individuals have sensory thresholds below the statistical average. Furthermore, a stimulus that is subliminal for one person may not be so for another, just as a stimulus that is subliminal at one time for an individual may not be subliminal at another time.[1]

A stimulus could be below the threshold of awareness but not necessarily beneath the absolute threshold of the receptors involved. Galvanic skin responses have been reported to subliminally presented nonsense syllables that had been negatively reinforced earlier with an electric shock.[2]

This kind of **subception** is well accepted.[3] What causes controversy is the claim that subliminal stimulation can initiate subsequent goal-directed behavior.* In 1956, James Vicary, a theatre owner in New Jersey, is reported to have exposed his audience to two subliminal messages, "Drink Coca-Cola" and "Eat Popcorn" (flashed at 1/3000 of a second) over a six-week period and to have obtained large increases in the sales of Coca-Cola (18%) and popcorn (58%) compared to the previous six-week period.[4] These reports raised quite a flurry in marketing circles and among certain state governments, even though the experiment seemed to be quite crude and lacking in methodological controls. Furthermore, later attempts, not of an identical nature, have failed to produce similar results.[5]

One particularly interesting study conducted much later attempted to determine the effect of subliminal stimulation on drive level.[6] Haw-kins found that the subliminal presentation of the stimulus word COKE will produce significantly higher thirst ratings than the subliminal presentation of a nonsense syllable; the subliminal presentation of the command DRINK COKE will *not* produce significantly higher thirst ratings than the subliminal perception of the word COKE. Hawkins did not claim that any changes in behavior occurred, as the experiment was not set up to test this.

A second experiment by Hawkins found that a subliminal message did not exert a significant influence on brand choice and led to the suggestion that "the associations that result in brand images may depend entirely on supraliminal stimuli, even if not necessarily on conscious cognitive processes."[7] Of even greater relevance to marketers was a study that sought to determine the effect of subliminal stimulation on purchasing behavior.[8] Students exposed subliminally to the stimulus HERSHEY'S CHOCOLATE did not show any increase in purchases of that brand.

A more recent study also found that embeds (or embedded subliminal messages) had no significant effect on brand recall, although the possibility of effects on brand recognition was not discounted.[9]

At the heart of the controversy is the implication that not only does subliminal stimulation influence behavior but it does so with no interference or control from the perceiver. This implication no doubt expresses more of a fear than a reality. The evidence does not appear to support any such proposition.

There are, in fact, several reasons to support the view that subliminal stimulation, while it can and does occur, does not affect behavior. The period of stimulation is extremely brief, so that the content of any message is severely limited. This increases the possibility of error and perceptual distortion. It has not been demonstrated that subliminal stimuli are not subject to perceptual selectivity.

Recent writings have suggested, without proof, that there is a great deal of "subliminal adver-

---

*At least three kinds of subliminal stimulation have been claimed:

(1) Visual — briefly presented (using a tachistoscope) stimuli, such as words or images. Presentation is so fast that the viewer is unaware of their presence.

(2) Auditory — sub-audible messages such as the Seattle radio station that broadcast "TV's a bore" subliminally or the Toronto department store that employed subliminal auditory messages to deter shiplifters.

(3) Embedding — concealing words or images in pictorial advertisements in such a way that the viewer is not aware of them.

Other subliminal devices employed are incongruities (where the advertisement contains something that does not fit in with the picture and it is not evident upon first glance), and suggestiveness (where there is more to the ad than the explicit copy suggests).

tising" being employed today, mainly in the form of the **embedding** of phallic and other sex symbols, and of obscene words into advertisements. The basic hypothesis is that, in these cases, the appeal is made directly to unconscious, libidinal urges, which the organism presumably must satisfy.[10] The implication is that by breaking through to the unconscious, such material bypasses the control mechanisms of the individual. The current state of knowledge holds the view that such mechanisms as repression, distortion, and other forms of perceptual defence are mediated *at the unconscious level* by the individual's psychological make-up — needs, interests, attitudes, and values — so that selection is likely to occur at that level as well.

An example of the flights of imagination and fancy of which the proponents of subliminal advertising are capable is shown by Figure 6.1. In reaction to the ad (which appeared in *Time* Magazine on 9 May 1977) one respondent claimed:

The tall cylindrical glass on the far right is a phallic symbol. The cavity of the glass which holds the ice cubes, straws, and drink is shaped like the male sex organ. The orange slice on the rim of the glass represents the testicle. Together they portray the male genital organs. The small oval-shaped object underneath may be symbolic of an egg from the female. In fact, the dark shading in the lower half of the oval could be a fetus. The oval may also be interpreted as a drop of semen from the end of the penis.

The two other glasses are symbolic of a male and a female. The glass on the far left represents the female — it is smaller, slender, and more delicate-looking and the liquid is free of ice, suggesting smoothness or softness symbolic of the female. On the other hand, the glass in the middle is taller, heavier-looking, and sturdier, the ice cubes suggest ruggedness — all symbolic of the male. In the bottom of this glass, just behind the orange slice, there appears to be a pair of flesh-colored legs (in a horizontal position) which may be the lower part of a nude body. The possible subliminal message

FIGURE 6.1: An Example of Subliminal Advertising
Courtesy Dubonnet International, Paris, France

portrayed in this advertisement may be a sexual encounter with a lovely female friend if you drink Dry Dubonnet.*

Questions naturally follow, such as:
- How many viewers actually perceive those images?
- Why and how do these images bring about purchase of the product?

Key has suggested that such subliminal stimuli operate through some sort of subconscious psychological mechanism. However, "the notion of a separate super-powerful sensory system serving the subconscious (exclusively) cannot be accommodated by any theory of perception."[11]

In general, it seems that the issue of subliminal stimulation has been much overrated. Moore, in a recent review article, asserts: "While sub-

---

*Private report.

liminal perception is a bona fide phenomenon, the effects obtained are subtle and obtaining them usually requires a carefully structured context." Acknowledging the possibility of weak affective (emotional) responses, Moore concludes, "There is no empirical documentation for stronger subliminal effects, such as inducing particular behaviors or changing motivation."[12]

PRICE-QUALITY PERCEPTION

Some evidence suggests that, in the minds of consumers, there is a positive correlation between price and quality, so that price can serve as a cue or surrogate for quality. This relationship varies with the product. Lambert found, for example, that consumers selected the highest priced brands for stereos and tennis racquets but not for toothpaste, suntan lotion, or coffee.[13]

For some target groups the "you-get-what-you-pay-for" philosophy may be quite appropriate. A few years ago an advertisement for Michelob beer tried exactly this: "Michelob, America's highest priced beer." Figure 6.2 illustrates this approach very well.

Generally, "when price information is available and when the buyer is uncertain about product quality, it would seem reasonable to use price as a criterion for assessing quality."[14] Some researchers have shown that price is very important in brand choice where price is the only cue[15] and others that its salience declines where other cues, such as brand, are present.[16] Monroe concludes from his survey of the literature that there emerges "the suggestion that brand name is important and possibly dominates price for relatively inexpensive grocery products and beverages, whereas for clothing, there is an apparent increasing concern with price, although price may not always dominate the influence of brand name."[17]

Other studies have shown that, in the absence of brand identification, consumers of beer[18] and of pantyhose[19] were influenced strongly by price

FIGURE 6.2: An Advertisement Using the Price-Quality Relationship

Courtesy J.A. Henckels Zwillingswerk

in their perceptions of quality, even though the products were identical in quality.

There is also evidence that the accuracy of price perceptions varies with the consumer and with the product. Brown, for example, found that very price-conscious shoppers were more valid perceivers of price than non-price-conscious shoppers.[20] A study reported in *Progressive Grocer* found that among sixty products the percentage of correct prices stated ranged from 86% for Coca-Cola to 2% for shortening.[21]

In today's inflationary economy, with rapidly changing prices, the level of correct recall of prices may be considerably lower, even for products such as Coca-Cola. On the other hand, consumers may also be more sensitive to prices and therefore recall them better.

It seems that consumers think more in terms of a range of prices than in terms of an absolute price. "People apparently refrain from purchasing a product not only when the price is considered too high but also when the price is considered to be too low."[22]

Also worthy of consideration is the extent to which consumers are actually aware of the difference between two prices, particularly of competitive brands. Weber's law of the jnd is applicable here (see Chapter 5). The differential price threshold varies over different products and over different price levels.[23] Monroe makes two other interesting observations:

- While perception of price changes was independent of their direction, the dominance of reaction thresholds made respondents more sensitive to price increases; and
- Consumers are more sensitive to price changes for some products (i.e., have lower differential price thresholds).

Finally the price "last paid" has been suggested by some as a determinant of price perception — as a sort of adaptation level. And from this Emery has noted that:

- Price perceptions are relative to other prices and to associated use-values;
- There is a "standard price" for each discernible quality level for each product category;
- The "standard price" serves as an anchor for judgements of other prices;
- There is a region of indifference about a standard price such that changes in price within this region produce no change in perception;

- The standard price will be some average of the range of prices for similar products;
- Buyers do not judge each price singly, but rather each price is compared with the standard price and the other prices in the price range; and
- The standard price need not correspond with any actual price nor with the price of the leading brand.[24]

PERCEIVED RISK

Risk is a characteristic common to all behavior. It is certainly a pivotal element in consumer behavior. Since the outcome of choice can only be known in the future, every consumer action is attended by some degree of uncertainty.

Risk has been defined as the degree to which a consumer action will produce consequences that the consumer cannot anticipate with anything approximating certainty.[25] Any choice involves uncertainty about the outcome and uncertainty about the consequences.[26] Uncertainty of outcome relates to whether the product will match what was desired. This can be reduced by acquiring information. Uncertainty about the consequences involves the importance or seriousness of the possible failure of the product to provide the expected benefits. Consequences can refer to product performance or psycho-social loss or to the loss of time/money/effort invested in the attainment of one's goals. The greater the investment in striving for the goal, the more serious the consequences of failure to attain it.

Both types of risk are present in every choice but in varying importance to each other. In the same situation, individual consumers can perceive different proportions of outcome risk to consequences risk and adopt different risk-reducing strategies.[27]

Note the emphasis on the *subjective* element — not how much risk is actually involved but how much risk the consumer perceives in the situation. One may perceive risk that does not exist or not perceive risk that does exist. The marketer may know in clear terms what the product offers but knowing how the consumer perceives its potential for loss is imperative.

There are several reasons consumers may be uncertain about a product:

- insufficient information because it is new, or it has not been used or spoken about by others;
- negative previous experience with a similar brand or product;
- the product is expensive;
- the product is complex;
- finances are limited;
- there are strong quality differences among brands; or
- the product is considered very important.

The personality of the consumer (tolerance level) will influence the amount of risk perceived.[28] When the level of perceived risk exceeds one's tolerance limit, action will be taken to reduce the risk. Thus different individuals react differently to the same product. Because of this it is possible to segment consumers on the basis of perceived risk. Self-esteem and self-confidence have been found to influence perceived risk. A study by Hisrich, Dornoff, and Kernan involving store selection and product purchase concluded that "for each product studied, consumers' self-esteem and their self-assessed ability to choose a store in which to buy seemed to bear on how much risk they perceived."[29]

A later study designed to investigate how self-confidence, perceived product risk, and product importance affected choice between a specialty store for audio equipment and a department store found that "the specialty store customers were more self-confident (both generalized and product-specific), perceived less risk, and considered the product area to be of greater importance than did those who shopped for similar items in a department store."[30]

The study also found that the specialty store shoppers experienced less outcome risk but greater consequence risk, suggesting that in de-termining perceived risk it is better to measure the underlying dimensions than to merely obtain an overall risk score.

Kinds of Loss

It is important to identify the particular concerns that surround a given product. Not all products will be perceived as having the same risks nor will different market segments attach the same risk(s) or the same degree of risk to a particular product. The principal kinds of possible loss that a consumer may fear are:

- physical (or hazard) loss — where the product may be dangerous or harmful, either if it fails or in its normal functioning. For example, how safe is the microwave oven? Does it emit harmful radiation?
- financial loss — the possibility that the product will not be worth the money or time expended.
- social loss — the risk that the decision will be ridiculed or deprecated by acquaintances and others. This is particularly true of conspicuous products such as a car, lawn mower, or TV.

- performance loss — the possibility that the product (for example, a cold remedy) may not turn out to be as expected, in quality or effectiveness. Some standardized products will be quite low in performance risk, such as a new telephone or a pair of jeans. Where consumers lack information about a product, they are more likely to experience performance risk and, in order to reduce the risk, to seek more information. Where this is not practical or possible, price may be resorted to as an indicator of quality, as mentioned earlier.

Such lack of information also affects consumers who shop by telephone[31] or by mail.[32] It has been found that consumers using these methods are more likely to perceive greater risk than when buying in person.

- ego loss (psychological risk) — the concern that a particular purchase may reflect negatively on one's ability or taste and indeed affect one's self-perception.

Any product may be perceived as having one or more of the above types of risk. The combination and strength of the risks vary with the individual. The marketer should identify the risk or risks associated with his product, by segment if necessary. The telephone and the mail are likely, more for some products than for others, to generate higher levels of perceived risk than the personal buying situation.

Risk-Reduction Strategies

When risk is perceived, consumers resort to strategies designed to reduce uncertainty. Marketers also attempt to reduce the perceived risk by engaging in certain strategies to increase the attractiveness of their offering.

Consumer strategies include:
- brand loyalty — buying a brand one knows about;
- buying the most popular brand;
- information search (e.g., shopping around or using personal sources);
- buying a lower-priced brand;
- for some products, buying the most expensive brand; and
- buying a small amount.

The most common are buying a lower-priced brand and sticking with a brand used before. Related to the latter is the tendency to buy from the same retailer or supplier. This is especially true of high-risk perceivers.[33] They are also less likely to purchase a new product.[34] Consumers will rely on a popular or well-known brand, reasoning that "it must be good to be as popular as it is." Such a brand image is not necessarily the result of the product's attributes alone; promotional influence can contribute to such a perception. In the absence of knowledge about any brand, the consumer may choose the most expensive brand, assuming that the price is a good indicator of quality. Some consumers rely on the image of the store where the purchase is

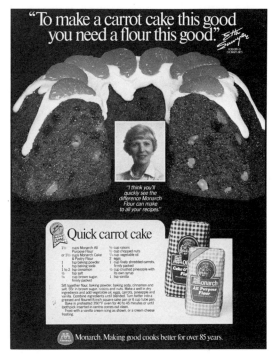

FIGURE 6.3: Use of Expert Endorsement to Reduce Risk
Courtesy Maple Leaf Mills Limited

made. They regard the store as reputable and dependable and therefore have confidence in the quality of the products it carries.

Some consumers attempt to reduce risk by seeking additional information about the product before purchase. They do so by talking with friends, acquaintances, or relatives, or by shopping around on their own. They attend to such sources as advertising (see Figure 6.3), salespeople, show-room displays, and packaging.

Word of mouth is a potent source of information and plays a significant role in risk reduction. In a study of headache remedies, fabric softener, and dry spaghetti (which had decreasing levels of perceived risk), Cunningham found that significantly more high-risk perceivers than low-risk perceivers were likely to talk about a product. High-risk perceivers were more likely to initiate talk about the product and to make brand recommendations.[35]

In a study of hairspray, Arndt also found that consumers relied on personal sources of in-

BEHIND OUR SIGN THERE'S MORE THAN A HOUSE FOR SALE

At A.E. LePage, real estate is our only business. That makes every one of our representatives a specialist.

They are people who pride themselves on listening to your needs and giving you sound real estate advice.

OVER 70 years OF SERVICE They are a highly trained team of real estate professionals with over 70 years of A.E. LePage experience on their side.

A.E. LePage people know the real estate market well, and can help you get the best possible price for your home . . . and get it quickly.

Behind our sign, there are thousands of satisfied A.E. LePage customers . . . and because they recommend us to their friends, you'll be seeing more of our signs than ever.

The name friends recommend

A.E. LePAGE
REAL ESTATE SERVICES LTD • REALTOR
NO. 3

FIGURE 6.4: Personal Sources of Information for High-Risk Products

Courtesy A.E. LePage Real Estate Services Ltd.

formation.[36] The word-of-mouth activity, however, decreased as experience with the product increased.

The finding that high-risk perceivers initiate product-related conversations implies that the marketer should implement a strategy that would encourage consumers of a high-risk product to seek advice from other consumers. For an ex-ample, see Figure 6.4, in which customers are claimed to "recommend us to their friends."

One researcher sought to rank a list of risk-relievers and found, for the situations tested, that "brand loyalty and major brand image evoked the most consistently favorable response."[37] He concluded that "buyers prefer some relievers to others depending upon the kind of loss involved, and that the attitude toward relievers can differ between different types of buyers. Perhaps a seller should first determine the kind of risk perceived by his customers and then create a mix of risk relievers suited for his combination of buyer type and loss type."[38]

Marketer-Generated Strategies

A marketer may attempt to reduce perceived risk by providing:

- free samples;
- small sizes;
- warranties;
- money-back guarantees;
- endorsements or testimonials by opinion leaders;[39]
- sufficient information about contents and use;
- government testing data; or
- private testing data.

Different kinds of strategies will be appropriate for different kinds of perceived loss. Government test data will be most effective for hazardous or potentially harmful products, such as medicines and toys. For products that are complex and need time for problems to show up (e.g., lawn mowers, electric razors, automobiles), guarantees and warranties may be most appropriate. One study found, however, that these strategies tended to reduce the consumer's perception of the financial risk but not the performance risk.[40] Endorsements and testimonials may be best for socially important, visible products. Private test sources such as the *Good Housekeeping* Seal of Approval, *Consumer Reports*, and newspaper and magazine editorials may be relied on for personal products. For other personal products (such as shampoos), free samples (or small sizes) may be most effective in permitting limited trial without any commitment or investment.

PERCEPTION OF CAUSALITY — ATTRIBUTION

With its beginnings in social psychology, attribution theory focusses on how individuals "attempt to explain the causes of the events they observe."[41] In essence, attribution is the psychological process by which an observer infers the cause of someone's behavior.

Attribution theory consists of three distinct paradigms, each seeking to explain how people make causal explanations concerning the behavior or performance of, first, other persons, second, objects around them, and third, themselves. In other words, attribution theory can be divided into three foci: person-perception, object-perception, and self-perception. The paradigms focus on how an individual attributes an effect (e.g., reaction to a product, the behavior of another person or one's own behavior) to the characteristics of the stimulus (i.e., the product, the other person, or oneself) or to conditions in the situation.[42]

Behavior may be attributed to internal, personal causes or to external forces. Individuals are generally biased toward internal attributions. In other words, observers tend to attribute an actor's behavior to that person's traits, preferences, and motives.

One researcher has suggested that an individual evaluates internal attributions by analyzing behavior on four dimensions:

- distinctiveness — if the behavior is attributable to an internal cause in all individuals, an internal attribution is plausible. It is also very plausible if there is:
- consistency over time — the actor behaves in the same way from one occasion to another;
- consistency over place — that is, in different situations; or

- consistency or consensus among observers about a disposition.[43]

If these are absent, the behavior can be attributed to external factors.

It has been suggested that in consumer behavior, the consumer is a social actor being observed by others. Such observations lead to attributions by others; that is, to inferences about the personal dispositions behind the behavior. Since these attributions are really judgements of the consumer, they influence how the observer reacts to the consumer so that, in turn, the observer's actions will influence the consumer. "Attributions thus provide a psychological basis, or reason, for the actions of influencers, something that is missing from 'group pressure' studies."[44]

Moreover, the consumer may be likely to behave in such a way as to evoke attributions that will be to his or her advantage. Influence may come not from the product but from what the consumer believes are the attributions observers make with respect to his or her behavior. "This," Calder and Burnkrant assert, "is a far more dynamic process than product-attribute social-influence conceptualizations imply."[45]

Attempts have been made to apply attribution theory in consumer research. One study sought to investigate the effect of certain factors on consumer confidence in advertising claims.[46] However, it has been quite heavily criticized on conceptual and methodological grounds.[47]

Another study, by Smith and Hunt, attempted to resolve the resulting issues surrounding past applications of attribution theory to promotional situations.[48] They claim to have:

- verified the existence of product claim attributions in promotional situations;
- found some support for the application of Jones and Davis' correspondence theory;[49] and
- demonstrated that product claim attributions do mediate the perceived credibility of the source.

In their review, Mizerski, Golden, and Kernan

reflect the focus of the application of attribution theory to the information-processing aspects of consumer decision making.[50] However, they suggest that attribution theory has many other applications in consumer research:

- as an alternative explanation to cognitive dissonance;
- as a formulation for assessing self-fulfilling prophecy and social-stereotype phenomena;
- as offering insights into group-influenced decision making;
- as a vehicle to reconcile the often opposing views of behaviorists and cognitivists in learning theory.

PERCEIVED IMAGE

Image is the total impression that an individual has of a given object. The image is composed of separate perceptions of that object on any number of relevant dimensions. It is the accumulation of experience qualified by personal factors. It can be accurate or inaccurate, to varying degrees; based on complete or incomplete information; or the result of either rational thought or emotion.

The principal marketing objects about which consumers acquire images include products, brands, brand users, and companies. Consum-

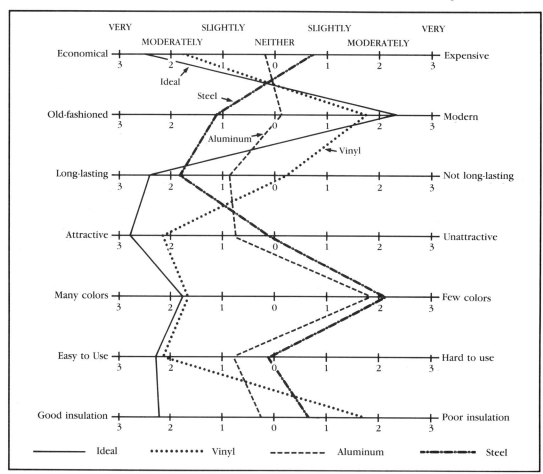

FIGURE 6.5: Profiles of the Ideal and of Aluminum, Steel, and Vinyl Sidings (Hypothetical)

Values shown represent median scale positions of the total sample.

ers also have images of themselves, just as they have images of other persons.

Product Image

In offering a brand to the public, it is important for the marketer to understand how the basic product is perceived so that generic limitations or deficiencies may be corrected *vis-à-vis* competitive products (e.g., aluminum siding versus steel siding versus vinyl siding).

The concept of the **ideal product image** is of particular significance here and involves what consumers think will be the best combination of the different attributes of the product concerned. Different consumers will, of course, have different ideal-product images. One result of this is the possibility of segmenting a market on the basis of three or four different ideals. In other words, through this approach the marketer may discover three or four consumer groups each wanting different versions of the product. These "versions" are shown as profiles in Figure 6.5.

The scale used is a seven-point *semantic differential scale*. A semantic differential scale is a bipolar adjectival scale. The midpoint is a neutral point and values increase toward the ends of the scale. Each point represents an increase in semantic strength as the distances from the zero point increases (see Chapter 12).

Consumers also develop images of different brands and marketers in turn try to make their brands match the ideal of their target market. This is referred to as **brand positioning**. Renault's attempts to position its Encore model for women is illustrated in Figure 6.6.

As illustrated in the first example in Chapter 5, the perceived brand profile is not necessarily what the marketer knows or intends the profile to be. Thus marketers should attempt to determine how consumers perceive their own and competitive brands. One way of achieving this is through **perceptual mapping**.[51] "A 'map' is prepared of an individual's perceptions of competitive brands on certain product attributes"[52]

FIGURE 6.6: Brand Positioning

Courtesy American Motors (Canada) Inc.

and one can develop perceptual maps showing the relative positions of different brands on two or more dimensions.

One study of MBA students determined their perceptions of six graduate business schools and produced the perceptual map shown in Figure 6.7. Perceptual mapping provides a picture of the relative positions of the different brands (schools, candidates) in a two- or three-dimensional space. The semantic differential scales yield a graphic profile of these same stimuli. In both cases, it is possible to compare these ratings with the corresponding ideal ratings and determine:

- whether significant segments exist;
- what the principal differentiating characteristics of these segments are; and
- into which of these segments it would be best to position one's brand.

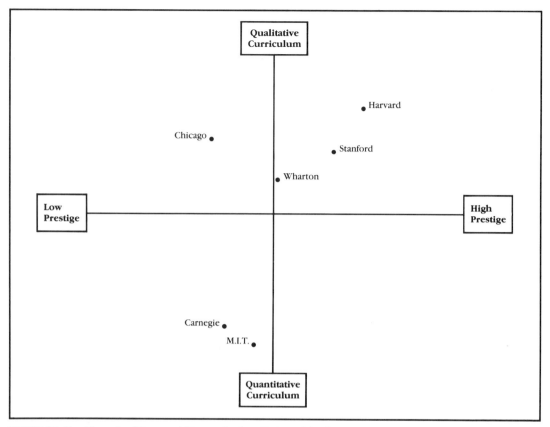

FIGURE 6.7: Two-Dimensional Perceptual Maps — Graduate Business Schools

SOURCE: P.E. Green, F.J. Carmone, and P.J. Robinson, "Nonmetric Scaling Methods: An Exposition and Overview," *Wharton Quarterly* (Winter-Spring 1968), pp. 27-41. Reprinted with permission of the American Marketing Association.

The development and maintenance of a good brand image are important because it is on the basis of that image, however acquired, that the consumer choice is made. The brand image can also be a useful tool for **brand extension** — where a company uses a successful brand name to launch product modifications or additional products — or for brand-name leasing (franchising).[53]

When Mrs. Paul's Kitchens added a new line of frozen fried chicken to its main product — frozen fried fish — it worried for a while over what name to use and eventually decided that since a chicken stick was just another flavor of fish stick, it was going to use the Mrs. Paul's name. Honda prominently displays its name on its new power lawn mower and General Foods

has named its dessert-on-a-stick Jell-O Pudding Pops.

An example of a perceptual map for product brands is shown in Figure 6.8.

"The consumer is suspicious of exaggerated claims and therefore trusts certain brand names," a marketing executive has been quoted as saying.[54]

John Deere, the farm machinery manufacturer, openly said so in its advertising for its line of insurance: "Our good name is the best insurance you can buy." (See Figure 6.9.)

Companies also license out their names to other manufacturers. Levi Strauss, for example, because of the success of its blue jeans, has sold the right to use the Levi name in boots, shoes,

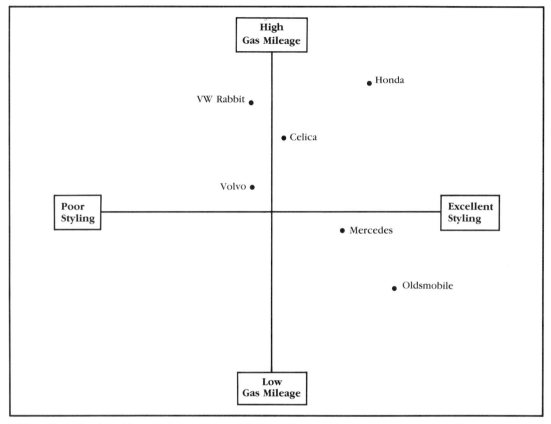

FIGURE 6.8: A Hypothetical Perceptual Map of Automobile Makes

shirts, and special models of American Motors' Jeeps. Of course, such strategies have their dangers:

- the new product may take sales away from the old (e.g., Maxim and Maxwell House instant coffees);
- the gap between the old and the new may be too wide (e.g., Arm and Hammer unsuc-

FIGURE 6.9: Brand Extension Strategy

Courtesy John Deere Insurance Co.

cessfully tried to stretch its baking soda name to include an underarm deodorant); or

- the new product may turn out to be such a failure that it may tarnish the original name (e.g., when Wyler added a line of low-priced flavored drink mixes to its established lemonade brand, not only did the new line fail but lemonade sales were affected).

Stronger companies with well-established images may be able to start over with a new name, as happened with Campbell's Soup. When in test markets it was found that a "Campbell's Very Own Special Sauce" for spaghetti was not accepted because it was perceived as soupy or watery, like tomato soup, Campbell's re-named it Prego ("please" in Italian) and it sold very successfully.

Corporate (Store) Image

Consumers develop images of other entities in marketing, such as manufacturing companies, retail food stores, department stores, TV stations, radio stations, newspapers, and magazines. The consumer may not be conscious of these overall impressions but they nevertheless influence reactions to the entities themselves and to the products and services they provide.

A product may be attributed with less risk, better quality, or better service because of the company that makes it. In this sense, we have an instance of the *figure-ground* phenomenon described earlier, with the corporate image serving as the ground against which the brand (figure) is perceived.

As with products and brands, measurements can also produce corporate profiles based on relevant descriptors such as interest in the customer, quality of service, price, product quality, salespersons, modernity, size, and reliability.[55] Once again, it is the perceptions of consumers that are of primary importance.

The semantic differential technique is widely used for measuring corporate images. Because numerical averages can be determined, it permits the development of profiles.

Companies may undertake deliberate promotional activities designed to create an image. Such activities may involve reference to specific facts or attributes or they may be as indefinite as "There's a definite difference at Dominion" or "At Canadian Pacific we are proud of yesterday . . . but we are planning for tomorrow."

Individuals also develop images of themselves. Not only do they try to understand their own behavior in the market place in order to determine whether their product reactions are based on their own "true" beliefs or on external factors;[56] but they also possess comprehensive self-concepts resulting from their socio-psychological experience. The self-image plays an important role in interpersonal behavior and in an individual's tastes and preferences. I discuss the self-image in greater detail, principally from the point of view of its significance as a motivating factor, in Chapter 10.

SUMMARY

This chapter has reviewed five broad examples of the perceptual process at work: subliminal perception, price-quality perception, perceived risk, perception of causality, and perceived image. Each covers an important area of consumer perception.

Subliminal perception concerns the problem of subliminal advertising and its effects. It seems that the issue has been much overrated and there is no evidence to support any claim that subliminal advertising influences motivation or behavior.

Depending upon the product and the individual, price can serve as a cue or surrogate for quality. Price sensitivity also varies with the product and the individual, as well as with economic conditions.

Perceived risk is a central element in consumer behavior. Five kinds of risk were discussed: physical, financial, social, performance, and psychological. Consumers resort to certain strategies to reduce risk, just as marketers use strategies to prevent or relieve the perception of risk.

Attribution theory seeks to understand how people make causal explanations of the performance (behavior) of objects, other persons, or themselves. It has particular relevance to the information-processing aspects of consumer decision making.

Finally, the perceived image deals with the total impression an individual has of an object. "Objects" can be products, brands, or companies.

QUESTIONS

1. What are some of the reasons why subliminal advertising does not affect behavior?

2. Describe the circumstances in which price is most likely to serve as a criterion for assessing quality.

3. Discuss some of the findings about price differences and price changes.

4. Under what conditions is a consumer more likely to perceive risk?

5. List the ways in which consumers seek to reduce risk.

6. Describe the five different kinds of risk. How are these important in the development of marketing strategy?

7. Internal attributions are arrived at by analyzing behavior on four dimensions. Describe these dimensions.

8. "Attributions provide a psychological basis for the actions of influencers, something that is missing from 'group pressure' studies." Discuss.

9. Discuss the significance of the ideal product image.

NOTES TO CHAPTER 6

[1] Bertrand Klass, "The Ghost of Subliminal Advertising," *Journal of Marketing*, 23: 4 (October 1958), p. 148.

[2] Richard S. Lazarus and Robert A. McCleary, "Autonomic Discrimination Without Awareness: A Study of Subception," *Psychological Review*, 58 (1951), pp. 113-22.

[3] N.F. Dixon, *Subliminal Perception: The Nature of a Controversy* (Toronto: McGraw-Hill, 1971), pp. 50.

[4] J.V. McConnell, R.L. Cutler, and E.B. McNeil, "Subliminal Stimulation: An Overview," *The American Psychologist*, 13 (1958), pp. 229-42.

[5] A.D. Calvin and K.S. Dollenmayer, "Subliminal Perception: Some Negative Findings," *Journal of Applied Psychology*, 43:3 (1959), p. 187; D. Bryne, "The Effect of Subliminal Food Stimulus on Verbal Responses," *Journal of Applied Psychology*, 43:3 (1959), p. 249.

[6] Del Hawkins, "The Effects of Subliminal Stimulation on Drive Level and Brand Preference," *Journal of Marketing Research*, 7 (August 1970), pp. 322-6.

[7] Ibid., p. 325.

[8] S.G. George and L.B. Jennings, "Effect of Subliminal Stimuli on Consumer Behavior: Negative Evidence," *Perceptual and Motor Skills*, 41 (1975), p. 845.

[9] J. Steven Kelly, "Subliminal Embeds in Print Advertising: A Challenge to Advertising Ethics," *Journal of Advertising*, 8 (Summer 1979), pp. 43-6.

[10] Wilson Bryan Key, *Subliminal Seduction* (Englewood Cliffs, New Jersey: Signet, 1973), p. 47. See also W.B. Key, *Media Sexpoloitation* (Englewood Cliffs, New Jersey: Prentice-Hall, 1976) and *The Clam-Plate Orgy* (Englewood Cliffs, New Jersey: Prentice-Hall, 1980).

[11] Timothy E. Moore, "Subliminal Advertising: What You See Is What You Get," *Journal of Marketing*, 46 (Spring 1982), pp. 38-47.

[12] Ibid., p. 46.

[13] Zarrel V. Lambert, "Product Perception: An Important Variable in Pricing Strategy," *Journal of Marketing*, 34 (October 1970), pp. 68-71; "Price and Choice Behavior," *Journal of Marketing Research*, 9:1 (February 1972), pp. 35-40.

[14] Kent B. Monroe, "Buyers' Subjective Perceptions of Price," *Journal of Marketing Research*, 10:1 (February 1973), pp. 70-80.

[15] D. Tull, R.A. Boring, and M.H. Gonsior, "A Note on the Relationship of Price and Imputed Quality," *Journal of Business*, 37 (April 1964), pp. 186-91.

[16] B. Enis and J. Stafford, "The Price-Quality Relationship: An Extension," *Journal of Marketing Research*, 6:4 (November 1969), pp. 256-8; J. Jacoby, J. Olson, and R. Haddock, "Price, Brand Name, and Product Composition Characteristics as Determinants of Perceived Quality," *Journal of Applied Psychology*, 55 (December 1971), pp. 470-9; D. Gardner, "Is There a Generalized Price-Quality Relationship?" *Journal of Marketing Research*, 8:2 (May 1971), pp. 241-3.

[17]Kent B. Monroe, op. cit., p. 73.

[18]J. Douglas McConnell, "Effect of Pricing on Perception of Product Quality," *Journal of Applied Psychology*, 52 (1968), pp. 331-4.

[19]George B. Sproles, "New Evidence on Price and Product Quality," *Journal of Consumer Affairs*, 11 (Summer 1977), pp. 63-7.

[20]F.E. Brown, "Who Perceives Supermarket Prices Most Validly?" *Journal of Marketing Research*, 8:1 (February 1971), pp. 110-3.

[21]*Progressive Grocer*, "How Much Do Customers Know about Retail Prices?" 43 (February 1964), pp. 104-6.

[22]Kent B. Monroe, "The Influence of Price Differences and Brand Familiarity on Brand Preferences," *Journal of Consumer Research*, 3 (June 1976), p. 42.

[23]Kent B. Monroe, "Buyers' Subjective Perceptions," p. 75.

[24]F. Emery, "Some Psychological Aspects of Price," in B. Taylor and G. Wills (eds.), *Pricing Strategy* (New York: Brandon/System Press, 1970).

[25]Raymond A. Bauer, "Consumer Behavior as Risk Taking," in Robert S. Hancock (ed.), *Dynamic Marketing for a Changing World* (Chicago: American Marketing Association, 1960), pp. 389-98.

[26]James W. Taylor, "The Role of Risk in Consumer Behavior," *Journal of Marketing*, 38 (April 1974), pp. 54-60.

[27]Ibid., p. 58.

[28]James R. Bettman, "Perceived Risk and Its Components: A Model and Empirical Test," *Journal of Marketing Research*, 10 (May 1973), pp. 184-90; and "The Structure of Consumer Choice Processes," *Journal of Marketing Research*, 8:4 (November 1971), pp. 465-71. See also Charles M. Schaninger, "Perceived Risk and Personality," *Journal of Consumer Research*, 3:2 (September 1976), pp. 95-100.

[29]Robert D. Hisrich, Ronald J. Dornoff, and Jerome B. Kernan, "Perceived Risk in Store Selection," *Journal of Marketing Research*, 9 (November 1972), pp. 435-9.

[30]Joseph F. Dash, Leon G. Schiffman, and Conrad Berenson, "Risk- and-Personality-Related Dimensions of Store Choice," *Journal of Marketing*, 40 (January 1976), pp. 32-9.

[31]Donald F. Cox and Stuart V. Rich, "Perceived Risk and Consumer Decision Making: The Case of Telephone Shopping," in Donald F. Cox (ed.), *Risk Taking and Information Handling in Consumer Behavior* (Boston: Division of Research, Graduate School of Business, Harvard University, 1967), p. 504.

[32]Homer E. Spence, James F. Engel, and Roger D. Blackwell, "Perceived Risk in Mail-Order and Retail Store Buying," *Journal of Marketing Research*, 7:3 (August 1970), pp. 364-9.

[33]Scott M. Cunningham, "Perceived Risk and Brand Loyalty," in Cox, op. cit., p. 513.

[34]Johan Arndt, "Role of Product-Related Conversations in the Diffusion of a New Product," in Cox, op. cit., p. 294.

[35]Scott M. Cunningham, "Perceived Risk as a Factor in Informal Consumer Communication," in Cox, op. cit., p. 274.

[36]Johan Arndt, "Word-of-Mouth Advertising and Informal Communication, in Cox, op. cit., pp. 188-239.

[37]Ted Roselius, "Consumer Rankings of Risk Reduction Methods," *Journal of Marketing*, 35:1 (January 1971), p. 58.

[38]Ibid., p. 61.

[39]Arch G. Woodside and M. Wayne DeLozier, "Effects of Word-of-Mouth Advertising on Consumer Risk-Taking," *Journal of Advertising*, 5 (Fall 1976), pp. 12-6.

[40]Terence A. Shimp and William O. Bearden, "Warranty and Other Extrinsic Cue Effects on Consumer Risk Perceptions," *Journal of Consumer Research*, 9 (June 1982), pp. 38-46.

[41]Richard W. Mizerski, Linda L. Golden, and Jerome B. Kernan, "The Attribution Process in Consumer Decision Making," *Journal of Consumer Research*, 6 (September 1979), p. 123.

[42]Robert A. Hansen and Carol A. Scott, "Comments on Attribution Theory and Advertiser Credibility," *Journal of Marketing Research*, 13:2 (May 1976), pp. 193-7.

[43]H.H. Kelley, "Attribution Theory in Social Psychology," in D. Levine (ed.), *Nebraska Symposium on Motivation* (Lincoln, Nebraska: University of Nebraska Press, 1967), p. 197.

[44]Bobby J. Calder and Robert E. Burnkrant, "Interpersonal Influence on Consumer Behavior: An Attribution Theory Approach," *Journal of Consumer Research*, 4 (June 1977), pp. 29-38.

[45]Ibid., p. 30.

[46]Robert B. Settle and Linda L. Golden, "Attribution Theory and Advertiser Credibility," *Journal of Marketing Research*, 11: 2 (May 1974), pp. 181-5.

[47]Hansen and Scott, op. cit.; Robert E. Burnkrant, "Attribution Theory in Marketing Research: Problems and Prospects," in M. J. Schlinger (ed.), *Advances in Consumer Research* (Chicago: Association for Consumer Research, 1974).

[48]R.E. Smith and S.D. Hunt, "Attributional Processes and Effects in Promotional Situations," *Journal of Consumer Research*, 5 (December 1978), pp. 149-58.

[49]E.E. Jones and K. Davis, "From Acts to Dispositions: The Attribution Process in Person Perception," in Leonard Berkowitz (ed.), *Advances in Experimental Psychology*, 2 (New York: Academic Press, 1965), pp. 219-66.

[50]Mizerski, Golden, and Kernan, op. cit., p. 137.

[51]P.E. Green, F.J. Carmone, and P.J. Robinson, "Nonmetric Scaling Methods: An Exposition and Overview," *Wharton Quarterly* (Winter-Spring 1968), pp. 27-41.

[52]Nariman K. Dhalla and Winston H. Mahatoo, "Expanding the Scope of Segmentation Research," *Journal of Marketing*, 40 (April 1976), pp. 34-41.

[53]Philip Kotler, *Principles of Marketing* (Englewood Cliffs, New Jersey: Prentice-Hall, 1980), p. 382.

[54]"Name Game — New Wine in Old Bottles," *Time* Magazine (31 August 1981), pp. 37-8.

[55]W.A. Mindak, "Fitting the Semantic Differential to the Marketing Problem," *Journal of Marketing*, 25 (April 1961), pp. 28-33.

[56]Daryl J. Bem, "Self-Perception Theory," in L. Berkowitz (ed.), *Advances in Experimental Social Psychology* (New York: Academic Press, 1972).

SHELBY CORN OILS LIMITED*

The Shelby Corn Oils Company produced a line of cooking oils, of which one brand was a leading seller nationally, although its market share varied considerably between different markets because of different cooking habits and because of the activities of competitors. In 1964, the company was considering a package label change as part of an overall company program of updating its labels. Before making the change, the company's research department was assigned the task of measuring its effectiveness against the old label as well as against the label of the company's leading competitor.

In considering how best to conduct such a test, the research department decided to set up the following criteria:

- visibility or brand recognition of each label as compared to one another;
- overall label preference (and reasons why);
- a comparative measure on various label attributes that are common to all three labels;
- a comparative measure on various product attributes as conveyed by the label.

It was decided to test the labels among a group of ninety housewives who currently used cooking oil. All respondents were interviewed individually in the offices of the independent research organization that was hired to undertake the study. In no case were any of the respondents told who the sponsor of the study was.

Random calls were made to local housewives asking them to come into the office to participate in a study. Appointments were made, where possible, at the convenience of the housewife, who usually tied in her appointment with a visit downtown. Housewives were offered ten dollars for cooperating in the study.

---

* *Adapted from* Harper W. Boyd, Jr., and Ralph Westfall, *Marketing Research*, rev. ed. (Homewood, Illinois: Richard D. Irwin, Inc., 1964), pp. 138-41. Copyright © 1964 Richard D. Irwin, Inc.

Each respondent was exposed to a visual testing device that was specifically designed to measure an optical stimulus. The technical name for the device is Tachistoscope. The device consisted of a box about three feet long that was completely sealed against light. The respondent looked into this box and was exposed, on a controlled basis, to material at the other end. The exposure was controlled by the amount of time the material was visible.

In this test, all labels were shown in pairs at a light flash interval of half a second. Each label's relative position, on the right or left hand side, was rotated.

Respondents were required to report, as exactly as possible, all that they remembered seeing — such as colors, words, designs, and drawings — and to indicate on which side (right or left) each item was seen.

Upon completion of the Tachistoscope test, respondents were shown all three labels, at which time overall preferences along with opinions regarding various label attributes, were obtained. The exposure and position frequency of each label paired-comparison for the sample were as follows:

Shelby new vs. Shelby current	15
Shelby current vs. Shelby new	15
Shelby current vs. major competitor	15
Major competitor vs. Shelby current	15
Shelby new vs. major competitor	15
Major competitor vs. Shelby new	15
TOTAL RESPONDENTS	90

Findings

Shelby Current Label Versus Shelby New Label

Twenty-four of the thirty respondents who were exposed to this particular combination played back a copy point. Both labels performed equally in terms of the amount of playback given. The predominant copy point given for each label was "corn oil."

All thirty respondents played-back a color or some combination of colors; however, twenty-one of them gave colors that were representative of the current label, as compared to fifteen who mentioned colors in connection with the proposed label. Shelby's current red and blue label received a higher degree of color playback than the proposed label, which was predominantly yellow.

Shelby Current Label Versus Major Competitor's Label

Twenty-seven of the thirty respondents played back a copy point. All twenty-seven mentioned the competitor's brand name, compared to fifteen who mentioned copy points in reference to the Shelby current label.

In the area of color playback, the competitor's brand again registered a higher recall with twenty-seven out of thirty as compared to fifteen out of thirty for the Shelby current label.

Shelby New Label Versus Competitor's Label

Twenty-seven out of thirty respondents played back a copy point. All twenty-seven mentioned the competitor's brand name while twelve gave a copy recall in reference to the Shelby new label. Among the twenty-one who mentioned a color or a combination of colors, fifteen were related to the Shelby new label and twelve referred to the competitor's label.

Label Preference and Reasons Why

When exposed to all three labels, respondents selected the competitor's label as the one *most* appealing. The average rank order preference score each label received was as follows:

	%
Competitor	92.2
Shelby's new	68.8
Shelby's current	48.2

These weighted average scores were computed by assigning the weight of 3 to a first place ranking, 2 to a second place ranking, and 1 to a last place. These accumulated totals were percentaged against 270, which represented a perfect score if every respondent ranked the same label in first place.

The reasons given most frequently for preferring the competitor's label were that its printing was larger and that its brand name stood out very plainly.

Reasons for preferring the Shelby new label were that the color combination was very attractive and the salad illustration was appealing.

Of the six respondents preferring the Shelby current label, three mentioned that the words "Corn Oil" stood out, while the other three liked the pictures on the label.

Respondents were then asked to rate the three labels using an eleven-point semantic scale. The results are shown in Exhibit 1. In each case, except in reference to economical/expensive, the competitor's label conveyed a stronger profile rating than either of the two Shelby labels. In comparison, the Shelby new label's image, in nearly all instances, was better than the current label, but not as good as the competitive label. The Shelby current label was very weak in color combination and not appealing. The current label left the impression that the product was more "oily" than the other two.

QUESTIONS

1. Evaluate the research design. What changes, if any, should be made?

2. What does this case illustrate about consumer perception?

3. Assuming the information obtained is adequate, what recommendations should be made regarding the Shelby new label?

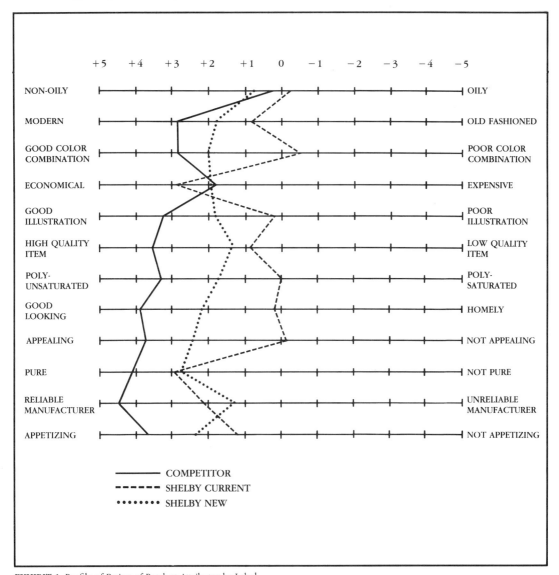

EXHIBIT 1: Profile of Rating of Product Attributes by Label

7

Symbolism

EXAMPLES

1. Canadian Logo Changes[1]

In recent months, a number of Canadian companies have modified their logos. There appears to be a considerable amount of confidence in the effectiveness of these signatures and in the ability of these corporate identities to reflect changes in ownership and direction.

What is interesting are the stated objectives given for the changes. For example, Island Paper Mills Ltd. adopted a new, corporate mark with "definite, flowing lines." It consists of a red sheet of paper, partly folded over to reveal a white underside, and a blue sheet next to it (A in Figure 7.1). It was felt that the style and colors projected an image of a young, energetic, innovative, dynamic company committed to success and strength. The assumption is that the blue, white, and red squares balanced on one corner symbolize all of these things.

Another product of the "image makers" is the striped, bold-face capital R with a T inside it that Royal Trustco has substituted for the letters R and T incorporated in a shield. RT's comments are interesting:

> The change has been undertaken to symbolize the new, dynamic, and aggressive character of the company.... The distinctive and unique symbol... continues to represent the reputation and integrity of Royal Trust as one of Canada's leading financial, trust, and real estate organizations... [and] to express to our customers, staff, shareholders, and affiliates a new style and commitment to quality, leadership, and growth.

It is of interest to note also the new look adopted by the Prudential Insurance Company of America — a stylized rock of Gibraltar (B and C in Figure 7.1). Often a new logo or a name change becomes necessary if a company adopts a different philosophy or approach or diversifies so far beyond its original business that the old logo or name

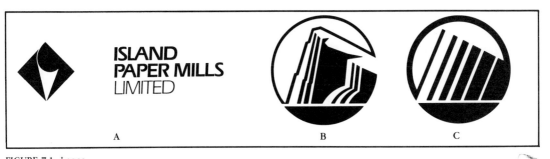

FIGURE 7.1: Logos

Courtesy Island Paper Mills Ltd. and the Prudential Insurance Company of America

no longer reflects the company's true nature. Sometimes such changes may have more to do with corporate cosmetics or even good old-fashioned hubris on the part of, say, a new president who decides he wants to set his own mark on the company.

2. A Story of O's: Sassoon Versus Sasson[2]

This story concerns a legal dispute in 1980 involving Vidal Sassoon, who has been called the father of modern hairstyling, and Sasson Jeans Inc., the jeans manufacturer whose television commercials feature peppy young people singing the praises of "Oo la la Sasson."

Vidal Sassoon Inc., which merchandises hair and beauty care products, objected because during these commercials Sasson (one "o") is sung as Sassoon (two "o's"). There was further objection to the commercial's on-screen hand forming a circular OK sign with thumb and forefinger within the "o" in Sasson. The consequences, Mr. Vidal felt, resulted in "confusion among consumers."

The man famed for the Sassoon cut in hair felt that he was being confused with the Sasson cut in jeans. So Vidal Sassoon Inc. brought a $25 million lawsuit against Sasson Jeans Inc. for "the appropriation of its name" and for "capitalizing on the reputation and credibility that Vidal Sassoon Inc. has spent over 25 years building." Then Sasson Jeans Inc. learned that Vidal Sassoon was taking steps to license *his* name on jeans. That, apparently, was hitting below the belt. The company filed a countersuit.

Under the settlement, agreed to with the help of New York Federal Judge Robert W. Sweet, the companies will "minimize or eliminate confusion with each other."

For Sasson Jeans Inc., that means the company is enjoined from employing its name "so that the last syllable of Sasson is pronounced as 'soon.'" The company was required to "explain to the public the change in pronunciation" as long as any explanatory advertising does not "disparage any other party." As for the company's "OK hand" logo, it may be used "so long as the appearance is not created that Sasson is spelled Sassoon."

As for Vidal Sassoon Inc., the settlement states that its use of the name Sassoon must be "preceded by the word 'Vidal' in substantially identical lettering and/or sound of the same size and prominence."

Paul Guez, president of Sasson Jeans Inc., answered, "Maurice Sasson, who was our original designer when we started making jeans in 1976, has always pronounced the last syllable of his name 'soon.' We feel that our business helped Vidal sell his shampoo."

A company spokesman for Vidal Sassoon said, "The settlement is exactly what we wanted and we can now undertake a vigorous licensing program."

Shown below is Sasson Jeans Inc.'s response to the agreement.

FIGURE 7.2: New Sasson Logo

Courtesy Sasson Jeans Inc.

3. Eye Influence on the Advertising Message[3]

Two studies in the early 1960s reported that pupil size seems to vary with degree of interest or positiveness. It was later reported that eye direction also appears to be related to the nature of the subject's reaction.[4] If the eyes turn to the left the response is emotional, if to the right, it is rational.

In an attempt to test these relationships as they might apply to promotional appeals, King carried out two studies with university students, arguing that

> Knowledge of these psychological characteristics of eye size and direction may have important implications for understanding nonverbal communication between the eyes of a person in an advertisement and the viewer. The message mediated by eyes is usually communicated unintentionally, without any conscious action on the artist's part. Although viewers may not be consciously aware of the subtleties involved, both pupil size and eye direction of models in advertising photographs may be important in shaping consumer attitudes about the product advertised.

He cites another study, which found that when men and women were shown semi-nude pictures of the opposite sex, their pupils dilated considerably more than when they observed members of the same sex.[5] He further notes that subsequent studies indicate that in some cases pupil response may be a more valid measure of attitude than verbal response. In questions concerning prejudice and race relations, verbal and visual responses were inconsistent. Some respondents insisted they were not prejudiced and were strongly opposed to discriminatory practices; however, their eyes revealed a strong constriction to photos of minority groups.

The consensus from later research appears to question the validity of pupillary dilation and constriction in detecting affective valence.[6] Pupillary response may reflect a number of other psychological processes such as arousal and attention and may be more useful in indicating the magnitude of a subject's responsiveness. Pupillary responses may also be more reliable in tests involving senses other than sight. For example, one study concluded that "sensitivity of eye response can indicate differences in taste preference which are so slight that respondents may not be consciously aware of them."[7]

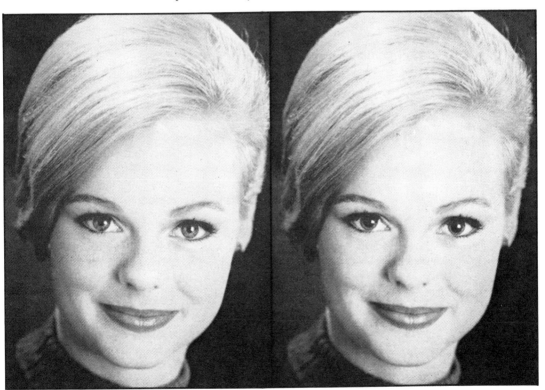

FIGURE 7.3: Two photographs, almost identical, except for the fact that one had been retouched to make the woman's pupils enlarged (right) and the other to make them very small (left)

Photo credit Hess, 1965, © Globe Photos, Inc., New York

Study 1 — Pupil Size and Message Appeal: Fifty students in an advanced marketing research course were shown two seemingly identical photographs of a young woman (Figure 7.3). The photos were identical except that one was modified to make the pupil size of the eyes much larger than in the other. None of the students noticed the specific way in which the photos were different. Interestingly, while over half of them felt there was some difference, none could identify it.

All subjects selected the woman with the enlarged pupils as prettier and more appealing.

Study 2 — Eye Direction and Message Appeal: It appears that individuals are characteristically left- or right-lookers and that there are important personality differences between the two groups.[8] Lateral directions of the eyes appear to indicate which hemisphere of the brain is dominant. In general, left-lookers tend to be more relaxed, sociable, imaginative, subjective, yielding to suggestion, less quantitative, and more affectionate than right-lookers. Also, they tend to exhibit greater fluency in writing, and are likely to show greater interest in philosophy, music, art, and the humanities than right-lookers, who show more scientific inclinations. It also seems that there are some individuals whose thought is equally dominated by both left- and right-shifting eye movements.

The basic differences imply that eye direction also serves as an unintentional cue conveying rational or emotional appeal. This suggests a possible relationship between eye direction and message appeal. It should be noted that, although a left-looking model is gazing to the viewer's right, the viewer, in effect, mentally transposes the picture and still "sees" the model as left-looking.

Two similar photographs, in one of which the eyes were aligned to the right and in the other to the left, were shown to 106 undergraduates at Kansas State University. The students were first asked to select the photo with stronger appeal and then interviewed by another experimenter who, in the course of posing a number of questions, classified them as right- or left-movers. The results are shown in Figure 7.4.

Subjects Photographs	Left-Movers*	Right-Movers	Total
Left direction	31	14	45
Right direction	20	41	61
Total	51	55	106

$x^2 = 13.52$ df = 1   P < .001

FIGURE 7.4: Pattern of Eye Movements and Photo Selection

*Subjects classified as either left- or right-movers on the basis of eye response to two out of three questions.

Right-lookers saw the photo with the eyes directed to the right as significantly more appealing, whereas left-lookers favored the photo with the eyes to the left. None of the subjects could specify the reason for selecting one photo over the other.

King makes the following general conclusion: nonverbal messages conveyed by the eyes in pictorial advertisements may be an integral aspect of what is communicated to a viewer. If this nonverbal cue is perceived by the viewer in a manner inconsistent with the advertiser's intended message, it may inhibit the reception of that message. How an advertiser treats eye size and eye direction in advertisements may affect the effectiveness of the advertising appeal.

In the last chapter perception was described as the process by which an individual gives meaning to a stimulus. The perception is the result of subjective factors (personality, needs, attitudes) and the stimulus characteristics. What I want to emphasize in this chapter is that the contribuion of the stimulus comes not only from its physical properties but from its associations and connotations.

SYMBOL DEFINED

All human communication is done through symbols: words, figures, numbers, images, or gestures serve to express a message that others, for whom those symbols have the same meaning, will perceive correctly. In a sense, "the vehicle of perception is the symbol."[9] We live in the midst of symbolical representations, from the ceremonies celebrating the joy of birth to rites expressing the sorrow of death. Symbols are an important form of human communication and because they "are very often a shorthand for expressing complex thoughts, they hold the potential for increasing the efficiency of a commercial mass communications system."[10]

Strictly speaking, those words or images that "do no more than denote the objects to which they are attached" may be called signs. The term symbol I will reserve for those that "may be familiar in daily life, yet possess specific connotations in addition to [their] conventional and obvious meanings."[11]

They are symbols because, as Jung would explain, they imply "something more than [their] obvious and immediate meaning. [They have] a wider 'unconscious' aspect that is never precisely defined or fully explained."[12]

This "unconscious aspect" should be emphasized. While an individual may be conscious of the denotative meaning of a stimulus, he or she is most likely to be unaware of other connotative meanings it may have that will also influence reactions to it. In most instances in marketing, the same words or objects or images serve as both signs and symbols, so their use in communication requires care and knowledge. Words come to acquire additional, symbolic meanings, as do images and objects. For example, brand names are chosen for their literal meanings but also for what they suggest or connote; entire products take on a significance far beyond their original purpose (Cadillac and Rolls-Royce cars, Chivas Regal whisky). Numbers, gestures, facial expressions, and even entire behavioral sequences (e.g., rites) can have symbolic value.

Symbol is a general term for all instances where experience is mediated rather than direct; where an object, action, word, picture, or complex behavior is understood to mean not only itself but also some other ideas or feelings.[13]

GENESIS OF SYMBOLS

Symbolic meanings may be established by accident or by intention. Words or images may happen to become associated with certain emotions or values; or certain agencies (e.g., advertisers) may deliberately generate and foster particular associations with given stimuli. In any event, these meanings are acquired through personal or societal experience. A stimulus could have symbolic meaning for an individual because of that individual's experience with it, in which case the symbolism is specific and personal; or it could have a wider meaning shared by large numbers of individuals (even though they may not be conscious of this fact). Although symbols are frequently limited to a particular culture or society, some have a common significance across cultures. Some have withstood the rigors of time and continued to have the same meaning; some have disappeared and later reappeared in modified form; others are entirely new and relevant to our technological age.

SYMBOLS AND THE MARKETER

In employing symbols, marketers must be aware of the symbolic meanings of words and images, and recognize that the same stimulus can have different meanings for different persons. As Levy notes,

> The same person may see several meanings and different people may see different meanings. A picture of a skier shows a man standing on two sticks: this may signify a pleasant sport, a dangerous sport, an expensive pastime, new ways of leisure in America, superior social status at an elegant resort, the competitiveness of the Olympics, even a cause of perspiration (in a deodorant advertisement).[14]

As mass communicators, marketers search for those stimuli with broad, social meanings in order to communicate with groups of individuals. Marketers must ensure that the symbols they employ will convey the intended meaning to their target audience and be constantly mindful that the goods and services consumers buy are seen as symbolic of personal attributes and goals. Levy puts it this way:

> The product will be used and enjoyed when it joins with, meshes with, adds to, reinforces the [consumer's self-perception]. In the broadest sense, each person aims to enhance his [or her] sense of self, to behave in ways that are consistent with a set of ideas he [she] has about the kind of person he [she] is or wants to be.... Because of their symbolic nature, consumer goods can be chosen with less conflict or indecision than would otherwise be the case.... Our choices are made easier ... because one object is symbolically more harmonious to our goals, feelings, and self-definitions than is another.... There is then more well with the world when the bathroom tissue is pastel blue.[15]

... and, he might have continued for our world of the 1980s, the car small and foreign-made, the trousers blue jeans.

Some social observers have remarked on the pervasiveness of symbolism in marketing in affluent societies. Consumers do not choose to buy a particular product, but rather the functional expectations they attach to it. They buy these expectations as tools "to help solve the problems of life.... Whether we are aware of it or not, we in effect expect and demand that advertising create these symbols to show us what life might be, to bring the possibilities that we cannot see before our eyes, and screen out the stark reality in which we must live."[16]

In the next section I discuss the basic sources of the symbolism employed by marketers — the attributes that can invest words and images with overlays of symbolic meaning. These include colors, words, objects, sound, shape or form, and typography. Expressions of their application may appear in the shapes and colors of packages or labels, in trademarks and brand names, in the color of the product, in the decor and atmosphere of retail outlets, in TV, magazine, billboard, or newspaper advertising or in other promotional material.

COLOR SYMBOLISM

Colors come to be associated with particular objects so that, through experience, we expect certain things to have certain colors. We expect snow to be white, just as we expect raw beef to be red or carrots to be yellow. When consumers inspect merchandise, they seem to compare it with an accepted color or range of colors. Bread that is too dark may be overbaked; apples and tomatoes that are too green are not mature; packages must have the familiar colors or negative perceptions may result. For example, if the colors of the package are too pale, the consumer may think that the package has been left on the shelf too long and the contents may be spoiled.

Marketers attempt to correct for some of these possibilities in many ways — they use synthetic additives to produce the colors consumers expect, and create the kind of lighting environment that enhances appearance. It has been found, for example, that fluorescent lamps give meat an unpleasant greenish tinge, suggesting putrefaction, while other lamps make it appear redder than it is.

Beyond these physiological characteristics of color, it has been found that colors have symbolic meanings. Some experts believe that these meanings are derived from experience and tradition, others that the symbolic significance is the result of inherent properties of the color. As we shall see, in many instances associative learning may be responsible for the meanings some colors have, but it is also possible that the electromagnetic waves (which are the physical components of color) may be related to the generation of certain psychological states or experiences in the individual.[17]

It has been found that:[18]

- **Red** means heat, excitement, danger, rage, fire, and blood. The underlying notion of heightened anticipation (danger) or activity (excitement) could be related to the effect of the long wavelengths in the red part of the spectrum on human mental activity. In addition, many objects that we know to be "hot" are red — hot peppers, hot iron, fire. A good example in marketing is Tabasco — a hot pepper sauce that is red and is shown on the package as a red bottle on a white background. There are, however, other things that are red and soothing — tomatoes, watermelon.
- **Orange** is associated with forcefulness, exuberance, autumn, and a certain richness (see Plate II in the color-plate section).
- **Yellow** means warmth, sunlight, vitality, and brightness. It can also mean cowardice.
- **Green** symbolizes coolness, freshness, peacefulness, nature, and water. Mark the number of brands of menthol cigarettes that have taken advantage of this symbolism. Green can also mean envy or guilt.
- **Blue** means coldness or sadness, loneliness, and depression. It can also mean high quality, modernness, and pleasantness. (See Plate III.) Some years ago it was found that the identical detergent was rated better when taken from a blue box than from a box of another color. Soon almost all detergent brands appeared in blue boxes, at which point blue lost its differential advantage[19] and many brands switched to other colors, such as Tide (Orange), Fab (Yellow), and Sunlight (Yellow). Cheer is a major brand that has retained a basically blue box.
- **Violet** is associated with coolness and with royalty and dignity (quality). An excellent example is the color used in advertisements for Seagram's Crown Royal, particularly the color of the pouch (violet) and the gold cord (both of which are being dispensed with, presumably for economic reasons).
- **White** symbolizes purity, cleanliness, and peace.
- **Black** symbolizes death, mourning, emptiness, and generally seems to possess negative

connotations. In marketing, however, it is widely used to convey sophistication, expensiveness, high quality — Black Velvet Rye (Figure 7.5), Johnny Walker Black Label (Figure 7.6), and Black Tower — all brands of alcohol!

McNeal points out that the colors with the longer wavelengths (red, orange, yellow) "are symbolic of heat" and those with the shorter wavelengths (green, blue, violet) "are associated with cold."[20] Tests have shown that a red product appears warmer and a blue or green product cooler;[21] and that a red room is perceived as warmer than a blue room of the same temperature.[22]

Some colors have masculine associations and others feminine.[23] The primary colors (red, green, blue, brown) are seen as masculine and pastels as feminine. The use of primary colors

in the label of a beer for men was noted in Example 1 in Chapter 5. In western society, pink is for baby girls and blue for boys.

Colors are also associated with **weight**. It appears that such colors as red, purple, blue, and black are heavy and yellow, orange, white, and pastels are light. Some colors seem to give the impression of greater solidity and substance and thus may be experienced as heavier.

Color preferences seem to vary among social classes in our society. The upper classes are reported to prefer delicate hues and the lower social classes bright, pure hues.[24] Differences of this kind may also be found among age groups or life-style groups.

Color is also used to generate moods and emotions. In Plate IV, for example, a clever combination of color shades has been put together to create feelings of elegance and romance and to give the scene an ethereal, dream-like quality.

**Stare at this picture for fifteen seconds.
Now name the rye.**

The first thing you notice is that it is very black. And certainly it looks very much like velvet. Did you guess? Of course you did. Black Velvet.

FIGURE 7.5: Black in Advertising
Courtesy Gilbey Canada Inc.

There's one colour that always identifies fine Scotch.
EXTRA SPECIAL OLD SCOTCH WHISKY

FIGURE 7.6: Black in Advertising
Courtesy John Walker & Sons Ltd.

The symbolic meanings of the different colours are not the same from one culture to another. For example, while in the western world white suggests purity, in China it symbolizes death. Purple is the color of mourning in parts of Asia and Latin America; it is black in most of Europe, the U.S., and Canada.

This phenomenon of cultural variation is of particular importance to the marketer because of its implications for international marketing. Preferences for and symbolic meanings of different colors should be noted and their use in products, packages, labels, logos, or advertising guided accordingly.

The story is told of a brewery in Southern Ontario that was contemplating a label change. Concerned about the influence of prior experience on reactions to the new label, the advertiser decided to test it in Southern California, where he felt he would get "pure" reactions. The problem was that Californians might prefer different colors and color combinations and the results could be quite inapplicable.

The variation in color preference and meaning across cultures no doubt is due in part to geographical differences. Green labels and packages may not have much influence in getting farmers to buy your goods. They see so much green that it hardly registers with them. And yet societies in warmer climates with verdant, colorful vegetation seem to prefer bright, basic colors. "Internationally, Scandinavians seem to favor bright greens and blues while Mexicans and Italian are fond of warm reds."[25]

It is reported that "an oil company that exported its products to India for use in oil lamps was informed that the natives loved red and had reverence for monkeys. The company therefore had a red monkey painted on the oil containers that were distributed to India. Needless to say, the business was fine."[26]

WORD SYMBOLISM

Repeat aloud the words, "The Golden Road to Samarkand" and you won't fail to grasp how ordinary words and sounds can evoke glorious images and wondrous feelings. The ability to use words and images in that way is the essence of successful communication in marketing or in any other field.

Such connotative or symbolic meanings of words may be said to emanate from three main sources:

- the "objects" that they represent;
- the sociological or psychological context in which they are used; and
- the inherent sound or rhythm of the word.

Words such as Cougar, Mustang, and Thunderbird come to symbolize power, speed, and sleekness. In some cases, these connotations may be intercultural, in others it may be characteristic of a group within a society.

Other words derive their connotations, not from the properties of the objects they represent, but from sociological and psychological circumstances. For example, "housewife" has negative connotations for some who reject it and prefer "homemaker" or "householder." The current "fad," in this observer's opinion, of exorcising the word "man" from the language and replacing it with "person," relates directly to the connotations such words as "chairman" are seen to possess. Other examples are dinner (versus supper) and napkin (versus serviette), which have social class connotations.

Some words possess an inherent phonetic quality that gives them unconscious symbolic meanings (e.g., quarterback, lumberjack, supersonic, safari, space age, exotic).

One source has claimed that there are tall, skinny words, and short fat ones, and strong ones and weak ones, and boy-words and girl-words.[27] For example:

- tall — title, peninsula, ellipsis
- short, fat — hot, bomb, plump, sop, acne
- feminine — tissue, cute, peek, nude
- masculine — rupture, oak, naked
- hard — edge, point, corner
- soft — lip, thud, stuff, drum

BRAND-NAME SYMBOLISM

Traditionally, although companies spend a great deal of time and money on new product ideas, they do not invest too much in the choice of a brand name. This has been changing, however, as more and more marketers recognize that a well-chosen name can considerably enhance the image and desirability of a brand. Now there are companies that deal exclusively with name selection. One of these is NameLab, who describe themselves as "name consultants." Ira N. Bachrach, its founder, feels that name selection should not result from the boss' inspiration or a contest among the secretaries.

An excellent example of a good name is American Honda's popular Civic automobile, which, according to Bachrach (although he was not involved with that car), "is made for urban driving and . . . it's socially responsible — 'civic-minded' — because it doesn't pollute too much or waste gasoline."

A name that he did have something to do with was Nissan's Sentra, which, explains a Nissan executive, "doesn't mean anything." It developed from the fact that the car was the central model in the Nissan line and it also reminded consumers of "sentry."

When entrusted with creating a name, NameLab starts with a list of the qualities the client wants to convey. Mr. Bachrach and two linguists then make a list of related root words from Latin, Greek, Anglo-Saxon, and other languages and another list of words that describe what the product is or does.

NameLab looks for mnemonic factors, the qualities that make certain words stick in the mind. Names that tell what a product *does* are especially good. "A name like Theragram-M is more expensive to stuff into a vitamin buyer's head," says Mr. Bachrach, "than a name like One-A-Day." Words like Coca-Cola are memorable simply for their sounds. Name consultants work with onomatopoeia, assonance, and mnemonic devices. In essence, the task is to make deodorant sound wholesome, lipstick sensual, and frozen potato exciting.

Also prized are words with "episodic encoding" — words that remind people of emotional or physical experiences like childbirth. The name Mustang for a car, as an example, causes emotional responses in men, associated with the excitement of being a cowboy.

In addition, potential names are judged for unusualness and "flicker perception," that is, the way a name is regarded as it is flashed across a screen.

A short, reduced list of potential names is tested with likely buyers of the product in order to determine the final choice.

An excellent example of what a company tries to accomplish with a name is what lay behind the name changeover from Allegheny Airlines to USAir in 1979. Marketing Research had shown that Allegheny was perceived as a small regional carrier (even though it was the sixth largest airline in the United States), and that small airlines were not good, in such areas as experienced pilots, safety, maintenance, and dependability.

In the face of such a serious image problem, management decided to adopt a name that would suggest an airline of national scope and character, and the official change was made after the company had expanded its service in order to be consistent with the connotations of the name. A massive advertising campaign was undertaken to publicize and reinforce the name change. The media mix was changed, with an emphasis on television and an increase in magazine advertising; radio commercials, personal field staff calls, outdoor signs, and a wide variety of specialty advertising were used to support the campaign — all at a total cost of $3 million.

OBJECT SYMBOLISM

The advertisement in Figure 7.7 is an excellent example of how objects may be used to suggest ideas to the viewer. While many objects have inherent connotations (e.g., a baby suggesting innocence), in many others symbolic meanings may be generated and fostered over time (e.g., the Rolls-Royce symbol on an automobile). Symbolic use is made of humans (of all ages), animals, as well as both animate and inanimate natural objects.

Babies suggest innocence, love, care, affection; children fun, togetherness, "carefree-ness"; teenagers can symbolize growth, optimism, potential, and excitement; older persons may mean contentment and wisdom. As social values change, symbols also need to change in order to reflect acceptable norms.

The human figures in Figure 7.7 clearly suggest a certain life-style, and particular class connotations, with which the service is being associated.

Pictures of animals are widely used. Kittens are soft and cuddly; birds are gentle; dogs are masculine and "man's" best friend. The mouse symbolizes meekness and quiet; the tiger is fast and sleek; the lion powerful and dominant; the cow is gentle, quiet, and patient; the fox is sly and quick.

Trees may be used as symbols of strength and growth, of freshness and good health; rivers and lakes may suggest a setting that is clean and refreshing, just as mountains symbolize loftiness, challenge, permanence, and even coolness (snow-covered peaks).

Your first minute at Marriott.

Marriott Hotels.

FIGURE 7.7: Object Symbolism
Courtesy Marriott Corporation

Cherubic but Not as Chubby

Campbell's pudgy kids of the 1920s are now trimmer and athletic

For 79 years the dimpled dumplings known as the Campbell's Soup kids have been among the most familiar and successful symbols in advertising. When the kids first appeared in posters on New York City trolley cars, Cy Young was on the mound for the Boston Somersets (now the Red Sox) and Enrico Caruso was winding up his first American opera season. Cherubic and definitely chubby, the kids have always conveyed the message that children raised on "M'm! M'm! Good!" Campbell's soups will grow up healthy and happy.

But times are changing, and so are the kids. Realizing that thin is in and fitness is the fashion, the Campbell Soup Co. has made its pudgy pixies taller, trimmer and more athletic. The transformation is part of the company's drive to convince the yogurt-and-vitamin crowd that soup from a can is as nutritious as anything found in a health-food store. As part of the effort, Campbell is sponsoring the U.S. figure-skating team and has managed to get its products designated the "official soups" of the 1984 Winter Olympics in Sarajevo, Yugoslavia. The new, thinner Campbell kids are appropriately garbed as skaters, skiers and bobsledders. Admits Paul Mulcahy, Campbell's managing director for advertising: "We've slimmed them down a bit, and we'll gradually slim them down a bit more." He vows, however, that "the kids will never be skinny."

Many companies have a long tradition of making cosmetic changes in their advertising symbols. Psyche, the winged goddess who has adorned the labels of White Rock beverages for 89 years, has grown steadily more svelte. In 1894, says the company, she was 5 ft. 4 in. tall, weighed 140 lbs. and sported measurements of 37-27-38. Now she is 5 ft. 8 in., 118 lbs. and 35-24-34. She was always topless until 1975, when White Rock switched from paintings and started using photographs of a real, filmily clad woman in some promotional materials. Betty Crocker, the imaginary supercook at General Mills, has had five facelifts since 1936 to make her look younger and trendier. Careful observers may have noticed that Aunt Jemima seems to have joined Weight Watchers in recent years.

Some famous advertising figures, of course, have so far escaped the fitness fad. The jolly old Quaker of Quaker Oats is as rotund today as when his paunchy figure first appeared in 1877.

Psyche in 1894, top, and today

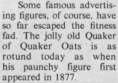

Betty Crocker in 1936 and her updated images in 1965 and 1980

An Example of Symbol Adaptation to Changing Social Values

SOURCE: *Time* Magazine (4 April 1983), p. 57. Reprinted with permission from *Time*, Campbell Soup Company Ltd., General Mills Ltd., and White Rock Products Corp.

Inanimate objects abound in marketing material. Their connotations develop out of the customs and values of a particular society. In Figure 7.7 it does not take long to identify the message being conveyed by the ad (lighting, models, dress, briefcase, doorman, plants, the Rolls-Royce, chauffeur, layout) about the hotel and its clientele (note the style of lettering on the entrance). As the ad says, "One minute should be more than enough to show you why Marriott stands apart from every other hotel company in the world." This is very important. From the wide variety of carefully chosen symbolic stim-uli, the viewer quickly and unconsciously arrives at a general, unified impression of Marriott.

Figure 7.8 illustrates the use of objects in more subtle ways to convey ideas about a product. The table top, the fireplace, the pen on what is obviously a legal document all suggest upper-class status for the advertised brand. It is used by professional, affluent, well-dressed men (the French cuffs, the shirts, the cuff link, the signet ring on the finger) who are elegant and sophisticated (a well-manicured hand holding the snifter in the right way).

The figures are obviously facing the fire in a

SIGNED. SEALED. SAVOUR IT!

COURVOISIER

Le Cognac de Napoléon

FIGURE 7.8: Object Symbolism
Courtesy Corby Distilleries Ltd. and Courvoisier S.A.

quiet, easy sharing of a pleasurable, relaxed moment as a reward for a job completed. Even the position of the hands and fingers is suggestive of the relaxation and friendship that is the ambience of the scene.

SOUND SYMBOLISM

Pause sometime when you are watching a movie. Concentrate on the *musical background* behind the images and consider how much the music is contributing to your perception of the mood, feelings, relationships, and future of the characters. It anticipates and recalls, it supports and contradicts. A great deal of time is spent by gifted composers in the creation of the musical background to movies (recall the figure-ground phenomenon described in the Chapter 5). Music is used to set a mood not only in commercials but also in shopping malls, stores, offices, and factories.

Sounds surround us and different sounds come to represent certain feelings, emotions, and images. The human voice is among them. Within a given culture one can usually distinguish from an individual's voice whether he or she is angry, pleased, rushed, or relaxed. This ability is not infallible, nor is the relationship of voice and meaning the same from one culture to another.

Have you noticed how often you may hear the same male voice and/or see the same model (announcer) in several different advertisements for different products? You are sure to find that the voice, if male, is low and resonant, pleasant rather than harsh, and perhaps even sexy. Not only does it attract attention, but it unconsciously conveys other messages such as confidence, trustworthiness, authority, reliability, intelligence, and masculinity.

Other sounds can take on symbolic meanings. Cars, for example, should sound a certain way. Many years ago a researcher found that car doors that sounded "heavy" impressed potential customers. An appliance company found that a silent mixer did not give the homemaker the feeling of work and so had to "introduce" more "noise" into it to achieve that end. Sounds are nostalgic or reminiscent of experiences and can be effective communicators — the "pop" of the champagne bottle, the "effervescence" of a ginger ale, or the "gurgling" of a bottle of beer being poured into a glass.

SHAPE/FORM SYMBOLISM

Like the other phenomena we have been discussing, shape and form are also transferred by individuals into the experience of other sense modalities. A given shape may be associated with a particular kind of sound or suggest a certain taste.

A delightful example of a transfer from shape to the sound of a name was given by a German psy-

FIGURE 7.9: Shapes and the Sounds They Symbolize

chologist. He drew the two designs [in Figure 7.9] and asked people which they would rather call "takete" and which "maluma"; the decision was easy.[28]

Shapes can suggest certain feelings or images. The hourglass may suggest a woman's figure, and even the shape of the sun can have symbolic significance. Several dishwashing-liquid containers are claimed to look like the figure of a woman and many shampoo "bottles" have been "accused" of looking like phallic symbols.

The shape of the package and the label significantly affect the perception of a brand.

> The product package is often spoken of as the 'silent salesman.' A good package has the ability to attract (and stimulate) the customer's attention. The size of the package, its color, and its design may be influential even though the consumer may think himself [herself] interested only in price, brand name, or contents.[29]

Some shapes come to evoke, over time, certain qualities. Companies generate and foster these associations. A prime example is the Mercedes-Benz symbol shown in Figure 7.10.

Other shapes appear to possess *inherent* connotations. Chrysler's Pentastar (see Figure 7.10), made up of five triangles that form a pentagon, is claimed to "provide an image of precision, strength, integrity, and unity."[30]

The basic geometric shapes are also considered to have symbolic meanings. The point (or dot) should not be underestimated. The point tends to freeze the eye and is a valuable attention-getter in packaging or advertising.

Depending upon how they are drawn, *lines* can be strong and decisive, weak and timid, or thin and precise. Dark angular lines generally symbolize strength, smoother flowing lines femininity, straight lines formalism, and kinky lines informality.[31]

Lines drawn in a certain fashion can suggest movement or force or emotion. A vertical line can symbolize growth, spiritual uplift, poise, or honesty; a horizontal line repose or stability; the diagonal line instability, action, and excite-

Trademark "Threepointed Star in a Ring" *Courtesy* Mercedes-Benz Canada, Inc.; trademark registered for Daimler-Benz AG, Stuttgart, Federal Republic of Germany.

Courtesy Chrysler Canada Ltd.

FIGURE 7.10: Shapes as Symbols

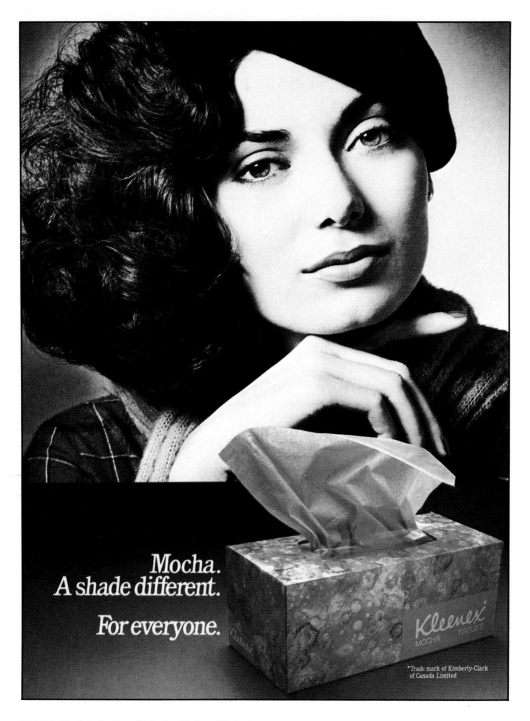

PLATE I: The Selective Use of Color in a Black-and-White Context

Courtesy Kimberly-Clark of Canada Ltd.

The beginning of a beautiful past.

PLATE II: The Use of Orange to Produce a Feeling of Exuberance

Courtesy Houbigant Inc.

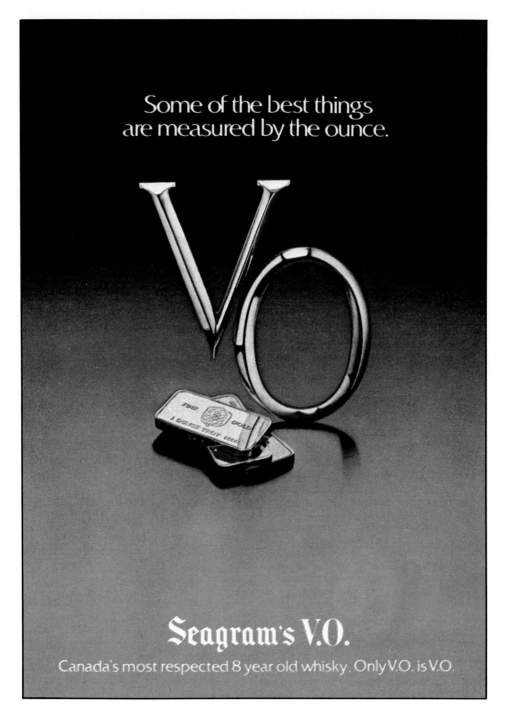

PLATE III: The Use of Color to Convey Quality

*In every woman there's a place
where life and vision interlace.
Where you look back to see
how far you've come,
and you know the best has just begun.
This is the place.
This is the Emeraude of your life.*

*Emeraude
Perfume by Coty.*

PLATE IV: The Use of Color to Create a World of Fantasy,
Romance, and Dreams

Courtesy Coty Division, Pfizer Inc.

ment (because it appears to be falling from an upright position).

> Lines... that lead the eye out from the package make the package appear larger than it is, but lines that lead the eye inward cause the package to appear smaller. Lines that run up and down the package make it appear taller than it is.[32]

Angles indicate direction. The sharper the angle the more forceful it becomes. The radial (or sun-burst) tends to take the eye away from the center and to generate a feeling of space (see Figure 7.11).

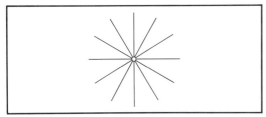

FIGURE 7.11: Radial

The square suggests solidity or unity. A true square does not appear square because a vertical line is seen as longer than a horizontal line of the same length.

The triangle suggests spirit and animation. The circle as the simplest form of continuous movement, is soft and feminine. The oval is the most aesthetically pleasing shape and has balance and gentleness. Many brand names make use of the oval (see Figure 7.12).

TYPOGRAPHICAL SYMBOLISM

Just as handwriting is claimed to reflect character (graphology),[33] so the style, arrangement, or appearance of the printed word (typography) can invest a word with additional connotative meanings. The width, height, style, thickness, and slant, and the space between letters and between words can all contribute to the word's symbolic meaning. Typography generates a mood or atmosphere. The way a word is printed may symbolize social class, progressiveness, modernity, tradition, masculinity, femininity, expensiveness, cheapness, dignity, economy, luxury, or strength, which are transferred to the brand or company.[34] Some typefaces are more appropriate for certain products than for others.

Typography reinforces the image that the marketer wishes to project, which is reflected in other marketing activities and materials as well. Figure 7.13 presents a selection of company names with different typefaces. Note, for example, the contrast between *The Globe and Mail* and Brian Winston, one staid, old-fashioned, long-established; the other free, modern, progressive, chic. Note too the modernity of the RCA and the MICOM typefaces and the computerish, space-age images evoked by the characters. The CN Rail typeface is noteworthy for its first two letters, which possess a fluidity and continuity, a

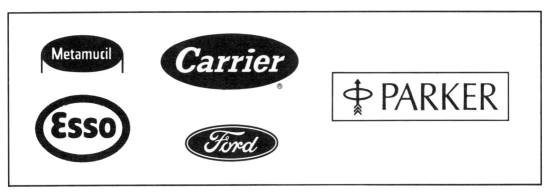

FIGURE 7.12: The Oval

Courtesy G.D. Searle & Co. of Canada Ltd., Imperial Oil Limited, Ford of Canada, Carrier Canada Ltd., The Parker Pen Company

FIGURE 7.13: A Selection of Different Scripts

Courtesy The Globe and Mail, Winston Public Relations, Inc., Philips Information Systems Ltd./ Micom Co., RCA Corporation, Canadian National Railways, Harmony TV & Applicances, Firestone Canada Inc.

smoothness and ease, movement and efficiency that are desirable attributes for a railway company. Harmony and Firestone both project long-established, quality images.

THE ETHICS OF SYMBOLISM IN MARKETING

Questions have been raised about the use of symbolism by marketers to create product differentiation when no product differences exist.

> It is often to the advantage of firms to spend vast sums on promotion to differentiate commodity products such as bread and aspirin in order to gain market control and pricing latitude. But is it beneficial to consumers or to society?[35]

For example, through the use of color, name, or objects, brands are invested with qualities they do not possess to any greater degree than do other brands, and there is no justification, from the point of view of product benefits, for the higher prices such brands may demand.

On the other hand, it has been argued that symbolic enhancement of a package or advertisement yields psychological benefits to the consumer that increase the satisfaction derived from the product. In other words, satisfaction comes from the physical as well as the psychological properties of the stimulus. For example, it has been pointed out that perfume and cosmetic companies spend a great deal of money on packaging, brand name, and brand image, often much in excess of the cost of the product, because those elements are ego-satisfying to the consumer. A perfume manufacturer is selling not just a physical essence but a promise, a hope.

Other questions have been raised about the nonverbal presentation of the life-styles and identification models by brands of cigarettes, alcohol, and beer. How close to the truth are these stereotypes and, if they are wishful ideals, should marketers be permitted to make use of them and, by implication, acquire greater legitimation of the use of their products? Is this not, in fact, false or misleading advertising? Furthermore, if the associations are false, do they not have the potential to influence, to the degree that such advertising can, the values that come to exist in that society? For example, is lifestyle advertising that depicts specific groups consuming a product in certain situations likely to lead others to believe that such individuals do indeed use that product and that the behaviors they exhibit are desirable and normative?

These are important questions that marketing needs to confront. In response to the criticisms of consumer groups, governments are beginning to show concern and to take some action about these matters. The Ontario government is currently considering legislation that would place limitations on, if not abolish, lifestyle advertising.

SUMMARY

The possibilities for nonverbal communication in marketing appear almost limitless. The manipulation of colors, words, objects, sounds, shapes, and typography can greatly enhance the scope and efficiency of commercial messages. Symbols generate moods, feelings, and atmosphere, as well as add to the attractiveness and attention-getting quality of promotional material.

The many uses and meanings of colors; the versatility of words, especially for brand names; the connotations of objects, animate and inanimate; the nuances of sounds; the suggestions from shapes and form; and the impact of styles of print were described with examples.

Reference was made to the questions raised about the use of symbolism in marketing for psychological product differentiation and for doubtful life-style associations.

QUESTIONS

1. Using Example 2, why would Vidal Sassoon Inc. be so concerned about such use of their name? Do you think the court's decision was fair? Why?

2. Think of two examples in each of the following product classes with significant symbolic meaning and indicate what they symbolize:

   (a) automobiles   (c) liquor

   (b) cigarettes   (d) watches

3. "The same stimulus can have different symbolic meanings for different persons." Discuss.

4. Find half a dozen color print ads that illustrate the various symbolic meanings color can have.

5. In addition to those mentioned in the chapter, what other symbolic elements can you identify in Figure 7.7? Can you think of a similar stimulus that represents a different set of symbolic meanings?

NOTES TO CHAPTER 7

[1]Adapted from John Partridge, "Boom for Image Business May Just Be Starting," *The Globe and Mail* (14 May 1984), p. B-1.

[2]Adapted from Ron Alexander. "The Story of O's: Settling a Fight Over 'Sassoon'," *The New York Times* (4 May 1980), p. 76.

[3]Adapted from Albert S. King, "Pupil Size, Eye Direction, and Message Appeal: Some Preliminary Findings," *Journal of Marketing*, 36:3 (July 1972), pp. 55–8.

[4]Eckhard H. Hess and James M. Polt, "Pupil Size as Related to Interest Value of Visual Stimuli," *Science*, 132 (5 August 1960), pp. 349–50; "Attitude and Pupil Size," *Scientific American*, 212 (April 1965), pp. 46–54; "Pupillometrics A Method of Studying Mental, Emotional and Sensory Processes," in N.S. Greenfield and R.A. Steinbach (eds.), *Handbook of Psychophysiology* (New York: Holt, Rinehart and Winston, 1972). Merle E. Day, "Eye Movement Phenomenon Relating to Attention, Thought and Anxiety," *Perceptual and Motor Skills*, 19:2 (1964), pp. 443–6.

[5]Michael A. Cann, "Pupil Size and Sexual Dichotomy," unpublished doctoral dissertation, University of Chicago, 1953.

[6]Paul J. Watson and Robert J. Gatchel, "Autonomic Measures of Advertising," *Journal of Advertising Research*, 19 (June 1979), pp. 15–26.

[7]Eckhard H. Hess and James M. Polt, "Changes in Pupil Size as a Measure of Taste Difference," *Perceptual and Motor Skills*, 23 (July 1966), pp. 451–5.

[8]Paul Bakan, "The Eyes Have It," *Psychology Today*, 4 (April 1971), pp. 64–5.

[9]James U. McNeal, *An Introduction to Consumer Behavior* (New York: John Wiley & Sons, 1973), p. 97.

[10]Ronald R. Gist, *Marketing and Society* (Hinsdale, Illinois: Dryden Press, 1974), p. 419.

[11]Carl G. Jung, *Man and His Symbols* (New York: Dell, 1978), p. 3.

[12]Ibid., p. 4.

[13]Sidney J. Levy, "Symbols for Sale," *Harvard Business Review*, 37 (July-August 1959), pp. 117–24.

[14]Sidney J. Levy, "Symbolism and Life Style," in Frederick D. Sturdivant et al. (eds.), *Perspectives in Marketing Management* (Glenview, Illinois: Scott, Foresman, and Company, 1971), pp. 112–8.

[15]Sidney J. Levy, "Symbols by Which We Buy," in James U. McNeal (ed.), *Dimensions of Consumer Behavior*, 2nd ed. (New York: Appleton-Century-Crofts, 1969), pp. 100–1.

[16]Norman Kangun, *Society and Marketing — An Unconventional View* (New York: Harper and Row, 1972).

[17]R. Claus and K. Claus, *Visual Environment* (Toronto: Collier-Macmillan, 1971), pp. 18–20.

[18]Faber Birren, *Selling With Color* (New York: McGraw-Hill, 1945).

[19]Larry J. Rosenberg, *Marketing* (Englewood Cliffs, New Jersey: Prentice-Hall, 1977), p. 141.

[20]James U. McNeal, *An Introduction to Consumer Behavior* (New York: John Wiley & Sons, 1973), p. 99.

[21]Charles E. Osgood, George J. Suci, and Percy H. Tannenbaum, *The Measurement of Meaning* (Urbana, Illinois: University of Illinois Press, 1957), pp. 299–301.

[22]Louis Cheskin, "The Nature of Color and Its Effect on Human Behavior," *Contacts*, III (November 1959), p. 341.

[23]Louis Cheskin, *Why People Buy* (New York: Liveright, 1959), Chapter 3, "Imagery and Color in Packaging."

[24]S. Watson Dunn, *Advertising: Its Role in Modern Marketing* (New York: Holt, Rinehart and Winston, 1969), p. 352.

[25]Louis Cheskin, *How to Predict What People Will Buy* (New York: Liveright, 1957), p. 189.

[26]Louis Cheskin, *Colors — What They Can Do For You* (New York: Liveright, 1948), p. 189.

[27]An advertisement by Marsteller Incorporated, an advertising/public relations firm with offices in New York and worldwide, 1969.

[28]Cited in Fred T. Schreier, *Modern Marketing Research* (Belmont, California: Wadsworth, 1963), p. 271.

[29]C. Glenn Walters and Gordon W. Paul, *Consumer Behavior* (Homewood, Illinois: Richard D. Irwin, 1970), p. 284.

[30]*Business Week*, "Chrysler Corporation Assembles a New Identity" (29 April 1967), p. 62.

[31]Sybil Emerson, *Design* (Scanton: International Textbook, 1957), p. 57.

[32]Louis Cheskin, *Colors — What They Can Do*, p. 182.

[33]Stephen Kurdsen, *Graphology, the New Science* (Washington: Acropolis Books, 1971).

[34]John S. Wright, Daniel S. Warner, and Willie L. Winter, Jr., *Advertising* (New York: McGraw-Hill, 1971), p. 449.

[35]Harold H. Kassarjian and Thomas S. Robertson, *Perspectives in Consumer Behavior* (Glenview, Illinois. Scott, Foresman, and Company, 1973), p. 4.

THE MOOSE THAT ROARED*

Since 1978, the St. John, New Brunswick brewery owned by the Oland Family has been the font of America's fastest-growing imported beer. Just twenty months after its introduction into the US, Moosehead is a legend in the business. In the intensely competitive $1.5 billion imported beer market, it has leaped into seventh place among the more than 225 imports sold there. Its sales have eclipsed those of mighty Carling O'Keefe, which until recently held seventh spot, and are rapidly closing in on Molson Breweries and John Labatt, which occupy the lofty second and third positions respectively. (Molson's produces three brands, and Labatt's two, for the American market.) The Olands sold more than twice as much Moosehead in the US last year as they did the year before, and today you can buy it in forty-nine states.

Moosehead has caught fire in Atlanta, Memphis, Detroit, New Orleans, and Boston. In Texas, automobile bumper stickers bear the slogan, "The Moose is Loose." Sales of other Moosehead bric-à-brac are soaring. Its fans have snapped up more than a million Moosehead T-shirts. Country music star Willie Nelson wore one in the recent film *Honeysuckle Rose*. It is, in the words of America's voice of the trade, *Beer Wholesaler* magazine, "an amazing success story."

History

Moosehead Brewery is run by Philip Warburton Oland, sixty-nine years old, a formal, rather reserved figure clad in old-fashioned pinstripes and highly polished black Oxfords. He is the patriarch of the fourth generation in the business. "Moosehead," he says, "is a good name for our beer. In New Brunswick, the moose is recognized as the king of animals."

In 1971, Olands in Halifax sold their brewery to Ontario beer giant, Labatt, and the threat of outside competition increased. It was about

---

* *Adapted from* Stephen Raikes, "The Moose that Roared", *Canadian Business* (February 1981), pp. 42-6.

this time that Paul Lohmeyer, president of All Brand Importers, of Roslyn Heights, New York, came into the picture. Lohmeyer is a veteran beer man whose company already carried some of beer's great names — Pilsner Urquel (a Czechoslovakian beer often said by aficionados to be the world's best), Foster's Lager from Australia, and the leading brands of Mexican beer. But he lacked a Canadian product.

Canadian beer has long had a good reputation in the US. Ours is a little stronger and has a bit more body without tasting quite as different as some foreign brands, such as British ales. In the early 1970s beer importing was a pioneer business. Transportation costs and tariffs made the imports substantially more expensive, and in 1970 they accounted for a miniscule 0.6% of the market. Even Lohmeyer hesitated to predict that by the end of the decade 25 million drinkers would be hooked on imported brew. But he knew the market would grow. "Beer drinkers were travelling more," he says, "and it seems to me inevitable that they would want to buy foreign brands when they got back home."

Strategy

It wasn't until about 1976 that Lohmeyer could overcome the Olands' skepticism. The Olands insisted on the final word on any proposed marketing strategy. They quickly agreed that Moosehead should be sold on the image of the wide Canadian outdoors, the clean air, the virgin forests, the unspoiled wilderness — all those qualities that foreigners love about our country.

The beer would be a lager, in contrast to the Moosehead ales sold in the Maritimes, but similar in taste to one of the company's existing brands, Alpine Lager. A few changes in the brew formula were made to give the beer a longer shelf life. But the real change was in the packaging. The stubby, brown bottle used for virtually all beer destined for Canadian throats simply did not have enough class for the US premium market. A number of different shapes and colours were tried in mock-up, and the end result was a tall, elegant, green bottle, similar in design to the best-selling import, the Dutch brand Heineken.

It was the label that presented the toughest challenge. Because of the vast size of the US beer market and the relatively small slice of it occupied by imports, media advertising on any scale is not really justifiable except for the very biggest sellers. So promotional budgets tend to be spent on packaging, point-of-sale material, and trade advertising. The original Moosehead label had to go, and the new label was crucial. Eventually, Lohmeyer's advertising agency came up with the design that graces Moosehead Canadian Lager bottles today: a moose head against a field of matte green with a cross-hatched centre.

One feature that remained unchanged was the name. Moosehead was perfect. "More than the label, the name has a big role in customer selection," Lohmeyer argues. "Where else but Canada could a beer named Moosehead come from? It's outdoors, clean air — all that good stuff."

Today the beer is on the verge of achieving cult status. Grayden Carter, a staff writer on *Time* Magazine's Living section, and therefore a man presumed to have his finger on the pulse of national taste, reports that Moosehead is on a par with McSovely's (a brew sold under the auspices of the oldest bar in Manhattan) in status. He terms it "delicious — more body than US beer. Becoming pretty popular in NYC."

It's possible that within five years Moosehead will be selling more beer in the US than it does at home. In the fifth generation of brewing Olands, Derek and Richard, the beer business is not quite the parochial gentlemen's trade it once was. The moose is not just loose; it's on the rampage.

QUESTIONS

1. Why do you think Moosehead has been such a success in the US?

2. Identify the principal symbolic elements that were effective in communicating with the US market.

3. What evaluative criteria seem to have been particularly significant?

4. Evaluate the marketing strategy that was decided upon. Comment on the image projected.

8

Learning

EXAMPLES

1. Diffusion of an Innovation: The Microwave Oven in Canada[1]

In 1980, questions were being asked about whether the microwave oven, long considered a luxury extra of the kitchen appliance industry, was finally coming into its own. The spinoff industries were beginning to think so. Many makers of cookbooks, cooking utensils, food wraps, frozen foods, and other food products were testing the waters of the microwave cooking market by either adapting their products to suit microwave ovens or introducing new ones.

FIGURE 8.1: New Product Trends in Microwave Oven Industry

Courtesy Supreme Aluminum Industries Ltd.

It seems that the industry's best hopes have been realized, judging from developments in the spinoff industries (see Figure 8.1) and from sales of the microwave oven.

Sales are well in advance of projections. In 1980 it was predicted that there would be one million Canadian microwave owners by 1984. According to Statistics Canada that figure had been surpassed by May 1983 (1,055,000).

Microwave oven owners consume more frozen products than the average consumer and companies are adapting to the needs resulting from the new technology. One company introduced Micro Baste, a product intended to cure the common complaint that meats cooked in microwave ovens do not brown. Others have changed their packaging to include microwave directions or at least inform consumers that the products can be used in microwave ovens.

Geographical Diffusion

Microwave oven saturation levels vary considerably among the provinces of Canada (Figure 8.2). Alberta appears to be the trendsetter, with more than a quarter of the households (27.3%) having microwave ovens in mid-1983, followed by Saskatchewan (24.8%), British Columbia (17.9%), and Manitoba (17.2%). Interestingly, these are all western provinces. The eastern provinces are relatively lower: Ontario (11.2%), the Maritimes (7.0%), and Quebec (5.5%).

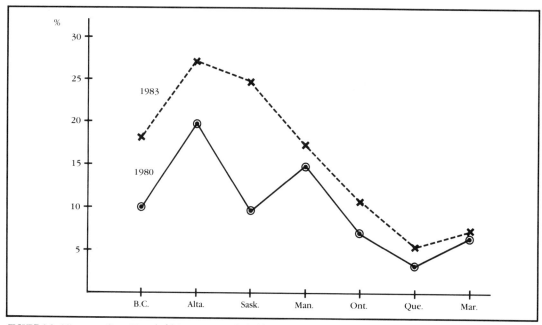

FIGURE 8.2: Microwave Oven Household Saturation Levels (%) by Provincial Regions in Canada — mid-1980 and mid-1983

Based on statistics from *Statistics Canada*, 1983, Cat. No. 64–202.

Between 1980 and 1983, the increase in penetration was relatively small (between 2% and 4%) in the eastern provinces and Manitoba. There were significant increases in the western provinces — all at least 7.7%. In Saskatchewan the penetration level almost tripled (from 9.5% to 24.8%).

2. Relevance and Learning[2]

A few years ago Esso, the sole sponsor of "Hockey Night in Canada," decided to share sponsorship with Molson's, a national brewery. In its first advertising series, Molson's chose as its theme the rapid and impressive growth of transportation media in Canada, the underlying purpose being to associate the development of Molson's with that remarkable record of progress.

The first fifteen to twenty seconds of every sixty-second commercial were devoted to a kaleidoscopic pictorial presentation of transportation media — from sailing vessels to large boats to ocean liners; from early locomotives to steam engines to modern diesels; from single-engine airplanes through to the large modern jetliners, and likewise for cars and trucks.

It was decided to test the impact of this advertising approach after six weeks — mainly to determine the extent to which consumers were aware of Molson's sponsorship of the program. The results were very discouraging. Esso dominated and Molson's identification was very low. But awareness of the commercials (recall of jetliners, etc.) was high. It seemed the brewery had inadvertently reinforced association with its co-sponsor by emphasizing a theme that was decidedly relevant to gasoline, since it was the prime source of energy for the modes of transportation depicted. Employing a theme that was characteristic of the brewing industry (or, at least, less typical of the gasoline industry) might have avoided such confusion.

3. Learning from Advertising[3]

While the following article may be an exaggeration of fact, it nevertheless illustrates the plethora of commercial claims and learning situations to which the contemporary consumer is exposed from morning till night.

Jane got up early, feeling *Pepsi light* all over after a good *Posturepedic* night. In the bathroom, she washed her face and applied *Oil of Olay* so she'd be smoother, softer, younger-looking. Then she brushed her teeth with *Crest* for the protection she knew must last and which was, she thought, a real ego-booster because in extending the same protection to all her family, she was a real *miracle mom*. In fact, she reflected, it gave her the same good feeling she had about fighting *static cling* with *Downy*.

After her shower Jane had a moment of doubt — should she apply her *Secret, which was strong enough for a man but made for a woman*, or should she dab away with a little extra *Avoid* for that something between her and her clothes? She opted for the *Secret* and added a little of her favorite perfume, *Ocean Spray*, to go with it.

This was a regular routine with Jane since she never ever wanted to *wonder about her neighbors' reactions*. And besides, who knew when the *Man from Glad* would turn up . . .?

Rushing back to the kitchen she prepared an *instant breakfast* for the family, pausing for a second to get a *cup of Salada* tea, which always gave her that little lift when she needed it. Then it was more rushing . . . to make sure the kids drank their *100% orange juice* and that her husband got his favorite brand of coffee — the one that *made him better, not bitter*.

Then, carefully, she put in her purse her *Dietac* tablets, her *One-a-Day* vitamins, her *Valium* in case her *extra-strength pills for tension headaches* didn't work, her *Signal mouthwash* for strong mouth odors, her *Wet-ones* towelettes, and her *New Silhouette romance novel*.

After waving goodbye to her husband and children, Jane got her breath back with *Scope*, and put all the dishes in the sink along with a good dollop of *Ivory Liquid* because she knew the suds would last until she got back. Driving to work, Jane considered the birthday gift she would buy for her eldest son. She thought the *Polaroid Presto* camera might be the answer, but she knew he wanted the *new electronic Brain Baffler*, which might be alright since it always bleeped and tweeted to let you know right from wrong.

Jane's boss was in a good mood and she decided it was due to *Rolaids* or *Tums*, which she had suggested for his acid indigestion, or perhaps it was . . . his *anti-perspirant*.

At lunch she was careful to consume just one cup of 97% *decaffeinated* coffee. Better wise than sorry. Lunch might have been perfect, except for Louisa, who kept asking questions. How many hours of TV commercials do children see before they arrive at kindergarten? How insidious is the commercial on young minds? Do kids start to think, write, and search out material that's as easy to understand as a commercial?

After work Jane drove to the office of her *psychiatrist*, who combined a small private practice with a drop-in centre for put-down women. Jane, who had seen him three times a week for three years, stretched herself out thankfully on the couch, "Honestly, Doctor," she said, "I don't think I have much more to discuss. For the first time I have that deep-down clean feeling that I have absolute control of my life."

4. Learning of a Social Practice[4]

The management of Kingston Cigarettes were concerned about the long-term effects of restrictions imposed by the major cigarette companies on advertising directed to persons under twenty-one. They wondered when individuals do begin smoking, and whether the lack of exposure to cigarette advertising and the failure to smoke in the teens would carry over into later years and result in a lower porportion of smokers; or whether beginning to smoke would simply be delayed a few years.

From a large consumer survey, the company found that:
- more than half of the smokers began smoking before the age of 16; and
- 70% had at least one parent who smoked.
  A review of other studies also indicated:
- teenagers are inclined to smoke or start smoking in certain kinds of stressful social situations, such as meeting a new acquaintance, or entering a room full of strangers;
- heavy smoking may be related to unhappy childhoods; and
- a taste for cigarettes was acquired over time.

Marketers are very interested in how the consumer organizes and interprets the various stimuli (brands, labels, advertisements) they inject into the environment. But they are even more interested in how much of these communications the consumer retains or learns. From all the information to which the consumer is exposed, only some will be comprehended, and even less retained. What is learned helps to simplify the consumer decision process by providing solutions to the problems faced by the consumer.

Learning is, therefore, of fundamental interest to marketers. It is at the core of their basic purpose, which is to provide information in such a way that there will be effective consumer learning. Brand choice and repeat purchasing will be facilitated. Thus the central questions become, "What are the factors that determine which perceptions and behaviors are learned by the consumer?" and, more pragmatically, "*What* messages should I send and *how* should I present them so that they will be retained in long-term memory?"

DEFINITION OF LEARNING

Learning involves changes in behavior. It will be recalled that I defined behavior as involving both overt and covert acts, so that learning involves changes in the physical as well as the mental responses of the individual. Individuals learn to act differently and to think differently. "In the broadest terms, learning refers to the effects of experience, either direct or symbolic, on subsequent behavior."[5] Another writer defines it as "any change in an individual's response or behavior resulting from practice, experience, or mental association."[6]

Changes that take place with maturational processes or reflexes (or instincts) or that are artificially induced (for example, through drugs or fatigue) are not to be regarded as learning.

Psychologists are also very concerned with the process of learning that underlies any change. Learning cannot be observed directly and is therefore an *inferred* process. It is also a *dynamic* process, which appears to possess neurological correlates, but exactly how these physiological changes occur is not well understood. Some interesting postulations, however, have been offered. Hebb has suggested that learning brings about lowered synaptic resistances in certain brain cells so that cell connections or associations are set up and are more easily reactivated when similar situations recur.[7] The cell-assemblies are arranged in certain phase sequences that are characteristic of each response of the organism.[8]

These "interconnected electrochemical circuits" have also been referred to as engrams. "Like the lightbulbs in a moving sign that spells out news headlines, each neuron may be turning on and off in an infinite number of engrams."[9]

It appears, too, that memory traces are located in specific areas of the brain and can be evoked with appropriate techniques. The great Canadian neurosurgeon, Wilder Penfield, found that, by electrically stimulating parts of the cerebrum, he could evoke vivid, exact, detailed recall of events in the individual's life, suggesting the possibility that the human-brain-computer, with its ten billion cells, records every experience of the organism.[10] While things may be forgotten, they are not eliminated and are capable of recall with appropriate techniques. The phenomenon of hypnosis would tend to support this hypothesis. But even if this is true, it has been suggested that, upon retrieval, the "filling-in" process still occurs. Loftus claims that electrical stimulation of the brain produces the same mix of fiction and fact found in most unassisted attempts at recollection.[11]

LEARNING IN MARKETING

One of the primary characteristics of learning is its **selectivity**. While the individual responds to a large number of situations, some responses are retained and others are discarded, mainly on the basis of the ability of the response to satisfy the individual's needs. We are constantly learning, modifying, and making adaptations in such a way as to improve our performance in our environment.

As in the many roles that the individual plays, the role as a consumer calls for selecting and

making the right response. So far as the marketer is concerned, the right response occurs when the consumer buys the marketer's product. The marketer's communications (advertising, public relations, sales promotion, corporate image, pricing, retail outlets) aim to have people learn things about the product that will lead to that choice. Essentially, learning is the establishment of links or connections between certain stimuli (products) and the cues that represent them (e.g., color, symbol, name) on the one hand, and consumer preference-responses on the other. On the basis of consumer studies, the marketer identifies the cues that mean satisfaction or reduction of need, and, through marketing activities, attempts to link the product with those cues so that the right response will be made.

What does learning theory have to offer the marketer that will help in successfully establishing these bridges or links? I will first take a look at the kinds of learning involved in marketing, and then discuss the factors that affect what and how much we learn. I will then review the concept of forgetting, and the basic ways in which consumers learn. Finally, I will examine the kinds of models that have been developed to explain the structure and operation of memory followed by the principal theories of how learning takes place.

KINDS OF LEARNING

Human beings are constantly exposed to new situations and ideas so that they are constantly learning. The consumer is no exception as the recipient of communications from business, government, and social sources. The nature of the information is a good way of classifying the kinds of learning in which the consumer engages. These are:

Factual

The consumer learns about new products, changes in products or packages, or the consumer may acquire information about a company and its operations or where and when a product is available.

Value-Related

There are several ways in which changes in our values may occur. We may come to want a particular style of dress as a result of the influence of our reference group or of other individuals in our neighbourhood. From such sources as well as from marketing sources we may develop our **choice criteria**; that is, the considerations on the basis of which we will differentiate and choose among different products or brands. Similarly, we come to adopt the attitudes, beliefs, mores, and norms of our social groups, as was illustrated in Example 4 with the influence of parents and peers in the acquisition of the cigarette-smoking habit.

Associative

The consumer learns to associate certain attributes or benefits with certain products or brands. What is more important, certain cues (color, brand symbol) that represent the product or brand may themselves come to be associated with those attributes. The latter are referred to as sign-expectancies. In some cases the consumer may use price as a cue for quality or be influenced (unconsciously) to prefer the taste of one sample of ice cream because it was cream-colored over another sample that was white. These sign-expectancies can operate at either the conscious or the unconscious level. In addition, such associations can be culture-bound, so that a given stimulus-element will not have the same significance or expectancy from one culture to another. We referred to a number of these, particularly in relation to color, in the chapters on perception and symbolism.

In advertising, this kind of associative learning frequently occurs with the repetition of a slogan with a brand name and serves mainly as a reminder of the brand (e.g., "Why do most Canadians Shop at Dominion — Mainly Because of the Meat").[12]

The association that takes place between a benefit (relaxation) and a response (buying X brand of cigarettes) can become so strong that whenever the need arises, the individual will automatically make that response. In such a case, a **habit** can be said to have been formed and is the ideal relationship each marketer hopes to achieve. Habit simplifies the task of the shopper. It would be extremely demanding if the consumer had to engage in the entire decision process whenever a purchase was made.

In those cases where the association involves a stimulus and the emotions it evokes, the term **affective learning** is used.

Sensory

This occurs when the individual's sensory modes eventually respond in a manner that is quite different from their original response. We learn to like the taste of olives or Scotch whisky or caviar. Without this adaptability, it is not likely that cigarettes would have reached the level of popularity they enjoy today. Consumers' original reaction to the taste would have doomed cigarettes to failure. But we learn to like certain tastes with repeated exposure.

Other evidence of such **habitative** learning includes such delicacies enjoyed by one culture and recoiled at by another culture as frog legs, snails, chocolate-covered insects, blood-pudding, beef, and whale blubber.

Perceptual

Not only do our senses adapt to different stimuli with time but the meanings that we attach to our sensations and our ability to differentiate among different patterns or arrangements can be refined and improved by training or experience. Thus our taste in clothing, architecture, interior decoration, or art may change (through the influence of others or self-education); biological training will enable us to identify cells and tissues in what was previously a "blob" of shapes and colors. In short, we learn **perceptual discrimination**.

Integrative

The individual's ability to think and to evaluate logically grows and develops so that his or her problem-solving activities become more efficient. Such changes can result from the influence of business sources or social institutions. A good part of learning in marketing is integrative learning: the formation or modification of attitudes, the development of preferences (e.g., the categorizing of brands as described in Chapter 9), the comprehension of advertising appeals.

THE FACTORS THAT AFFECT WHAT AND HOW MUCH WE LEARN

It is important for the marketer to know under what conditions learning occurs and how it can be facilitated. Psychologists agree that most learning will not occur in the absence of motivation. Drive energizes the individual to respond. When the response provides satisfaction, it is reinforced and becomes a learned response. In consumer terms, there must be a need or reason for acquiring a product, or learning about it will not take place.[13]

Drive may not always be necessary for learning. A motorist on the way to work may unconsciously note the location of a vegetable market and recall it on a weekend shopping trip. Learning in the form of a perceptual reorganization had occurred even though the information was not needed at the time. Such **latent learning** is supported by the phenomenon of hypnosis. It has been found that a student who is unable to report the color of the shirts worn by the two persons beside him or her in an earlier class will almost always give the correct answer under hypnosis.

Krugman has also drawn attention to the existence of "low involvement" learning and compares it to latent learning.[14] Subjects are reported to have "learned a TV message better when hearing the audio and watching unrelated video than when they watched the speaker giving the message directly, i.e., video and audio together." He suggests that "apparently the distraction of watching something unrelated to the audio message *lowered* whatever resistance there might have been to the message." The significance of this phenomenon of **passive learning** for low-involvement decisions was discussed in Chapter 4.

Secondly, it bears repeating that *learning is a selective process*. Just as consumers selectively perceive from among the multitude of stimuli to which they are exposed, so they are selective in what they learn.

Reinforcement is a central concept of most learning theories today. Of all the responses that can be made to a stimulus situation, the response that brings satisfaction (or, in other words, drive-reduction) is likely to be repeated when that situation arises again. Repetition of the response leads to a strengthening of the response in that the more it is repeated the greater the likelihood of the response being made. That strengthening is, in fact, the reinforcement of the stimulus-response association.

The terms **reward** and **reinforcement** are sometimes used interchangeably even though they can be distinguished clearly. Reinforcement is the strengthening of the response and reward is the benefit derived from the making of the response. Thus, if the need for the "dry, clean look" is satisfied with the purchase of a particular brand of shampoo, then with every purchase the response of buying that brand will be reinforced and the reward will be dry clean hair and the benefits it brings (e.g., social approval, admiration from friends). Psychologists have also used the term "incentive" in this context to refer to the desired object or product that provides the sought reward.

Three major implications flow from the concept of reinforcement. First, a response that is not reinforced will not be repeated. This is of extreme importance to the marketer because it suggests that if the buying of a product is to be repeated, then that product must provide satisfaction. It cannot survive on advertising or brand name or package or promotion alone. The product itself has to be good. Thus to those who claim that "advertising can make people buy things they do not need," the answer seems very clear — a marketer will not succeed in getting consumers to *adopt* a product if it does not satisfy a need. The consumer may *try* it once, maybe twice, but it is doomed to eventual failure. Those who voice such a criticism may be thinking of the apparent failure of the product to satisfy the obvious need, not recognizing that there may be other needs (perhaps psychological and therefore less obvious) that account for the repeated purchases of the product. Second, the greater the reward-value of the response, the stronger will be its association or learning. Third, the greater the strength of the need or drive, the greater will be the reinforcement of a satisfactory response and therefore the association or learning will be stronger. The timing of advertising is strongly influenced by this phenomenon — for example, Coca-Cola beach ads are most effective in the summer.

Learning psychologists tell us that the more often the learning situation is presented, the greater will be the amount of learning.[15] According to this "weak effects" hypothesis, "the effect of any one exposure (to an advertisement, for example) is slight and only very substantial levels of repetition 'ingrain a stimulus in the mind'." However, it appears that advertising may not actually work this way. To quote the same researchers cited above:

In contrast to this incremental theory of association . . . [it seems that] a "strong effects" hypothesis is more appropriate to order the findings of field research on the effects of advertising repetition. The strong effects hypothesis implies that the effectiveness of an ad depends on the events occurring during the first few exposures to it.

Subsequent exposures lead to a phenomenon known as **wearout**, the occurrence of a decrement in the recall of a message while the message is gaining a higher level of exposure.

This research study found that "when the level of repetition was three times that needed to learn the brand names, subjects exhibited significantly poorer recall than when repetition was only twice that needed for learning" and further suggested that "the wearout . . . most probably was caused by subjects' inattention to the stimuli (that is, in the later presentations) and their reactance when very high levels of repetition were employed."[16] (Reactance is the tendency of people to increase their resistance as greater pressure to influence them is applied. In this case, brand recall would be very low because of the increasing amounts of influence input.)

Important implications to the marketer were then pointed out. When high exposure campaigns are planned, steps should be taken to enhance attention — such as varying the execution of the campaign theme or introducing several claims; after a certain point, mere repetition can be counter-reproductive. An interesting exception is the Maytag Company. Many advertisers switch commercials from year to year but Maytag's advertisements featuring "Old Lonely" — the Maytag repairman who has nothing to repair — has been the company's mainstay since 1967.

The use of day-after recall to measure advertising effectiveness may be misleading because differences between ads may not become evident until more than twenty-four hours has elapsed. Similarly, post-tests carried out after too long a delay may also reveal no differences because of the inhibiting factors that produce wearout.

The researchers conclude that "to avoid misinterpretation of retention data, it is suggested that recall be measured at several points in time after stimulus presentation."

In this context the question of measuring learning is an important one. Generally, psychologists have found that recognition measures tend to yield higher values than recall measures, so that preference between the two will depend on the purpose of the test.[17]

Psychological research studies have found that, assuming the same total amount of exposure, learning is greater when the message to be learned is presented over a longer time with longer intervals between repetitions than when it is presented in a shorter time with very short periods between presentations. Psychologists refer to the former as distributed practice and the latter as massed practice. "The superiority of distributed over massed practice is not confined to the learning of skills, but has been observed in a wide variety of learning situations, from simple instrumental conditioning through rote memorizing to the study of symbolic materials."[18] Obviously, there will be an optimum total period and an optimum interval that will produce the greatest learning. Generally, it has been found that massed practice yields faster learning and distributed practice results in longer-lasting learning. For example, massed exposure may be appropriate, to achieve quick awareness and stimulate trial, at the introductory stage of a new brand and distributed exposure suitable for a product in the growth or maturity stage. The choice will also depend on the type of product and the nature of the message to be conveyed. High-involvement products such as automobiles, houses, and furniture, which usually require complex decision making and also make use of more detailed and less simple advertising messages, will likely benefit more from the distributed approach.

These generalizations were supported by a recent study that found that of five different television advertising schedules (ranging from every four weeks to fifty-two weeks and with varying intensities of advertising) the thirteen-week period (massed) yielded the highest un-

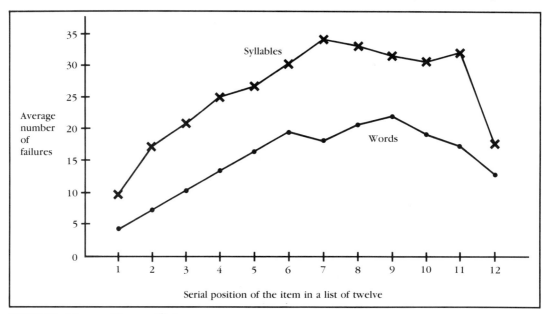

FIGURE 8.3: Primacy and Recency Effects

SOURCE: Leo J Postman and Lucy Rau, "Retention as a Function of the Method of Measurement," *Publications in Psychology*, 8:3 (Berkeley, California: University of California Press, 1957), p. 236.

aided recall (24%) and that at the end of a year the fifty-two week schedule achieved the best recall (8%).[19]

Originally, tests conducted with nonsense syllables indicated that from a list of such items, those at the beginning (primacy) and those at the end (recency) of the list were better learned than those in the middle. Figure 8.3 shows this effect.

The more meaningful material was generally better remembered so that, where advertising is concerned, message content and execution could modify these results. Nevertheless, it would be well for the marketer to take note of this general serial-position phenomenon and to avoid assigning middle positions to important product claims or advertising appeals. How many of us have found, when trying to reconstruct a mental shopping list, that we more easily remember the items at the beginning and at the end of the list and have greater difficulty recalling those in the middle?

Psychologists have long spoken of the phenomenon of **generalization** in learning. This occurs when an individual who has learned to associate a given stimulus with a given response makes the same response to a *similar stimulus* or to an extension of the original object. The former is called **stimulus-generalization** and the latter **response-generalization**. An example of stimulus-generalization is a consumer who buys a GE refrigerator, also being inclined to buy a GE air conditioner. Response-generalization could be said to occur if, for example, a consumer, who, as a result of a bad experience with a suit of clothing, regards it as badly made, and also comes to think of it as made of poor materials. This phenomenon is known in sociology as **stereotyping**.

In marketing, generalization is a common occurrence. In any product category, the consumer may be inclined to make the same buying response to more than one brand, though with different levels of probability. Brand K may be the preferred brand and would be chosen first but if it were not available, then Brand L might be chosen next (probability of .70). Similarly Brand M could have a probability of .30 and Brand N of .10. The ordering of these probabilities on a graph produces a **generalization gradient** (Figure 8.4). The level of generalization of a brand is really a measure of its **substitutability**.

The stronger the need for the product, the greater will be the possibility of generalization. The greater an individual's need or desire for

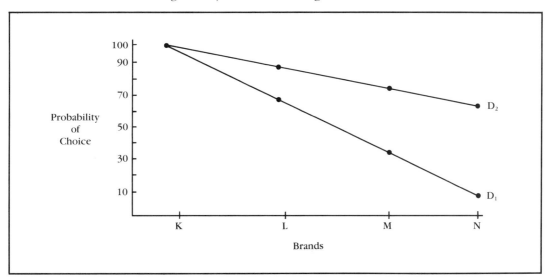

FIGURE 8.4: Gradient of Generalization

a beer, the more likely she or he will be to select a substitute for a preferred brand that is not available. The probabilities of choosing the other brands increase (line D_2 in Figure 8.4) and the gradient of generalization becomes less steep.

This phenomenon has serious implications for the marketer. It means that if marketing activities increase the desire for a product, they increase its substitutability and automatically make it more vulnerable to other brands. Thus the beer company that in midsummer decides to promote the satisfying, thirst-quenching qualities of its brand could be exposing itself to quite some risk if it cannot ensure adequate, uninterrupted distribution. Every marketer knows that creating a situation in which the users of one brand have the opportunity or are forced to try another brand is diligently to be avoided.

A common application of stimulus generalization is **family branding**, where the marketer is relying on the carryover of the positive attributes of one of the company's products to others (e.g., automobiles, appliances). Of course, the marketer should recognize that such generalization can work the other way as well, transferring the negative attributes of one product to the company's other products. An example of this risk was the decision by General Motors to produce a compact Cadillac. What effect is a subcompact Cadillac likely to have on the general Cadillac image?[20]

Generalization is a basic principle of all behavior and can be applied usefully in consumer behavior. Sometimes, a smaller company may seek to benefit from generalization by presenting its brand with similar colors, or a similar name, or in a similar advertising format to the most popular brand so that consumers may generalize from the popular brand. This may work but research seems to suggest that usually such promotional tactics tend to backfire, as they are associated with the popular brand. For example, advertising for Heinz soups may be found to be associated with Campbell's soups.

Discrimination and generalization are, in a sense, opposites. During our development we learn both the similarities (generalization) and differences (discrimination) among stimuli. **Discrimination learning**, therefore, is "learning to detect and respond to differences among stimuli. . . . the child has to learn that oranges and lemons both belong under the concept "fruit," but . . . that one is sweet and the other sour."[21]

In marketing, discrimination learning comes into play in the consumer's ability to differentiate among brands of products. Procter and Gamble is an excellent example of a company that has used discrimination very successfully. It manufactures several brands of household detergent, which it has managed to position in different market segments and to identify as independent brands (Bold, Cheer, Tide).

The exact nature of the material to be learned will also affect how well it is learned. Meaningful material is better learned than non-meaningful material and, as we shall see later when we discuss learning theories, insight and understanding of the relationships between ideas also make for better learning.

Marketers often seek to enhance learning by introducing completely new stimuli, which grasp the attention of the consumer and, because of their catchy quality, are better remembered. Sometimes brand names are formed from letter combinations that may be appealing and nice-sounding but not necessarily denotative of anything. Examples are Exxon, Kodak, and the term *pizzazz*, which was introduced to express the unique quality of Pontiac cars.

The reverse can also happen. Words that were once effective cease, through overuse, to have their original impact. It is equally important for marketers to be alert to this phenomenon, since hundreds of thousands of dollars may be saved by avoiding or not relying too heavily on such words as *discount, improved, cut-rate, new*. They have been used so widely that consumers no longer pay much attention to them; nor do they possess the credibility they once enjoyed.

Another major example of such **semantic satiation** that marketers have not yet attempted to avoid is the description of package sizes in detergents, toothpaste, and cigarettes.

As part of the notion of meaningfulness, the pertinence of the message will affect learning. Example 2 provided a good illustration of the human tendency to associate elements that, by their essential nature, are more compatible with each other. Transportation is so much more closely related to fuel and gasoline that the failure to associate it with beer is entirely understandable.

Learning is also more likely to be efficient if the language and the graphic symbols employed in advertising messages are consistent with the level of education and the frame of reference (values, attitudes, social class, customs) of the recipient of the message. Figure 7.7 in Chapter 7, showing an advertisement for Marriott Hotels, is an excellent example of the use of symbols appropriate to the intended target market.

The notorious case of the failure of the Edsel car provides another interesting example of the important principle of facilitating understanding and identification by using relevant and familiar symbolism. It has been said that one possible reason for its failure was the freestanding vertical grille, which, reminiscent of the grilles of earlier classic cars, was greatly admired by knowledgeable individuals within the industry but was unimpressive to the general market.

It is not surprising that the source from which the message emanates can have an important influence on its reception. A message that is presented by a credible expert source is more likely to be persuasive and to be retained than a message from a low-credibility source.[22] A high-credibility source inhibits thoughts for counterarguing with the communicator's message whereas with a low-credibility source, the audience is likely to counterargue and not be persuaded by the message.[23]

"Source" is a very broad term in marketing and can refer to the type of medium (e.g., radio, TV, print), the particular vehicle within the medium (e.g., TV program, or magazine), the company sending the message, or the individual "mouthing" the message. All of the elements can have an effect on the believability and acceptability of the message.

To recapitulate, there are a number of key factors that affect learning:

- drive level;
- reinforcement of the response;
- frequency of exposure to the message;
- the pattern of exposure to the message;
- primacy and recency (order of presentation);
- generalization;
- discrimination;
- the nature of the message; and
- the source of the message.

FORGETTING

Learning is selective — everything that is learned is not necessarily retrievable. The better a message is learned, the longer it will be before forgetting occurs. It is reasonable that an individual will not retain all that has been learned in a lifetime. Forgetting serves a very important function in that it enables the individual to place less important information in the background.

It has been claimed that a college graduate makes active use of only about 5% of the information learned in school. Another interesting characteristic of forgetting is that nothing is really eliminated from the mind. As described earlier in the chapter, material may fall from consciousness but it appears to make permanent traces in the brain.

Researchers suggest that forgetting occurs because subsequent learning tends to weaken or partially redirect earlier neural brain pathways so that, in a sense, the later learning serves to inhibit ready recall of the earlier learning.[24] Psychologists label this phenomenon *retroactive inhibition*. It is one of many explanations for forgetting: (a) memory trace fading or decay; (b) memory trace distortion through metabolic brain changes that have been used to explain forgetting even after a short period of time; (c) changes in motivation; (d) inhibition; and (e) a failure of the retrieval process due to inadequate coding, transfer, or placement (discussed in the next section).

With inhibition, forgetting is attributed to interference of two kinds:
- **retroactive inhibition**, where subsequent activities or the learning of new material affect the retention of earlier learning; and
- **proactive inhibition**, where previously learned material affects what is retained from material learned later.

Several significant, though not surprising, facts should be noted:
- interference or inhibition increases with the similarity between the two sets of materials;
- the shorter the time between learning two sets of material, the greater the inhibition;
- the more meaningful the material, the less the interference; and
- overlearning reduces interference.

In seeking to induce learning, the marketer should attempt to make the learning experience as strong as possible and subsequently to maintain recall with reminder advertising. Furthermore, to optimize learning, a message should be presented in such a way as to avoid potentially inhibiting material that is too similar or too closely spaced. Forgetting is most rapid in the first twenty-four hours after learning and declines with the meaningfulness of the material.

Psychologists have also found that forgetting does not occur in a regular, passive way like a fading photograph. "Remembered material undergoes systematic and meaningful changes reflecting, as in perception, tendencies to select, organize, and interpret."[25] For example, meaningless or irrelevant elements tend to be dropped; elements that may add to the material's meaningfulness or consistency may be invented.

With slightly incongruous elements, two things could happen:
- they may be eliminated or shortened — called *levelling*; or
- they may be exaggerated — called *sharpening*.

Both of these mechanisms are influenced and guided by the individual's attitudes, values, and needs (which affect perception) as well as by her or his expectations or set.

It has also been pointed out that:
- Hearing memory is apparently stronger than touch, sight, or smell memory. Patients who have been under total anaesthesia can sometimes recall words spoken during an operation.
- Alcohol and other drugs seem to affect information storage more than retrieval.
- Most people can easily remember no more than six or seven items in a series — a fact that explains the difficulty individuals have with remembering their nine-digit social insurance numbers.

It is important for the marketer to take into account not only the motivations of the audience but also its expectations or prior conceptions. Put another way, the marketer should ensure that the motivations and expectations of the audience are compatible with and likely to enhance the proper perception and retention of the message.

WAYS IN WHICH WE LEARN

I have emphasized before that there can be no learning without motivation of some kind (conscious or unconscious). The best methods or the highest intelligence will count for little if there is no incentive to learn. Reinforcement and reward are also basic to learning.

Individuals acquire "information" in three basic ways — imitation, participation, and training.

Imitation

We tend to change our attitudes or actions to conform more closely to individuals we admire and look up to. We tend to like and purchase what star athletes or movie stars or our peers or our parents use or tell us is good. Individuals imitate those persons or social groups who serve as models of what they are like or what they want to be like. The human urge to conform and thus be accepted by relevant others is a significant factor in human behavior.

Participation

It is well accepted among psychologists that playing an active role in the learning process by participating in the task to be learned results in faster and greater learning.[26] Actually participating in operations, as exemplified by medical internships or business games, makes for better learning than just being told how to do something.

Marketers employ several means of creating or simulating this kind of participation:

- Free samples, coupons, trial offers, and refunds are some of the ways of getting consumers to participate in the use of the product without any financial risk;
- TV commercials that are so realistic that they generate in the viewer a state of mind that comes quite close to the actual experience. Examples of such covert involvement include the Coke or Pepsi beach scenes, and some of the ads for swimming pool companies or for health spas.
- Another kind of TV commercial generates participation but with much less involvement. Because they show individuals using a product, actually "look over the actor's shoulders," they tend to increase learning through a sort of vicarious practice on the part of the viewer. Good examples of this are the Black and Decker ads showing how to use their drills, saws, collapsible work bench, and other tools.

- Advertising that makes use of the Gestalt principle of closure (see Chapter 5) results in better learning because in seeking to complete the deficient perceptual situation, individuals get more involved in the message than they ordinarily might and they consequently remember more of it.
- Contests and games are also ways of encouraging consumer participation. While the possibility of direct gain exists in the form of prizes, the greater attention-getting aspect coupled with the heightened interest and involvement inevitably result in greater learning. At the same time, these "promotools" should not become so dominant that they overwhelm the consumer and drown out the center of the exercise — the product message.

Training

People learn in formal instructional situations. Marketers seek to benefit from such learning with procedures that approximate the true training session (e.g., Avon training groups, or Tupperware parties). How-to advertising is also helpful for certain kinds of products that are not too complicated to assemble or use.

THE STRUCTURE OF MEMORY

Memory affects consumer choice in a number of ways. Not only does it serve as a storage place for learned material, but what is held in memory and how it is organized influence the interpretations given to and the inferences drawn from subsequent incoming material. In addition to some of the questions raised earlier, other important questions involving memory concern:

- the length of time and the number of repetitions necessary for learning some piece of information; and
- the types of information already in memory that are likely to facilitate retention of new information.

Recent research has put forward some potentially useful insights with respect to the structure and operation of memory.[27]

There are currently three different models of memory. **Multiple-Store Theory** postulates that there are different types of memory storage systems: a set of sensory stores (SS), a short-term memory store (STS), and a long-term memory store (LTS). Basically, what happens is that information received through the sense organs is passed to the appropriate sensory store and is rapidly lost if it is not processed further and thus transferred to STS. There, the information is interpreted, in the light of what is already in LTS, and can be held briefly. The STS is where incoming information is actively processed. Continued processing will lead to the transfer of the information to LTS.

Most researchers have not found the notion that there are several distinct memory stores too attractive. Another model is the **Level of Processing Model**, which suggests that there is one basic memory with limited processing capacity, which is allocated in accordance with the level of processing needed for the kind of information being received. Sensory analysis (e.g., noting that a given element was red) will require lower levels of processing, and deeper analysis in terms of interpretations on the basis of existing cognitions will require deeper levels of processing. The latter, according to this model, leads to memory storage. This model would suggest that advertisements should generate both sensory *and* semantic and cognitive processing if claims and other cognitive information are to be remembered. This model also has been criticized for the vagueness of the notion of "depth" of processing.

The **Activation Model** also postulates one memory store but only portions of it can be activated at a particular time. Current processing will occur only in the activated portion. If activation is shortlived, the information will die out; if it is continued, the information will be held in memory. The concept of activation has been explained as one of rate or intensity and is thus not different from the level of processing model.

All three models share the basic notion of limited processing capacity, especially if we concede that the multiple-store model does not necessarily call for physiologically separate locations. In other words, it seems justifiable to think of one memory system and to identify three functions: sensory memory (SM), short-term memory (STM), and long-term memory (LTM).

Sensory memory is shortlived and related mainly to the physical characteristics of stimuli. The short-term memory function is central to memory, because it is the locus of ongoing information processing from which data may be stored or dropped. It has limited capacity and can process only about five items or chunks at a time.[28] An example of a chunk is a brand name. Chunks can be expanded by adding information to them, such as adding new attributes to a brand name.

It seems that to transfer information from STM to LTM takes about five to ten seconds, if the information is to be recalled later.[29] For recognition, it will require only two to five seconds. This difference derives from the fact that the recall task involves a reconstruction of the stimulus, whereas recognition demands only the differentiation or discrimination of a previously encountered stimulus from others. Recall is more likely to be characteristic of high-involvement decisions, where "deeper" information processing occurs. Recognition is more likely in low-involvement decisions.

Long-term memory is regarded as a permanent, unlimited repository of semantic, visual, and auditory information. Its primary contents are semantic concepts and their interrelationships, including events, objects, processing rules, and attributes of objects and events. The interrelationships, referred to as "memory schemata," involve all information relevant to a concept, such as the organization of new incoming information around previous experience. Long-term memory is generally agreed to involve a network of nodes and links, where the nodes are the concepts and the links the connections among them.[30] This new information is stored by linking it with already stored concepts.

It is important for the marketer to distinguish between *external* and *internal* memory. External memory refers to information "stored" in packages, shopping lists, point-of-purchase displays; internal memory, to what is held, so to speak, within the individual. External memory can serve as a significant aid to internal memory. For example, detailed or complex data may be better used by the consumer if it is provided through external memory rather than internal memory. It is also noteworthy that the information in internal memory can influence the interpretation of external memory data (selective perception).

There are a few key strategies, called control processes, by which individuals determine what to process and how, and how to retrieve information from LTM. These are rehearsal, coding, transfer, placement, retrieval, and response generation.

Rehearsal, referred to earlier, is the processing effort devoted to incoming information in STM. Rehearsal more likely occurs in high-involvement decisions because it implies active, cognitive consideration of stimuli. Continued rehearsal of information in STM leads to storage in LTM.

The significance of rehearsal lies not just in the time spent but, more importantly, in the form of the rehearsal itself. Form can mean either simple repetition or more detailed analysis. Thus a consumer may remember a price not as a result of repetition but by relating it to the price of another brand.

Coding involves the associations the individual constructs with the stimulus during rehearsal in order to facilitate memory. Encoding strategies such as images and mnemonics are used for either recall or recognition. Thus a brand name such as Autumn may be associated with a fall scene.[31]

Transfer controls what is stored in memory and how it is stored. It depends on the nature of the information and how the individual intends to use it. For example, a consumer exposed to detailed information about the chemical components of a drug product may transfer to LTM the basic fact that the ingredients are impressive and can be found on the label. When and if the need arose to purchase that product the consumer would rely on examining the label in the store.

Placement refers not to any physical location of information but rather to the association structure in which it is placed. Its significance lies in the greater likelihood of retrieval if the associations can be easily reconstructed. In Example 2, the linking of transportation with Esso made it more difficult to establish any links between Molson's and transportation.

Retrieval is a crucial process because that is the purpose of generating learning. The more effective the coding, transfer, and placement, the easier the retrieval. If LTM is permanent, forgetting must be viewed as a failure to retrieve stored information and not as the result of some loss or decay.

Response Generation is consistent with what we have said about selective comprehension. What is recorded in LTM is not retrieved in exactly the form in which it was entered. "Memory may be subject to biases, since reconstructions will be based partly on what was and partly on individuals' expectations or schemas for what must have been."[32]

It bears repeating that the marketer must recognize that what a consumer records and retrieves from memory can be very different from the original information. The subjectivity of the learning process demands close attention to the reconstructions consumers impose on messages and necessitates testing and re-testing of communications until a most satisfactory level of retrieval is assured.

THEORIES OF LEARNING

The dynamics of learning discussed in this chapter come from two main schools of thought in psychology — the stimulus-response and the cognitive schools.

Stimulus-response (S-R) theories are, basically, connectionist theories that regard learning as the formation of connections or associations between stimuli and responses. They are also called **behaviorist** theories.

There are two S-R theories:

- **classical conditioning**, first developed by Pavlov, who found that by ringing a bell at the same time as he presented his dogs with meat, he was able to elicit the salivation response. The dogs had become conditioned to the ringing of the bell in association with the presentation of the meat (see Figure 8.5). Classical conditioning relies on the principles of *contiguity* in time and space, and *repetition*.

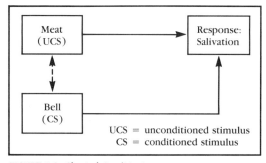

FIGURE 8.5: Classical Conditioning

- **instrumental conditioning** introduces the concept of reinforcement and postulates that a satisfactory response that leads to a reduction of need will be repeated and thus learned (see Figure 8.6).

The stimulus may be the need itself or a cue such as an advertisement or a package. Much of human learning may be of this type. It should be noted, however, that a response that ceases to provide the expected reward will be **extinguished**. Thus purchase of a product that ceases to provide satisfaction will, in spite of promises in advertising or packaging, eventually be extinguished. Where reinforcement is continuous the probability of repurchase increases and eventually a habit is formed.

Instrumental conditioning underlies the technique of **shaping** in marketing, that is, the rewarding of successive approximations of behavior until the desired behavior is attained:

> Such a series might begin with the use of a free sample. . . . A coupon would be included in this sample for a large discount on the first purchase and in the first purchase the consumer would find a coupon for a smaller discount on later purchases. As these incentives are reduced, the behavior approximates repeat purchase of the product at its full retail price.[33]

It is important that the reward be derived from the product (the primary reinforcer) and not from the coupon or other tool (the secondary reinforcer) or the response will be extin-

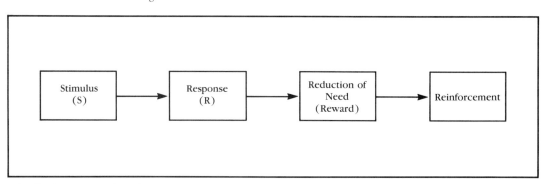

FIGURE 8.6: Instrumental Conditioning

guished as soon as the secondary reinforcers are removed.

Cognitive theories regard learning as a change in the way a situation is perceived. On the basis of new insights into the relationships between stimuli and responses, **perceptual reorganization** (or learning) occurs. To cognitive theorists behavior is **purposive**, that is, guided and influenced by personal goals and objectives. Thus, to understand behavior one has to consider the entire psychological field of the consumer — perception, needs, attitudes, personality, and cultural and social forces. This approach is reflected in the model that informs this book.

All three approaches — classical conditioning, instrumental conditioning, and cognitive learning — are useful in the study of consumer behavior. They are complementary to each other, rather than exclusive. Each theory may be relevant to certain kinds of learning.

Classical conditioning, relying primarily on contiguity and repetition, explains the effects of such marketing phenomena as the repetitive scheduling of advertising, brand associations, and passive learning.

Instrumental conditioning is useful in explaining behavior in trial-and-error situations, in which reinforced responses are learned and repeated.

Both of these theories appear to be most relevant to low-involvement purchasing.

Cognitive learning theory is most relevant to complex decision making, which originates in a need and involves information search and evaluation.

SUMMARY

Learning is the acquisition of new responses or changes in behavior as a result of experience. It is a dynamic, inferred process that is identifiable by its results. Learning is of fundamental importance to the marketer because all marketers aim to get their customers to learn information about their offerings.

Some of the processes by which individuals store information and the nature of such storage were reviewed. As shown in previous chapters, consumer treatment of information is very selective. So far as learning is concerned, they engage in a number of kinds of learning — factual, value-related, associative, sensory, perceptual, and integrative.

What and how much we learn is influenced by many factors: reinforcement, repetition, pattern of exposure, generalization, discrimination, and the nature and the source of the message.

Forgetting was defined as partly decay or interference but primarily the failure of retrieval. Several considerations were provided for reducing the possibility of forgetting.

For the most part (except for latent or incidental learning) learning will not take place without motivation. It seems that individuals acquire information in three basic ways — imitation, participation, and training.

Three theories of learning were reviewed and found to be complementary to each other in their relevance to marketing. The behaviorist theories of classical conditioning and instrumental conditioning were viewed as more relevant to low-involvement purchase decisions and cognitive learning theory to high-involvement purchase decisions.

QUESTIONS

1. Based on the findings reported in Example 4, what would you say are some of the factors that influence the acquisition of the smoking habit?

2. Obtain the most up-to-date information you can on the market penetration of the microwave oven and try to account for the differences of these data with those reported in Example 1.

3. Define internal memory, external memory, recognition, and recall and show how they can be related to high- and low-involvement decisions.

4. Relate the concept of reinforcement to shaping, continuous reward, and primary and secondary reinforcers in marketing.

5. Distinguish between generalization and discrimination and discuss their marketing implications, with examples.

6. Define forgetting and show some of the ways in which the marketer may attempt to reduce it.

7. Define (a) semantic satiation, (b) counterargumentation, (c) covert involvement, (d) rehearsal.

8. Describe the differences between the three models of memory and show how they are basically compatible.

9. "The three theories of learning are useful, each in its own way, in explaining consumer learning." Discuss.

NOTES TO CHAPTER 8

[1] Adapted from Peggy McCallum, "Microwave Oven Coming Into Its Own," *The Globe and Mail* (7 June 1980).

[2] Personal communication.

[3] Adapted from Angela Colingwood, "How Does She Know? The Commercials Told Her So," *The Spectator* (28 May 1980), p. 75.

[4] Roger D. Blackwell, James F. Engel, and David T. Kollat, *Cases in Consumer Behavior* (New York: Holt, Rinehart and Winston, 1969), pp. 44–8.

[5] Bernard Berelson and Gary A. Steiner, *Human Behavior: An Inventory of Scientific Findings* (New York: Harcourt, Brace and World, 1964), p. 135.

[6] Jack A. Adams, *Learning and Memory: An Introduction* (Homewood, Illinois: Richard D. Irwin, 1976), p. 6.

[7] D.O. Hebb, *Organization of Behavior* (New York: John Wiley & Sons, 1949), pp. 69–74.

[8] Ibid., pp. 98–100.

[9] Roy Rowen, "That Filing System Inside Your Head," *Fortune*, 98:4 (28 August, 1978), p. 82.

[10] W. Penfield, "The Interpretive Cortex," *Science*, 129 (1959), pp. 1719–25.

[11] Elizabeth Loftus, *Memory: Surprising New Insights Into How We Remember and Why We Forget* (Reading, Massachusetts: Addison-Wesley, 1980).

[12] Herbert E. Krugman, "What Makes Advertising Effective?" *Harvard Business Review*, 53 (March-April 1975), pp. 96–103; Howard Kamin, "Advertising Reach and Frequency," *Journal of Advertising Research*, 18 (February 1978), pp. 21–5.

[13] John A. Howard, "Learning and Consumer Behavior," in Harold H. Kassarjian and Thomas S. Robertson, *Perspectives in Consumer Behavior*, rev. ed. (Glenview, Illinois: Scott, Foresman, and Company, 1973), pp. 77–78.

[14] H.E. Krugman, "The Impact of Television Advertising: Learning Without Involvement," *Public Opinion Quarterly*, 29 (1965), pp. 349–65.

[15] C. Samuel Craig, Brian Sternthal, and Clark Leavitt, "Advertising Wearout: An Experimental Analysis," *Journal of Marketing Research*, 13 (November 1976), pp. 365–72. Reprinted with permission of the American Marketing Association.

[16] Ibid.

[17]R.S. Woodworth and H. Schlosberg, *Experimental Psychology* (New York: Holt, Rinehart and Winston, 1960), p. 724.

[18]Berelson and Steiner, op. cit., p. 159.

[19]H.A. Zielske and Walter A. Henry, "Remembering and Forgetting Television Ads," *Journal of Advertising Research*, 20 (April 1980), pp. 7–13.

[20]Leonard M. Apcar, "Detroit's Future Rides on New Small Autos It Plans to Unveil Soon," *Wall Street Journal* (28 August 1980).

[21]Robert M. Goldenson, *The Encyclopedia of Human Behavior* (Garden City, New York: Doubleday, 1970), p. 337.

[22]W. McGuire, "The Nature of Attitudes and Attitude Change," in G. Lindzey and E. Aronson (eds.), *The Handbook of Social Psychology*, 2, 2nd ed. (Reading, Massachusetts: Addison-Wesley, 1969), pp. 136–314.

[23]Brian Sternthal and C. Samuel Craig, "Fear Appeals: Revisited and Revised," *Journal of Consumer Research*, 1 (December 1974), p. 27.

[24]Goldenson, op. cit., pp. 470–1.

[25]Berelson and Steiner, op. cit., p. 183.

[26]O.H. Mowrer, *Learning Theory and Behavior* (New York: John Wiley & Sons, 1960), p. 16.

[27]James R. Bettman, "Memory Factors in Consumer Choice: A Review," *Journal of Marketing*, 43 (Spring 1979), pp. 37–53.

[28]Herbert A. Simon, "How Big is a Chunk?" *Science*, 183 (February 1974), pp. 482–8.

[29]Herbert A. Simon, *The Science of the Artificial* (Cambridge, Massachusetts: MIT Press, 1969), p. 39.

[30]Allan M. Collins and Elizabeth F. Loftus, "A Spreading-Activation Theory of Semantic Processing," *Psychological Review*, 82 (1975), pp. 407–28.

[31]Kathy A. Lutz and Richard J. Lutz, "Effects of Interactive Imagery on Learning: Application to Advertising," *Journal of Applied Psychology*, 62 (August 1977), pp. 493–8.

[32]Bettman, op. cit., p. 41.

[33]Michael L. Rothschild and William C. Gaidis, "Behavioral Learning Theory: Its Relevance to Marketing and Promotions," *Journal of Marketing*, 45 (Spring 1981), pp. 70–8.

LUMPKIN'S COSMETICS, INC.*

Lumpkin's Cosmetics, Inc. is a large "personal care" firm established over sixty years ago by John Lumpkin for the manufacture of cosmetics for women of all ages. During the 1970s the company's sales were seriously affected by intense competition from Revlon and other domestic and foreign firms. Profits were not suffering but they definitely had levelled and Robert Lumpkin (who had inherited the firm from his father in 1968) feared that a period of decline was imminent.

Lumpkin hired Janice Morris, an executive from his advertising agency. He was very impressed with her credentials. He felt that an imaginative female was needed to advise him and his staff on the kinds of products they produced — lipsticks, hand lotions, mascara, eye shadows, eye liners, rouges, base make-up, moisturizers, cleansers, and other related products.

Strategy Decision

A few years later, Lumpkin's was still in stalemate. Some product lines had improved slightly, while others had declined. Lumpkin realized that an advance in traditional markets or product lines would be costly. He felt satisfied to hold present market shares for his company's products if new markets could be developed to improve corporate sales and profits.

Lumpkin called his executive board together to discuss expansion, diversification, and potential markets for present products. All agreed that an increase in market shares of present products in present markets would not be worth the cost and effort. Thus, new proposals were suggested for consideration. Ms. Morris suggested that present lines of make-up, mascara, lipsticks, facial creams, and moisturizers be reformulated and packages redesigned for the male market.

---

* *Adapted from* M. Wayne De Lozier, *Consumer Behaviour Dynamics—A Casebook* (Columbus, Ohio: Charles E. Merrill, 1977), pp. 38-40.

Harry McQuillen objected most strenuously to her proposal, as did other male members of the board. "Men do not use make-up, lipstick, mascara, and other lines that we produce."

Morris believed her idea was sound and would create a totally new market for their present lines of products without the costs of adding new product lines or acquiring new production facilities for diversification. In her proposal she stated the following:

Traditional male-female product barriers have broken down — not to the extent they could, but nevertheless have broken down. Who in the 1950s would have dreamed that men would, a few years later, use hair spray? Who in the 1960s would believe that men would carry purses, make appointments for hair styles, or buy hair dryers? Along with feminine hygiene deodorants came male hygiene deodorants (Braggi, for example).

Men are just as concerned as women are about their personal appearance — perhaps more so. They are just as vain as women are about how they look. Sex barriers have been broken down. All we would be doing is extending a trend in the unisex revolution.

Male actors use make-up. They use cleansing creams, moisturizers, rouge, lipstick, powders, eye make-up. They are opinion leaders. We could use them and athletes in ads to show it is not effeminate to use our personal care products to improve personal appearance.

We can show them that a little dab here and a little dab there covers up blemishes, wrinkles, and highlights their best facial features.

Remember, gentlemen, that our forefathers wore wigs and used powders. What we have to do is break down the prior learning experiences of men that these products are for "females only" — that they are effeminate! We must educate the mass male market that these are personal care products, not feminine products. They deserve, and indeed owe it to themselves to look their best. We must emphasize that women will find them more appealing and that other men will not consider them effeminate.

Through the socialization process, men have learned what is masculine and what is feminine. This is a lot of hogwash. We must educate the male market that there is nothing wrong and that it is all right for them to use personal grooming products to enhance their appearance. Lumpkin's will go down in history as the personal-care company that broke down the sex barriers and developed a new market for personal care products.

If we are to expand and innovate, we must be willing to take risks.

Tom Robertson: "As vice-president of marketing, I am most interested in innovation and expansion. But I am afraid that by implementing this proposal, we'll go down in history as the 'queer' company in the personal care market!"

Robert Lumpkin: "Tom, I understand your concern, but I believe that Janice has come up with an idea that we should explore. As she has pointed out, other traditionally female products have come into popular use by the male market.

"My initial inclination is to go along with her proposal. After all, we have expanded as far as we can in our present markets. Her idea has merit. I feel we should study it."

QUESTIONS

1. This case suggests several behavioral notions. Attitude change is one. However, Janice Morris believes that a change in prior learning is the basis for changing attitudes. Discuss the relationship between learning and attitude change and attitude formation.

2. How easy or difficult is it for a company to change consumers' prior learning, both in general and specific product situations?

3. What principles of learning would you suggest to Morris' and Lumpkin's marketing management as useful for educating the male market for cosmetics?

9

Important Learning Phenomena in Consumer Behavior

A number of aspects of consumer behavior are characterized by fairly involved learning processes. In this chapter, four principal examples will be examined:

- Categories of Awareness;
- Loyalty — brand, corporate, store;
- Adoption and Diffusion of Innovations; and
- Fashion Acceptance.

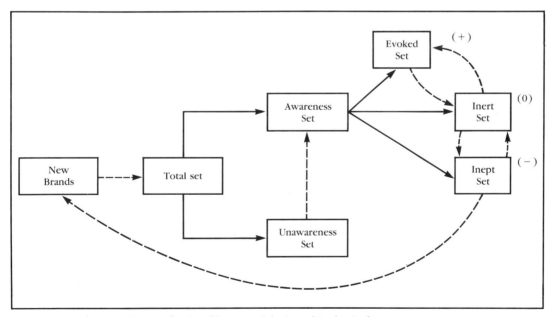

FIGURE 9.1: An Alternative Conceptualization of Consumer Behavior and Product Performance

SOURCE: Chem. L. Narayana and Rom J. Markin, "Consumer Behavior and Product Performance: An Alternative Conceptualization," *Journal of Marketing*, 39 (October 1975), pp. 1-6. Reprinted with permission of the American Marketing Association.

CATEGORIES OF AWARENESS[1]

A consumer is either aware or unaware of the existence of any product class. The set of brands in a given product class of which the consumer is aware is denoted by the awareness set. It is from among the brands in the awareness set that the consumer makes a purchase choice.

Figure 9.1 illustrates the relative positioning of brands within the consumer's perception.

The **total set** is comprised of all brands within a product category in the market. However, a consumer may not be aware of all the brands that exist. This leads to the concepts of **awareness set** and **unawareness set**. If a given brand is in the unawareness set of a consumer, the chance of that brand being considered for purchase is non-existent, although this situation may change. Thus, the marketer's first job is to ensure that the consumer knows about the availability of his or her brand. But even among those brands of which the consumer is aware, there are many that would not be considered for different reasons. It appears that the consumer seeks to simplify the choice by narrowing the awareness category further.

The **evoked set**, which consists of only a few brands, are those the consumer considers in the purchase choice. They are evaluated positively (+).

The **inert set** consists of those brands about which the consumer has neither a positive nor a negative evaluation (0). The consumer may not have enough information about them or may not perceive any advantage in buying them. Most brands fall into this set.

The **inept set** consists of those brands the consumer has rejected from purchase consideration (—), perhaps because of an unpleasant experience with them or of negative feedback from other sources, or of lack of information about them. There are generally only a few brands in this set.

Note that changes in brand perception occur and the brand position may be altered, as indicated by the broken arrows. For example, a new brand could enlarge the total set and enter either the awareness or unawareness group; consumers may become aware of certain existing brands, which thus move from the unawareness to the awareness set; and brands may move among the three sub-sets. The ideal direction of movement, of course, is toward the evoked set. These movements can be affected by changes in advertising content and format, change of name, changes in quality, competitive activities, new information, trial, or changes in needs and preferences.

This exploratory study suggested two interesting generalizations:
- the evoked and inept sets are usually quite small, so that consumers consider far fewer brands than they are aware of;
- the inert set is usually larger than the other two, so that consumers appear to ignore a large number of brands in a product category.

This conceptualization is a useful one because it tells marketers more than just whether consumers are aware of their brands or not. If they are in the evoked set, marketers can concentrate on differential advantages in order to get non-users to buy their brands; if in the inert set they at least know that the task is not as difficult as if their brands were in the inept set; comparative advertising or free samples might easily "do the trick." For a brand in the inept set, corrective advertising strategies might work, or a modified or "new" brand might be required. The crucial necessity would be to determine why consumers perceive the brands as they do, assess the probability of achieving the desired shift (if necessary), and develop appropriate strategies.

LOYALTY

A response that provides satisfaction is likely to be repeated the next time the same or a similar situation arises. Repetition of the response leads to reinforcement and learning can be said to have occurred. Such learning is a necessary feature of loyalty, as it is of habit. In fact, learning, habit, and brand loyalty are closely related.

"Both learning and brand loyalty are processes which are manifested over a period of time, and in both cases, there arises a habitual course of action which is dominant in a given situation."[2] Furthermore, both habit and brand loyalty are characterized by less information seeking and less brand evaluation.

Loyalty Defined

There has been a great deal of controversy around the subject of loyalty and little agreement about its definition. One source describes the research on brand loyalty as "inconclusive, ambiguous, and contradictory."[3] The controversy involves whether loyalty should be defined in terms of how it is expressed or in terms of internal dynamics. It is argued that loyalty consists of both behavioral and attitudinal components and that, since it is a multidimensional concept, the definition should reflect this characteristic. The two basic approaches to defining loyalty are the behavioral (operational) and the dynamic.

The behavioral approach considers that repeat purchasing results from reinforcement. On the assumption that the greater the number of purchases, the greater the reinforcement and therefore the greater the probability of repurchase, researchers have developed **stochastic** (or probabilistic) models to explain brand loyalty.

The dynamic approach argues that loyalty is more than behavior and involves *commitment.* For example, a consumer may continue to purchase a brand not because it is preferred but because it is the only one available in the store. Day refers to this as spurious loyalty.[4]

When others become available, the consumer may switch to a brand that is preferred. Continuous purchasing of the latter type would be regarded by the cognitive approach as loyalty. Thus the models based on such internal consumer characteristics as attitudes and preferences are called **deterministic** models — for example, the model of complex decision making (see Chapter 3).

The Behavioral Approach

Behavioral definitions have been at the root of the contradictory findings on the subject, because different researchers have applied different definitions employing different criteria, such as:

- percent of purchase (e.g., in the following twelve-trial sequence – AABAACAADAAE – the consumer would be described as loyal to Brand A);
- sequence of purchase — most such definitions would require at least three consecutive purchases, so that on this basis the consumer above would not be regarded as loyal to any brand; and
- number of brands purchased — some would maintain that the kind of loyalty revealed in a five-brand sequence as above would be different from sequences involving different numbers of brands (e.g., two or three).

Behavioral definitions thus emphasize repeat purchase over time.

The Dynamic Approach

The other approach takes the position that loyalty is something more than repeat purchase behavior. One source asks if the consumer, who always buys Brand A because it is the cheapest, is "loyal" in the same sense as the consumer who buys Brand A because he or she prefers it. What of the consumer who buys Brand A because it has the most favorable shelf space or because it is the only nationally advertised and distributed brand carried by the store in which the buyer shops?[5] Loyalty should also consider the reasons underlying repeat purchase behavior. Both aspects should be included in a proper definition of loyalty. Day refers to these as "intentional loyalty" (reasons) and "spurious loyalty" (repeat purchase).[6]

Jacoby and Kyner went on to develop exactly such a definition, which specifies *brand* loyalty but can easily apply to other objects (products, stores). "Brand loyalty is the biased (i.e., non-random), behavioral response (i.e., purchase) expressed over time, by some decision-making unit, with respect to one or more alternative brands out of a set of such brands and is a function of psychological (decision-making, evaluative) processes."[7]

Degrees of Loyalty

Brand loyalty is not easy to measure but attempts made to distinguish among different degrees of loyalty are usually described in terms of:

- the purchase sequence: undivided (AAAAA), divided (ABABAB), unstable (AAABBB); or
- consumer types: hard-core loyals (who show undivided purchase sequences), soft-core loyals (unstable), and switchers (divided).

It is important to recognize that the degree of loyalty is not necessarily related to volume of purchase (although some researchers have tried to combine both).[8] Hard-core loyals are not necessarily the heavy users of a brand and the marketer would be well advised to try to get current heavy users of the brand to become hard-core loyals or to get more hard-core loyal types to adopt the brand. In the latter case, it would be necessary to determine who, what, and where they are in order to improve advertising content and direction.

Characteristics of Loyal Consumers

Because of the variations in the definitions of loyalty by different researchers, it is hard to come up with any definitive descriptions or correlates. A few generalizations are possible:

- Loyalty varies among individuals but it also varies across products. Thus it cannot be said that an individual who exhibits undivided loyalty in one product category will be likely to behave similarly with all product purchases. Loyalty is product-specific.
- It has been suggested that loyalty is greater with increased perceived risk, as occurs with high-involvement products. Thus an individual who is very concerned about product outcome and consequence will be likely to buy the biggest brand or a national brand or shop at a prestigious store. This suggestion has intuitive appeal, even though the evidence on this point is not conclusive.
- It has also been suggested that the less one knows about a product or the less confident one is about the purchase, the more likely one is to stick to a well-known brand. The individual who does not have any clear choice criteria will be likely to behave in that way.
- A household's store choice strategy is closely linked to its brand choice strategy. For example, Carman found that store loyalty and brand loyalty are strongly related.[9]
- A recent study of deal proneness (or less loyalty) suggests that "the households most likely to be deal prone are homeowners, car owners, households with no children under six, and households without working wives."[10]

Brand Loyalty Models

From the attempts to understand loyalty behavior, two basic kinds of models have emerged: *stochastic* models, which are based on probability determined by past behavior, and *deterministic* models, which seek to take into consideration the variety of factors that influence choice. Some of these models will be reviewed in the chapter on consumer behavior models (Chapter 19).

Brand Loyalty and Involvement

With a high-involvement product there is greater commitment and self-identification so that loyalty will be based on cognitive variables. Preference for the brand developed with use and with evaluation over time leads to loyalty. Change in such loyalty is difficult to achieve and occurs only with significant shifts in brand positioning or brand image.

With low-involvement products, loyalty is more likely to be superficial or spurious since there is repeat purchasing without commitment. Repeat purchasing is the result of familiarity rather than any strong feelings regarding the brand. Information search and brand evaluation are not justified and brand switching will occur where price cuts, deals, coupons, or other promotional incentives are attractive.

ADOPTION AND DIFFUSION

Two very important questions in consumer behavior are: "How does a consumer come to try and use a new product?" and "How does an innovation come to be accepted by the market at large?"

The first question relates to individuals; the second to the spread of a new product from one individual to another throughout a market.

The individual process is known as **adoption**: the acceptance and continued use of a new product or brand by an individual.

The group process is known as **diffusion**: the adoption of a new product or brand by consumers in a market over time.

Marketers introducing new products are most interested, not only in how these processes work but in *accelerating* them so that they can reach, with a new product, the greatest number of people in the shortest possible time.

Two different kinds of learning are involved here — one is at the individual level and the other at the social. But before we look at the factors involved, let us define what an innovation is. There are several different ways of defining an innovation:

- *market-oriented*, based on the length of time a product has been on the market or on the proportion of the potential market that has purchased it. In either case, the marketer would need to specify the limits of time or

market share after which a product is no longer an innovation;

- *consumer-oriented*, based on consumer perception of the product — a product is new if it is new to the consumer;
- *firm-oriented*, where the newness of a product is based on how it is perceived by the firm — if it is new to the company, it is a new product. This view is quite limited, because while it may be useful to a company in evaluating company performance, it does not take into account the consumer viewpoint; and
- *product-oriented*, based on the impact of the product on established usage patterns.

One product-oriented approach takes into account user satisfaction and defines newness in terms of the amount of satisfaction the product gives, compared to an older product.[11] This approach identifies *artificially* new, marginally new, and genuinely new products.

Another product-oriented approach, which appears to be the most widely used among researchers, differentiates among new products or services (e.g., retail outlets) on the basis of their *disruptive effect* on current behavior.[12] It identifies three types of innovations — continuous, dynamically continuous, and discontinuous:

- **A continuous** innovation has the least disrupting influence on existing patterns, as exemplified by modified products rather than a totally new product (e.g., gel toothpaste, fluoride toothpaste, new car models, light beers and wines, and menthol cigarettes). These products do not really alter the behavior surrounding the originals from which they were derived. Most new products fall in this category.*

---

* Food companies have been more cautious in introducing new brands in the past couple of years. After topping 1,000 a year in the mid-1970s in the US, the number of new brand introductions slumped to 744 in 1978 and recovered only somewhat to 912 in 1979," according to A.C. Nielsen. Lawrence Ingrassia, "There's No Way To Tell If a New Product Will Please the Public," *The Wall Street Journal* (26 February 1980), p.1.

- A **dynamically continuous** innovation has more disruptive effects than the continuous innovation but it still does not alter patterns of buying or use. It may involve the creation of a new product or the modification of an existing product — e.g., electric toothbrushes, touch-tone telephones, color TVs, pocket calculators, and microwave ovens.
- A **discontinuous** innovation involves an entirely new product that brings about significantly different behavioral patterns — e.g., the automobile (about eighty years ago), television (about thirty years ago), computers, and snowmobiles. Discontinuous innovations are rare and come infrequently.

Reference above to the number of years suggests the need to emphasize the dependence of the classification of an innovation on the cultural context. For example, it is possible that currently in some third-world countries TV or even the automobile may be discontinuous innovations.

Within recent years the home-entertainment industry has developed a number of innovations, some of which have been very successful while others have failed. The videocassette recorder (VCR) diffused more rapidly than color TV; personal home computers and video game systems have also experienced rapid growth. On the other hand, the videodisc did not find high consumer acceptance. In April 1984, RCA announced its discontinuation. In the United States the company had lost over half a billion dollars since the introduction of its videodisc player in 1981.

Part of the reason for the failure was the cheaper rental fee for videocassettes. Other reasons were the ability of VCRs to record broadcasts as well as play pre-recorded tapes and the inferior quality of the video images. One marketer of videodiscs commented: "It was a dinosaur from the beginning. There was never really a strong need for it."

However, recent developments in videodisc technology using a more advanced system based on lasers may ensure the survival of the disc, particularly for applications in industry and education. For example, several firms are planning to use discs as data-storage devices for computers.[13]

The grouping of innovations sheds some light on adoption and diffusion. Generally, the less disruptive the product, the faster and wider its acceptance is likely to be. Other product characteristics also play a role.

Product Characteristics and Acceptance

A number of product characteristics have been found to facilitate new product acceptance.[14] Some of the principal attributes are relative advantage, ease of use, compatibility, divisibility, and communicability. Two things should be emphasized. First, we are speaking about consumer perceptions of these characteristics, and, second, the product must satisfy a need before those other attributes will influence acceptance.

Relative advantage is the extent to which consumers perceive the new product to be superior to the product it is intended to replace. This is a crucial element in achieving acceptance. Frequently a marketer may change a product (color, form — powder, liquid, flake) but if the change adds no perceivable advantage to the product, it will likely fail. Fluoride toothpastes are an outstanding example of a product that was perceived to have a clear advantage.

It seems, too, that the clearer the benefit (that is, the less time it takes to show up), the greater the likelihood of acceptance. "Some food products fail because they simply don't *taste* good enough. No one sets out to make a bad product but, in an effort to make a product convenient and inexpensive, too much quality can be sacrificed. Recently, Pillsbury had an idea for a new dessert — apples in cinnamon sauce with a crunchy streusel topping — which they called Appleasy. After good initial consumer test results, however, they began skimping on apples because the price of apples more than doubled. The product became less Appleasy and more starch and sugar. There was no problem with convenience but lots of problems with quality. . . . It was a magnificent flop."[15]

A new product that is *easy to use* has a greater likelihood of being accepted. A product that has complex instructions for use will find slow acceptance.

Compatibility is the degree to which the new product fits in with the consumer's existing values, attitudes, and behavioral patterns and does not require abrupt changes in behavior. In other words, the more disruptive the innovation, the less likely it is to find acceptance. Some years ago an analgesic (Analoze) that could be taken without water found little acceptance because potential consumers had difficulty believing that this tablet would work without water.

Recently Green Giant was sure of success with Oven Crock baked beans, which came already sweetened in the can. But it was a disaster in a test market because it was found that "people who ate heavily flavored baked beans added their own fixings to the bland variety and didn't want somebody to do it for them."

In another case, Pillsbury dropped plans to market a high-quality frozen croissant because "people didn't know *when* to eat it. The reaction was: 'It sure tastes good but I don't know what it is. Do I eat it for dinner or breakfast?'"[16]

A new product that can be purchased in small amounts ("trialability") is more likely to be accepted. There is much *less risk* than if a large quantity had to be purchased. The risk and investment are avoided when marketers provide free samples. And they are at least reduced when coupons or introductory cents-off deals are offered. The same reasons lie behind the "ten-day" trial offer or money-back guarantees frequently made for expensive or durable products (e.g., major appliances, encyclopedias).

The more easily the advantages of a product can be *communicated* or observed, the greater the likely success of the innovation. Thus, for example, pre-emergent herbicides have been slow to find acceptance because, by their very nature, the extent of their effectiveness is not demonstrable or observable. Products with high social visibility, such as fashion items, appear to be more communicable.

Communication as a Factor

The two most important types of communication that influence the acceptance of an innovation are marketer-dominated sources (such as advertising, publicity, sampling, sales promotion, and retail sales personnel), and non-marketer-dominated or informal sources (such as friends, acquaintances, and opinion leaders).

Marketer-Dominated, Formal Sources

Mass communications are most effective in the early stages of a new product's life by establishing awareness. The type of product or service may have a bearing on this. One group of researchers found that print media may be more important for a service than for a new product, and that television may be important for both.[17]

For some products, sampling is very effective, and, in general, personal sales staff are very important as a source of information to potential customers.[18]

Informal Sources

Word-of-mouth communications are increasingly recognized as a strong influence in the acceptance of an innovation, particularly in the later stages of evaluation and trial. Consumers tend to turn to someone who has purchased the product previously or to an expert. This tendency is more pronounced with products of high perceived risk.[19]

It has been found that such interpersonal contacts are more likely to be initiated by the recipient of the information and that in the relationship the opinion leader is not the dominant element holding forth to a passive recipient.[20] This has been referred to as the "two-step flow hypothesis," wherein information from the advertiser through mass media reaches the innovator, from whom it is then transmitted to the potential adopter.[21]

Consumer Characteristics and Acceptance

The acceptance of an innovation is influenced by the society in which it is introduced. The values, needs, attitudes, and norms of the social system may facilitate or militate against certain innovations. Then, within the system, there will be differences among individuals based on such characteristics as personality, need, and education.

For the successful introduction of an innovation, the marketer should first attempt to determine how the society will likely react to it and which groups of individuals within it will be disposed to accept it. The product concept, as suggested earlier, should be compatible with existing values, beliefs, and attitudes. Other features, such as communications media and level of technological advancement, should also be consistent with the efforts necessary for the successful innovation.

The Two Learning Processes

Both learning processes — adoption and diffusion — are influenced by the attributes of the product (disruptive impact, advantage, compatibility, ease of use, divisibility, communicability), the modes of communication available, and the characteristics of the consumers and the social system involved. More, however, seems to be known about the adoption process than about the diffusion process.

The adoption process involves essentially the stages through which the consumer passes in deciding whether or not to try and then continue or discontinue buying a new product. E.M. Rogers, a sociologist, has suggested five such stages:

- awareness;
- interest;
- evaluation;
- trial; and
- adoption/rejection.[22]

The marketer must employ the kinds of media and messages that ensure that the consumer knows about the new product (recall the discussion of selective perception in Chapter 5). More information will increase interest and lead to a consideration of its merits (in terms of its attributes as described earlier). In a sense, the evaluation is a kind of "mental trial" after which the consumer may or may not decide to try the product. If trial occurs, then the experience (or a repeat experience) will provide the information for adopting or rejecting the product. Adoption occurs when the consumer decides to continue using the product.

I have already discussed the roles played by mass media (marketer-dominated) and informal sources of communication at different stages of the adoption process. This no doubt varies with the product, so that each marketer should attempt to determine his or her role *vis-à-vis* the particular product in order to be successful in taking potential consumers through to the final stage.

Several criticisms have been levelled at Rogers' paradigm — from the lack of emphasis of a need for the product, through the implication that evaluation takes place at one — and not every — stage, to the notion that it deals mostly with discontinuous innovations. Some of these may be rather pedantic — clearly, awareness implies selective perception, which we know is strongly affected by need; evaluation cannot take place without information, and it permeates each stage even to a (not stated) post-adoption stage. Its limitation to the discontinuous innovation may be the most serious criticism, especially since most marketing innovations are of the continuous or dynamically continuous types. But the principal benefit of the paradigm lies in its ability to alert the marketer to the different strategies necessary at the different stages.

A revised paradigm — the **innovation decision process** — has sought to correct for some of these limitations.[23] It suggests four stages:

- knowledge;
- persuasion;
- decision; and
- confirmation.

The model telescopes the earlier model and introduces the post-adoption confirmation stage. It seems to omit trial, which is an intrinsic part of the adoption process for any product.

Other formulations of this process are the "Hierarchy of Effects Model" and the "AIDA Model," whose basic components are compared with the "Adoption Process Model" discussed earlier (see Figure 9.2).

A Summary Model proposed by Robertson combines all of these features and takes into account a few others (see Figure 9.3).

- the information–attitude–behavior conceptualization is kept;
- feedback effects are included with broken lines; and
- problem perception and dissonance are two new stages added to the process to account more fully for the possible sequences that may occur.

Robertson notes that rejection can occur at any stage. He has also omitted the interest and evaluation stages of the APM. He feels that interest is a prerequisite for the occurrence of every stage. That may be true but if after initial awareness the idea was not sufficiently appealing, the process would likely end. In a sense, his "attitude" stage represents that "interest" stage. Similarly, he feels that evaluation occurs at every stage and suggests "legitimation" instead. Note that the process begins with the perception of a problem. The introductory presentation of the

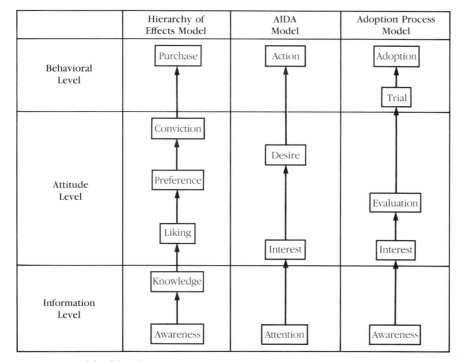

FIGURE 9.2: Models of the Adoption Decision Process

SOURCE: Thomas S. Robertson, "A Critical Examination of 'Adoption Process' Models of consumer Behavior," in Jagdish N. Sheth (ed.), *Models of Beyer Behavior* (New York: Harper and Row, 1974), pp. 271-95. Reprinted with permission of Harper and Row, Publishers, Inc.

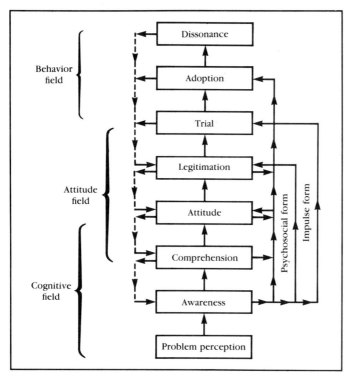

FIGURE 9.3: Summary Adoption Decision Process Model

SOURCE: Thomas S. Robertson, "A Critical Examination of 'Adoption Process' Models of Consumer Behavior," in Jagdish N. Sheth (ed.), *Models of Buyer Behavior* (New York: Haper and Row, 1974), p. 290. Reprinted with permission of Harper and Row, Publishers, Inc.

product or idea must, of course, be clearly related to a consumer need. Comprehension, following awareness, is an important stage since the marketer must ensure that the "consumer's conception of what the product is and what functions it can perform" is in accordance with what he or she intends.

The diffusion process is also affected by the various factors described earlier but how it actually occurs has not so far been described with any precision. The closest we have come to a treatment of the mechanics of the diffusion process has been with the two-step flow of communication hypothesis (described earlier in this chapter) and the trickle-down theory.

The trickle-down theory, dealing with women's fashions, holds that acceptance flows from upper to lower classes. This view has more or less been replaced by the "two-step" hypothesis, which suggests that diffusion takes place horizontally from opinion leaders to others within the same group.[24]

Rogers has represented the nature of the diffusion of an innovation in the social system as a normal distribution curve to which perhaps many, but certainly not all, products may conform.[25]

Figure 9.4 is illustrative of many important characteristics of adoption. It takes place over time. Only a small number first accept an innovation (innovators), and the number increases from adopters to a majority group; that is, the pace of adoption increases. The growth in acceptance then begins to fall again.

The rate of adoption, it should be noted, is a function of the *social system* — its orientation, its values and norms, its level of technology (e.g., kitchen devices). The social climate and attitudes toward innovations play an important role. For example, the current attitudes to health

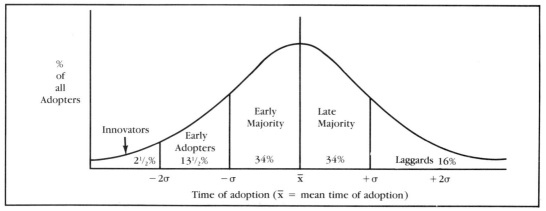

FIGURE 9.4: Market Segments by Time of Adoption

SOURCE: E.M. Rogers, *Diffusion of Innovations* (New York: Free Press, 1962). Reprinted with permission of Macmillan Publishing Company, Inc. Copyright © 1962 by the Free Press of Glancoe, a division of Macmillan Publishing Company.

in the US and Canada have fostered the growth of numerous health-related products (e.g., natural health foods, jogging equipment, and sports facilities).

The rate of adoption is also affected by the frequency of purchase of the product. An innovation in a category that is purchased frequently (such as cigarettes) will diffuse much more rapidly than an innovation that is purchased infrequently (e.g., a TV).

It is interesting to note that our society appears to be characterized by rapidly shortening product life cycles and a concomitant increase in the rate of diffusion of innovations.[26]

Innovator Characteristics

Researchers have suggested some important characteristics of innovators. Compared to non-innovators, they have a higher income and occupational status; they are younger and better educated; they read more, are more socially active, and more venturesome.[27] One study of adopters of the touch-tone telephone found the innovators to be significantly more venturesome, socially mobile, socially integrated, financially privileged, impulsive, active, and dominant. They were also found to "engage in more new product discussions and exert greater opinion leadership."[28]

A recent study investigating the profile of a technological innovation, the home computer, found it to be "similar to that of the adopter of many other types of innovations: middle-aged, higher income, more education, opinion leader, information seeker, and so on."[29] The authors conclude that the characteristics of the adopter of an innovation are a function of the characteristics of the innovation itself. For example, the adopters of home computers appear to have had more experience with a variety of technical products and services than non-adopters.

According to Rogers, the innovators are a very small "avant-garde" group who are not necessarily influential on others; it is the "early adopters" who are relied upon and serve as the "opinion leaders" others follow in the adoption of the new product.

The variable nature of the **rate of diffusion** is well illustrated by Example 1 in Chapter 8, dealing with the acceptance of the microwave oven in Canada. A number of factors influence the varying rates of adoption in the different provinces of the country.

Although theorizing on the mechanics of diffusion is sparse, a number of models have been developed for predicting the diffusion of new products; that is, predicting the number of consumers likely to accept a new product and the time it will involve. These models do not contain any behavioral constructs. Essentially they are concerned with the relationship between time and new product sales (actual from a previous period or assumed).[30]

The Implications of Adoption and Diffusion Research

For marketers, a better understanding of both the adoption and the diffusion processes can offer many advantages. Even outside the consumer behavior field, in government and social services, for example, such knowledge provides numerous benefits.

Marketing Significance

One of the biggest and most expensive problems in marketing is the number of new products that fail to gain market acceptance. Estimates vary widely but leave no doubt that the proportion of new product failures is high. This is one way in which better knowledge of the dynamics of adoption and diffusion may contribute to an improvement in product success rate, to the growth and survival of our modern companies (dependent as they are upon growth), and to a reduction in the waste of resources resulting from the large number of failures.

The adoption process deals with the adoption and *continued use* of a product, unlike the general models in consumer behavior, which focus on a single decision.[31] This, along with the fact that innovation research usually analyzes generic products rather than specific brands, adds a valuable dimension to the study of consumer behavior.

The emphasis of diffusion research on the social dynamics involved in communication has the potential for a broader understanding of consumer choice.

Significance Outside Marketing

Just as innovation research may help in achieving better rates of acceptance of new products,

so too it offers the possibility of improving upon society's reaction to new ideas and measures — whether in birth control, farming techniques, politics, energy conservation, or pollution. I discussed this subject in Chapter 1 under the heading of "Societal Marketing."

FASHION ACCEPTANCE

A particularly interesting example of the adoption and diffusion of innovation is women's fashions. In an excellent article, Sproles reviewed "the evolution and the current state of fashion theory," emphasizing the cyclical nature of fashion phenomena — with stages of introduction and adoption by fashion leaders, increasing public acceptance, mass conformity, and decline.[32]

While clothing is clearly the classic product of fashion-oriented behavior (and indubitably comes first to mind when one speaks of fashion), many other consumer products show similar characteristics, ranging from automobiles and housing to foods and music.

General Fashion Theory

Current theory appears to take both a long-term and a short-term view of fashion phenomena.

The long-term view proposes that fashions show a certain historical continuity of change, progressing from one extreme to another every thirty to fifty years (e.g., dress lengths changing from short to long and back to short).

Some have suggested that changes in fashion silhouettes can be attributed to the desire of women to shift attention to different parts of the body to attract the opposite sex.[33] In essence, each new fashion is seen as a relatively small change to the earlier fashion rather than a revolutionary or visually dramatic modification and is more likely to be favored by both producers (less risky) and consumers (less faddish).

The study of long-run data could involve "decades of data" that reveal only the gross, broadly defined parameters of change. On the other hand, marketing decisions are in fact made within a year-to-year or season-to-season framework and variations involving ornamentation, color, fabric, and trim are at times quite radical or random.

The short-term view focusses on a single fashion cycle, which typically lasts several years and sometimes from five to ten years. Styles that last a short time, sometimes only weeks or months, are termed *fads*. Those which are accepted for many years — ten or more — are called classics. Fads may be bizarre or exotic and adopted by only a small part of the population or perhaps by a single subculture. Classics, on the other hand, receive wide acceptance and are perceived to have basic, enduring aesthetic quality.

The Dynamics of Fashion Diffusion

The initiation and propagation of new fashions have been attributed to two primary sources: designers and the fashion industry, and consumer groups.

The fashion industry is widely perceived as having a most powerful, almost dictatorial control over fashion trends, particularly the well-publicized high-fashion designers and the trade media (e.g., the British *Women's Wear Daily*). In recent years, the growth in the number of fashion designers and their wide use of mass communications have no doubt served to increase industry impact on fashions. By offering dominant trends and certain styles, mass retailers have also begun to exert some considerable control, allowing consumers little choice "except perhaps in colors and less conspicuous design details."

Sproles asserts, "It is hard to deny that the industry has a role in persuading, if not coercing, the direction of fashion trends."[34] But objective evidence of this influence is lacking and the possibility of significant influence of other factors on such a complex phenomenon must be recognized. Take, for example, the case of the midi dress, introduced in 1969–70.[35] Al-though heavily promoted by the fashion press and "decreed" by some as sure to catch on, it was rejected by consumer opinion leaders and failed to gain mass acceptance.

Certain social and industry factors may have tended to enlarge consumer influence on fashion diffusion:

- the variety of styles available;
- current permissiveness surrounding socially appropriate dress;
- a highly competitive industry; and
- the importance of individuality to modern consumers.

Exactly how consumers propagate fashion is not agreed upon. In fact, four theories have been proposed:

The Trickle-Down Theory suggests that fashions are first adopted by the upper class and then trickle down progressively to the lowest class. Historically, this was probably true, for as the leisure class became more wealthy they sought increasingly to display their wealth, most notably with clothing. It appears, though, that fashion-conscious social groups have grown in influence and that a strong horizontal flow within social classes has resulted from greatly accelerated fashion cycles, mass production, mass communications, and changing life-styles.

The Mass Market Theory proposes that modern marketing has made new styles and information about new styles available simultaneously to all socio-economic classes, so that diffusion of fashion is more of a trickle-across than of a trickle-down phenomenon. Fashion leadership comes from within an individual's social class and peer groups. However, the role of industry and of social leaders in influencing the acceptance of certain broad trends cannot be overlooked.

The Subcultural Leadership Theory. In a society of dynamic changes in values and tastes, many new fashions have originated with specific subcultural groups — such as blacks, youth, and ethnic minorities —- striving for individuality and identity. Those styles with creativity and artistic excellence may spread beyond the subculture and, after adoption by the upper class, trickle down to the other classes or, with mass marketing, trickle across the dominant culture.

The Theory of Collective Selection contributes to the origin of fashions mainly by suggesting that the collective tastes of many people lead to the evolution of new styles that compete for acceptance by consumers and that those styles that best reflect existing trends in consumer tastes become fashionable. The theory then accepts the propositions of the other theories regarding the roles of innovators, prestige leaders, and historical continuity in the diffusion of fashion, but it does not specify how collective tastes are formed and how collective selection actually occurs.

A number of other theories offer some interesting insights into why fashions change:

- **sex appeal**: fashions serve to play up sex appeal, which is enhanced by the shifting of erogenous zones; that is, by using new fashions to shift attention to different parts of the body;
- **self-identity**: through fashions, individuality is attained, whether the means are social deviancy or masquerading;
- **social and economic changes**: new styles reflect social and economic trends (e.g., skirt lengths rise and fall with the business cycle and new life-styles generate new fashions);
- **history**: fashions are usually resurrections from the past;
- **culture**: new styles originate when different cultures come together; and
- **modernism**: new, changing life-styles necessitate new, changing fashions.

Limitations

Fashion theory offers many useful insights into understanding how and why consumers accept new styles, but there are still a number of areas not adequately treated:

- the process underlying fashion decline: forces such as market saturation, overuse, boredom, the desire for novelty, loss of prestige or exclusivity, planned obsolescence, and social obsolescence have been identified, but details on the process are limited;
- of the large number of **market segments** that may be identified over the fashion life-cycle — innovators, opinion leaders, innovative communicators, other fashion-conscious consumers, followers, laggards (late adopters, those favoring classics), deviants (non-conformists, subcultures), disintegrators (whose acceptance or termination of use may indicate decline), and non-adopters — only a few (the first four mainly) have been properly delineated;
- the **perceptual processes** by which consumers identify and react to new styles have not been explored. We need answers to such questions as: How much change is required before a new object is perceived as different from its predecessor? How much change will be tolerated before overstimulation occurs (i.e., the style is perceived as too innovative)? Do perceptual processes differ among aesthetic components of silhouette, color, and design details? Answers to these questions would significantly advance fashion theory.

Sproles summarizes a number of general principles encompassing our present knowledge of fashion acceptance:[36]

- new styles originate from centers of prestige and creativity, including both creative entrepreneurs and fashion-conscious consumers;
- both groups also interact to give public exposure to new styles via social groups;
- a new style is most likely to receive substantial acceptance if it is first adopted by a discernible proportion of fashion-conscious consumers and if it is also consistent with the relevant style trends in historical continuity;
- fashions will diffuse within social groups sharing similar social class, prestige, life-style, need, and value characteristics as a result of

marketing strategy (communication and pricing), massed availability in all types of retail stores, and appropriateness to the relevant life-style. These collective forces of the mass market are more powerful than processes of upper-class leadership and social competition between classes for symbols;

- once acceptance of a fashion is substantial, mass acceptance will depend upon the pressures of social conformity and upon the extent to which the style is featured exclusively by mass marketing; and
- decline and termination begin when overuse and consumer boredom become evident and when industry designers and producers and consumer innovators and opinion leaders start to experiment with new, different styles.

Fashion is under-researched, both in the scholarly literature and in industry. Research so far has involved the identification of fashion leaders, consumer style preferences, and dress, but little related to the fashion life-cycle framework. Similarly, while manufacturers and retailers may intuitively apply the fashion-cycle concept and think in terms of designs and preferences, the fashion business is organized around seasonal or annual merchandising cycles, not around fashion life-cycles.

SUMMARY

Four examples of learning in consumer behavior were examined in this chapter: categories of awareness, loyalty, the processes of adoption and diffusion, and fashion acceptance.

Not all brands in a product class are in a consumer's awareness set and not all brands in the latter are considered at the time of purchase. Only those in the evoked set are. Thus it is not enough for marketers to determine whether consumers are aware or not aware of their brands; it is necessary for them to know whether or not their brands are in the evoked set.

A great deal of controversy has surrounded the concept of loyalty, mainly because of the two different approaches to defining loyalty: the behavioral and the dynamic. The dynamic appears to be preferable because it takes into account attitudes to products or brands, and not just repeat behavior. Loyalty varies with the individual and with the product. Some individuals are more inclined to be loyal than others and an individual may be loyal to one or two products and not to others.

Adoption and diffusion deal with how a product achieves acceptance. The adoption process concerns how an individual comes to accept a new product; the diffusion process how adoption spreads from one individual to another in a market. Three kinds of innovations were identified: continuous, dynamically continuous, and discontinuous. A number of product characteristics affect acceptance such as relative advantage, complexity, compatibility, divisibility, and communicability.

The adoption process consists of five basic stages: awareness, interest, evaluation, trial, and adoption. The diffusion process appears to follow the normal distribution curve. Two theories attempt to explain it: the two-step flow hypothesis and the trickle-down theory.

Fashion acceptance theory was reviewed from the long-term and the short-term viewpoints. It was shown how both the fashion industry and consumers influence fashion diffusion. A number of theories of fashion diffusion were discussed and areas worthy of further exploration identified.

QUESTIONS

1. What is the broad significance of the various categories of awareness? What are their implications for marketing strategy?

2. Discuss the merits of the operational and conceptual approaches to brand loyalty.

3. Relate the concepts of brand loyalty and involvement.

4. Classify the following products into types of innovations:

   home computers   video games
   Stripe toothpaste   Carnation Instant
   videotape recorders   Breakfast

   snowmobiles   Sizzlelean
   Starch-eze   microwave ovens
   electric cars

5. Discuss the importance of relative advantage as a factor in influencing adoption.

6. Describe the nature of the controversy among the different paradigms of the adoption process, stating your position on the roles of interest, trial, evaluation, and confirmation.

7. In your opinion, what are the primary dynamics underlying fashion adoption?

NOTES TO CHAPTER 9

[1]Chem L. Narayana and Rom J. Markin, "Consumer Behavior and Product Performance: An Alternative Conceptualization," *Journal of Marketing*, 39 (October 1975), pp. 1-6.

[2]Jagdish N. Sheth, "How Adults Learn Brand Preference," *Journal of Advertising Research*, 8 (September 1968), pp. 25-36.

[3]J. Jacoby and D.B. Kyner, "Brand Loyalty and Repeat Purchasing Behavior," *Journal of Marketing Research*, 10 (February 1973), pp. 1-9.

[4]George S. Day, "A Two-Dimensional Concept of Brand Loyalty," *Journal of Advertising Research*, 9 (September 1969), pp. 29-35.

[5]Ibid.

[6]Ibid.

[7]Jacoby and Kyner, op. cit., p. 20.

[8]Robert C. Blattberg and Subrata K. Sen, "Market Segments and Stochastic Brand Choice Models," *Journal of Marketing Research*, 13 (February 1976), pp. 34-45; John A. Howard and Jagdish N. Sheth, *The Theory of Buyer Behavior* (New York: John Wiley & Sons, 1969), p. 249; Jagdish N. Sheth, "Measurement of Multidimensional Brand Loyalty of a Consumer," *Journal of Marketing Research*, 7 (August 1970), pp. 348-54.

[9]James M. Carman, "Correlates of Brand Loyalty: Some Positive Results," *Journal of Marketing Research*, 7 (February 1970), pp. 67-76.

[10]Robert Blattberg, Thomas Buesing, Peter Peacock, and Subrata Sen, "Identifying the Deal Prone Segment," *Journal of Marketing Research*, 15 (August 1978), pp. 369-77.

[11]James H. Donnelly, Jr. and Michael J. Etzel, "Degrees of Product Newness and Early Trial," *Journal of Marketing Research*, 10 (August 1973), pp. 295-300.

[12]Thomas S. Robertson, "The Process of Innovation and the Diffusion of Innovation," *Journal of Marketing*, 31 (January 1967), pp. 14-19.

[13]*Time* Magazine (16 April 1984), p. 45.

[14]E.M. Rogers and F. Shoemaker, *The Communication of Innovations* (New York: Free Press, 1971), pp. 137-57.

[15]Lawrence Ingrassia, "There's No Way to Tell if a New Product Will Please the Public," *Wall Street Journal* (26 February 1980), p. 1.

[16]Ibid.

[17]Robert T. Green, Eric Langeard, and Alice C. Favell, "Innovation in the Service Sector: Some Empirical Findings," *Journal of Marketing Research*, 11 (August 1974), pp. 323-6.

[18]Ronald P. Willett and Allan L. Pennington, "Customer and Salesman: The Anatomy of Choice and Influence," in Raymond M. Haas (ed.), *Science, Technology and Marketing* (Chicago: American Marketing Association, 1966), pp. 598-616.

[19]Johan Arndt, "Perceived Risk, Sociometric Integration and Word of Mouth in the Adoption of a New Food Product," in Donald F. Cox (ed.), *Risk Taking and Information Handling in Consumer Behavior* (Boston: Division of Research, Graduate School of Business Administration, Harvard University, 1967), pp. 289-316; Jagdish N. Sheth, "Word of Mouth in Low-Risk Innovations," *Journal of Advertising Research*, 11:3 (June 1971), pp. 15-8.

[20]James H. Myers and Thomas S. Robertson, "Dimensions of Opinion Leadership," *Journal of Marketing Research*, 9 (February 1972), pp. 41-6.

[21]Elihu Katz and Paul H. Lazarsfeld, *Personal Influence: The Part Played by People in the Flow of Mass Communications* (New York: Free Press, 1955).

[22]E.M. Rogers, *Diffusion of Innovations* (Glencoe, Illinois: Free Press, 1971), pp. 81-6.

[23]Rogers and Shoemaker, op. cit., pp. 100-33.

[24]Charles W. King, "Fashion Adoption: A Rebuttal to the 'Trickle-Down Theory,'" in Stephen A. Greyser (ed.), *Toward Scientific Marketing* (Chicago: American Marketing Association, 1964), pp. 108-25.

[25]E.M. Rogers, *Diffusion of Innovations* (New York: Free Press, 1962).

[26]Richard W. Olshavsky, "Time and the Rate of Adoption of Innovations," *Journal of Consumer Research*, 6 (March 1980), pp. 425-8.

[27]Thomas S. Robertson, *Innovation and the Consumer* (New York: Holt, Rinehart, and Winston, 1971).

[28]Roger D. Blackwell, James F. Engel, W. Wayne Talarzyk, *Contemporary Cases in Consumer Behavior* (Hinsdale, Illinois: Dryden Press, 1977), pp. 257-67.

[29]Mary Dee Dickerson and James W. Gentry, "Characteristics of Adopters and Non-Adopters of Home Computers," *Journal of Consumer Research*, 10 (September 1983), pp. 225-34.

[30]Philip Kotler, *Marketing Decision Making: A Model Building Approach* (New York: Holt, Rinehart, and Winston, 1971), Chapter 17; Vijay Mahajan and Eitan Muller, "Innovation Diffusion and New Product Growth Models in Marketing," *Journal of Marketing*, 43 (Fall 1979), pp. 55-68; David B. Learner, "Profit Maximization Through New-Product Marketing and Control," in Frank Bass (ed.), *Application of the Sciences in Marketing Management* (New York: John Wiley & Sons, 1968), pp. 151-67; Vijay Mahajan and R.A. Peterson, "Innovation Diffusion in a Dynamic Potential Adopter Population," *Management Science*, November 1978, pp. 127-46.

[31]Thomas S. Robertson, "A Critical Examination of 'Adoption Process' Models of Consumer Behavior," in Jagdish N. Sheth (ed.), *Models of Buyer Behavior* (New York: Harper and Row, 1974), pp. 271-95.

[32]George B. Sproles, "Analyzing Fashion Life Cycles — Principles and Perspectives," *Journal of Marketing*, 45 (Fall 1981), pp. 116-24.

[33]John Carl Flugel, *The Psychology of Clothes* (London: Hogarth Press, 1930); Edmund Bergler, *Fashion and the Unconscious* (New York: Robert Brunner, 1953).

[34]Sproles, op. cit.

[35]Fred D. Reynolds and William R. Darden, "Why the Midi Failed," *Journal of Advertising Research*, 12 (August 1972), pp. 39-44.

[36]Sproles, op. cit.

THE BATTLE FOR THE RAZOR MARKET: GILLETTE VERSUS BIC*

The battle between Gillette and Bic for the rich razor-blade market provides some dramatic illustrations of the goings-on in the world of innovation.

It has taken Gillette twenty years to start lashing back at Bic, the French-owned upstart. It is now more of a vicious street fight, in which price slashing is the main weapon and market share the main prize.

With about $2 billion in sales, Gillette is more than three times as large as Bic ($600 million) but the smaller company has been a thorn in Gillette's side, first with disposable ballpoint pens, then disposable lighters, and most recently with disposable razors.

In the early 1960s, when Bic entered the US market with its pens, Gillette executives regarded the French company more as a nuisance, confident that Bic's nineteen-cent throwaway pen was no match for their higher-priced, best-selling Paper-Mate. Soon, however, Bic sales were outstripping those of Gillette's ninety-eight-cent product. Ten years later, Bic's entry into the disposable cigarette-lighter business trounced Gillette's Cricket brand. But Gillette was still not too bothered because pens and lighters have never accounted for more than 15% of sales or pretax profits.

But the $1-billion world-wide razor-and-blade market was a different matter. It is the very core of Gillette's business — 30% of its sales, 70% of pretax profits, and perhaps 100% of corporate pride. Since 1976 the Bic razor, priced at "$19\frac{3}{4}$ cents," has captured a 9% share of the market. What really alarms Gillette is the fact that Bic has been working on the low-priced end of the shaving market — the area where Gillette could get hurt the most.

Beginning with the Super Blue Blade in 1960, Gillette has been moving consumers to more sophisticated and expensive blades. Every few years — or so it seems — the company would announce a new

---

* *Adapted from* Linda Snyder Hayes, "Gillette Takes the Wraps Off," *Fortune* (25 February 1980), pp. 148-50.

shaving product at a premium price. In 1971, for example, it introduced the Trac II razor, which features a twin-blade shaving cartridge. Six years later came the Atra, with twin blades mounted on a pivoting head.

Today, the blades for these two razors are the most popular shaving products in the US, together accounting for more than a quarter of all blades sold, and constituting Gillette's most profitable products.

A vital part of Gillette's current marketing strategy is simply to "out-Bic" Bic. Even before the French company was ready to launch its razor in the US, Gillette brought out its own disposable razor, Good News, which, it argued, was worth its twenty-five-cent price because, unlike Bic's single blade, it featured a twin blade.

"Gillette never really hoped to sell very many of these razors," explains Brenda Lee Landry, security analyst at Merrill Lynch. "The last thing in the world the company wanted was to see consumers switch away from its other blades." While the Good News is priced considerably lower than the Atra or Trac II blade, it actually costs much more to manufacture. Its intended role was to undermine Bic's most effective marketing ploys. In the past, Bic's success in selling its inexpensive, disposable products had stemmed largely from its ability to convince consumers that its products were as good as, or better than, anything the competition had to offer. By offering a disposable with a twin blade, Gillette cast doubt on Bic's claim.

While Bic feel that their product *is* as good as Gillette's, they concede that Gillette's twin-blade claim does sound logical and is difficult to counter. Although Bic holds a 9% share of the US market (compared to 11% for Good News) it has paid dearly for that "honor" — $7 million annually for advertising compared with only $2 million for Good News. Moreover, during the past three years Bic has *lost* $25 million on its razor (roughly one-half of its pretax profits) while Gillette has consistently made money on its disposable.

In addition to keeping the pressure on in the razor market, Gillette appears to be putting the squeeze on Bic's other businesses. Although Bic brought out its disposable lighter after Gillette's Cricket in 1972, each soon had about 40% of the market. Instead of sitting back and enjoying short-term profits, Bic decided on the big play. In mid-1977 it slashed its wholesale price by 32%. Because of higher costs, Gillette waited before reducing its own price, only to be matched by a further reduction by Bic — and a ferocious price war ensued.

By the end of 1978, Bic had gained nearly 50% of the market, with Gillette holding 30%; Bic reported a $9.2 million pretax profit for its lighter division while Gillette suffered a loss of almost the same amount. In spite of continuing losses, in 1979 Gillette reduced its Cricket lighter to 10% lower than the Bic price. While this hasn't substantially hurt Bic's market share, it has cut into profits and thus the amount of money Bic can keep pouring into razors.

Gillette has counteracted with a cheaper pen to match Bic's top seller in the office-supply market. Both companies are "going at" each other on several fronts. Bic does not appear to be wilting, especially since its disposable razor is doing so well.

In addition, Bic has another innovation up its sleeve. Far from being daunted by Gillette, Bic appears to be spoiling for yet another fight. It is test-marketing in Canada a rolling-ball marker, the Bic Roller. It appears to have considerable potential. If Bic introduces the product in the US, Gillette will surely take counter-measures. The competition between the rivals is no longer just a matter of one pen or one lighter or one razor against another. It is a war on all fronts.

The ramifications of innovational strategy are quite complex. Development costs for an innovation can be considerable and promotional costs may be high but the commitment does not end there. Competition can become extremely serious and involve the entire weight of all corporate resources and corporate pride.

QUESTIONS

1. Evaluate the strategies and counter-strategies applied by Gillette and Bic in their battle of innovations.

2. The male razor market appears to be very receptive to innovations. Why do you think this is so?

3. What is the current status of the battle between Gillette and Bic for the razor market in the US? In Canada?

10

Motivation

1. Baby Food Containers

Some years ago, a large Canadian producer of prepared baby foods sought to determine likely consumer reactions to a changeover from cans, in which the product was currently sold, to glass jars.

A research study conducted with a sample of mothers of babies in urban Southern Ontario uncovered a wide variety of motivations in favor of the jar. These included:

- easier to open;
- safer — no risk of cutting oneself on the rough edges of the top of the can;
- no risk of contamination with tiny pieces of tin that may fall in upon opening the can;
- easier to re-close and refrigerate leftovers;
- looks better feeding the baby from a glass jar than from a can;
- can be put to other uses; and
- makes possible checking of the food in the jar for freshness before purchasing.

What was surprising was the variety of reasons: from practical reasons such as "easier to open" to aesthetic reasons such as "looks better to serve from" to economic reasons such as "leftovers can be kept." Many of them did not occur to the marketing manager, emphasizing the desirability of consumer input. Needless to say, the reactions were so overwhelmingly positive that the changeover was quickly made by the company and adopted by the industry not long after.

2. The Honda[1]

The people who sell Hondas seem to have a perennial problem. They do not seem to have nearly enough to satisfy demand. A primary motivation for its subcompacts is their outstanding gas consumption.

It is so important a criterion that buyers are willing to wait months for delivery. Mileage became particularly important after the energy crisis brought on by the Arab oil embargo in 1972. In the United States, Honda sales accelerated from eleventh among foreign imports in 1972 to third place in 1978 and through to 1983. In Canada, sales have steadily increased, reaching close to 45,000 units in 1983, representing the largest share of all imports (23%). And, as of April 1984, Honda has remained the leader.

It appears that low fuel consumption may not be the only reason for Honda's popularity. Honda's cars also offer a combination of ingratiating features: they are equipped with front-wheel drive (but most other cars now also have front-wheel drive); the engine is mounted sideways and it runs smoothly and quietly; they come with independent suspension so that they take bumps better than most small cars.

Honda cars also get high marks for quality of craftsmanship, attention to detail, and for various little amenities, such as a coin box built into the dashboard, which is very useful on toll highways, for example (see Figure 10.1).

This is a good example of how economic or social conditions can affect the kinds and importance of criteria consumers will use for making a choice. It also attests to the basic common sense of the consumer, who can take into account numerous practical reasons for purchase, as well as social or psychological reasons. Undoubtedly, in such a large number of motivations the consumer is guided by an attribute hierarchy in which some motives have priority over others.

FIGURE 10.1: An Example of Honda's Advertising
Courtesy Honda Canada Inc.

3. Metrecal[2]

Metrecal, the first diet food, was introduced in 1959. In the beginning, it emphasized its strong medical associations: manufactured by a pharmaceutical firm (Mead, Johnson, and Company), sold through drug stores, and medically accepted. Ads also stressed that consumers consult with their family doctor before taking Metrecal.

It was soon found, however, that the medical appeal was far less effective than the approach of competitors who increased the size of their package, introduced new flavors, and emphasized girlish figures and slimming down for summer fashions. Metrecal was forced to switch to a *social approach* ("Metrecal-for-lunch bunch") and to recognize that different kinds of diets were preferred by different groups — "crash diets" of unusual foods; regulated, extended diets of normal foods; carefully controlled diets for short periods of time; as well as low-calorie foods as a supplement to help prevent unwanted weight gains.

Dieters' motivations are interesting. There are:
- medical dieters — based on medical advice;
- deprivational dieters — depriving themselves of food to purge feelings of guilt, reminiscent of religious fasting;
- attention attractors — such as among high-school or college students who conform, for example, to fads; and
- social interaction dieters — who diet in order to fit social norms.

Conversely, there are societies in which obesity is desirable, because it is regarded as evidence of prosperity and success.

The complexity of motivation is apparent in this case — a combination of rational and emotional motives (convenience, personal appearance) as well as conscious and unconscious motives (variety, health, conformity, social approval, guilt).

4. J&B Scotch[3]

Because of stagnant sales, the top-selling brand of Scotch whisky in the US, J&B, is changing its advertising. In place of the J&B bottle and glass will be a view of an isolated Scottish farmhouse, surrounded by a moor and a quiet, blue lake. Superimposed on the water is J&B's label. The ad copy reads: "*J&B. It whispers*".

They hope that this will suggest lightness. The new ads do not give any explicit reasons, except that J&B has known all along that it owes much of its popularity to its lighter color and taste.

The idea is to set a scene in which people can be relaxed and comfortable. Here is an attempt to appeal to motives (lightness, "refreshingness") through imagery rather than through words.

5. American Can's Paper Towel, Bolt[4]

Quality sells. Products can always be improved. Consumers will pay more if they perceive good value. Like nearly all name-brand marketers, American Can accepts these precepts as gospel but the company's faith is being tested. Its trial: paper towels. Will consumers buy paper towels that are so strong and absorbent that they're difficult to throw away?

American Can thinks so and is backing its belief with Bolt, a paper towel that, the company asserts, "actually looks and performs like cloth." But the big question is whether there really is a need for such a product. Does the world really want a bullet-proof paper towel? One expert believes that, while in other days consumers thought that more was always better, now many people are looking for the product that simply is good enough for the job.

These examples have presented a wide range of motivations for buying. Example 1 illustrates the variety of reasons that can lead to brand preferences and the desirability of consumer research. The example of the Honda car also highlights the influence of economic and social conditions on choice criteria and their priorities.

The Metrecal example illustrates the varying complexity of motives. J&B Scotch relies on emotional motives stimulated by imagery and symbolism. Bolt, on the other hand, points to the basic good sense of the consumer and the wisdom of not making exaggerated claims. Through the contrast effect, consumers are likely to reject promises that offer too much. Sometimes it is better to be realistic and make a product that is just good enough.

WHAT IS MOTIVATION?

In the preceding chapters I discussed how individuals learn responses to particular stimuli — the factors that affect what is learned and how much is learned — but a more basic question is why learning takes place. The factors acting together to bring about such learning make up the motivational dynamics of the individual. Most, if not all, learning in consumer behavior is motivated. There are some types of human learning that can occur without motivation. Cognitive psychologists point to the possibility of "perceptual reorganization" of a situation or problem in the absence of motivation (e.g., latent learning).

Krugman has referred to this phenomenon in consumer behavior as **passive learning**, which was discussed in an earlier chapter. The crucial question for us is what causes the individual to put what has been learned into practice? While learning establishes the associations between stimuli and responses and while these associations may be retained or registered in the long-term memory, behavior may not necessarily follow. In some instances, learning takes place with the results being stored in memory for future use. In others, learning may be followed by a behavioral response so that, as part of the same situation, both learning and behavior are influenced and directed by the same motivations.

The learning of responses that takes place through instruction, vicarious practice, or nonaction will be applied later by the individual. Those responses that provide satisfaction will be reinforced, so that in similar situations the motivations that initially produced the responses will call them forth again. Motivation, then, is at the heart of consumer behavior for it refers to the reasons that lie behind behavior.

Motivation is one area in which marketers have borrowed heavily from psychologists. Out of a desire to simplify (and, unfortunately, also out of inadequate understanding of psychological concepts), marketers have tended to broaden and combine concepts so that the subject of motivation in consumer behavior shows some degree of confusion and ambiguity.

To start with, the term "motivation" itself is used by some to denote the state of being driven to act and by others as a general term for any of the elements underlying, or having a causal relationship with, behavior — such as need or drive.

It is unfortunate, too, that "motivation" comes from the word "motive," which is only one of the components of motivation, at least as we shall attempt to employ it. Many authors use "motive" interchangeably with such terms as need, drive, and want but I feel (and shall try to show) that, like many of the others, it can be meaningfully separated from the others so as to be of practical significance to the marketer.

The tendency to group all of these concepts together is evident in the writings of a number of marketing scholars and, contrary to what some of them say, attempting to distinguish among these terms is not merely "considering the finer points of distinction."[5] Here are some examples of the tendency to use "motives" as a substitute for "motivations," in an all-embracing sense:

[motives are] all those inner striving conditions variously described as wishes, desires, needs, drives, and the like.[6]

Motive, goal, need, drive and want will be used interchangeably here — even though these terms tend to be used in slightly different ways in the psychological literature. . . .[7]

But why does he act at all? What is the driving force behind his behavior? Or, more simply, what are his motives?[8]

We shall return to this later and attempt to show how and why "motive" should be used in a specific sense in marketing.

Definition

The definition of motive by Myers and Reynolds quoted above expresses exactly the point of view of this book, except for the broad use of the word "motives." Adapting the drift of their statement, I define **motivation** as the state of the organism involving all those inner strivings or conditions variously described as needs, motives, wants, goals that initiate, sustain, and direct behavior.

This point of view recognizes that motivation:
- is an inner state;
- is multifaceted;
- determines whether or not the individual will act;
- influences how and toward what goal the individual will act; and
- includes both overt and covert acts.

The Difficulty of Determining Motivation

A health educator was asked what the expected response would be if a teacher were to catch a seventh-grader smoking. He suggested that the ensuing dialogue might run something like this:

"Oh, you shouldn't do that!"

"Why not?"

"Why, because it's *bad* for you. You'll get heart disease, lung cancer, and emphysema."

Then he pictured the teacher running off to the principal to get help in arranging for a series of films to be shown to the seventh grade. Films, naturally, on heart disease, lung cancer, and emphysema!

But could the problem be dealt with more effectively? His answer was that the teacher should try to find out why the child had taken up smoking and deal with that *basic cause*. Usually one of two reasons will come out. Either the child will say, "I want to be like Dad and Mom," or "My friends will call me 'chicken' if I don't."

So what is actually needed? Obviously not a lecture on the diseases attributed to cigarette smoking. The children who are having this very real problem need to know how to be like Mom and Dad, without ruining their lungs. Or what to do when someone calls them "chicken." Health educators need to know how to get right to the heart of the problem. Then they need to learn how to bring about a change in behavior, using the strongest possible motivation.[9]

Motivation is *multifaceted* and *multitiered*, so that the analyst is confronted by difficulties in determining not only the particular facet or facets involved but also the deeper and deeper levels of causation. Example 3 about Metrecal illustrates these characteristics of motivation very well. Motivations underlying the use of such a product range from convenience and variety to conformity, social acceptance, and popularity, to vanity and achievement, to guilt and self-punishment. The more basic the motivation identified, the better the understanding of the behavior. The behaviorists, as we shall see, do not believe that understanding is necessary to achieve behavioral change (which is often the aim of the marketer); the psychoanalysts, on the other hand, hold the view that real change cannot occur without identifying basic causes.

Group Motivation

This discussion of motivation is in terms of single individuals, but it must be remembered that in actual practice the marketer is interested in groups of individuals, since marketing strategy is directed at markets and market segments.

When we speak of motivation we are really referring to groups of similar individuals. Societies and groups within a society are marked by varying degrees of homogeneity in their values and needs, so that it is possible for the marketer to identify relatively homogeneous segments and, on the basis of an understanding of individual motivations, make useful generalizations about the market segment as a whole.

BASIC MOTIVATIONAL CONCEPTS

Looking at the root of the word, motivation (Latin *movere* — to move) is what impels the individual to action. It may be viewed as a process that starts with a need and consists of a number of interrelated constructs within the psychological make-up of the individual. The unfilled need creates a state of arousal,* which can bring about behavior designed to reduce or fulfill the need.

The model in Figure 10.2 indicates that a **stimulus**, whether internal or external, will be interpreted by the individual, on the basis of the current psychological and physiological state, and could lead to arousal of a need, which will increase in strength until it is strong enough to cause the individual to begin to do something about it. A need and its related drive may also be aroused by the current state of the individual, without any external stimulus.

As an example, let us take an advertisement for hamburgers. Exposure to the advertisement could result in the interpretation that the individual needs lunch (**arousal**) until eventually behavior is focussed (**drive**) on filling the need. The need and its accompanying drive could also have been aroused by the internal physiological state (hunger pangs). The behavior is directed by the desire to satisfy certain aims (**motives**), depending upon the individual. In this case the economy motive may dominate and lead to the

---

* As we shall see later, there are other causes of arousal as well.

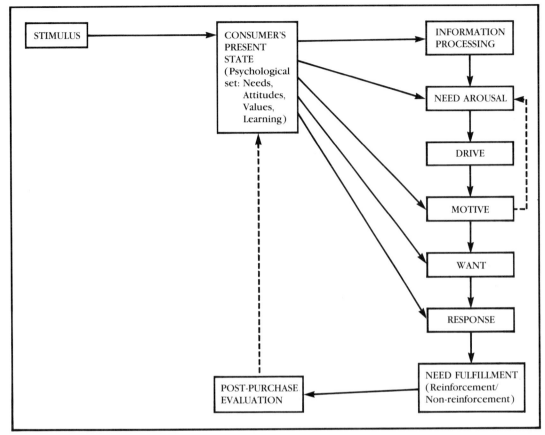

FIGURE 10.2: The Basic Motivational Model

selection of a fast-food product (**want**). It could have been convenience or social conformity (friends wanted to go there) or habit or any number of other motives. If the response to purchase the hamburger leads to need fulfillment, it will be **reinforced**, leading to a positive evaluation of the goal object that becomes registered in LTM (consumer's present state) for later use. Non-reinforcement leads to a negative evaluation and extinction of the response.

Needs

The unfilled need is the discrepancy between an actual state and a desired state. This state may be biological, psychological, or social and the need could be conscious or unconscious (that is, the individual may not be aware of the discrepancy).

Needs may be divided into two main types:

(a) physiological, or organic or biogenic. These needs are *innate* and are based on "physical conditions that drive the organism to activity."[10] They may be broken down into two subtypes:

- those that depend on physiological need (hunger, thirst, warmth, elimination, and pain) and those based to a somewhat lesser extent on physiological need (sex and maternal drives); and

- those that stem from unspecified (so far) physiological conditions (activity, manipulation, investigation, and stimulation).

(b) psychological, social, or psychogenic. These are *learned* through experience, although they may in some cases be indirectly derived from physiological need. Some of these appear to be quite universal (gregariousness, imitation), probably because they begin to appear in childhood and are deeply rooted in feelings of helplessness and dependence. Some are cultural, such as social approval and cooperation.

The learned needs are far more numerous than the innate. Needs vary in strength among themselves and among individuals. Maslow has proposed a hierarchy of needs that consists of five levels of saliency:[11]

- Physiological needs (e.g., food, water);
- Safety needs (e.g., security, shelter);
- Social belongingness and love needs (e.g., affection, identification);
- Ego or esteem needs (e.g., prestige, success, self-respect); and
- Self-actualization needs (e.g., the desire for self-fulfillment).

Once "lower" needs are satisfied, "higher" needs emerge; when these in turn are satisfied other needs emerge, and so on, so that *an organism is never really in a fully satiated state*. With psychological growth and social development, the individual's "catalogue of wants and goals increases in number and variety as he ascends the ladder from belly to brain."[12]

Figure 10.3 illustrates the characteristics of this hierarchy.

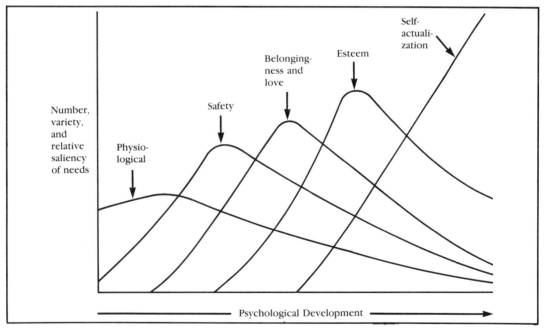

Note: The peak of an earlier main class of needs must be passed before the next "higher" need can begin to assume a dominant role, and that as psychological development takes place, the number and variety of needs increase.

FIGURE 10.3: Maslow's Hierarchy of Needs

SOURCE: David Krech, Richard S. Crutchfield, and Egerton L. Ballachey, *Individual in Society* (New York: McGraw-Hill, 1962), p. 77. Reprinted with permission of McGraw-Hill Book company, Inc., New York.

In our society, increasing affluence has engendered a large number of psychological needs. Note the complexity of motivations, of rational, emotional, conscious, and unconscious motives involved in the dieting behavior described in the Metrecal example at the beginning of the chapter.

Maslow's need classification lends itself well to other methods of classification. For example, the physiological needs may be described as primary and the acquired needs as secondary. These terms refer not to their importance but rather to their origin. The **primary** needs would include Maslow's first and second levels or innate needs and the **secondary** needs would comprise the other three levels. Another author has referred to social needs as affectional needs and has subdivided ego needs into ego-enhancing and ego-defensive needs.[13]

The essential point to keep in mind is that needs constitute the start of the motivational chain and can be either physiological or psychological.

Rational versus Emotional

The tendency to regard economic, observable reasons as rational and emotional reasons as irrational still lingers in the minds of some. A decision is a good one if it is based on facts, on objective considerations. But it must be recognized that an emotional (or psychological) reason or need, such as status, prestige, or social approval, can also be purposeful and rational. Psychological needs can be as worthy of satisfaction as basic needs.

Needs may originate from physiological conditions so that they are innate and other needs may be learned, in the sense that the culture, society, reference groups, and individuals will influence the ideal state and in that way generate certain need states, which an individual will seek to fulfill.

When those circumstances arise, **need arousal** occurs. When a need is aroused, it energizes the organism as a preliminary to action, a readiness to respond.[14] Arousal is a general effect, not specific to a particular brand or product. The strength or urgency of the need will directly influence the level of arousal and the likelihood of response.

Needs can be aroused and decision making initiated in a number of ways:

- **internal stimulation** such as through physiological needs (food, sex, water) or through learned needs and motives;
- **external stimulation**, through a number of different influences, such as
  - *other individuals* (e.g., a neighbor's or a friend's new car);
  - *social influences* (e.g., changes in cultural norms and values or in reference group behavior); and
  - *economic changes*, which may bring about a re-evaluation of **choice criteria** (e.g., the rapid change, as described in our first example about the Honda, that brought mileage to the top of the **attribute hierarchy** as a result of the energy crisis in 1973);
- **autistic processes** where, for example, thinking of an object and the pleasurable experiences surrounding it can itself lead to need arousal.

Need arousal energizes the individual to respond and this tendency begins with increased attention to and search for relevant information. Arousal leads the individual to search for information relevant to the decision, that is, the "selective regulation of information."[15]

Drive

Drive denotes the level of need arousal at which the individual is impelled to seek need satisfaction. For example, the physiological stimulus of hunger pangs will initiate the need arousal for food, which will persist for some time before it reaches the intensity necessary to trigger the drive and generate goal-seeking behavior.

Motives

Motives, like needs, are reasons for behavior, but they are derived reasons — derived from or related to the needs. In that sense, motives are second-order reasons. For example, in order to satisfy a need for social approval, one individual may try to excel at college, another at sports, or another as an author (involving in all cases an achievement motive); someone else may seek to accomplish that same end by collecting art or buying antique furniture (acquisition); yet another may become class president or captain of the college football team (popularity). The possibilities are numerous.

Needs generate the response tendency, motives direct the response. Thus motives are closer to the response. In the Metrecal example, numerous motives were identified as serving the terminal values[16] of the need for food and the need for security (a healthy body) as well as the social need for acceptance. Among these motives were conformity, achievement, popularity, variety, convenience, avoidance of guilt, and attention-seeking. The latter may be described as **instrumental**, because they serve the basic needs and through them those terminal values are fulfilled.

The motives that come into play when a need is aroused are the result of thinking processes and of previous learning. They are connected to or are served by the perceived product attributes or choice criteria, which are "the mental counterparts of the attributes by which a consumer judges a brand."[17] For example, with automobiles the economy motive will be served by good fuel economy, performance by smooth ride and fast pick-up, comfort by roominess and quality of craftsmanship. Motives are, therefore, extremely important in consumer choice because they direct the response toward certain wants (product, brand) perceived as possessing the attributes necessary to satisfy them.

Motives are essentially of two kinds: person-related (such as achievement, conformity, status) and product-related (such as economy, variety, performance).

The number of needs may be relatively limited but, as we move to the right in the model, the number of choices proliferates (see Figure 10.4). In the figure, the need for social approval, once aroused, may be directed by a number of different motives, such as achievement, acquisition, and affiliation. Different individuals will choose different **motive paths**. The student who selects the achievement path to attain social approval may seek to obtain high grades and/or membership on the college basketball team and/or write a novel. In each of these choices, several kinds of behavior will be possible. For each need there are a number of motives and for each motive an even greater number of possible wants to satisfy it, and an even greater range of response behaviors.

At the level of motives, considerable motivational differentiation occurs, allowing for a sharper identification of consumer groups. For this reason motives should be differentiated from needs. For every response, one should identify *at least* one motive and one related need. Greater emphasis should be placed in marketing strategy on the more salient elements of each of these two levels. For example, of the needs filled by Metrecal, the need for security (health) and social acceptance would be emphasized in marketing strategy and even greater stress would be placed on such motives as conformity, achievement, popularity, and variety. The marketer would need to determine the salience of the needs and motives involved in order to develop proper strategies.

Sometimes the marketer is faced with the problem of determining not only the salience of a motive but also its intensity. For example, with American Can's paper towel, Bolt, it was important to determine not only the salience of absorbency and strength but also what level of absorbency and strength were most desirable. Similarly, with the individuals cited in Figure 10.4 as satisfying their need for social approval in widely different ways, it would not be sufficient to employ social approval as the important motivation. It would be far more helpful to identify segments characterized by

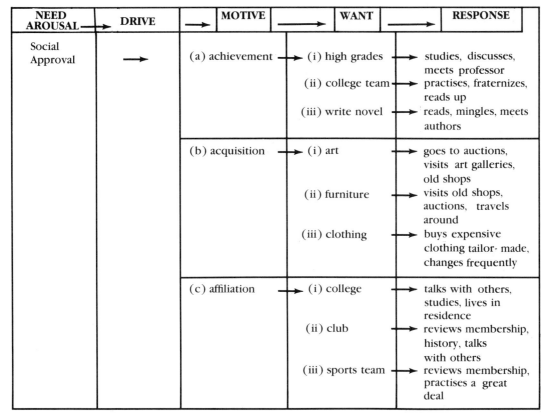

NEED AROUSAL →	DRIVE →	MOTIVE	WANT		RESPONSE
Social Approval	→	(a) achievement →	(i) high grades →		studies, discusses, meets professor
			(ii) college team →		practises, fraternizes, reads up
			(iii) write novel →		reads, mingles, meets authors
		(b) acquisition →	(i) art →		goes to auctions, visits art galleries, old shops
			(ii) furniture →		visits old shops, auctions, travels around
			(iii) clothing →		buys expensive clothing tailor- made, changes frequently
		(c) affiliation →	(i) college →		talks with others, studies, lives in residence
			(ii) club →		reviews membership, history, talks with others
			(iii) sports team →		reviews membership, practises a great deal

FIGURE 10.4: An Example of the Basic Motivational Process

NOTE TO FIGURE 10.4: The above example illustrates the kinds of proliferation that are possible as we move to the right in the model. The illustrations are not exhaustive and many more possibilities in each instance may be developed. Note, too, that the cues (which have been left out) will add to the variety of the "want" category.

each motive and appeal to them in those specific ways.

As a very important link in the motivational chain, motives and their relationships should be clearly understood. Let us review briefly the arguments just presented.

(a) A need may express itself through one or more of several possible motives.
(b) Conversely, one motive (e.g., convenience) may be the means through which several needs are expressed. There is no one-to-one relationship between needs and motives.
(c) There is no one-to-one relationship between a motive and a want since one or more of a number of wants may satisfy that motive.

(d) Similarly, a particular response may be related to more than one motive. The situation will help determine the operant motives in a particular case.
(e) As with needs and wants, the motive or motives underlying an individual's response will not remain the same from one time to another.

Motives Are Learned

Motives are socially acquired or learned factors. As Maslow suggested, once the basic needs of an individual are satisfied, the higher-order social and ego needs come into play. An affluent society in which the physical needs of individuals are, for the most part, well satisfied, has the psychological and economic potential for the development of other ways of allocating resources and providing satisfaction. That is, the potential for the growth of learned needs and motives is vast. In such a context, the marketer hopes to provide the wants that will satisfy those need/motive complexes. I indicated earlier how motives express the values held by an individual. I will show in Chapter 11 how motives influence the number and importance of the criteria by which products or brands are evaluated. Through advertising and other promotional activities, the primary aim is to *establish links between motives and products, in the broad context of the relevant need or needs*. In other words, the greater the correspondence between the consumer's perception of the product attributes and his or her motives, the greater the likelihood that the consumer will prefer that product.

The Role of the Marketer

While marketers focus primarily on that objective, they may also, through their activities, affect the salience of the motives by accentuating their importance. But they cannot affect the basic needs. They cannot affect the strength of the need for liquid intake, but they certainly can affect the intensity of the sociability motive. Secondary or psychological needs (such as affection and social approval), which are learned, may clearly be affected by input from marketers, but the extent of the contribution to their strength and intensity may be only marginal, in view of the number of other sources in our society (such as parents, schools, peer groups, religious groups, TV programs, books, magazines, newspapers, movies) from which the flow of information and influence is far more consistent, long lasting and intensive. These certainly will have a lot more to do with the psychosocial development of the individual by inculcating the appropriate values, attitudes, and needs that from time to time may be marginally affected by the marketer.

Marketers are neither capable of nor interested in affecting individual needs. Their main objective is to build the bridges between their product and the appropriate motives so that the consumer will be conditioned to reach for that product when the need arises. Of course, it is not this simple. The conditioning may take place but the response will be repeated only if it is reinforced.

It must be remembered that in attempting to find motives, the marketer is hoping for *commonalities* — that is, motives shared by groups or market segments, because only then can efforts at mass marketing be successful. Fortunately, motives are learned through the agency of social forces so that large numbers of individuals in a culture share common motives and wants.

It should be noted, too, that the product–motive association differs among cultures. Thus while a Cadillac may be associated with achievement in American society, it may have a totally different significance in an African society.

Cues

A cue is generally a representation of the whole or a component part of an object (e.g., a brand). Examples of cues are advertisements, signs, symbols, labels — any stimuli that convey some impression of the brand. These stimuli may be weak or strong. Advertising serves to direct the response of the consumer to a particular product or brand (e.g., the golden arches of McDonald's Restaurants). *Cues communicate certain attributes* to the potential consumer (such as convenience, economy, and good taste) and they are learned.

Cues may also result in the arousal of the organism and, in that sense, initiate behavior — such as when the golden arches first remind individuals that they haven't had lunch and then direct their response.

The cue is of considerable significance to the marketer since it is directly related to brand selection. Through the cue, the marketer is able to direct motives to specific brands, because the cues can be employed to suggest or "promise" attributes or satisfactions offered by those brands. These were described in Chapter 8 on learning.

Goal or Want

The goal or want is the specific goal-object that is perceived as likely to satisfy the need-motive complex, and to which the cue directs the motive. Note that want, in our model, does not refer to the need state of the individual. It is used specifically to denote the entity that is considered likely to satisfy the need (e.g., the Big Mac).

Most, if not all, marketing communication is concerned with establishing the link between a motive and a particular want. Several wants may exist with the potential to satisfy the motive, just as several motives could be satisfied by a single want.

The cue serves to epitomize the motive-want relationship for ready, instantaneous recall, so marketers deliberately seek to *create wants* by building up a preference for their products.

Response

The response is the expression of the final choice the consumer makes from among the various wants available. Most commonly, the response may be to buy, although the decision not to buy is just as much a legitimate response.

A response that leads to **need-fulfillment** (which includes satisfaction of the motives) will be reinforced and have a high probability of repetition in similar circumstances. A response that is not reinforced will not be learned. An already learned response that is not reinforced will eventually be extinguished.

Motivation and Involvement

The basic motivational model in Figure 10.2 will be most applicable in complex decision making. High-involvement products will be accompanied by stronger needs, drives, and motives with greater search and evaluation before the brand is chosen.

With low-involvement products, on the other hand, need arousal is likely to be followed by purchase behavior, without much consideration of motives and evaluative criteria. Purchase is the result of familiarity and habit. Neither the needs nor the motives are particularly important.

Where there is brand differentiation, variety-seeking behavior may occur; where there is no brand differentiation the motives are likely to be based on promotional incentives.

Motivation and Situational Effects

It is logical to expect that consumer motivations will vary with the situations or circumstances in which a product is used or bought. A marketer cannot assume that, so far as the product is concerned, the needs and motives will remain the same from situation to situation. This basic notion underlies the concept of segmentation: different segments reveal different motivations, preferences, and purchasing behaviors. In turn, marketers adapt their strategies to these groupings by varying their products, their promotions, their distribution, and their pricing.

Unfortunately, while segmentation has been based on product benefits, on consumer characteristics, and on heaviness of usage, not enough attention has been placed on the *usage situation*. For example, a consumer who uses coffee will have different motives, different product criteria, and prefer different brands depending on whether the coffee is for everyday home use or for social occasions.

Basically, there are three types of situations:[18]
- the **consumption** situation (e.g., coffee for home or for entertaining; or buying a product as a gift or for oneself);
- the **purchase** situation (e.g., the impact of such factors as out-of-stock, ease of shopping, deals); and
- the **communications** situation (e.g., whether a TV commercial is seen by the viewer when alone or with others).

The motivations, attitudes, and criteria can vary with the situation, *particularly the consumption situation*, and marketers should attempt to apply this kind of segmentation to a greater extent in developing their strategies.

THEORIES OF MOTIVATION

Because of the complexity of human motivation, it is not surprising that many theories have arisen to attempt to explain and understand it. From our treatment of the subject, it may be apparent that no single theory is sufficient to explain all motivational phenomena. Essentially, I have made use of the three most influential theories — behavior or drive-reduction theory, the theory of unconscious motivation, and cognitive theory.

Behavior (Drive-Reduction) Theory

Behavior theory is based on the idea that internal biological states activate behavior, either through physiological deficits or painful external stimuli. The state creates a tension or drive that the individual seeks to reduce and thereby restore balance. Behavior theory also postulates the principle of reinforcement, where a response that satisfies the need is rewarded and learned.

Both the Gestalt or field theory approach and Skinner's behaviorism (behavior strictly controlled by external rewards or punishments) fall in this category.

Because drive-reduction theory rests primarily on a few drives, it has been considered to be too limited in its scope. Since it is based essentially on tension-reduction, it does not allow for the existence of stimulus-seeking (curiosity, exploration) or purposive behavior.

In many cases, an increase, rather than a reduction, in drive can be rewarding. For example, going to a horror movie or riding a roller coaster implies that fear can be pleasant.[19] Consequently, although drive theory has contributed significantly to our understanding of some forms of human behavior, some writers have suggested that it should be replaced.[20] Two alternatives have been put forward: incentive theory and arousal theory.

Incentive theory basically claims that motivation is produced by the expectation of reaching goals. Anticipating something desirable is positive incentive motivation, and anticipating something not desired is negative incentive motivation.

The second alternative theory is **arousal theory**, which suggests that motivation comes from the level of physiological arousal or excitement generated by the task or situation.[21]

It is clear that both alternatives attempt to avoid the problem of behavior that does not result in drive reduction and instead results in an increase in drive. But the essential notions of tension and tension-reduction appear to be an inherent part of motivation.

Theory of Unconscious Motivation

The theory of unconscious motivation "focuses on impulses of which we are not aware rather than on the expression of drives in overt behavior."[22] I will discuss in Chapter 13 the unconscious mechanisms of defence elaborated by Sigmund Freud in his development of psychoanalysis.

There is no doubt that unconscious motivation is a real phenomenon, as demonstrated by experiments in hypnosis conducted over forty years ago.[23] Differences exist about the extent of its operation, going from one extreme to the other. Some psychologists believe all motivation must exist in the conscious; others, like Maslow, not only believe that motives can be unconscious but also go so far as to say that "on the whole . . . they are more often unconscious than conscious" and that "unconscious motivations would, on the whole, be rather more important than the conscious motivations."[24]

Unconscious motives have been described as expressing themselves in everyday life in slips of the tongue, slips of memory (e.g., forgetting an appointment with an individual we unconsciously dislike), dreams, defence mechanisms, and unconscious conflicts of motives.

It seems clear that this theory has added significantly to our understanding of certain kinds of human behavior, regardless of the controversy surrounding the extent of its contribution.

Cognitive Theory

The third theory used in building up a system for understanding behavior is cognitive theory. It relates motivation to our thinking processes and regards behavior as purposive, problem-solving, and goal-oriented. Cognitive theory does not reject unconscious motivation or biological drive-reduction as determinants of behavior; it expands motivational theory to include certain other important features of human behavior.

The **level of aspiration** is an important concept in cognitive theory. It involves the goals and the level of performance that one sets for oneself. Levels of aspiration are set on the basis of an assessment of one's abilities and interests, the processing of relevant information, a weighing of alternatives, and long- and short-term goals — all of which are influenced by one's self-concept (discussed in Chapter 13).

A basic tenet of cognitive theory is that the individual is constantly striving to achieve *consistency* among his or her cognitions; in other words, to reduce or remove dissonance. I will deal with this aspect in greater detail in the next chapter.

The cognitive theory views human beings as intelligent, rational individuals with both biological and socio-psychological needs. Rather than replacing the other theories, it complements them — a view I have tried to present in this chapter.

TWO WIDELY USED MOTIVATIONAL APPROACHES IN MARKETING

"A good part of the history of life can be written in terms of fear."[25] "Humor has been a subject of endless discussion by writers and philosophers."[26] As these quotations indicate, fear and humor have been pervasive elements of human existence, touching every individual in one way or another. It is no surprise that in their communications, particularly advertising, marketers make widespread use of fear and humor.

Fear Appeals

Fear appeals are used in communications "designed to stimulate anxiety in an audience with the expectation that the audience will attempt to reduce this anxiety by adopting, continuing, discontinuing, or avoiding a specified course of thought or action."[27] The anxiety relates to the threat to one's social image and self-concept as well as to the physical self (see Figure 10.5).

Such advertisements as "Ring Around the Collar" and those relating to bad breath and body odor, for example, emphasize the threat

FIGURE 10.5: An Example of Fear Appeal

Courtesy Allstate Insurance Co.

to one's social image. The cancer and smoking ads of a few years ago are a good illustration of threat of physical harm. In the former case, the fear appeals are being used to get the consumer to use the sponsor's product in order to *avoid* the feared condition; in the latter to *discontinue* a specific course of action. Toothpaste ads may be said to evoke fear by elaborating the consequences of failure to perform certain practices.

Fear appeals should be distinguished from **positive appeals**. "The critical difference . . . is that [fear appeals] contain a *deliberate* attempt to arouse anxiety. While a positive appeal may also arouse anxiety, it is usually incidental to the main thrust of the message, which is a presentation of the product's motive-satisfying attributes. For example, a tire manufacturer using a fear appeal began [an] ad by portraying the plight of a woman stranded along a dark road with a flat tire. The message seemed to say, 'Would you allow your wife to get into this situation through your failure to properly equip the family car?' On the other hand, a positive appeal for automobile tires may contain primarily a series of claims about the safety, reliability, and price of the company's product without attempting to stimulate anxiety."[28]

Several problems have been pointed out in connection with fear appeals: Since psychologists have found that anxiety is conditionable, concern has been expressed that, in the words of Spence and Moinpour, "the continued bombardment of consumers by fear appeals transmitted through mass media may be creating new fears and anxieties or exacerbating old ones."[29]

It has been argued that if a single high-fear appeal can have negative effects, then perhaps multiple exposures to messages, each just below the anxiety-producing level, may also have similar effects.

The ethical question has been raised of whether marketers should be *allowed* to employ fear appeals if such advertising creates anxiety in consumers, since "the complexity and pace of contemporary social life [already] creates many situations that are potential sources of anxiety"[30] — such as a deteriorating physical environment, the increasing incidence of violent crime, international confrontations, overpopulation, and the threat of nuclear war. Advertising that uses fear appeals may just further increase the general level of an individual's anxiety.

Referring to bad breath and body odor advertising, those authors note that "advertisers have not played a totally passive role. . . . While [they] are not the cause of the odor and stigma problems, they do appear to play a role in establishing and perpetuating their existence as standards of social comparison and, thus, perhaps make them more persistent and important than they might otherwise be."

Apart from the ethical question, the effectiveness of fear appeals has not been conclusively demonstrated. Early studies suggested that there was a negative relationship between fear arousal and persuasion[31] but, as Sternthal and Craig observe, "the majority of recent investigations have found a positive fear-persuasion relationship."[32] It appears that the effect is greater on attitude than it is on intentions or subsequent behavior.

Some have felt that this may be due to the nature of the behaviors recommended. When the advocated actions are perceived to be effective and when the course of action is outlined specifically, behavior is more consistent with attitude. A cancer–smoking ad may be quite persuasive but it may fail to get compliance because the recommended action is too general.

Fear research has been marred by a number of deficiencies, including the difficulty of ascertaining the comparability of fear levels across studies, and the difficulty of establishing whether differences in substance or in reduced fear level account for differences in the persuasiveness of messages labelled high and low threat.

The evidence is not conclusive that fear appeals are any more effective than positive appeals. One can only assume that, since marketers continue to use the fear approach, its effectiveness must be showing up in balance sheets. Or, perhaps, marketers may just intuitively feel that fear appeals have greater impact.

It appears, too, that the characteristics of the source delivering the fear appeal, those of the audience receiving it, and the situation in which it is presented can have a significant influence on its effectiveness. Sternthal and Craig point out that:

- high-credibility sources are more persuasive when they employ strong rather than mild fear-arousing messages because counter-argumentation is inhibited;
- a source is more persuasive if it presents arguments that are both supportive and damaging *vis-à-vis* its position than if only supportive arguments are advanced;
- some kinds of individuals may be more susceptible to fear appeals (e.g., those low in self-esteem or high in vulnerability); and
- placing a straightforward persuasive message delivered by a moderate or low-credibility source in a fear-arousing context may enhance its persuasiveness.[33]

A recent study conducted in the field "to assess the effect of a fear promotion on attitudinal and behavioral response to a new group health insurance plan" discovered both curvilinear and levelling-off relationships.[34] The researchers concluded that "a response to fear is probably specific to the situation, topic, person, and criterion. Thus the form of the relationship will vary across combinations of these four factors. This implication provides additional support for the use of a segmentation strategy in the investigation of fear appeals."

Fear appeals have not been conclusively demonstrated to be more effective than positive appeals in producing compliant behavior. The research may be at fault because of the possibility of a variety of errors in measurement, but in the absence of any positive proof of its impact, the fear appeal approach is questioned on the ground of its likely effect on the mental state of society, even if marginal. Some are inclined to feel that "some members of the advertising industry view the fear approach as extremely risky and better left unused." They regard this evidence as "premature" and "unfortunate because an analysis of the findings to date suggests that some may offer promise."

The applied situation does not appear to conform to this view. There is wide use of fear appeals, regardless of the nature of the evidence about their effectiveness.

Humor

Humor is another approach widely used by marketers to improve the effectiveness of their communications in establishing links between motives and responses. One study found that 15% of TV commercials made use of the humorous approach (cartoons, jokes, slices of life), but there is little or no systematic evidence of its effectiveness.[35] Unlike fear appeals, humor has been the subject of only a limited amount of research.

General and sometimes opposing views exist about the use of humor in advertising. Some argue that humor is universal and "humanizes advertising"; others that it is not universal, indeed quite regional. Some feel that its effect wears out with repetition; others that it takes too much of the commercial's time.

In one literature review, the authors drew a number of conclusions, with the qualifications that "their basis is often laboratory experimentation" and that "these conclusions are necessarily tentative."[36]

(a) Humorous messages attract attention. The authors report that advertisers appear to agree that humor enhances audience attention (see Figure 10.6). The question that naturally arises is how rapidly does this effect wear out with repetition?

(b) Humorous messages may lower comprehension. It is felt that even though humor may improve attention, it may inhibit com-

FIGURE 10.6: An Example of Humor

Courtesy Global Communications Ltd.

prehension and thus reduce overall message reception.

In general, the data *appear* to indicate that humor does not affect message comprehension differently from serious communications.

(c) Humor may distract the audience, yielding a reduction in counter-argumentation and an increase in persuasion. But distraction studies do not seem to have directly addressed the question of whether the persuasive effect of humor is attributable to its distraction quality.

(d) Humorous appeals appear to be persuasive, but the persuasive effect is at best no greater than that of serious appeals.

(e) Humor tends to enhance source credibility. It was found that a source was considered to have relatively greater attributes of character when delivering a humorous rather than a serious message. And this greater credibility ultimately increases the persu-

asiveness of the appeal. Another study found that the addition of humor enhanced audience reception of the source's character only when a communication was dull, not when it was already interesting.

(f) Audience characteristics may confound the effect of humor. The research on this subject is deficient. However, it seems obvious that such variables as age, education, and involvement with the message issue would mediate the persuasive effects of humor.

(g) A humorous context may increase liking for the source and create a positive mood. This may enhance the persuasive effect of the message. To the extent that this is true, it may be advantageous to frame a TV commercial, for example, in a humorous format.

(h) Regarding the editorial or program context in which a humorous communication is most effective, a recent study found that, because of the contrast effect, humorous television commercials were better recalled when presented in non-comedy environments.[37]

A report by an advertising practitioner has made some interesting suggestions about the effectiveness of humor:[38]

● brand identification must be made in the first ten seconds or, as Sternthal and Craig concluded, comprehension and recall may be inhibited;

● the humor should be neither extreme nor derogatory of the prospective user; and

● humorous appeals that are more compatible with the product are more effective.

Studies have shown that the appreciation of humor is also influenced by social pressures. Group approval seems to set standards for execution and content,[39] even though there may be individual differences in the reaction to humor.

It should also be recognized that humor serves many psychological functions, some of which it may be useful for the marketing communicator to understand:[40]

- enjoying a joke with others increases our sense of *belonging* and *social acceptance*; the idea of the "in-joke" epitomizes group identification;
- understanding a joke, especially a subtle one, enhances our self-confidence;
- laughing provides a release of pent-up emotional energy.

As with fear appeals, the use of humorous appeals may offer certain benefits (attention, persuasion, and certain psychological gains) but it is also fraught with significant dangers (lower comprehension, lack of group approval, wear-out). Very importantly, the tastes and preferences of the society, in addition to segment characteristics, must be considered. The notion of humor creating a positive mood may be a very significant one but its susceptibility to the erosive effects of wear-out will seriously detract from its usefulness.

MOTIVATION RESEARCH

A brief note on **motivation research** is in order here mainly because of the considerable degree of confusion regarding its nature and role in consumer research.

While the term denotes any research conducted to determine motivation, it is largely associated with the kinds of motivation research (MR) that are based on psychoanalytic approaches. The reason is primarily historical since some of the earliest attempts to delve into the motivations of the consumer were made by a Vienna-born psychoanalyst, Ernest Dichter.[41]

Considerable controversy has surrounded this approach over the years. It reached its heyday in the late 1950s and early 1960s and has since declined significantly in popularity.

MR is regarded today as most useful for exploratory rather than conclusive research, for the development of new ideas and new copy appeals, and for discovering the emotional factors underlying behavior. It makes use of such techniques as focus groups and projective tests (free association, thematic apperception, sentence completion).[42]

Because it is expensive, time-consuming, and requires the expertise of trained psychologists, MR is limited to small samples and cannot, therefore, justifiably make generalizations about the larger population. Admittedly, there are times when the insights and understanding achieved may have such consensual and logical validity that generalization does not appear to be unreasonable.

In any event, this approach should not be dismissed, precisely for the kinds of considerations discussed earlier regarding the operation and significance of unconscious motivation. Question-and-answer surveys perhaps rely too much on the conscious, verbalizable responses of consumers and a middle-of-the-road position that takes into account insights and interpretations based on such things as rationalizations, projections, and fantasy may be amply warranted.

SUMMARY

The study of motivation is crucial to an understanding of consumer behavior, since motivation deals with the reasons that lie behind the behavior. Motivation may be defined as "the state of the organism involving all those inner strivings or conditions variously described as needs, motives, wants, goals that initiate, sustain, and direct behavior."

Motivation is a complex phenomenon, because it is multifaceted and multitiered. The model presented in the chapter identified a number of motivational concepts and suggested that:

(a) every behavioral sequence begins with a need, and sometimes more than one. For example, the purchase of a car may have begun with both a transportation need and a social status need;

(b) the options increase as we get closer to the response;

(c) any response may be traced back to one or more of several motives;

(d) a motive may be satisfied by any of several wants and may be initiated by one or more of several needs; and

(e) it is a serious mistake to consider needs, motives, and wants as interchangeable. In fact, identifying the specific role that motives play is of extreme significance to the marketer.

It should be noted that motivation varies with involvement and with the situation.

A number of theories have been developed to explain motivation, including drive-reduction theory, incentive theory, arousal theory, unconscious motivation, and cognitive theory. They each help explain certain aspects of behavior and are quite complementary to each other.

The two most widely used motivational approaches in marketing are fear appeal and the humor appeal, both of which have remained quite controversial with respect to their effectiveness.

QUESTIONS

1. What are some of the problems that have characterized the definition of motivation? Which concept appears to warrant specific treatment? Why?

2. "Motivation is multifaceted and multitiered." Explain this statement using the Metrecal example.

3. "Need arousal represents the beginning of decision making." How is such arousal brought about?

4. What is the usefulness of the concept of drive?

5. "Cues may be regarded as primary elements in marketing communications." Discuss the significance of this statement.

6. Write a short essay on the ethical implications of the use of fear appeals in advertising.

7. Discuss some of the problems that have been associated with fear appeal research. What impact have they had on demonstrating the effectiveness of fear appeals?

8. Overall, what is your opinion of the effectiveness of humor in advertising?

9. Select three print ads that illustrate the fear approach and three the humor approach, and analyze them for their content, execution, and possible effectiveness.

NOTES TO CHAPTER 10

[1]Adapted from *Fortune* (30 July 1979), pp. 92-9; "The Automobile Importers of Canada" (May 1984).

[2]Adapted from Roger D. Blackwell, James F. Engel, and David T. Kollat, *Cases in Consumer Behavior* (New York: Holt, Rinehart, and Winston, 1969), pp. 3-9.

[3]Adapted from "J&B Scotch Scuttles Old Ads to Put Kick Into Stagnant Sales," *The Wall Street Journal* (18 September 1980), p. 33.

[4]Adapted from Bill Abrams, "What Happens if the Product Offers More Than Users Need," *The Wall Street Journal* (25 September 1980).

[5]James H. Myers and William H. Reynolds, *Consumer Behavior and Marketing Management* (New York: Houghton Mifflin, 1967), p. 80.

[6]Ibid.

[7]John A. Howard and Jagdish N. Sheth, *The Theory of Buyer Behavior* (New York: John Wiley & Sons, 1969), p. 991.

[8]Harold H. Kassarjian and Thomas S. Robertson, *Perspectives in Consumer Behavior*, rev. ed. (Glenview, Illinois: Scott, Foresman, and Company, 1973), p. 113.

[9]Leo R. Van Dolson, "Better Isn't Bitter," *Life and Health* (September 1976), p. 27.

[10]Based on Robert M. Goldenson, *The Encyclopedia of Human Behavior* (Garden City, New York: Doubleday, 1970), p. 833.

[11]Abraham H. Maslow, *Motivation and Personality*, 2nd ed. (New York: Harper and Row, 1970), pp. 35-46.

[12]David Krech, Richard S. Crutchfield, and Egerton L. Ballachey, *Individual in Society* (New York: McGraw-Hill, 1962), p. 77.

[13]James A. Bayton, "Motivation, Cognition, Learning — Basic Factors in Consumer Behavior," *Journal of Marketing*, 23 (January 1958), pp. 282-9.

[14]John A. Howard, *Consumer Behavior: Application of Theory* (New York: McGraw-Hill, 1977), p. 25.

[15]Ibid., p. 142.

[16]"Values guide behavior.... [They] can be separated into terminal values ['being'] and instrumental values ['doing']. Terminal values are closer to the ultimate end, which is self-concept.... Instrumental values are closer to the 'means' which is purchase." Ibid., p. 92.

[17]Ibid., p. 28.

[18]Fleming Hansen, *Consumer Choice Behavior* (New York: Free Press, 1972).

[19]Henry L. Roediger III, J. Phillipe Rushton, Elizabeth D. Capaldi, and Scott G. Paris, *Psychology* (Toronto: Little, Brown, 1984), pp. 415-20.

[20]R.C. Bolles, *Theory of Motivation*, 2nd ed. (New York: Harper and Row, 1975).

[21]R.J. Andrew, "Arousal and the Causation of Behavior," *Behavior*, 51 (1974), pp. 135-65.

[22]Goldenson, op. cit., p. 835.

[23]M.H. Erickson, "An Experimental Investigation of the Possible Anti-Social Use of Hypnosis," *Psychiatry*, 2 (1939), pp. 391-414.

[24]Abraham H. Maslow, *Motivation and Personality* (New York: Harper and Row, 1954), p. 101.

[25]Goldenson, op. cit., p. 451.

[26]Ibid., p. 564.

[27]H. Spence and R. Moinpour, "Fear Appeals in Marketing: A Social Perspective," *Journal of Marketing*, 37 (October 1973), pp. 12-8. Reprinted with permission of the American Marketing Association.

[28]Ibid., p. 12.

[29]Ibid.

[30]Ibid.

[31]J. Janis and S. Feshback, "Effects of Fear-Arousing Communications," *Journal of Abnormal and Social Psychology*, 48 (January 1953), pp. 78-92; A. de Wolfe and C. Governale, "Fear and Attitude Change," *Journal of Abnormal and Social Psychology*, 69 (July 1964), pp. 119-23; M. Goldstein, "The Relationship Between Coping and Avoiding Behavior and Response to Fear-Arousing Propaganda," *Journal of Abnormal and Social Psychology*, 58 (March 1959), pp. 247-52.

[32]Brian Sternthal and C. Samuel Craig, "Fear Appeals: Revisited and Revised," *Journal of Consumer Research*, 1 (December 1974), pp. 22-34.

[33]Ibid.

[34]John J. Burnett and Richard L. Oliver, "Fear Appeal Effects in the Field: A Segmentation Approach," *Journal of Marketing Research*, 16 (May 1979), pp. 181-90.

[35]J. Patrick Kelly and Paul J. Solomon, "Humor in Advertising," *Journal of Advertising*, 4 (Summer 1975), pp. 31-5.

[36]Brian Sternthal and C. Samuel Craig, "Humor in Advertising," *Journal of Marketing*, 37 (October 1973), pp. 12-8.

[37]John H. Murphy, Isabella C.M. Cunningham, and Gary B. Wilcox, "The Impact of Program Environment on Recall of Humorous Television Commercials," *Journal of Advertising*, 8 (Spring 1979), pp. 17-21.

[38]Harold L. Ross, Jr., "How to Create Effective Humorous Commercials Yielding Above-Average Brand Preference Changes," *Marketing News* (26 March 1976), p. 4.

[39]Goldenson, op. cit., pp. 564-5.

[40]Ibid., p. 565.

[41]See, for example, Ernest Dichter, *Handbook of Consumer Motivations* (New York: McGraw-Hill, 1964); Rena Bartos, "Ernest Dichter: Motive Interpreter," *Journal of Advertising Research*, 17 (June 1977), p. 8; Ernest Dichter, *The Strategy of Desire* (Garden City, New York: Doubleday, 1960).

[42]Fred D. Reynolds and Deborah K. Johnson, "Validity of Focus Group Findings," *Journal of Advertising Research*, 18 (June 1978), pp. 21-4; George J. Szybillo and Robert Berger, "What Advertising Agencies Think of Focus Groups," *Journal of Advertising Research*, 19 (June 1979), pp. 29-33; Theodore J. Gage, "Theories Differ on Use of Focus Group," *Advertising Age*, (4 February 1980), pp. 19-22; R. Ferber and H.G. Wales (eds.), *Motivation and Market Behavior* (Homewood, Illinois: Richard D. Irwin, 1958).

COTTONS AND MMMUFFINS*

Two young Canadians seem to have a nose for what the consumer wants and to have parlayed that ability into enormously successful businesses that have become instant hits on the franchise circuit. Melanie Stephens, who never completed high school, is a small-town girl who backed into business. Michael Bregman, big-city son of a millionaire baking giant, has a Harvard Business School degree and a calculated, well-financed marketing strategy.

Stephens produces 100% cotton clothes and Bregman oven-fresh muffins and croissants from the finest basic ingredients. Not only are these products more than merely "natural" material and foods, but they may also be said to appeal to a cultural elitist taste. The "baked in front of you" and the "hand sewn" quality of both products gives the feeling that they are custom-made. Yet both entrepreneurs have entered into franchising their products. They are betting on the notion that people are tired of renting cars from the same salespeople, tired of golden arches, tired of hotel rooms that look the same in Tahiti as they do in Timmins. "The consumer has become more quality-conscious than ever before, and is willing to pay extra," says Bregman. "It's not health food — it's life-style."

Stephens and Cotton

Melanie Stephens has parlayed a cottage industry into a company whose twenty-five franchises will gross about $2.5 million this year. Four years ago, she was making a living near her native town of Port Stanley, Ontario, sewing bed comforters for a local store. She rented a room to work in, beneath a yacht broker's office in St. Thomas, and soon found that the broker's customers, attracted by the sound of her sewing machines, were asking her to make tote bags for them.

---

* *Adapted from* Allan Gould and Philip Marchand, "Franchising Good Feelings," *Canadian Business* (September 1983), pp. 32-6, 125-6.

Sales were so good that she opened a store in Port Stanley to sell canvas bags. She wanted to call the store "the Kettle Creek Canvas Bag Company" (after a creek running through the town) but was persuaded to leave out "Bag." Three weeks before her tiny fourteen square metre store opened in May 1979, she made some sample clothes — cotton drawstring pants and so on — to help fill the empty shelves. The clothes turned out to be her hottest-selling items, and Stephens decided to specialize in them.

The concept she subsequently developed was simple. She would sell nothing but 100% cottons, solid colors, no prints; clothes that could be worn equally well on the deck of a sailboat or to a job interview. "We didn't have any particular kind of person in mind when we first started doing the clothing," she insists. "I've seen New Wave rock bands in our clothes, as well as sixty-year-old women on the golf course. What we had in mind, I guess you'd call it, was a state of mind."

Today the clothes are designed by David MacDonnell, whose responsibility is to make sure the designs stay "acceptable," a responsibility he fulfills mainly by working in basic shapes so that "the clothes will fit and look good on a variety of age groups and sizes." Simplicity and lack of ornamentation are major characteristics, although, as MacDonnell says, "we're extending our reach by dressing up the clothes a bit more."

"Other than switching colors from season to season," Stephens says, "we probably don't change more than 25% of the line from year to year." The clothes are manufactured by forty-five home sewers.

Stephens sold $68,000 worth of goods in her first year. In the second year she opened a store in London, Ontario and grossed $129,000. By 1982, the third year, she was considering expansion and chose the franchise route rather than wholesaling to big retailers. ("We were offered wholesaling accounts — Eddie Bauer, Eaton's, Simpson's, big companies in the U.S. — but we refused because in the long term we would have lost our business. You mix our products with ready-mades in the stores and the idea of Kettle Creek is gone, because what we're selling is a concept.")

In November 1982, the first franchise outside Ontario opened in Calgary. That store, like all Kettle Creek stores, is decorated in light-colored pine and with minimal ornamentation, in keeping with the simplicity of the merchandise. Business is good, even though the nautical flavor of the clothes jars slightly with the cowboy ambience of Calgary, and even though Kettle Creek firmly adheres to a policy of holding no price-cutting sales. This lends credibility to the product.

Recently the company placed a $15,000 ad in *Vogue* magazine, which resulted in a deal with Bamberger's, a subsidiary of Macy's, to open Kettle Creek boutiques in Bamberger stores in twelve American cities. Nonetheless, Stephens has no plans for large-scale exporting. Because her items are handmade, she does not get volume economies. "I think if we're going to have a big impact in the U.S., it probably makes sense to produce there," Stephens says. "After four years, it's starting to be nice now. The hard part's over."

Mmmuffin Man

Michael Bregman owns one of the highest-grossing stores, per square metre, in Toronto's Eaton Centre. It's a tiny little thing, and it brings in around $400,000 a year. He does this from selling 65¢ to 75¢ muffins.

Bregman opened that muffin store (spelled Mmmuffins), his first, less than four years ago. In late 1983 a happy franchiser opened the sixtieth in Sherbrooke, Quebec. Bregman has also franchised five of the ten bakery-restaurants known as Michel's Baguette French Bakery Cafe. The eleventh opens in November in Palm Beach, Florida.

This year Mmmuffins Inc. will gross around $17 million, up from $4 million in 1981. The company is so successful that prospective franchisees are almost tripping over each other to open a Mmmuffins store but Bregman is very conservative and anxious to maintain his standards.

Basically, Bregman sells flavor and variety at premium prices. He produces fifty-five kinds of muffins, from chocolate fudge to oatmeal and raisin, and from banana to carrot nut. They're large, tasty, and hot from the ovens, which the customers can see behind the giant, bright-colored posters depicting all Bregman's luscious muffin ingredients.

After Harvard, Bregman worked for Loblaw's, the grocery chain, for a while, under the tutelage of another Harvard graduate, Dave Nichol. Loblaws was the ideal place to learn consumer tastes and preferences. "I discovered that the public is far more appreciative of good quality than I had expected," Bregman says. "Consumers were extremely sensitive to price when it came to basic necessities" — but not when it came to so-called specialty items like muffins.

In 1979, Bregman was working on improving the supermarket's bakery department, and he tried out some giant 45¢ muffins at a few affluent stores. They took off. "People didn't mind spending an extra buck on high quality," he says. But what really gave Bregman a glimpse of the future was when these premium-price muffins also took off in Oshawa, Ontario, a GM factory town. "Then I realized that muffins had mass appeal."

The first Mmmuffins store opened in December 1979. From the start Bregman had planned Mmmuffins as a franchise operation and soon after came a store in the Yonge-Eglinton Centre in Toronto, and others in Oshawa, Winnipeg, Thunder Bay, Longueuil, Quebec, Red Deer, Ottawa, Calgary, Hamilton, Edmonton, Kamloops, and Regina.

Bregman got the idea for Michel's Baguette when he and his wife were honeymooning in France in 1978. They fell in love with the croissants and baguettes they ate there, and vowed to try a bakery-restaurant if the muffins concept succeeded.

Bregman maintains control through in-store training of all owner-operators and bakers. For its franchises, head office identifies all suppliers and has established a national network for paper products, flour, coffee, and other items. (Eggs and milk are locally obtained.) It also assembles most of the dry ingredients in advance. Bregman constantly tests new products to keep up consumer interest, though they don't all work out. One flop was a flat bran muffin, called a "muffinwich". He regularly hops around to different cities, looking at new concepts in food. He reads all the industry journals and walks endlessly around shopping malls in quest of new sales techniques. He says he doesn't worry about muffin saturation, though pointing out that while it's true that a lot of muffin stores have gone bankrupt, his have soared in number and profits.

QUESTIONS ■━━━━━━━━

1. Identify the trends that may be taking place in consumer motivations and preferences to account for the successes described in the case.

2. Define the image that Kettle Creek sought to project and describe the strategy pursued to maintain and reinforce it.

3. What comments can you make about the concepts of "need identification," "motive arousal," and "reinforcement" as they apply to the Mmmuffins Inc. case?

4. Why did franchising appear to be a more acceptable strategy to Mmmuffins Inc. than to the Kettle Creek Canvas Co.?

11

Attitudes

EXAMPLES

1. Determining Attitude Causation: A Canadian Supermarket Example

A study conducted for a new supermarket in Thunder Bay found that consumers were not flocking to the store in the expected numbers because they did not feel comfortable in the store. It turned out that their negative feelings were engendered by the in-store layout. The aisles were too narrow and the high shelves (which many could not reach) made consumers feel uneasy. One got a claustrophobic feeling of walking from one canyon to another.

Another study carried out for a food store in Mississauga found that the positive attitudes consumers held for the store were considerably enhanced by the pleasant aromas emanating from the on-premise bakery.

2. The Toronto Blue Jays[1]

The Blue Jays came into existence in 1977 and were financially successful from the very beginning in spite of terrible win-loss records. For example, in 1977 they lost more games than any other team that year but were about $4 million in the black. Though their record has been improving, it remained quite bad until 1983, when they were contenders for the division pennant until late in the season.

A good part of the reason for the positive public attitude to the Blue Jays was their president, Peter Bavasi. Very aware of the importance of media acceptance, he groomed his players accordingly. Not only did they appear clean-cut and conservative but they avoided controversy and adhered to high personal standards of conduct, so that media attitudes and public attitudes started out and remained very positive.

3. The Impact of a Single Incident[2]

"DC-10" has burrowed into the language as a synonym for air disaster in much the same way that "Central Park" has come to stand for urban crime. This has persisted in spite of the time that has passed since the 1979 crash of a DC-10 at Chicago's O'Hare Airport, killing 275 people in the worst single-plane disaster in US history; and although the FAA concluded that neither the design nor the manufacture of the plane was at fault.

A survey conducted just over a year after the crash found that 10% of the public continued to believe that the airplane itself was the primary cause of the Chicago disaster.

Very much aware of public doubts about the DC-10, the airlines reacted swiftly. For example, American Airlines shifted DC-10s from the New York to Los Angeles run, where they had been competing head-on with TWA's L-1011s and 747s, to the New York to San Francisco route, where the competition flies DC-10s as well.

These examples illustrate the importance of determining not just how consumers feel but particularly why they feel the way they do about products, brands, companies, and advertising.

As in the Blue Jays example, public attitudes sometimes have to be carefully moulded; sometimes one significant incident, such as the DC-10 crash, can swiftly polarize public attitudes. Even though the Federal Aviation Agency in the United States had cleared the plane of all blame, negative attitudes based on strong doubt about its safety persisted.

Attitudes, therefore, have important implications for action. Attitudes are not motivational. They do not initiate or generate behavior. They determine how an individual will respond to an object. Thus attitudes direct the response tendency. They indicate an individual's predisposition toward a specific object — in marketing terms, a readiness to buy. One researcher has defined an attitude as "a learned predisposition to respond in a consistently favorable or unfavorable manner in respect to a given object."[3]

THE RELATIONSHIP AMONG VALUES, ATTITUDES, BELIEFS

The relationship among values, attitudes, and beliefs is hierarchical. Values represent the broad, general orientations an individual holds toward the environment and are not directed to specific objects. Each value can provide the frame of reference for a number of attitudes or predispositions to specific objects.[4] For example, a value such as conservatism could influence the attitudes an individual has on a variety of issues — social welfare, education, labor unions, taxes, fluoridation, defence, import tariffs, and quotas (see Figure 11.1). This is why attitudes are described as "having structure"; ideally, attitudes to related objects are similar and consistent with relevant basic values.

In turn, **beliefs** are the building blocks of attitudes. They are the specific knowledge that the individual has about an object; and attitudes are based on these beliefs. Thus consumers'

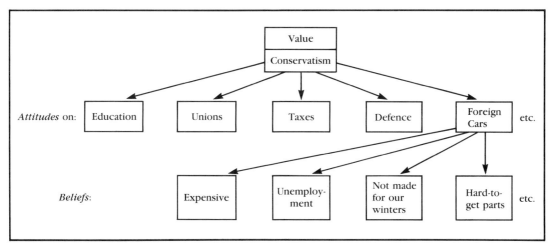

FIGURE 11.1: Relationship of Values, Attitudes, and Beliefs

attitudes to GM's Buick (whether positive or negative and how much so) will be based on what they believe about Buick *vis-à-vis* each of its characteristics or their sets of evaluative criteria, such as economy, acceleration, durability, servicing, design, and interior. Remember, too, that these evaluative criteria and their importance are determined by the *motives* of each individual. For example, the individual with a strong status motive will be likely to place a high importance on such criteria as styling, interior, and price.

What this suggests for marketers is that, when determining consumers' attitudes, they should uncover all the specific beliefs about their product — what consumers know (or do not know) about the different attributes of the product and how they evaluate the product in terms of these attributes. This exercise is especially useful when the beliefs the individual holds are based on insufficient or inaccurate information. The course for the marketer is clear in such a case — to make sure that the market is fully and properly aware of the product's merits.

Importance to the Marketer

Why would marketers be interested in attitudinal data? Because, basically, they want to know how consumers feel about their brand, company, advertising, and other strategic components.

There are several reasons for this:

1. Marketers assume that attitude affects response behavior. We shall see that the correlation between attitude and behavior has not been particularly impressive so that *prediction* of behavior is not very good. Part of the reason for this is that the behavior depends on the nature of the product. It will be recalled that in high-involvement decision making, information search and evaluation and the formation of attitudes occur *before* the purchase decision, whereas in low-involvement decisions, purchase is more likely to occur on very limited information and attitudes are more likely to develop *after* behavior.

2. In addition to individual consumer attitudes, generally held attitudes can influence the consumption habits of an entire society. Thus society's attitudes to leisure, working women, and dress and the changing attitudes in these cases have a strong impact on marketing strategy.

3. The possibility of **segmenting** a market on the basis of attitudes, describing segments in

terms of their favorability/unfavorability to a brand, and thus making general inferences about likely brand acceptance is always attractive.

4. Because attitudes reflect how consumers feel about an object, they can be used to determine the overall impact of marketing strategies involving current products, new products, advertising, or the company.

Why Do We Have Attitudes?

We have attitudes because they are useful. They perform definite functions in helping to determine "how efficiently consumers solve problems and achieve their goals." In brief, attitudes serve mainly to simplify our decisions by providing, for the most part, ready predispositions toward or away from any object. Underlying this, attitudes reflect and fulfill certain psychological needs of the individual.

Katz has suggested that attitudes can serve four functions: adjustment, knowledge, value-expressive, and ego-defensive.[5]

These functions are not fixed and any attitude can serve a different function from one individual to another. In any event, a better understanding of why an attitude is held clearly facilitates strategies for attitude change.

The Adjustment (Utilitarian) Function

Attitudes can serve a practical purpose of permitting individuals to have likes and dislikes so that they can choose the "objects" to which they are favorably disposed (which, in other words, provide satisfaction) and reject those to which they are negatively disposed (that is, those that do not provide satisfaction).

In a social situation, we acquire those attitudes that will bring about group approval, if that is what we want.

The Knowledge Function

Generally, by providing "standards and frames of reference"[6] with which to categorize and evaluate, attitudes help us to understand the world around us. For example, we may have the attitude that all the brands in a particular product class are alike, so the purchase decision is simplified and will be likely to be based on other criteria.

For this reason some have referred to this attitudinal structure as the individual's "map of the world." Quite often these knowledge-attitudes may be based on false, inaccurate, or inadequate information but they are nonetheless real because of their influence on behavior. They often take the form of stereotypes or generalizations.

Stereotypes can be quite strong and difficult to change. People do not associate fine jewelry with variety stores or high-quality boxed chocolates with grocery stores. Frequently, marketers come up against such attitudes and encounter considerable difficulty, and may even be thwarted in their attempts to change them.

Similarly, a consumer who "knows" that she or he prefers wool to synthetic fibres will have a far simpler decision to make when purchasing a sweater or other garment. The knowledge function of attitudes is also exemplified in brand loyal behavior. Based on experience, the consumer develops a very positive attitude to a brand and thus avoids re-evaluation each time a purchase decision has to be made.

Viewed another way, it may be said that the competitor seeks to disturb the complacency of loyal behavior by attempting to force re-evaluation and possible attitude change through the introduction of new cognitions (e.g., a "new" brand, price deals), or creating new emotional associations, or even forcing trial.

The Value-Expressive Function

Attitudes often reflect the individual's self-concept, basic values, and beliefs. A consumer who is conservative or very patriotic may have negative attitudes to foreign-made products. The ecology-conscious person will prefer small automobiles or even a bicycle. The products we buy often serve as expressions of how we perceive ourselves — what we are and *what we believe in*.

The Ego-Defensive Function

Sometimes one develops certain attitudes in order to protect oneself from anxiety or threat. The attitudes may be rationalizations or perceptual distortions; that is, mechanisms of defence against unacceptable needs or drives.

For example, when a sample of cigarette smokers were asked if the US Surgeon-General's report had proven the link between cigarettes and cancer, it was found that the heavier the smoker, the greater was the level of denial that such proof had been provided.

Positive attitudes to expensive liquors, clothing, and cars may frequently reflect compensatory behavior for unconscious feelings of insecurity or inferiority. The attitudes to these products thus serve an ego-defensive function. They are more ego-involving and therefore more difficult to change.

It is important to understand the particular function or functions that an attitude fills, because only then will there be some chance of influencing it. Identifying the underlying psychological need will be of considerable help in developing communications strategy. The same attitude can serve more than one function; the same attitude can serve different functions in different individuals or different attitudes can serve the same function in different individuals. There is no one-to-one relationship and proper identification depends upon the particular context. In Figure 11.2, Lutz has provided some examples of the application of these attitude functions in advertising. Advertising such as "Crest whitens teeth" serves the utilitarian function by focussing on an appeal that will enhance the perception of the brand's utility. "Pepsi drinkers think young" appeals to the value of

youthfulness to which significant segments of our society today subscribe. For those who have guilt feelings or anxiety about cigarette smoking, the advertising message "Marlboro smokers are masculine" will help allay those feelings by reinforcing their masculinity.

Function	Advertising Message
Utilitarian	"Crest whitens teeth."
Knowledge	"Pringles potato chips are different."
Value-expressive	"Pepsi drinkers think young."
Ego-defensive	"Marlboro smokers are masculine.'

FIGURE 11.2: Application of the Four Attitude Functions in Advertising

SOURCE: Richard J. Lutz, "A Functional Theory Framework for Designing and Pretesting Advertising Themes," in John C. Maloney and Bernard Silverman (eds.), *Attitude Research Plays for High Stakes* (Chicago: American Marketing Association, 1979), p. 43.

A study done with members of two Houston tennis associations and university students enrolled in tennis classes sought to determine if the attitudes players held toward tennis served a variety of functions across the sample.[7] It found that attitudes to tennis were based on different reasons and served different functions. Interestingly, the study also showed that only a small percentage of the sample (23.7%) held an attitude that served only one function and that the value-expressive function seems to be the most important single function served by the attitude. The study also suggested that "this approach to attitudes could be particularly useful for segmenting markets or designing mass communication messages."

In summary, an attitude can be best understood by knowing the beliefs on which it is based, by identifying the value and thus the other attitudes to which it is related, and by ascertaining the function (utilitarian, value-expressive, ego-defensive, or knowledge) it fulfills for the individual (that is, the psychological need it serves).

HOW ATTITUDES ARE FORMED

The definition of attitude emphasizes one key aspect of attitudes — they are learned. Attitudes develop throughout an individual's lifetime on the basis of personal experience and of information acquired from such personal and non-personal sources as the family, teachers, peer groups, other reference groups, religious organizations, and commercial and other media.

Attitudes are also subjective. They are dependent on the individual's needs, values, and other characteristics.

> In the consumer's cognitive structure, attitudes are interrelated with the other psychological variables.... they are affected by selective perception and, in turn, influence new perceptions.... attitudes are subject to different motivations and help determine how efficiently consumers solve problems and achieve their goals.[8]

If acquired information is processed through a subjective filter, exactly how do consumers arrive at their attitudes? Two types of models have been proposed, a compensatory model and a non-compensatory model.

The **compensatory model** claims that a consumer considers all of the attributes of a brand together so that the strengths compensate for the weaknesses.

One subtype is the **expectancy-value model**, which combines the degree to which the consumer believes the brand to possess an attribute (the expectancy dimension, sometimes also called instrumentality) with the importance of that attribute to the consumer (the value dimension). The total from all the attributes yields an overall attitude measure. Figure 12.5 in Chapter 12 provides an example of how an attitude index to Sony televisions is calculated from the four attributes considered. Figure 12.6 illustrates how the same can be done for three competitive brands of automobiles.

Not only do these data yield the overall attitude index but they also indicate the strengths and weaknesses of each brand.

Figures 12.5 and 12.6 are discussed further in the section on attitude measurement in the next chapter.

The **attribute adequacy model**, another subtype, suggests that, while compensation among attributes does take place, each attribute is judged in relation to some "ideal" level.

Noncompensatory models suggest that the strengths of one attribute do not compensate for the weaknesses of another. There are three such models: (a) **conjunctive**, where each attribute must reach at least a certain minimum level. Brand attitude will be negative even if only one attribute falls below the acceptance level; (b) **disjunctive**—the opposite of conjunctive—where a brand that reaches the minimum level on at least one desirable attribute is accepted; (c) **lexicographic**, where the consumer ranks the attributes in order of importance and the brand with the best value on the top attribute obtains the most positive attitudinal rating. Two brands receiving equal ratings are then rated on the next most important attribute, and so on.

Research seems to indicate that most consumers follow the lexicographic model.[9] The expectancy-value method comes next. There is also evidence that in some circumstances both compensatory and non-compensatory approaches may be used. It was found that consumers may first use non-compensatory rules to reduce a large number of brands to perhaps three or four, and then apply a compensatory approach to make their final choice.[10]

It is noteworthy that the lexicographic method is the only one that suggests that the consumer arrives at a brand attitude by processing information by attribute rather than by brand, a strategy that, it has been argued, is easier for the consumer.[11]

If this finding holds up, it could have important implications for marketing strategy. Most current advertisements and other promotions emphasize brand. It may be far more advantageous to stress preferred attributes first and then brand.

THE CHARACTERISTICS OF ATTITUDES

Attitudes are made up of three components: cognitive, affective, and conative.[12] The **cognitive** component consists of what the individual believes or knows about the object, which can be descriptive (e.g., good fuel economy or high vitamin content) or evaluative (e.g., relating to product benefits such as economy, prevents cavities).

The **affective** component is whether the individual likes or dislikes the object. The two components are related because we often like or dislike an object on the basis of what we believe about it. Sometimes how we feel about it is contrary to what we believe. The affective component may have a deeper origin.

The **conative** (or behavioral) component is the tendency to respond, measured by intention. Intention to buy may not lead to purchase because of other factors, such as situational or social restraints (e.g., nonavailability or price).

A given attitude may lead to a number of behavioral expressions in different individuals, just as several attitudes may find expression in a particular response by a number of individuals. Because of this, the identification of behavior with underlying attitudes can cause difficulty and make the prediction of behavior risky.

Some of the other characteristics of attitudes also lead to a better understanding of whether and how marketers are able to make use of them in developing strategies. For example, *valence* is the positiveness or negativeness of the attitude; *intensity* is the strength of the attitude or the degree of positiveness or negativeness. Determining the intensity of an attitude has clear implications for the ease with which

it may be changed. Also related to attitude intensity is the importance of the attitude, often referred to as its **centrality**. Centrality measures the extent to which the attitude is important to the individual, the extent to which it is ego-involving. The more central an attitude, the more difficult it is to change. On the other hand, rather than trying to change an attitude, a marketer will seek to emphasize the benefits associated with a central attitude and show how a particular product provides these benefits. Attempts can sometimes be made through advertising to increase the perceived saliency of a product benefit to enhance the acceptance of a brand.

Finally, the **complexity** of an attitude affects the ease with which a marketer is able to make use of the attitude. The more complex an attitude, the greater the number of elements it contains and the greater the care necessary in applying it. For example, an individual's attitude to a brain surgeon will be the result of a greater number of beliefs based on more complex information than the attitude to a brand of toothpaste.

ATTITUDES, INTENTION, AND BEHAVIOR

It seems reasonable to expect that attitudes will correlate highly with behavior. In some cases, this may be true and behavior can be predicted from a knowledge of attitudes. In other cases, behavior is inconsistent with attitude for a number of possible reasons, such as social norms, price, availability, advertising, personality, economic circumstances, competition, family decision, and store environment.[13]

Almost twenty years ago, Fishbein observed that after more than seventy-five years of attitude research, no strong correlation between attitude and behavior had been clearly established.[14]

He suggested that, while researchers were inclined to attribute these results to invalid measurement techniques, the true reason may be a simplistic view of the causes of behavior. He felt that behavior was the result of not only attitudes but also "motivational, situational and personality" factors.

It was the reaction to the early simplistic attitude-behavior relationship that led to the development of the **multi-attribute** attitude models. Instead of seeking to measure a single, global attitude concept that involved the affective component,[15] it was felt that better results would come from measurement of the cognitive elements of the attitude.

Thus arose the **expectancy-value** models of Rosenberg and then of Fishbein. Their basic conceptualization was the same but there were some differences, mainly regarding measurement.

Rosenberg postulated two components: (1) the importance of the attributes or evaluative criteria and (2) perceived instrumentality (the extent to which the brand possesses the attribute) as indicated below:

$$A_o = \sum_{i=1}^{N} (VI_i)(PI_i)$$

where A_o = the attitude to alternative o

VI_i = the importance of the ith attribute

PI_i = the perceived instrumentality of alternative o with respect to attribute i

N = the number of salient attributes.[16]

Fishbein also postulated two components of attitudes: (1) the belief about the object — the extent to which the product (brand) possesses a particular attribute, and (2) whether the attribute is considered to be good or bad. His model is represented by:

$$A_o = \sum_{i=1}^{N} B_i a_i$$

where A_o = attitude toward the object

B_i = the ith belief about the object

a_i = the evaluation (goodness or badness) of the attribute

N = the number of attributes.[17]

The difference between the two formulations lay in the evaluative component of the attribute. Rosenberg rated its importance; Fishbein, developing his model outside of consumer behavior, sought to determine how good or bad the attribute was perceived to be, as in:

Evaluate the following:
    Fast acceleration in a car is:

Good— — — — — — —Bad

Which of these two approaches, the belief/importance approach of Rosenberg, or the belief/evaluation model of Fishbein, is more effective in consumer research appears to depend on the type of product and the consumer. The evidence available falls on both sides of the question. In one study, it was found that "the Fishbein approach to attitudes seems to be relatively more valid. . . . Subjects respond much more heterogeneously to the (belief/importance) task than to the Fishbein task."[18] In particular, subjects were able to deal with "very bad" in the Fishbein model but many seemed uncertain about how to deal with "not at all important" in Rosenberg's model. On the other hand, a study by Mazis and Ahtola found the Rosenberg model to be a better predictor of intention.[19]

Whichever model is used in a particular instance, the result is a summation of ratings on all relevant attributes weighted for importance or goodness/badness. Thus, for example, attitude to the Buick car will be determined by summing the ratings of the probability (beliefs) that Buick possesses of each of those attributes considered relevant, such as fuel economy, acceleration, styling, comfort, and durability. Each attribute is weighted on the basis of the importance or evaluation rating assigned to it.

Fishbein later noted that one of the reasons why the attitude-behavior correlation had been low was that attitude measurement failed to take into account the *situational influences* on the consumer decision. In addition, he suggested that rather than determining attitude to the object (which did not predict behavior well), it might be better to measure the attitude toward the act (in the consumer case, the act of buying). This concept of the attitude to the act he labelled *behavioral intention*. Accordingly, he modified his belief/evaluation model in two significant ways:

- he introduced the concept of behavioral intention; and
- he took into account two social components, the expectations of significant others or social referents (normative beliefs) and the individual's motivation to comply with those normative beliefs.

The resulting formulation is called Fishbein's Extended Model or Fishbein's Intentions Model:

$$B \sim BI = \sum_{i=1}^{n} B_i a_i(w_o) + \sum_{j=1}^{k} NB_j MC_j(w_1)$$

where B = a specific overt behavior, such as a product purchase

BI = the behavioral intention to perform or not perform the specific behavior

B_i = a belief (the probability or improbability) that performing the behavior will lead to an ith outcome. For example, that consuming a product will produce a particular sensation

a_i = the evaluative aspect of B_i; that is, the negative or positive feeling or evaluation toward the ith outcome

n = the number of salient outcomes

NB_j = a normative belief; that is, the belief that a jth relevant other expects the individual to perform or not perform the behavior. For example, that a dentist expects usage of a particular brand

MC_j = the individual's motivation to comply or not comply with the expectation of the jth other

k = the number of relevant other persons or groups

w_o and w_1 = empirically determined standardized regression coefficients (beta weights).[20]

Thus behavior is postulated to be an approximation of the behavioral intention that is the result of multiplicative and additive relationships between the attitude to the act and the social variables of normative belief and motivation to comply. Note that the attitude to the act takes the same form as the attitude to the object. The difference between them lies in the questions used to assess the B and a components.

A paper by Ryan and Bonfield provides a good illustration of the types of measurement employed.[21] Such measures and others will be discussed in greater detail in Chapter 12.

It is important to note that with such a formulation it is entirely possible that what others expect the individual to do or what the individual should do in a situation may be so strong (high w_1 and low w_o) as to outweigh the attitude; as a result, behavior can be contrary to an expressed or identified attitude.

This is an extremely important proposition. It means that the marketer should not rely solely on attitude data in attempting to measure likelihood of purchase of a brand. As earlier research indicated, attitude was not a good predictor of behavior. Behavioral intention is a better measure, because it takes into account the other factors.

Even where the normative and motivational components cannot be measured, attitudinal measures may be helpful if those components are recognized and allowed for in an enlightened fashion. In other words, before attempting to predict behavior on the basis of attitudes, one needs to determine whether and how the individual is motivated to act.

Fishbein's formulation also seems to indicate that, unlike what consistency theory would suggest, behavior does not have to be consistent with attitudes. However, this may be too hasty a conclusion.

When behavior is not consistent with the "relevant" attitude, it could mean that other attitudes (situational and motivational) relating to the event are likely more salient and, consequently, the individual seeks consistency in that direction rather than in the purchase-attitude relationship.

Fishbein's Intentions Model appears to predict behavior far better than the A_o model.[22] A recent review concludes that "the evidence suggests the model is theoretically sound . . . . and has been shown to have predictive validity in a real-world marketing application."[23]

There are, however, a number of issues that need clarification.[24] A particularly important one is the "additive assumption" of the model. Others have suggested that "the root of the problem" is that Fishbein has not "taken account of the full range of situational influence."[25] Specifically, "*anticipated circumstances* such as financial status, availability of goods, access to retail stores, and general attitudes or optimism or pessimism toward the future financial picture all function to shape intentions." Ryan and Bonfield also indicate the desirability of a "disaggregation" of the attitudinal ($B_i a_i$) and normative (NB_j, MC_j) variables that "may reveal which attitudinal outcomes ($_i$) or normative referents ($_j$) *more strongly* influence intentions."[26]

For example, as the model now stands, it cannot be used to identify the most important outcomes or the most important referents that would make for more effective promotional

strategy; there are doubts about the validity of the relative weights of the cognitive and social variables (w_o and w_1); there are questions about the additive assumptions of the variables; and there are doubts about whether the measurement of the normative component is valid.

Overall, it appears that the Fishbein Intentions Model may be leading us in the right direction. Unfortunately, its applications have been almost entirely theoretical. The practical and financial difficulties of measurement could make it even harder to be accepted by industry than were the multi-attribute attitude models.

THE MARKETING IMPLICATIONS OF MULTI-ATTRIBUTE MODELS

While the single attitude measure is effective in predicting usage in many instances,[27] there are several advantages derived from the expectancy-value models:

- Like the single-scale measures, they also yield a summary attitude index that can be derived for current company brands, competitive brands, new brands, or any other objects. Although measurement involves the weighted summation of ratings on a number of attributes, the task is not as hard as it may seem. Only the expectancy components need to be determined for each object; the value component needs to be measured only once.
- The expectancy (beliefs) component can identify those attributes in which a brand is strong and those in which it is weak. Moreover, these can be related to the strengths and weaknesses of competitive brands.
- The value component can help identify what is important or desirable to a particular market segment, so that products can be positioned in accordance with their strengths and weaknesses.
- Use of Fishbein's extended model permits determination of behavioral intention, which

has been found to be a better indicator of behavior.

- From the extended model, the marketer will also be able to disaggregate the social component to determine the relative roles of different social referents in influencing attitude.

- Theoretically at least, from Fishbein's Intentions Model it is possible to determine how influential attitude to the act is, compared to the social variables of normative beliefs and motivation to comply.

SUMMARY

An attitude is a learned predisposition to respond to a given object in a consistently favorable or unfavorable manner. Attitudes simplify decisions by providing ready predispositions toward objects. They serve specific psychological needs and have their origin in the experience and knowledge of the individual.

Determining consumer attitudes is very important to the marketer because it can help to predict behavior, can permit market segmentation, and can also be used to measure the impact of marketing strategies.

Individuals arrive at these attitudes by processing information in either a compensatory or a non-compensatory way.

Attitudes are made up of three components: cognitive, affective, and behavioral. Other char-

acteristics are their intensity, centrality, and complexity.

There does not appear to be a strong correlation between attitudes and behavior. Attributing this to the failure to consider situational factors, Fishbein introduced the concept of behavioral intention, which he defined as the result of the attitude to the act (not the object) and the social variables of normative beliefs (i.e., the influence of what others expect) and the motivation to comply.

This model and the basic multi-attribute expectancy-value model offer many advantages to the marketer over the single-measure attitude score.

QUESTIONS

1. Why are marketers interested in attitude data?

2. Discuss the relationship among values, attitudes, and beliefs. Why is it important?

3. Describe the functions that attitudes fill and show how this classification is useful to the marketer.

4. What are the different ways by which consumers are thought to arrive at their attitudes?

5. Explain and give examples of what is meant by (a) the complexity and (b) the centrality of attitudes?

6. What considerations led to the development of Fishbein's Intentions Model? How did he modify the expectancy-value model?

7. In what ways is the attitude index obtained from the expectancy-value model superior to that devised from single-item attitude measures?

NOTES TO CHAPTER 11 ▄▄▄▄▄▄▄▄

[1]Adapted from Wayne Lilley, "Losers Take All," *Canadian Business* (April 1981), pp. 37-43.

[2]Adapted from Lee Smith, "McDonnell Douglas is Flying Scared," *Fortune* (25 August 1980), pp. 41-2.

[3]M. Rokeach, *Beliefs, Attitudes, and Values* (San Francisco: Jossey-Barr, 1968), p. 110.

[4]Donald E. Vinson, Jerome E. Scott, and Lawrence M. Lamont, "The Role of Personal Values in Marketing and Consumer Behavior," *Journal of Marketing*, 41 (April 1977), pp. 44-50.

[5]D. Katz, "The Functional Approach to the Study of Attitudes," *Public Opinion Quarterly*, 24 (1960), pp. 163-204.

[6]Ibid., p. 175.

[7]William B. Locander and W. Austin Spivey, "A Functional Approach to Attitude Measurement," *Journal of Marketing Research*, 15 (November 1978), pp. 576-87.

[8]Harold W. Berkman and Christopher C. Gilson, *Consumer Behavior* (Encino, California: Dickenson, 1978), p. 307.

[9]James R. Bettman, "Issues in Designing Consumer Information Environments," *Journal of Consumer Research*, 2 (December 1975), pp. 169-77.

[10]Denis A. Lussier and Richard W Olshavsky, "Task Complexity and Contingent Processing in Brand Choice," *Journal of Consumer Research*, 6 (September 1979), pp. 154-65.

[11]James R. Bettman, "Data Collection and Analysis Approaches for Studying Consumer Information Processing" (Working Paper no. 41, Center for Marketing Studies, University of California, Los Angeles, July 1976).

[12]David Krech, Richard S. Crutchfield, and Egerton L. Ballachey, *Individual in Society* (New York: McGraw-Hill, 1962), p. 140.

[13]George Day, *Buyer Attitudes and Brand Choice Behavior* (New York: Free Press, 1970).

[14]M. Fishbein, "Attitude and the Prediction of Behavior," in M. Fishbein (ed.), *Attitude Theory and Measurement* (New York: John Wiley & Sons, 1967), p. 477.

[15]See for example, Russell I. Haley and Peter B. Case, "Testing Thirteen Attitude Scales for Agreement and Brand Discrimination," *Journal of Marketing*, 43 (Fall 1979), pp. 21-30.

[16]Milton J. Rosenberg, "Cognitive Structure and Attitudinal Effect," *Journal of Abnormal and Social Psychology*, 53 (1956), pp. 367-72.

[17]Martin Fishbein, "An Investigation of the Relationships Between Beliefs About an Object and the Attitude Toward That Object," *Human Relations*, 16 (1963), pp. 233-40.

[18]James R. Bettman, Noel Capon, and Richard J. Lutz, "Cognitive Algebra in Multi-Attribute Attitude Models," *Journal of Marketing Research*, 12 (May 1975), pp. 151-64.

[19]Michael B. Mazis, Olli T. Ahtola, and R. Eugene Klippel, "A Comparison of Four Multi-Attribute Models in the Prediction of Consumer Attitudes," *Journal of Consumer Research*, 2 (June 1975), pp. 38-52.

[20]Martin Fishbein and Icek Ajzen, *Belief, Attitude, Intention, and Behavior: An Introduction to Theory and Research* (Reading, Massachusetts: Addison-Wesley, 1975); Icek Ajzen and Martin Fishbein, *Understanding Attitudes and Predicting Social Behavior* (Englewood Cliffs, New Jersey: Prentice-Hall, 1980).

[21]Michael J. Ryan and E.H. Bonfield, "Fishbein's Intentions Model; A Test of External and Pragmatic Validity," *Journal of Marketing*, 44 (Spring 1980), pp. 82-5.

[22]For example, David T. Wilson, H. Lee Matthews, and James W. Harvey, "An Empirical Test of the Fishbein Behavioral Intention Model," *Journal of Consumer Research*, 1 (March 1975), pp. 39-48.

[23]Ryan and Bonfield, op. cit., pp. 83-4.

[24]Richard J. Lutz, "Conceptual and Operational Issues in the Extended Fishbein Model," in B.B. Anderson (ed.), *Advances in Consumer Research*, 3 (1976), pp. 469-76; Paul W. Miniard and Joel B. Cohen, "Isolating Attitudinal and Normative Influences in Behavioral Intentions Models," *Journal of Marketing Research*, 16 (1979), pp. 102-10.

[25]James F. Engel, Roger D. Blackwell, and David T. Kollat, *Consumer Behavior*, 3rd ed. (Hinsdale, Illinois: Dryden Press, 1978), p. 403.

[26]Ryan and Bonfield, op. cit., p. 84.

[27]Haley and Case, op. cit., pp. 21-30.

12

Attitude Change and Measurement

1. Canadian Attitudes to Imported Cars[1]

The attitude that the quality of imported cars is superior to that of domestic cars dies hard; so much so that Chrysler Canada is out to promote the quality of its passenger cars and explode a few myths about imports at the same time in its latest round of advertising.

According to the advertising manager, the "Myths" campaign was developed "from the fact that we were hearing from so many sources that imported cars were of superior quality."

Chrysler is the only auto-maker offering a five-year, 80,000-kilometre warranty and the ads point out that their cars have had fewer problems than any of the imports. The campaign is part of Chrysler's continuing theme of "Best built, best backed," which the company has been using since early 1984 to promote its quality and the warranty program.

2. The Dairy Bureau of Canada and Attitudes to Butter and Margarine[2]

The three Fleischmann's margarine advertisements to appear in newspapers across the country have raised a few eyebrows in advertising circles and in the dairy industry.

At issue is the way research material and clippings from newspaper stories on a recent Lipid Research Clinic report were used in advertisements for Fleischmann's margarine (Figure 12.1). The ads point to the relationship between low cholesterol and "risk to heart" and shout that "new medical facts are going to change all our eating habits." The Dairy Bureau of Canada has responded with bold ad headlines "Fleischmann's is wrong!", refuting the implied message that eggs and butter can be linked to heart disease.

The origin of the storm is the use being made of an independent research report on the effects of cholesterol and such substances on

FLEISCHMANN'S IS WRONG!

In recent newspaper advertising, Fleischmann's Margarine suggests that the Lipid Research Clinic study says that eating butter is linked to heart disease.

Can you really believe Fleischmann's claim when you get the true facts?

FLEISCHMANN'S CLAIM:
"And it (the study*) outlines the danger of foods that are high in animal fats such as eggs and butter."**

TRUE FACTS:
The study* stated that it "...was not designed to assess directly whether cholesterol lowering by diet prevents coronary heart disease." In fact, the purpose of the research was to study the effects of a drug and not daily eating habits. *Fleischmann's is wrong* because the study never mentions butter. While the study researchers feel that cholesterol lowering by diet would be beneficial, the same researchers state that "...it is unlikely that a conclusive study of dietary-induced cholesterol lowering for the prevention of coronary heart disease can be designed or implemented."

FLEISCHMANN'S CLAIM:
"New medical facts* are going to change all our eating habits."**

TRUE FACTS:
The study* does not refer to the eating habits of members of the public at large. The study specifically recruited only men who were at high risk for coronary heart disease and suggests its findings could be applied to some other groups. *Fleischmann's is wrong* to suggest that normal healthy people need to change their eating habits as a result of the study.

We encourage you to read all the facts and decide for yourself,
keeping your own interest at heart ...not someone else's.

For all the true facts, not just Fleischmann's interpretations, we offer you
a free copy of the complete Lipid Research Clinic Study
as published in the Journal of the American Medical Association.

Write to: Dairy Bureau of Canada
20 Holly Street, Suite 400
Toronto, Ontario
M4S 3B1

 Dairy Bureau of Canada

*Lipid Research Clinic Study. Jan '84.   ® Registered trademark of the Dairy Bureau of Canada   **Quoted from Fleischmann's advertisements

FIGURE 12.1: Claim and Counterclaim: Fleischmann's versus the Dairy Bureau of Canada
Courtesy Dairy Bureau of Canada

heart disease to influence public attitudes. Critics of the Fleischmann's ads claim that newspaper and magazine headlines used in the advertisements do not accurately portray the facts surrounding the Lipid Research Project or its conclusions. It is interesting to note that some feel that, by using headlines containing the word "cholesterol," Fleischmann may have breached guidelines set out under the Food and Drugs Act. According to the guidelines, ad copy that could be linked to the "treatment, prevention, or cure for any of the diseases . . . . mentioned in Schedule A [heart disease falls under Schedule A] may not be used in advertisements."

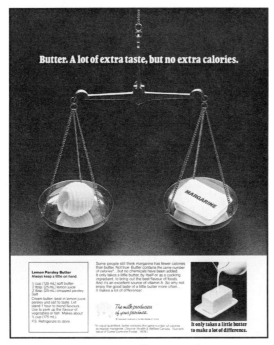

FIGURE 12.2: An Attempt to Change Attitudes to Margarine and Butter

Courtesy Dairy Bureau of Canada

The legal question, however, is a separate issue. The issue of attitude change and its effects on the dairy industry is the significant problem. The Dairy Bureau of Canada represents 50,000 dairy farmers and serves a $3.6 billion industry.

The Dairy Bureau has also made use of comparative advertising in which it raised the question of calorie content (see Figure 12.2). It cited a 1979 report by Health and Welfare Canada to claim that margarine does not have fewer calories than butter. It obviously hopes to influence attitudes to butter and margarine by employing a credible, reliable source to support its claim that "butter contains the same number of calories" with "a lot of extra taste."

Chapter 11 was devoted to a definition of the concept of attitude, and to a description of the formation, roles, and salient characteristics of attitudes.

This chapter begins with an examination of theories that seek to explain how attitudes work. With this as a background, various approaches to achieving attitude change are presented. The chapter concludes with a treatment of attitude measurement.

ATTITUDE CHANGE

In the application of attitude data, two strategic possibilities are open to the marketer:
* an adaptive strategy that seeks to reinforce

and maintain existing positive attitudes; and

- a change strategy that attempts to change existing attitudes, either to increase their positive valence or to change their valence from negative to positive.

Suggestions for adaptive strategies were made throughout the last chapter, particularly in terms of segmentation on the basis of attitudes, new product positioning and existing product repositioning. The importance of understanding the functions of attitudes in the development of more effective communications strategy was emphasized.

Adapting to existing attitudes is easier than attempting to change them. Because attitudes vary in intensity, in complexity, and in centrality, some are more difficult to change than others. Some are impossible to change. Before turning to a closer examination of attitude change strategies, it will be useful to review the principal theoretical explanations for why individuals change their attitudes.

UNDERLYING THEORIES

The theory that has the most significant implications for attitude change is **functional theory,** which was explained in Chapter 11. It suggests that attitudes fulfill people's psychological needs. Four needs were identified: utilitarian, knowledge, value-expressive, and ego-defensive needs. Before changing an attitude, it is important to understand what needs are served by the attitude. For example, if a consumer's negative attitude to imported cars were found to be based on a personal conviction that Canadians should buy Canadian-made cars, one could try to change that attitude by showing, for instance, that buying an imported car helps create jobs for Canadians.

Another theory that is helpful in understanding why individuals may change their attitudes is **consistency theory**. It suggests that individuals strive to achieve consistency in their attitudes and behavior in order to remove the tension created by an inconsistency. As far as attitudes are concerned, there can be inter-attitude inconsistency (that is, attitudes that disagree or are inconsistent with each other) and intra-attitude inconsistency (where there is inconsistency among the cognitive, affective, and behavioral components).[3]

Because attitudes express basic values, they tend to form clusters with other attitudes that express the same value. Tension arises when attitudes that are related to a value do not all reflect that value. It has been observed that the greater the consistency among an individual's attitudes, the greater the stability and maturity of that individual's personality.[4]

With regard to intra-attitude inconsistency, tension will arise where, for example, an individual's affective valence (like or dislike) is in conflict with cognitive valence (i.e., knowledge about the object). Such tension exists in the individual who dislikes Jews despite the wealth of favorable information he or she has about them.

Cognitive dissonance theory is a variant of consistency theory that is specific to post-purchase situations. It refers to the psychological discomfort or tension that occurs after a decision has been made when there is inconsistency between two cognitions. A cognition is any knowledge, opinion, or belief about an object. The source of such conflicting cognitions can be internal (such as afterthoughts about the strengths of rejected alternatives) or external (such as use of the product, the opinions of others, or advertising).

Dissonance is more likely to occur:

- the greater the financial or psychological value of the purchase;[5]
- the larger the number of desirable choices available;[6]
- the greater the extent to which the choices have attractive features;[7]
- the greater the similarity (cognitive overlap) among the choices;[8] and
- the greater the extent to which the respon-

sibility for the decision is unshared and of free volition. For example, if the decision is made under outside pressure or on the advice of another individual, dissonance is likely to be less.[9]

Cognitive dissonance theory suggests that the greater the dissonance, the greater the likelihood of attitude change. Unfortunately, this is not so. Attitude change is only one of the possible responses to dissonance. The discrepancy between the two cognitions may be so great and the attitude so central that the dissonance cannot be removed through attitude change to the object.

There are a number of other ways of resolving inconsistency:

- discrediting the source of the message, so that attitude to the object remains the same while the attitude to the source is changed. The source (announcer, medium, sponsor), for example, is regarded as dishonest or unreliable and the message is not believed;[10]
- downrating or minimizing the issue, thus reducing the strength of the inconsistency. The consumer may understate the time spent considering the decision and regard the purchase as unimportant;
- revoking the decision;
- seeking new information to support the current position;
- explaining away the inconsistency through

rationalizations (spurious reasons) such as "it is better for my health" or "my doctor smokes too";
- accepting the inconsistency, especially if it is not too great.

Research evidence suggests that the influence of cognitive dissonance on attitude change is substantial, although not unequivocal.[11]

Finally, some useful insights into attitude change are provided by **social judgement theory**, which takes into account the magnitude of message discrepancy.[12] It postulates that of all the possible attitudes toward an object, some will fall within the individual's **latitude of acceptance** (i.e., the range of attitudes acceptable to the individual), some will fall in a **latitude of non-commitment** (which represents a neutral zone), and the rest will fall in the **latitude of rejection** (those attitudes not acceptable to the individual).

The typology is viewed as a continuum, so that an expansion of one zone leads to a reduction in one or both of the other two, and vice versa (Figure 12.3).

For example, a salient, central attitude will have a very narrow latitude of acceptance (zone A). It will allow only small discrepancies. The latitude of rejection (R) will be large and the latitude of non-commitment (NC) will be small.

With a peripheral or less important attitude, A will be large, NC will also be quite large and R will be very restricted.

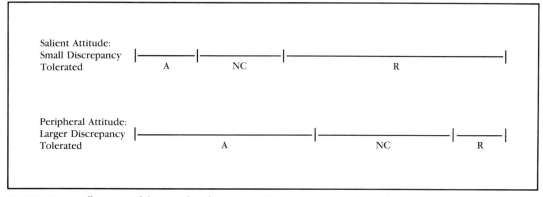

FIGURE 12.3: An Illustration of the Latitudes of Acceptance, Non-Commitment, and Rejection.

The theory thus emphasizes two factors as being important in achieving change — the *magnitude of the discrepancy* and the *degree of involvement* (centrality, saliency, importance) of the attitude.

A message that is too discrepant and falls in the latitude of rejection has no chance of acceptance. One that is not too discrepant will likely fall in the latitude of acceptance and thus attitude change is possible. Where the message falls in the latitude of non-commitment, it could possibly move to the acceptance zone if, for example, the marketer decides to use a highly credible source.

On the other hand, the greater the involvement of the individual in the issue or the more committed he or she is, the more restricted will be zone A and the more remote the likelihood of change.

Social judgement theory is somewhat clearer than cognitive dissonance theory as regards message discrepancy, in that it specifies a limit beyond which a discrepant message will fail to persuade. It also postulates involvement or commitment as the underlying factor that determines the sizes of the different zones.

In addition, the topographical nature of the theory makes obvious the possibility of market segmentation on the basis of consumer position on the attitude continuum.

From the theories just reviewed, functional theory, consistency and dissonance theories, and social judgement theory, a number of useful guidelines may be outlined, describing the conditions under which attitude change should be attempted:

1. Understanding the personal need behind an attitude will help to determine if attitude change should be attempted. For example, if an attitude is found to be related to a deeply held value or need, change in attitude is not likely to occur, unless the product itself is appropriately changed.

2. There is a basic tendency to seek consistency, balance, and harmony, but attitude change is not the only way of achieving that state.

3. Strategies for change will be greatly assisted if the source of the inconsistency is clarified — whether it comes from conflict with other related attitudes or it is due to inconsistencies among the cognitive, affective, or behavioral components of the attitude.

4. Balance theory suggests that a highly credible source will decrease the possibility of discrediting the source and increase the probability of attitude change.

5. Dissonance theory suggests that providing appropriate information after the purchase can reduce or even avoid dissonance and establish positive attitudes.

6. Social judgement theory suggests that attitudes that are less central and less ego-involving will have wider latitudes of acceptance and will therefore be more susceptible to change.

7. It also suggests that the less discrepant a message is from the individual's current position, the more likely it is to fall within the latitude of acceptance and thus be accepted. The marketer would be well-advised not to seek to bring about large shifts in consumer attitude all at once.

CHANGE STRATEGIES

Change strategies involve two kinds of situations:

- changing attitudes *before* the purchase, in order to persuade consumers to try the brand; and
- attempting to prevent or reverse possible negative changes in attitude *after* purchase. The objective is to induce repurchase.

Change Strategies Before Purchase

Multi-attribute models provide a useful basis for changing attitudes. They make use of the three components of attitudes and involve four possible strategies. Using the multi-attribute model of the attitude to the object:

$$A_o = \sum_{i=1}^{n} B_i a_i$$

the four strategies are:
- changing brand beliefs (B_i);
- changing attribute evaluation (a_i);
- adding a new attribute ($B_i a_i$); and
- changing the overall attitude.[13]

Changing Brand Beliefs

This involves changing the consumer's perception of a particular attribute of a brand. This is by far the most common pre-purchase attitude change strategy pursued by marketers. In Example 2, Fleischmann's is seeking to change attitudes to the low cholesterol content of margarine.

It should be noted that attitude change will not hold in the long run if the claim is not true; that is, if the product turns out not to possess the attribute claimed. Also, attempted change should not be too drastic, since extreme changes tend to be exaggerated and thus rejected (assimilation-contrast theory). Finally, the attitude is not likely to be affected if the attribute is relatively unimportant. In other words, if the a_i value is relatively low, changing that belief will not have a significant effect on brand attitude. An attribute that is important but taken for granted should not be used for attitude change because all brands are assumed to possess it. For example, an airline advertising safety is not likely to change consumer attitudes, because normally safety is not perceived to vary among airlines.

Because of the inter-connectedness of attitudes, successfully changing the B_i component of one attitude could cause a negative change in a related belief. For example, while successfully convincing consumers that a brand is low in price, a marketer may bring about the perception that it is also low in quality. It is im-portant to understand the relationship among attitudes.

Changing the Evaluation of an Attribute

Attempts may be made to convince the consumer that an attribute is more (or less) important than currently perceived. For example, a toothpaste marketer may try to show consumers who emphasize white teeth that decay prevention is more important. By so doing, the marketer hopes to increase market share by convincing part of the "whiteness" segment that they should stress decay prevention.

Pringles potato chips are an excellent example of increasing the importance of packaging, which could be shown to have a significant effect on freshness, a very desirable feature of the product.

Changing the importance of product attributes is closely tied to the ability to change choice criteria and, for that reason, it is not easily accomplished. Consumers' evaluative criteria and motives are rooted in their needs and their life-style, and they are not easily changed. Attempts at attribute evaluation change may be more successful with those attributes that are not related to deep-seated social and cultural needs. In addition, it is easier to bring about change in existing criteria than to establish new criteria.

Adding a New Attribute

This (a new $B_i a_i$ combination) can be accomplished and can succeed in producing attitude change in some circumstances. The new attribute may be a previously ignored attribute or may be an innovation. It may be difficult for a previously ignored attribute to lead to change, because it is very likely to have been considered previously by the consumer; the true innovative feature is more likely to succeed. Unfortunately, such technological or product changes do not occur very frequently and this strategy for bringing about attitude change is not often feasible.

It is important that a new attribute be associated with a real need, or its ability to lead to attitude change will be minimal and temporary. For example, the introduction of stripes in Stripe toothpaste failed to affect brand attitudes because it possessed no real consumer benefit. On the other hand, Head and Shoulders shampoo, with its new conditioning formula, is more likely to succeed.

Katz's model of the *functions of attitudes* (see Chapter 11) provides specific examples of how the strategy of adding new attributes may be applied. Recognizing the needs served by attributes can lead to the identification of new product attributes that could change attitudes to the brand. For example, recent advertising by Arm and Hammer seeks to enhance attitudes by presenting a series of utilitarian functions that baking soda can serve: as a tooth powder, indigestion reliever, cleaning agent, refrigerator deodorizer, and bath salt.

Understanding that attitudes serve a knowledge function, by which information is organized and classified, suggests that new, clear, unambiguous product information can lead to favorable attitudes if it improves the positioning of the brand and clarifies its advantages over the competition.

For example, Shield deodorant soap, positioned as an extra-strength deodorant soap that was more effective against odor, was clearly seeking to change attitudes through the knowledge function; so did Carnation Instant Breakfast, which was directed at a specific segment (those with limited time) for a specific purpose (a quick breakfast that was nutritious).

Similarly, by identifying the *values* that an attitude serves, it is possible to change (or reinforce) the attitude by appealing to the right values. If attitudes represent deep-seated orientations in the individual's life, they are difficult to change and it would be better to accept and adapt to them than try to change them. This approach would be even more appropriate with

the *ego-defensive function* of attitudes, because such attitudes are far more likely to be highly ego-involving and difficult to change.

Changing the Overall Attitude

Marketers can also attempt to change attitudes to a brand by concentrating on changing overall preference rather than on specific attributes. Such a strategy involves a broad, general type of appeal that seeks to arouse a particular emotion or mood or to claim distinction for the brand, such as "largest selling," "most popular," or "long-established." Beer commercials generally tend to attempt attitude change through the use of life-style or mood commercials.

Forced Behavior

Fishbein's extended multi-attribute model suggests another strategy for changing attitudes. It is possible to provide the circumstances for forced (attitude-discrepant) behavior that may lead to attitude change. For example, non-preferrers of a brand may be induced to try it (through a free sample, a low-price offer, or a coupon) and change their attitudes to the brand. Behavior preceded the positive attitude and accomplished what other strategies had failed to do. Psychologists refer to this phenomenon as **role playing**. Forced to carry out roles counter to their attitudes, people end up feeling positively about those roles.[14]

Balance theory also provides a basis for effecting attitude change. It postulates that in situations of conflicting attitudes, individuals tend to act in the direction of achieving consistency and balance among their attitudes.[15]

Consider a typical marketing situation in which a TV personality presents a favorable brand message to a consumer. If the consumer already has a positive attitude no change is expected. However, if the consumer's initial attitude is negative or weakly positive, what are the possible relationships and reactions, according to balance theory? There are two possibilities: one in which the consumer is highly positive to the TV personality (Figure 12.4a) and one in which the consumer is negative to the TV personality (Figure 12.4b).

According to balance theory, "balance exists if the product of all the signs is positive, imbalance if the product is negative."[16]

Thus, in Figure 12.4(a) there is imbalance and the consumer's attitude is likely to change, depending on the degree of admiration for the personality and the strength of the appeal.

On the other hand, in Figure 12.4(b) the product of the signs is positive and the situation is one of balance. The consumer doesn't like the brand or the personality and is unlikely to change.

Balance theory suggests that attitudes to the message source (advertiser, endorser, announcer, friend, or medium) should be highly positive if attitude change is to occur. The more credible or trustworthy the source, the greater the effectiveness of the message. Attributes that make for credibility are impartiality, expertness, and integrity.

A study of the influence of **source credibility** suggests initial opinion of the receiver is an important factor in determining the "persuasive power" of a highly credible source, compared to one of lower credibility.[17]

In the first of two experiments, the subjects, who were known to have a favorable initial opinion toward the issue, "were presented with an appeal that was attributed to either a high or moderate credibility source. For half of the subjects in each treatment the communicator was identified prior to the message, while for the remainder his identification was delayed until the end of the communication."

The second experiment, instead of manipulating the timing of source identification, held that variable constant (both sources were identified prior to the message) and varied the initial opinion of the subjects (positive and negative).

Three major findings emerged:
- when initial opinion was positive, the moderately credible source was more persuasive than the highly credible source (found in both experiments);
- when the source was identified after the message, credibility had no systematic effect on attitudes, support argumentation, or counter-argumentation; and
- when initial opinion was negative, the highly credible source induced more agreement than the less credible source.

Explaining the results in cognitive terms, the researchers felt that the moderately credible source, when identified before the message, and when initial subject opinion is positive is more persuasive "presumably because message recipients felt a need to bolster support for a position they favored when the communicator was of questionable credibility. They felt less

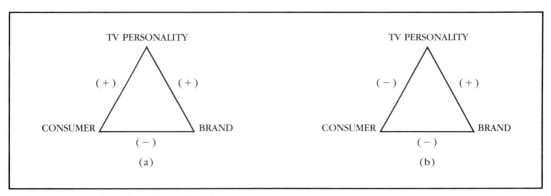

FIGURE 12.4: Triangular Relationships in Typical Advertising Situations

inclined to engage in this cognitive work when a highly credible source was presenting a favored position. In contrast, there was no source credibility effect when source identification followed the message because the credibility cue was made available too late to mediate the thought generation process." When subjects were not grouped according to initial opinion, source credibility had no systematic effect on thought generation or on attitudes.

These findings suggest that the highly credible source is not always more persuasive; the moderately credible source is more persuasive if initial opinion is already favorable; and the highly credible source is more persuasive when initial opinion is negative.

For the marketer, the findings imply that:

- it is important to ascertain the initial opinion of the target in order to select the appropriate communicator;
- the source should be identified (or identifiable) *prior* to the message; and
- in situations of high initial positiveness, it is more effective to use a moderately credible source and avoid overkill with a highly credible source.

SPECIFIC TECHNIQUES FOR ATTITUDE CHANGE BEFORE PURCHASE

Apart from choice of the specific source, there are a number of techniques that can be employed to bring about attitude change. They involve the content and structure of the message.

Message Content

Several aspects of message content are important.

Message Discrepancy

First among these is the discrepancy between current beliefs and the position advocated in the message. Social judgement theory suggests that there's a limit to the size of discrepancy that will be persuasive. Two factors become important:

- the greater the *credibility* of the source, the greater the discrepancy that will be accepted; and
- the greater the ego-involvement or commitment with the product, the smaller the discrepancy (i.e., the more restricted the latitude of acceptance) that will be tolerated, because discrepancy causes dissonance and tension, which increase with involvement.

Related to this concept of involvement is that of centrality — the more involved the individual is with the issue, the more important or central it is to him or her. With an ego-involving issue, a highly discrepant message is not likely to be successful. There is evidence to suggest that to be successful a message should fall at least near the edge of the latitude of acceptance.[18] Beyond that it could lead to selective perception and rejection of the message.

In fact, a widely discrepant message may be successful only with an issue of low involvement but, at the same time, commitment to the issue may be so low that the individual may not be moved to change in any event.

It should be noted that extremity of position on an attitude (high positive or negative valence) does not necessarily mean high commitment. Valence and centrality are two separate concepts. The individual may feel strongly about a particular attribute but the attribute may not be central to the self-concept, and therefore not very ego-involving.

Message Treatment

One of the most widely used message treatments is the **fear appeal**, which has been a controversial subject for over twenty years. We reviewed fear appeals in Chapter 10, concluding that more recent studies show a positive relationship between fear and persuasion.[19] It also appears that the effect of a fear appeal may be mediated by high source credibility.[20]

It should also be noted that the vast majority of studies on which our conclusions are based have dealt with threats of physical consequence.

Humor is another widely used message treatment, ranging from cartoons to "slice of life episodes" ("Please Don't Squeeze the Charmin," "Flick My Bic"). This subject was also covered in Chapter 10.

Distraction

Distraction means some element or elements that detract from attention to the main message. This may be accomplished through the use of humor, background music, noise, persons, or objects. It is supposed to inhibit or reduce counter-argumentation with a message and improve the chances of message acceptance. Not only are such tactics questionable but they also run the risk of lower attention to and reduced comprehension of the message.[21]

It has also been suggested that counter-argumentation occurs when commitment is high and the individual resists change. Since, for the most part, consumer brands rarely attain such high degrees of commitment, it would appear that the main consequences of distraction would be a decline in attention and comprehension, thus making a distraction tactic of little or no value in producing attitude change. This conclusion should be distinguished from the effects of distraction or passive learning of generalized brand identification.

Message Structure

A number of variations in message structure have been described as influencing attitude change, including repetition, sequence of arguments and one-sided versus two-sided appeals.

The **repetition** of messages should lead, according to learning theory (see Chapter 8), to better learning. Repetition can strengthen weak impressions, reinforce drives, affect saliency, and thus possibly influence behavior, if only through increasing awareness and knowledge.

Not much is known about the effects of repetition on attitude. Claims that repetition leads to positive attitude change may be more true for verbal than for behavioral responses.

Repetition is reported to result in wearout, or decrease in impact after a certain level of repetition. One kind of wearout is a loss of meaning suffered by words (semantic satiation).[22] Other consequences are loss of interest, annoyance, and boredom. It has been suggested that these conditions may be alleviated by varying themes and treatments.[23]

The *sequence* in which arguments are presented in a message has been related to the question of one-sided versus two-sided messages. Studies have shown that a source is significantly more persuasive if both supportive and detractive arguments are presented than if only supportive arguments are given.[24] This relationship depends on the sequence of the arguments. It holds when the detractive arguments are presented first, include only information familiar to the audience, and are presented in a compelling manner.[25]

Empirical evidence of the acceptance and use of these approaches is lacking. It does not seem likely that advertisers will be persuaded to mention some of the negative attributes of their product.

AFTER-PURCHASE ATTITUDE-CHANGE STRATEGIES

The need to develop attitude-change strategies after a purchase can arise in many ways including:

- new information about the product (from competitive advertising or word of mouth) may conflict with prior attitudes and lead to doubt in the consumer's mind (causing cognitive dissonance);

- the product may be unsatisfactory (discomfirmation of expectations);
- general awareness, with no formed attitudes, may lead to behavior (product trial) from which attitudes will eventuate (passive learning); and
- positive attitudes may need to be reinforced after trial of a new product (novelty).

Cognitive dissonance theory suggests marketers must provide consumers with positive information about the brand to reduce dissonance by reinforcing positive attitudes and avoiding negative attitudes. This can be done in several ways:

- advertising that provides supportive information about the product's quality and other desirable attributes in order to reassure the consumer;
- warranties and guarantees that reduce risk or doubt;
- follow-up contacts to ensure proper product use and maintenance;
- brochures and enclosures in the packaging to provide reassurance of satisfaction with the purchase and further information about use and maintenance; and
- post-purchase services and follow-ups on complaints.

Some of these strategies will be especially necessary when the purchase involves a new product, with which there was no previous experience.

All of the strategies discussed so far apply to high-involvement products, for which search, evaluation, and attitude formation occur before the purchase and with which the possibility of post-purchase dissonance always exists. The **theory of passive learning** suggests that for low-involvement products (Chapter 4), general awareness is followed by purchase and attitude formation occurs after. It is, therefore, in the interest of marketers to attempt to ensure positive attitudes after the purchase. Since involvement is low, interest and attitudes are weak, particularly from the point of view of brand preference. One way to generate brand preference and brand loyalty is to increase the level of involvement. Several strategies for doing so were reviewed in Chapter 4.

THE MEASUREMENT OF ATTITUDES

Since detailed treatment of the measurement of attitudes is beyond the scope of this book, only a general review of the subject will be attempted. A brief discussion of the main problems of attitude identification and measurement will be presented first, followed by description of the principal techniques employed.

Main Problems

Modern attitude measurement is based fundamentally on the Rosenberg-Fishbein multiattribute model. The expectancy-value concept is transformed in the consumer behavior context to evaluative criteria and their importance. Marketers measure the extent to which the consumer perceives the product to possess each attribute or evaluative criterion; instead of a simple positive or negative evaluation of each attribute, *importance ratings* of each attribute are obtained.

The identification of evaluative criteria is a problem. Because marketing researchers "attempt to identify a small number of attributes that correlate with consumer preferences or behaviors, such as buying a given brand or choosing between competing brands. . . . [these] evaluative criteria . . . . need not correspond to the salient beliefs about the product class nor to the salient beliefs about particular brands within the class."[26] In attempting to reduce the number of attributes to a relatively small and manageable set, marketers may eliminate salient beliefs.

Another problem is that marketers typically use attitudes toward brands and products to predict preferences or actual choice behavior. While some correlation does exist, for some products it is quite obvious that preference does not mean choice (see Chapter 11). For example, the Mercedes and the Jaguar may be the most preferred cars and yet they may be the least likely to be purchased. In other words, it might be better to measure, instead, attitudes toward the *act* of buying a product — that is, the purchase intention, which, according to Fishbein's extended model, is the result of the attitude toward the act and normative beliefs.

Other problems concern the **validity** of the actual measures taken. How questions are worded and in what context they are asked may influence the consumer's responses. For example, a direct question — "Do you like 7-UP?" — is likely to evoke a positive answer because the consumer's first reaction is to express agreement. The attitude expressed can be affected by the context in which an item is presented — in a list of products, for example. The attitude reported may be affected by the **halo effect** — where an object's specific attributes are judged in line with an overall positive evaluation of the object — or may be actually based on one feature to the exclusion of others, perhaps because of incomplete information, or of perceptual distortion. Frequently, therefore, indirect measures of attitude such as depth interviews, projective techniques, or group discussions yield better measures of attitude.[27] These techniques are also very useful in identifying the relevant criteria to measure attitudes.

The increasing application of the multi-attribute model has provided information about the beliefs and the evaluations behind the attitude and permitted an understanding of the causes of the attitude. For the marketer, such measures give insights into the extent to which current attitudes are based on incorrect or incomplete information — situations that should not be difficult to correct.

Principal Techniques

Application of the multi-attribute approach $(A_o = \sum_{i=1}^{n} B_i a_i)$ involves the following kinds of measures:[28]

Expectancy or Brand Instrumentality (B_i)

This describes the extent to which a brand is perceived to possess each of a number of evaluative criteria. Some also refer to this as the **satisfaction measure**. A typical question would be:

With respect to natural color, Sony color television sets are:
Extremely Unsatisfactory ——:——:——:——:——:——:—— Extremely Satisfactory
−3 −2 −1 0 +1 +2 +3

This is the format of the *semantic differential* developed by Osgood et al., which some consider to be by far the most important new contribution to attitude measurement.[29]

Sometimes the points in the scale are given verbal, rather than numerical tags:

With respect to natural color, Sony color television sets are:

Unsatis- factory	—:—:—:—:—:—:—	Satis- factory
	Extreme- Quite Slightly Neither Slightly Quite Extreme ly -ly	

Or a scale such as that shown below may be used:

With respect to natural color, Sony color television sets are:

Very Satisfactory						Very Unsatisfactory
1	2	3	4	5	6	7

A more popular form of the semantic differential employs polar adjectival opposites to describe the brand, a store, a company, or any other "object." Such measures for a number of attributes yield an image profile. One of the advantages of this approach is that the profile can be depicted in graphic form (see Chapter 6), which makes it easy to identify differences among brands. Examples of a few scales are given below:

How would you rate Sony color television sets on the following scales?

Natural color	— — — — — — —	Color not natural
Good value	— — — — — — —	Poor value
Reliable	— — — — — — —	Unreliable
Well made	— — — — — — —	Not well made
Expensive	— — — — — — —	Inexpensive

Other forms of these scales may include numerical and/or verbal tags, as shown above in the satisfaction measures.

Another type of scale that is widely used is the **Likert agreement scale**. Ratings are obtained on a five-point scale for one or more descriptive statements about the product or brand. In effect, each measure is a measure of B_i. In the example below, responses to the statements can be combined to produce a total attitude score.

	Strongly Agree	Agree	Neither Agree nor Disagree	Disagree	Strongly Disagree
Sony color TV sets are well made	—	—	—	—	—
Sony color TV sets are expensive	—	—	—	—	—
Sony color TV sets are good value	—	—	—	—	—

Value/Importance (a_i)

Attribute-importance may be measured with a scale like:

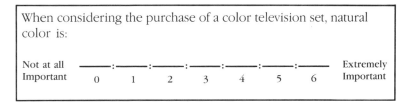

As with the B_i measures, verbal tags for each point may also be included.

Another approach is the use of **rank-order scales**, where a list of (say) seven attributes are ranked from most important (1) to least important (7). Ranking of too large a set of criteria (ten or more) can become unreliable.

The Likert scale can also be used to measure importance:

> Natural color is important in a television set:
>
> Strongly   Agree   Neither Agree   Disagree   Strongly
> Agree   nor Disagree   Disagree
> _____   _____   _____   _____   _____

The Total Attitude Index (A_o)

This scale is derived from combining the belief (B_i) and the importance (a_i) measures. Figure 12.5 provides an example of the derivation of the overall attitude index for a brand.

(Compensatory Processing)

Evaluative Criteria	Sony Belief Ratings (Semantic Differential) ($+3$ to -3) (B_i)	Importance of Criterion (7-point Scale) (a_i)	Belief × Importance ($B_i a_i$)	Maximum Possible
Natural Colors	$+2.5$	6	15	18
Price (Reasonable)	$+1$	3	3	9
Reliability	$+2$	2	4	6
Appearance	$+2.5$	1	2.5	3
		Overall Attitude =	24.5	36

FIGURE 12.5: Computation of Overall Attitude to Sony Televisions (Hypothetical)

Adapted from Icek Ajzen and Martin Fishbein, *Understanding Attitudes and Predicting Social Behavior* (Englewood Cliffs, New Jersey: Prentice-Hall, 1980), p. 154.

The determination of this overall attitude index permits:

- a comparison of the score with the maximum possible (in this example, Sony's rating was quite high); and
- the identification of the brand's strengths and weaknesses.

Ratings for several brands in a product category can provide an overall comparison of the various brands as well as point out their relative strengths and weaknesses (Figure 12.6).

Evaluative Criteria	Attribute Importance (Maximum = 7) (a_i)	Makes of Automobile (Max. = 7)						Maximum Rating Possible
		A		B		C		
		B_i	$B_i a_i$	B_i	$B_i a_i$	B_i	$B_i a_i$	
Styling	3	4	12	4	12	6	18	21
Fuel Economy	6	6	36	5	30	6	36	42
Acceleration	3	4	12	5	15	6	18	21
Low Maintenance	5	5	25	3	15	4	20	35
Reliable Starts	6	4	24	3	18	6	36	42
Roominess	4	4	16	2	8	6	24	28
TOTALS			125		98		152	189

FIGURE 12.6: Attitude Ratings of Three Makes of Automobile (Hypothetical)

Note that C came closest to the ideal. Except for maintenance costs, C was highly rated on all criteria. Car A's main strengths were its good fuel economy and relatively low maintenance costs. Car B was weakest on maintenance costs, roominess, and reliable starts.

Where the Fishbein Intentions Model is used, there are several variables to be measured, as shown below:

$$B \sim BI = \sum_{i=1}^{n} B_i a_i (w_o) + \sum_{j=1}^{k} NB_j MC_j (w_1)$$

These variables are:

B_i = a belief (the probability or improbability) that performing the behavior will lead to an ith outcome

a_i = the negative or positive feeling (or evaluation) toward the ith outcome

n = the number of salient outcomes (e.g., the results or benefits of using a product)

NB_j = a normative belief, that is, the belief that a jth relevant other expects the individual to perform or not perform the behavior

MC_j = the individual's motivation to comply or not comply with the expectation of the jth other

$$k = \text{the number of relevant other persons or groups}$$

$$w_o \text{ and } w_1 = \text{empirically determined standardized regression coefficients (beta weights)}$$

$$BI = \text{the behavioral intention to perform or not perform the specific behavior.}$$

Note that in this case the attitude component $(B_i a_i)$ is not the attitude to the object but rather the attitude to the act of purchasing. *Beliefs* will be expressed as a probability that the act will give certain outcomes. For example:

How likely do you feel it is that Brand X camera does not require you to make your own setting for light and distance?

Likely   +3   +2   +1   0   −1   −2   −3   Unlikely
       ___:___:___:___:___:___:___
       Extreme- Quite Slightly Neither Slightly Quite Extreme-
       ly   ly

Sometimes the scale is reduced to six points by dropping the middle ("neither") category. The *evaluation* of the outcome is also measured in terms of a good/bad scale with either seven or six points.

How good do you feel it is that Brand X camera does not require you to make your own setting for light and distance?

Good   +3   +2   +1   0   −1   −2   −3   Bad
      ___:___:___:___:___:___:___
      Extreme- Quite Slightly Neither Slightly Quite Extreme-
      ly   ly

These **salient outcomes** are generated from a preliminary sample of respondents from the relevant population. The respondents are asked questions such as, "What do you see as the advantages/disadvantages of buying Brand X?" Behavioral belief statements are then constructed linking the act (of purchase) to each modal salient outcome selected.

Normative Beliefs

In the interview with the preliminary sample, questions are also asked about **salient referents** (questions such as, "Are there any groups of people who would approve/disapprove of your purchasing Brand

X?") and from the responses obtained, normative belief statements with respect to each salient referent are constructed. For example:

> How likely do you feel it is that your spouse wants you to buy a camera like Brand X?
>
> Likely   +3   +2   +1   0   −1   −2   −3   Unlikely
>
>   Extreme-   Quite   Slightly   Neither   Slightly   Quite   Extreme-
>   ly   ly

The same would be done for other salient referents — such as, in this case, other members of the family or close friends.

Motivation to Comply

The motivation to comply is asked with respect to *each* salient referent about whom a normative belief statement is constructed. For example:

> To what extent do you think you would comply or not comply with what your spouse would like you to do?
>
> Comply ——:——:——:——:——:——:—— Not comply
>   3   2   1   0   1   2   3

Another format would read as follows:

> I intend to comply with what my spouse would like me to do:
>
>   True ——:——:——:——:——:——:—— False

Behavioral Intention

It is possible to statistically derive the behavioral intention measure by combining the weighted belief/evaluation component and the normative belief/motivation-to-comply component.

This can also be empirically determined by asking respondents a direct question, such as:

> How likely do you feel it is that you will buy a Brand X camera in the next thirty days?
>
> Likely   +3   +2   +1   0   −1   −2   −3   Unlikely
>
>   Extreme-   Quite   Slightly   Neither   Slightly   Quite   Extreme-
>   ly   ly

Response Reliability

In order to determine the reliability of the responses, it is possible to measure each variable in three different ways, permitting an estimate of internal consistency.[30] For example, in addition to measuring beliefs on a likely/unlikely scale, two other scales may be used: possible/impossible and probable/improbable. Phrasing of the question is appropriately changed.

The same could be done for normative beliefs and behavioral intention.

The evaluation variable could use beneficial/harmful and wise/foolish, in addition to good/bad. The motivation-to-comply question could also be asked using obey/not obey and conform/not conform scales.

SUMMARY

This chapter examined attitude change and attitude measurement.

A number of theories attempt to explain why individuals change their attitudes, including functional theory, consistency theory, cognitive dissonance theory, and social judgement theory. These were reviewed and their implications for attitude change discussed. Specific change strategies applicable before purchase were outlined in terms of multi-attribute models, and functional and balance theories. Specific techniques — such as those involving the content and structure of messages, fear and humor appeals, repetition, sequence of arguments, and one-sided versus two-sided messages — were evaluated.

The relevance of cognitive dissonance theory for attitude change strategies after purchase,

particularly for high-involvement decisions, was emphasized. The theory of passive learning was shown to be applicable to low-involvement situations.

The identification of evaluative criteria and the low attitude-behavior correlation pointed out significant problems in attitude measurement. It was suggested that Fishbein's extended model may be a more effective approach to attitude measurement because it determines behavioral intention.

The chapter concluded with a brief review of the principal techniques employed in measuring expectancy and importance where attitude-to-the-object multi-attribute models are used. It also examined the techniques used to measure the key variables when the Fishbein extended model is applied.

QUESTIONS

1. Define cognitive dissonance. In what kinds of circumstances is it likely to occur?

2. "Attitude change is but one of the ways in which the individual resolves inconsistency." Discuss.

3. What are the contributions of social judgement theory to the question of attitude change?

4. To what kinds of attitude change strategies does the multi-attribute model lend itself?

5. Show how understanding the functions that attitudes serve can be very useful in attempting attitude change.

6. What is the effect of source credibility on attitude change? Discuss with reference to the research evidence reviewed in the chapter.

7. How can message content and structure be used to effect attitude change?

8. Write an essay on the strengths and weaknesses of attitude measurement in consumer behavior.

NOTES TO CHAPTER 12

[1] Adapted from "Chrysler Sets Out to Explode Import 'Myths' in Latest Ad Round," *Marketing* (7 May 1984).

[2] Adapted from Frances Phillips, "The Fleischmann's Fuss Jolts Advertising Industry," *Financial Post* (31 March 1984).

[3] Peter Suedfeld (ed.), *Attitude Change: The Competing Views* (Chicago: Aldine Atherton, 1971), pp. 1-7.

[4] David Krech, Richard S. Crutchfield, and Egerton L. Ballachey, *Individual in Society* (New York: McGraw-Hill, 1962), pp. 144-5.

[5] C.A. Kiesler, "Commitment," in R.P. Abelson et al. (eds.), *Theories of Cognitive Consistency: A Sourcebook* (Chicago: Rand, McNally, 1968), pp. 448-55.

[6] J.W. Brehm and A.R. Cohen, "Re-evaluation of Choice Alternatives as a Function of Their Number and Qualitative Similarity," *Journal of Abnormal and Social Psychology*, 58 (1959), pp. 373-8.

[7] H.T. Greenwald, "Dissonance and Relative vs. Absolute Attractiveness of Decision Alternatives," *Journal of Personality and Social Psychology*, 11 (1969), pp. 328-33.

[8] Brehm and Cohen, op. cit.

[9] A.R. Cohen, J.W. Brehm, and W.H. Fleming, "Attitude Change and Justification for Compliance," *Journal of Abnormal and Social Psychology*, 56 (1957), pp. 276-8.

[10] A sub-set of consistency theory, *balance theory*, explains such a response in terms of the relationships in a given person's experience between the person, some other person, and some event, idea, or object. If, because of the relationships, attitude to the object cannot change, then attitude to the other person will, in order to establish balance or harmony. See R.B. Zajonc, "The Concepts of Balance, Congruity, and Dissonance," *The Public Opinion Quarterly* 24 (Summer 1960), pp. 280-96; A. Rodrigues, "Effects of Balance, Positivity, and Agreement in Triadic Social Relations," *Journal of Personality and Social Psychology*, 5 (1967), pp. 472-6.

[11] William H. Cummings and M. Venkatesan, "Cognitive Dissonance and Consumer Behavior: A Review of the Evidence," *Journal of Marketing Research*, 12 (August 1976), pp. 303-8.

[12] C.W. Sherif, M. Sherif, and R.W. Nebergall, *Attitudes and Attitude Change* (New Haven, Connecticut: Yale University Press, 1961).

[13] Richard J. Lutz, "Changing Brand Attitudes Through Modification of Cognitive Structure," *Journal of Consumer Research*, 1 (March 1975), pp. 49-59; "An Experimental Investigation of Causal Relations Among Cognitions, Affect, and Behavioral Intention," *Journal of Consumer Research*, 3 (March 1977), pp. 197-208; Andrew A. Mitchell and Jerry C. Olson, "Are Product Attribute Beliefs the Only Mediator of Advertising Effects on Brand Attitude?" *Journal of Marketing Research*, 18 (August 1981), pp. 318-32.

[14] Robert E. Matfey, "Attitude Change Induced by Role Playing as a Function of Improvisation and Role-Taking Skill," *Journal of Personality and Social Psychology*, 24: 3 (1972), p. 343.

[15] Bobby J. Calder, "Cognitive Consistency and Consumer Behavior," in James U. McNeal and Stephen W. McDaniel (eds.), *Consumer Behavior: Classical and Contemporary Dimensions* (Boston: Little, Brown, 1982), pp. 78-92.

[16] Ibid., p. 80.

[17] Brian Sternthal, Ruby Dholakia, and Clark Leavitt, "The Persuasive Effect of Source Credibility: Tests of Cognitive Response," *Journal of Consumer Research*, 4 (March 1978), pp. 252-60.

[18] Martin Fishbein and Icek Ajzen, *Belief, Attitude, Intention and Behavior: An Introduction to Theory and Research* (Reading, Massachusetts: Addison-Wesley, 1975), Chapter 11; J. Whittaker, "Opinion Changes as a Function of Communication/Attitude Discrepancy," *Psychological Reports*, 13 (1963), pp. 763-72.

[19] M. Ray and W. Wilkie, "Fear: The Potential of an Appeal Neglected by Marketing," *Journal of Marketing*, 34 (1970), pp. 59-62.

[20] Brian Sternthal and C. Samuel Craig, "Fear Appeals: Revisited and Revised," *Journal of Consumer Research*, 1 (December 1974), pp. 26-7.

[21] M. Venkatesan and G.A. Haaland, "The Effect of Distraction on the Influence of Persuasive Marketing Communications," in J. Arndt (ed.), *Insights into Consumer Behavior* (Boston: Allyn and Bacon, 1968), pp. 55-66; D.M. Gardner, "The Distraction Hypothesis in Marketing," *Journal of Advertising Research*, 10 (1970), pp. 25-30.

[22] Harriett Amster, "Semantic Satiation and Generation: Learning? Adaptation?" *Psychological Bulletin*, 62 (1964), pp. 273-86.

[23]C. Samuel Craig, Brian Sternthal, and Clark Leavitt, "Advertising Wearout: An Experimental Analysis," *Journal of Marketing Research*, 13 (November 1976), pp. 365-72.

[24]E.W. Faison, "Effectiveness of One-Sided and Two-Sided Mass Communications in Advertising," *Public Opinion Quarterly*, 25 (1961), pp. 468-9; Robert B. Settle and Linda L. Golden, "Attribution Theory and Advertiser Credibility," *Journal of Marketing Research*, 11 (May 1974), pp. 181-5.

[25]R. Haas and D. Linder, "Counterargument Availability and the Effects of Message Structure on Persuasion," *Journal of Personality and Social Psychology*, 23 (August 1972), pp. 219-33.

[26]Icek Ajzen and Martin Fishbein, *Understanding Attitudes and Predicting Social Behavior* (Englewood Cliffs, New Jersey: Prentice-Hall, 1980), p. 158.

[27]Gilbert A. Churchill, *Marketing Research*, 2nd ed., (Hinsdale, Illinois: Dryden Press, 1979), pp. 167-74.

[28]Much of this discussion is adapted from: M. Fishbein and I. Ajzen, *Belief, Attitude, Intention, and Behavior: An Introduction to Theory and Research* (Reading, Massachusetts: Addison-Wesley, 1975); Icek Ajzen and Martin Fishbein, *Understanding Attitudes and Predicting Social Behavior* (Englewood Cliffs, New Jersey: Prentice-Hall, 1980); James F. Engel, Roger D. Blackwell, and David T. Kollat, *Consumer Behavior*, 3rd ed. (Hinsdale, Illinois: Dryden Press, 1978), pp. 400-2; and Michael J. Ryan and E.H. Bonfield, "Fishbein's Intentions Model: A Test of External and Pragmatic Validity," *Journal of Marketing*, 44 (Spring 1980), pp. 82-95.

[29]C.E. Osgood, G.J. Suci, and P.H. Tannenbaum, *The Measurement of Meaning* (Urbana, Illinois: University of Illinois Press, 1957).

[30]Ryan and Bonfield, op. cit., pp. 86, 92-3.

ATTITUDES TOWARD PRODUCT CHANGE (MARTHA VINE COMPANY)*

The Martha Vine Company produced a line of cosmetics including cold cream, facial cleanser, and hand lotion. Hand lotion was the largest seller in the company's product line. Over the past two years, sales of the company's hand lotion had declined 19.8%, whereas total industry sales of this product had remained the same or shown a slight increase. Martha Vine executives were concerned about this situation and were looking for some way in which to improve the sales of their hand lotion. The advertising manager proposed the blending of Vitamin A to the present lotion as a way of providing a product change that could be effectively dramatized in advertising.

The advertising manager believed that adding Vitamin A to the hand lotion would make the product more desirable because of the favorable public image of vitamins. Vitamin additives to cosmetics were not an entirely new idea, but in his opinion improper exploitation of the idea was the reason for its negligible use in hand lotions.

Other company executives felt that a vitamin additive to the lotion would have little, if any, appeal to users of the product. They pointed out that the use of vitamins was not usually associated with any external application and might make the company look ridiculous. Furthermore, some felt that the addition of Vitamin A might have an adverse effect on the product image among women who would tend to regard it as a non-essential ingredient for which they might be asked to pay a price premium. Others thought that a vitamin additive would increase production costs and perhaps place the company at a competitive disadvantage. A few also questioned whether the vitamin feature could be effectively dramatized in the company's advertising so as to have any real sales appeal.

When asked whether it would be feasible, cost-wise, to add Vitamin A to the company's hand lotion, and whether its addition would create

---

* Adapted from Stuart Henderson Britt (ed.), *Consumer Behavior and the Behavioral Sciences* (Toronto: John Wiley & Sons Canada, 1967), pp. 149-50.

any production problems, the company's chief chemist indicated that such an additive would create no manufacturing problem and that the cost would be negligible. In the light of this opinion and also the objections that had been raised, the advertising manager discussed the idea with the firm's advertising agency and the company's account supervisor. The latter suggested that before discussing the matter further the agency should make some effort to find out from lotion users what they thought of the idea. The advertising manager agreed that this type of inquiry would be worthwhile.

The agency research director had an outside interviewing firm make a survey on this problem among a sample of three hundred housewives who were representative of three metropolitan markets. Respondents were asked whether or not they thought Vitamin A would do any good in a hand lotion and whether the addition of such an ingredient would interest them personally. The research director's written report to the Martha Vine account supervisor concluded as follows:

- 37% of the respondents believed Vitamin A would do some good in a hand lotion. Of this number about half said they would be interested in trying the newly prepared hand lotion.
- Those respondents who stated that the addition of Vitamin A to the hand lotion would do little or no good gave as their reason the opinion that for vitamins to be effective they would have to be taken internally rather than used externally.

The findings of the survey were presented to the Martha Vine advertising manager, together with the account supervisor's recommendation to go ahead with the idea. The account supervisor, in his discussion of the matter said: "After all, 37% of the women queried indicated that the addition of Vitamin A would do some good in a hand lotion, and none of them indicated that it would do any harm. This ingredient should lend itself to effective product promotion and dramatic advertising copy appeal. It should be another plus factor in our favor. Our present appeals include such facts as (1) our hand lotion gives longer protection than competing ones; (2) the user requires a smaller amount for application; (3) our lotion has faster absorption qualities, and (4) it is less greasy than other lotions. Adding the Vitamin A to our present product would certainly enhance the product's desirability to users of hand lotion."

QUESTIONS

1. Evaluate the marketing research design employed in the consumer study. How does it affect your interpretation of the results?

2. Identify the relevant consumer behavioral concepts (mainly attitudinal) and outline what other kinds of information would be desirable.

3. What recommendation would you consider making to the advertising manager of the Martha Vine Company? Give reasons.

13

Psychographics: Personality and Life-Style

EXAMPLES

1. Sheaffer Pens

Figure 13.1 provides an example of a marketer's attempt to match the product with the consumer's self-image:

" . . . . the pen you choose say(s) a lot about you . . ."

"Choosing a Sheaffer shows you appreciate a superior pen that makes a gift of distinction."

2. The Canadian Cigarette Industry

One of the responses of advertisers to the cigarette broadcast advertising ban in the early 1970s was to take advantage of the health concerns of smokers by expanding and broadening their product lines to include a variety of low-tar, low-nicotine cigarettes.[1] Almost all brands now have a *light* equivalent.

The large number of brands and the strong reliance on advertising for brand differentiation suggests that choice among brands is based on non-product characteristics. One possibility is the appeal that the different marketing combinations (product + brand name + promotion) have for different personality types. Export A, for example, appeals to the strong, traditional smoker who likes a full-flavored cigarette. This is matched in the US by the preference of the virile outdoorsman for Malboro.

3. The Canadian Beer Industry

The Canadian beer industry is also characterized by a large number of brands, with an increasing proportion of light brands. Light-tasting

FIGURE 13.1: Product Choice and Self-Image
Courtesy Sheaffer Eaton Textron

US brands, such as Budweiser and Miller High Life, were introduced in 1983. There are also special premium brands, Bock beers, and European brands manufactured in Canada (Amstel, Lowenbrau). With all of these additions, the total number of domestically produced brands available is close to fifty.

Beer taste tests frequently cannot distinguish among certain brands and yet consumers develop preferences for and loyalties to specific brands. Much of this is attributable to advertising and other promotional activities. Three of the top ten advertisers in Canada are breweries — Carling, Labatt, and Molson. Until early 1984, they had little that could be used to differentiate their brands. All beer was sold in identical bottles, at the same price, and the product was essentially the same. The influx of US and European-style brands brought the introduction of new bottles.

Nevertheless, brand choice in the beer industry is very much a result of the match between brand image created by advertising and consumer self-image or life-style. The examples of beer brand advertising described below reflect this relationship:

- Molson Export — "Like an old friend." The boys get together for some type of activity and then enjoy an Ex or two.[2]
- Molson Golden — "The with-it crowd." Young achievers at poolside parties having fun and enjoying Golden.
- Labatt '50 — "Cutting out of here," and going to relax with the boys.

These examples illustrate how marketers' offerings, fortuitously or by design, appeal to different kinds of individuals. It is only common sense to expect that different consumers, as different "bundles of needs," will seek to satisfy these needs with different products or different "bundles of satisfactions."[3] It is plausible that different personalities will seek and want different products.

The exact composition of those satisfactions will vary from one buyer to the next, even for the same object. Some of the utilities sought in the purchase may relate directly to the physical performance of the object, but even when they do, they may not offer the greatest value for some of the buyers, other satisfactions may be gained solely because of learned associations, and some may inhere in the place and manner of sale. Even when the components of satisfaction are the same for two buyers, each may place the emphasis on different components in the set and value each differently. Any single physical product is therefore many market products.[4]

What Is Personality?

Despite this "obvious connection" between personality and product choice, the research evidence does not demonstrate its objective existence in consumer behavior. Before we address this problem, however, let us agree on what we mean by personality.

When I use the expression "different kinds of individuals" I mean their psychological rather than physical characteristics. Psychologists agree that internal "make-up" does affect behavior, whatever system they use to identify different make-ups. In the most general sense, I define personality as *the characteristic ways in which an individual copes with the environment*. This includes both action and thought (overt and covert behavior), as stated by Allport: "Personality is the dynamic organization within the individual of those psychophysical systems that determine his [her] characteristic behavior and thought."[5]

Personality is, therefore, an integrative concept; it brings together, in unique combinations, different needs, motives, abilities, interests, values, attitudes, and behavioral and emotional patterns.

WHY STUDY PERSONALITY IN CONSUMER BEHAVIOR?

From the marketer's point of view, the primary significance of personality lies in the extent to which:

- different types of personality can be identified;
- these types are homogeneous;
- these types are numerically large enough; and
- these types behave differently as consumers.

The major potential usefulness of studying personality in consumer behavior resides in its ability to **segment** a market.

If personality segments are easily and clearly identifiable and offer real target markets, then the efficiency of marketing strategy will be enhanced:

- "product bundles" will be more closely tailored to the requirements of the consumer (product positioning);
- product appeals will be more likely to be on target (advertising);
- proper demographic and behavioral data about the segment will mean improved media selection;
- better psychological understanding will enhance the appropriateness and effectiveness of promotional messages by permitting the development of moods and emotions that will be more relevant to and compatible with the segment;
- the identification of certain consumers with unmet needs will lead to opportunities for developing and offering new products.

PERSONALITY STUDIES IN CONSUMER BEHAVIOR

In an earlier section, I referred to the lack of evidence of a significant correlation between personality and consumer behavior. This section reviews the existing evidence and then considers some of the reasons for its failure to support what appears to be a logical relationship.

Marketing Evidence

In a review of the literature on consumer behavior and personality, Kassarjian concluded that "these dozens of studies and papers can be summarized in the single word, *equivocal*."[6]

As an example, he referred to the "landmark study" by Evans who "could find no differences between Ford and Chevrolet owners to an extent that would allow for prediction."[7] The study was criticized for its sample, the cars rated, and the analysis, until Evans decided to replicate the study. Different analytic manipulations were attempted but the facts did not change much.

> The final conclusion that seems to trickle through is that personality does account for some variance but not enough to give much solace to personality researchers in marketing.[8]

As another example, Kassarjian reported a study by Koponen with a panel sample of nine thousand respondents.[9] His results indicated a positive relationship between cigarette smoking and certain personality characteristics and differences between filter and non-filter smokers. Using the same data, Massy, Frank, and Lodahl found that personality accounted for a very small percentage of the variance in the purchase of coffee, tea, and beer.[10]

Employing the notion that there is a congruence between the symbolic image of a product and a consumer's self-image, Birdwell studied automobile owners to test if their image of their car was congruent with their self-image and if a specific car is perceived differently by the owners of different cars.[11] As Kassarjian observes, "the hypotheses were confirmed with varying degrees of strength. However, this does not imply that products have personalities and that a consumer purchases those brands whose images are congruent with his self-concept; Birdwell's study did not test causality. It could very well be that the owner begins to perceive a product as an extension of his own personality, only after he has purchased it."[12]

Kassarjian's entire review underlines the contradictory results that have been obtained by different researchers. Another important finding is that, even where positive correlations were obtained between personality and purchase behavior, the correlations were such as to account for between only 5% and 10% of the variance.

In summary, "a few studies indicate a strong relationship between personality and aspects of consumer behavior, a few indicate no relationship, and the great majority indicate that if correlations do exist they are so weak as to be questionable or perhaps meaningless."[13]

Why Personality Studies in Consumer Behavior May Have Failed

The possible reasons for the equivocal results obtained from personality studies range from the characteristics of the personality-testing instruments to the conditions under which they are administered to the relevance of the respondents whose personalities are measured.

As we consider them, the results so far obtained may not be so surprising after all. The reliability and validity of the instruments used for measuring personality have not been high enough. In applying such tests, marketers seem to have ignored reliability and validity data. For example, a "good" instrument may have a validity coefficient anywhere from .40 to .70 so that, when correlated against a criterion variable, it may account for about 20% to 40% of the variance. Considering that these borrowed

tests were developed for specific populations (e.g., college students), for specific purposes (e.g., mental hospital admission), and that they are now being applied to the general population, one should be prepared to accept lower values.

One author cited the Edwards Personal Preference Schedule (EPPS) as "the personality test most frequently used in consumer personality research" and suggested that too often marketing researchers not only have ignored the technical characteristics of standard personality tests but have been influenced by such factors as simple scoring, and the availability of results for comparison purposes.[14] Because it measures intraindividual differences, the EPPS cannot be used for interindividual comparisons. Consequently, Horton notes that all such tests are not appropriate for consumer behavior research, which typically requires such comparisons.[15]

The test is likely to be given under conditions quite different from those that were intended. Most of the personality tests were intended for the clinic or office of a psychotherapist or counsellor and not for the classroom, doorstep, or living room. In addition, the respondents do not have the same attitudes as the individual in a clinical or therapeutic situation. The latter, most likely, wants help and is far less inclined to falsify or mislead. On the other hand, consumers, in such a situation, could have a greater tendency to indicate what they want others to think they are or what they would like to be.

Personality tests in marketing have possibly been unsuccessful because they are often abbreviated or modified to fit the circumstances. Items may be taken out of context, words changed, and items dropped; this lowers the efficacy of the instrument because:

- the items that normally precede and follow a given item may be dropped and this could, for example, make the purpose of the item more obvious and facilitate faking;
- changing words may alter the meaning and validity of the item.

Correlations can be weakened by invalid measurement of the criterion variable, which, because it is based on the report of the consumer, may be inaccurate. For example, such a simple measure as brand used regularly may, for social reasons, be reported incorrectly.

In most, if not all, cases, personality tests measure broad general traits, such as sociability and emotional stability. "It is a different story to use them to predict whether a shopper would buy a particular brand of toilet paper"[16] or purchase a washing machine.

Marketers may have been "too microscopic" in their attempts to uncover personality differences by testing such closely related and similar products as Chevrolets and Fords. They may be more successful with a product category or with brands that are clearly quite different (Chevrolet versus Volkswagen), particularly with specially designed instruments.[17]

Marketers have tended to make the assumption that product choice is the decision of the buyer or owner. This is not always the case. For example, automobiles purchased may not be significantly correlated with the personality of the male head of the household (the owner) because product choice is a family decision and does not necessarily reflect the needs, preferences, and attitudes of the owner alone.

Finally, consumer behaviorists have been unrealistic and have expected too much of personality measures.

Social scientists do not get upset that personality is not the only relevant variable or that the portion of the explained variance is merely 20% or 10% or 5%. Yet personality researchers in consumer behavior much too often ignore the many interrelated influences on the consumer decision process, ranging from price and packaging to availability, advertising, group influences, learned responses and preferences of family members, in addition to personality. *To expect the influence of personality variables to account for a large portion of the variance is most certainly asking too much.* What is amazing is not that there are many studies that

show no correlation between consumer behavior and personality, but rather that there are any studies at all with positive results. That 5% or 10% or any portion of the variance can be accounted for by personality variables measured on ill-chosen and inadequate instruments is most remarkable, indeed![18]

How Marketers Should Measure Personality

Like Kassarjian (if we read between the lines correctly), I am confident that the intuitive plausibility of a behavior-personality correlation is matched by the possibility of its objective measurement, *with the right kinds of instruments.*

Consumer behaviorists should not rely on measures developed by others. They "must develop their own definitions and design their own instruments to measure the personality variables that go into the purchase decision."[19] Marketers should build tests making use of marketing-related items. Activities, Interests, and Opinion (AIO) inventories (which I discuss later in this chapter under Life-Style Research) are a step in that direction but they too suffer from their generality.[20] The mere fact that they seek to correlate over three hundred items with a large number (thirty to forty) of different products reduces their ability to discriminate within products. Measures are meaningful only when they are situation- or product-specific and not of a generalized nature. "For example, instead of searching for the general trait of self-confidence, it is better to determine the extent to which consumers are self-confident in evaluating (and choosing) different brands within the product category."[21]

Once it is determined whether personality measures in consumer behavior can be generalized across product and service classes or are product-specific, researchers can turn their attention to how to use such data — market segmentation, segment description, or the creation of advertising and promotional programs.

APPROACHES TO DESCRIBING PERSONALITY — THEORIES OF PERSONALITY

While the existence of many personality types may be incontrovertible, there is no agreed-upon basis for classification. In the course of the development of psychology, several different approaches have evolved to explain differences in character or temperament.[22]

> A successful theory must weave together the various strands descriptive of individuality into a fabric that has enduring, identifiable features, unique for each individual yet permitting individuals to be compared to each other. There are many theories — partly because personality is so loosely defined that all theories do not deal with the same subject matter, partly because the facts upon which a finished theory must rest are not yet well enough known.[23]

Each of these theories reflects a different philosophy of human nature and attempts to provide an integrated explanation of the consistencies in human behavior. Four personality theories have been most influential in consumer behavior: trait theory, psychoanalytic theory, socio-psychoanalytic theory, and self-concept theory.

Trait Theory

Trait theory has been more widely used in marketing than any other personality theory. **Trait** generally denotes a basic characteristic or underlying predisposition to respond in a particular way. Personality types are described as combinations of different traits.

Perhaps the most attractive feature of trait theory, and no doubt the reason for its extensive application in consumer behavior studies, is its ease of measurement and quantification. The marketing studies discussed earlier all made use of trait theory. Indeed, most of the psycho-logical personality inventories are based on trait theory.

Several things should be noted about trait theory. It describes but does not explain personality. Trait theory is also referred to as *factor theory* because, through statistical procedures, a large number of measured traits may be reduced or related to a smaller number of more basic, underlying traits. Because of the amorphous nature of the concept of trait, different researchers develop different lists of traits — and the number of traits is considerable.

Here is an example of one list of traits that were grouped on the basis of different aspects of the personality:[24]

- **Drive traits**: activity, sensory awareness, and sexuality;
- **Temperamental traits**: emotionality, optimism, and expressiveness;
- **Perceptual traits**: thinking, extroversion, speed of closure, and flexibility of closure;
- **Self traits**: self-extension, self-confidence, and self-insight;
- **Value traits**: economic, religious, scientific, aesthetic, and liberal values;
- **Problem-solving traits**: ambition, emotional control, orderliness, and intelligence;
- **Human-relations traits**: gregariousness, dominance, warmth, and conformity.

Each trait is measured using a Likert-type agreement scale (with five or seven points) or a true-false response to a number of statements. For example, for the activity trait, statements such as the following would be used:

> I spend myself freely, since I have plenty of energy.
> I am extremely active in my everyday life.
> I like long periods of physical exertion.
> I am a restless person.
> I get restless when I have to wait for very long.
> I am very tense about the things that interest me.[25]

Personality types identified by trait theory are based on the deeper, underlying traits derived from the factor analytic procedures. Cattell refers to these as "source traits."[26] Examples of such personality types are reserved/outgoing, humble/assertive, sober/happy-go-lucky, self-assured/apprehensive, relaxed/tense.[27]

Psychoanalytic Theory (Freud)

The psychoanalytic theory of personality developed by Sigmund Freud has had a profound influence in psychology and psychotherapy. Over the last thirty years it has also had a significant impact on marketing, particularly with reference to unconscious motives, sexuality, and conflict of motives.

Underlying Personality Make-Up

According to Freud, the personality consists of three components — the id, ego, and superego. The **id** consists of basic innate instincts or urges. It has no direct access to the environment and operates through the **ego**, which, on the basis of experience, directs, restrains, and controls the urgings of the id. In other words, the ego, when functioning properly, exercises rational control and determines the environmental objects that will gratify the desires of the id. The **superego** is that part of the personality that exercises moral control on the behavior of the individual. Unlike the ego, which is the executive, rational part of the personality, the superego derives its authority from the unconscious.

This conceptualization of the personality should not be interpreted as suggesting an objective existence to the three parts within the organism; it should be viewed as expressing dynamic relationships among psychological processes. It points to a few basic characteristics of personality:

- unconscious motives;
- rational control;
- unconscious control; and
- conflict of motives.

In summary, the id, ego, and superego may be viewed as having the relationships shown in Figure 13.2.

Component	Source	Aim
id ego supergo	biological psychological social	pleasure reality ideal (perfection) (moral)

FIGURE 13.2: Characteristics of the Freudian Theory of Personality

Personality Development

Freud believed that the first few years of life were the formative years in the development of an individual's personality. The young organism's sensitivity changed from one zone of the body to another as time progressed; the satisfactions and frustrations experienced at each stage laid the groundwork for the adult personality. He identified five important stages:

- oral — source of pleasure is the mouth (0 to eighteen months);
- anal — primary pleasure comes from relieving anal tension (elimination), (eighteen months to three years);
- phallic — pleasure from the newly discovered sex organs (three to five years);
- latency — sexual instincts are dormant and no important personality changes take place (five to adolescence);
- genital — heterosexual pleasure (puberty and adolescence).

Personality Types

In the course of the psychological development of the individual, the interaction between the id, ego, and superego at the various developmental stages results in the persistence of certain kinds of behavior related to the particular stage at which the organism experienced frustration. Freud called this **fixation** because the solutions the individual applies to the removal of anxiety seem to become the basic pattern for all of the individual's later adjustment to the world. Freud identified broad types related to the developmental stages: oral, anal, phallic, and genital.

Within each of these there may be subtypes, such as "anal expulsive" (aggressive, mean, emotional, as in the elimination process) and "anal retentive" (very strict toilet training that led to the postponement of elimination and later to a compulsive, stingy, obstinate, extremely neat personality).

I referred above to the handling of **anxiety**. Anxiety is a basic concept in Freudian theory; it is the apprehensive reaction that occurs when the ego feels threatened, faced with a situation that must be handled. Such situations can be motive conflicts within the personality or internal-external conflicts. Where the ego cannot handle the situation directly through behavioral change, it will seek to falsify or distort the situation before resolving it. The mechanisms it resorts to are called mechanisms of defence.

The basic defence mechanism is **repression**, which seeks to remove or alleviate anxiety by forcing the threatening impulses into the unconscious. They may not re-enter consciousness but they may be expressed in dreams, and neurotic reactions, such as rationalization, projection, regression, compensation, denial, fantasy, identification, displacement, and sublimation.[28] Because they are unconscious, they cannot be tapped by standard marketing research techniques.

Rationalization finds an acceptable reason for behavior rather than the real one, which is usually a motive that is threatening to the individual. For example, the consumer who purchases a fur coat for status reasons may justify the purchase with rationalizations such as "it is warmer than cloth," or "it will not go out of style." In such a case, it may be wise for the marketer to employ the rationalizations in advertising and to imply the "irrational" reason.

Projection occurs when an individual attributes to others the inner urges that he or she finds unacceptable.[29] For example, those uncomfortable with their sexual desires may see sexual improprieties in others. Marketing researchers sometimes attempt to make use of projection by asking consumers to indicate what they think are the reasons for the actions of others.

In defence of the self or in frustrating situations, an individual may find it less threatening or frustrating to "redefine" the situation and **regress** to childish or immature behavior. For example, a consumer may react with uncontrollable rage if a favorite product is not available, or an individual may react to frustration by turning to chocolates (because of the reward value they had in childhood years). When this kind of defence is indicated, marketers can make use of mood advertising intended to evoke happy experiences of earlier times.

Individuals tend to engage in **compensatory** behavior when other responses are frustrated. For example, the high consumption of butter and Scotch whisky by US blacks has been described as compensation for the social status frustrations they suffer in other areas of their lives.[30]

Denial is the tendency to shut out reality. In situations of cognitive dissonance, for example, a consumer may resolve the problem by "denying" any inconsistency.

Fantasy is another mechanism by which an individual escapes present frustrations and makes life easy to bear. Personal products (such as furs, cosmetics, perfume, luxury cars, and clothing) provide effective vehicles for fantasy (see Plate IV).

As a defence mechanism, **identification** provides a solution to frustration by making it possible for an individual to obtain satisfaction through the experiences of others. Sports heroes, movie stars, and rock singers provide outlets for identification and are used extensively in advertising.

Displacement and **sublimation** were considered by Freud to be the healthiest defence mechanisms. Displacement involves displacing unacceptable desires into more acceptable forms.[31] The overweight consumer, for example, is tempted to order apple pie *à la mode* for dessert but chooses yogurt instead. Sublimation is a special form of displacement, wherein baser libidinal urges are channelled into higher cultural values.

Psychoanalytic Theory (Jung)

Carl Gustav Jung was another psychoanalyst who made significant contributions to the understanding of human behavior; some of his insights have been helpful in consumer behavior, although most of their potential usefulness is yet to be realized.

Carl Jung and Sigmund Freud were associates at one point and together founded, early in their acquaintance, an international psychoanalytic society. But it soon became clear that Jung's ideas deviated quite considerably from Freud's, to the point where Freud insisted that Jung cease calling himself a psychoanalyst. Jung eventually referred to himself as "an analytical psychologist." Jung placed less importance than did Freud on the sexual character of the libido and disagreed with Freud on infantile sexuality.

Structure and Types

In Jung's theory, the psyche is composed of the conscious and the unconscious, one complementary to the other. This is only one of several **polarities** (introversion/extroversion, thinking/feeling, sense perception/intuition).

Jung's concept of the unconscious allows for deeper and deeper layers. The least deep is the **personal unconscious** (composed of material repressed by the individual, as Freud pointed out, and of material forgotten or learned unconsciously). Deeper than this lies the **racial** or **collective unconscious**, which makes use of the actions and thoughts of countless generations, manifested mainly through symbols and behaviors.

The collective unconscious includes the instincts (Freud's id) and what Jung calls **archetypes**. Archetypes are primitive ways of thinking and show up in dreams, children's fantasies, delusions of the insane, and fairy tales and myths. Jung emphasized the importance of tapping the collective unconscious in the attainment of self-fulfillment or self-actualization.

Two of Jung's main archetypes are the **animus/anima** (animus = the male archetype in a woman; anima = the female archetype in a man) and the **persona** (the image that people attempt to create in social situations).

Socio-Psychoanalytic Theories (Neo-Freudians)

Another school of personality theory has made important contributions to the understanding of human behavior and has had some influence on consumer behavior. Some analysts who started out as Freudian psychoanalysts later developed their own theories based on differences with "the master." They are collectively known as the "neo-Freudians."

Neo-Freudians shift the orientation of psychoanalysis from the physiological to the social. They hold that the source of human motives lies in the social situation, in the interrelationships among individuals.

Adler and "Individual Psychology"

Alfred Adler, an early associate of Freud, differed from Freud in emphasizing the importance of early environment and the ego rather than the libido as the basic motivating force. Adler felt that every individual is driven toward **compensation** of one kind or another and strives for power, dominance, and superiority arising from feelings of inferiority.[32]

In response to early situations, the individual develops a certain **style of life** (a term coined by Adler), which is maintained throughout his life. Adler also coined the term **inferiority complex**.

The Cultural Influence

Abram Kardiner and Erich Fromm stress the importance of the society in the development of individual personality. Kardiner believes that social institutions influence human personality and that, in general, each society possesses a characteristic cultural personality.[33]

Fromm emphasizes that human beings are social beings and that personality develops from a child's dealings with the whole social environment.[34]

Karen Horney, influenced by the work of Fromm, also abandoned Freud's biological premises and argued for the importance of social environment in individual development. Horney disagreed most with Freud's conception of the unconscious — in particular, with the repression and re-emergence of isolated events.

> We recognize that the connection between later peculiarities and earlier experiences is more complicated than Freud assumed: there is no such thing as an isolated repetition of isolated experiences; but the *entirety* of infantile experiences combines to form a certain character structure, and it is this structure from which later difficulties emanate.[35]

This **character structure** (compare it with Adler's "style of life") results from the home environment of the child and its relationship with the parents. Unfavorable treatment creates a "basic anxiety" that the external environment is hostile and threatening. The defences that develop "crystallize" along three main lines — moving *toward, against,* or *away from* people. These she referred to as: compliance needs (C), aggressive needs (A), and detached needs (D).[36]

The socio-psychoanalytic theories have not received much application in marketing, although they appear to possess considerable potential for understanding consumers and for market segmentation. One study was reported in which an attempt was made to apply Horney's CAD typology.[37] Cohen sought, with a sample of undergraduate students, to correlate brand preference for eleven product categories and frequency of usage for four with personality type as determined in a test of compliance, aggressiveness, and detachedness. Significant cor-

relations were found for men's dress shirts, mouthwash, men's deodorant, cologne, and aftershave lotion, toilet or bath soap, razors, tea, and television viewing. Cohen concluded:

> Personal grooming products appear to differ initially among themselves in relevance to interpersonal goals and values. In addition, the ability of a specific brand to attract compliant, aggressive, or detached people may reflect the application of a consistent and enduring program of marketing and advertising emphasizing one or another set of interpersonal values.

Understanding the values of a segment who had adopted a product can assist in developing the attributes to be stressed in promotional material.

> The aggressive person should desire more distinctive brands of personal grooming products. Acceptance by others is not enough. He wants to establish his separate identity and style of behavior . . . . He may, for example, choose an especially manly deodorant. . . . The detached person should not be overly concerned with products or brands that help ensure his interpersonal attractiveness. . . . The compliant person should want reassurance that he is capable of being liked by others.

Regarding television and magazine preference, Cohen states: "In general, the results are in agreement with the expectation that programs and magazines having a compatible format will be preferred by each interpersonal group."

A recent study however, raised "serious questions about the usefulness of the CAD instrument in its present form."[38] It called for further development and refinement but did not suggest its rejection. The approach appears to have promise for classifying actual and potential users of a product to permit better identification of the product attributes to be emphasized for each group, better selection of media for promotion, and better understanding of the roles that could be played by each type in the diffusion of information and the adoption of new products.

Self-Concept Theory

The number of different motives that affect behavior is considerable. How does one try to understand why different individuals are influenced by different motives? It is generally agreed that an individual's entire psychological make-up is centered around a *self-concept*; that is, on how one sees oneself in relation to the environment. All of the inner strivings of an individual (all needs, motives, values, goals) are dependent on this self-concept. "The self-concept, or self-structure, may be thought of as an organized configuration of perceptions of the self which are admissible to awareness."[39]

One marketing scholar has expressed it well: "Your self-concept is how you view and think about yourself. Just as you have a concept of a brand, you have a concept of yourself. . . . There is a connection between self-concept and buying behavior — indeed, between self-concept and all behavior."[40]

The self-concept is the sum of the perceptions one has about oneself. It gives unity and stability to them because it serves to integrate the individual's motivations into a meaningful whole. The self develops over time through the process of social experience, a cumulative evolution based on the reactions of other individuals, such as parents, peers, and teachers.

Another basic element in self-concept theory is self-enhancement, the process by which an individual seeks to improve the self-concept over time. It depends on the reactions of significant others: ". . . self-enhancement requires favorable reactions from those persons who are admired."[41]

A third element is symbolic interaction. An individual seeks enhancement through those products that will convey the desired meanings to others as well as to the individual.

There are a number of approaches to the components of the self.[42] Several of these have been investigated in consumer behavior.[43] For example, Dolich examined the relationship between perceived self-image and brand image

for beer, cigarettes, bar soap, and toothpaste; Landon investigated the concepts of self and ideal-self in relation to purchase intentions; and Birdwell studied the relationship between self-image and automobiles.

The relationship between self-image and brand varies according to the situation. For example, the self-image that is operant in a social situation may be quite different from that in a business situation.[44]

The three significantly useful aspects of the self in consumer behavior will be reviewed here: the actual self-image, the ideal self-image, and the looking-glass self (the perception of an individual by others).

The Actual Self-Image refers to the perceptions one has about oneself derived, as described earlier, from past experience. Most products reflect this aspect of the self. Because of the need for enhancement, this self-image is not always accurate. An individual, for example, may think of himself or herself as sexy and tend to purchase products likely to enhance that image. The self-image involves every facet of an individual's life, ranging from the social group to the home and residential area.

The Ideal Self-Image encompasses what and how the individual would like to be. Behavior expressing the ideal self will involve responses to the aspirations of the individual.

Some researchers have identified what may be called an intermediate concept between the actual and the ideal self-images.[45] From a pragmatic point of view, it may be more attainable than the ideal and therefore of greater use to the marketer. They have labelled it the *expected* self.

To some extent, cigarette, beer, automobiles, clothing, jewelry, and perfume reflect the ideal self-image. Landon found that some products are more closely related to the ideal self.[46]

The Looking-Glass Self or the Social Self is how the individual believes others perceive him or her. Consumers are strongly influenced by what others think and, since they strive to maintain or enhance the self, this aspect of the self has an important effect on product purchases.

Sometimes an individual may behave in such a way as to seek to change the social image in accordance with some ideal social self.[47]

In spite of the difficulties of measurement, particularly of the ideal, marketers have made extensive use of self-concept theory in promotion and segmentation.

HOW PERSONALITY DATA CAN BE USED

There are three basic ways in which personality data can be used in studying consumer behavior: as an independent variable, as a moderator variable, and as an intervening variable.

Personality as an Independent Variable

Personality has not proved to be an adequate segmentation criterion because the measures used so far have been general and not oriented to marketing. "For example, instead of searching for the general trait of self-confidence, it is better to determine the extent to which consumers are self-confident in evaluating different brands within the product category."[48] That is, a product-specific approach to personality measurement may be more effective in identifying personality segments. No studies of this kind, to the best of this writer's knowledge, have appeared in the literature.

Personality as a Moderator Variable

Even if personality *is* product-specific, it may at times not be useful for segmentation because of the particular situation. The situation will determine which personality characteristic will be brought into play. For example, a thrifty consumer who is price-conscious when buying some

food products may consistently purchase the most expensive brand of wine or perfume. A study by Brody and Cunningham found that personality variables had negligible value for explaining relative loyalty to a family's favorite brand. "However, when trying to discriminate the brand choice of people most likely to have perceived high performance risk and to have high specific self-confidence, personality variables were very useful."[49] Another study reported that "personality variables . . . appear to have considerable potential for improving understanding of the psychological basis of brand choice."[50] The perceived differences among brands can be identified, and then a decision made on what personality variables seem relevant to choice.

Personality as an Intervening Variable

Perhaps the most useful application of personality data is in describing and differentiating among market segments. The segments are first determined by common criteria such as age, income, and heaviness of usage and then the data are examined for personality differences.

An excellent example of this approach is provided by the Flavorfest Company (fictitious name), the manufacturer of a bottled spice product.[51] It first segmented the market by extent of usage and then differentiated among the segments on the basis of demographic and personality characteristics.

The heavy using group were found to be very progressive, with a strong desire to be creative and to express their individuality. They enjoyed the product's exciting, exotic taste. The light/moderate users possessed a strong desire to express their individuality through creative cookery but seemed to be constrained by an inclination to be traditional and to satisfy family tastes. The desire to experiment seemed to be inhibited by a lack of confidence. The product was therefore limited to one type of food. The non-users were very traditional, older, lower in income, and non-venturesome, with no inclination to experiment. The image of the product was too exotic and too modern.

The insights obtained from the personality data suggest that the company's greatest opportunity was with the light/moderate users, whose desire for individuality and inclination to experimentation could be excellent platforms for presenting a product already perceived favorably. The possible obstacles — the desire to maintain tradition and stick with family preferences, the restricted view of the product, and the lack of confidence — could be overcome through promotion emphasizing the variety of dishes in which Flavorfest might be used and through providing "fail-safe," family-tested recipes, which would enhance confidence and ensure satisfaction.

Essentially, one of the primary applications of personality would be in market segmentation: on the basis of the insights obtained, useful contributions can be made to the creation of advertising appeals and to the development of better product positioning.

Better media selection could result from reliable personality data. Few studies have been reported in this area. One such study identified five segments on the basis of the type of TV show most frequently watched and measured the psychographic and demographic characteristics of each segment.[52] Although the approach appears to have potential, the general conclusion was that audiences were relatively heterogeneous in terms of personality and life-style characteristics and "that it will be difficult, if not impossible, to identify television audiences where people with such characteristics are concentrated."

LIFE-STYLE RESEARCH

Life-style research seeks to assess psychological expressions rather than psychological dynamics and is therefore confined mainly to activities, interests, and opinions (AIO). It has also been referred to as **psychographics**, although such life-style measures are but one kind of psychographic (literally, "drawing of the mind") description. Personality profiles are another.* So far, life-style research has shown the following characteristics:

- it is quantitative in that it employs large samples (as opposed to the attempts of motivation research to arrive at consumer typologies using small samples);
- it measures responses on a large number of items;
- it may be general or product-specific, although recent research suggests that the product-specific approach may be more helpful to marketers; and
- the data are quantifiable and can be subjected to statistical analyses of varying complexity (such as factor, discriminant, and multivariate analyses).

As Wells has put it, psychographic research "combines the objectivity of the personality inventory with the rich, consumer-oriented descriptive detail of the qualitative motivation research investigation."[53]

An Evaluation of Life-Style Research

Life-style research seeks to group consumers on the basis of commonalities in their activities, interests, and opinions, in order to identify life-style patterns. The assumption is that the behavior of the consumer will also vary among these groups.

A comprehensive review of the field by Wells evaluated the basic types of life-style research currently being carried out (Figure 13.3).[54]

A good example of the **single profile** based on general life-style dimensions (there are actually two profiles but the non-user group is

---

* Howard makes this same distinction: "Psychographic studies focus on more abstract, theoretical personality traits; life-style studies focus more on specific activities, interests, attitudes, and values, which are held to be more directly tied to consumer behavior," in John A. Howard, *Consumer Behavior: Application of Theory* (New York: McGraw-Hill, 1977), p. 161.

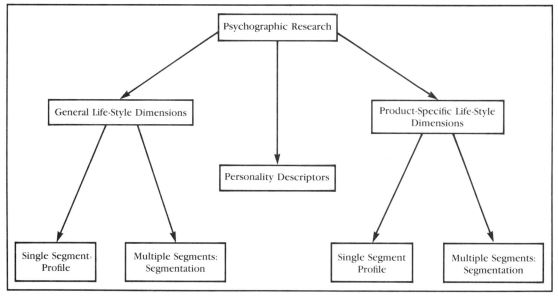

FIGURE 13.3: The Different Approaches to Psychographic Research

the obverse of the user group) is the shotgun study, in which a large number of questions were asked about a wide range of activities, interests, and opinions. There were questions about shotgun ammunition along with questions about approximately one hundred other products and services so that the study was not designed around shotgun users or around the users of any other product. It was concluded that the life-style data, though general in nature, provided useful insights into the shotgun user and added significantly to the demographic data.

This approach was first applied by Wells and Tigert, who employed a self-administered questionnaire containing, in addition to the usual demographics, questions about a large number of different products and three hundred AIO statements.[55] "The statements covered a wide variety of topics — including day-to-day activities, interests in media, the arts, clothes, cosmetics and homemaking; and opinions on many matters of general interest" and were administered to a sample of one thousand homemakers.

All in all, this approach seems to improve significantly on the demographic data normally employed to provide segment profiles. Figure 13.4 presents a sampling of the kinds of AIO statements employed in such a study. Each statement is usually rated on a six-point agree/disagree Likert-type scale, where one equals definitely disagree and six equals definitely agree.

In *General Life-Style Segmentation* studies, a large sample is given a long psychographic questionnaire of the type discussed above and, through Q-factor analysis, placed in segments. The study reported by Wells identified eight psychographic segments.

Another approach dealt with the use of personality traits to describe ecologically concerned consumers, the type of personality study discussed at the beginning of the chapter. In fact, it revealed the same order of relationship as most such studies.

The *Product-Specific Single Profile* relies on a "limited number of relevant, product-related dimensions" and is therefore less cumbersome than the general approach.

Finally, the *product-specific segmentation* study also employs product-related material but its purpose is to identify different segments. For the most part, items of a general nature are

Price-Conscious
- I shop a lot for "specials"
- I usually watch the ads for announcements of sales
- A person can save a lot of money by shopping around for bargains

Fashion-Conscious
- I usually have one or more outfits that are of the very latest style
- An important part of my life and activities is dressing smartly
- I often try the latest hairdo styles when they change

Child-Oriented
- My children are the most important things in my life
- I try to arrange my home for my children's convenience
- I take a lot of time and effort to teach my children good habits

Compulsive Housekeeper
- I usually keep my house very neat and clean
- I am uncomfortable when my house is not completely clean
- Our days seem to follow a definite routine, such as eating meals at a regular time

Cook
- I love to cook
- I am a good cook
- I love to bake and frequently do

Self-Confident
- I am more independent than most people
- I think I have a lot of personal ability
- I like to be considered a leader

Sports Spectator
- I like to watch or listen to baseball or football games
- I usually read the sports page in the daily paper
- I would rather go to a sporting event than a dance

Housekeeping
- I really don't like household chores
- I enjoy most forms of housework
- My idea of housekeeping is "once over lightly"

Homebody
- I would rather spend a quiet evening at home than go out to a party
- I am a homebody

Community-Minded
- I do volunteer work for a hospital or service organization on a fairly regular basis
- I like to work on community projects
- I have personally worked in a political campaign or for a candidate or an issue

New Brand Tryer
- When I see a new brand on the shelf I often buy it just to see what it's like
- I often try new brands before my friends and neighbors do
- I like to try new and different things

Canned Food
- I depend on canned food for at least one meal a day
- I couldn't get along without canned food
- Things just don't taste right if they come out of a can

Finances
- Our family income is high enough to satisfy nearly all our important desires
- I will probably have more money to spend next year than I have now
- Five years from now the family income will probably be a lot higher than it is now

Arts
- I enjoy going through an art gallery
- I enjoy going to concerts
- I like ballet

FIGURE 13.4: Examples of AIO Statements

Based on William D. Wells and Douglas J. Tigert, "Activities, Interests, and Opinions," *Journal of Advertising Research*, 2:4 (August 1971), pp. 27-35.

recast into product-specific form. For instance, "I worry too much" was translated (in a study of stomach remedies) into "I seem to get stomach problems if I worry too much."

The discrimination produced by the product-specific approach is somewhat sharper than the discrimination produced by the more general segmentation. . . . When the segmentation is based upon the dimensions upon which brands differ, it is almost certain to discriminate more sharply among brands than when it is based upon more general considerations.[56]

A major problem with this approach is the selection of psychographic items. One way, as done above, is to transform general personality descriptions or general AIO items. A recent study suggested a basic framework of four areas of consumer behavior for selecting product-specific items — role perceptions, value orientations, buying style, and communications reactions. These were defined as follows:[57]

Role Perceptions — the manner in which individuals behave in order to give positive expression to the type of people they are or perceive themselves to be (e.g., social entertainer, creative cook);

Value Orientations — an enduring belief that a particular mode of conduct or a particular end-state of existence is personally and socially preferable to alternative modes of conduct or end-states of existence (e.g., weight watchers);

Buying Style — differences in shopping behavior even when buyers are confronted with the same purchasing environment (e.g., conformist, impulsive);

Communications Reactions — includes habits, reactions to advertising, and communications with or from other sources (e.g., tendency to give advice to friends).

A test of this schema was subsequently conducted with a sample of 341 adult male respondents, who rated 29 psychographic items chosen on the basis of an earlier exploratory study.[58] Analysis identified significant group differences among a number of dependent variables, such as preferred brand, media habits, sports interest, and basic demographics.[59]

As was pointed out for personality research, it would appear that the product-specific approach may be more effective than the general approach for segmentation. It achieves a high level of segment clarity (45% of the variance), and provides significantly different segment profiles for promotional and other strategies such as product positioning.

The question of whether such typologies are generalizable is not settled. Current knowledge would suggest that in consumer behavior, personality functions either as a moderator variable — so that the aspect of an individual's personality that comes into play is largely dependent upon the particular situation — or as an intervening variable for elaboration of already identified segments.

At least the studies just cited point a way toward some kind of generalizability in that, no matter what the product, the consumer analyst has a theoretical framework from which to generate psychographic descriptors that are relevant to any product or service.

Applications of Psychographic Research

A 1979 paper described life-style measures as a "popular means of identifying consumers and describing their differences along psychological dimensions."[60] Psychographics have been used to identify and provide life-style profiles for opinion leaders, credit-card users, store-loyal consumers, outshoppers, private-brand buyers, brand images, and media habits.[61]

Others have claimed psychographics were very helpful in the selection of advertising themes and media for a wide variety of products —

Chevrolet Vega, Colgate-Palmolive's Irish Spring, Dewar's White Label Scotch, Jack Daniel's Whiskey, Kentucky Fried Chicken, Lava Soap, Nescafé, Schlitz Beer, Sony Betamax, Taster's Choice Coffee, Tums, and Union 76 Gasoline.[62]

Some recent studies demonstrate the relevance of life-style to various kinds of consumer decisions. For example, Roberts and Wortzel investigated the effect of life-style on food shopping and preparation behavior.[63] They found that employment status was not as strong a predictor of food preparation as was age. Another study was concerned with the correlation between life-style and media decisions.[64]

A number of studies have applied psychographic segmentation in the retail shopping context.[65]

Assael reports a study by a leading food manufacturer that used life-style data to segment the snack food market.[66] It identified six snacking segments on the basis of life-styles and needs: nutritional snackers (concerned about health, self-confident, and controlled); weight watchers (outdoors types, emphasize quick energy and few calories); guilty snackers (highly anxious, emphasize taste and feel they overeat); party snackers (sociable, serve to guests); indiscriminate snackers (heavy snackers, emphasize taste); and economical snackers (self-assured, price-oriented).

The marketing implications of the study were many:
- the segment(s) to concentrate on;
- the advertising to use for each segment;
- the appropriate media for reaching each type of snacker;
- products preferred by the segments;
- packaging decisions; and

- new products that may be considered necessary for certain segments.

PERSONALITY AND RISK BEHAVIOR

Risk is a crucial element in consumer behavior. Since consumer behavior is essentially choice behavior and "since the outcome of a choice can only be known in the future, the consumer is forced to deal with uncertainty or risk."[67]

Of the many factors that affect the perception of risk (see Chapter 6) and the consumer's reaction to it (e.g., the outcome of the choice, its consequence), the personality of the individual plays a central role. In particular, the consumer's level of self-esteem affects both the amount of risk perceived in a particular situation and the methods used to alleviate risk (Chapter 6).[68]

Self-confidence and anxiety are essential aspects of self-esteem. It has been found that the lower the self-esteem, the greater the perception of risk and the experience of anxiety.[69] Self-esteem also varies with the specific choice situation, age, and sex.

Research has shown that the lower the self-esteem, the less the likelihood of innovative behavior and the greater the tendency to be brand loyal.[70] Store choice also appears to be influenced by self-confidence. A recent study found that, among the purchasers of relatively expensive audio equipment, those who had purchased from a specialty store were more self-confident (both generalized and product-specific) than those who purchased from a department store.[71]

SUMMARY

Two important psychographic measures in consumer behavior are personality and life-style. Personality is an integrative concept and represents the total of all the individual's life in-

fluences as expressed in enduring characteristic patterns of thought and behavior. So far, empirical studies in marketing have not been very successful in demonstrating a significant relationship between personality and consumer choice. A number of possible reasons were discussed. However, the potential applications of personality data to marketing strategy are many: segmentation, product positioning, advertising content, media selection, and distribution. Personality measures in marketing may be more useful if they are based on tailor-made inventories, rather than on borrowed psychological inventories.

A number of personality theories were reviewed: trait theory, which is the most widely used in marketing; psychoanalytic theories (Freud, Jung); socio-psychoanalytic theories (Adler, Fromm, Horney); and self-concept theory. Unconscious motivation, as postulated by Freud, was cited as a potent factor in consumer behavior, particularly the various mechanisms

of ego-defence to which individuals resort — rationalization, projection, regression, compensation, fantasy, and identification, each of which could represent a segment to be approached appropriately.

Finally, the roles of personality as a moderating variable and as an intervening variable in consumer behavior were emphasized.

Life-style measures are based on activities, interests, and opinions. Two kinds of life-style studies — general and product-specific — were identified. The latter would appear to have greater promise in isolating consumer types.

The final section of the chapter underlined the importance of personality as a factor in risk behavior, a central determinant of consumer behavior.

QUESTIONS

1. Using the examples of perfume, cigarettes, and beer, explain the relevance of personality characteristics to product and brand choice.

2. Distinguish between psychographics, life-style, AIO, personality, and self-concept.

3. Explain why the empirical evidence in marketing does not demonstrate a significant relationship between personality and behavior.

4. Which theory or theories of personality have contributed most to our understanding of consumer behavior? Justify your answer.

5. Self theory holds that individuals try to protect or enhance their self-concept (that is,

they make decisions that are most consistent with self or ideal-self images). Which of these is more useful in developing marketing programs? Why?

6. Try to explain how the following unconscious mechanisms of ego-defence may be applied by the marketer: rationalization, compensation, projection, fantasy.

7. Discuss some of the main advantages and disadvantages of the application of life-style data in consumer behavior.

8. Relate personality and risk-involved behavior and explain the significance of the relationship between the two.

NOTES TO CHAPTER 13

[1]Sandra J. Teel, Jesse E. Teel, and William O. Bearden, "Lessons Learned from the Broadcast Cigarette Advertising Ban," *Journal of Marketing*, 43 (January 1979), pp. 45-50.

[2]Philip Kotler and Gordon H.G. McDougall, *Principles of Marketing*, Canadian ed. (Toronto: Prentice-Hall, 1983), pp. 439-40.

[3]Chester R. Wasson, Frederick D. Sturdivant, and David H. McConaughy, *Competition and Human Behavior* (New York: Appleton-Century-Crofts, 1968), p. 6.

[4]Ibid., p. 4.

[5]G.W. Allport, *Pattern and Growth in Personality* (New York: Holt, Rinehart and Winston, 1967), p. 28.

[6]Harold H. Kassarjian, "Personality and Consumer Behavior: A Review," *Journal of Marketing Research*, 8 (November 1971), pp. 409-18. Reprinted with permission of the American Marketing Association.

[7]Franklin B. Evans, "Psychological and Objective Factors in the Prediction of Brand Choice," *Journal of Business*, 32 (October 1959), pp. 340-69.

[8]Kassarjian, op. cit., p. 412.

[9]Arthur Koponen, "Personality Characteristics of Purchasers," *Journal of Advertising Research*, 1 (September 1960), pp. 6-12.

[10]William F. Massy, Ronald E. Frank, and Thomas M. Lodahl, *Purchasing Behavior and Personal Attributes* (Philadelphia: University of Pennsylvania Press, 1968).

[11]Al E. Birdwell, "Influence of Image Congruence on Consumer Choice," *Proceedings*, Winter Conference, American Marketing Association, 1964, pp. 290-303; "Automobiles and Self Imagery: Reply," *Journal of Business*, 41 (October 1968), pp. 486-7.

[12]Kassarjian, op cit., p. 413.

[13]Ibid., p. 415.

[14]Raymond L. Horton, "The Edwards Personal Preference Schedule and Consumer Personality Research," *Journal of Marketing Research*, 11 (August 1974), pp. 335-7.

[15]Ibid., p. 337.

[16]Nariman K. Dhalla and Winston H. Mahatoo, "Expanding the Scope of Segmentation Research," *Journal of Marketing*, 40 (April 1976), pp. 34-5.

[17]Raymond L. Horton, "Some Relationships Between Personality and Consumer Decision Making," *Journal of Marketing Research*, 16 (May 1979), pp. 223-46.

[18]Kassarjian, op. cit., p. 416.

[19]Ibid., pp. 415-6.

[20]William D. Wells and Douglas J. Tigert, "Activities, Interests, and Opinions," *Journal of Advertising Research*, 11 (August 1971), pp. 27-35.

[21]Dhalla and Mahatoo, op. cit., p. 37.

[22]Calvin S. Hall and Gardner Lindzey, *Theories of Personality* (New York: John Wiley & Sons, 1957).

[23]E.R. Hilgard and R.C. Atkinson, *Introduction to Psychology* (New York: Harcourt, Brace, 1967).

[24]Henry Clay Smith, *Personality Adjustment* (New York: McGraw-Hill, 1961), p. 31.

[25]Ibid., p. 99.

[26]R. Cattell, *The Scientific Analysis of Personality* (Chicago: Aldine, 1965), pp. 62-5.

[27]R.B. Cattell, H.W. Eber, and M.M. Tatsuoka, *Handbook for the Sixteen Personality Factor Questionnaire* (Champaign, Illinois: Institute for Personality and Ability Testing, 1970), pp. 16-7.

[28]Robert M. Goldenson, *The Encyclopedia of Human Behavior* (Garden City, New York: Doubleday, 1970), pp. 300-1; Anna Freud, *The Ego and the Mechanisms of Defense* (New York: International Universities Press, 1957).

[29]Henry L. Roediger III, J. Philippe Rushton, Elizabeth D. Capaldi, and Scott G. Paris, *Psychology* (Boston: Little, Brown, 1984), pp. 473-4.

[30]J.E. Stafford, K.K. Cox, and J.B. Higginbotham, "Some Consumption Pattern Differences Between Urban Whites and Negroes," *Social Sciences Quarterly*, 44 (December 1968), pp. 619-30.

[31]Roediger, Rushton, Capaldi, and Paris, op. cit., p. 474.

[32]S.R. Maddi, *Personality Theories: A Comparative Analysis*, rev. ed. (Homewood, Illinois: Dorsey, 1972), p. 111.

[33]A. Kardiner, *The Individual and His Society: The Psycho-Dynamics of Primitive Organization* (New York: Columbia University Press, 1939); R. Linton, C. Dubois, and J. West, *The Psychological Frontiers of Society* (New York: Columbia University Press, 1945).

[34]Erich Fromm, *The Sane Society* (New York: Rinehart and Company, 1955).

³⁵K. Horney, *New Ways in Psychoanalysis* (New York: W.W. Norton, 1939), p. 9.

³⁶K. Horney, *Our Inner Conflicts: A Constructive Theory of Neurosis* (New York: W.W. Norton, 1945).

³⁷J.B. Cohen, "An International Orientation to the Study of Consumer Behavior," *Journal of Marketing Research*, 4 (August 1967), pp. 270-7. Reprinted with permission of the American Marketing Association.

³⁸Jon P. Noerager, "An Assessment of CAD — A Personality Instrument Developed Specifically for Marketing Research," *Journal of Marketing Research*, 16 (February 1979), pp. 53-9.

³⁹Carl R. Rogers, *Client-Centred Therapy* (Boston: Houghton-Mifflin, 1951), p. 492.

⁴⁰John A. Howard, *Consumer Behavior: Application of Theory* (New York: McGraw-Hill, 1977), pp. 89-90.

⁴¹Terrence V. O'Brien, Humberto S. Tapia, and Thomas L. Brown, "The Self-Concept in Buyer Behavior," in James U. McNeal and Stephen W. McDanied (eds.), *Consumer Behavior: Classical and Contemporary Dimensions* (Boston: Little, Brown, 1982), p. 211.

⁴²M. Joseph Sirgy, "Self-Concept in Consumer Behavior: A Critical Review," *Journal of Consumer Research*, 9 (December 1982), pp. 287-300.

⁴³A number of studies have investigated some of these relationships: A.E. Birdwell, "Automobiles and Self-Image: A Reply," *Journal of Business*, 41 (October 1968), pp. 486-7; I.J. Dolich, "Congruence Relationships Between Self-Images and Product Brands," *Journal of Marketing Research*, 6 (February 1969), pp. 80-4; E.L. Grubb and H.L. Grathwohl, "Consumer Self-Concept, Symbolism, and Market Behavior: A Theoretical Approach," *Journal of Marketing*, 31 (October 1967), pp. 22-7; J. Ross, "Self-Concept and Brand Preference," *Journal of Business*, 44 (January 1971), pp. 38-50; E.L. Landon, "Self-Concept, Ideal Self-Concept and Consumer Purchase Intentions," *Journal of Consumer Research*, 1 (September 1974), pp. 44-51.

⁴⁴Robert E. Burnkrant and Thomas J. Page, Jr., "On the Management of Self-Images in Social Situations: The Role of Public Self-Consciousness," in Andrew Mitchell (ed.), *Advances in Consumer Research*, 9 (Ann Arbor, Michigan: Association for Consumer Research, 1982), pp. 452-5.

⁴⁵Humberto S. Tapia, Terrence V. O'Brien and George W. Summers, "Self-Concept and Consumer Motivation," *Proceedings*, Fall Conference, American Marketing Association, August 1975.

⁴⁶Landon, op. cit.

⁴⁷M. Joseph Sirgy, "Self-Concept in Relation to Product Preference and Purchase Intentions," in V.V. Bellur (ed.), *Developments in Marketing Science*, 3 (Marquette, Michigan: Academy of Marketing Science, 1980); J. Michael Munsen and W. Austin Spivey, "Assessing Self-Concept," in Jerry C. Olson (ed.), *Advances in Consumer Research*, 7 (Ann Arbor, Michigan: Association for Consumer Research, 1980), pp. 598-603.

⁴⁸Dhalla and Mahatoo, op. cit., p. 37.

⁴⁹Robert P. Brody and Scott M. Cunningham, "Personality Variables and the Consumer Decision Process," *Journal of Marketing Research*, 5 (February 1968), p. 56.

⁵⁰Joseph N. Fry, "Personality Variables and Cigarette Brand Choice," *Journal of Marketing Research*, 8 (August 1971), pp. 298-304.

⁵¹James F. Engel, Roger D. Blackwell, and David T. Kollat, *Consumer Behavior*, 3rd. ed. (Hinsdale, Illinois: Dryden Press, 1978), pp. 202-5.

⁵²Kathryn E.A. Villani, "Personality/Life Style and Television Viewing Behavior," *Journal of Marketing Research*, 12 (November 1975), pp. 432-9.

⁵³William D. Wells, "Psychographics: A Critical Review," *Journal of Marketing Research*, 12 (May 1975), p. 196.

⁵⁴Ibid., pp. 196-213.

⁵⁵William D. Wells and Douglas J. Tigert, "Activities, Interests, and Opinions," *Journal of Advertising Research*, 2: 4 (August 1971), pp. 27-35.

⁵⁶Wells, op. cit., p. 202.

⁵⁷Dhalla and Mahatoo, op. cit.

⁵⁸W.H. Mahatoo, "Product-Specific Psychographics in Market Segmentation for Product Positioning," *Proceedings* (Chicago, Illinois: American Statistical Association, 1977), pp. 747-52.

⁵⁹W.H. Mahatoo, "Product-Specific Psychographic Inventories: A Schema for Generating Test Items" (in press).

⁶⁰Alvin C. Burns and Mary Carolyn Harrison, "A Test of the Reliability of Psychographics," *Journal of Marketing Research*, 16 (February 1979), pp. 32-8.

[61]Ibid.

[62]Leon G. Schiffman and Leslie Lazar Kanuk, *Consumer Behavior* (Englewood Cliffs, New Jersey: Prentice-Hall, 1978), p. 142.

[63]Mary Lou Roberts and Lawrence H. Wortzel, "New Life-Style Determinants of Women's Food Shopping Behavior," *Journal of Marketing*, 43 (Summer 1979), pp. 28-39.

[64]J.E. Teel, W.O. Bearden, and R.M. Durand, "Psychographics of Radio and Television Audiences," *Journal of Advertising Research*, 19 (April 1979), pp. 53-6.

[65]William R. Darden, and William D. Perrault, Jr., "Identifying Inter-Urban Shoppers: Multiproduct Purchase Patterns and Segmentation Profiles," *Journal of Marketing Research*, 13 (February 1976), pp. 51-60; William O. Bearden, Jesse E. Teel, Jr., and Richard M. Durand, "Media Usage, Psychographic, and Demographic Dimensions of Retail Shoppers," *Journal of Retailing*, 54 (Spring 1978), pp. 65-74; Danny N. Bellenger and Pradeep K. Kakkar, "Profiling the Recreational Shopper," *Journal of Retailing*, 56 (Fall 1980), pp. 83-92.

[66]Henry Assael, *Consumer Behavior and Marketing Action* (Boston, Massachusetts: Kent, 1984), pp. 259-64.

[67]James W. Taylor, "The Role of Risk in Consumer Behavior," *Journal of Marketing*, 38 (April 1974), p. 54.

[68]Stanley Coopersmith, *The Antecedents of Self-Esteem* (San Francisco: W.H. Freeman, 1967).

[69]Charles M. Schaninger, "Perceived Risk and Personality," *Journal of Consumer Research*, 3 (September 1976), pp. 95-100.

[70]Johan Arndt, "Role of Product-Related Conversations in the Diffusion of a New Product," *Journal of Marketing Research*, 4 (August 1967), pp. 291-5; Ted Roselius, "Consumer Ranking of Risk Reduction Methods," *Journal of Marketing*, 35 (January 1971), pp. 56-61.

[71]Robert D. Hisrich, Ronald J. Dornoff, and Jerome B. Kernan, "Perceived Risk in Store Selection," *Journal of Marketing Research*, 9 (November 1972), pp. 435-9; Joseph F. Dash, Leon G. Schiffman, and Conrad Berenson, "Risk- and Personality-Related Dimensions of Store Choice," *Journal of Marketing*, 40 (January 1976), pp. 32-9.

PURITEEN COSMETICS*

Background

Puriteen, a cosmetics company based in Atlanta, acquired a small, faltering perfume and cologne company located in Orangedale, Florida (a suburb of Jacksonville).

Puriteen has produced several cosmetics lines since 1946. By year-end 1975, they had become a leader in cosmetics in the southeast US with $125 million in sales.

A small producer, Henri's, was started by Henri and Marie Duprey in 1972. They began in their garage, turning out two fragrances, "Henri's" and "Marie," but after four years of struggling they were forced to admit defeat.

Expansion

A few years ago, Puriteen's top management decided to expand their lines by entering the perfume and cologne market. Long-range plans were to enter the shaving cream and deodorant markets as well. Raymond Dozier, vice-president of marketing, had defined their business as a personal care business and believed that these and other products were essential to long-term growth.

Thus recently Puriteen acquired Henri's, and Dozier began to consider plans for marketing the two newly acquired perfumes.

"Henri's" and "Marie" perfumes were fresh, new fragrances to the market. Both rated very highly in consumer smell preference tests and had tremendous potential. However, Dozier knew from his experiences and those of other companies that the success of such products depended upon the creation of an appealing *image* for the brand.

Entering the Perfume Market

Because Henri's and Marie are produced with natural ingredients they are more expensive to make and thus higher in price than many of

---

* Adapted from M. Wayne De Lozier, *Consumer Behavior Dynamics — A Casebook* (Columbus, Ohio: Charles E. Merrill, 1977), pp. 84-92.

the more popular brands of perfume. To whom should these products be directed — and how?

After having taken a course in Consumer Behavior at the university, Dozier had become very interested in the notion of developing brands that were based on consumer *self-concepts*. He decided to develop a marketing program on the basis of self theory. He constructed a semantic differential questionnaire to measure the self and ideal-self images of female consumers and the images they held for three (fictitious) perfume brands.

The Marketing Research

The tests were conducted in New Orleans, Tallahassee, Atlanta, Raleigh, and Memphis. Four hundred and ninety-six personal interviews were conducted (approximately one hundred per city). Subjects were given semantic differential scales on which to describe their self- and ideal-self concepts, and then perceptions of each of three perfume brands on the basis of three advertisements presented to them. Each perfume advertisement was a videotaped version of a proposed Henri's advertisement, each featuring a fictional name. The order of presentation of the ads and self-concepts was randomized. Subjects were asked at the end of each session to select the brand they preferred and told that, if their number was selected at a later drawing, they would receive the brand chosen as a prize. The results of the tests are presented in Exhibits 1 to 4.

The advertised "brands" were given three different themes. One used a sensual theme, the second a romantic theme, and the third a prestigious, regal theme, with an appropriate model and picture sequence to match each theme. The following is a partial reproduction of each theme:

Nakū. "Nakū — the naked scent. Unadorned, primitive, sensuous Nakū. Nakū is for the woman who has a mind of her own; for the woman who goes her own free and feminine way. It's for the woman who understands that perfume is feminine power! Nakū — the naked scent. It is the essential you!" (sensual theme)

Rumäns. "Fragrance admittedly triggers emotions, but science doesn't know why. The whole wide world of scents is full of mysteries. However, Rumäns has captured the one scent that can make your world come alive with excitement and romance.

"Rumäns is a word of endearment, full of affection. Like dew sparkling, brooks babbling, stars smiling, lovers meeting, Rumäns goes about its business of making its wearer feel spirited, airy, romantic.

"Wear Rumäns day and night, because love comes without warning!" (romantic theme)

El Primo. "Once she was the *only* woman in the world allowed to wear this perfume. The queen of Navarre commissioned the most famed alchemist in Paris to create a perfume of magical potency and bewitching powers. A perfume so irresistible, it disarmed her competitors. A perfume so feminine, it intensified her legendary appeal,

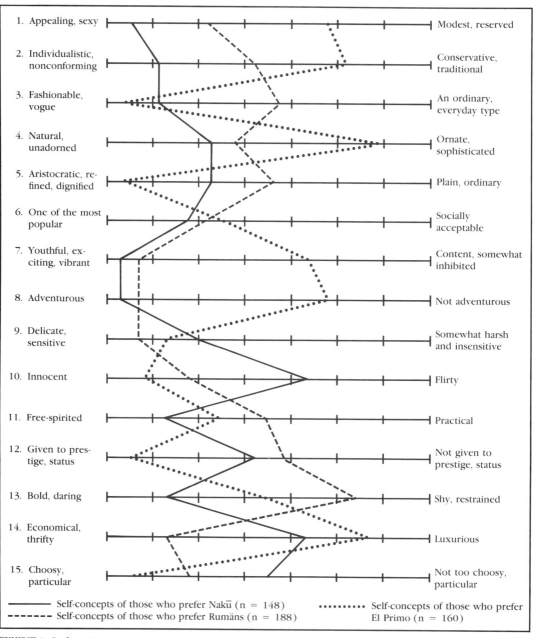

EXHIBIT 1: Perfume Images

drawing the great and the glorious to her court. This magical perfume was El Primo. Unchanged since 1572, it casts its spell for great women today. El Primo, the perfume made for a queen!" (prestigious, regal theme)

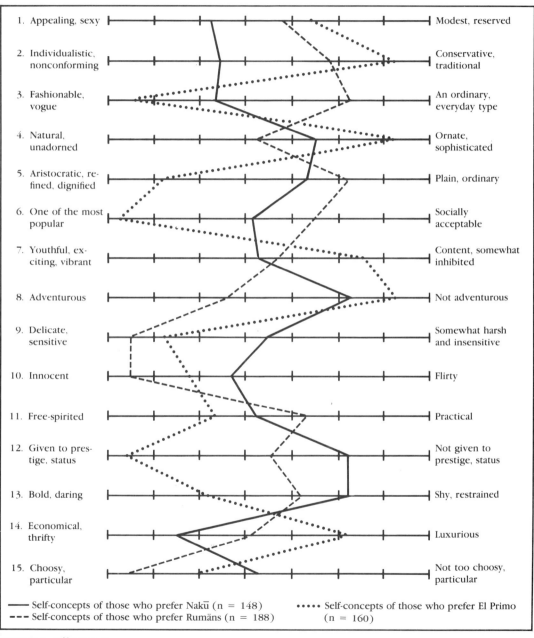

1. Appealing, sexy	Modest, reserved
2. Individualistic, nonconforming	Conservative, traditional
3. Fashionable, vogue	An ordinary, everyday type
4. Natural, unadorned	Ornate, sophisticated
5. Aristocratic, re-fined, dignified	Plain, ordinary
6. One of the most popular	Socially acceptable
7. Youthful, ex-citing, vibrant	Content, somewhat inhibited
8. Adventurous	Not adventurous
9. Delicate, sensitive	Somewhat harsh and insensitive
10. Innocent	Flirty
11. Free-spirited	Practical
12. Given to pres-tige, status	Not given to prestige, status
13. Bold, daring	Shy, restrained
14. Economical, thrifty	Luxurious
15. Choosy, particular	Not too choosy, particular

—— Self-concepts of those who prefer Nakū (n = 148)   ••••• Self-concepts of those who prefer El Primo
--- Self-concepts of those who prefer Rumäns (n = 188)   (n = 160)

EXHIBIT 2: Self-Concepts

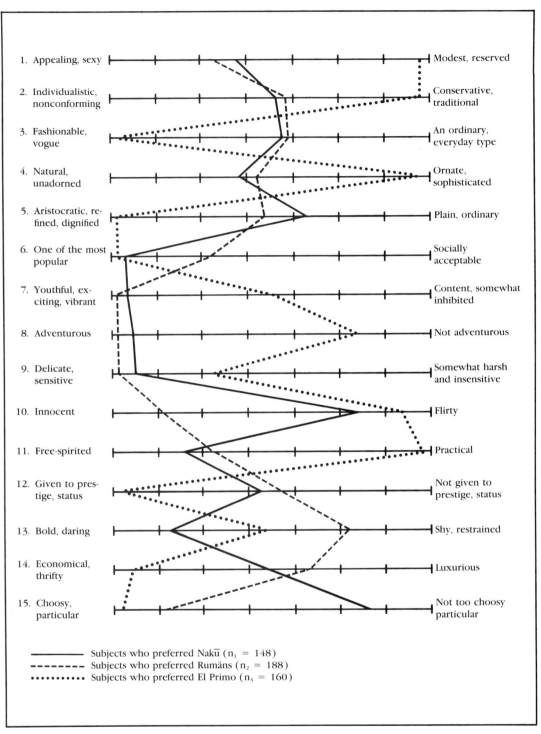

1. Appealing, sexy		Modest, reserved
2. Individualistic, nonconforming		Conservative, traditional
3. Fashionable, vogue		An ordinary, everyday type
4. Natural, unadorned		Ornate, sophisticated
5. Aristocratic, refined, dignified		Plain, ordinary
6. One of the most popular		Socially acceptable
7. Youthful, exciting, vibrant		Content, somewhat inhibited
8. Adventurous		Not adventurous
9. Delicate, sensitive		Somewhat harsh and insensitive
10. Innocent		Flirty
11. Free-spirited		Practical
12. Given to prestige, status		Not given to prestige, status
13. Bold, daring		Shy, restrained
14. Economical, thrifty		Luxurious
15. Choosy, particular		Not too choosy particular

——————— Subjects who preferred Nakū ($n_1 = 148$)
- - - - - - - Subjects who preferred Rumäns ($n_2 = 188$)
•••••••••• Subjects who preferred El Primo ($n_3 = 160$)

EXHIBIT 3: Self-Ideal Concepts

Family Income	Nakū Age Categories				Rumäns Age Categories				El Primo Age Categories				Totals
	18-25	26-35	36-49	50 and over	18-25	26-35	36-49	50 and over	18-25	26-35	36-49	50 and over	
$6,000-9,999	2	22	2	—	18	12	1	—	3	—	—	1	61
$10,000-14,999	5	30	15	—	33	8	15	1	2	6	2	4	121
$15,000-19,999	3	15	17	4	29	14	14	3	18	6	14	22	159
$20,000 and over	1	27	2	3	15	6	13	6	19	8	19	36	155
Totals	11	94	36	7	95	40	43	10	42	20	35	63	
Grand Total	148				188				160				496

EXHIBIT 4: Ages and Family Incomes of Subjects Preferring Each Brand

QUESTIONS

1. What kinds of analyses do you think should be performed on the data?

2. Evaluate the dimensions used in Dozier's semantic differential. How would you improve on them?

3. What additional information would you want to develop a program for Puriteen?

4. Self theory holds that individuals try to protect or enhance self-concept — that is, they make decisions that are most consistent with their self- or ideal-self images. Given this theory, what marketing plan should Dozier recommend to the board of directors of Puriteen?

5. Do certain products lend themselves to self-theory congruence? If so, what are the characteristics of those products?

6. Which self-concept is more useful — self or ideal-self — in developing marketing programs? Defend your answer.

7. How does the use of consumer self-concept differ from the use of consumer personality traits as a basis for developing brand images? Explain.

IV

External Influences — Cultural and Social Factors

Part IV deals with the characteristics of the environment within which the human individual functions.

It devotes separate chapters to the influence of:

- culture and subculture;
- reference groups and social class; and
- the family group

on human behavior, specifically consumer behavior.

Because business influences, though external, are somewhat different in nature and origin, being marketer-generated and controlled, they will be treated in the next section, Part V.

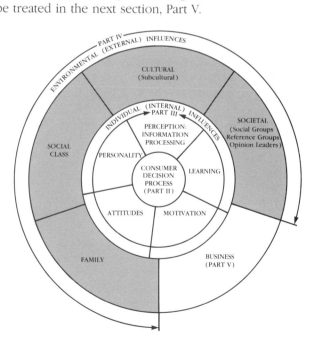

14

Culture and Subculture

EXAMPLES

1. The Non-Alcoholic Beverage Market in Canada

Judging by what the executives at Canada Dry Limited were quoted as having said, the company may be looking forward to big sales increases in the 1980s.[1] The postwar Boomies are now over thirty and they want a different beverage. Preferences change with age, they explain.

"... when they're twelve or thirteen, kids are oriented toward flavors — orange, grape — the sweetest they can get." Between fourteen and eighteen "they climb on the cola bandwagon. But after that, their palates mature and they want something lighter. The situation we have now is that the 25-to-35 age group is growing. This is our major market." (See Figure 14.1.)

Attitudes to non-returnable bottles have also changed significantly. The return to returnables has been quite rapid, especially in Quebec where the non-returnables never did reach a high level of popularity.

There also appears to be a boom in the bottled water business. It is estimated that 85% of the bottled water sold in Canada is consumed in Quebec — which, according to one executive, "reflects the typical French-Canadian preoccupation with the liver." Some of the 85% and most of the remaining 15% is sold to European immigrants, to whom drinking bottled water is a natural part of keeping healthy.

2. Cultural Taboos

Some years ago, a Quebec brewery decided to change the label of its main brand of ale in an attempt to increase brand share by developing greater identification among Quebecers. The new label employed the

FIGURE 14.1: Adapting to the End of the Boomie Era

Courtesy Canadian Imperial Bank of Commerce

colors of the Quebec flag, made liberal use of the fleur-de-lis, and even designed the initial letter of the brand name in such a way that it resembled a cross (over 80% of the Quebec population is Catholic).

Within a few days of the appearance of the label, there was little doubt of its rejection by the public. The Jean Baptiste Society, an organization dedicated to preserving French Quebec's heritage, was strong and loud in its protests. It ran ads in the major French-language daily newspapers vociferously protesting the transgressions of the brewery and exhorting its compatriots to boycott the brand. It claimed that the label had violated not only Quebec's political emblems but also its religious symbols.

The company's response was immediate. Shocked at having so badly misread Quebec sentiment, it quickly recalled all of its bottles and replaced the offending label with a hastily designed substitute. Unfortunately, the damage was considerable and, as it turned out, irreparable. Within a few years the brand was dead.

3. The Canadian Consumer and Coupons[2]

As an example of how behavior reflects social values, the use made of coupons varies in different regions of Canada. It is estimated that the rate at which Canadian marketers are using cents-off coupons to promote their products is increasing at about 20 to 25% a year. The two billion coupons distributed by manufacturers in 1980 was double the number distributed in 1975 and 23% higher than the 1.63 billion in 1979. In 1981 it increased by 25% to 2.5 billion. In 1983 the total number distributed was 3.14 billion.

It is estimated that a further billion or so were distributed by retailers in newspaper advertisements and that the average Canadian household receives about three hundred coupons a year.

The per-capita redemption rate is highest in Quebec.

4. Cultural Norms

The marketer needs to be aware of the norms of behavior in a culture. The following example illustrates the risks of importing advertising appeals from another culture.

A few years ago, an advertisement for canned fish directed at the French-Canadian market showed a young woman dressed in shorts playing golf with her husband. The ad copy pointed out the convenience of the product suggesting that the housewife could play golf all afternoon and still have time to prepare a delicious fish dinner. The advertiser failed to realize that the scenario presented was not typical of his target market. A French-Canadian wife would not be likely to play golf with her husband or to be wearing shorts on the golf course and "she would not be serving the particular kind of fish as a main course."[3]

All of these examples illustrate the importance of cultural factors in the practice of marketing — such factors as population and taste trends (Example 1), social customs and taboos (Example 2), and social values and norms (Examples 3 and 4) — and how they influence the development of appropriate strategies.

Not only is such an adaptive approach necessary for the particular culture (and its sub-cultures) in which the company is located, but the growth of multinational corporations and increasing international marketing have made it almost mandatory that companies seek to understand the values, attitudes, and needs of the foreign cultures in which they operate, if they are to reduce the chances of failure.

The context in which consumers live and work has a direct bearing on their behavior. External or environmental factors influence and even determine the internal workings of the individual. The intra-individual determinants so far discussed (perception, learning, needs, motives, wants, values, beliefs, attitudes, and personality) are not separate, independent forces but, rather, they operate within and are influenced by cultural and social forces.

This chapter examines the ways in which culture influences, determines, and interacts with those individual factors and at the same time, how the individual influences the environment. These phenomena are considered primarily as they relate to consumer behavior and as they are useful to the marketer.

WHAT IS CULTURE?

Attempts to answer this question have led to numerous definitions — one source cited 164 definitions of culture[4] — but behind them all is the notion of a society coping with its environment. In our view, then, culture may be defined as those characteristic ways in which a society has come to solve the problems generated by its environment. According to Ralph Linton, a distinguished anthropologist, it is behavior and the results of behavior that are learned, shared, and transmitted by members of a society.[5]

Culture is part of every member of a society. All individual variants can be traced to certain basic, underlying commonalities — and in different parts of the world, different cultures have evolved to solve the problems faced by each group.

The term "culture" has no definite boundaries, so that who belongs in what culture is not an easy question to answer. It can be applied in a number of different ways, depending upon the frame of reference. Thus one may speak of Western (versus Eastern) culture, and, within that, of American, German, Spanish, or Canadian culture; and within some of these one may refer to component cultures — for example, French-Canadian culture. At an even broader

level — so to speak, at an interplanetary level — it is conceivable that some day one may use such terms as "Earth Culture" or "Venusian culture" or "Martian culture." The essential point is that, at whatever level, a cultural group shares certain basic elements. The broader the frame of reference the fewer the basic attributes that characterize each group.

HOW DOES CULTURE DEVELOP AND FUNCTION?

All cultures develop in similar ways and fulfill certain basic functions or purposes. The solutions a society evolves for its problems include three kinds of elements (cultural symbols):

- **material** (e.g., such artifacts as machines, tools, movies, computers, buildings);
- **psychological** (e.g., values, attitudes, beliefs, ideas — in short, knowledge); and
- **kinetic** (e.g., behaviors that have come to be accepted as necessary, useful and productive by the society and are subject to certain rules or standards).

The interrelatedness of these components should be clear. The consumer, for example, will engage in certain kinds of approved behavior (job, dress, shopping), guided by certain motives or drives that reflect the values and norms held by the individual. It should also be clear that for different societies, different combinations of the three kinds of components develop as appropriate for their own situation.

In that sense, culture is an adaptive' social phenomenon. It is dynamic, constantly changing to suit the needs (material, cognitive and behavioral) of the situation. Societies are characterized by different rates of change, frequently slower than they should be (**cultural lag**). On the other hand, change may also be very rapid, as a result of environmental or technological developments. Kenneth Boulding has, for example, made the following observations about today's world:

As far as many statistical series related to activities of mankind are concerned, the date that divides human history into two equal parts is well within living memory.... The world today... is as different from the world in which I was born as that world was from Julius Caesar's. I was born in the middle of human history, to date, roughly. Almost as much has happened since I was born as happened before.[6]

Changes are taking place around us with such rapidity that, in Alvin Toffler's opinion, we seem to be suffering from **future shock**, which he defines as "the dizzying disorientation brought on by the premature arrival of the future.... It is culture shock in one's own society."[7]

How do the members of a society acquire the particular material/psychological/behavioral orientations developed by the society? They **learn** from others of the same generation and values, norms, and knowledge are also transmitted from one generation to another. This learning of one's culture is called **socialization**. Learning a new culture (by immigrants, for example) is called **acculturation**.

A related concept is **assimilation**, which is the degree to which an acculturated individual is accepted by the dominant society. It is possible for someone to be acculturated and yet not be assimilated or for someone to be assimilated without being acculturated. The northern black in the United States, for example, is probably more acculturated than assimilated.

For a better understanding of the motives and reactions of social groups, the marketer should note that:

● there are several types of assimilation — groups may not be accepted to the same extent in all spheres of their lives. For example, marital assimilation has been found to follow residential assimilation, which comes after occupational;[8]

● the speed with which a group is assimilated will determine the rate of acculturation of that group.

The influence of social groups is of particular importance in the learning of a culture. The family is central in the socialization of the individual, because, among other things, it performs such a significant function in the formative years of the individual. Many other types of social groups (such as work groups, peer groups, and other reference groups) and social institutions (e.g., educational and religious institutions) are also important in the interpretation and transmission of culture.

The integrating of these characteristics of culture — its social, adaptive, learned, and transmissive functions — is well summarized in the following excerpt:

In the process of social evolution, people find certain behaviors and values to be adaptive and helpful; others, non-adaptive and even harmful. Helpful practices are *shared* and rewarded; harmful practices are discarded and discouraged. Over a period of time, useful behaviors, values, and artifacts become institutionalized and incorporated as part of the cultural traditions. The individual *internalizes* these institutionalized practices and often forgets their origin.[9]

In our society, change seems to be very rapid and adaptation has also accelerated but perhaps not sufficiently. Marketers must recognize people's inherent resistance to change, especially for "knowledge" acquired early in life. They need to assess carefully the degree of lag and the strength of resistance before strategies are implemented. Sometimes they may assume, wrongly, that adaptive change has occurred; at other times it may be wiser to conform to certain strongly held ideas than to seek to change them.

The development of culture serves two other important functions. Cultural phenomena are retained when they satisfy or *gratify* biological and human social needs. The more important the need of the society, the greater is the esteem given to those traits that bring about its gratification. In a sense, the survival of the society, as its most basic goal, engenders the highest rewards and status in a society. Thus the physician, the jurist, the educator, and the priest all rank very high in status in our society, as do the witch-doctor, the aged, and the warrior in a less developed society.

The last function is the **integrative** quality of culture. All the cultural traits of a society seem to form a configuration that marks it out from other societies — this is sometimes known as the **cultural personality**:

> ... every society has its own basic personality type and its own series of status personalities differing in some respects from those of any other society.[10]

To summarize, culture makes use of symbols that are transmitted within and between generations. It is an adaptive, social phenomenon that is cumulative (adds new elements as time goes) and progressive (achieving greater control over the environment). All of these characteristics serve to satisfy biological and social needs and to lead toward greater security for human beings.

Cultural Norms

A society develops certain standards by which to judge other individuals. These standards of behavior reflect the values and attitudes of the society. Anthropologists have distinguished four kinds of *norms*: laws, mores, customs, and folkways.

Laws are explicit standards of behavior and sanctions that are enforced by the society and that must be obeyed. They usually involve behavior that is threatening or harmful to the society. Laws must be obeyed and are broken only on pain of punishment. Punishments vary according to the severity of the infraction, which is directly related to the centrality of the behavior.

Mores are sanctions that do not have the force of law but may at times exert stricter control than the law. They involve such moral issues as "the seven sins."

Customs are behaviors that are faithfully and traditionally practised but carry no legal or moral requirements. Customs can undergo change with time and with changes in values and attitudes. Examples are nine-to-five office hours, three meals a day, turkey at Christmas, and pants for men and skirts for women.

Folkways are behaviors that do not require any strong degree of conformity but are carried out by large numbers of the society. These behaviors are most susceptible to changing tastes and preferences. Examples are wearing a tie, or wearing tailored slacks at lectures (now denim jeans are "in").

Such a distinction among the different standards of behavior in a society can be very useful to a marketer. Where, for example, behavioral change is involved, it will be possible to assess the likely degree of resistance that may occur.

Thus, attempting to make turkey a year-round food (custom) would likely be more difficult to accomplish than getting women to wear the midi skirt (folkway). Such a schema would be particularly helpful in international marketing where certain behaviors may be judged by completely different standards in the new market compared to the domestic market.

Cultural Values

The values that lie behind the behavioral norms represent the beliefs shared by a society that certain general states of existence are personally and socially worth striving for.[11] These values are basic orientations and goals and they influence the attitudes and motives that guide behavior.

Rokeach has listed eighteen *terminal values* (or end-states).[12] Some of these are:

- a comfortable life;
- a sense of accomplishment;
- a world of beauty;
- equality (brotherhood, equal opportunity);
- freedom;

- inner harmony;
- mature love (sexual and spiritual intimacy);
- national security;
- self-respect; and
- social recognition.

He has also listed eighteen *instrumental values*, the intermediate ends (or the means) by which the terminal values are achieved. Examples are:

- ambition (willingness to work hard);
- capableness (competence);
- cleanliness (neatness, tidiness);
- courage (willingness to stand up for beliefs);
- honesty (truthfulness);
- imagination (daring, creativity);
- independence (self-reliance);
- cheerfulness (joyfulness);
- logic (consistency);
- responsibility (dependability); and
- self-control (restraint).

Not all values are shared to the same degree by the members of society. Because of the individual differences that exist, marketers are able to develop separate strategies for groups that share similar values. It is particularly important to uncover and evaluate cultural changes and trends in order to develop more effective long-range strategies.

In the absence of any works specifically about Canada, this review will paint with a broad brush those values considered relevant to western industrialized society, attempting wherever possible to indicate how and to what degree Canadian society is different.

That, unfortunately, is more easily said than done. Canada, perhaps more than any other country in the world, is a diverse nation, with two official languages, many separate cultures, and a large minority strongly bent on maintaining its traditions. In such a context it is clearly difficult to identify core values that reflect a mainstream Canadian culture. In addition, some of the contradictions in our society often make the identification of values confusing. Both ends of a continuum (e.g., individualism/conformity) may be held at the same time by different seg-

ments of the population, so that characterizing the society is a difficult task.

The values to be discussed will serve as a broad base from which the marketer may seek to understand the motivations and behavior of Canadian society.

Materialism

There is a strong emphasis in our society on possessions. The great majority of families in Canada own telephones, television sets, and automobiles, for example. Owning more and more material things and the importance of others knowing about them (conspicuous consumption) are dominant thrusts in our society, no doubt attributable to the unprecedented level of affluence. Marketers have made full use of the opportunities thus presented by providing consumers with dishwashers, microwave ovens, TV games, home movie cameras, videotapes, and home computers, to name a few. Immediate gratification, leisure, and the "good life" have been described as significant personal motives that business has not only catered to but fostered and encouraged.

Within recent years, changing economic conditions — inflation, product shortages, rising prices, and wage restraints — may have reduced society's materialism.

Competitiveness

The quality of competitiveness expresses itself in a number of ways: in the urge to achieve and succeed and in an emphasis on progress, growth, and expansion.

The personal need to achieve is associated with a strong degree of **individualism**, which values the individual's independence and self-respect. A great deal of advertising emphasizes personal status, uniqueness, self-esteem, and achievement. The consumer is reminded of the rewards of success and how products serve as symbols of success (see Figure 14.2).

The emphasis on progress and growth is shown by the attitudes to innovations and new

FIGURE 14.2: An Appeal to Individualism

Courtesy John Walker & Sons Ltd.

The caption on the image reads: *Be recognized by your taste in Scotch.*

products. In Canada, progress may be judged more in terms of social programs and social well-being than, as in the US, in terms of technological advance that becomes the source of strong national pride.

Conformity

Though individualism may be quite strong, there is at the same time a tendency to group standards and expectations. Individualism and conformity are not mutually exclusive. Each is important in different circumstances, although the pendulum seems to swing from one period to another. It would appear that individuality is becoming somewhat submerged in the mid-1980s and, in the face of nuclear fear, the population explosion, pollution, and other general threats, is giving way to a wider struggle for security and the promise of strength that resides in group cohesion.

Activity

Though perhaps not as strong as it is in the US, another relevant value in Canada is the emphasis on activity. Much after the pattern of the US, Canadians enjoy shorter work weeks and smaller families; greater discretionary income has been translated into an expansion of hobby activities, do-it-yourself tasks, cultural activities, travel, and even fast-food outlets. The desire for convenient meals has led to the popularity of "Egg McMuffins" and, at the same time, to the decline in egg consumption. As indicated earlier, it should not be thought such trends are characteristic of the whole society. They are segment-specific.

Youthfulness

The period of glory for the ideal of youthfulness was probably the 1960s and the 1970s, when the society's youth seemed to dominate its life. For example, university students around the world from Montreal and Los Angeles to Paris and Tokyo had serious effects on policies and ideas. Young people influenced environmental control, clothing, music, family concerns, sexual relationships, and many other aspects of personal and social life, for their peers as well as for older generations. All kinds of products — soaps, shampoos, skin creams, sun-tan lotions, hair driers, Levi's, soft drinks, and liquid diets — sang the glories of the "Pepsi generation" and exhorted us to "think young," and look young (Figure 14.3). While youthful attitudes and goals will remain a justifiable ideal for many, their predominance is already declining. The increasing proportion of the 35 + age group threatens to restore some balance to our perspective (see Figure 14.1).

Health and Nutrition

Related in part to youthful ideals and in part to an increasing sensitivity to personal welfare and self-fulfillment, another significant trend over

FIGURE 14.3: An Appeal to Youthfulness

Courtesy Germaine Monteil Cosmetiques Corporation

FIGURE 14.4: An Appeal to Good Nutrition

Courtesy Canada Packers Inc.

the last few years has been the phenomenal growth in health-related activities. Canadians have taken to jogging, running, and various sports of all kinds in large numbers and there seems to have developed a greater awareness of and interest in diet and nutrition (see Figure 14.4).

In a broad sense, all of these expressions of self-enhancement are related to the need for security — for a safer, cleaner, more satisfying life. Marketers have made good use of these needs in such advertising appeals as "Ring around the collar" (fear of social disapproval) and "The closer you are, the better we look" (fear of social unattractiveness).

Rationalism

A strong tendency to be practical, logical, and efficient exists in our society. Generally speaking, anything that saves time and effort is highly valued. Dishwashers, microwave ovens, trash compactors, and food processors are some examples of how industry has responded to this characteristic.

Time is a valued commodity because being efficient is important. Our lives are run by our watches, which must be accurate. The contrast with other societies in terms of the respect for promptness and the allotment of time for specific activities is well described by Hall.[13] Time always seems to be in short supply. We are always on the run, doing something.

Conservatism

Canadians have been described as quite conservative, more so than Americans.[14] Horowitz describes the conservatism as being less egalitarian, emphasizing "aristocratic responsibility." According to Lipset, the open American frontier fostered notions of equality and opportunity whereas Canada, with no revolution or "wild" West, was more tolerant of inequality.[15]

This orientation has led to a system of education in Canada (except Quebec) that is "elitist," that emphasizes not so much individual or national success as maintaining British Empire tradition.[16] In the United States, on the other hand, education stresses a definition of "Americanism" and American individual and national success. Horowitz holds the view that this Canadian conservatism at one end of the scale has left room for a socialist alternative at the other extreme, thus accounting for the development of socialist views and a social democratic party in Canada.

CURRENT SHIFTS IN CULTURAL VALUES

We live in an age of rapid change. Satellite telecommunications, home computers, wonder drugs, and revolutionary medical techniques are a few examples of technological change. Attitudinal and social changes are equally significant for the marketer, who needs to be especially tuned to such trends in order to compete successfully.

The economy and society in general are becoming increasingly complex, and changing conditions are becoming part of our normal operating environment. Executives are recognizing the need to plan, not so much to help them make future decisions,

but to help them see the future implications of today's decisions.[17]

It is necessary for the marketer to assess not only the *directions* of the changes taking place but also their *rate* and *patterns*.

Changing economic conditions and technological developments in communications, in manufacturing processes, and in materials are a few of the factors behind cultural shifts. The gasoline shortage of 1974, earlier shortages of sugar and coffee and increasing prices all served to bring about changes in consumer orientations. At one stage in the 1960s and 1970s certain changes occurred with a rapidity that was rather startling and gathered such force among young adults that some referred to this phenomenon as the "counterculture." The effects of this orientation on dress, music, living habits and foods were just short of traumatic to the society.

This impact has subsided but there is no question that the changes wrought on society are here to stay. The importance of identifying cultural value trends cannot be overemphasized. A number of research agencies, using questionnaire surveys, attempt to measure cultural values and trends in the United States on a regular basis. Two key ones are the Yankelovich Monitor and the SRI Values and Life-styles Program.[18] There are apparently no comparable services in Canada. Occasional *ad hoc* social surveys have been conducted by some research agencies, such as the Canadian Gallup Poll.

Prediction is always hazardous and difficult, particularly in non-mathematical matters. Where social trends are indicated, questions persist about their exact nature, their duration, and their eventual course. Nevertheless, some trends appear quite evident:

Frugality

There appears to be a trend away from the strong emphasis on materialism and a de-emphasis of material possessions, at least on the part of a significant minority. This was no doubt brought about by the unfavorable economic conditions since the 1970s and is reflected, for example, in the sales of small cars. At the same time, larger cars cannot be said to be disappearing from the market. Indeed, there appears to be a new surge of interest in the middle- and large-size automobiles, which are promising luxury and elegance with fully electronic instrument panels (see Figure 14.5).

FIGURE 14.5: An Appeal to Materialistic Values

Courtesy General Motors Limited

Self-Fulfillment

Our society also seems to be moving from the strong emphasis on achievement and success. There is a trend in the lives of many toward self-enhancement, self-understanding, and personal creativity. Individualism, in the sense of strong self-interest, may be giving way to a need for life experiences, for cultural self-expression, and for meaningful work. Competitiveness is being submerged by greater community involvement and in a simplification of life that

means turning away from complicated products, services, and ways of life.[19]

This trend may be leading to a return to nature for the enjoyment of the natural beauty of our surroundings and of our planet (see Figure 14.6). This is reflected in the increasing trend to move away from our cities and to visit other countries. Canada is known for its interest in and its willingness to help other (particularly third world) countries, for its sensitivity and generosity, and for its genuine desire to improve the lives of others, as exemplified by Norman Bethune and Chester Ronning, both Canadians who are revered and respected by the Chinese; by Cardinal Leger, who spent years in Africa; and by missionaries in Central and South America and other parts of the world.

Liberalism and Conservatism

A good part of the liberalism of the 1960s and 1970s fostered by the women's liberation movement may be here to stay. For example, sex-role stereotypes may not return to the traditional guidelines typical of the Victorian era and the greater equality of the sexes may be maintained (see Figure 14.7).

On the other hand, sexual attitudes could move away from the permissiveness of the 1960s and 1970s toward greater conservatism. Already such threats as AIDS and herpes have forced a re-evaluation of sexual attitudes, so that greater caution and care may be exercised in sexual matters. This turnaway from sexual adventuring may be only a part of a larger phenomenon of society going through a sober, responsible phase.

Feminism is also here to stay. Women will play increasingly important roles in our society — in politics, law, education, religion, and business. The functions and occupations in which they engage will pose fewer and fewer restrictions and will be limited only by their physical capabilities. The cars they drive, the games they play, the clubs they join, and the clothes they wear will get closer and closer to those of men

FIGURE 14.6: An Appeal to Enjoyment of Nature

Courtesy Ontario Heritage Foundation, Ministry of Citizenship and Culture

and will be different only when unavoidable (see Figure 14.8).

This is, in fact, a true expression of egalitarianism. The belief that fulfillment for women comes from homemaking as well as from more challenging and productive work will lead to increasing female careerism. Already women make up about half of the labor force, of whom approximately one-half are married.

Health, Athleticism, Activity

Emphasis on physical fitness is also on the rise. Increasing numbers of Canadians of all ages are jogging, exercising, joining aerobic classes, participating in sports, spurred on by personal initiative, by clubs and groups, and even by the federal government (see Figure 14.9).

The interest in nutrition and diet is likely to grow as Canadians continue to spend more time, effort, and money on improving their physical appearance. Greater sensitivity to foods and their ingredients could have serious consequences for the fast-food industry.

At the same time, experts are showing some concern about the *mental* health of a genera-

FIGURE 14.7: Changing Sex-Role Stereotypes

Courtesy Watleys Ltd., Wine Merchants, representing Cointreau

FIGURE 14.8: Trends in Women's Clothing

Courtesy Jockey International Inc. and Harvey Woods Limited

tion of teenagers growing up in a world of anxiety over nuclear war, environmental pollution, and all of the other ills that beset our society. A 1984 study conducted in Metro Toronto with a sample of 1,012 students between twelve and eighteen found that the threat of nuclear war was the greatest source of fear and anxiety, far more than unemployment or career problems.[20] The nuclear threat affected their plans for the future. Twenty-eight percent said they wondered whether they would want to get married; 24% indicated a desire to live for the present and forget the future. Such attitudes can have far-reaching effects on the future course of our society.

Multiculturalism

Canada is a multicultural society and there is every indication that it will become even more so. Since 1950, immigrants to Canada have numbered about 1.5 million every ten years.[21] In

FIGURE 14.9: The Government's Physical Fitness Program

Courtesy PARTICIPaction, a private nonprofit organization promoting fitness in Canada, funded by the Government of Canada

1982, a total of 121,147 foreign nationals came to Canada, from all over the globe: the UK (14%), Eastern Europe (14%), the Caribbean and Guyana (13%), South Asia (9%), the Philippines (4%), Viet Nam (4%), Central and South America (4%), Hong Kong (4%), Portugal (3%), Korea (2%), Italy (2%), Iran (2%), Greece (1%), Cambodia (1%), Israel (1%), Taiwan (1%), other European countries (7%), other Asian countries (5%), and other Middle Eastern countries (1%). All of these national and ethnic groups will undoubtedly keep Canada as a true cultural mosaic and make the identification of Canadian cultural values more difficult.

It is clear that Canada will remain an internationally oriented society whose values and attitudes will be in constant change. It is worth noting that Ontario is perhaps the most dynamic of the provinces in this regard. In 1982 almost half (44%) of all immigrants to Canada settled in Ontario.

An attempt has been made in this section to delineate some of the current value trends in our society. They are more indicative than definitive. Differences of opinion will exist, particularly in a society as heterogeneous and diverse as Canada's. What is important is that the marketer recognize the dynamism of our society and seek to become aware of developing shifts so that strategic planning can take them into account.

INTERCULTURAL MARKETING

The international framework of world trade and finance (e.g., trade restrictions such as tariffs, quotas, embargos or trade agreements such as the European Economic Community or the General Agreement on Tariffs and Trade), and the economic and politico-legal environments in each market are usually well understood by the marketer. Too frequently, however, the cultural environment is taken for granted. It is ignored or assumed to be no different from the home market.

Responsible for such faulty management is a basic short-sightedness, described by sociologists as **ethnocentrism**, whereby individuals tend to judge another culture by the standards and norms of their own culture and, indeed, to consider other cultures as inferior to their own. The simple fact is that marketers, even when correct, are not social reformers and cannot and should not seek to change cultural preferences and behaviors. Rather, they should adapt to them and judge them from the point of view of their origin in a different cultural context (**cultural relativism**). This is true of not only discrete politico-national groups but also subcultural groups within the same national boundaries.

Examples abound in cross-cultural marketing of errors and misjudgements made by myopic marketers in every facet of marketing strategy, where marketers failed to recognize and adapt to local habits of behavior and thinking.

Product

Consider the case described in Example 2 of the Quebec beer company that attempted to introduce a new label showing the colors of the Quebec flag and presenting the initial letter of the brand name in such a way that it resembled a cross. Not only was it unwise to employ the national colors on the label but it was objectionable to commercialize the society's religious symbol.

The story is told of a drug company's failure with a pain-killer similar to aspirin (Analoze) that could be taken without water. What seemed like a "sure thing" because of its convenience (it could be taken in the car, bus, or subway, at your desk, or in the classroom) did not find acceptance, it was later determined, because of the widespread belief that such analgesics would not work without water.

Product names should be carefully checked for translation into other languages or disastrous consequences can result. While names such as "Matador" or "Nova" may have exotic, romantic associations, their translations in Spanish ("killer" and "does not go") spelled failure in Spanish-speaking countries. The introduction of Coca-Cola in China led to a translation of the name to Kekou Kele, which communicates the universal claim of Coca-Cola and is close to the English in sound.

Literally, it means "happiness (delightful) in the mouth." In Hong Kong, Pepsi Cola was translated "Pak Si Hall Lok," which meant "delightful for everything you do," and was very close to the English. Other examples:

Baume & *Mercier* Watch → Ming Si = Famous person, dignitary

Wrangler → Wai Gha = Dignity and Class
Citizen Watch → Sing Zun = Morning Star (old measure of time)
Sanka → Sun Gar = New and Better

Marketers have also found surprising national product preferences — General Foods' Tang orange powder in the jar was very successful in the US and a failure in Canada; their pouch pack revealed the exact opposite. McDonald's McChicken sandwich failed in the US while it was a success in Canada. The per capita consumption of soft drinks in Quebec is among the highest in the world, even higher than economically comparable areas in tropical or sub-tropical regions. Brandy is the most popular drink in Hong Kong, which has the highest per capita brandy consumption in the world. In the UK large refrigerators are quite uncommon because they are not needed — shopping is done several times a week and there is little need for storage space. In Spanish and Latin American countries the lack of refrigerative facilities means that perishable goods such as butter cannot be stored and, as a consequence, most cooking is done with cooking oil rather than with butter.

Although the tangible characteristics of a product may be perceived by all consumers in the same way, the consumption patterns of that product are likely to vary widely from one country to another. For example, most North Americans like cold beer, whereas the English prefer their beer near room temperature. These varying consumption patterns naturally have a bearing on advertising strategies and must be considered in evaluating the standardization of promotional activities across cultures.

Promotion

General Motors' slogan, "Body by Fisher," when rendered into Flemish, emerged as "Corpse by Fisher." Pepsi Cola's slogan "Come alive with Pepsi" emerged from the translation into Chinese as "Pepsi brings back your ancestors" and from the German as "Come out of the grave."

Promotional difficulties involve not only linguistic translations but also the use of symbols, colors, models (French Canadians complained that the models in some commercials did not look like Quebecers), and background. Strategy should take note of the *media structure* in a foreign market so that TV commercials are not planned for a country dominated by radio, or, as another example, a national TV campaign is not prepared in one language for a country in which several different languages are spoken (for example, India has sixteen different languages).

Advertisements that do not reflect the local life-style are for the most part ineffective (unless the contrast in life-style is intentional). For example, the American-owned General Mills Corporation introduced a breakfast cereal to the English market with a picture of a grinning, red-haired, crew-cut "All-American Boy" on the box designed to capture the attention of English children. However, English housewives refused to purchase the cereal because they thought the grinning boy on the package was "banal" — a precocious youngster did not appeal to the more formal ideal of a well-disciplined child upheld by the English.

Place

In countries such as Spain or Latin America or even the UK, the grocery shopping trip fills a social function. Shoppers look forward to meeting their friends and exchanging news and they prefer the personal relationships with the grocer and the grocery clerks. In such a setting, supermarket retailing is not likely to expand very rapidly.

In Quebec, small "Mom-and-Pop" corner grocery stores account for over 60% of the retail food trade, compared to about 30% in Ontario.

Every aspect of marketing can be different in an outside culture and the marketer, to avoid the kinds of errors described above, must acquire a thorough understanding of the behaviors, preferences, values, and other cultural characteristics of the host society.

One source has drawn up an outline for systematically analyzing a foreign market in order to develop appropriate strategy.[22] Figure 14.10 is based on that outline.

These are useful points to be considered before the marketer decides to enter a foreign market. They could form the basis for extensive consumer research or at least for a critical evaluation of the proposed market on the basis of existing information.

CULTURAL UNIVERSALS

Intercultural studies have led to the suggestion that in many instances different markets can have much in common and that, in designing their strategy, marketers can make good use of such *cultural universals*. One study found that black and grey were considered "bad" in twenty-three different cultures, while white, blue, and green were considered "good."[23]

For the cross-cultural marketer, there is always the problem of the balance between what some have called "standardization and localization." Although localization is a safer approach, there appears to be a trend toward greater standardization, possibly due to the pervasiveness and speed of modern media and to the dominance of American values in many countries. Sorenson and Wiechmann found that

---

1. Determine Relevant *Motivations*:
   - What needs will the product fill?
   - How are these needs currently being satisfied?
   - What *unique* need(s) will the product fill in that society?
   - Do members of that society readily recognize these needs?

2. Determine *Behavior Patterns*:
   - What are the characteristic purchasing patterns?
   - Who in the family decides? Who buys?
   - Frequency of purchase.
   - Size(s) preferred.
   - Are any conflicts expected with regard to the use of this product?
   - What could be done about them?

3. Determine Broad *Cultural Values* Relevant to the Product:
   - What values in the society about work, religion, family life, etc. relate to the product?
   - Does the product conflict with any of these values?
   - How can it be resolved? (Product change; emphasis on positive values with which product may be identified.)

4. Forms of *Decision Making*:
   - Sources of information — friends, opinion-leaders, family, media?
   - What criteria do members of the society use in evaluating offerings?

5. Evaluate *Promotion* Methods:
   - Role of advertising.
   - Relative roles of different media.
   - Significance of themes, symbols, words, illustrations? Which are taboo, which acceptable?
   - What kinds, if any, of salespeople are acceptable?

6. Determine Appropriate *Institutions*:
   - Types of retailers and other intermediaries available.
   - What services do consumers expect?
   - Do these intermediaries provide such services?
   - How are various types of retailers regarded by the consumer?
   - Are changes in the distribution structure likely to be accepted?

FIGURE 14.10: Cross-Cultural Analysis of Consumer Behavior

Adapted from James F. Engel, Roger D. Blackwell, and David T. Kollat, *Consumer Behavior*, 3rd. ed. (Hinsdale, Illinois: Dryden Press, 1978), p. 90.

among twenty-seven multinational companies operating in Europe (including Coca-Cola, General Foods, Procter and Gamble, Revlon, and Unilever), 63% of the marketing programs were regarded as "highly standardized."[24]

The answer, it seems, lies in a marketing program that combines standardized with localized elements. In order to ensure proper assessment of the localized elements, companies are making greater use of local executives. Standardization is probably inadvisable if the symbolic content of a product type varies among countries — a bicycle company may successfully promote its most basic product as a recreational vehicle in North America, but it would need to take an entirely different approach in Asia where the bicycle is a more important means of transportation than the automobile.

If a product violates traditions or customs in some of its uses in certain countries but not in others, standardization of promotion may be ill-advised — a distiller in the US or Canada may employ ads depicting women drinking alcoholic beverages, but would need to use a different campaign in a country where women are not supposed to be seen drinking in public.

Consumers also tend to have *national product stereotypes*, that is, they have specific attitudes to the products made in a given country. For example, American businessmen tended to evaluate Japanese products as "inexpensive, technically advanced, mass produced, and distributed worldwide."[25]

The same study also identified consumers who had favorable attitudes toward foreign products as being characterized by "low status concern, low conservatism, low dogmatism, and high educational attainment."

A related issue is the *relative importance* of consumers' perceptions of all foreign products, their national product stereotypes, and their evaluations of specific products from a given country. The authors in that study concluded that consumers show differences between national product stereotypes and their perceptions of specific products from that country. It

seems that a multinational company would be advised to carry out marketing research to determine foreign consumer attitudes to particular product types before committing itself to an advertising campaign. An American automobile manufacturer should determine British attitudes to American cars rather than attitudes toward American products or foreign products in general before finalizing the promotional programs in the British market.

It is reasonable to expect that cultural universals will involve products with common universal appeal. For example, most people everywhere, from Argentina to Zaire, want a better way of life for themselves and for their families.

The "desire to be beautiful" is universal, as are such appeals as "mother and child," "freedom from pain," "glow of health." *It is the specific avenues that such needs and motives take that make the difference, and even where the avenues are similar, the language of the advertisement must be translated into the idiom of the culture or subculture in which it is to appear.*

Some outstanding examples of companies using standardization or cultural universals are Esso ("Tiger in the Tank"), McDonald's ("We Do It All For You"), and Coca-Cola ("The Real Thing").

SUBCULTURES

Subcultures are subgroups within a culture that, while sharing the values and norms of the dominant culture, exhibit certain significant differences of their own — differences that are sufficient to warrant the development of separate strategies in certain instances. The term has come to be applied to a wide variety of groups in the society:

The list only begins with (1) socioeconomic strata — such as the lower class or the poor. It goes on to include (2) ethnic collectives — e.g., Negroes, Jews; (3) regional populations — Southerners, Midwesterners; (4) age grades — adolescents, youth; (5) community types — urban, rural; (6) institutional complexes — education, penal establishments; (7) occupational groupings — various professions; (8) religious bodies — Catholics, Muslims, and even (9) political entities — revolutionary groups, for example. Yet this does not exhaust the catalog, for one also finds (10) genera of intellectual orientation, such as "scientists" and "intellectuals"; (11) units that are really behavioral classes, mainly various kinds of "deviants"; and (12) what are categories of moral evaluation, ranging from "respectables" to the "disreputable" and the "unworthy" poor.[26]

Marketers have perhaps used all of these classifications at one time or another to identify segments, such as lower middle class, French-Canadians, Maritimers, "the youth culture," rural consumers, and so on.

In doing so, marketers have fallen prey to some dangerous assumptions. For example, in the United States studies on the black or Negro market have tended to generalize the results to all blacks. Clearly, it should be recognized that there are wide differences of attitude, value, and behavior within the black community, primarily due to varying degrees of assimilation, and that it is folly to generalize in that way. In fact, it may even be true that too much has been made of the differences and too little of the similarities between subcultures and the dominant culture.

The same may be said of subcultures in Canada. Though one may speak of French Canadians or English Canadians, it is a gross oversimplification to think that there is little difference within each group. For example, it is a mistake to regard all English Canadians as quite similar. The fact that they speak the same language in Atlantic Canada, Ontario, the Prairie provinces, and British Columbia does not mean that they make up a homogeneous market.

As was suggested for intercultural marketing, it is necessary to understand the needs, motivations, decision-making behavior, purchasing and consumption patterns, attitudes, and media habits of a subculture so that appropriate marketing strategies may be developed. With this in mind, the remainder of the chapter will treat a number of important subcultural groups — first, French Canadians (the major subculture in Canada), and an increasingly important group, Italian Canadians. I will continue with a review of age subcultures in our society and conclude, with a brief treatment of the two major subcultures in the US — black Americans and Hispanic Americans.

French Canadians

Canada presents an interesting situation, in that it contains a distinct subculture of significant size that is almost entirely concentrated in one region — French-speaking Canadians in Quebec. According to Statistics Canada, French Canadians will number about 6.6 million or 25.6% of the Canadian population in 1985, with about 88% residing in Quebec, approximately 8% in Ontario, and another 4% in New Brunswick.[27] Francophones make up about 33% of the population in New Brunswick.[28]

While comparisons may be made with the black subculture in the United States, there are a number of important differences that should be pointed out:

● French Canadians make up a larger proportion (26%) of the national population than do blacks in the US (12%);
● they speak a distinctly different language and have an older, well-established, more developed cultural heritage;
● they are concentrated in one region and not, like the US blacks, dispersed throughout the country; and
● their economic standards are higher.

The presence of such a large and different subcultural group in Canada has resulted in many differences for the marketer. For example, labels and packages must, by law, be bilingual. Advertising presents serious problems. Marketing executives have to decide whether advertising used in English Canada (frequently the US version) should be altered in content for Quebec. Of course, such advertising also needs to be translated into French, a fact that has been the source of many difficulties. Ten to fifteen years ago ads were, for the most part, quickly rendered into French (transliterated more than translated) and blunders were common. Today, primarily because of separatist activism, much greater attention is paid to the needs and differences of the Quebec market, as evidenced by the increasing number of Francophone advertising agencies qualified to prepare advertising for that market in French.

Consumption Attitudes and Practices

The French-Canadian life-style is reported to be characterized by a *joie de vivre* — compared to English-speaking Canadians, they tend to eat more, drink more, and party more.[29] Two full-course meals a day are common.

A study conducted several years ago found that French Canadians spend more per capita on food than do their English-speaking counterparts.[30] This was also found in a more recent study by Chebat and Hénault.[31] They are more frequent users of packaged soups, cake mixes, instant coffee, decaffeinated coffee, cosmetics, meat sauces, molasses, soft drinks, and sandwich spreads; and less frequent users of canned fish or meat, frozen foods, pancake mixes, margarine, potato chips, canned milk, hot breakfast cereals, chocolate chips, pickles, tea, and dietetic foods.[32] Instant-type meal products such as wieners and beans, chili con carne, and spaghetti are not very popular among French Canadians.

The French-Canadian consumer makes significantly greater use of cosmetics, such as perfumes, hand creams, colognes, and men's shampoos and of medications, such as cold tablets, headache remedies, cough syrups, and nose drops. These findings suggest an almost hypochondriac trait, a strong concern with health and particularly with digestion.[33]

With almost 26% of the national population, Quebec accounts for 30.2% of furniture and appliance sales, and 38.2% of hardware sales, even though home ownership is relatively low in Quebec (50% compared to 64% in Ontario).[34]

In Quebec, ale makes up 95% of the beer consumed, the remaining 5% being lager. By contrast, in Ontario the ratio is 55:45, while at the other end of the country, in British Columbia, it is of the order of 10:90. Quebec also has the highest per-capita consumption in Canada of soft drinks, cough syrup, maple syrup, and molasses—the Quebecer's sweet tooth requires a different formulation of sweet products.[35] Chocolate, butterscotch, and *tarte au sucre* are preferred flavors. Lemon is not.[36] Quebec accounts for almost one-half of Canada's sales of dry soup — used to make homemade soup that is served in 80% of all French-Canadian homes in a given week.[37]

Further, regarding consumption attitudes and practices it has been found that:[38]

- the French-Canadian woman prides herself on being a good cook, so that ready-made products do not sell as well as products that require some preparation; she is more oriented toward the home and the family;
- the major meal of the day is lunch, so that lighter foods are served at dinner;
- on the average, the French-Canadian female is more curious and hence more innovative in product choices than her English-speaking counterpart;
- Francophones prefer better quality clothing; they are less price-conscious, less likely to shop for bargains or watch for sales but more likely to be conscious of brand names;[39]
- The French-Canadian female is more concerned about personal and home cleanliness, and is more fashion-conscious;
- Francophones display a more luxurious taste in automobiles. They choose larger cars and use less regular gasoline (more recent re-

search, however, suggests a trend toward smaller cars);[40]

- Francophones are becoming more mobile and, though still less than Anglophones, are spending more on travel and vacations;
- Francophone leisure habits are quite distinct: a larger proportion of French Canadians than English Canadians attend movies (42% to 30%), plays, ballet, and operas (20% to 16%).

Shopping Behavior

Francophone shopping patterns differ widely from those of the Anglophones:[41]

- whereas large retail chains and shopping malls appeal to the English, the French prefer small, independent retail stores and face-to-face contact with sales staff.
- Francophones prefer door-to-door sales.

Media Habits

Because of language differences, US-based regular and cable networks do not affect Quebec as much as they do other parts of Canada. It is worth noting that:[42]

- French Canadians are the heaviest TV watchers in the world and are more receptive to TV advertising;
- radio is far more popular in Quebec than in English Canada: Quebecers listen to about five hours more in the average week;[43]
- the average Francophone spends less time reading the newspaper, compared to the average Anglophone, and also reads fewer books;
- local weekly newspapers by far dominate the larger city dailies — 70% of the French never read a daily but depend instead on the local weekly paper.

While some claim that the technological revolution will not have much effect on Quebec,[44] change is inevitable. Indeed, the French consumer is gradually changing while the society as a whole is undergoing drastic sociological,

political, economic, and psychological changes. In some cases, change has been surprising. Boisvert points out a number of contradictions as well as basic changes.[45]

- although Quebec is a bastion of Catholicism, French-Canadian women were very receptive to birth control pills: per capita consumption is among the highest in Canada;
- contrary to what it was in the past, Quebec's birth rate (15.1) is now below the national average (15.3);
- post-secondary and university enrolments now match the national average;
- the French-Canadian family spends more on groceries than its English-Canadian counterpart — 62% spend more than $50 a week compared to 51%;
- the French-Canadian male is not much more involved in the shopping decision than his English-speaking counterpart (38% to 33%);
- reading habits are changing — Quebec is experiencing a magazine boom; and
- French Canadians concentrate on their own Quebec TV stars.

In addition to the fact that appropriate product, place, promotion, and price strategies need to be developed for French Quebec, it should be noted that government regulations in Quebec are far more restrictive, in many ways, than in other parts of Canada. For example, commercial advertising to children is forbidden, contest and lottery prizes used as promotional gimmicks are taxable, the alcohol and tobacco industries are severely restricted in the content, time of day, and frequency of their advertising, and all business in Quebec must be done in French.[46]

The Acadians

The French market of New Brunswick is usually either forgotten or lumped with the Quebec market. The Acadians, however, are a distinct group and resent Quebec-directed ads.[47] Acadian consumers are more fashion-conscious and dine out more frequently than Quebec Francophones. In addition, they are more price-conscious and prefer medium-priced items. Strategies designed for the Acadian market should acknowledge their growing sense of identity and their distinctness from Quebec. Advertising material should be in the French language but should not mention Quebec.

OTHER ETHNIC SUBCULTURES

Unlike the United States, where people of different ethnic origins seem to have blended into a "melting pot," Canada consists of what has been called a "cultural mosaic," in which several ethnic subcultures live together but tend, in large measure, to maintain their cultural identity — a fact that makes the task of the marketer more complicated but at the same time more interesting.[48]

Only one ethnic group in Canada is of sufficient size and concentration to warrant possible separate national marketing treatment — the Italian subculture.

Italian Canadians

The Italian-Canadian subculture is a vibrant, rapidly expanding market segment that is heavily concentrated in Toronto. It is sufficiently large, cohesive, and different to warrant separate attention from marketers. The most recent figures from Statistics Canada show that in 1980 there were 747,970 Canadians of Italian origin, of whom 297,205 resided in Toronto, mainly in the west-central sector of the city. In total there were 487,310 Italian Canadians residing in Ontario.

Another major center with a large Italian population is Montreal, sometimes referred to as "the cradle of Italians in Canada," followed by Hamilton, Ontario. With continued immigration, the Italian-Canadian population has probably crossed the one million mark.

A fundamental characteristic of the Italian-Canadian population is that the majority are involved in a double transition — moving from their country of origin to a different culture and adjusting to an urban society from rural beginnings.

Age Distribution

If the forty-five to fifty-nine and sixty-plus age groups are combined, Italian Canadians show an age distribution that is very similar to the overall Canadian distribution (see Figure 14.11).

Language and Education

Language has been cited as one of the principal problems facing the Italian community in Canada. As far as acculturation is concerned, the largest stumbling block is often their limited knowledge of English, coupled with a low level of education.[49]

Sociology

The Italian ethnic group is reported to be one of the most segregated in Toronto, so that most of their daily contacts are with other Italians.

	Under 15	15-19	20-24	25-44	45-59	60+	Total	Total Persons
Italian Canadians	20.8	10.2	9.8	29.3	20.1	9.8	100	747,970
All Canadians	22.7	9.6	9.7	29.7	15.2	13.1	100	24,083,495

FIGURE 14.11: Age Distribution of Italian Canadians (Percentages)

SOURCE: Statistics Canada, *1981 Census*, Cat. 92-911, Table 3.

Residential ethnic enclaves are replete with a multitude of ethnically distinctive restaurants, stores, newspapers, and social, recreational, and cultural organizations.... The majority of Italian immigrants are laborers and have jobs where co-workers are largely Italian.[50]

The Italian community is characterized by a lack of social integration, internal factionalism, and institutional fragmentation. There is no strong tradition of Italian ethnic identity and they tend to identify mainly on a local level (when outside the family circle) with fellow Italians from the same hometown or village. Consequently, it is not surprising that Italian ethnic identity tends to decrease sharply with length of residence or duration of contact.[51]

Italian immigrants are highly stereotyped to fit the job roles of laborer and construction worker. In 1971, Italians in Canada were distributed as follows by occupation (in rank order):[52]

1. Construction
2. Production
   Fabrication
   Assembly
   Repair
3. Service
4. Processing
5. Machining
6. Managerial
   Administration

In a study done in Toronto, 35.5% of all Toronto males were in managerial, professional, or clerical positions while only 11.4% of male Italian Canadians held such positions. On the other hand, 37.2% of all Toronto males were craftsmen, production workers, or laborers, compared to 67.6% among male Italians.[53]

Media

A survey conducted in Toronto found that Italians have a daily newspaper, a weekly newspaper, a monthly magazine, a radio station, and several daily and weekly programs on various TV stations.[54] Almost half of them (45%) read an English-language daily, the largest number reading the *Toronto Star* (30%).

Consumer Characteristics

Studies by Multifax Corporation of Montreal and Data Mart Research Associates of Toronto indicate that:

- there are about 150,000 Italian households in Southern Ontario;
- 91% occupy detached or semi-detached homes;
- 89% own their own homes;
- 79% own at least one automobile, 22% own two or more;
- 48% of the households have more than one kitchen;
- 62% own at least one storage freezer; and
- total disposable income is $3 billion.[55]

Surveys suggest that Italians are very individualistic and that the use of personalities as "opinion leaders" would probably not be worthwhile.[56] It might be better to rely on other sources.

AGE SUBCULTURES

Two age groups will be selected for examination — the youth subculture and the elderly subculture — because they are both undergoing significant changes in numbers, attitudes, and potential.

The Youth Subculture

This market consists of all those young persons between fifteen and twenty-four years of age. Projections are that in 1985 this group will number approximately 4.4 million or 17.1% of the Canadian population,[57] but that it will begin to decline so that by 1990 the numbers will reach 3.9 million or 14.2 % of the national population.

Apart from the significant changes in life-style that have marked this group in the last two decades, there are several reasons why they constitute a desirable market for the marketer:

- the development of their purchasing patterns is in its formative stage;
- they have increasing amounts of discretionary income at their disposal;
- their influence on other market segments is considerable; and
- their interest in new products is high and brand loyalty is low.

The 1960s saw the rise to extreme prominence of the influence and power of our young people. Not only in Canada but all over the world — in the US, Japan, Britain, Germany, France, Scandinavia, even Russia — youth profoundly affected manners, dress, sexual morality, music, recreation, and notions of rights and freedom. They brought about significant changes in the outlook, values, and behavior of society. So dominant was this influence that the trend toward imitation and emulation of youthfulness attained considerable force and pervasiveness.

Marketers reacted to these developments with an amazing range and variety of products from Levi jeans, t-shirts, and hair styles to rock records, jogging paraphernalia, and youthful TV and movie stars; from hair dryers and cosmetics to stereos, tape cassettes, and transistors.

What marketers need to note most about this market is its fluidity and dynamism — its rate of change. Constant examination and anticipation of trends are essential if costly errors are to be avoided.

Not only do life-styles, values, and product preferences change with extreme rapidity, but so do the symbols and language of communication. New words and expressions are coined, old words are given new meanings and, so as not to offend and alienate, the marketer must be "hip" to the latest jargon.

Because of its affluence and the unprecedented exposure to and acceptance of electronic information systems, the youth market can be effectively reached through TV and radio and through magazines, particularly when TV

and music stars are used. Even more importantly, this huge market lends itself to effective segmentation on the basis of age, region, sex, and social class.

The Elderly Market

In size this market, which includes all individuals sixty-five years of age and over, is projected to include over 2.5 million, or 9.88% of the Canadian population in 1985 and to increase to 2.9 million (or 10.64%) by 1990. Two primary reasons make it important to the marketer. First, it is a segment that is increasing in size, due mainly to advances in medicine, to better health care, and better nutrition. Second, it is characterized by special needs and interests to which marketers can cater with specific products. For example, pharmaceutical companies have catered to the elderly with vitamin supplements, digestive aids, and salt substitutes; food companies and retailers can develop special sizes and formulations to suit the needs of the elderly; and builders and social agencies have established retirement communities and homes for the elderly.

One of the principal motivations of this group is the desire for meaningful social involvement, particularly with their peers. Another is to remain financially and physically self-reliant.

US SUBCULTURES

The two major subcultural groups in the US are black Americans and Hispanic Americans.

The Black Subculture in the US

A great deal has been written about black consumers in the US, but much of it is inconsistent. The problem may be the tendency to regard all blacks as sharing the same values, attitudes and preferences, rather than as consisting of different subgroups with different characteristics. It must be recognized that the black market consists of different segments, just as does the larger white market, and generalizations from one limited study about all blacks are likely to be incorrect.

As a whole, blacks, compared to whites, are characterized by lower average annual incomes and lower average educational and occupational status.[58] The average age is much lower than for whites (median of 21.4 years versus 28.7 years). Almost half of the black population in the US is under 18.

Blacks are described as showing greater family instability based on such criteria as proportion living with spouse, illegitimate births, and children living with both parents.[59]

This market in the US is changing rapidly. It is growing faster than the white population; the average income, occupational, and educational levels are rising, and the average age is declining. Along with these, changes in social acceptance, though slow, will have a significant impact on the consumer behavior of blacks. Such sociological phenomena as forced housing will yield to a freer choice of residential location and affect all aspects of the lives of blacks. For example, the reliance on other status products (in lieu of housing) such as expensive cars, liquors, clothing, and appliances will likely decline.

The question of how to reach the black market increasingly bothers marketers as that market increases in size and economic power but it does not appear that any safe generalization can be made. Strategies may depend upon the particular product category and the specific target market involved.

Hispanic Americans

Hispanic Americans include immigrants from Mexico, Puerto Rico, and Cuba. In 1977 the number of legal and illegal Spanish-speaking immigrants in the United States was estimated at between 12 million and 15 million.[60] It was also noted that including the large number of illegal entrants may raise that estimate to 20 million. More recent estimates are close to 22 million — 10% of the population — so that, in fact, Hispanic Americans may now outnumber blacks in the US.[61]

Hispanic Americans tend to differ in a few significant ways from mainstream American culture. Strong family ties and a patriarchal dominance characterize Hispanics. The "macho man" is very much a reality. As a cohesive group that is proud of its traditions and values, Hispanics are likely to change slowly.

Currently a $50 billion market, it increased by about 60% between 1970 and 1980, even though the population increase was only 6%.[62]

Hispanics place a great deal of emphasis on quality and brand loyalty. Expenditures on packaged goods are above average. They are more likely to watch TV than the average American.

The median age among Spanish Americans is twenty-three, well below that for the total population. This difference reflects the above-average birth rate in the Spanish-background population. Since the large proportion of Americans of Spanish origin are in the younger age groups and since their numbers are expected to continue to grow from immigration and the high birth rate, their presence in the population, in the labor force, and in school enrolments will continue to mount. Income and education are below average but both are rising rapidly. Families of Spanish origin have an average of over four members, compared to 3.5 in the total population.

The ten largest metropolitan areas with significant Spanish-speaking populations are Chicago, New York, Miami, Houston, San Antonio, El Paso, San Bernardino, Los Angeles, San Jose, and San Francisco. In fact, Hispanic Americans are heavily concentrated in metropolitan areas, as shown in Figure 14.12.

A more detailed distribution by city is given in Figure 14.13.

The composition of the Hispanic markets in eight major metropolitan areas reveals a concentration of Mexicans in the west, in California and Texas — in such cities as San Francisco,

Los Angeles, Sacramento, Fresno, Houston, and El Paso. Cubans are concentrated in the southeast, mainly in Miami, and Puerto Ricans in the north and northeast, in New York and Chicago.

Hispanics from other countries (Central and South America) are widely distributed in New York, San Francisco, Los Angeles, Chicago, and Miami.

	Spanish Language Total	Mexican	Puerto Rican	Cuban
In metropolitan areas	83.8%	83.5%	95.6%	96.4%
In central city	52.0	47.4	83.0	56.4
Outside central city	31.8	36.1	12.6	40.0
Outside metropolitan areas	16.2	16.5	4.4	3.6

FIGURE 14.12: Place of Residence For Spanish-Language Population

Adapted from William D. Costigan, "The Spanish Heritage Ethnics," in *Proceedings*, American Statistical Association, 1977, pp. 744-6.

	Mexican	Cuban	Other (Central/ South America)	Puerto Rico	Total
Los Angeles	79.8%	4.7%	12.6%	2.9%	100%
San Francisco	65.2	2.4	25.6	6.8	100
Fresno	96.7	0.2	2.0	1.2	100
Sacramento	88.1	1.3	7.7	2.9	100
Miami	1.1	81.2	10.5	7.3	100
San Antonio	95.9	0.6	2.0	1.5	100
Chicago	45.8	7.3	11.2	35.7	100
New York	0.8	10.4	28.4	60.4	100

FIGURE 14.13: Ethnic Composition of the Spanish Markets

Adapted from William D. Costigan, "The Spanish Heritage Ethnics," in *Proceedings*, American Statistical Association, 1977, pp. 744-6.

SUMMARY

Culture is the broadest level of influence on consumer behavior, representing the material, psychological, and behavioral solutions a society has developed to solve its problems. These expressions of culture are dynamic, adaptive, and transmitted from one generation to another. Cultural values and behavior are learned through a process of socialization and several different groups and institutions are involved, such as peer groups, social groups, families; religious and educational institutions; commercial media; books and movies.

The primary values in our society include materialism, youthfulness, individualism, security, and competitiveness. It was pointed out that while these values are important in analyzing consumer behavior, it is equally important to consider the shifts in values that are taking place, particularly in the rapidly changing conditions of modern society.

The benefits of cultural relativism in international marketing were emphasized and examples of strategic applications in different cultures were discussed.

Subcultures were defined as subgroups that, while sharing the values and norms of the mainstream culture, exhibited certain differences of their own. The French-Canadian subculture, making up about 26% of the Canadian population, was described as a significant element in Canadian marketing. The Italian-Canadian subculture was reviewed briefly, followed by a discussion of the youth and elderly markets.

The two largest subcultures in the US — the Hispanics and the blacks were described in the final section of the chapter.

QUESTIONS

1. Define "culture" and discuss its most relevant characteristics to marketing.

2. Write an essay on the different expressions of culture, and show how they are interrelated and how they are of interest to the marketer.

3. Discuss some of the major changes that are taking place in our cultural values. How are they likely to affect marketing strategy for (a) the food industry, (b) clothing, (c) automobiles?

4. Write an essay on the importance of cultural relativism in international marketing.

5. Define "cultural universals." What is your assessment of the standardization/localization controversy? Justify.

6. What are some of the factors you would consider in each case if, as marketing manager of your company, you were going to enter the following markets in Quebec: (a) dessert, (b) women's clothing, (c) packaged soup?

7. Describe some of the main obstacles that would be confronted by a company that was attempting to introduce a new brand of tomato paste to the Italian-Canadian market.

8. What are some of the key questions that a cross-cultural marketer should address before entering a foreign market?

NOTES TO CHAPTER 14

[1] Doug Fetherling, "The Drugstore That Made Canada Famous," *Canadian Business* (June 1978), pp. 67-9, 100-4.

[2] Adapted from "Use of Coupons Increases Twenty-three Percent," *The Globe and Mail* (8 January 1981); "Newspaper Coupons Strong in 1981," *The Globe and Mail* (13 January 1982); *The Financial Post*, "Canadian Markets, 1981 and 1982"; A.C. Nielsen Company, Toronto.

[3] Charles Winick, "Anthropology's Contributions to Marketing," *Journal of Marketing*, 25 (July 1961), p. 60.

[4] A.L. Kroeber and Clyde Kluckhohn, *Culture: A Critical Review of Concepts and Definitions* (New York: Random House, 1963).

[5] Ralph Linton, *The Cultural Background of Personality* (London: Routledge and Kegan Paul, 1945), p. 21.

[6] Kenneth Boulding, quoted in Alvin Toffler, *Future Shock* (New York: Bantam, 1971), p. 13.

[7] Ibid., p. 11.

8M.M. Gordon, *Assimilation in American Life* (New York: Oxford University Press, 1964).

9Kenneth E. Runyon, *Consumer Behavior*, 2nd ed. (Columbus, Ohio: Charles E. Merrill, 1980), p. 94.

10Ralph Linton, op. cit., p. 130.

11Milton J. Rokeach, "The Role of Values in Public Opinion Research," *Public Opinion Quarterly*, 32 (Winter 1968), pp. 547-9.

12Milton J. Rokeach, *The Nature of Human Values* (New York: Free Press, 1973), p. 28.

13Edward T. Hall, *The Silent Language* (Greenwich, Connecticut: Fawcett, 1959).

14G. Horowitz, *Canadian Labour in Politics* (Toronto: University of Toronto Press, 1968), pp. 19-21.

15Seymour M. Lipset, *The First New Nation* (New York: Basic Books, 1963), p. 25.

16H. Blair Neatby, *The Politics of Chaos: Canada in the Thirties* (Toronto: Macmillan, 1972), p. 12; Horowitz, op. cit. pp. 3-57.

17Larry J. Rosenberg, *Marketing* (Englewood Cliffs, New Jersey: Prentice-Hall, 1977), p. 105.

18*The Yankelovich Monitor* (New York: Yankelovich, Skelly, and White); *Values and Life Styles*) Menlo Park, California: SRI International).

19James G. Barnes and Lessey Sooklal, "The Changing Nature of Consumer Behavior: Monitoring the Impact of Inflation and Recession," *Business Quarterly*, 48: 2 (Summer 1983), pp. 58-64.

20Study presented at Meeting of International Physicians for the Prevention of War, Helsinki, Finland, June 1984. Conducted by the Toronto Board of Health.

21Ministry of Citizenship and Culture, Government of Ontario, 1982.

22James F. Engel, Roger D. Blackwell, and David T. Kollat, *Consumer Behavior*, 3rd ed. (Hinsdale, Illinois: Dryden Press, 1978), p. 90.

23Francis M. Adams and Charles E. Osgood, "A Cross-Cultural Study of the Affective Meanings of Color," *Journal of Cross-Cultural Psychology*, 4: 2 (June 1973).

24Ralph Z. Sorenson and Ulrich E. Wiechmann, "How Multinationals View Marketing Standardization," *Harvard Business Review,* 53 (May-June 1975), pp. 38-56.

25M.J. Etzel and B.J. Walker, "Advertising Strategy for Foreign Products," *Journal of Advertising Research*, 6 (1974), pp. 41-4.

26C.A. Valentine, *Culture and Poverty* (Chicago: University of Chicago Press, 1968), p. 105.

27Statistics Canada, 1985 Projections; *Handbook of Canadian Consumer Markets, 1979* (Ottawa: The Conference Board in Canada, 1979), pp. 28-9.

28Gail Chiasson, "The French Market Today," *Marketing* (1 June 1981), p. 11.

29Lisette Ross, "Vive La Différence! A Quebecer's Look at Les Anglais," *Homemakers' Digest* (January/February 1969), pp. 28-9.

30"1963 Survey of the Canadian Daily Newspaper Association," cited in N.K. Dhalla, *These Canadians* (Toronto: McGraw-Hill, 1966), pp. 290-8.

31Jean-Charles Chebat and Georges Hénault, "The Cultural Behavior of Canadian Consumers," in V.H. Kirpalani and R.H. Rotenberg (eds.), *Cases and Readings in Marketing* (Toronto: Holt, Rinehart and Winston, 1974), pp. 176-84.

32"1963 Survey of the Canadian Daily Newspaper Association," op cit.; Frederick Elkin, *Rebels and Colleagues: Advertising and Social Change in French Canada* (Montreal: McGill-Queen's, 1973), p. 73.

33Dhalla, op. cit., p. 289.

34Marcel Boisvert, "Is the French-Canadian Consumer Really Different?" *Sales and Marketing Management in Canada*, 24: 2 (February 1983), pp. 10-11, 20.

35Bruce Mallen, "The Present State of Knowledge and Research in Marketing to the French-Canadian Market," in D.N. Thompson and D.S.R. Leighton (eds.), *Canadian Marketing: Problems and Prospects* (Toronto: John Wiley & Sons Canada, 1973), pp. 100-1; M. Brisebois, "Industrial Advertising and Marketing in Quebec," *The Marketer*, 2: 1 (Spring/Summer 1966), p. 11.

36Gerald B. McReady, *Canadian Marketing Trends* (Georgetown, Ontario: Irwin-Dorsey, 1972), pp. 64-5.

37Brisebois, op. cit.

[38]Chebat and Hénault, op. cit.; M. Saint-Jacques and B. Mallen, "The French Market Under the Microscope," *Marketing* (11 May 1981), p. 10.

[39]Marilyn Stewart, "For Direct Marketing Success You Have to Understand the Rules," *Sales and Marketing Management in Canada*, 24: 2 (February 1983), pp. 12-13.

[40]Boisvert, op. cit.

[41]Ibid.

[42]Michel Claudios, "Media Watch: The Technical Revolution Won't Hurt One Bit," *Marketing* (1 June 1981), p. 20.

[43]Lucien Roy, "How Do We Motivate the French-Canadian Buyer?" cited in McReady, op. cit., p. 50.

[44]Claudios, op. cit., p. 20.

[45]Boisvert, op. cit.

[46]Robert Legault, "Legal Lowdown on Advertising in Quebec," *Marketing* (1 June 1981), p. 16.

[47]Raymond Bourque, "The Forgotten French Market," *Marketing* (1 June 1981), p. 14.

[48]John Porter, *The Vertical Mosaic* (Toronto: University of Toronto Press, 1965).

[49]J.L. Elliott, *Immigrant Groups* (Scarborough, Ontario: Prentice-Hall, 1971), p. 214.

[50]D.R. Hughes and E. Kallen, *The Anatomy of Racism: Canadian Dimensions* (Montreal: Harvest House, 1974), p. 176.

[51]Ibid., pp. 176-9.

[52]J.L. Elliott, *Two Nations, Many Cultures* (Scarborough, Ontario: Prentice-Hall, 1979), p. 390.

[53]T. Grygier, "Integration of Four Ethnic Groups in Canadian Society," in Paul M. Migus (ed.), *Sounds Canadian* (Toronto: Peter Martin Associates, 1975), pp. 158-89.

[54]Leo Driedger, *The Canadian Ethnic Mosaic* (Toronto: McClelland and Stewart, 1978), p. 312.

[55]Sandy Fife, "Piercing the Ethnic Barrier," *Financial Times of Canada* (8 August 1983), p. 3.

[56]Clifford J. Jansen, "Community Organization of Italians in Toronto," in Driedger, op. cit., p. 323.

[57]Statistics Canada, 1985 Projections, *Handbook of Canadian Consumer Markets, 1979* (Ottawa: The Conference Board in Canada, 1979), p. 22.

[58]R.A. Bauer and S.M. Cunningham, "The Negro Market," *Journal of Advertising Research*, 10 (April 1970), pp. 3-13.

[59]Reynolds Farley and Albert I. Hermalin, "Family Stability: A Comparison of Trends Between Blacks and Whites," *American Sociological Review*, 36 (February 1971), pp. 1-17.

[60]William D. Costigan, "The Spanish Heritage Ethnics," in *Proceedings*, American Statistical Association, 1977, pp. 744-6.

[61]Mark Watanabe, "A Profile Grows to New Heights," *Advertising Age* (6 April 1981), pp. 8-23.

[62]Al Hartig, "Cultural Differences Offer Rewards," *Advertising Age* (7 April 1980); Danny N. Bellenger and Humberto Valencia, "Understanding the Hispanic Market," *Business Horizons* (May-June 1982), pp. 47-50.

THE NINE NATIONS OF NORTH AMERICA

Joel Garreau, an editor of the *Washington Post*, has put forward an interesting new way of segmenting North America (covering Canada, the US, Mexico, and the Caribbean) that crosses international boundaries and creates nine distinct "nations" on the basis of "economic, social, cultural, political, topographical, and natural-resource factors."

Exhibit 1 illustrates the location of the nine nations. The labels Garreau has given them are as follows:

(1) the industrial "Foundry";
(2) the Maritimes and New England;
(3) "Dixie," the southern states;
(4) the Intermountain West or the Empty Quarter;
(5) the Hispanic Southwest and Mexico or "MexAmerica";
(6) the Pacific Northwest or "Ecotopia";
(7) the Great Plains or the "Breadbasket";
(8) the Latin American Rim or the "Islands"; and
(9) Quebec.

Garreau's view is that "each region has its own way of *dealing with the present and planning for the future*" and the differences among the divisions are far more than just geographical. They are more in the nature of motivations, attitudes, and preferences.

Below is a summary of the main characteristics of the nine "nations".

The Foundry

Area: Southeastern Ontario, New York (excluding Manhattan), Pennsylvania, Ohio, New Jersey, N.E. Illinois, N. Indiana, Michigan (excluding the northwest), S.W. Connecticut, N. Virginia, N. Maryland, E. Wisconsin, N. Delaware, N. West Virginia.

Characteristics: "The whole point of living in the Foundry," says Garreau, "is work. No one ever lived in Buffalo for its climate or Gary for its scenic vistas."

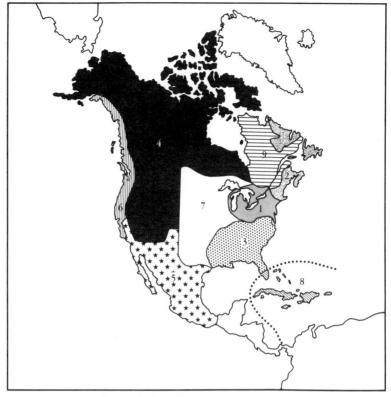

EXHIBIT 1: The Nine "Nations" of North America

Based on a paper presented by Joel Garreau, editor, *Washington Post*, at the Third Annual Marketing Research Conference of the American Marketing Association in Denver, Colorado, October 1982; *Marketing News* (21 January 1983), pp. 1, 18-20.

The Foundry is marked by loss of population and jobs and by "urban prison camps," decaying infrastructure, heavy trade unionism, obsolete technologies, and racial friction. It is a nation in decline, due to soft demand for autos, steel, rubber, and its other major products. It is no longer dominant in a business or social sense, even though it is home to ninety million people. The Foundry's major asset is water.

The Maritimes and New England

Area: Nova Scotia, New Brunswick, Prince Edward Island, Newfoundland, Labrador, Massachusetts, Maine, New Hampshire, Vermont, Rhode Island, E. Connecticut.

Characteristics: With virtually no energy or new materials, little agriculture, few basic industries, high taxes, and expensive home fuel and auto gas, New England is the poorest of the nine "nations." It includes the oldest and most civilized Anglo "nation." It is once again a land of pioneers, rebounding, as a post-industrial society, through the influx of high-tech industries.

Dixie

Area: Georgia, Alabama, Mississippi, Louisiana, Arkansas, Kentucky, Tennessee, North Carolina, South Carolina, S. Virginia, S. Maryland, S. Illinois, S. Indiana, S. Missouri, N. and C. Florida, E. Texas, S.E. Oklahoma, S. West Virginia, and S. Delaware.

Characteristics: "Forever underdeveloped," according to Garreau, Dixie is an emotion, an idea embodied in calling oneself a "Southerner," the Confederate flag, and waving to strangers.

Dixie is undergoing the most rapid social and economic change on the continent, though still below the national average. The people are among the most optimistic about the future. But "Dixie isn't the sunbelt."

The Empty Quarter

Area: N. Ontario, N. Manitoba, N. and S.W. Saskatchewan, Alberta, E. British Columbia, Northwest Territories, Yukon, N. Alaska, N.W. New Mexico, E. Washington, E. Oregon, N. Arizona, E. California, W. Colorado, Wyoming, Nevada, Montana, Utah, Idaho.

Characteristics: A pristine environment of wide-open spaces (the true west) with energy (oil, gas) and minerals (gold, silver, copper, zinc, iron, uranium). It consists of the largest land area with the smallest population. There's plenty of fresh air but the land is high and dry.

There is wide belief in the "frontier ethic" but Garreau thinks this "nation" will undergo radical change over the next twenty years, resulting in significant growth in employment and population, due mainly to development by outsiders.

Mexamerica

Area: S.W. and S.C. California, S. Arizona, W. New Mexico, S. Texas, S. Colorado, and Mexico.

Characteristics: Its language, culture, economics, food, politics, and life-style are under heavy Hispanic influence. Houston, bordering Mexamerica on the east, is the world's new energy capital. Mexamerica is a watershed of the future, but its main problem is lack of water.

Mexamerica is rapidly becoming the most influential of all the "nations." It evinces a strong entrepreneurial spirit as "northern" influences are creeping in. The southwestern "sombrero, siesta"; the Los Angeles "hot tub, laid-back, flakiness"; and the Houston "all (oil) well, cowboy hat" stereotypes are no longer accurate.

Ecotopia

Area: W. British Columbia, S.E. Coastal Alaska, W. Washington, W. Oregon, and N.W. California.

Characteristics: Blessed with adequate water and renewable resources. Home of "Silicon Valley," computer chips, aluminum, timber, hydroelectric power, fisheries, bioengineering, environmentalism, outdoor nature lovers, energy conservation, and recycling. "Quality of life" is a religion in the great Pacific Northwest. Strongly anti-nuclear, Ecotopians have as their motto: "Leave. Me. Alone."

Residents want clean, high-tech industries and will cling to the "small-is-beautiful" ideology. Unlike the eastern part of the US and Canada, which is Europe-oriented, Ecotopia looks to Asia for its future, particularly Pacific Rim nations.

The Breadbasket

Area: Central Ontario, S. Manitoba, S.E. Saskatchewan, W. and C. Illinois, Minnesota, Iowa, Kansas, North Dakota, South Dakota, Nebraska, N. Missouri, W. Wisconsin, N.W. Michigan, W. and C. Oklahoma, E. New Mexico, E. Colorado, N. and C. Texas.

Characteristics: Marked by agricultural industries. Mainstream America — conservative, hard-working, religious, the ratifiers of social change. "Ideas still must 'play' in Peoria before they become accepted," Garreau explains.

The Breadbasket is stable, its economy prosperous and renewable. The Great Plains have acquired great political power because of the strategic world importance of food. But farmers are being hurt financially by their own productivity.

The Islands

Area: S. Florida, Cuba, Jamaica, Bahamas, Puerto Rico, Virgin Islands, Dominican Republic, Haiti, N. Colombia, N. Venezuela, and dozens of smaller Caribbean islands.

Characteristics: S. Florida looks south for its future, and the Caribbean north to Miami. The major industries are the $55 billion illegal drug trade, trade with the "Latin American Rim," and non-Anglo tourism. The Latin American influence is strong and pervasive.

Garreau describes this nation as "weird and hard to track." Southern Florida has very little in common with the rest of the state, let alone Dixie.

Quebec

Area: Province of Quebec.

Characteristics: French speaking, steeped in history, tradition, ethnic pride, and a homogeneous culture. It is blessed with plentiful hydroelectric power, prosperous transportation industries, minerals, a diversified economy, and an inclination to high technology.

The Québécois feel they are different not only from the rest of Canada but also the rest of the world. They are fiercely independent and determined to maintain their own culture.

Studies conducted to test the "nine-nation theory" have described it as "very useful" and an "interesting paradigm."

In one study, a large international advertising agency, Ogilvy and Mather, found a great deal in common between the Ecotopians and the Inner Directeds isolated by VALS (the Values and Life-Style measure of SRI International, Menlo Park, California). Essentially, they revealed a "disenchantment with the traditional ways that we market and advertise our products and services."

Another research study by the same agency "found that consumer views of attitudes about life in America differ significantly in Dixie and the Foundry. For example, people in Dixie are optimistic; they're twice as likely to think 'the average person is better off today' than not. People in the Foundry aren't nearly so positive."

QUESTIONS

1. Briefly describe the trends that characterize each "nation."

2. What kinds of impact do you think these cultural trends may have on the attitudes and behavior of consumers in the different "nations"?

3. What sort of correlation do you think there might be between "Nine Nations" and VALS data?

4. Where do such concepts as "the suburban housewife" and "the suburb" fit in the Garreau scheme? Or, for that matter, such regions as the "Sunbelt," the "MidWest," or the "West Coast"?

5. What implications does the theory have for marketing research in North America?

15

Social Factors — Reference Group and Social Class Influences

EXAMPLES

1. The Toronto Home Building Industry*

The house building industry has always been sensitive to public attitudes. It is often the first industry to suffer or benefit from economic, political, or social change. Within recent years many home builders in the Toronto area have detected a drop in public confidence in their ability to live up to promises of performance and some have developed imaginative ways to counteract this perception, such as turning to public personalities to speak on their behalf.

One company that has done this is Runnymede, who have hired Lynne Gordon, a well-known consumer advocate, to build confidence in Runnymede homes. In a full-page newspaper advertisement for the firm's Pickering project, Glendale (some twenty miles east of Toronto), Ms. Gordon warns, "Don't be sold on hype. Look for honest value, not double talk."

Is Ms. Gordon believable when she endorses a Runnymede home? Does Bill Cosby really drink Coke? Says Ms. Gordon, "I would not have entered into a contract with Runnymede unless the company had agreed to take my recommendations regarding consumer complaints." (See Figure 15.1.) In order to maintain her credibility in the eyes of the consumer, Ms. Gordon had the builder agree to the condition that buyers of Runnymede homes could write to her about any problems they might have and that she would then meet with company representatives to help solve the problems.

Some endorsers can take their responsibility very seriously. Ms. Gordon seems to have done so. Before taking the job she toured Pickering, visited the site several times, checked out Runnymede's financial status, and even checked Glendale's competition.

---

*Adapted from Karen O'Reilly, "High Profile Draws Buyers to Glendale," *The Globe and Mail* (12 May 1984), p. H1.

FIGURE 15.1: Reference Group Influence: Expert Power

Courtesy Runnymede Development Corp. Ltd.

The sales manager for Runnymede's Glendale site says that the company is ecstatic about public reaction to Ms. Gordon. "With Ms. Gordon, sales at Glendale took off like a bat out of hell." But surely spokesmen are only as good as the product they push. Bill Cosby isn't the only reason we drink Coke, and Peter Ustinov isn't the only reason we use American Express.

2. Advertising and Identification Models*

Pepsi-Cola Canada is launching a new ad campaign built on big names in contemporary music. It is using the band Rough Trade, featuring lead singer Carole Pope, a less-known Toronto rockabilly group, Willie English, and the Quebec band, Spa Romance.

The groups perform their trademark styles of music in thirty-second commercials that borrow from the fast-cut technique of rock videos.

Pepsi director of marketing said that they decided to use the music format in an effort to improve the image of Pepsi among young people. "We want the Pepsi image to be at the forefront of attracting the attention of teens today. And in order to do that we needed to talk in a language that is relevant to them," he said.

Having established with its Coke-challenge commercials its taste credibility through a rational, comparative approach, "we are now

---

Adapted from Mark Smyka, "Pepsi Drops Challenge in Favor of Rock Stars," *Marketing* (19 March 1984), p. 1.

extending a campaign that said Pepsi tastes good with an emotional sell," he added.

3. Appealing to Class*

Montreal's Corby Distilleries is aiming its English-language campaign for Courvoisier cognac at the upscale, prestige-oriented consumer. In the ad, a number of status symbols are used to emphasize the fact that Courvoisier cognac is of the quality that matches the buyer's sophisticated taste (see Figure 7.8).

Because consumer research indicated that the Quebec Francophone market feels intimidated by appeals to status, Corby's decided to retain its French-language ads that portray a strong Napoleonic association with the brand.

The product's demographic target is male, aged thirty-five to fifty-nine, well-educated, with a household income of over $25,000. Psychographically, the cognac consumer's life-style/attitudinal classification is that of joiner-activist, a well-rounded, committed, liberal-minded and influential person. The English ad is running in *Time, Maclean's* urban center edition, *Quest*, and *Financial Post Magazine*. The French ad appears in *L'Actualité, Montréal Ce Mois-ci, Affaires, Commerce, La Caducée, Place des Arts*, and in Société des alcools du Québec posters.

Courvoisier holds 20% to 25% of Canada's cognac market. Corby's have allocated a budget of over $500,000 to promote the brand.

Adapted from "Courvoisier Takes Aim at Upscale English Canadians," *Marketing* (19 March 1984).

REFERENCE GROUPS

Social Groups

A social group is not just a random collection of persons, such as the people riding on a public bus, but rather an aggregation of individuals who share common goals and needs. It consists of two or more individuals who interact to accomplish a stated objective.

There are many kinds of social groups — political clubs; families; educational, friendship, work, religious, neighborhood, and recreational groups.

Each of them is potentially a **reference group**: that is, a group used by the individual in determining and evaluating values, attitudes, behavior, and self-perceptions. Reference groups vary in the extent of their influence on group members, some being more important than others.

Individuals are influenced not only by groups to which they belong but also by groups to which they do *not* belong. Such groups may be ones to which they aspire or whose values they emulate. Similarly, people can have *negative* reference groups — groups with which they do not want to be identified (e.g., a motorcycle gang), called **avoidance groups**.

The three most important criteria for classifying positive reference groups are:

- membership;
- extent of interpersonal relationships or contacts; and
- structure of group relationships.

These are illustrated in Figure 15.2.

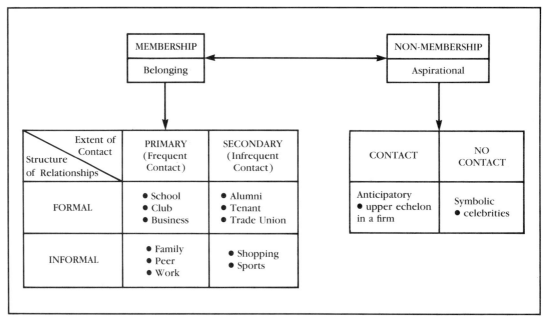

FIGURE 15.2: Classification of Reference Groups

Based on membership, there can be belonging groups (those of which the individual is a member) and aspirational groups (those of which the individual is not a member).

So far as extent of contact is concerned, there are primary and secondary groups. A primary group is characterized by regular contact among its members, a variety of roles and interests for each member, and possible strong emotion. Examples of primary groups are peer groups, school groups, and the family. Because of the frequent close contact, primary groups exert a great deal of influence on their members' attitudes, preferences, and opinions — and thus on their behavior as consumers.

In secondary groups, contact is infrequent and the influence on members' purchasing behavior is less strong and sometimes minimal, as in tenant or alumni groups. Shopping groups are more likely to exert some influence on buying behavior. Secondary groups are also characterized by less emotion, and less spontaneous and fluid behavior. Other examples are trade unions and religious groups or such aggregations as book clubs.

Groups can also be formal or informal in structure. A formal group is one with a defined structure in which the interrelationships are specified (e.g., a group with a president, a secretary, a treasurer). Informal groups are less structured and usually arise because of closeness or shared interests.

Among membership groups, therefore, there can be primary informal groups, primary formal groups, and secondary informal and formal groups.

Primary informal groups, such as the family and peer groups, are clearly the most influential because of the frequency and closeness of contact. They are often used by marketers to portray acceptance and belongingness (e.g., a Molson's Golden commercial showing a poolside party with a group of young adults).

Primary formal groups, such as school class groups or business groups, can be portrayed when the marketer wishes to win approval.

Secondary informal groups, such as shopping or sports groups that meet infrequently, can also have a direct influence on purchases, mainly because of the pressures of conformity.

One researcher found that among "single shoppers, 58.9% purchased as many items as planned, while only 26.6% of the (shopping) parties including three or more persons purchased as many items as planned."[1] He also found that parties containing children tended to purchase less than planned and those without tended to purchase more than planned.

Secondary formal groups, such as business clubs and tenant groups are least influential, since personal interaction is very restricted.

Aspiration Groups

Both the anticipatory and the symbolic aspiration groups can be important to the marketer — the anticipatory group because the individual may have direct contact with it and may indeed one day be a member. It represents progress, achievement, and the enhancement of power, prestige, and money (e.g., clothing, jewelry, automobile, and a rising company executive); the symbolic group because it represents the ideal to which some individuals strive, in terms of material, psychological, and behavioral characteristics (e.g., Bjorn Borg advertising a particular make of tennis racquet or Wayne Gretzky advertising GWG jeans). They are not likely ever to belong to such a group.

THE FUNCTIONS OF REFERENCE GROUPS

Reference groups are very important to the marketer because, whether primary or secondary or membership or aspirational, they determine the attitudes, preferences, and norms of behavior that the individual accepts.

Reference groups bring about the individual's **socialization**; this is the process by which the individual acquires the values, norms, attitudes, and behavioral patterns of the group. In this process, two concepts are significant. Individuals become part of the group through **identification** with the others in the group in the sense that they accept the expectations of the group and come to think of themselves as being "like" the group. Secondly, not only do they identify with the group but they also accept the norms and values of the group as their personal norms and values. At that point, they have **internalized** the group's standards.

One of the principal aspects of socialization is the development in the individual of the *self-concept* (see Chapter 10).

The family is especially important in this regard, since it exerts its influence from childhood but other groups such as school and religious groups also play their part.

I discussed in Chapter 10 how the self-concept influences the behavior of the individual as a consumer — studies were cited that showed the relationship between the self-concept and preference for automobiles, cigarettes, soap, beer, and other products. Basically, through lifestyle the individual expresses the self-concept or the ideal self to the reference group. Advertisers make use of such influence in testimonial advertising that arouses identification in terms of either the self-concept or the ideal self.

Reference groups also serve to exert influence in achieving behavioral **compliance** with the expectations and norms of the group. The nature of such conformity can vary with the purpose it serves, as described below:[2]

1. Informational: when the group, either verbally or behaviorally, provides the consumer with information that influences what the consumer does. It is based on the consumer's desire to make informed decisions. For example, observing what products or brands others use; seeking information about brands from professionals or experts; finding out about a brand's performance from friends, neighbors, relatives, associates; noting sources of approval such as endorsements from government testing services or from private testing agencies.

2. Evaluative or comparative: when consumers judge or evaluate their self-concept and their behavior by comparison with the norms of the group. They tend to accept positions expressed by others in order to show others what they are or would like to be (as a parent, athlete, neighbor); because the group possesses characteristics they would like to have or that will enhance their image in the eyes of others; or even because they want to be like the person shown using the products in advertisements.

3. Utilitarian or normative: when a member of a group behaves in a certain way because the group expects it and also behaves in that way. Individuals will comply with the wishes of others in order to achieve rewards or approval and to avoid punishment.

The individual is largely a product of the group insofar as socialization and the development of self-concept are concerned; he or she becomes very dependent on the group for the satisfaction it provides. Compliance with the group, in other words, satisfies many of the needs and motives of the individual, although the group will likely satisfy different needs and motives for different individuals.

The pressure to conform can be so great as to lead sometimes to quite surprising behavior. In a classic study conducted many years ago, Asch sought to determine "the social and personal conditions that induce individuals to resist or to yield to group pressures when the latter are perceived to be contrary to fact."[3]

Groups of eight individuals were given a simple task — they were asked to match the length of a given line with one of three unequal lines (as illustrated below) and to announce their judgements *publicly*. This was repeated several times.

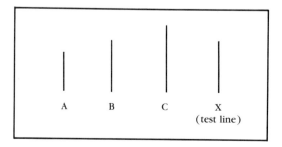

The group in question had, with the exception of one member, previously met with the experimenter and received instructions to respond at certain points with wrong — and unanimous — judgments. The errors of the majority were large and of an order not encountered under control conditions. The outstanding person — the critical subject — whom we had placed in the position of a minority of one in the midst of a unanimous majority — was the object of investigation. He faced, possibly for the first time in his life, a situation in which a group unanimously contradicted the evidence of his senses.[4]

The study was done with male college students and involved a total of fifty critical subjects. In each case, eighteen trials were conducted. In six of these the majority responded correctly (the *neutral* trials) and the remaining twelve trials were the critical ones in which the majority responded incorrectly. It was found that:

(a) one-third of all the estimates in the critical group were in line with the distorted estimates of the majority. The control group, who recorded their estimates in writing, was virtually error-free; the other two-thirds of the critical group were not influenced by the majority;

(b) personality differences play a large part in compliance — one-quarter of the critical subjects were completely independent; at the other extreme, one-third of the group tended to yield to the estimates of the majority.

Experimental variations also disclosed that

(c) a disturbance of the unanimity of the majority markedly increased the independence of the critical subjects. For example, the presence of one "true partner," who always announced estimates *before* the critical subject, resulted in a drop in the yielding to the unanimous majorities from 32% in the basic experiment to 5.5%; and

(d) the effects of group size on conformity seem to increase up to a majority of six or seven.[5]

The majority effect grows stronger as the stimulus situation diminishes in clarity. The more similar the lines, the greater the likelihood of yielding to the majority estimates.

Group pressure can thus play a significant role in an individual's behavior; the perceived amount of social support or of social opposition can be crucial in this regard. Apart from becoming what one is as a result of the socializing influence of reference groups, the individual is also subjected to certain pressures inherent in the group situation per se.

Factors That Affect Reference Group Influence

A number of factors determine the degree of influence a reference group exerts on the purchasing behavior of the individual: characteristics of the group itself, characteristics of the individual, and certain attributes of the particular product.

Cohesiveness

The more cohesive and stable the group, the greater the pressure on its members to conform to its norms. The longer established the group, the greater the interpersonal relations and contacts among its members, and the greater the extent to which values and attitudes are shared, the more cohesive the group will be.

Attractiveness

The goal and purpose a group has set itself and the characteristics of its operation and of its members can make it very attractive. The more attractive belonging to a group is to the individual, the greater the likelihood of group conformity.

In other words, the greater the rewards (acceptance, approval, status) and the smaller the sanctions and losses (social and psychological mainly), the greater the tendency to conform.

Credibility

The more trustworthy, reliable, and knowledgeable the members of a group are perceived to be, the more persuasive they will be in achieving conformity. Consumers seeking information about a product are more likely to follow the suggestions of the group if they consider it to be very credible.

Power

Groups can also influence the behavior of the individual because of the power they exert over the individual. Such power can come from different sources, four of which are relevant to marketing.

Reward Power Reward power comes from the ability of the group to reward the individual. Rewards reinforce the individual's response and increase the likelihood of repetition of the response. Rewards may be material rewards (such as quality products or services, price discounts, coupons, or deals) or psychological (such as praise, approval, or recognition). All of these rewards will, in the marketing situation, lead to repurchase (see Figure 15.3).

Coercive Power Linked to reward power is the power of the group to generate certain responses by the threat of disapproval or physical harm. Marketers apply such coercive power when they make use of fear appeals — for example, "ring around the collar" and social disapproval; and the fear of cancer from cigarette smoking.

Expert Power Individuals or groups with experience, knowledge, and high accomplishment in a given area of activity exert expert power. Because of their expertise, their opinions and recommendations are very likely to be heeded (see Figure 15.4).

Marketers may seek to demonstrate expert power by creating their own experts. General

FIGURE 15.3: An Example of Reward Power: An Appeal to Social Approval

Courtesy Armstrong World Industries Canada Ltd.

Mills created Betty Crocker and presented her as the "First Lady of Food," just as General Motors created Mr. Goodwrench.

Referent Power This is based on the degree of the consumer's identification with the individual or group. That is, the greater the extent to which the consumer shares or would like to share the attitudes and behaviors of the referent individual or group, the greater the referent power (see Figure 15.5).

Referent power should be distinguished from reward power and coercive power. A person who is influential through the fear of ridicule or disapproval is exercising coercive power. If that person is influential because he or she offers praise or approval or recognition, the power is reward power. And if that person is admired or emulated, then referent power is involved.

FIGURE 15.4: An Example of Expert Power

Courtesy Kraft Limited

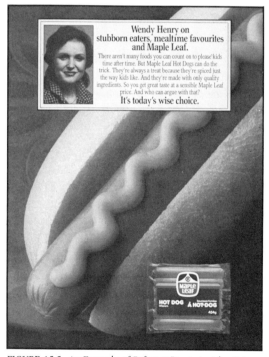

FIGURE 15.5: An Example of Referent Power in Advertising

Courtesy Canada Packers Inc.

These three sources of power appear to correspond to the three types of group influence described in an earlier section, as shown in Figure 15.6.[6]

Type of Influence	Source of Power
Informational	Expert
Comparative	Referent
Normative	Reward

FIGURE 15.6: Types of Group Influence and Source of Power

Experience

Among the characteristics of the individual that affect reference group influence is experience. The more an individual knows about a product or service or the more easily obtainable the relevant information, the less will be the influence of the group on that individual.

Confidence

Asch's experiment demonstrated that some subjects were more likely to conform in the "line-judgement" test. Yielders were less confident and lower in self-esteem.

Risk

Studies have shown that self-confidence is related to perceived risk.[7] Basically, the greater a shopper's self-confidence, the less the perceived risk. Thus the more self-confident an individual, the lower the perceived risk, and the less the influence of the group.

It appears that risk perception may be reduced by discussions with a group prior to a purchase,[8] although this may vary with the product involved,[9] probably related to whether the product is high- or low-involvement. There is a greater willingness to accept more risk for low-risk products and less risk for high-risk products.[10]

Product Conspicuousness

So far as the product is concerned, group influence appears to vary according to the conspicuousness of the product. Conspicuousness can be defined in terms of visibility (public versus private) and of exclusiveness (luxury versus necessity). Choice of less conspicuous products (e.g., toilet soap, canned peaches) is less likely to be influenced by reference groups than choice of conspicuous products (e.g., clothing, automobiles).[11]

CELEBRITIES IN MARKETING

Frequent use is made in marketing of celebrities whose power derives from the fact that consumers would like to be like them. The underlying process is identification with an aspiration group. Celebrities used by marketers range from movie stars, television personalities, and sports stars to entertainment figures.

Celebrities are used in a number of ways:[12]
- to give testimonials, where they have personally used the product or service (e.g. Maurice Richard and Grecian Formula or Bruno Gerussi and Monarch Flour;
- to give an endorsement, where the celebrity simply approves of the product, not necessarily as an expert (e.g., Wayne Gretzky and 7-UP or Lynne Gordon and Runnymede Homes in Example 1);
- as an actor in a scenario concerning the product (e.g., Harold Ballard and Ed Mirvish in a Ford television commercial); and
- as a spokesperson where the celebrity delivers the message for the company (e.g., Lorne Greene for the Olympic Fund or Anne Murray for the Canadian Imperial Bank of Commerce, see Figure 15.7).

As with any other reference group, credibility, particularly trustworthiness, is an important characteristic of celebrities, because they are usually not expected to be experts, except per-

FIGURE 15.7: Advertising with a Celebrity Spokesperson

Courtesy Canadian Imperial Bank of Commerce

haps for sports celebrities presenting messages about the sport in which they excel.[13]

In the last few years, an increasing number of top executives have played the role of spokesperson for their companies. Some were not known at all but the identification of their position and a reliance on their ability to project trustworthiness and sincerity led them to assume this role (e.g., Dave Nichol of Loblaws).

REFERENCE GROUP INFLUENCE IN MARKETING

There is little empirical evidence to show that reference groups have a significant influence on consumer behavior. However, if the frequency of their use (in advertising) is any indication, then there is no doubt that they are in fact very effective.

The difficulty of measuring these effects is illustrated by a study done about twenty years ago in which it was shown that the choice of brand of bread was influenced by informal neighborhood groups.[14] A recent replication of the study contradicted the earlier study's findings.[15] It found that products low in visibility, complexity, and perceived risk (such as bread) are less susceptible to group influences than products high in those characteristics.

Another study found that reference group influence varies with the product involved and with the types of individuals. It found that college students were more susceptible to reference group influence than were housewives, for twenty products tested.[16] The danger in generalizing its findings to other products and to other populations is clear.

Bearden and Etzel recently sought to measure the influence of reference groups on brand preference and on product preference.[17] Employing Bourne's original proposition that group influence is a function of conspicuousness and that conspicuousness consists of two components, exclusiveness and visibility, the researchers found the relationships shown in Figure 15.8.

The four groups of products shown in Figure 15.8 were derived from the two components of conspicuousness. The first condition, which affects product decisions, is that the item must be exclusive. If virtually everyone owns it, it is not conspicuous. Accordingly, exclusiveness was operationalized as the distinction between luxuries and necessities. The second condition that affects brand decisions is visibility, which is operationalized as publicly consumed versus privately consumed. Those brand decisions involving products that are publicly consumed are more susceptible to reference group influence.

The results of the study confirmed the relevance of the two forms of conspicuousness and "the substantial differences in consumer perceptions of reference group influence across the four product categories represented by the

	Public	
Product / **Brand**	**Weak Reference Group Influence** (−)	**Strong Reference Group Influence** (+)
Strong Reference Group Influence (+)	*Public Necessities* Influence: Weak product and strong brand Examples: 　Wristwatch 　Automobile 　Men's suit 　Women's dress	*Public Luxuries* Influence: Strong product and brand Examples: 　Golf clubs 　Snow skis 　Sailboat 　Tennis racquet
Weak Reference Group Influence (−)	*Private Necessities* Influence: Weak product and brand Examples: 　Mattress 　Floor lamp 　Refrigerator 　Blanket	*Private Luxuries* Influence: Strong product and weak brand Examples: 　TV game 　Trash compactor 　Ice maker 　Pool table

Necessity ———————————————————————— Luxury

Private

FIGURE 15.8: Reference Group Influence on Product and Brand Decisions

Adapted from William O. Bearden and Michael J. Etzel, "Reference Group Influence on Product and Brand Purchase Decisions," *Journal of Consumer Research*, 9 (September 1982), pp 183-94.

specific products used in the study."[18]

The study also investigated the nature of the influence (informational, comparative, or normative) on the product and brand decisions and found that in a particular case,

> ... it would seem reasonable to find one type of influence operating and the others absent. For example, in the purchase of a man's suit, comparative influence might play a much larger role than either informational or normative influence.[19]

Generally, the influence on product decisions was more likely to be informational and on brand decisions comparative or normative. It was also suggested that reference group influence is probably more effective in stimulating selective demand (i.e., brand decisions).

The Influence of Opinion Leaders

Another facet of the social influence of groups is the opinion leader, that is, "the individual within a group to whom others turn for information and advice."[20] He or she is not necessarily the formal leader of the group; any member of the group can be an opinion leader.

Misconceptions

A few common misconceptions about opinion leaders have existed for a long time, perhaps because of their common-sense appeal:
(a) opinion leaders are persons of high prestige in religion, education, business;
(b) opinion leaders belong to the higher social classes; and

(c) an individual who is an opinion leader is influential in most product areas.

Characteristics

Research studies, however, have shown that opinion leaders:
(a) can be anyone who influences the purchasing behavior of others;
(b) can be found in all social classes and that their influence is horizontal within their own class rather than vertical;[21]
(c) vary according to the product category. It is now felt that opinion leaders tend to be influential in related product areas.[22] In the six product categories studied, King and Summers found:

> Opinion leaders in 2 or more categories 46%
> in 3 or more categories 28%
> in 4 or more categories 13%

> Other research has also supported this view that *opinion leadership parallels consumer interests*.[23] The general conclusion is that the correlations are quite weak and influentials can be found in all demographic categories;[24]

(d) are more gregarious and socially active and, although they are more exposed to mass media than are non-opinion leaders, they are more influenced, because of their social contacts and accessibility, by others with whom they associate than by the mass media.[25] They also seem to talk to others more than do non-opinion leaders about products of interest;
(e) are more innovative and tend to have more favorable attitudes to new products;[26]
(f) can be identified by life-style characteristics. A study done in Canada found that opinion leaders were more involved in community affairs, and were more price-conscious and more style-conscious.[27]

One source has suggested that underlying these behavioral characteristics are other reasons or motivations that explain why certain individuals are opinion leaders.[28] They may be more product involved, more self-involved, more concerned about others, or more message (or advertising) involved — and so they are more likely to discuss products or services with others. Self-involvement may mean that an individual talks about a product in order to gain attention, show his or her knowledge, or suggest status or assert superiority by, for example, implying possession of inside information.

It has also been suggested that, in some cases, opinion leaders may be motivated to discuss products with others in order to reduce their own post-purchase dissonance by getting others to buy the product.

Opinion Leaders and Marketing

There are no generalized opinion leaders — they vary by product type and there is overlap among related products. They are very interested in the particular area, they are innovative and gregarious, and have more exposure to mass media and to other consumers. There seems little doubt that they are an important part of the marketing process. Indeed, the identification of the opinion leader led to the formulation over thirty years ago of the **two-step flow hypothesis**, which suggested that information is not transmitted directly from the mass media to the consumer but that it goes through an intermediary step — the opinion leader — thus the *two-step* hypothesis (see Figure 15.9). It seems simple enough that all the marketer needs to do is direct a message to the opinion leaders and, from them, to the rest of the market. This could be quite effective since several studies have found that about half of word-of-mouth communications are initiated by consumers seeking advice from opinion leaders.[29]

Unfortunately, it is not as simple as that. There are a number of problems that make it difficult. Identifying relevant opinion leaders is not easy — because the "leadership" is casual, it is quite "invisible and inconspicuous";[30] most methods for identifying opinion leaders are verbal and

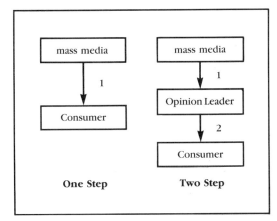

FIGURE 15.9: Information Flow

can be quite unreliable; it can also be quite expensive to locate opinion leaders.

There is evidence to suggest that the two-step model may not be an accurate representation of interpersonal influence; that, in fact, a multi-stage model may be more appropriate. An example is Sheth's study of interpersonal influence in the purchase of stainless steel blades.[31]

The two-step approach is still applied, however, in many instances in marketing. Samples are sent to selected individuals — farm products or demonstrations to successful farmers, lawn-care products to certain homeowners, fashion and personal grooming products to college and high-school leaders (class presidents, football team members).

Rogers has distinguished between the innovator and the opinion leader (see Chapter 9).[32] The innovators are the first 2.5% of the individuals to adopt a new product. The next 13.5% are referred to as the early adopters and it is from this group that the opinion leaders come.[33]

Strategies Using Opinion Leaders

Several different approaches have been developed by marketing to make use of opinion leaders, in spite of the problems (identification, expense, limited information) that exist.

Identifying and Reaching Opinion Leaders

It is sometimes possible, in such small markets as institutions or individual industries, to locate opinion leaders and direct strategies specifically to them — for example, advertisements in the mass media or direct mail or messages sent to individuals on mailing lists identified as including high proportions of opinion leaders (*Time* subscribers, physicians, high-school coaches). A company may also send samples to such leaders.[34] Take, for example, the shoe company that selected two small college campuses that were quite similar. To one campus they sent sample pairs of shoes to leaders such as class presidents, team captains, and student council members. On the other campus, distribution of the same kinds and number of samples was random. Subsequent checks indicated a significantly higher level of sales on the first campus.

Companies may also use identified leaders as advisors in the selection of new products. These advisors may help indirectly in the adoption of the products by others.

Simulating Opinion Leadership

This is a strategy used where advertisements suggest that the product is accepted and used by leaders (e.g., two women discussing a feminine hygiene product with one playing the "role" of the opinion leader).

Using "Proxy" Opinion Leaders

Where it is very difficult to identify opinion leaders (and this is quite often), the marketer may make use of individuals who are very likely to be influential, such as persons who are innovative or have a great deal of public exposure. Examples in the latter group are disc jockeys, stewardesses, hotel bellhops, and cab drivers.

Creating Opinion Leaders

In a sense, this strategy is a variant of the last, in which "proxy" opinion leaders were used. Better-known individuals in the community are selected, exposed to new information, and encouraged to discuss it with friends and acquaintances (opinion leadership role). In one study, high-school class presidents, cheer leaders, sports captains, and secretaries were asked to join a panel to evaluate rock and roll records. They were asked to discuss their choices with friends before giving their final vote. As a result the company had several hit records in the test cities but not in any other cities.[35]

All of these approaches suggest the considerable importance of interpersonal communication and personal influence in purchasing decisions. In a social climate of increasing consumer skepticism and distrust, marketers may have to rely more on such personal sources of influence. I consider these broader problems of communication in a later chapter.

SOCIAL CLASS

Another aspect of social influence comes from certain broad groups that result from the stratification of the society; that is, large social groups characterized by different social status — social classes.

In a country such as Canada or the US in which egalitarianism is an important value, it is difficult to accept the notion that some members are ranked higher than others "so as to produce a hierarchy of respect or prestige."[36] Some may even deny that such stratification exists, but the reality of social classes, as defined, is incontrovertible. In order to survive, a society needs to distribute its tasks and responsibilities in such a way as to achieve the greatest efficiency.

> The hierarchical evaluation of people in different social positions is apparently inherent in human social organization. Stratification arises with the most rudimentary division of labor and appears to be socially necessary in order to get people to fill different positions and perform adequately in them.[37]

Stratification may be based on a variety of criteria that vary from time to time and from place to place. Examples are authority, power (political, economic, military), income (amount, type, source), life-style, occupation, education, kinship (ancestry), ethnic status, religion, race. It is important to recognize that these characteristics are not always evaluated in the same way in all societies. For example, in the United States the significance of kinship connection is less important than it is in China or Great Britain.

On the basis of some of these criteria, sociologists have stratified society into a number of social classes, which vary in status and power, and in attitudes, preferences, and behavior. Social classes are important to marketers because they may be useful in identifying significant differences in their consumers' behavior. For our purposes their salient characteristic is that each class shares a similar life-style.

Indicators of Social Class

Some of the best indicators of social class are occupation, income, education, type of dwelling, area of residence, possessions, personal interactions, influence, and class consciousness.

Occupation is considered the best single indicator because it correlates highly with most of the other indicators and, important to marketers, an individual's occupation strongly influences the individual's life goals and life-style. The prestige accorded an occupation is, generally speaking, directly proportional to the contribution that occupation makes to the survival of the society. Thus, the ranking by Canadians of 204 occupations in terms of prestige showed government leaders, physicians, professors, and the legal profession to enjoy the highest prestige ratings (Figure 15.10). There were some English-French differences but these were not drastic. There was an extremely high correlation of 0.98 with corresponding US data.

It has been found, too, that there is a high degree of stability in occupational prestige over time.[38]

Income and *education* also indicate social class. They are highly correlated with occupation. With regard to income, some feel that source of income may be a better indicator than amount of income.[39]

Type of dwelling, area of residence, and *possessions* are strongly related to economic power and influence. The area in which an individual chooses, and is able to afford to reside, the type of house, and how it is furnished and equipped are all indicators of social class.

	National Sample	National English Sample	National French Sample
N =	793	607	186
1. Provincial Premier	89.9*	88.7	93.6
2. Physician	87.2	87.5	86.1
3. Member of Canadian Senate	86.1	86.0	86.1
4. Member of Canadian House of Commons	84.8	84.9	84.5
5. University Professor	84.6	86.1	79.9
6. Member of Canadian Cabinet	83.3	84.2	82.4
7. County Court Judge	82.5	81.0	87.4
8. Lawyer	82.3	81.6	84.4
9. Mayor of Large City	79.9	80.6	77.5
10. Architect	78.1	77.6	79.6
11. Physicist	77.6	79.9	69.3
12. Psychologist	74.9	76.0	71.3
13. Chemist	73.5	73.3	73.9
14. Civil Engineer	73.1	72.6	75.1
15. Catholic Priest	72.8	71.5	77.2
16. Mathematician	72.7	73.7	69.5
17. Biologist	72.6	73.4	69.7
18. Physiotherapist	72.1	72.3	71.3
19. Dept. Head of City Government	71.3	74.5	60.4
20. Bank Manager	70.9	72.1	67.1
21. Colonel in Army	70.8	71.6	68.4
22. Owner of Manufacturing Plant	69.4	69.8	67.9
23. Druggist	69.3	68.5	72.0
24. General Manager of Manufacturing Plant	69.1	70.4	64.9
25. Admin. Officer in Federal Civil Service	68.8	69.9	64.9
30. Veterinarian	66.7	66.7	66.6
31. High School Teacher	66.1	67.8	60.4
32. Airline Pilot	66.1	67.4	61.6
33. TV Star	65.6	67.7	58.7
35. Registered Nurse	64.7	66.1	59.9
38. Accountant	63.4	62.9	65.4

* Mean rank scores were transferred to a 0-100 scale.

FIGURE 15.10: Occupational Prestige Rankings in Canada (1966)

SOURCE: Peter C. Pineo and John Porter, "Occupational Prestige in Canada," in James E. Curtis and William G. Scott (eds.), *Social Stratification: Canada* (Montreal: The Canadian Review of Sociology and Anthropology, 1967), pp. 205-20.

Social Class Measurement

There are three general approaches to social class measurement — the reputational, the subjective, and the objective.

The **reputational method** determines in intensive interviews the social class of an individual by asking others who know him or her to indicate the person's social status. Since it can only be done for persons known to the raters, this method is best for small communities. It is interesting that even persons who claim not to be class conscious end up, through these interviews, categorizing community members into different social status groups. It should be noted, too, that this method thus obtains *perceived* rather the actual social status. This may not necessarily be a negative feature, since how individuals are perceived by others will determine how the latter behave toward them and also indicate those members who will make good models for testimonial advertising, for example.

The **subjective method** relies on individuals' self-ratings on social class. Because of its very nature — subjective — this method has two main drawbacks: most individuals tend to overrate themselves and they tend to avoid placing themselves in "upper" or "lower" categories and the "middle class" accordingly becomes exaggerated.

This happens because the vast majority of persons with whom Canadians interact are, just as they themselves are, members of the middle class.

> The middle class insulate themselves from extremes of wealth and poverty. Our working experiences and our residential communities are remarkably homogeneous, such that we only associate with people like ourselves.... As we travel from home to work and back, to shopping centres, movie theatres, we do so in our private capsules along routes that never penetrate the slums or the exclusive communities of a city.[40]

Obviously, the subjective method is not very useful for classification purposes.

The **objective method** is the most widely used in consumer research. Instead of requiring ratings on social class groupings, it obtains a scale value on a variable or variables presumably correlated with social class — for example, occupation or income. Objective methods can be of two kinds — single-item and multiple-item.

For single-item indexes, occupation is a widely used variable. This is not surprising since, as discussed earlier, occupation greatly influences the income earned, the possessions acquired, personal associations, influence and, in general, the life-style of the individual.

Several occupational scales such as the Trieman Scale indicate status indexes for different occupations.[41] Other single indicators — such as possessions, personal associations, or income — have been used but limitations exist and vary according to the situation. Income will be discussed at some length in a later section of this chapter.

Multiple-item indexes seek to improve the measure of social class by employing several variables chosen on the basis of theory or experience. Every individual is assigned a score on each variable and the scores are combined (usually weighted) to yield a single index of social status.

Some of the more widely used composite indexes are those developed by Warner and Coleman.

Warner's ISC (Index of Status Characteristics)

The best-known method for measuring social class was developed by the sociologist W. Lloyd Warner over thirty years ago and the six social classes he identified have become part of our everyday knowledge.[42] The ISC is a weighted measure of four variables: occupation, source of income, house type, and dwelling area. Originally included, size of income and education were later omitted because they did not significantly affect the predictive power of the index. Warner assigned weights to each variable as follows:

Occupation	4
Source of income	3
House type	3
Dwelling area	2

For each variable, an individual is rated on a seven-point scale and the rating is multiplied by the appropriate weight. The products are added to yield the index score.

Warner's *occupation* categories range from professionals and proprietors of large businesses (1), semi-professionals and officials of large businesses (2), clerks and such workers (3), to skilled workers (4), proprietors of small businesses (5), semi-skilled workers (6), and unskilled workers (7).

The seven points for *source of income* range from inherited wealth (1) and earned wealth (2) to private relief (6) and public relief (7). *House type* is rated from excellent (1), through very good (2) to poor (6) and very poor (7). Finally, *dwelling area* is rated from very high, exclusive neighborhood (1), through average (4) to low, run-down, semi-slum (6) and very low, slum (7).

Coleman's IUS (Index of Urban Status)

Similar to Warner's ISC, the IUS employs Warner's four variables as well as two others — education and associations.[43] Education ratings are obtained for both spouses and associations cover formal and informal relationships. The IUS is used primarily in marketing research studies by the Social Research Institute of Chicago.

The two objective methods discussed and other variations all seem to produce similar results, identifying anywhere from five to seven social classes.[44] Warner's has remained the most widely used.

Among the criticisms of the composite measurement approaches is the fact that it would be very expensive, time-consuming, and inefficient to collect the data from an entire population. They are more suitable, it is argued, for some communities or for a representative sample of the population. An alternative approach is to analyze existing statistics, such as those provided by Statistics Canada, for such factors as occupation, education, income, or housing. Two of these factors, education and/or income, have generally been used to provide indicators of stratification.[45]

In Canada, Blishen has used educational requirements and associated incomes for identifiable occupations to approximate class-like divisions, although it can be seen that three indicate graduations within the middle class and three within the lower or working class (see Figure 15.11).[46]

It is felt that approaches such as Blishen's "serve to identify real differences in Canadian society. They do not identify real classes, in the sense of integrated and conscious groups. But they do approximate such identification."[47]

Social Class Characteristics

Social classes are not really discrete divisions but are part of a *continuous* system that is divided up arbitrarily and for convenience. Individuals fall on the fringes of two classes on both sides of a dividing line that is dependent upon the number of sub-classes identified.

This has led some researchers to differentiate those individuals at the upper fringes of a social class and those at the lower fringes. In terms of money, the former group will earn incomes above the average of their class and the latter incomes below their class-average. Accordingly, these groups have been referred to as the over-privileged and the under-privileged of their class.[48]

While these subgroups share the same general orientations as the rest of their class, they tend to exhibit different purchasing patterns, in

Class	Occupation	Socio-Economic Index	Overall Ranking
1 (Index 70+)	Administrators, teaching and related fields	75.2846	1
	Physicians and surgeons	74.2246	6
	Chemical engineers	70.8910	10
2 (Index 60.00 to 69.99)	Petroleum engineers	69.7069	21
	Writers and editors	62.8184	64
	Sociologists, anthropologists, and related social scientists	60.5728	83
3 (Index 50.00 to 59.99)	Officials and administrators unique to government	58.8662	94
	Inspectors and regulatory officers, non-government	54.2791	131
	Bookkeepers and accounting clerks	50.7098	160
4 (Index 40.00 to 49.99)	Photographers and cameramen	49.5214	175
	Musicians	43.3157	240
	Tellers and cashiers	40.4164	274
5 (Index 30.00 to 39.99)	Bookbinders and related occupations	38.8055	291
	Paper products fabricating and assembly occupations	35.2914	329
	Plasterers and related occupations	30.4749	387
6 (Index Below 30)	Hotel clerks	30.0380	393
	Bartenders	26.4920	449
	Farmers	23.0227	480

FIGURE 15.11: Examples of Blishen Rankings, 1971 Census Data

Adapted from B. Blishen and H. McRoberts, "A Revised Socioeconomic Index for Occupations in Canada," *CRSA*, 13 (February 1976), pp. 71–9.

line with their relatively different income. This has been referred to as the **Relative Occupational Class Income** (ROCI) and is the ratio of total family income to the class median.[49] In fact, a subsequent study suggests that, for certain products, ROCI groups in all classes tend to behave similarly, implying that the market for quality products is not confined to the upper or upper-middle class but extends to the over-privileged of all classes.[50]

Social class is not static; there is the possibility of intergenerational mobility from one class to another. All communities do not exhibit the same class distribution because of differing conditions. An industrial city may include a pre-dominance of individuals in the lower-class categories and a university town may consist of a high proportion of upper-middle or upper-class groupings.

Members of a social class tend to behave in similar ways. Social class is a hierarchical concept in that some members are considered superior or inferior to others, or to have higher or lower social status.

Figure 15.12 presents the distribution of these classes for Warner's ISC and for Coleman's Social Standing Class Hierarchy.

Two distributions for Canada are shown in Figure 15.13. It should be noted that, unlike the US stratification, which is based on objective

Class	Warner* (%)			Coleman and Rainwater** (%)	
Upper-Upper	1.4	Upper	3.0	0.3	1.5
Lower-Upper	1.6			1.2	
Upper-Middle	10.2	Middle	38.3	12.5	44.5
Lower-Middle	28.1			32	
Working: Upper-Lower	32.6	Lower	57.8	38	54
Lower-Lower	25.2			16	

FIGURE 15.12: Social Class Distribution in the United States

*Adapted from W. Lloyd Warner, Marchia Meeker, and Kenneth Eells, *Social Class in America: Manual of Procedure for the Measurement of Social Class* (New York; Harper and Brothers, 1960).

**Adapted from Richard P. Coleman, "The Continuing Significance of Social Class Marketing," *Journal of Consumer Research*, 10 (December 1983), p. 267.

Class	National (1965) (%)		Ontario and Quebec (4 cities) (1971) (%)	
Upper	2.0		1.0	
Upper-Middle	12.9	61.8	13.4	60.3
Middle	48.9		46.9	
Working	30.4		27.4	
Lower	2.1		0.3	
No Answer	3.7		11.0	

FIGURE 15.13: Social Class Distribution in Canada

Adapted from John C. Goyder and Peter C. Pineo, "Social Class Self-Identification," in James E. Curtis and William G. Scott (eds.), *Social Stratification: Canada* (Scarborough, Ontario: Prentice-Hall of Canada, 1979), p. 434.

measures, the Canadian distribution is based on subjective measures. Also, one of the distributions is based on a national interview study conducted in 1965, and the other on a questionnaire survey of four cities in Ontario and Quebec, conducted in 1971.[51] In both cases, the question asked was, "If you had to pick one, which of the following five social classes would you say you were in . . . ?"

Both Canadian distributions probably indicate the upward bias of subjective measures.

It should be noted that:
- the upper classes are very small;
- the lower-middle (or middle) and the upper-lower (or working) classes make up the great majority of the population. They are the *mass market* in which marketers are primarily interested; and
- a major source of error in marketing is the failure of those communicating (advertising managers and advertising agencies who belong to higher social classes) with the mass

market to "speak" in the language and use the symbolism of the class to which they are directing their efforts.

SOCIAL CLASS PROFILES

Some broad generalizations about the life-styles of the different social classes serve as guides for the marketer in understanding the important values, attitudes, and behavior that characterize these groups. It must be kept in mind that "a diversity of family situations and a nearly unbelievable range in income totals are contained within each class."[52] I will use the popular Warner system, recognizing that it can be easily adapted to a seven-strata distribution (Coleman and Rainwater, Figure 15.12) or to a five-class system (Figure 15.13).

The upper-upper class consists of the social elite, of the prominent, established families, most

Contrary to popular belief, we will sell Gibson's finest to any Tom, Dick or Harry.

FIGURE 15.14: An Appeal to Family Tradition and to Social Class

Courtesy Schenley Canada Inc.

of whom live on inherited wealth. Many financiers and top business executives belong to the group (see Figure 15.14).

What is notable about this group in the 1970s and 1980s, according to Coleman, is that more change has occurred in their life-styles and self-conceptions than in the classes below. Some may still pursue a traditionally aristocratic life-style and identify with British nobility, but significant numbers are less conventional and less uniform. There is now a vibrant mix of many life-styles, including counter-cultural, intellectual, and conventional. For targeting messages and goods these variations are more important for the marketer than the older horizontal notion of a single class and single status.

The lower-upper class consists of professionals or businesspeople who have achieved their status through acquired wealth, not inheritance. They are inclined to show off their wealth in flamboyant fashion. This class too is now a lively mix of many life-styles.

The upper-middle class is likely to be made up of the families of successful but less wealthy professionals and businesspeople. They are career-oriented and their goals are success and advancement. They are well-educated and place great emphasis on education for their children. It seems that they still lead a country- and service-club existence.

In his new classification, Coleman combines these three groups into an *upper class*, whose life-styles and self-conceptions all appear to have changed.[53] While they consist of many subdivisions, however, they still subscribe heavily to bourgeois values. They still prize quality merchandise and prestige brands and greatly emphasize self-expression.

The lower-middle class, referred to by Coleman as the *middle class*, includes the top half of the mass market, the "white collar" workers, and small businesspeople. They still want "to do the right thing," buy what's popular, and follow media "experts" in fashion. For the most part, better living means a nicer home and a nicer neighborhood, and there is a constant concern over the appearance of the home.

However, in the 1980s life seems to be more fun. There is less stuffiness expressed in more relaxed dress codes, more eating out, and so on. Possessions-pride has yielded a bit to activity-pleasure and deferred gratification is not so often practised. There is a better balance between self-denial and self-indulgence.

The group, therefore, also consists of a variety of life-styles: traditional and liberated, possessions-oriented, and pleasure-oriented. Their gaze is still upward, which accounts for the increasing enrolments in local universities and community colleges.

The upper-lower or *the working class* (Coleman), consists of "blue collar" families. They are characterized by limited horizons: socially, psychologically, and geographically. Their locational narrowness is exemplified in such matters as sports heroes, who are generally chosen from local amateur or professional teams. They prefer local segments on the TV news; and for vacations they are likely to stay at home or take a trip to a lake or resort within two hours' driving time. They exhibit a strong emphasis on family ties and are very dependent on relatives for advice on purchases, support in times of trouble, and so on.

They show a chauvinistic devotion to nation and neighborhood. For example, they still show the lowest ownership of imported cars (economy or luxury). They prefer standard-size and larger domestic cars, which for the males of this group are a "macho" symbol of roadway conquest.

It is claimed that for this group change has occurred more with possessions than with values. There is still a sharp sex-role division, emphasis on peer groups and on kin, and masculine camaraderie. In brief, they are marked by a strong pride in family, place, and country.

*The lower-lower class (*or *the real poor)* consists of the families of unskilled workers and the poorly educated, with limited economic means. They have been described as alienated from society, as fatalistic, and as living lives of frustration and anger. To escape their life of hopelessness, they are likely to overreach themselves and engage in "compensatory consumption," as if out of a desire to taste a better way of life.

PROBLEMS WITH THE SOCIAL CLASS CONCEPT

Many problems exist with the concept of social class that create doubts about its usefulness to the marketer for segmentation and product positioning.

1. There seems to be a common tendency to perceive social class as being equivalent to income. It is not. To some degree income may discriminate among social classes but it should by no means be thought that individuals earning the same income necessarily belong to the same social class. The axiom "A rich man is a poor man with more money" is certainly not true. From our earlier definition, it is the *life-style* that matters. A steel worker, an accountant, and a school teacher can all earn $35,000 a year and yet belong to different social classes because of their different life-styles.

2. The notion that social stratification is breaking down and that the differences among classes are decreasing[54] seems to have evolved into a recognition that social class has not disappeared but rather has changed. We may not have the same classes now as we did two or three decades ago and different variables may need to be employed to measure social class.[55] The use of variables such as occupation, education, neighborhood, and/or house type may be out of date and predicated on a society that no longer exists. The time seems to be ripe for the development of new scaling devices suitable for the 1980s.

3. Because of both geographical and social mobility, it is difficult to categorize people within

specific social classes; as a result the boundaries among the classes appear to be more blurred than they actually are.

4. There are no discrete lines separating one class from another. Social classes are essentially continuous, with those in the core of each category being quite similar to each other and those at the upper end of a stratum not clearly distinguishable from those at the lower end of the next higher category. There is a wide variation of status within each social class.

5. The concept of social class clearly involves families rather than individuals. Thus the assumption that a husband's social class is a good indicator and the sole determinant of a household's class position is not tenable. In addition to augmenting the family's purchasing power, wives by their employment status and by their educational achievements must have some effect on the family's social class standing.[56]

6. In addition, it has been assumed that consumer behavior can be explained by *present* social class, without regard to one's class in the family of orientation. The fact that a correlation of only 0.4 has been found between the occupational status of fathers and sons indicates a significant degree of status modification and mobility from one generation to another.

One's present values, beliefs, and attitudes are partially attributed to recent acculturation but, in addition, are in large part the result of the childhood enculturation process. Since behavior is partly a function of deep-seated values, beliefs, etc., it follows that consumption behavior is largely determined by past social position in addition to present position.[57]

In other words, while the measurement of social class through observable, external criteria may yield a certain stratification, it should not be assumed that the underlying values, attitudes, and tendencies have necessarily changed.

Another limitation of social class is the problem of social class *incongruence*, such as when an individual is rated high on one criterion and low on another, resulting in a distortion of the social class index. A good example is the medical intern, who gets a high rating on occupation and a low rating on income and thus obtains the same overall index as someone with a middle rating in occupation and income. It is clear that these two individuals live different life-styles and belong to different social classes, but the objective measurement does not correct for the incongruency. It would appear that if, in measuring the social class of a large group, such incongruency is likely to be frequent, it would be better to employ a single-index measure, such as occupation.

SOCIAL CLASS AND MARKETING STRATEGY

The most important contribution of the concept of social class to marketing is in the area of *segmentation*, that is, in its ability to identify significant market groups different in life-styles and purchasing behavior.

Theoretically, social class data, by yielding information about consumers' life-styles, goals, and attitudes, can also provide direction to marketers for:

- *product positioning* (i.e., directing current products or developing new products to suit the needs and attitudes of different segments);
- *promotion* (such as for advertising appeals, for message treatment, for media selection, and for determining the appropriate language and symbols for different social classes);
- *distribution* (deciding on the appropriate retail outlets for the marketer's products, in accordance with the attitudes and perceptions of the different classes).

The next section reviews a number of studies to illustrate these specific applications. Unfortunately, some of the results are not as clear-cut as one would wish, largely attributable to the problems discussed in the preceding section. Nor are they as up-to-date as desirable, for several reasons. There was a noticeable lack of fresh evidence on the marketplace impact of social class in the literature of the latter 1970s and in the 1980s social class seems forgotten. A good part of the reason is "that much of what has been learned about the social class role in consumption choices has remained the private property of research houses and their clients."[58]

Social Class and Consumer Behavior

Applications of social class in consumer behavior have not been extensive. They have covered furniture, retail store patronage, leisure activities, and media behavior.

Products

A study done to determine the ownership of specific types of living-room furniture found that the upper-class families prefer traditional home furnishings and the lower-upper are inclined toward expensive but modern furnishings.[59] It was also found that lower-class families are likely to have their television sets in the living room while middle- and upper-class families are likely to place theirs in the family room.

A study of automobile buyers found that "the buying behavior of relatively well-off, blue-collar workers is more like that of affluent, white-collar and professional workers than that of less well-off, blue-collar workers."[60] Generally, the "over-privileged" owned more medium-sized and large cars.

Retail Store Patronage

A study of the retail store preferences of social classes found that consumers in the higher social strata are more likely to exhibit "patronage mix" tendencies, preferring to patronize department and specialty stores for products of

high social risk and to use discount stores for products of low social risk.[61] Those in the lower social strata are inclined to use discount stores for all kinds of products.

A study done in Newcastle, England, found that there was a higher frequency of shopping for groceries among middle-class women than among lower-class respondents but that middle-class housewives shopped with their husbands significantly less often than did lower-class women.[62]

The notion that retail stores are attributed with social class status is an old one, so that some are seen as catering to the higher social classes (e.g., Creeds, Birks Jewellers) and others to the lower classes (e.g., Woolworth's, K-Mart) (see Figure 15.15). Shoppers prefer to go to a store that they perceive as catering to their so-

FIGURE 15.15: Status Appeal by a Retailer
Courtesy Ritz•Carlton, Montreal

cial class, where they feel relatively at ease, and where they are treated in a satisfactory manner.

Leisure Activities

Preference for leisure activities varies with social class. It has been suggested that the upper classes prefer activities that are less time-consuming and yet more physically demanding, such as tennis, swimming, and bicycling; lower classes prefer bowling, fishing, bingo, and television.[63]

Media Habits

Media habits and perceptions appear to vary with social class. Lower-class individuals are less likely to read newspapers and magazines than higher-class persons.[64] They are more likely to read such magazines as *True Story* and *Photoplay*, which essentially provide an outlet for their fantasies through stories of romance and of celebrities.

Lower-class callers over a radio or telephone hot-line are also more likely to complain about practical problems, service, or repair while upper-class consumers are more likely to complain about deception or disliked advertising.[65]

THE SOCIAL CLASS VERSUS INCOME CONTROVERSY

For many years, a controversy has persisted over the relative usefulness of social class versus income in differentiating among consumer groups (i.e., as bases for market segmentation).

Proponents of the social class concept argue that it is a superior method because it takes into account the psychological differences among individuals. As Martineau observed, "a rich man is not simply a poor man with more money."[66] The lower-class person thinks, acts, and behaves differently from the upper-class person and these differences profoundly influence behavior in the market place.

Wasson later supported Martineau's position, basing his conclusions on more complete data.[67] He claimed that whatever validity income had for segmentation purposes was due to a very rough and now disappearing correlation with occupational status.

A number of other studies also reported income to be a better correlate of buyer behavior.[68] All of this occurred in the 1960s and early 1970s, after which the controversy seemed to be dormant.

It appears that one of the reasons for the conflicting results regarding the association of social class with product usage was that no distinction has been made between use or non-use of a product and how often the product was used.[69]

A recent re-examination of the social class/income question has supported this observation and suggested that:

- social class is superior to income when frequency of usage is examined for low-expenditure (food and non-soft drink/non-alcoholic beverage grocery) items;
- income is generally superior for products that require substantial expenditure, such as major kitchen and laundry appliances, perhaps because they no longer serve as symbols of status; and
- combined social class and income is superior for highly visible, fairly expensive items, such as clothing, make-up, automobiles, and television, which can serve as symbols of status within class.[70]

Another review of the controversy makes two further suggestions:

- that "new stratification scales" be developed for present-day life-styles; and
- that research should take greater account of the role of stratification on the value and communication systems that underlie consumption systems.[71]

Further empirical studies will need to be conducted to substantiate these observations.

SUMMARY

Reference groups can exert significant influence on the behavior of the consumer, both membership and aspirational reference groups. Other classifications of reference groups are primary and secondary groups, and formal and informal groups. The most influential groups are the primary informal groups such as the family and peer groups, because of the close relationship among their members and their frequent contact.

Reference groups serve a number of functions — socialization, development of the self-concept, and behavioral compliance or conformity. Basically, the reference group exerts its influence on the individual through three sources of power: expert power, reward (and coercive) power, and referent power.

Definitive evidence of the role of reference groups in influencing consumer purchases is lacking. It appears that reference groups vary in their influence not only according to the products involved but also depending upon the individuals concerned.

Opinion leaders are important members of reference groups because of the role they play in influencing others. Several misconceptions about opinion leaders were discussed. For example, opinion leaders are not generally influential over a wide range of products. Their impact is quite product-specific or, at most, extends to related products (e.g., appliances).

Several characteristics of opinion leaders were reviewed. In spite of these, it is very difficult to identify opinion leaders so that marketing strategy using opinion leaders is quite restricted. Most times marketers may resort, in their advertising, to simulating opinion leadership (by having one model play the role of the opinion leader), to using "proxy" opinion leaders (e.g.,

disc jockeys, stewardesses), or to creating opinion leaders (by selecting specific individuals and pre-exposing them to new products or information).

The concept of social class stratifies a society into groups of individuals of equal status and power who share certain values, attitudes, and behaviors, that is, a common life-style. Criteria commonly used for determining social class are occupation, education, and income. Because a social class exhibits similar preferences, attitudes, and behavior, marketers can identify market segments and tailor their product, promotional, and distribution strategies to the different social groupings.

The most widely accepted method of social class measurement is Warner's Index of Status Characteristics. On this basis, Warner identified six social classes, each exhibiting different values, media behavior, shopping patterns, and store preferences.

A number of problems with the concept and measurement of social class were identified. Primary among them were the notion that social class distinctions are disappearing and the inadequacy of measurement when specific conditions create incongruency among criteria. Several qualitative class differences were also discussed — for example, lower-class individuals are more likely to seek immediate gratification; middle-class persons are more likely to be concerned with respectability and morality; lower-class individuals are more concerned with the present and the past, middle-class show concern and interest in the future. Such insights can also be useful to the marketer for developing promotional appeals and for product strategy.

QUESTIONS

1. Define reference group and identify, with examples, the different kinds of membership reference groups.

2. Discuss the principal functions filled by reference groups.

3. Relate the kinds of influence exerted by a group to the different sources of group power.

4. Write an essay on the factors that influence group conformity.

5. Discuss and evaluate the evidence in marketing on the influence of reference groups on consumer behavior.

6. Outline the main findings of the Bearden and Etzel study and comment on its implications for marketing strategy.

7. Describe the main characteristics of opinion leaders, pointing out the misconceptions that may exist about that group.

8. "Several different approaches have been developed by marketing to make use of opinion leaders." Discuss.

9. Define social class and describe its main manifestations.

10. What are some of the chief problems with the social class concept?

11. Write an essay on the income/social class controversy in consumer behavior.

12. Discuss the applicability of social class data in the development of marketing strategy.

NOTES TO CHAPTER 15 ▬▬▬▬▬

[1]Donald H. Granbois, "Improving the Study of Customer In-Store Behavior," *Journal of Marketing*, 32 (October 1968), pp. 28-33.

[2]C. Whan Park and V. Parker Lessig, "Students and Housewives: Differences in Susceptibility to Reference Group Influence," *Journal of Consumer Research*, 4 (September 1977), p. 105.

[3]Solomon E. Asch, "Effects of Group Pressure Upon the Modification and Distortion of Judgments," in H. Guetzkow (ed.), *Groups, Leadership, and Men* (Pittsburgh: Carnegie Press, 1951).

[4]Ibid.

[5]D.A. Wilder, "Perception of Groups, Size of Opposition, and Social Influence," *Journal of Experimental Social Psychology*, 13 (1977), pp. 253-68.

[6]Robert E. Burnkrant and Alain Cousineau, "Informational and Normative Social Influence in Buyer Behavior," *Journal of Consumer Research*, 2 (December 1975), p. 207.

[7]Joseph F. Dash, Leon G. Schiffman, and Conrad Berenson, "Risk- and Personality-Related Dimensions of Store Choice," *Journal of Marketing*, 40 (January 1976), pp. 32-9; Robert D. Hisrich, Ronald J. Dornoff, and Jerome B. Kernan, "Perceived Risk in Store Selection," *Journal of Marketing Research*, 9 (November 1972), pp. 435-9.

[8]Arch G. Woodside, "Informal Group Influence on Risk Taking," *Journal of Marketing Research*, 9 (May 1972), pp. 223-5.

[9]Arch G. Woodside, "Is There a Generalized Risky Shift Phenomenon in Consumer Behavior?" *Journal of Marketing Research*, 11 (May 1974), pp. 225-6.

[10]Daniel L. Johnson and I. Robert Andrews, "Risky-Shift Phenomenon as Tested With Consumer Products as Stimuli," *Journal of Personality and Social Psychology*, 20 (August 1971), pp. 328-85.

[11]V. Parker Lessig and C. Whan Park, "Promotional Perspectives of Reference Group Influence: Advertising Implications," *Journal of Advertising*, 7 (Spring 1978), pp. 41-7.

[12]Joseph M. Kamen, Abdul C. Azhani, and Judith R. Kragh, "What a Spokesman Does for a Sponsor," *Journal of Advertising Research*, 15 (April 1975), p. 17.

[13]Hershey H. Friedman, Michel J. Santeramo, and Anthony Traina, "Correlates of Trustworthiness for Celebrities," *Journal of the Academy of Marketing Science*, 6 (Fall 1978), pp. 291-9.

[14]James E. Stafford, "Effects of Group Influence on Consumer Brand Preferences," *Journal of Marketing Research*, 3 (February 1966), pp. 68-75.

[15] Jeffrey D. Ford and Elwood A. Ellis, "A Re-Examination of Group Influence on Member Brand Preference," *Journal of Marketing Research*, 17 (February 1980), pp. 125-32.

[16] C. Whan Park and V. Parker Lessig, "Students and House-wives: Differences in Susceptibility to Reference Group Influence," *Journal of Consumer Research*, 4 (September 1977), pp. 102-10.

[17] William O. Bearden and Michael J. Etzel, "Reference Group Influence on Product and Brand Purchase Decisions," *Journal of Consumer Research*, 9 (September 1982), pp. 183-94.

[18] Ibid, p. 189.

[19] Ibid.

[20] Harold H. Kassarjian and Thomas S. Robertson, *Perspectives in Consumer Behavior*, 3rd ed. (Glenview, Illinois: Scott, Foresman, and Company, 1981), p. 219.

[21] George P. Moschis, "Social Comparison and Informal Group Influence," *Journal of Marketing Research*, 13 (August 1976), pp. 237-44.

[22] Charles W. King and John O. Summers, "Overlap of Opinion Leadership Across Consumer Product Categories," *Journal of Marketing Research*, 7 (February 1970), pp. 43-50.

[23] David B. Montgomery and Alvin J. Silk, "Clusters of Consumer Interests and Opinion Leaders' Spheres of Influence," *Journal of Marketing Research*, 8 (August 1971), pp. 317-21.

[24] James H. Myers and Thomas S. Robertson, "Dimensions of Opinion Leadership," *Journal of Marketing Research*, 9 (February 1972), pp. 41-6.

[25] Paul F. Lazarsfeld, "Who Are the Marketing Leaders?" in James U. McNeal and Stephen W. McDaniel (eds.), *Consumer Behavior: Classical and Contemporary Dimensions* (Boston: Little, Brown, 1982), pp. 317-23.

[26] John O. Summers and Charles W. King, "Interpersonal Communication and New Product Attributes," in Philip R. McDonald (ed.), *Marketing Involvement in Society and the Economy* (Chicago: American Marketing Association, 1969), pp. 292-9.

[27] Douglas J. Tigert and Stephen J. Arnold, *Profiling Self-Designated Opinion Leaders and Self-Designated Innovators through Life-Style Research* (Toronto: Faculty of Management Studies, University of Toronto, 1971).

[28] Ernest Dichter, "How Word-of-Mouth Advertising Works," *Harvard Business Review*, 44 (November-December 1966), pp. 147-66.

[29] Johan Arndt, "Selective Processes in Word-of-Mouth," *Journal of Advertising Research*, 8 (June 1968), pp. 19-22; Carol A. Kohn Berning and Jacob Jacoby, "Patterns of Information Acquisition in New Product Purchases," *Journal of Consumer Research*, 1 (September 1974), pp. 18-22.

[30] Paul Lazarsfeld, "Who are the Marketing Leaders?" in McNeal and MacDaniel, op. cit., p. 318.

[31] Jagdish N. Sheth, "Word-of-Mouth in Low-Risk Innovations," *Journal of Advertising Research*, 11 (June 1971), pp. 15-8.

[32] Everett M. Rogers and F. Lloyd Shoemaker, *Communication in Innovations* (New York: Free Press, 1971).

[33] Steven A. Baumgarten, "The Innovative Communicator in the Diffusion Process," *Journal of Marketing Research*, 35 (October 1971), pp. 48-53.

[34] John H. Holmes and John D. Lett, Jr., "Product Sampling and Word-of-Mouth," *Journal of Advertising Research*, 17 (October 1977), pp. 35-40.

[35] Joseph R. Mancuso, "Why Not Create Opinion Leaders for New Product Introduction?" *Journal of Marketing*, 33 (July 1969), pp. 20-5.

[36] Bernard Berelson and Gary A. Steiner, *Human Behavior: An Inventory of Scientific Findings* (New York: Harcourt, Brace and World, 1964), p. 453.

[37] Ibid.

[38] Peter C. Pineo and John Porter, "Occupational Prestige in Canada," in James E. Curtis and William G. Scott (eds.), *Social Stratification: Canada* (Montreal: The Canadian Review of Sociology and Anthropology, 1967), p. 206.

[39] Stephen J. Miller, "Source of Income as a Market Descriptor," *Journal of Marketing Research*, 15 (February 1978), pp. 129-31.

[40] Dennis Forcese, *The Canadian Class Structure*, 2nd ed. (Toronto: McGraw-Hill Ryerson, 1980), p. 25.

[41] Nan Lin and Daniel Yauger, "The Process of Occupational Status Achievement: A Preliminary Cross-National Comparison," *American Journal of Sociology*, 81 (1975), pp. 543-61.

[42]W. Lloyd Warner, Marchia Meeker, and Kenneth Eells, *Social Class in America* (Chicago: Science Research Associates, 1949), pp. 11-15.

[43]Richard P. Coleman and Lee P. Rainwater, with Kent A. McClelland, *Social Standing in America: New Dimensions of Class* (New York: Basic Books, 1978).

[44]Richard P. Coleman, "The Continuing Significance of Social Class to Marketing," *Journal of Consumer Research*, 10 (December 1983), p. 267.

[45]Forcese, op. cit., p. 17.

[46]B. Blishen and H. McRoberts, "A Revised Socioeconomic Index for Occupations in Canada," *Canadian Review of Sociology and Anthropology*, 13 (February 1976), pp. 71-9.

[47]Forcese, op. cit., p. 19.

[48]R.P. Coleman, "The Significance of Social Stratification in Selling," in Martin Bell (ed.), *Proceedings of the 43rd National Conference of the American Marketing Association* (Chicago: American Marketing Association, 1960), pp. 171-84.

[49]William H. Peters, "Relative Occupational Class Income: A Significant Variable in the Marketing of Automobiles," *Journal of Marketing*, 34:2 (April 1970), pp. 74-7.

[50]R. Eugene Klippel and John F. Monoky, Jr., "A Potential Segmentation Variable for Marketers: Relative Occupational Class Income," *Journal of the Academy of Marketing Science*, 2 (Spring 1974), pp. 351-6.

[51]John C. Goyder and Peter C. Pineo, "Social Class Self-Identification," in James E. Curtis and William G. Scott (eds.), *Social Stratification: Canada* (Scarborough, Ontario: Prentice Hall of Canada, 1979), p. 434.

[52]Coleman, op. cit., p. 268.

[53]Ibid., p. 270.

[54]S.D. Feldman and G.W. Thielbar, *Life Styles: Diversity in American Society* (Boston: Little, Brown, 1972); R.A. Nisbet, "The Decline and Fall of Social Class," in R.A. Nisbet (ed.), *Traditional Revolt* (New York: Random House, 1968).

[55]Denis Gilbert and Joseph A. Kabl, *The American Class Structure: A New Synthesis* (Homewood, Illinois: Dorsey Press, 1982).

[56]Terence A. Shimp and J. Thomas Yokum, "Extensions of the Basic Social Class Model Employed in Consumer Research," in Kent Monroe (ed.), *Advances in Consumer Research*, 8 (Ann Arbor, Michigan: Association for Consumer Research, 1981), pp. 702-7; Gerald Zaltman and Melanie Wallendorf, *Consumer Behavior: Basic Findings and Management Implications* (New York: John Wiley & Sons, 1979).

[57]Shimp and Yokum, op. cit., p. 704.

[58]Coleman, op. cit., p. 270.

[59]Edward O. Laumann and James S. House, "Living Room Styles and Social Attributes: The Patterning of Material Artifacts in a Modern Urban Community," *Sociology and Social Research*, 54 (April 1970), pp. 321-4.

[60]William H. Peters, "Relative Occupational Class Income: A Significant Variable in the Marketing of Automobiles," *Journal of Marketing*, 34 (April 1970), pp. 74-7.

[61]V. Kanti Prasad, "Socioeconomic Product Risk and Patronage Preferences of Retail Shoppers," *Journal of Marketing*, 39 (July 1975), pp. 42-7.

[62]Gordon R. Foxall, "Social Factors in Consumer Choice: Replication and Extension," *Journal of Consumer Research*, 2 (June 1975), pp. 60-4.

[63]Doyle W. Bishop and Masaru Ikeda, "Status and Role Factors in the Leisure Behavior of Different Occupations," *Sociology and Social Research*, 54 (January 1970), pp. 190-208; Robert B. Settle, Pamela L. Alreck, and Michael A. Belch, "Social Class Determinants of Leisure Activity," in William L. Wilkie (ed.), *Advances in Consumer Research*, 6 (Ann Arbor, Michigan: Association for Consumer Research, 1979), pp. 139-45.

[64]Leah Rozen, "Coveted Consumers Rate Magazines over T.V.: MPA," *Advertising Age* (20 August 1979), p. 64.

[65]"Consumer Problems and Consumerism: Analysis of Calls to a Consumer Hot Line," *Journal of Marketing*, 40 (January 1976), pp. 58-62.

[66]Pierre Martineau, "Social Classes and Spending Behavior," *Journal of Marketing*, 23 (October 1958), pp. 121-30.

[67]Chester R. Wasson, "Is it Time to Quit Thinking of Income Class?" *Journal of Marketing*, 33 (April 1969), pp. 54-6.

[68]James H. Myers, Roger P. Stanton, and Arne F. Haug, "Correlates of Buying Behavior: Social Class Vs. Income," *Journal of Marketing*, 35 (October 1971), pp. 8-15; James

H. Myers and John F. Mount, "More on Social Class Vs. Income as Correlates of Buying Behavior," *Journal of Marketing*, 37 (April 1973), pp. 71-3.

[69]Robert D. Hisrich and Michael P. Peters, "Selecting the Superior Segmentation Correlate," *Journal of Marketing*, 38 (July 1974), p. 63.

[70]Charles M. Schaninger, "Social Class Versus Income Revisited: An Empirical Investigation," *Journal of Marketing Research*, 18 (May 1981), pp. 192-208.

[71]Louis V. Dominquez and Albert L. Page, "Stratification in Consumer Behavior Research: A Re-Examination," *Journal of the Academy of Marketing Science*, 9 (Summer 1981), pp. 250-71.

GRIFFITH INSURANCE AGENCY*

Background

Avery Griffith, Chartered Life Underwriter, started out as a broker for several medium-sized life insurance companies and for seven years served a broad range of clients. In the past three years, since he became a CLU, the nature of his clientele had begun to shift and become largely high-income, high social-class persons.

Griffith decided that he could continue to expand his volume only if he were to start an independent agency in which other salespeople and service personnel could assist in the work. He selected a wealthy Chicago suburb, Lake Forest, and rented space in Market Square, a fashionable shopping center located in the center of the town. Market Square was a prestige area containing small shops and offices and a Marshall Field department store. The Marshall Field branch was very small and was rumored to exist primarily for the personal convenience of the Field family, who lived in Lake Forest, and of their close friends of similar status. Actually, the store was a favorite shopping place for many Lake Forest residents.

Griffith Insurance Agency

The new agency would offer a complete insurance planning service as well as numerous additional financial services and it would be designed to appeal to the specific social classes who dominated the area.

Staff

In addition to Griffith, there would be Alan Williams, a Chartered Property and Casualty Underwriter. Williams' duties, apart from relieving Griffith in his absence, included supervision of the office, and

---

Adapted from Roger D. Blackwell, James F. Engel and David T. Kollat, *Cases in Consumer Behavior*, pp. 126-33. Copyright © 1969 by Holt, Rinehart and Winston Inc. Reprinted by permission of Holt, Rinehart and Winston, CBS College Publishing.

research on new developments in the insurance field. Williams was confident of his technical knowledge about insurance but was somewhat apprehensive about how his background would fit in with the clients in Lake Forest, having come from a working-class family whose head had been a union official. He had attended a large state university in the South.

Griffith also employed two salesmen — Edwin P. Corkin, a middle-aged former salesman for a local heating and air-conditioning firm; grayed and distinguished-looking; active in civic organizations and respected by many people.

The other salesman — Jonathan T. McCormick, son of a socially prominent family in Lake Forest — was twenty-two and a recent Yale graduate with a major in history. Academically, McCormick had just barely made it through Yale, but he was personable, and he viewed the insurance field as an attractive career.

Services

Griffith planned two divisions: the Griffith Insurance Agency (GIA), which would provide complete planning and service for all types of insurance (including mutual funds at a later time); and Griffith Investment Brokers (GIB) to handle common stocks. Thus Griffith would become a complete financial counselling service.

Target

Griffith felt that the highest potential for insurance existed in the upper social classes — a fact that was especially true in Lake Forest. Thus he wanted to develop the image of the agency as one that served the upper social classes and his entire marketing mix (services, personnel, advertising, physical surroundings) would be determined that way.

Market

GIA would serve Lake Forest and the adjacent village of Lake Bluff. Other high-income suburbs from which Griffith expected to draw some clients were Highland Park and Libertyville.

Both Lake Forest and Lake Bluff were areas of very high income but Griffith felt that income was not as reliable an indicator of social class as other measures.

Chicago's Community Renewal Program published a ranking of the most desirable communities on a socio-economic basis, using the criteria of percent of professional workers, average years of schooling, and family income. On a weighted scale, Lake Bluff was ranked fourth among the Chicago suburbs. Lake Forest had a higher family income but a considerably lower rating on education and percent of professional workers, giving it a ranking of thirty-second.

Griffith's opinion was that Lake Forest was among the highest status suburbs in the Chicago area and much higher than Lake Bluff; and that it didn't show up because Lake Forest was a much more heterogeneous community — there were significant numbers of domestics, clerks, school teachers, and service workers serving the higher-income, invested-wealth families.

Griffith also found considerable heterogeneity of living areas and housing types in Lake Forest and relative homogeneity in Lake Bluff. Most houses in Lake Bluff were selling between $75,000 and $110,000; in Lake Forest house sale prices varied from $35,000 to $800,000 and more.

Griffith felt that Lake Forest was one of the highest status suburbs in Chicago, but he was somewhat troubled by the fact that other suburbs ranked higher in status from a statistical perspective. As a further check on his beliefs, Griffith examined each issue of the *Chicago Sun* for the past two years. He found that Lake Forest was mentioned as the site of parties among the upper-uppers of the Chicago Metropolitan Area or as the home of persons attending important social events almost every day, and more than any other suburb of Chicago.

Promotional Strategy

After a few months in a temporary office, Griffith was ready to move into the new quarters in Market Square. He planned to prepare a promotional program to announce the opening, to create awareness of the agency, and to establish its image. His stated policy would be to get across that GIA was designed for the upper-middle, lower-upper, and upper-upper social classes. He hoped not only to reach this market but also to serve other social classes in the area. Griffith believed that if the image were attractive to upper classes, the middle classes would also want to do business with the agency. If he designed it as a middle-class agency, however, he believed that the upper classes would not be attracted to the agency. To accomplish this goal, an introductory promotional program was prepared.

The Campaign

To introduce his service, Griffith planned a number of activities:
(a) a series of seminars to run for ten weeks on personal financial planning. He doubted that attendance would be high but he felt it would cause readership of his advertising, create awareness of the agency, inform the public of GIA's intention to be a complete financial service, and provide a vehicle for establishing an image

for the agency. Ten distinguished seminar speakers — including two university professors, a tax consultant, an investment broker, a local bank president, and the senior vice-president of a major insurance company — would cover timely financial topics of interest to high income people;

(b) a twelve-week advertising program in local newspapers and on radio stations in nearby Highland Park. The *Lake Forester* reached 89% of the households in Lake Forest, and the *Lake Bluff Review* 95% of the Lake Bluff households. The radio stations were new and Griffith was not sure of their reach;

(c) a pre-seminar meeting to be advertised by direct mail, consisting of a carefully selected mailing of engraved invitations to the social elite of Lake Forest. This pre-seminar was the direct responsibility of McCormick, who selected the guests, arranged for an appropriate meeting place (the Onwentsia Club), and arranged for appropriate refreshments and the program; and

(d) once-a-week sponsorship of the five-minute business news on the radio stations beginning three weeks before the seminar.

Creative Strategy

(a) The advertising art work had to connote an upper social class image. Accordingly, a highly respected Chicago advertising art studio was hired to prepare high-quality cuts far above the quality of the typical newspaper ad. The tone of the ad was formal, the type was light, and there was a great deal of white space. Photographs of each speaker were the prominent feature of the ad and were lined up horizontally through the middle of the space.

(b) The headline stated in formal type, "You are cordially invited to attend a series of seminars presenting ten distinguished speakers from leading financial institutions..." Phrases such as "considering the subject" were used instead of "speaking on," and the copy was as formal as might be expected on an invitation from an important government officer to attend a formal reception. The ad included a contemporary but subdued logo in the lower right corner of the ad, with the inclusion of the phrase, "Comprehensive financial services."

Perhaps the most interesting aspect of the advertisement was its non-conventional use of lower-case type. Only a few key words — the more important ones — contained capital letters. The overall image was formal and reserved, which Griffith believed appropriate for the community.

The entire tone of the ad was not pushy, but dignified and reserved. Griffith was very pleased with the advertising and felt that it developed exactly the image he wanted.

Problem

Griffith showed the advertising plans to an account executive for a Chicago advertising agency. His friend felt strongly that Griffith was making a big mistake. He argued that upper classes preferred to purchase insurance from long-time associates and friends. Griffith felt his superior and comprehensive service would overcome this. Also, he would be satisfied to get the middle groups in Lake Forest – Lake Bluff. In addition, 30% of the population in these two suburbs moved each year so that he expected to have new potential customers moving into the area in large numbers.

His friend responded that the upper-class image he wanted to create would be interpreted by the middle classes as a "snob" appeal and they would not patronize GIA for fear that they were not really wanted and that they would feel uncomfortable with Griffith personnel.

In summary, the advertising executive felt that the campaign would not reach the upper groups. It would alienate the middle groups and should therefore not be undertaken.

Griffith was not sure what to do. He believed the series could still be cancelled without expense to him. So he was considering not only changing his advertising but also re-evaluating his whole approach to the market.

QUESTIONS

1. Cite from the case instances of social class behavior, attitudes, and symbolism, indicating their significance.

2. Evaluate Griffith's current marketing plan. Should Griffith proceed with the series designed to interest high-income families? Should the proposed advertising be run? Give reasons for your suggestions.

3. What research would be useful and economically feasible for Griffith to conduct in evaluating his decisions?

4. Develop, to the best of your ability, considering the evidence at hand, a strategy that you think Griffith should adopt.

16

Family Influence

1. Family Role Stereotypes

A Canadian advertising agency, in carrying out a pre-test of an advertisement for a brand of baby food, was surprised at the strength of consumer reaction to the perceived roles among the models in the ad. The ad showed a baby sitting in a high chair in the foreground. The baby was being fed by an older lady, who was obviously its grandmother. In the background stood a young woman (obviously the mother) looking on with an approving, satisfied smile.

The pre-test found that what might have been accepted in another day was not found to be appealing. Mothers, who acted as the respondents in the study, felt that the illustration gave the impression that the young mother was lazy and had pressed her mother into a job that the younger woman should be doing. They thought that they would prefer to feed their own babies because "a lot had changed since [grandmother] had looked after her own kids."

The solution was to switch the roles around. The revised ad again showed the baby being fed in the foreground, this time by the younger woman. The older woman was standing in the background with a proud, approving smile on her face.

2. Adapting to Family Needs*

Mrs. Sandra LeMaistre of Fredericton, New Brunswick, used to complain to her husband James about having to hold their seven-month-old daughter while doing the household chores, until he made a child carrier for her from a pile of discarded leather scraps he found. LeMaistre cut them into straps and invented the Superkodler (see Figure 16.1). It consists of four straps and a shoulder pad. Two of the straps form

---

*Adapted from Ann Silversides, "Superkodlers, Snuglis Face off in Quest for Better Baby Carrier," *The Globe and Mail* (19 December 1983), p. B3; David Folster, "A Baby-Carrying Sling," *Maclean's* (16 January 1984), p. 50.

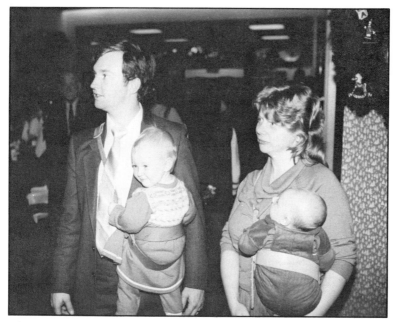

FIGURE 16.1: The Superkodler

Brian Willer/*Maclean's*

the adjustable shoulder harness, another fits under the baby's bottom, and the fourth wraps around its back. Unlike other carriers, which hold a baby against a parent's chest or back, the Superkodler holds the child against the hip, which is where most mothers naturally tend to hold their babies. The sling allows the mother to carry her baby comfortably and have her arms free.

After making the first model for his wife, LeMaistre quickly sold several hundreds locally and in a few months, by the fall of 1983, large retailers like Eaton's and Reitman's had placed orders. The LeMaistres expected to sell 20,000 carriers in their first year in business.

3. Cycles and the Family Life-Cycle*

The target audience for the advertising of motorcycles, once the symbol of youthful rebellion, was the eighteen-to-twenty-five-year-old age group. Apparently, the age of the audience has moved upward. As the affluent post-war generation shifts gears into middle age, motorcycle dealers are looking to them to take up the slack left by the younger market.

In an advertisement for a $9,000 to $10,000 upscale touring bike, the message evoked images of sexuality and elusive youth and was

---

Adapted from Marian Stinson, "Cycle Ads Shift to Higher Gear," *The Globe and Mail* (16 May 1984), p. B10.

directed to the thirty-to-fifty-year-old, married with a family and an income of $35,000 or more. The ad was described as suggesting, in essence, one more chance at freedom and romance. Judging from the powerful, costly motorcycles clustered in the corners of parking lots in Toronto's financial district, these ads seem to be working.

All of these examples illustrate certain facets of the consumer dynamics of the family — family role expectations, product innovation based on family needs and behavior, and adapting advertising appeals to different stages in the family life-cycle. This chapter discusses these and a number of other family characteristics that affect the behavior of the family as a whole and of family members in their role of consumer.

THE FAMILY

The influence of the family on its individual members — their acculturation, personality, motivation, values, and attitudes — is pervasive and profound. The family is the principal reference group for most individuals. It is characterized by emotional involvement, face-to-face interaction, and interpersonal influence. The attitudes and motives of every member affect and are affected by those of the other members. The family is also a social organization in that each member has certain roles, responsibilities, and power.

Kinds of Families

Understanding the dynamics of families would be greatly facilitated by examining how families can be differentiated. Two of the main categorizations are:

- Nuclear/Extended: The **nuclear family** is the basic family group, consisting of two parents and their natural or adopted children. Sometimes it consists of only one parent or a couple with no children. The **extended family** includes the nuclear family and its relatives, such as grandparents, uncles, aunts,

in-laws, cousins. The extended family is more characteristic of older societies (e.g., in Europe) than of the newer industrialized societies of North America.
- Procreation/Orientation: The **family of procreation** is the family one establishes by marriage and is roughly equivalent to the nuclear family — that is, a husband, a wife, and their children. This is the family in which younger members of the population are socialized. The **family of orientation** is the family into which one was born.

A household should be distinguished from a family. A household includes all those persons, related or unrelated, who occupy a housing unit, such as a house or apartment.

THE FAMILY IN INDUSTRIALIZED NORTH AMERICA

Most of the discussion in this chapter concerns the nuclear family, which is the characteristic family structure in industrialized North America and has led to a number of developments in Canada and the United States that were previously unknown. These developments have brought with them important consequences for marketing:

- Older generations form separate consuming units and become identifiable markets. Where people can no longer look after themselves, the society makes available a number of services — such as senior citizen homes, medical insurance, and housing developments for the retired. Modern medicine has made the elderly market an expanding one that is increasing in size and marketing significance — medicines, special foods, vacations etc.

- Every generation creates, upon marriage, new households — needing housing space, furnishings, appliances, transportation, heating and lighting energy, and so on. Economies of size (for food, energy, space, and attire) are lost with the absence of the extended family.

- In the absence of grandparents and traditional wisdom, young families look to others for guidance (e.g., opinion leaders and information media). They rely more on their own resources and engage in more consultation with friends and associates, which may at times even lead to a rejection of parental influence. Some young women, for example, deliberately use different brands and styles from those their mothers use.

- Because of the small average household size (an average of about four people), many products have been scaled down — dinette sets, refrigerators, washers, and food packages.

- The new nuclear family, separated from its roots, lacks established status and must establish its own. This need is increased by the high rate of mobility in our society, involving movement to distant communities, where the new family, left alone to establish its status, pursues activities likely to imply the status it desires. This perhaps accounts, in part, for the emphasis in our society on materialism, and specifically on *conspicuous consumption* — to impress acquaintances and accidental neighbors with our symbols of status (e.g., houses, cars, clothing, gadgets, appliances).

- Establishing a new family upon reaching adulthood is a far more serious and responsible undertaking than simply bringing a new spouse to an established family. Some feel that this greater change necessitates a clearer *rite of passage* and our society does this by recognizing a transition period between

childhood and adulthood that serves as a training ground for later responsibilities. This is the youth culture, which has assumed considerable marketing importance in the last decade or two.

The marketer must recognize that in our society the family is both an earning and a consuming unit. Indeed, the trend is increasing — more wives are in the labor force and more of the older children find employment not only in summer vacations but as part-time help during the school year. These trends have an enormous impact on product decisions within the family, since more members make direct contributions to the family finances and consequently expect to participate in how they are used. The marketing researcher would therefore be well advised to obtain *family* data when seeking to determine income class. The marketer should also be alert to the possibility of

FIGURE 16.2: Family Role Stereotypes

Courtesy Ralston Purina Inc.

a widening web of influence within the family on purchase decisions, due in large part to the investment that members other than the husband are making in the resources and goals of the family.

Not only does the family apply standards (norms) to its members but it also serves to filter and interpret the norms of the wider social system. Family norms are particularly important because they are the children's introduction to the **socialization** process and prepare them for relationships controlled by societal norms (Figure 16.2). The family is thus both a training ground and a mediator for the norms of the culture, subculture, social class, and other large groups.

Because of close personal interaction, limited financial resources, exposure to similar information sources, and shared consumption needs, family members tend to *converge* and become quite homogeneous, at least more so than if they had belonged to different families. They develop similar evaluative criteria, motives, attitudes, purchasing patterns, and, some say, even personalities.

Another characteristic of the family is the natural development of conflicting needs and motives among its members, so that compromises often have to be made on the disposition of the family's resources, especially on family decisions. Although the father may be regarded as the leader for most things, particularly major decisions, leadership rotates. Certain decisions are made by the wife and others by children; all members of the family can be said to play some role in the various decisions.

These roles may be summarized as follows:

1. Initiator — the individual who recognizes the need for the item;

2. Information gatherer — the member who is most knowledgeable about the product and about how and where to seek information;

3. Influencer — the individual most aware of the evaluative criteria for the product and is

most influential in brand evaluation and choice (not necessarily different from the information gatherer);

4. Decision maker — the member or members who make the final decision;

5. Purchaser — the person who does the buying (not necessarily the decision maker or any of the others); and

6. User — could be one or more of the family members.

One or more or all of those roles could be filled by the same family member.

FAMILY MEMBER ROLES IN THE PURCHASING PROCESS

The fact that different family members play different roles in the purchasing process (**role differentiation**) has important implications for the marketer. It means that the planning of various marketing elements (such as the design and labelling of packages, the naming of brands, the type of retail outlets, shelf location, store displays, sales approaches, media strategies, advertising messages) must take into account the family member or members most likely involved in that aspect of the process.

A purchase often is the result of influences from several or all family members, all of whose motivations must be considered if the marketer is to understand the dynamics of the decision. Yet marketing researchers continue to study *individuals* and make inferences about family decisions. One writer has attempted to explain the low correlations found between personality measures and buying behavior by pointing out the flaw in the assumption that an individual's motivations will be highly correlated with family purchase decisions.

A husband may buy a station wagon, given the reality of having to transport four children, *despite* his strong preference for sports cars .... A housewife bases product and brand decisions to some extent on orders or requests from family members and on her judgment of what they like or dislike and what is good for them. Even preferences for products individually consumed are likely to be influenced by feedback from members of the family — e.g., "Gee, Mom! That dress makes you look fat," or "I like the smell of that pipe tobacco." . . . Researchers trying to develop and test various theories often link, without apparent concern, individual-based, independent variables to group-based, dependent variables.

. . . The same point of view characterized investigations of brand loyalty and consumer studies. . . . Since these data often reflect purchases by several family members as well as their brand preferences, why should one expect the housewife's brand attitudes or personality to predict household purchases?[1]

Types of Family Role Differentiation

Different families are characterized by different kinds of **role specialization**; that is, families go about making their purchase decisions in different ways. Four types of role structures can be identified:

- **Husband-dominant** — most of the decisions are made by the husband;
- **Wife-dominant** — where most of the decisions are made by the wife;
- **Autonomic** — when each spouse makes an equal number of decisions, but each decision is made by one spouse or the other; and
- **Syncratic** — where most of the decisions in the family are made jointly by the husband and wife.

It should be noted that no account is taken of the role of children in the nuclear family for this categorization — no doubt a serious omission because of the increasing knowledgeability, awareness, and active participation of children in family affairs.[2]

One attempt has been made to correct this situation. Sheth put forward a model that recognizes the individual differences (such as different perceptions, biases, attitudes, motives, evaluative criteria) that each member brings to decisions within the family; that decisions can be separate or joint; and that consumption can be for the family as a whole or for members or groups of members.[3] It is, unfortunately, only a rudimentary step that hardly takes us beyond the obvious and leaves completely untouched the central questions of the nature and extent of the interrelationships and influence among family members. We need to get beyond the flow-chart stage.

It appears that there are certain kinds of situations in which joint decision making is more likely to occur:

- when the perceived risk is high;
- when the decision is important to the family;
- when there is little time pressure;
- with certain groups of individuals, such as the middle income groups, younger families, and families in which only one spouse is working; and
- where there are no children in the family.[4]

Factors Affecting Role Structures

A number of factors influence family role structures:

- the type of product;
- sub-decisions of the purchase act;
- the stage in the decision process;
- stage in the family life-cycle;
- resource contributions of each spouse;
- relative investment;
- personality of family members; and
- location.

These factors operate within the broader context of the culture, the subculture, and the reference group, which may all impose general prescriptions or requirements for the division of labor within a family — what has been called "a traditional role ideology."[5] These are external to the family. Within the family, the father has traditionally tended to be primarily concerned with external family matters and to play a task-oriented role. The wife has been more likely to look after internal matters and to play a social/emotional/aesthetic role. The male was more likely to fix the family car, for example, and the female to decide on furniture and draperies.

These patterns have undergone considerable change in our society. Men and women are increasingly performing both task-oriented and expressive functions.[6]

Subcultural ethnic groups may also impose certain roles on family members, although these seem to weaken with acculturation over time. Sometimes, behavioral patterns within the social class or peer group environment may be more influential than other norms.

Type of Product

Husband-wife involvement varies widely by product category. For example, there is more joint decision making with higher-priced products and separate decisions for lower-priced products. The latter may follow cultural or other group norms or may be based on the individual's competence. One study found the husband to be dominant 69% of the time in the decision on when to buy an automobile and only 16% of the time regarding when to buy furniture.[7]

Sub-Decisions

A purchase decision is not simply a buy or no-buy choice. It can consist of several sub-decisions, such as when to buy, where to buy, how much to spend, what make/kind to buy, what model/style to buy, what color to buy, and so on.

Munsinger et al., studying house purchasing, identified seven sub-decisions and found consistent patterns of role differentiation among them.[8]

Three conclusions emerge from these studies:

- the marketer should identify in his or her own case what the important sub-decisions are and how the responsibility for each decision is allocated;
- role differentiation appears to occur in clusters and these clusters generally seem to be consistent with the task-oriented (husband) – expressive (wife) dichotomy usually associated with family role differentiation; and
- there is considerable disagreement about the roles of the husband and the wife when independent reports from each are compared. This suggests that researchers should be very careful before deciding whether to interview one or both spouses regarding the purchase decision for a particular product.

The Stage in the Decision Process

As was discussed in Chapter 3, a complex purchase decision is not just a single act of buying but a series of steps or a process. Apart from consisting of many component sub-decisions, the purchase act is preceded and followed by other significant considerations. The process starts with the recognition of a need (or problem), followed by the search for information, the evaluation of alternatives, and then the decision to purchase or not purchase. A positive decision is followed by a post-purchase (in-use) evaluation of the product.

Research has shown that role differentiation can occur through the various stages of the process. Woodside demonstrated this with a number of durable products and Hempel with housing.[9] Hempel found, for example, that husbands are more involved at the recognition and initiation stage and wives in the search stage.

In another study, Davis and Rigaux, pointing out that "researchers either oversimplify their conceptualization of the decision-making process (who discussed the purchase and who then bought it), or construct very detailed models of the decision-making process either lacking

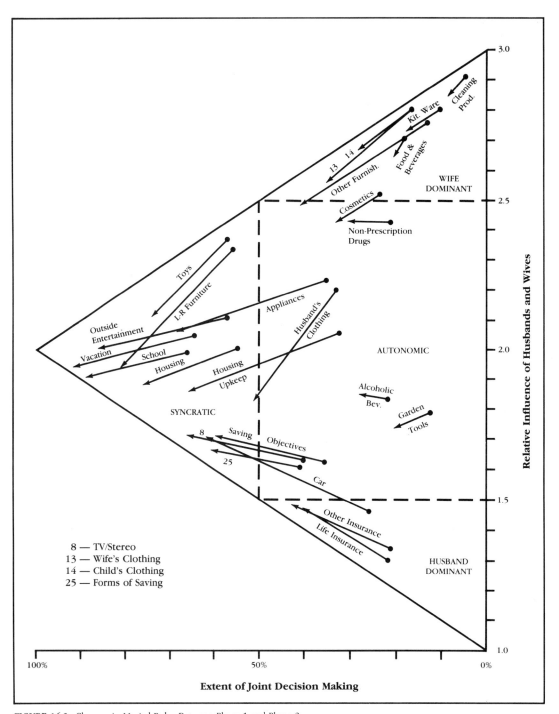

FIGURE 16.3: Changes in Marital Roles Between Phase 1 and Phase 2

SOURCE: Harry L. Davis and Benny P. Rigaux, "Perception of Marital Roles in Decision Processes," *Journal of Consumer Research*, 1 (June 1974), p. 56. Reprinted with permission of The Journal of Consumer Research, Inc.

any empirical validation or limited to a small number of product categories," set out to answer two questions:

- do marital roles in consumer decision-making differ by phase of the process? and
- to what extent do husbands and wives agree in their perception of roles at the various phases?[10]

Employing a three-phase schema — problem recognition, information search, and final decision — they found that marital roles do vary throughout the three phases of the decision process (see Figures 16.3 and 16.4). Figure 16.3 shows the original role differentiation for twenty-five different products as well as the shift toward greater specialization from the problem recognition to the search stage. Figure 16.4 indicates the shift back in the direction of syncratic decision-making in the final decision stage.

Note the location of different products. The vertical axis indicates the extent of husband/wife dominance, with husband dominance at the bottom (from 1.0 to 1.5), wife dominance at the top (from 2.5 to 3.0), and autonomic decisions in between (1.5 to 2.5). The further to the left on the horizontal axis, the greater the extent of joint decision making.

Note that husbands dominate decisions for insurance, wives decisions for food, household products, children's clothing, and cosmetics. Decisions for husband's clothing, alcoholic beverages, and garden tools are made by either spouse and joint decisions are made for housing, vacations, and school.

These data suggest different strategies for marketers. A product in the husband- or wife-dominant category would require strategies (e.g., appeals, media, packaging) directed to one spouse or the other. A product in the syncratic category would require strategies directed at both spouses.

Autonomic products would no doubt require separate advertising appeals to husbands and wives. For decisions that cover longer periods of time (e.g., months in the case of vacations), it may be wise for the advertiser to consider the times of the year when a given stage most likely occurs. A travel agency wishing to promote winter vacations might, in the early fall, advertise the advantages of taking a winter vacation to both husbands and wives. It might follow this a month or so after with search information (alternative plans) directed separately at husbands and wives and yet later, toward year-end, revert to "joint" advertising to encourage couples to make the final decision.

Incidentally, it was also found that there was a high level of agreement between the responses of husbands and wives in the aggregate. However,

> the level of consensus within families, although higher than chance, was nevertheless lower than one might assume if comparing husbands' and wives' responses as groups .... The methodological implications of these findings for researchers who want to collect data about household economic behavior relate to both interviewing and question construction. Depending upon the objectives and budget of a research project, the use of either husband or wife would be appropriate if the analysis was limited to gross descriptions of marital decision roles.[11]

A similar study done a few years later with US consumers also explored shifts in husband/wife decision making during the same three stages of the decision process.[12] For most of the products not much change seemed to occur over the three stages. However, items such as washing machines, living-room drapes, and insurance seemed to move in the syncratic direction. These were the opposite of the results in the Belgian study, which may indicate the existence of cultural differences. Nevertheless, that family member roles can differ from one stage of the decision process to another is well demonstrated.

It is important for the marketer to identify who the key decision maker is at each stage to plan a strategy accordingly — from the design and packaging of the product, to the creative appeals, the media mix, the timing of appeals,

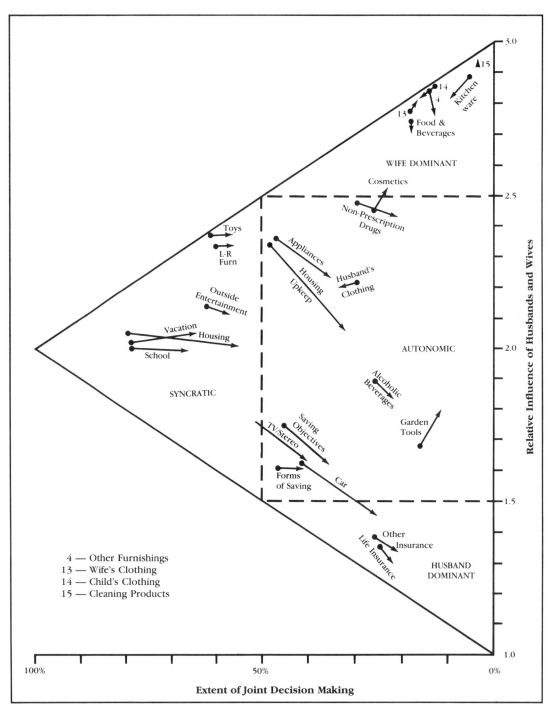

FIGURE 16.4: Changes in Marital Roles Between Phase 2 and Phase 3

SOURCE: Harry L. Davis and Benny P. Rigaux, "Perception of Marital Roles in Decision Processes," *Journal of Consumer Research*, 1 (June 1974), p. 57. Reprinted with permission of the Journal of Consumer Research, Inc.

the types of retail outlets, the sales personnel, and in-store displays and decor.

For example, assume a marketer found that the decision to purchase a color television set was characterized by significant role differentiation at the various stages of the process. Suppose that problem recognition occurs jointly (no doubt including children), internal search is also "joint," external search is husband-dominant (mainly visiting showrooms, talking with salespeople, and picking up printed material), and alternative evaluation and the final decision are "joint." While need recognition advertising might be directed separately at different members of the whole family, external search information (sales staff, appeals, decor and displays in stores) would be geared to the male, and brochures and other literature to both husband and wife for evaluation and final decision.

Stage in the Family Life-Cycle

It has also been found that family-member decision roles vary according to the stages in the life-cycle of the family. A family's needs, resources, attitudes, behavior, and motives change over time and appear to go through a number of stages. I will discuss these in a later section. At this point it should be stated that there is some evidence that the early stages of the family life-cycle are characterized by joint decision making and that, as the spouses get to know each other better and acquire more and more responsibilities, there is a tendency toward specialization.[13]

Resource Contributions of Each Spouse

Resource contributions include not only income but also education, occupational prestige, social status, and decision-making ability.

Working wives tend to play a greater role in decision making than non-working wives, but overall, it seems that power is based not so much on the value to one spouse of the contributions of the other as on the value placed on these contributions *outside the family*. In

other words, the greater the value placed on the resources (or potential contributions) of the wife outside the family, the greater will be her influence in decision making.[14] This has been referred to by some as the **least-interested-partner** hypothesis. The partner with the higher level of education would also tend to dominate.

One study found that attitudes to marital roles are an important factor in husband/wife dominance. In families where the wife has contemporary attitudes toward the female role, there is less husband dominance in decision making. The husbands of liberal wives make fewer purchasing decisions on their own than husbands of either moderate or conservative wives. It was suggested that this pattern may be product-specific rather than generalized. Thus the liberal wives seem to play a significantly greater role in deciding the amount of money to spend on purchases than moderate or conservative wives.[15]

Relative Investment

This implies that each spouse has a particular decision domain because, typically, the outcomes of a decision do not fall evenly across all family members.[16] While the resources explanation defines the potential to exert influence, investment defines the motivation to exert influence and in specific instances rather than in the general family authority structure.

Personality

It is possible, too, for personality to influence the roles played by family members in decision making. Authoritarian individuals with a strong need for power will tend to dominate and those with a strong need for affection may tend to yield in decision-making situations.

Location

Role specialization may also vary by geographical location. For example, joint decision making may be more common in rural areas than in urban areas.

CHANGING HUSBAND/WIFE ROLES

There is a great deal of evidence to support the claim that husband/wife roles in our society are changing rapidly. The women's liberation movement, accompanied by the increases in the proportion of women in the labor force, has brought about considerable overlap in the roles played by men and women.

It is to be expected that major shifts in societal role structures will affect buying behavior patterns, particularly within families. Thus the increased status and autonomy of the modern wife will lead to an increased frequency of wife dominance and a decline in the power of the husband in family purchasing decisions.

Cunningham and Green found, for example, that more effective family planning and labor-saving appliances have freed the modern housewife for more activities outside the home.[17]

Marketers should recognize that changes are taking place in family-member roles in purchase decision making and should also be aware that not all women holding contemporary attitudes are necessarily "liberated" or more autonomous in their buying decisions, and that such attitudes may have a more pronounced impact on some products than on others.

A study of "the significance of the changing roles of women to consumer research" focussed on three groups of women designated as traditionalists, moderates, and feminists.[18] Feminists and moderates were found to be younger than traditionalists, generally more educated, and more likely to be employed fulltime. More traditionalists labeled themselves "housewives" and more feminists preferred the term "co-head of household." No differences were found among the groups by income or marital status.

As far as differences in life-style were concerned, a large number of psychographic statements were given to the respondents and these were reduced to ten basic factors, as shown below:

1. Sex Stereotyping — e.g., "I would like to see more and more girls play with mechanical toys."

2. Self-Confidence — e.g., "I feel capable of handling myself in most social situations."

3. Television Viewing — e.g., "I watch television to be entertained."

4. Fashion and Personal Appearance — e.g., "I like to feel attractive."

5. Life Simplification — e.g., "I consider it essential for most families to own a dishwasher."

6. Leisure-Work Attitude — e.g., "Leisure activities are more satisfying than a job."

7. Innovative Behavior — e.g., "I often try new ideas before my friends do."

8. Active-Leisure Behavior — e.g., "During leisure time I like to relax by reading a book or listening to music."

9. Opinion Leadership — e.g., "My friends or neighbors often come to me for advice."

10. Frozen Food Consumption — e.g., "I couldn't get along without frozen foods."

Based on group differences, the life-style data indicated the kinds of appeals that might be used to advantage with certain groups and those that should be avoided.

For example, under Sex Stereotyping, it was found that feminists (80%) were very much more likely to agree that boys and girls should play with the same kind of toys, compared to moderates (64%) or traditionalists (30%). Traditionalists, on the other hand, agreed with the statement, "Advertisements seem to have recognized the changes in women's roles" to a significantly greater degree (48%) than did moderates (33%) or feminists (22%).

Under Self-Confidence, feminists (57%) were significantly more likely to agree with the statement, "I am rarely at a loss for words when I am introduced to someone" than were moderates (50%) or traditionalists (40%). Traditionalists (23%) were more inclined to agree that "in group discussions I usually feel my opinions are inferior" than were moderates (13%) or feminists (14%).

Working Wives

One of the principal reasons for the changing roles of men and women in our society with regard to shopping habits, household tasks, and decision making is the working status of an increasing number of wives. This has also affected such other areas of family life as family consumption habits and family attitudes. As of April 1984, 47.2% of Canadian married women were officially in the labor force (see Figure 16.5).

	Population (15 years and over) (000's)	Labor Force Participation Rate (%)
Married Women	5,892	47.2
15–24	529	54.0
25–44	3,481	58.1
45–64	1,829	39.8

FIGURE 16.5: Estimate of Married Women in Canadian Labor Force, April 1984

SOURCE: Statistics Canada, *The Labour Force, 1984*, Catalogue No. CA1 B571 C001.

As can be seen, the percentage of women participating in the labor force is particularly high (58%) in the 25 to 44 age group and around 40% among the 45 to 64 age group. The rate is likely to continue to increase.

There are a variety of reasons why a wife works outside the home: of course, to add to the family's income, but also to escape the dullness of housework, to sharpen her own talents and skills, to meet and get involved with others, and to prepare for when she may be single again.[19]

It has been found that as consumers, working wives' families do not spend differently from non-working wives' families for such durables as dishwashers, washers, dryers, refrigerators, stoves, TVs, and furniture.[20] Time-saving durables also did not show any significantly different patterns. For example, the microwave oven (owned by only 13% of the sample) was not significantly related to wives' labor-force status. It appears that once the impact of wives' earnings in raising family income is taken into account, income and stage in the life-cycle are more important determinants of purchase and ownership of such items than employment status.

Another area likely to be affected by women's changing roles is the portrayal of women in advertising. Early studies criticized the role portrayal of women in advertising as limited, unrepresentative, and stereotyped.[21] More recent research reports improvement in such portrayals.[22] However, attitudes to role portrayal, especially among women, still appear to be quite negative.[23]

OTHER WAYS OF VIEWING FAMILY CONSUMER DECISIONS

Examining the roles played by family members in decision making can be very helpful to the marketer, but there are a number of other perspectives from which the family may be analyzed that can be extremely useful. These include:

- stage in the family life-cycle;
- family orientation or life-style; and
- demographic composition.

These are, in other words, different ways of segmenting families in the target market to determine the most effective way for discriminating among them.

Stage in the Family Life-Cycle

The concept of the **family life-cycle (FLC)** is based on the developmental changes that a family goes through in its needs, resources, motivations, and behavior. Starting as early as the 1930s, a variety of schemes have been put forward regarding the number, as well as the determinants, of the "stages" of the FLC. One of the most widely accepted is the nine-stage cycle proposed by Wells and Gubar (see Figure 16.6) It is based on the ages of parents and children and employment status.

Other research studies on specific FLC stages have made some interesting observations. For example, "young singles" have been described as increasingly oriented toward personal growth and enriching personal experience rather than mate searching and marriage preparation. The emphasis is on household durables as expressions of one's individuality and accomplishments.[24]

STAGE IN LIFE-CYCLE	BUYING OR BEHAVIORAL PATTERN
1. *Bachelor stage:* Young single people not living at home	Few financial burdens. Fashion opinion leaders. Recreation-oriented. Buy: basic kitchen equipment, basic furniture, cars, equipment for the mating game, vacations.
2. *Newly married couples:* Young, no children	Better off financially than they will be in near future. Highest purchase rate and highest average purchase of durables. Buy: cars, refrigerators, stoves, sensible and durable furniture, vacations.
3. *Full nest I:* Youngest child under six	Home purchasing at peak. Liquid assets low. Dissatisfied with financial position and amount of money saved. Interested in new products. Like advertised products. Buy: washers, dryers, TV, baby food, chest rubs and cough medicines, vitamins, dolls, wagons, sleds, skates.
4. *Full nest II:* Youngest child six or over	Financial position better. Some wives work. Less influenced by advertising. Buy larger-sized packages, multiple-unit deals. Buy: many foods, cleaning materials, bicycles, music lessons, pianos.
5. *Full nest III:* Older married couples with dependent children	Financial position still better. More wives work. Some children get jobs. Hard to influence with advertising. High average purchase of durables. Buy: new, more tasteful furniture, auto travel, nonnecessary appliances, boats, dental services, magazines.
6. *Empty nest I:* Older married couples, no children living with them, head in labor force	Home ownership at peak. Most satisfied with financial position and money saved. Interested in travel, recreation, self-education. Make gifts and contributions. Not interested in new products. Buy: vacations, luxuries, home improvements.
7. *Empty nest II:* Older married couples, no children living at home, head retired	Drastic cut in income. Keep home. Buy: medical appliances, medical-care products that aid health, sleep, and digestion.
8. *Solitary survivor, in labor force*	Income still good but likely to sell home.
9. *Solitary survivor, retired*	Same medical and product needs as other retired group; drastic cut in income. Special need for attention, affection, and security.

FIGURE 16.6: An Overview of the Life-Cycle and Consumer Behavior

SOURCE: William D. Wells and George Gubar, "Life Cycle Concept in Marketing Research," *Journal of Marketing Research*, 3 (November 1966), p. 362. Reprinted with permission of the American Marketing Association.

Criticisms of the Traditional FLC Model

In the light of social trends, it has been suggested that the FLC needs to be updated. Some of the evidence cited include:

- the length of time within stages is changing because women are beginning childbearing later and finishing sooner;[25]
- the number of children per family is declining;
- the traditional FLC does not include families broken up by separation or divorce;
- the traditional FLC does not include couples who never have children;
- it does not include one-parent families;
- it places undue emphasis on the age of children;
- it stresses the importance of the changing role of the father/husband but not that of the mother/wife;
- the traditional FLC does not include older families with children under six; and
- it does not include older individuals who marry late in life.

Because of these trends, which seem to have altered the typical family both in its composition and life-style, a new, modernized FLC has been proposed.[26] It seeks to correct for some of the demographic shifts by including divorced individuals, middle-aged marriages, and units without children. However, it does not take into account:

- cohabitative couples (because the proportion is very small);
- single mother families;
- separated married couples, except for those who eventually divorce (who are in the majority);
- young and middle-aged widowed husbands and wives and their families.

It consists of five major categories, with the last three divided into a total of eleven subcategories. Because of the limitations of Statistics Canada data, Figure 16.7 presents these stages but grouped in accordance with the data available for Canada. The table also shows the (approximate) distribution for the traditional FLC.

The modernized FLC included 1.1 million more Canadians than did the traditional FLC, an increase of 5.8% of the total Canadian population. The comparable figure provided by Murphy and Staples for the United States was 11.8 million or 6.1% of the total population.

Limitations of the FLC Concept

Researchers have noted two principal limitations in the use of the FLC concept:

1. significant disagreement in defining the stages so that there is a wide diversity of classifications; and

2. interpretation of the stages assumes that families in a particular stage are homogeneous in attitudes, etc. The categories cover a wide range, are based on demographic variables, and are likely to contain families with different psychological and expenditure characteristics.[27]

Derrick and Lehfeld suggest that stages be dispensed with and that the identifying variables be used to describe families. However, the advantages of a system that summarizes family characteristics must not be overlooked. The life-cycle concept certainly should be improved rather than dispensed with. If explaining family behavior is based on currently used variables as well as other variables, as suggested by Derrick and Lehfeld, then perhaps those additional variables could be incorporated into an FLC model that will be more discriminating.

From the description of the various stages in the family life-cycle given earlier, it can be seen that the primary benefit of the FLC concept is the possibility of market segmentation, providing data on the needs, attitudes, and usage patterns of consumers. Such information will be useful in developing strategies for packaging,

MODERNIZED FLC				TRADITIONAL FLC		
	Stage	No. of Individuals (000's)	% of Cdn. Pop.	Stage	No. of Individuals (000's)	% of Cdn. Pop.
	1. Young single*	4,488	23.8	1. Bachelor	4,488	23.8
	2. Young married without children			2. Newly married		
15-34	3. Other young:	4,235	22.5		4,235	22.5
	a) young divorced w/out children					
	b) Young married with children	139	0.7			
	c) Young divorced with children			3. Full Nest I		
	4. Middle-aged:					
	a) Married w/out children	6,412	34.0			
	b) Divorced w/out children					
	c) Married with children			4, 5. Full Nest II, III	5,810**	30.8
35-64	d) Divorced with children					
	e) Married w/out dependent children	322	1.7			
	f) Divorced w/out dependent children			6. Empty Nest I		
	5. Older:					
	a) Older married	1,303	6.9	7. Empty Nest II	1,303	6.9
65+	b) Older unmarried:					
	Divorced	39	0.2			
	Widowed	805	4.3	8, 9. Solitary Senior	805	4.3
	All other	1,119	5.9	All other	2,221	11.7
		18,862	100.0		18,862	100.0
	Under 15	5,481		Under 15	5,481	
		24,343			24,343	

* Starts at 15, unlike US statistics, which start at 18.

** Based on the assumption that the percentage of middle-aged without children is the same for both married and divorced persons. Figure derived as follows:

Total ever married = 6,734,000

Total ever married without children = 632,450 = $\frac{632,450}{6,734,000} \times 100 = 9.4\%$

∴ Full Nest II and III + Empty Nest I = 6,412,000 − 9.4% = 5,810,000

FIGURE 16.7: Comparison of Canadian Population Distributions for the Modernized and the Traditional Family Life-Cycles (1981)

SOURCE: Statistics Canada, *1981 Census*, Catalogue 92-901, Table 5, and Catalogue CA1 B592 C906, Table 4.

retail outlets, store hours, new products, and advertising appeals.

Family Orientation

In order to extend our understanding of the motivations and behavior of families, it may be useful to examine their basic orientations — their values and preferences, or the goals that influence their behavior and attitudes or their life-styles. Four such types of orientation may be described:[28]

(a) *Consumption-oriented*: includes families that emphasize the ownership of things. They spend a large proportion of their time and money on products and services related to enjoying life and having a good time. Expensive sports equipment, cars, the latest appliances, saunas, and expensive vacations are typical of such products. "Conspicuous consumption" may be an apt description of their behavior.

(b) *Career-oriented*: families in which everything is geared to the advancement of the career of the head(s) of the household — the type and location of the home, the furnishings, the car, and the clothes they wear will all be consistent with the family goal of career enhancement and success. Products that symbolize status are also characteristic of such families. With such individuals, marriage may be delayed and children postponed and, where one exists, even the family may be "neglected." Such families may be described as having a high degree of "upward mobility."

(c) *Family-oriented or child-oriented*: In many ways, such families are the reverse of the career-oriented families. All of the family's activities, interests, and purchases are centered around the children and the family as a unit. Being together is a prime goal. Products such as games, books, and recreational equipment and activities such as trips and going to shows together are characteristic of this type of family. In such families, the marriage likely occurred at a young age and children arrived early.

(d) *Socially oriented*: In these families the emphasis is on social interaction. In some ways, they are superficially similar to the career-oriented families. In the career-oriented family, social interactions are determined by their ability to contribute to career enhancement; the socially-oriented family, on the other hand, is more likely to participate in social activities for their own sake. Such families can be very influential in their social groups because they have many friends and see a lot of them.

The above types are not mutually exclusive and a family does not belong exclusively to a certain group but, rather, may be described as predominantly in a certain category. There also may be families that cannot be described in terms of one specific orientation. Their emphasis and behaviors may be consistent with a combination of the above types. It is possible to have, for example, child-career oriented or child-consumption oriented families.

It should be re-emphasized that there is a great deal of overlap between categories and that each category represents the main focus or style of these families in terms of their values, attitudes, interests, preferences, and activities.[29]

It should also be understood that none of these classificatory procedures (role specialization, stage in the family life-cycle, family orientation) is sufficient as the sole basis for grouping or segmenting families. They are most likely complementary to one another in that each adds a certain kind and amount of insight that eventually "makes the picture clearer" for the marketer.

Demographic Composition

Apart from the demographic variables (age and employment status of the head of the household, age of children) already employed in the determination of stage in the life-cycle, there are others that should be taken into account in any analysis of family behavior. *Income trends* are reflected in the increasing economic power of individual households and affected by increasing numbers of working wives. The number of children in the average family is declining, which can have significant effects on package size, design of appliances and furniture, types of retail outlets, and so on.

HOW FAMILIES REACH DECISIONS

Most of the research in the field of family decisions focusses on the outcome of the decisions or on the roles played by family members (mainly the spouses) in decisions, but little has been done on the *process* by which families reach their decisions — the dynamics involved in the interplay among family members.

Davis has pointed out that family decisions are not always the result of *consensus*; they are often accommodative, involving the resolution of conflicts:

> Even if the group can agree about the likely consequences of each choice, there will be no way that one alternative can be satisfying to all. Bargaining, coercion and other means may be used to reach an acceptable solution.[30]

It would seem important for the marketer to know when decisions are consensual and when they are accommodative, since marketing strategy could be influenced by this knowledge. The relative frequency may vary by product, social class, race, or each spouse's employment status; and in the accommodative model "each spouse can engage in the same consumption behavior for different reasons."

The Context of Family Decisions

Consider how the family situation differs from other situations for the making of decisions. In contrast to laboratory groups in "ideal" conditions, family decisions are:

- made when energy levels are low — early in the morning or late in the day;
- more subject to distraction from non-task activities;

- influenced by the need to "assure continuance of the group," thus tending to avoid tension and rigorous (and what may also be invidious) analysis; and
- made in a context of other interrelated problems, where the thornier problems are probably left for later. "Families may be more solution-oriented than problem-oriented." Thus, for example, different family members may not perceive the problem (need) similarly because they are concentrating on different aspects of the problem.

These conditions do not appear to be conducive to objective problem solving. Rather, the interplay of emotional forces dominated by a motivation for survival leads the family into one or more of several strategies.

Strategies for Resolving Conflict

Where there is consensus about goals, decisions will be the result of expected roles, or accepted rules (budgets), or problem solving where options are evaluated for their merits.

Where there is conflict, two possible strategies exist — a persuasion strategy and a bargaining strategy, each of which permits a number of different tactics. Figure 16.8 summarizes these with examples and should be studied carefully. Davis concludes that the approach of consumer behaviorists should be "much broader than simply determining who is involved in various decisions and tasks. Research should be directed to these alternative decision strategies — to specifying the circumstances under which each will be used in the same family and how their use differs among families."[31]

> A recent study found that in general, people who are more traditional in their life styles and attitudes are more likely to use persuasive influence. A notable exception is the young, married individual with pre-school children. Those who are further along in the life cycle also tend to use less of the various types of influence.[32]

Goals	Strategy	Ways of Implementing (Tactics)	Examples
"Consensus" (family members agree about goals)	Role structure	The specialist	One member is accepted as having the expertise to decide in a particular area.
	Budgets	The controller	Limits agreed upon. Conflict and joint decision-making still possible.
	Problem solving	The expert	Knowledgeable one(s) decides on best choice.
		The better solution	The family pools its information and skill to come up with a "better solution."
		The multiple purchase	To avoid conflict two or more choices may be made [two black and white TVs (instead of one color), two vacations, two cars, two telephones].
Accommodation (family members disagree about goals)	Persuasion (getting someone to make a decision he or she would not otherwise make)	The irresponsible critic	The one without the authority can criticize freely and may often win out.
		Intuition	A spouse getting his or her way by playing on the weaknesses of the other.
		Shopping together	With both spouses having made the decision, the other person will find it harder to back out of the decision.
		Coercion	Unwilling agreement through threat. Possible when there are big differences in authority.
		Coalitions	Agreeing members will tend to bring dissenters into line.
	Bargaining (willing agreement)	The next purchase	The other spouse will have his or her way the next time.
		The impulse purchase	Make the purchase first, bargain later.
		The procrastinator	Delaying a purchase that has been agreed on in the hope that new information or a changed situation may result in a new decision.

FIGURE 16.8: Alternative Decision-Making Strategies

Adapted from Harry L. Davis, "Decision Making Within The Household," *Journal of Consumer Research*, 2 (March 1976), pp. 254-6.

THE ROLE OF CHILDREN IN FAMILY DECISIONS

The volume of promotion addressed to children suggests, since there is very little published evidence, that marketers must have other evidence of a proprietary nature of the importance of children in family purchase decisions. It is possible, of course, that much of it may be attributed to "intuitive good sense."

Roles Children Play

Children are important in marketing in three ways:

(a) They are consumers and purchasers *in their own right* and "represent an economic force of considerable consequence. Based only on an assumed average weekly allowance of 40¢ for the almost 20 million children ages five to nine in the United States, the potential expenditure of this age group in one year is over $400 million."[33]

(b) They exert considerable influence over expenditures made by other family members, particularly for certain products, such as food, clothing, entertainment, toys, vacations, and even certain appliances. This influence may be exerted indirectly ("passive dictation") such as when mothers settle upon a brand or product type on the basis of their children's likes and dislikes, even though the children may not explicitly say what they would like.

(c) Children may also play an active role and make direct attempts at influencing the family decision. A recent study found that children attempt to influence preferences in the in-store situation, particularly for products of interest to them but also for products that may not be too related to their interests.[34]

Studies of Children's Influence

One set of studies has investigated the interaction between mother and child. Berey and Pollay selected a product (ready-to-eat breakfast cereals), in which the mother-child relationship seemed predominant, and interviewed eight-to-eleven-year-old students, their mothers, and their teachers. Two hypotheses were tested: (a) the more assertive the child and (b) the more child-centered the mother, the greater the likelihood that the mother would purchase the child's favorite brands of cereal.[35] Neither relationship was found to hold. The child's degree of assertiveness had little effect on the brands purchased; and there was indeed a significant negative correlation between child-centeredness and favorite brand, suggesting that the mother who is more child-centered has a greater tendency to purchase what she thinks is good for the child and not what the child would like.

Another study, which sought to measure parental yielding to children between five and twelve years of age for twenty-two different products, did not produce any surprises regarding the products for which children attempt to exert some influence (breakfast cereals, toys, games, toothpaste, candy, snack foods, soft drinks).[36] It did reveal, however, that older children (eight to twelve) make fewer attempts to influence their parents, and parental yielding tends to increase with the age of the child. Caution should be exercised in generalizing from these results because the sample was a very specific one — skewed toward the upper and upper-middle classes and restricted to the Boston area. Furthermore, it was a convenience sample and the data was generated through self-administered questionnaires completed by a small sample of 109 mothers. It should be noted that both studies were conducted twelve to fifteen years ago and could be out of date.

A few other studies have attempted to investigate the relative roles of parents and peers in adolescent purchase decisions or in adolescent influence on family purchase decisions. They were no doubt reflecting the view that parents have a decreasing influence on older children, who turn to their peer groups for norms and values. But there is some evidence that parents continue to be more influential than peers with adolescent children.[37]

Evaluation

All of the above studies are indicative of certain relationships, but the whole area of children's influence in family purchase decision remains inadequately examined. Even those studies that have been reported rely, for the most part, on information from parents. The difficulties of securing information from children may be great but not insurmountable. Studies of the influence of TV on mother-child interactions have so far been contradictory;[38] but the reality cannot be denied. The role of children in the purchase decision process may be far greater than we even suspect, especially considering the high level of exposure to marketing and other information that children in our society have nowadays, which makes them far more informed and aware than children a decade or two ago.

MARKETING IMPLICATIONS OF FAMILY DECISION MAKING

I have looked at family purchase decisions from a number of different points of view. I have reviewed how different family members perform different roles, how these roles can vary by product, stage in the decision process, stage in the family life-cycle and other factors, and I have discussed the influence of family goals and values and taken a look at the strategies by which families arrive at decisions. Although good, reliable information on these topics is scanty, it is not difficult to see how such information could be used in the improvement of marketing strategy. Every phase of marketing activity would be influenced:

- **whom** to direct messages to: whether husband and/or wife and/or children;
- **what** to say — whether appeals will say different things to different family members be-

cause they are involved at different stages in the decision, have different evaluative criteria or values, or employ specific strategies for arriving at decisions;

- the selection of appropriate **media** based on the individual's media habits;
- the overall **time scheduling** of communications for purchase decisions that cover months at a time;
- the selection of appropriate **retail outlets** — the approaches and personality of salespeople; the decor and in-store displays; store hours;
- the types of **products**; the sizes, colors available; package design and brand name choice; and
- **pricing** strategy — is the decision maker influenced by coupons, for example? Who makes the how-much-to-spend sub-decision?

All of these factors are interrelated and a properly developed strategy would take them all into consideration. Generalizations are difficult; each marketer will need reliable data on which to segment the market and examine the dynamics of the families involved in the particular segment of interest. The marketer will also need to recognize that the market is not likely to remain static, so that strategies will also have to change over time.

FAMILY TRENDS IN OUR SOCIETY

An earlier section discussed some of the demographic changes taking place with the family in Canada and the United States:[39]

1. the declining size of the family;
2. fewer marriages and increasing cohabitation;
3. later marriages;
4. rising divorce rates; and
5. the increasing proportion of wives in the labor force and its effects on shopping be-

havior, consumption habits, household roles, decision making.

These alone will bring about such consequences as product size changes, changes in family goals and values, possible role structure changes, the increased development of nurseries and day-care centers and even earlier school starts.

In addition, other changes of a socio-psychological nature are occurring that are also likely to have profound effects on marketing. For example:

6. The family is becoming *less cohesive*. Fathers in some segments are said to spend less time with their children because they bring home work from the office. The increasing incidence of *single-parent families* is leading to an attenuation of the socializing function of the family. With increasing *exposure to television*, children are slowly being indoctrinated more by the mass media than by family standards of value and behavior. Some have observed that there is an increasing reliance on outside sources of influence, such as peer groups, school, and church, because of the decreasing cohesiveness of the family unit. In many ways, it is frightening to think of the extent to which marketers (through mass advertising, particularly on television) may influence the values, attitudes, behavior, preferences, and decision processes of consumers one or two decades hence. Recently, the Quebec government, through its Consumer Protection Act, explicitly banned all advertising to children. But will this achieve what obviously lies behind the decision? Will children watch less television or enjoy less exposure to TV advertising? Would it not perhaps be more effective to do something about the programs to which children are exposed — programs that may have a great deal to do with the values, attitudes, and other psychological characteristics that they develop?

7. The slowly shrinking work week of other segments of the population has brought with it increased leisure time, which is sure to have a significant impact on the roles, goals, and activities of those families and their family members.

8. The women's liberation movement has placed in sharper focus the relative roles and responsibilities of husbands and wives. For one, the leadership role of husbands is less pervasive and women and children are becoming increasingly independent.

9. Urbanization has thrown large numbers of people together, thus adding to the opportunities for exposure to and reliance on outside associations and influences.

10. High fuel prices will likely continue to reduce the mobility of family members and lead to a variety of possible consequences — families rediscovering themselves; a greater reliance on mass media, particularly television, and all that goes with it; decreased travel and less eating out (with considerable impact on motel chains and fast-food outlets). This will be more true of single-earner families; as the proportion of working wives increases, this trend is likely to decline.

The possibilities are enormous and exciting. The crux of the matter is that marketers must be ever mindful of the phenomenal accelerative thrust of today's society and the consequent need for generating current data. Our capacity to manage "information" may be exploding, but so is our tendency to generate it.

SUMMARY

In Canada and the US, the nuclear family is the predominant family structure, a fact that has had profound effects on marketing in these countries. The family, however, still serves an important socializing function, in addition to being the basic earning and consuming unit in society.

It is important to recognize the specialization of decision-making roles among family members and that this specialization is affected by a number of factors — product, purchase sub-decisions, stage in the decision process, stage in the family life-cycle, resource contributions, relative investment, personality, and geographical location.

Four types of decision-making families were identified — husband-dominant, wife-dominant, autonomic, and syncratic. These may be considered as potential segments. Other useful, general family segmentation approaches include the family life-cycle (FLC), and family life-style orientation. The latter includes the consumption-oriented, the career-oriented, the child-oriented, and the socially oriented family.

Spousal roles are changing rapidly. Increasing numbers of wives are joining the labor force and more husbands are shopping for groceries and doing household chores.

The inadequacies of the traditional FLC model were discussed and a modernized version reviewed. Applied to Canadian population data, the latter included 5.8% more of the population than did the traditional FLC.

Basically, families reach purchase decisions either by consensus or by accommodation, the latter perhaps being the more common and involving the resolution of conflicts.

Not enough is known about the role of children in family decision making. The increasing influence of advertising (in particular, television) on children and their socialization creates a situation in which comprehensive, valid research is urgently needed.

Most of the data discussed in the chapter deal with families in Canada or the United States. It should be recognized, however, that family attitudes, behavior, and preferences vary among cultures so that marketers in international companies will need to determine the differences from one society to another.

QUESTIONS

1. Define (a) nuclear family, (b) extended family, (c) family of procreation. Which is the most relevant in consumer behavior? Explain.

2. Describe the principal ways in which Canadian or US families are different from the family structure in the old countries. What impact have these differences had on marketing?

3. Discuss the primary functions filled by the nuclear family and how it is different from larger reference groups.

4. Explain the different kinds of role specialization and indicate, with explanation, how it varies with the type of product.

5. Discuss how family member roles vary by the stage in the decision process. What are some of the marketing implications of such differences?

6. Write an essay on changing spousal roles. What are the implications of the findings of some recent research?

7. What are the main deficiencies of the Family Life-Cycle as pointed out by Murphy and Staples? How did they try to correct for some of these?

8. What is the marketing usefulness of viewing families from the point of view of their overall orientation?

9. What strategies do families follow to reach decisions? How does the family situation differ from other situations in the making of decisions?

10. How would you sum up what we know about the role of children in family decision making?

11. Discuss the possible applications of family decision making data to marketing strategy.

12. Write an essay on the changes in family attitudes and behavior taking place in our society and how they are likely to affect marketing strategy.

NOTES TO CHAPTER 16

[1]Harry L. Davis, "Decision Making Within the Household," *Journal of Consumer Research*, 2 (March 1976), pp. 241-2.

[2]James U. McNeal, "Children as Consumers: A Review," *Journal of the Academy of Marketing Science*, 7 (Fall 1979), pp. 346-59.

[3]Jagdish N. Sheth, *Models of Buyer Behavior* (New York: Harper and Row, 1974), pp. 22-3.

[4]Pierre Filiatrault and J.R. Brent Ritchie, "Joint Purchasing Decisions: A Comparison of Influence Structure in Family and Couple Decision-Making Units," *Journal of Consumer Research*, 7 (September 1980), pp. 131-40.

[5]Davis, op. cit., p. 250.

[6]John Scanzoni, "Changing Sex Roles and Emerging Directions in Family Decision Making," *Journal of Consumer Research*, 4 (December 1977), pp. 185-8.

[7]F.K. Shuptrine and G. Samuelson, "Dimensions of Marital Roles in Consumer Decision-Making: Revisited," *Journal of Marketing Research*, 13 (February 1976), pp. 87-91.

[8]Gary M. Munsinger, Jean E. Weber, and Richard W. Hansen, "Joint Home Purchasing Decisions by Husbands and Wives," *Journal of Consumer Research*, 1 (March 1975), pp. 60-6.

[9]Arch G. Woodside, "Effects of Prior Decision-Making, Demographics, and Psychographics on Marital Roles for Purchasing Durables," and Donald Hempel, "Family Role Structure and Housing Decisions," both in M.J. Slinger (ed.), *Advances in Consumer Research* (Association for Consumer Research, 1975), pp. 81-92 and 71-80.

[10]Harry L. Davis and Benny P. Rigaux, "Perception of Marital Roles in Decision Processes," *Journal of Consumer Research*, 1 (June 1974), pp. 51-62.

[11]Ibid., op. cit., p. 60.

[12]E.H. Bonfield, "Perception of Marital Roles in Decision Processes: Replication and Extension," in H. Keith Hunt (ed.), *Advances in Consumer Research*, 5 (Ann Arbor, Michigan: Association for Consumer Research, 1978), pp. 302-5.

[13]D.H. Granbois, "The Role of Communication in the Family Decision Process," in S.A. Greyser (ed.), *Proceedings of the American Marketing Association* (Chicago: American Marketing Association, 1963), pp. 44-57; Elizabeth H. Wolgast, "Do Husbands or Wives Make the Purchasing Decisions?" *Journal of Marketing*, 22 (October 1958), pp. 151-8.

[14]Scanzoni, op. cit.; Robert Ferber and Lucy Lee, "Husband-Wife Influence in Family Purchasing Behavior," *Journal of Consumer Research*, 1 (June 1974), pp. 43-50.

[15]Robert T. Green and Isabella C.M. Cunningham, "Feminine Role Perception and Family Purchasing Decisions," *Journal of Marketing Research*, 12 (August 1975), pp. 325-32.

[16]Davis, op. cit., p. 251.

[17]Isabella C.M. Cunningham and Robert T. Green, "Purchasing Roles in the U.S. Family, 1955 and 1973," *Journal of Marketing*, 30 (October 1974), pp. 61-4; William J. Qualls, "Changing Sex Roles: Its Impact Upon Family Decision Making," in Andrew Mitchell (ed.), *Advances in Consumer Research*, 9 (Ann Arbor, Michigan: Association for Consumer Research, 1982), p. 269.

[18]Alladi Venkatesh, "Changing Roles of Women — A Life-Style Analysis," *Journal of Consumer Research*, 7 (September 1980), pp. 189-97.

[19]Jeanne L. Hafstrom and Marilyn M. Dunsing, "Socio-economic and Social-Psychological Influences on Reasons Wives Work," *Journal of Consumer Research*, 5 (December 1978), pp. 169-75; "The Working Woman," *Media Decisions* (February 1976), pp. 53-4.

[20]Myra H. Strober and Charles B. Weinberg, "Working Wives and Major Family Expenditures," *Journal of Consumer Research*, 4 (December 1977), pp. 141-7; Myra H. Strober and Charles B. Weinberg, "Strategies Used by Working and Non-Working Wives to Reduce Time Pressures," *Journal of Consumer Research*, 6 (March 1980), pp. 338-48; Charles B. Weinberg and Russel S. Winer, "Working Wives and Major Family Expenditures: Replication and Extension," *Journal of Consumer Research*, 10 (September 1983), pp. 259-63.

[21]Alice E. Courtney and Sarah W. Lockertz, "A Woman's Place: An Analysis of the Roles Portrayed by Women in Magazine Advertisements," *Journal of Marketing Research*, 8 (February 1971), pp. 92-5; Louis C. Wagner and Janis B. Banos, "A Woman's Place: A Follow-Up Analysis of the Roles Portrayed by Women in Magazine Advertisements," *Journal of Marketing Research*, 10 (May 1973), pp. 213-4.

[22]Kenneth C. Schneider and Sharon B. Schneider, "Trends in Sex Roles in Television Commercials," *Journal of Marketing*, 43 (Summer 1979), pp. 79-84.

[23]William J. Lundstrom and Donald Sciglimpaglia, "Sex Role Portrayals in Advertising," *Journal of Marketing*, 41 (July 1971), pp. 72-8.

[24]Lawrence H. Wortzel, "Young Adults: Single People and Single Person Households," in William D. Perreault, Jr. (ed.), *Advances in Consumer Research*, 4 (Atlanta: Association for Consumer Research, 1977), pp. 321-9.

[25]Arthur J. Norton, "The Family Life Cycle Updated: Components and Uses," in Robert F. Winch and Graham B. Spanier (eds.), *Selected Studies in Marriage and the Family* (New York: Holt, Rinehart and Winston, 1974), pp. 162-7; Paul C. Glick, "Updating the Life Cycle of the Family," *Journal of Marriage and the Family*, 39 (1977), pp. 5-13.

[26]Patrick E. Murphy and William A. Staples, "A Modernized Family Life Cycle," *Journal of Consumer Research*, 6 (June 1979), pp. 12-22.

[27]Frederick W. Derrick and Alan K. Lehfeld, "The Family Life Cycle: An Alternative Approach," *Journal of Consumer Research*, 7 (September 1980), pp. 214-7.

[28]C. Glenn Walters, *Consumer Behavior — Theory and Practice*, 3rd ed. (Homewood, Illinois: Richard D. Irwin, 1978), pp. 346-8.

[29]Joseph T. Plummer, "The Concept and Application of Life Style Segmentation," *Journal of Marketing*, 38 (January 1974), pp. 33-7.

[30]Davis, op. cit., p. 252. Most of the discussion in this section is based on Davis's excellent review.

[31]Ibid., p. 256.

[32]Rosann L. Spiro, "Persuasion in Family Decision-Making," *Journal of Consumer Research*, 9 (March 1983), pp. 393-402.

[33]Jacob Jacoby and David B. Kyner, "Brand Loyalty Versus Repeat Purchasing Behavior," *Journal of Marketing Research*, 10 (February 1973), pp. 3-4.

[34]Charles K. Atkin, "Observation of Parent-Child Interaction in Supermarket Decision-Making," *Journal of Marketing*, 42 (October 1978), pp. 41-5.

[35]Lewis A. Berey and Richard W. Pollay, "The Influencing Role of the Child in Family Decision Making," *Journal of Marketing Research*, 5 (February 1968), pp. 70-2.

[36]Scott Ward and Daniel B. Wackman, "Children's Purchase Influence Attempts and Parental Yielding," *Journal of Marketing Research*, 9 (August 1972), pp. 316-9.

[37]George P. Moschis and Roy L. Moore, "Decision Making Among the Young: A Socialization Perspective," *Journal of Consumer Research*, 6 (September 1979), pp. 101-12.

[38]Pat L. Burr and Richard M. Burr, "Parental Responses to Child Marketing," *Journal of Advertising Research*, 17 (December 1977), pp. 17-20; Edward T. Popper, "Mother's Mediation of Children's Purchase Requests," and Daniel B. Wackman, "Family Processes in Children's Consumption," both in Neil Beckwith et al. (eds.), *Proceedings of the American Marketing Association Educators' Conference*, Series #44 (1979), pp. 645-52.

[39]Murphy and Staples, op. cit., pp. 12-22.

FEMININE ROLE PERCEPTIONS AND FAMILY PURCHASING DECISIONS*

Introduction

The last decade has witnessed a substantial change in the role of women, as indicated by the momentum attained by the feminist movement. The diminishing distinction in the roles that men and women perform in society has resulted in the merging of the traditional sex roles. Women are increasingly performing tasks traditionally assigned to men, and vice versa.

The changes occurring in the woman's role should have a major impact upon the performance of tasks within the family. Major shifts in societal role structures should be reflected in the marketplace. These changes will present many new opportunities for marketers, and they could either positively or negatively affect several existing products and marketing practices.

The study reported examines differences that exist in consumption-related aspects of family decision making between families in which the wife is characterized by varying attitudes toward the woman's role. The primary objective of the study is to examine the potential impact that changes in the female role have upon family purchasing patterns.

Earlier studies have shown that decisions regarding some products (e.g., groceries) tend to be the domain of the wife, while the husband makes decisions on another set of products (e.g., life insurance, automobiles). The purchase of a third set of products is characterized by joint husband-wife decisions (e.g., housing and vacations).

The Study

A randomly selected sample of 257 married women in Houston, Texas, completed a self-administered questionnaire. Respondents were pre-

*Adapted from Robert T. Green and Isabella C.M. Cunningham, "Feminine Role Perception and Family Purchasing Decisions," *Journal of Marketing Research*, 12 (August 1975), pp. 325-32, with permission of the American Marketing Association.

sented with a list of ten products and services together with a number of specific decisions that have to be made when purchasing each product and service (Exhibit 1). They were asked to:

1. provide basic demographic data (income, age);

2. indicate whether each decision was usually made by the wife, the husband, or both the husband and wife;

3. rate each item of an attitude inventory on a seven-point scale ranging from "strongly agree" to "strongly disagree." The items measure the extent of agreement with statements concerning aspects of the woman's role in society (e.g., "The word 'obey' should be removed from the marriage ceremony"). On the basis of their scores the respondents were divided into three groups: conservatives (traditional), moderates (intermediate), and liberals (contemporary).

Groceries
When to shop
How much to spend
Which store
Which grocery products to buy

Furniture
When to buy
How much to spend
Where to buy
Which piece of furniture to buy
Which style
What color and fabric

Major Appliances
When to buy
How much to spend
Where to buy
Which brand
Which model

Life Insurance
When to buy
Amount to buy
From whom to buy
Type of policy

Automobile
Which make
Which model
What color
When to buy
Where to buy
How much to spend

Vacation
When to go
How much to spend
Where to go
How long to take
Form of transportation

Family Savings
When to save
How much to save
How to invest savings

House or Apartment
Size
Price
Location
Who selects the family doctor?
Who keeps track of money and bills?

EXHIBIT 1: Products and Product-Related Decisions Employed in the Study

Findings

The mean number of decisions made by conservatives, moderates, and liberals on each product and service and across all products and services are presented in Exhibit 2:

1. the husbands of liberal wives tend to make fewer purchase decisions than husbands of conservative and moderate women;

2. on five of the products and services, the purchase decision patterns of husbands and wives are the same for the three groups — grocery decisions are wife-dominant; life-insurance husband-dominant; furniture is basically a jointly decided item, with a substantial wife influence; family-savings decisions are split between joint and husband influence; and housing decisions are joint;

3. the products that provide the greatest contribution to the total difference between groups are major appliances, vacations, and particularly automobiles;

4. regarding the "how much to spend" decision, overall, liberals are characterized by less husband and more wife decisions than are moderates and conservatives (Exhibit 3), except for groceries, major appliances, life insurance, and vacations (which showed no group differences);

5. among upper-income liberals there is significantly less husband decision making (Exhibit 4) — major appliances, family savings, vacations, and housing; for life insurance and automobiles there is more joint decision making among liberals;

6. middle-income liberals exhibit significantly more wife decisions than the other groups;

7. no group differences were found among lower-income respondents;

8. liberals in the under-thirty-five age category report significantly less husband decision making than moderates and conservatives (Exhibit 5); for vacations liberals in this age group also report more wife decisions;

9. within the middle-age category, liberals indicate significantly fewer husband decisions and more wife decisions than moderates and conservatives for major appliances, family savings; automobiles are characterized by fewer husband and more joint decisions among middle-age liberals;

10. the fifty-and-over category does not show any differences among the three attitudinal groups.

	Conservatives (n = 32)	Moderates (n = 158)	Liberals (n = 66)	F-ratio
Groceries				
Husband	.38	.18	.30	1.33
Both	.91	.58	.48	1.47
Wife	2.69	3.25	3.21	2.29
Furniture				
Husband	.50	.47	.26	1.34
Both	3.59	3.33	3.29	.25
Wife	1.91	2.18	2.45	.86
Major Appliances				
Husband	1.47	1.03	.64	3.70[a]
Both	2.94	3.22	3.26	.37
Wife	.59	.77	1.12	2.12
Life Insurance				
Husband	2.56	2.65	2.59	.05
Both	1.34	1.23	1.17	.12
Wife	.09	.15	.24	.56
Automobile				
Husband	3.31	2.70	1.94	5.36[b]
Both	2.28	3.02	3.41	2.97[a]
Wife	.41	.30	.65	4.06[b]
Vacation				
Husband	1.47	.97	.73	3.16[a]
Both	3.44	3.63	3.65	.20
Wife	.06	.40	.55	2.23
Family savings				
Husband	1.06	1.06	.80	1.00
Both	1.72	1.53	1.62	.31
Wife	.19	.42	.53	1.43
House or apartment				
Husband	.56	.32	.26	1.98
Both	2.06	2.37	2.24	1.27
Wife	.38	.27	.45	1.24
Family doctor				
Husband	.03	.04	.00	1.51
Both	.57	.35	.26	2.22
Wife	.50	.59	.74	3.34[a]
Money and bills				
Husband	.34	.25	.30	.61
Both	.22	.30	.14	2.99[a]
Wife	.44	.49	.56	.71
Total purchase decisions				
Husband	12.03	9.64	7.89	4.89[b]
Both	18.16	19.44	19.11	.41
Wife	7.44	10.16	10.83	.64

[a] $p \leq .05$.
[b] $p \leq .01$.

EXHIBIT 2: Mean Number of Purchase Decisions for Conservatives, Moderates, and Liberals

	Conservatives	Moderates	Liberals
Husband	38.7%	31.1%	25.1%
Both	46.5	53.4	51.4
Wife	14.8	15.5	23.4
(number of cases)	(256)	(1266)	(525)

$x^2 = 27.27$, d.f. $= 4$, $p < .0001$.

EXHIBIT 3: Percent of "How Much to Spend" Decisions by Conservatives, Moderates, Liberals

	Conservatives	Moderates	Liberals	F-ratio
Lower income (Less than $10,000)				
Husband	9.20	7.80	10.11	.36
Both	22.40	21.10	16.44	1.11
Wife	6.20	9.00	10.56	.99
(n)	(5)	(20)	(9)	
Middle income ($10,000 to $19,999)				
Husband	11.15	8.99	8.00	1.21
Both	20.15	20.33	19.03	.38
Wife	6.69	8.58	10.97	4.08[a]
(n)	(13)	(86)	(30)	
Upper income ($20,000 and above)				
Husband	13.58	11.79	7.23	6.24[b]
Both	14.67	17.35	19.92	2.19
Wife	8.83	15.69	10.73	.27
Husband	(12)	(43)	(26)	

[a]$p \leq .05$.
[b]$p \leq .01$.

EXHIBIT 4: Mean Number of Purchase Decisions Within Income Groups for Conservatives, Moderates, and Liberals

	Conservatives	Moderates	Liberals	F-ratio
Less than 35 years old				
Husband	14.78	9.18	8.43	5.13[b]
Both	16.44	21.38	20.60	2.67
Wife	5.67	7.36	8.97	2.37
(n)	(9)	(55)	(30)	
35–49 years old				
Husband	13.00	10.03	5.92	5.84[b]
Both	16.25	18.39	18.67	.45
Wife	8.75	9.39	17.96	3.81[a]
(n)	(12)	(59)	(24)	
50 years old and above				
Husband	7.10	9.48	9.92	.59
Both	22.80	18.93	15.67	1.86
Wife	8.00	17.05	11.67	.24
(n)	(10)	(44)	(12)	

EXHIBIT 5: Mean Number of Purchase Decisions Within Age Groups for Conservatives, Moderates, and Liberals

QUESTIONS

1. Evaluate the research design of this study — respondents, sample composition, validity of the data, analysis. On the basis of your comments and considering that the study was done over ten years ago, how generalizable would the results be to the present? to the future?

2. Outline the marketing significance of the major findings of the study.

3. Take any two of the ten items and, on the basis of what you've learned about family decision making from the study, develop a suitable promotional strategy for each.

V

External Business Influences

Part V examines the main non-product activities that business firms pursue with the intention of influencing consumer decisions. In particular, it reviews two such sources of influence — communications and retailers.

Chapter 17 discusses mass communications. Chapter 18 deals with strategies pursued by retail stores that influence choice of store, product, and brand. It also considers the influence of the customer-salesperson interaction on such decisions.

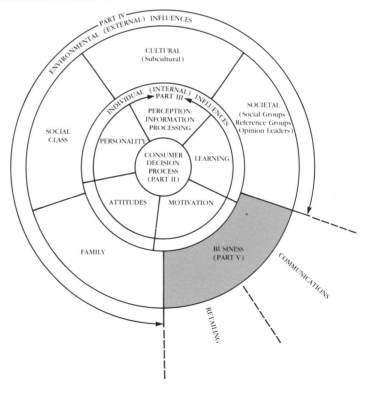

17

Communications

EXAMPLES

1. Fifteen-Second Ads[1]

It appears that the high cost of television advertising will speed up the advent of the fifteen-second commercial. There are fears, however, that the CRTC will object to the clutter it may cause and that viewers may even show their displeasure by tuning them out. Fifteen-second commercials will most likely take the form of two-product thirty-second spots. Media agents report that over 90% of Canadian stations are likely to accept them. It is also rumored that several major advertisers are seriously interested in the piggyback concept.

It appears that the government-owned CBC is firmly opposed to the fifteen-second commercial, but is more agreeable to what they call "integrated 30s" — that is, two piggy-backed fifteen-second commercials in which such things as voice, background, and product category are "essentially the same." They warn, however, that significant increases in the rate structure are likely to follow.

Many broadcasters and advertisers recall the irate response of viewers to the introduction of the piggybacked thirty-second commercials in the late 1960s. Viewer protests eventually subsided but this time it may not be the same. "It is entirely possible that television may self-destruct as a result of all of this," said Rolf James, secretary of the Association of Canadian Advertisers. "It may trivialize commercials to the extent that no one [will care] enough to bother with them." It is also possible that viewers may not just be turned off by the plethora of messages but also remember less and less of the commercials so that message dilution will end up costing far more than advertising dollar dilution.

2. Testing Ad Copy

The Toronto ad agency for a Canadian cooking oil company knew what it wanted to say about its client's product but wasn't quite sure about whether the copy it had developed would get the message across. The strategy was to emphasize the suitability of the brand for frying foods (pork chops, french fries, chicken) without getting them greasy.

The creative department came up with several possible descriptions, from among which two were chosen for the final selection: "dry fry" and "quick fry." "Dry fry" would clearly denote the absence of greasiness but would it do more than that? "Quick fry" had the potential to do as well but were there any negative connotations that it might evoke?

In the consumer copy tests that followed, two versions of the same advertisement, each incorporating one of the two phrases, were shown to two matched samples of housewives. A number of questions were asked about the advertisement, among which were some designed to determine the message received about the food prepared with the advertised product.

The original doubts were justified. "Dry fry," while denoting "no greasiness," was found also to connote "overcooked" or "no juiciness" ("dried out," so to speak). On the other hand, "quick fry" suggested an effective oil that did its job so fast that the end-product retained its natural moisture. Its quick action prevented the absorption of excess oil and thus kept the food from becoming greasy. How easy it is to use the wrong word in communications!

3. Ads Ignoring Grammar

A recent study reports that advertisers are breaking the rules of grammar and spelling in three-quarters of the commercials on television.[2] Such grammatical irregularities as "a real nice feeling on the road" (Chevrolet), a soft drink (Pip) that "goes down good," and a bandage that "Don't ouch us" (Curad) are perpetrated deliberately for effect. The most frequent reason, it appears, is the desire to be remembered. The researcher claims that advertisers do not have any evidence to show that such misuse of the language is actually more effective.

In another study it was pointed out that advertisers choose words and syntax in accordance with what they think is appropriate for their target audience.[3] They choose to use "the language of the people" as opposed to correct grammar, as a device to attract attention. The authors suggest that, "wittingly or unwittingly, advertisers are contributing to changes in the English language," because of the pervasive and repetitive nature of advertising.

It was found that out of 455 commercials analyzed, almost three-quarters contained at least one syntactic or stylistic irregularity. Sixty-four percent had more than one irregularity.

There is some concern about the effects of such misuse, particularly on children, and the suggestion was made that perhaps the industry should attempt some self-regulation out of a recognition of their social responsibility.

ELEMENTS OF THE COMMUNICATION PROCESS

It is not enough to develop a good product and expect "customers to beat a path to your door." Their perception of the product may be quite different from what the marketer intends or hopes for and is based on information (maybe misinformation) and impressions that come from every possible source — the product, its advertising, the company name and brand name, packaging, employees, and friends. Each of these elements communicates something, consciously or unconsciously, to the consumer — the reputation of the president, a speech he made to the local Kiwanis Club, and so on.

The sources from which impressions can be derived are myriad and each makes a contribution to the perception or image that the consumer has of the product or service offered. It is the task of the marketer to ensure, as far as is possible, that all the elements of communications eventuate in the total impression that is intended.

This chapter examines the role each of the following plays in the communication process:

- the product;
- promotional activities, with particular emphasis on mass advertising, and such ele-

ments as the communicator (source), the message, the execution, and the media; and
- the receivers.

THE COMMUNICATION PROCESS

The communication process consists of a sender, a message, and a recipient; but many other elements can intervene so that the process may look more like that illustrated in Figure 17.1.

While the large number of elements themselves can present many problems, communications become even more complex when one takes into account that for any one product, the process may be repeated (problems and all) for a number of different sources or media.

Let us examine some of the possible obstacles that can beset the marketer.

The sender, the originator of the message, knows the target market to be reached and the message to be delivered. The latter is the intended message, which is expressed in words and/or pictures and/or sound — that is, it is encoded. The encoded message (which, it is hoped, correctly represents the intended message) is then transmitted through the communications medium considered most likely to

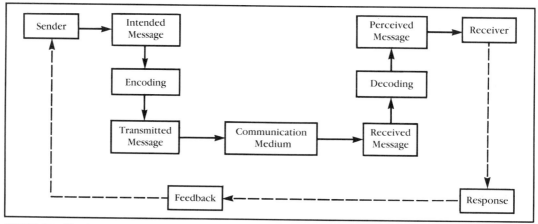

FIGURE 17.1: The Communication Process

reach the target audience. The message needs to be put in a form appropriate to the medium and the sender must ensure that, through that medium, the message will reach the target.

The message that emerges from the medium becomes the received message, which is not necessarily the same as the transmitted message because the character of the medium itself could transform the message. For example, an advertisement appearing in *Popular Mechanics* may not deliver the same message as when it appears in *Playboy*. In any event, the message that is received now "enters the mind" of the receiver to be decoded.

Every symbol (word, picture, sound) will be interpreted or understood in a certain way, obviously in accordance with the background, knowledge, needs, and personality (see Chapter 5) of the receiver. Because of these factors it is likely that the perceived message (subject to perceptual distortion) will be quite different from the intended message. Not only is it affected by the subjective characteristics of the receiver but the symbolism employed by the sender in encoding the message, even though expressing "perfectly" what the sender had in mind, could have different meanings for the receiver, in which case the response may not be the expected one. Noise or situational distractions and inattention are other possible reasons.

Discrepancy between the intended and the perceived message is probably more frequent than expected because of background differences between encoders and decoders. Reference was made to this in our discussion of social class, in which it was suggested that, because the encoders belong to the upper-middle or lower-upper class and they are communicating with the mass market, which is lower-middle or upper-lower, the differences in life-style and symbolism are quite likely to reduce the effectiveness of their messages. Where no discrepancy appears and the perceived message is thought to be exactly as intended, perfect communication may be said to have taken place.

The marketer, if possible, will set up the kind of system that will provide information about the responses of the receiver. With this kind of *feedback* the marketer can determine the discrepancies, if any, and institute corrective action to improve the accuracy of the message.

Procter and Gamble is an excellent example of the uses and benefits that can be derived from a well-organized feedback system, as illustrated in the following:

One day in 1879, a workman in Procter and Gamble's soap factory (in Cincinnati) went to lunch and forgot to turn off his mixing machine. When he came back, he found a frothy concoction that he considered throwing out. But he and his supervisor decided that the soap hadn't really been spoiled; so the batch was made into bars and sold.

A month later, consumers along the Ohio River (who had ended up with this soap) began pestering their storekeepers to reorder. 'Give us more floating soap,' the merchants told P&G, which traced those particular shipments back to the workman's mistake and determined that air bubbles whipped into the molten soap caused it to float.

Thus was born Ivory Soap. And so also began a dialogue between P&G and its customers that not only continues a century later but is growing at a tremendous pace. Giant P&G carefully nurtures this rapport with consumers, not to keep the Ralph Naders off its back but to remain the nation's biggest maker of everyday consumer products.

A lot of people think P&G "buys" its way into the market with big ad and promotion budgets . . . (but) the company simply is *tuned in to what consumers want* and it does a good job of making products to satisfy those wants.[4]

P&G operates a toll-free telephone operation to make it easier for customers to contact the company. Since the end of 1980 all of P&G's eighty brands, including six in test-marketing, have carried a toll-free phone number on the package or label. P&G also phones or visits some 1.5 million people in a year in connection with various research projects. These people are questioned extensively on their likes and dislikes about P&G products, including their names, packaging, and hundreds of other details. In addition P&G does an unusual amount of continuing basic research into how people go about washing clothes, preparing meals, doing the dishes, and other household tasks.

MAJOR FACTORS THAT AFFECT MARKETING COMMUNICATIONS

The product itself, no matter how good, cannot guarantee market success, because it is only one of the many factors that affect its acceptance. Consumers form their brand image from the impressions derived from numerous sources. Each source communicates something about the product. The image that the consumer finally acquires is the result of the consumer's perceptions of all of the communications. The consumer responds on the basis of his or her perceptions and the marketer needs to ensure that those perceptions (the perceived messages) are consistent with the intended messages. It is equally important to ensure that a message sent through different media (e.g., print, radio, TV) have the intended meaning so that impressions from different sources will support and reinforce each other. Obviously, the responsibility of communications in marketing is considerable. Once the offering is right, every source of impressions must be managed — employees, logo, retail outlets, etc. That is why some have said that "marketing *is* communications."[5]

Let us examine some of the main factors that have a bearing on the impact of communications.

The Product

In most cases, a product is purchased from a background of information accumulated from numerous sources. The product *per se* could have little to do with consumer perception of it. At the same time, it is reasonable to expect that non-product influences alone cannot sell a poor product. The product must reach a certain minimum level of quality. We discussed in the chapters on perception how attributes of the product itself, the package, the brand name, and the product symbol can affect the brand perception or brand image.

The case at the end of this chapter illustrates the effectiveness of a packaging change in increasing the market share of Nabob ground coffee in Ontario.

In communicating the nature of the product, several problems may arise. How do you communicate the benefits and advantages of the product? Encoding may be difficult. How do you communicate the product concept to achieve proper product categorization? Recall the problems the Monsanto company had with Starch-eze (see Chapter 5).

Promotion

Consumers gain impressions from every kind of promotional activity — sales promotions, publicity, and advertising.

Sales promotions can be a useful aid in marketing but they have to be handled with care. Too frequent price deals or couponing, for example, may begin to affect the perceived value or quality of the product and even bring into question the reliability and stature of the marketer. A department store such as Robinson's in Ontario, which continually offers discounts and sales (while implying it is not a discount house), is likely to erode the respectability and integrity of its image in the minds of the consumer.

Publicity, too, needs to be carefully managed so that consumers' perceptions are not distorted by misleading or ill-advised news or reports. Automobile companies, for example, are particularly sensitive to unfavorable reports and try not only to respond to the accusations of such consumer advocates as Ralph Nader but, even more, to minimize or eliminate their criticisms.

Companies generate publicity by organizing public relations activities and events that will create favorable news.

Advertising is the major and most directly controlled promotional activity of the marketer. Mass advertising involves six primary media — newspapers, television, direct mail, radio, magazines, and outdoor billboards. I will treat each of their common elements in turn: the communicator or sender, the message itself, the media for transmitting it, and the receiver.

The Communicator

A primary characteristic of the communicator or sender of a message that can affect the received or perceived message is **source credibility**. Opinion leaders and other social referents enjoy greater credibility than marketer-controlled advertising messages.

Research has demonstrated that highly trustworthy and expert spokespeople induce a greater positive attitude toward the position they advocate than do communicators with less credibility.[6] A more recent study showed that a high-credibility source — the New York State Public Service Commission — was more effective than a low-credibility source in inducing a reduction in the consumption of electricity for air conditioning.[7] It was suggested that once the receiver knows whether the source is high or low in credibility, little or no attention is paid to the arguments.[8] A cognitive response hypothesis, on the other hand, suggests that "a message recipient's initial opinion is an important determinant of influence."[9] Sternthal et al. argue that the finding that a highly credible source is more persuasive than a low-credibility source is "less than univocal" and that whether the recipient's initial opinion is favorable or negative is an important variable.

Other studies have pointed out that the effectiveness of source credibility increases for low-involvement products,[10] for products with which there is little experience,[11] or if the message is threatening (fear appeals).[12]

One study also pointed out that source credibility is increased if the communicator presents a two-sided message and does not appear to be totally biased.[13] Settle and Golden suggest that an advertiser may be more believable if it did not claim superiority over the competition on all features. It is difficult to visualize marketers being over-enthusiastic about this approach and few have so far been bold enough to try it.

Similarity between the communicator and receiver in terms of personality, background (racial, class) has also been suggested as increasing credibility.[14] This may be particularly relevant in salesperson-buyer situations.

It should be recognized that by "communicator" I mean not just the spokesperson but also the originator or initiator of the message — in our case, the marketer or the company. The size and reputation of a company can have a significant effect on the acceptance of a message as well.

Other sources are the *retailer*, who not only initiates some messages but also influences the credibility of the advertiser's message with the reputation of the store ("If Eaton's carries it, I am sure it's good"); and the *medium*, which exerts an influence similar to the retailer's in enhancing (or detracting from) the perception of the message.

All of these are impersonal sources. There are also interpersonal sources, which can be either informal (such as friends, family, colleagues, or neighbors) or formal (such as salesstaff or company representatives).

Interpersonal informal sources appear to be most important for most consumer goods, such as food, clothing, or small appliances.

The Message

Another factor that influences the effectiveness of communications is the message. Two aspects are important: content and execution.

Content

Content can be viewed in two ways: the claims or appeals used, and how they are expressed.

The nature of the appeals used will obviously influence the persuasiveness of an advertisement. Three attributes are very important for an effective message — **desirability** (the claim must involve something desirable about the product), **distinctiveness** (what it says should also be something other brands do not possess), and **believability** (the consumer should be able to accept it as true).[15]

Persuasiveness will, without doubt, be enhanced if the claims are simply constructed and clearly expressed. One must recognize the limited time available in an advertisement and also take into consideration all of the possibilities for distraction and distortion. The more direct and pointed the communications, the more effective they are likely to be.

It is worth noting, too, that an ad may contain too much information, present so many facts that the volume of its contents will detract from its communications effectiveness. No firm rules are available but communicators should always keep this in mind and exercise careful judgement. The controversy over information overload was discussed in Chapter 5.

Message Execution

Several different approaches have been used for presenting a message:

* one-sided versus two-sided appeals;
* implicit versus explicit conclusions;
* comparative advertising;
* agony and abrasive advertising;
* fear appeals;
* humor appeals; and
* majority versus minority group models.

One-Sided versus Two-Sided Appeals

The two-sided approach appears to be more effective in certain circumstances, although not much use has been made of it in marketing.[16] Evidence suggests that the one-sided ad may be more effective when the consumer knows less about the product, when the initial opinion is positive, and when the consumer is loyal to the brand advertised.[17]

The essential element appears to be the need for **counter-argumentation**. Better informed consumers are more receptive to two-sided arguments, while those who know less or are already committed are more susceptible to one-sided appeals. This suggests the possibility of increasing the use of two-sided presentations as consumers become better informed and are more inclined to evaluate product information.

There is some evidence that advertising that presents both sides of an issue in such a way that arguments against a product or perceived weaknesses are refuted (**refutational ads**) can be more effective than one-sided ads. An advertiser who knew the explicit arguments an opponent would use would be more able to resist those arguments by issuing a refutational advertisement rather than a supportive advertisement.[18]

A study that tested, for five products, the interaction of repetition with supportive and refutational ads against competitive ads (Figure 17.2) found that refutational ads were more effective and repetition was an important factor.[19] Sawyer concluded that refutational ads were more effective with people who had never used the advertised brand, as in the following situations:

* a new product that must overcome some consumer objections. For example, if consumers feel that the price of a trash compactor is too high, the advertiser could apply the refutational approach: "You may think it costs too much but remember how much space it will save you and it won't take too

Repeated Ad	Supportive Appeal	Refutational Appeal	Competitive Ad
Bayer aspirin	"Bayer works wonders. Relax with Bayer . . . Bayer is 100% aspirin."	"Buffer it, square it, squeeze it, fizz it, . . . Nothing has ever improved aspirin. Bayer is 100% aspirin."	Bufferin. "Take aspirin. I did but I still have a headache. Next time take Bufferin."
Lava soap	"For real dirty hands, reach for Lava—the soap that can really clean . . ."	"Lava—world's worst bath soap! Lava users have revolted. They argue that Lava is not only a good soap for hands but for anything else too . . ."	Phase III. "Both a deodorant and a cream soap . . ."
Parker pen	"Just one could be all you ever need. At $1.98 it's the best pen value in the world. Up to 80,000 words . . ."	"Why pay $1.98 for a ballpoint pen? You can get them for 49¢, 69¢, or for free. The kind that skip, stutter, etc. and run out of ink. You pay $1.98 for a Parker, but you never have to buy another."	Scripto. "Only 49¢."
Renault automobiles	"Sales are climbing. Renault's new features and fine construction are paying off . . ."	"Sure, they save money but I wouldn't want to take a long trip in one. Foreign cars are easy on the wallet but hard on everything else. Renault is changing all that."	Volvo. "The car that won't self-destruct in two years."
Slender diet drink	"The same appetite that made you fat can make you thin. Slender is a bona fide meal."	"A 225 calorie meal is easy. A good tasting 225 calorie meal is hard . . ."	Sego. "For the joy of a slender figure . . . Sego has more tasty flavors."

FIGURE 17.2: Repeated Supportive and Refutational Advertisements and Competitive Advertisements

SOURCE: Alan G. Sawyer, "The Effects of Repetition of Refutational and Supportive Advertising Appeals," *Journal of Marketing Research*, 10 (February 1973), p. 25. Reprinted with permission of the American Marketing Association.

long to pay for itself in the garbage bags you save."

- a brand with a low market share that wants to refute a large competitor's claims of superiority. Thus Avis admitted they were not Number One but claimed that they tried harder, implying their service would be likely to be better than Hertz's. This campaign was very successful.

- a high-selling brand able to isolate a segment that has a negative attitude toward it. For example, Allstate Insurance, though enjoying a large share of market, was unfavorably assessed by *Consumer Reports*. The readers of the magazine would be likely to be well-informed, so the company would be wise to make explicit reference to their anticipated counter-arguments and respond to them.

Sawyer also cited two hints gained from the research about a proper format for refutational ads:

- in order to help eliminate the danger of incomplete negative recall (as with advertising where exposure, attention, comprehension and learning are commonly unmotivated and often selective), advertisers should emphasize the refuting answer at least as much as the attacking statement, rather than, as is usually done, presenting the attacking statement or question in the headline and then proceeding to refute it in the body copy.

- the intrusiveness of TV and other broadcast media might be more successful than print media in completely communicating both sides of the refutational appeal.

Implicit versus Explicit Conclusions

The evidence on this approach is not very conclusive. In some cases it seems better for the communicator to make an explicit conclusion, in others it may be better to let the audience draw its own conclusions. Unless the situation is quite unstructured and the advertisement is directed at a number of segments, each of which can project its own motives into the situation, it is best for the source to draw the conclusion rather than run the risk of misperception.[20]

Comparative Advertising

There has been an increasing tendency for companies to name competitive brands in their advertising, to compare and refute claims (essentially two-sided advertisements).[21]

Part of the justification for using comparative ads has been that the users of brands mentioned (both the sponsor's brand and competing brands) will be more attentive to such an ad than they would have been otherwise.[22]

It has been suggested that for best advantage the ad should mention the competing brand(s) early in the message or display them prominently (see Figure 17.3). At the same time, initial attention is not the same as increased brand awareness and could benefit the competitors. Copy design is important, both to spark initial interest and to direct attention to the sponsor's brand and message:[23]

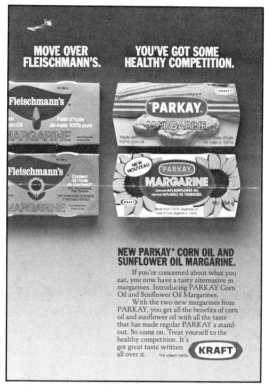

FIGURE 17.3: An Example of Comparative Advertising
Courtesy Kraft Limited

- Users of competing brands will develop clearer perceptions of the sponsor's brand.
- "Claims made in a comparison ad are more likely to be accepted as 'correct' than those in a standard ad."[24]
- Current users may also be better prepared with counter-arguments to refute possible later ads by competing brands.

The evidence on comparison advertising is not univocal. "Reactions . . . . have been mixed. Public policymakers, advertising agency representatives, professional associations, and other special interest groups have endorsed [it] on the assumption that it has the potential of being more beneficial to the consumer than traditional advertising . . . . Others, however, are skeptical about its potential, and have expressed concern about the ability of comparative advertising to convey deceptive and misleading information to the consumer."[25]

In her study "to investigate the relative effectiveness of comparative and non-comparative advertising for brands of antiperspirant," Golden concluded that "there is little published empirical research to clarify assumptions that have been made about its effectiveness . . . [and] . . . little is known about consumer perceptions of comparative advertising and the advertising situations most conducive to its use."[26]

Two studies found that comparative advertising may be more effective with shopping goods, such as appliances, than with packaged (convenience) goods.[27]

Comparative advertising is more complex than it appears at first and its effectiveness can be measured in terms of a number of variables — purchase intentions, claim believability, advertisement credibility, quantity of information and information usefulness, the advertiser's competitive position, claim substantiation, copy theme, and brand loyalty. Thus "the relative effectiveness . . . is not straightforward but multivariate and likely to be influenced by other variables in the advertising environment."[28]

More recent studies have found that comparative ads are no better than non-comparative ads so far as increasing brand awareness is concerned;[29] on the other hand, consumers appear to consider them less informative, though more interesting, than non-comparative ads.[30]

"Agony" and Abrasive Advertising

Both of these advertising execution techniques tend to draw negative consumer reactions, but they continue to be used because they seem to work.

Agony ads (which depict in detail the conditions of such things as heartburn, indigestion, plugged-up sinuses) appeal to a certain segment who give credit to the advertiser for recognizing what they really experience and are thus influenced by the message.

Abrasive advertising registers with consumers even though it may annoy or irritate. The negativity disappears with time and the main point of the message and the brand name seem to emerge more clearly (the **sleeper effect**).

RING AROUND THE COLLAR*

Whether or not advertisers should avoid irritating consumers, if they want their products to sell, has always been a question of major concern. But the experts do not appear to agree about this. Take the case of the "Ring Around the Collar" commercial for Wisk detergent. (Another campaign that falls in this category is Procter and Gamble's "Mr. Whipple" for Charmin toilet paper.)

In the view of some advertising professionals, "Ring" is the most obnoxious ad on television. It is irritating, insulting to women — especially the housewives who are Wisk's most important customers — and even harmful to advertising in general.

On the other hand, "Ring Around the Collar" can also be described as one of the greatest advertising campaigns ever. It resuscitated a troubled brand, which now holds an 8% share of the US detergent

*Adapted from Bill Abrams, " 'Ring Around the Collar' Ads Irritate Many, Yet Get Results," *The Wall Street Journal* (4 November 1982).

market and brings Lever Brothers Co., its manufacturer, more than $200 million a year. The campaign has lasted fifteen years and has outscored dozens of alternatives tested by Lever and its advertising agency. Competitors such as Procter and Gamble and Colgate-Palmolive have brought out their own liquid detergents but have never come close to Wisk's success.

The author of the slogan says, "It would be fair to call that commercial a screeching commercial, an abrasive commercial, an intrusive commercial but the one thing you can't call it is a bad commercial because the purpose of a commercial is to do a commercial job."

Other experts opine that "Ring" is insulting to the intelligence or that people hate it because they feel they are being talked down to. Defenders think that "Ring" has been successful because it appeals to consumers for whom "ring around the collar" is a real problem. Its critics, they say, perhaps belong to a different social class. They work in air-conditioned offices, send their shirts to the laundry, and are rarely troubled by dirty collars.

The line between making "Ring" a successful or an unsuccessful commercial appears to be very fine indeed. While *embarrassment* is a critical ingredient in its effectiveness, Lever has tried a number of different scenarios. For example, instead of embarrassing the wife by implying that the dirty collar was the result of her inadequacy, blame was shifted to competitors' detergents and the wife's moment of shame was cut. Some scenarios were too strong. When Lever recently experimented with a "hidden camera" ad in which ordinary consumers talked about "ring around the collar," Wisk sales fell in test cities.

However, it is likely that the basic format will be maintained, even though husband-and-wife versions may not always be used. For Lever, the "Ring" campaign still has a great deal to accomplish:

(a) there are new liquid detergents to fight,
(b) there are powdered-detergent buyers to convert;
(c) there are still a large number of consumers who haven't gotten the message — although the slogan is almost universally known, research shows that one out of every three viewers still doesn't associate it with Wisk.

Fear Appeals

The use of the fear motive in advertising is quite widespread (see Chapter 10). In general, it appears that moderate fear is more effective than strong fear, high credibility sources may be more persuasive when they employ strong rather than mild, fear-arousing appeals, and a source is more persuasive if it presents arguments that are both supportive and damaging *vis-à-vis* its position.

One study found that fear appeals are more effective with the users of a product than with non-users (in this case, insurance), suggesting that they may be more useful for product adoption than for brand switching.[31]

Fear research has been fraught with controversy over methodological problems and the evidence is not conclusive that fear appeals are more effective than positive appeals. The only strong evidence we have (and it is indirect) is the heavy use of fear appeals by marketers.

In summary, the findings of fear research have been mixed and the overall results remain quite equivocal. Burnett and Oliver identify a number of possible explanations:[32]

- fear research lacks a common vocabulary and conceptual structure across disciplines;
- there are questions about the accuracy of fear measures;
- there is uncertainty over whether the emotion used in the studies was fear or some other anxious state;
- the topic of fear messages used in prior studies has typically been health-related (e.g., smoking); and
- the majority of studies have been performed in classrooms with student subjects ranging from second grade to postgraduate educational levels.

Humor

Another widely used approach in marketing is humor (see Chapter 10). Here, too, there is little systematic evidence of the effectiveness of humor in increasing sales. What there is would suggest that (a) humorous messages attract attention (but how long does the effect last?); (b) humor may inhibit comprehension and thus reduce message reception; (c) because it distracts, humor may increase persuasiveness; (d) humor increases source credibility — at least, it creates a positive mood that is transferred to the communicator.

Thus, although humor is extensively used in marketing, sure evidence of its overall advantage is lacking.

Majority versus Minority Group Models

In a multicultural country such as Canada, advertisers are careful not to offend minority groups through the exclusive use of models from the majority group. This is particularly relevant where the minorities are "visible," such as Asians, native people, and blacks. Attempts are made to include representatives of such groups in ads (Figure 17.4). A proprietary study conducted by the author a few years ago found that French Canadians reacted negatively to the models used in an automobile ad because "they did not look French Canadian." The problem does not involve just color differences.

With the increasing numbers of immigrants into Canada from "visible minority" countries, greater attention will need to be given to the racial origin of models used in advertising. There does not appear to be any research done in Canada on this subject. However, work done in the United States can provide some guidance.

The growing black market in the United States has led to the need for marketers to make use

FIGURE 17.4: An Attempt at Integrated Advertising

Courtesy Allied Chemical Corporation

of black models in promotional material. While as a whole the research on the effects of black models on white consumers has been rather inconsistent, the bulk of the studies tend to indicate either neutral or positive reactions to black models. Very few negative reactions are reported.[33]

Bush, Hair, and Solomon, in replicating the only major inconsistent study in the literature (which found negative reactions among whites to black models),[34] refute the earlier study and conclude that "consumers' level of prejudice does not appear to affect response to ads containing all white, all black or black and white (integrated) models."[35]

They suggest that there may be a product type/level of integration interaction effect. In other words, for certain products, such as personal products (bras and tampons) or a socially conspicuous product (automobiles), negative reactions will increase with the number of black models employed. Thus "the type of product and the situational context of the ad may be useful to future researchers for understanding whites' reactions to black models." In general, however, "marketers should not fear a 'white backlash' or any negative consequences from the use of black models in promotional material."[36]

Regarding the reactions of black consumers to white models, the general conclusion appears to be that blacks do not respond unfavorably to integrated or all-white ads.[37] Nor do they react more favorably to black ads.[38]

The Media

I am not going to discuss here the importance of matching media used with the characteristics of the target audience in order to maximize reach. I am concerned in this section with how a medium can affect the transmitted message by reason of the medium's inherent characteristics. In such a case, the message that emerges at the other end of the "tube," so to speak, will be different from that transmitted.

While these transformations are all part of the "perceived message," one should recognize that some of the elements of the perceived message result from the nature of the medium itself and others from the characteristics of the receiver (see Chapter 5).

Television, for example, is more suitable than radio for advertising foods because the portrayal of color is important, or for products for which movement or action is influential. These might be called the inherent assets or liabilities of the particular medium. Magazines may be more suitable for lengthier messages that require greater attention.[39]

An interesting recent study found that consumers' processing of print advertisements is related to the structure and content of the advertisement.[40] An unframed picture yielded fewer evaluative thoughts. Differences were also found in the amount and direction of brand evaluation depending upon the type of claim made (objective, subjective, or characterization).

The most important inherent difference among media may relate to the amount of **involvement** they generate. Television, for example, has been described (along with radio, both as broadcast media) as "low-involvement," passive, or "cool" because exposure time is media-controlled and is limited.[41] Control of the pace is beyond the viewer's capability. On the other hand, print media are "high-involvement," active, or "hot" because the pace is set by the reader and time spent is not controlled by the medium.

I referred in an earlier chapter to the role of different magazines, because of their different images (based on different editorial content, subscribers, structure, and format), in influencing the comprehension of a message.[42]

The "transmitted message" can be subject to certain changes attributable to the medium that make it a different stimulus processed by the consumer.

The Receivers

As emphasized in Chapter 5, stimulus perception lies at the base of human response. How people process the information to which they are exposed determines what the resulting perceptions will be. In general, I identified two broad classes of influences that affect information processing:

(a) external — stimulus characteristics and environmental or situational factors;

(b) internal — characteristics of the perceiver.

The latter is our interest in this section.

Numerous characteristics were shown (in Chapter 5) to affect the perceived message in high-involvement decision making. These included physiological limitations, such as threshold, level of adaptation, differential threshold, and span and fluctuation of attention; psychological factors, such as selective perception, interests, needs, motives, expectations, and stereotyping; and symbolism, where words, form, shape, color, animals, persons, or objects can have different meanings for different individuals.

Other psychological motivations may also affect the response to communications. For example, the image of a source or medium will affect the perception of a message. I have already alluded to the fact that the same advertisement may be perceived differently when it appears in different sources because the vehicles themselves (whether two magazines or two newspapers or two TV networks) are perceived differently.[43] Also, it will be recalled that human beings tend to resist change. Overaggressive, hard-sell attempts of salespeople to persuade may elicit the opposite reaction because receivers react negatively to such strong approaches and ignore the arguments in favor of the behavior recommended (psychological reactance).

Children as Receivers

One area that has received considerable attention in recent years has been the impact of advertising (particularly television advertising) on children. The attention has come from researchers, marketers, and consumer groups. Literally hundreds of published papers on the subject have appeared in recent years in research journals; an increasing number of advertisements are being directed at children;* and criticism of the impact of advertising on children seems to grow stronger.[44]

Ten main areas of concern have been identified in the study of advertising effects on children:

1. ability to distinguish advertising from program material;
2. the influence of the mode of presentation itself on children's perceptions;
3. source effects and self-concept appeals;
4. children's information processing of commercial messages;
5. the effects of violence or unsafe acts in ads;
6. the effects of proprietary medicine ads;
7. the effects of food ads;
8. the effects of volume and repetition of ads;
9. the effects of advertising on the socialization process; and
10. the effects of ads on parent/child relations.

Not all of these problems have been examined. I will attempt to review briefly what has been done so far in this area. In general, the problems addressed have been either so esoteric or so specific that little generalizing can be done about them.

Products

About 50% of all commercials aimed at children are about food, about 10% vitamins, and 30% toys.[45]

Almost all of the food commercials are for snack food and sweetened products. In spite of widespread criticisms of these efforts, the research done is not sufficiently conclusive to lead to definitive action. For example, consumer

---

*An exception is the province of Quebec, which has banned all TV advertising directed at children.

groups have complained about the continued advertising of pre-sweetened cereals, claiming that the ads mislead children into thinking that sugared cereals are as good for them as other food. In February 1978, the Federal Trade Commission in the US recommended a ban on ads for sugared products directed at children under twelve, even though there were no studies that showed that pre-sweetened cereals cause tooth decay or that children who watch a lot of TV have more cavities (because they eat more sugared products) than those who watch less.

Toy ads have been seriously criticized for using false claims and other misleading techniques (such as size distortions, failure to provide information on what the toy is made of, how it works, what age group it is meant for, and even how much it costs).[46]

Attention

In terms of the cognitive child development theories of Piaget, it has been found that children between seven and ten pay more attention to the commercials than do older children between eleven and twelve,[47] partly because younger children often perceive the commercial as part of the program and, therefore, continue to watch.[48]

Information Processing

Children's processing of TV commercials may be viewed along four dimensions:[49]

1. cognitive-affective — whether differentiation of physical, emotional, or intellectual stimuli varies with age. Young children (two to seven) have "relatively simple cognitive structures (pre-operational), have a tendency to be bound perceptually in processing stimuli, and are more likely to focus on visual characteristics of message stimuli rather than on the more abstract meaning properties of message content."[50] The focus shifts to affective/symbolic elements with age and eventually to rational/thematic aspects.[51]

Most of this view is based on Piaget's conceptualization of children's cognitive abilities. An important limitation to Piaget's theory is its inability to explain how or why children process information within their limited capacities. A recent view, based on information processing theory, interprets age differences, for example, in children's reactions to television advertising in terms of cognitive abilities to store and retrieve information.[52] It distinguishes three types of processors:

- strategic — older children who possess and use the skills necessary to store and retrieve information;
- cue — younger children who are capable of using storage and retrieval strategies when prompted to do so; and
- limited — very young children who cannot use storage and retrieval strategies.

2. mode of assimilation — small children's recall is imitative (e.g., perfect recall of a whole jingle without understanding it); older children's is based on their responses to or association with stimuli; still older subjects remember on the basis of a commercial's content or purpose. According to Robertson and Rossiter, children are often not aware of the persuasive content of commercials.[53]

3. differentiation — the ability to distinguish fact from fantasy, products from advertisements, increases with age.

4. level of judgement — the stage of ego development or the ability to judge or be susceptible to a commercial message.

One of the significant findings is that children under seven do not distinguish between the commercial and the program.

Children often associated the program characters with the products being advertised. Marketers take advantage of this by using familiar characters to promote their products (e.g., the Flintstones and vitamins).[54]

Effects on Children

A possibly dangerous effect of advertising on children is the kind of *socialization* that advertising promotes. Donohue found that children regard pills and other proprietary medicines as the solution to any kind of illness.[55]

One particular mode of presentation — premiums — has come under careful scrutiny and has been the object also of Federal Trade Commission regulation in the US. Investigating the effects of premiums on children, two studies report no significant influence.[56] Price found no increase in product information recall or any overall influence on brand preference. Shimp, Dyer, and Divita also did not find any influence on recognition of product information or brand preference. A more recent study "complements" the Shimp et al. study in finding that "the effects of the advertising on behavior were minimal."[57]

Another study, which measured behavioral changes, suggests that there may be behavioral effects.[58] It found that "premium commercials showed a clear superiority over host-selling and announcer commercials, as measured by the percentage of children who selected the advertised product."

It has also been suggested that the effects of advertising on the socialization of the child may not be all bad. Children learn with age about the persuasive intent of commercials and, by the time they reach nine years of age, recognize that "products are not like (the) ads say they are."[59] Thus advertising may be said also to prepare children for modern-day life by developing the tendency to question and to evaluate.

Marketers would do well to avoid evoking any cynicism or distrust at such an early age, in view of the consequent attitudes and their effects later in life.[60]

There is some research on the effects of advertising on parent/child relationships. These were referred to in Chapter 16 and are admittedly quite superficial.

There is little doubt about the significance of this area of research. Exposure to television may determine the kind of society that will exist generations from now. This makes it all the more unfortunate that the studies done so far have been "simplistic and cannot be used for anything more than generating hypotheses for future research."[61] It must be borne in mind that advertising effects are only part of the problem. The broader problems of television effects on children (advertising *and* programs) must also be resolved — if not for our sakes, for our children's sakes.

"Canada is second behind Japan in the number of hours of programming produced or aired for children."[62] It has been estimated that by the age of eighteen, a child has spent 11,000 hours in school and 15,000 hours watching TV. "The average teenager has used up to two full years of his [her] life in front of the TV set."[63] There are over 50 million children under thirteen in the US and 6 million in Canada. The stakes are high and the opportunities enormous for the mercenary. But the question of the ethics of advertising to children, its effects on their development, and the broader problem of television in general must be resolved with urgency. They call not for a piecemeal, *ad hoc* approach but for an integrated, coordinated effort at obtaining reliable, practical insights, on which important decisions can be based.

SUMMARY

Everything that a marketer does is some kind of communication — and all such information goes to determine the consumer's total perceptions. A basic communications model was presented and its components discussed. The importance of proper encoding of the intended message before it is transmitted was emphasized, along with the transformation that can occur in the media so that the received image may be quite different from that which was intended. The decoding of the received message may result in a further distortion of the message that is eventually perceived. The significance of noise and feedback was also emphasized.

The rest of the chapter dealt with the major factors that affect marketing communications: the product, the promotion, the source, the message, the media, and the receivers.

The product itself and the package can affect communications. The nature of the product may render communications quite difficult.

All forms of promotion should furnish a unified, coordinated message. The main form of communications is advertising. Its primary elements — source, message, media, and receivers — were discussed.

Credibility was identified as a salient source characteristic that may be enhanced in certain ways. The content and its treatment of the message were reviewed. Several methods of treatment — one-sided versus two-sided messages, implicit versus explicit conclusions, comparative advertising, fear appeals, humor, ethnic origin of models — were considered.

With regard to media it was emphasized that the media used can affect how a message is perceived.

The chapter concluded by noting the importance of the characteristics of the receiver in information processing and its impact on message comprehension, and by reviewing the impact and significance of advertising on children. Three main effects were identified: (a) persuasion — because of their lack of cognitive resistance, (b) intra-family conflict over children's TV viewing and attempts to influence parents, and (c) socialization, the learning of undesirable as well as desirable values and behavior.

QUESTIONS

1. Discuss the importance of encoding in marketing communications.

2. What factors can affect a transmitted message by the time it is perceived by the consumer?

3. Review the P&G example cited in the chapter, identify the various kinds of communications involved, and comment on their effects.

4. Describe the role played by the product in influencing the effectiveness of communications.

5. Write an essay on the factors that can affect source credibility.

6. What conclusions have you come to about the usefulness of two-sided messages in marketing? Justify.

7. Similarly, what is your position on comparative advertising? What appear to be its advantages and disadvantages?

8. What are some of the main concerns that have been expressed with regard to the effects of advertising on children? Which of these have been examined in research and, generally, what has been found?

9. Write an essay on the information-processing characteristics of children.

NOTES TO CHAPTER 17 ▬▬▬▬▬

[1]Ben Fiber, "Don't Blink: Fifteen-Seconds Ads Near," *The Globe and Mail* (6 June 1984), p. B8.

[2]Robert G. Wyckham, "Ads Ignoring Grammar," paper presented at Annual Meeting of the Administrative Sciences Association of Canada, Learned Societies Conference, June 1984, Guelph, Ontario.

[3]Robert G. Wyckham, Peter M. Banting, and Anthony K. P. Wensley, "The Language of Advertising: Who Controls Quality?" *Journal of Business Ethics*, 3 (1984), pp. 47-53.

[4]John A. Prestbo, "At Procter and Gamble Success is Largely Due to Heeding Consumer," *The Wall Street Journal* (29 April 1980), pp. 1, 35. Reprinted by permission of *The Wall Street Journal*, © Dow Jones & Company, Inc. (1980). All rights reserved.

[5]Peter F. Drucker, *Management* (New York: Harper and Row, 1974).

[6]W.J. McGuire, "The Nature of Attitudes and Attitude Change," in Gardner Lindzey and Elliot Aronson (eds.), *The Handbook of Social Psychology*, 3 (Reading, Massachusetts: Addison-Wesley, 1969), p. 182.

[7]C. Samuel Craig and John M. McCann, "Assessing Communication Effects on Energy Conservation," *Journal of Consumer Research*, 5 (September 1978), pp. 82-8.

[8]R.A. Bauer, "A Revised Model of Source Effect," Presidential Address of the Division of Consumer Psychology, American Psychological Association, Chicago, 1965.

[9]Brian Sternthal, Ruby Dholakia, and Clark Leavitt, "The Persuasive Effect of Source Credibility: Tests of Cognitive Response," *Journal of Consumer Research*, 4 (March 1978), pp. 252-60.

[10]Richard W. Mizerski, James M. Hunt, and Charles H. Patti, "The Effects of Advertising Credibility on Consumer Reactions to an Advertisement," in Subhash C. Jain (ed.), *Proceedings of the American Marketing Association Educators' Conference*, Series #43 (1978), pp. 164-8.

[11]Ruby Roy Dholakia and Brian Sternthal, "Highly Credible Sources: Persuasive Facilitators or Persuasive Liabilities?" *Journal of Consumer Research*, 3 (March 1977), pp. 223-32.

[12]H. Sigall and R. Helmreich, "Opinion Change as a Function of Stress and Communicator Credibility," *Journal of Experimental Social Psychology*, 5 (1969), pp. 70-8.

[13]Robert B. Settle and Linda L. Golden, "Attribution Theory and Advertiser Credibility," *Journal of Marketing Research*, 11 (May 1974), pp. 181-5.

[14]Arch G. Woodside and J. William Davenport, Jr., "The Effect of Salesman Similarity and Expertise on Consumer Purchasing Behavior," *Journal of Marketing Research*, 11 (May 1974), pp. 198-202.

[15]Dik Warren Twedt, "How to Plan New Products, Improve Old Ones, and Create Better Advertising," *Journal of Marketing*, 33 (January 1969), pp. 53-7.

[16]Settle and Golden, op. cit.

[17]W.E.J. Faison, "Effectiveness of One-Sided Mass Communications in Advertising," *Public Opinion Quarterly*, 25 (1961), pp. 468-9.

[18]George J. Szybillo and Richard Heslin, "Resistance to Persuasion: Inoculation Theory in a Marketing Context," *Journal of Marketing Research*, 10 (November 1973), pp. 396-403.

[19]Alan G. Sawyer, "The Effects of Repetition of Refutational and Supportive Advertising Appeals," *Journal of Marketing Research*, 10 (February 1973), pp. 23-33.

[20]McGuire, op. cit., p. 209.

[21]Aimée L. Morner, "It Pays to Knock Your Competitor," *Fortune* (13 February 1978), p. 104.

[22]William L. Wilkie and Paul W. Farris, "Comparison Advertising: Problems and Potential," *Journal of Marketing*, 39 (October 1975), pp. 7-15.

[23]Ibid., p. 12.

[24]Ibid., p. 14.

[25]Linda L. Golden, "Consumer Reactions to Explicit Brand Comparisons in Advertisements," *Journal of Marketing Research*, 16 (November 1979), p. 517.

[26]Ibid., p. 530.

[27]V. Kanti Persad, "Communications-Effectiveness of Comparative Advertising: A Laboratory Analysis," *Journal of Marketing Research*, 13 (May 1976), pp. 128-37; Sawyer, op. cit.

[28]Golden, op. cit., p. 531.

[29]William Pride, Charles W. Lamb, and Barbara A. Pletcher, "The Informativeness of Comparative Advertisements: An Empirical Investigation," *Journal of Advertising*, 8 (Spring 1979), pp. 29-35.

[30]Terrence A. Shimp and D.C. Dyer, "The Effects of Comparative Advertising Mediated by Market Position of Sponsoring Brand," *Journal of Advertising*, 7 (Summer 1979), pp. 13-9.

[31]John J. Wheatley, "Marketing and the Use of Fear-Anxiety Appeals," *Journal of Marketing*, 35 (April 1971), pp. 62-4.

[32]John J. Burnett and Richard L. Oliver, "Fear Appeal Effects in the Field: A Segmentation Approach," *Journal of Marketing Research*, 16 (May 1979), pp. 181-90.

[33]James W. Cagley and Richard N. Cardozo, "White Responses to Integrated Advertising," *Journal of Advertising Research*, 10 (April 1970), pp. 35-9.

[34]Ronald F. Bush, Joseph F. Hair, Jr., and Paul J. Solomon, "Consumers' Level of Prejudice and Response to Black Models in Advertisements," *Journal of Marketing Research*, 16 (August 1979), pp. 341-5.

[35]Ibid., p. 344.

[36]Ibid., p. 345.

[37]Arnold M. Barban and Edward W. Cundiff, "Negro and White Response to Advertising Stimuli," *Journal of Marketing Research*, 1 (April 1964), pp. 53-6; Arnold M. Barban and Werner F. Greenbaum, "A Factor Analytic Study of Negro and White Responses to Advertising Stimuli," *Journal of Applied Psychology*, 49: 4 (1965), pp. 274-79; "The Dilemma of 'Integrated' Advertising," *Journal of Business of the University of Chicago*, 42: 4 (1969), pp. 477-96.

[38]John W. Gould, Norman W. Sigband, and Cyril E. Zoerner, Jr., "Black Consumer Reactions to Integrated Advertising: An Exploratory Study," *Journal of Marketing*, 34 (July 1970), pp. 20-6.

[39]Herbert E. Krugman, "The Measurement of Advertising Involvement," *Public Opinion Quarterly*, 30 (Winter 1966-67), pp. 583-96.

[40]Julie A. Edell and Richard Staelin, "The Information Processing of Pictures in Print Advertisements," *Journal of Consumer Research*, 10 (June 1983), pp. 45-61.

[41]Herbert E. Krugman, "The Impact of Television Advertising: Learning Without Involvement," *Public Opinion Quarterly*, 29 (August 1969), pp. 349-56.

[42]David A. Aaker and Philip K. Brown, "Evaluating Vehicle Source Effects," *Journal of Advertising Research*, 12 (August 1972), pp. 11-6.

[43]Ibid.

[44]S. Feldman and A. Wolf, "What's Wrong With Children's Commercials?" *Journal of Advertising Research*, 14 (1974), pp. 39-43; S. Ward, "Kids' T.V. Marketers on Hot Seat," *Harvard Business Review*, 50: 4 (1972), pp. 16-18.

[45]R.B. Choate, "The Sugar-Coated Children's Hour," *The Nation* (31 January 1972).

[46]R. Jennings, "Programming and Advertising Practices in Television Directed to Children," and F.E. Barcus, "Saturday Children's Television: A Report of Television Programming and Advertising on Boston Commercial Television," both in *Action for Children's Television*, unpublished monograph (July 1971).

[47]S. Ward, D. Levinson, and D. Wackman, "Children's Attention to Television Commercials," in E.A. Rubinstein, G.A. Comstock, and J.R. Murray (eds.), *Television and Social Behavior*, 4 (Washington, D.C.: U.S. Government Printing Office, 1972), pp. 491-515.

[48]S. Ward, "Children's Reactions to Commercials," *Journal of Advertising Research*, 12 (1972), pp. 37-45.

[49]J. Blatt, L. Spencer, and S. Ward, "A Cognitive Development Study of Children's Reaction to Television Advertising," in Rubinstein et al., op. cit., pp. 452-67.

[50]Scott Ward and Daniel B. Wackman, "Children's Information Processing of Television Advertising," in Peter Clarke, *New Models for Mass Communication Research*, 2 (Beverly Hills: Sage, 1973).

[51]Anees A. Sheikh, V. Kanti Prasad, and Tanniru R. Rao, "Children's T.V. Commercials: A Review of Research," *Journal of Communications* (Autumn 1974), pp. 126-36.

[52]Deborah L. Roedder, "Age Differences in Children's Responses to Television Advertising: An Information Processing Approach," *Journal of Consumer Research*, 8 (September 1981), pp. 144-53.

[53]T.S. Robertson and J.R. Rossiter, "Children and Commercial Persuasion: An Attribution Theory Analysis," *Journal of Consumer Research*, 1 (June 1974), pp. 13-20.

[54]T.R. Donohue, "Effect of Commercials on Black Children," *Journal of Advertising Research*, 15: 6 (1975), pp. 41-2.

[55]Ibid.

[56]G.H. Price, "The Effects of Premium Offers in Television Commercials on Children's Consumer Behavior," *Dissertation Abstracts International*, 37 (1977), 5841-2; Terence A. Shimp, Robert F. Dyer, and Salvatore F. Divita, "An Experimental Test of the Harmful Effects of Premium-Oriented Commercials on Children," *Journal of Consumer Research*, 3 (June 1976), pp. 1-11.

[57] Louise A. Heslop and Adrian B. Ryans, "A Second Look at Children and the Advertising of Premiums," *Journal of Consumer Research*, 6 (March 1980), pp. 414-20.

[58] Joseph H. Miller, Jr., and Paul Busch, "Host Selling Vs. Premium T.V. Commercials: An Experimental Evaluation of their Influence on Children," *Journal of Marketing Research*, 16 (August 1979), pp. 323-32.

[59] S. Ward, "Children's Reactions to Commercials," *Journal of Advertising Research*, 12 (1972), pp. 37-45.

[60] J.R. Rossiter and T.S. Robertson, "Children's T.V. Commercials: Testing the Defenses," *Journal of Communications*, 24: 4 (1974), pp. 137-45.

[61] Sheikh et al., op. cit., p. 133.

[62] *Marketing*, 83 (4 September 1978), p. 5.

[63] "Experts Can't Agree on Effects of T.V., Media Conference Told," *Marketing*, 82 (1 August 1977), p. 11.

NABOB FOODS LIMITED*

In January 1981, John Bell, the vice-president of marketing of Nabob Foods Limited, whose products include ground and soluble (instant) coffee, tea, jam, peanut butter, desserts, and fruit beverages, was evaluating the results of Nabob ground coffee's 1980 advertising campaign in Ontario. In a twelve-month period, Nabob ground coffee succeeded in more than doubling its sales in Ontario, and in moving from a struggling brand to a major force in the market.

In 1976, Nabob Foods Limited was purchased by Jacobs AG, Zurich, Switzerland, the largest coffee roaster in Europe. Jacobs accounted for 4% of all the coffee sold in the world in 1976, and was the coffee leader in France, Germany, and Austria. In addition, Jacobs held strong market shares in Belgium and Denmark. It is not surprising that on purchasing Nabob Foods, it decided to become both a high-profile, national packaged goods company and the leading ground-roast coffee marketer in Canada.

The Canadian Coffee Market

At the retail level, approximately $548-million worth of coffee was purchased and consumed by Canadians in 1980. Close to 52% of this total (approximately $284 million) consisted of instant (soluble) coffee; about 48% (approximately $264 million) consisted of roasted (ground) coffee.

Ontario, with 36% of Canada's population, accounted for 38% of the Canadian coffee market (40% of instant coffee sales — $114 million; and 36% of ground coffee sales — $95 million).

Previous Nabob Marketing Activities in Ontario

One of the advantages Nabob derived from its new Jacobs association was the latter's advanced coffee-packaging technology. Jacobs had pro-

---

*Adapted from John R.G. Jenkins, *Canadian Cases in Marketing Communications* (Toronto: Butterworth [Canada], 1983), pp. 248-55, with permission of Nabob Foods Limited, Vancouver, B.C.

duced a unique vacuum package that would protect the high-quality Nabob blend by sealing in freshness and sealing out air, which adversely affects coffee quality and taste.

The unique quality of the package lay in the fact that it was a foil package, as opposed to the more expensive metal containers already available in Canada and the US. In Ontario, 70% of all ground coffee products were sold in unprotected paper bags, including the leading brand, Maxwell House, marketed by General Foods.

In 1977, both Nabob and Maxwell House attempted to introduce versions of the new vacuum packs in Ontario. Both efforts failed, and Maxwell House subsequently withdrew its vacuum product. The failure of the Nabob vacuum pack was particularly disappointing to Nabob, because the product had established a clear superiority over Maxwell House in independent, blind taste tests among Ontario ground-coffee drinkers.

Subsequent Developments

Mr. Bell likened the activities of Nabob versus General Foods to "David fighting Goliath." "In retrospect," Mr. Bell observed, "our Ontario failure served as a lesson — and we were prepared to study Goliath and the territory a little more carefully before we took aim again." With ground-roast coffee retail sales as of January 1979 at about $100 million a year in Ontario, General Foods commanded a share of about 25%, followed by Chase and Sanborn (Standard Brands) with approximately 10%, and Nabob about 3 to 5%.

Although the Maxwell House Goliath was a formidable competitor, it had some visible weaknesses:

(a) consumer research had shown that the blend was inferior to Nabob's:
— in blind taste tests, Nabob was preferred 2:1 by all users and, more significantly, 7:3 by Maxwell House users;

(b) packaging: the unique Nabob vacuum pack ensured freshness while the Maxwell House soft bag was vulnerable to the staling effect of air;

(c) General Foods had historically directed all advertising funds to Instant Maxwell House, leaving Roast Maxwell House with only sales promotional support.

The Chase and Sanborn blend and package were very similar to those of Maxwell House and was thus considered by Nabob to have similar weaknesses.

As was indicated earlier, almost 70% of Ontario ground-roast coffee was sold in soft nonvacuum bags. The remaining 30% was sold in vacuum tins — at significantly higher prices. "Now," continued Mr. Bell, "Nabob was ready to seriously challenge the *status quo* of this market with a unique vacuum pack that was more expensive than the unprotected soft bags, but less expensive than tins to produce. And, don't forget that inside Nabob's unique pack was a superior quality blend."

The Test Markets: Nabob's Marketing Strategy

Working closely with their new advertising agency (Scali, McCabe, Sloves), Nabob developed their marketing plan for the test market that would help polish the final launch plan for the entire province. The prime elements of the strategy were as follows:

1. Product: a superior blend, vacuum-packed to preserve freshness, preferred to the market leader 7:3; the innovative package was not readily available to major Ontario competitors;
2. Price: primarily at par with the leader, Maxwell House;
3. Advertising: stimulate brand growth by creating consumer awareness of Nabob's unique packaging, which provides fresher, better-tasting coffee.

Because two distinctly different creative approaches evolved for the same strategy, it was decided to use not one but two test markets — Peterborough and Kingston. The start date for each was May 1, 1979 and the test-market medium was television. Mr. Bell explains, "Remember, this wasn't a reintroduction of Nabob coffee — distribution of product in the markets already exceeded 85%, and market share was in the 3% to 5% area. This was a test using a consumer marketing plan to meet a precise objective — to build market share. Our share goal in Year One was 10%, which equated to a 170% increase."

The Test Markets: Nabob's Creative Strategy and Implementation

The benefit claimed was that Nabob was a better, fresher-tasting coffee than coffee packed in soft paper bags. The "reason why" was the unique vacuum pack.

In Kingston, a thirty-second, slice-of-life commercial called "store" (an adaptation of the execution that successfully launched the vacuum pack in Western Canadian test markets in late 1978) was aired. It showed a shopper in a supermarket. She first picked up a Maxwell House soft bag, sniffed it, and put it back on the shelf. Then she picked up the Nabob pack, sniffed it, and looking puzzled, knocked her knuckles against it as she said to the manager, "I can't smell the Nabob coffee." And knocking the pack again she said, "It's as hard as a rock."

As the store manager explained about the vacuum pack, other curious shoppers crowded around and when he cut the pack open, everyone could hear the vacuum release and sniff the aroma of the Nabob coffee.

In the Peterborough market test, the thirty-second commercial that was used showed an authoritative presenter seated behind a desk in an office that exuded quality. "We picked a spokesman," Mr. Bell explains, "who we felt could tell the Nabob story with authority and dignity . . . and not be rejected by consumers as just another advertising pitchman. On the desk are three soft packs of coffee — including Maxwell House. The presenter's manner and delivery are direct and convincing. In his hand is the new vacuum pack which he introduces with, 'This is Nabob, Canada's leading coffee.' "

Research Findings

(a) *Advertising Research.* Regarding advertising recall, the slice-of-life commercial "came out strong" with a 34% D.A.R. (Day-After-Recall) score, well above the average of 19% and better than the "Presenter" commercial with 26%.

However, the results of a diagnostic communications test (product rating, sales rating, believability) showed the "Presenter" commercial to be more effective. Scores for product and sales ratings were almost double those of the slice-of-life commercial. In addition, the strategic message had a communication level of over 85%.

Negative comments to the hard-sell, comparative approach of the "Presenter" commercial were few and everything seemed to point to it as a very persuasive approach.

(b) *Brand Image.* A number of tracking studies, consisting of one pre-advertising wave and two post-advertising waves of three and six months, were conducted in both cities to measure brand awareness, advertising awareness, trial, repeat purchase, and shifts in brand image.

Not only did the "Presenter" commercial outperform the slice-of-life commercial but it also surpassed Nabob's highest expectations. As Mr. Bell stated, "Ad awareness grew from a precampaign level of 14% to 60%. Nabob's image as 'best quality coffee' increased from 33% to 58% while other coffee attributes, such as aroma and freshness showed similar significant upward shifts."

(c) *Market Share.* Both approaches showed dramatic share gains but in the Peterborough test (the "Presenter" commercial) share surged ahead, with the brand reaching number one with a 24.0% share in the June/July period over Maxwell House at 18.4%. By October 1979, Nabob had settled into a solid number two position, and the decision was made to roll out the Peterborough program province-wide starting January 1, 1980.

(d) *The Ontario Market Launch.* Because of the test market performance, Year One share goals were changed from 10% to 13%. An introductory thirty-second television commercial explained the packaging concept and it was followed up with a 60-second commercial. A second thirty-second commercial emphasized Nabob's basic selling position.

The "Presenter" commercials were supported by four informative and dramatic full-page ads inserted in a number of leading Ontario newspapers, in order to speed up awareness and add impact to the early trial-generating period. Other promotions included a four-page insert with a store coupon and egg carton coupons targeted at major chains.

Maxwell House responded with price-cuts accompanied by some advertising for Roast Maxwell House in the spring of 1980 — the first advertising for the brand in many years. Using the TV and movie star Ricardo Montalban, General Foods emphasized "full-bodied goodness" and "taste."

All of this marketing activity resulted in considerable consumer movement in trial, repeat purchase, and loyalty. Nabob and Maxwell House gained; Chase and Sanborn and other brands suffered losses. However, Nabob's gain was nearly two-thirds higher than that of Maxwell House and there was every likelihood that even bigger gains could be expected once prices returned to normal.

In the August/September 1980 period, Maxwell House was down to a 20.4% share, their lowest in recent years; Nabob reached 20.0% — almost number one in the province, and the top in the competitive Toronto market. In spite of a strike at Nabob toward the end of the year, Nabob's average performance over the year was 15.3%, which exceeded the objective by 2.3% and represented an increase of 101% over the previous year.

QUESTIONS ▬▬▬▬▬▬▬

1. Discuss the major factors you think were responsible for Nabob's extraordinary success.

2. Identify the consumer behavioral concepts that help explain Nabob's impressive performance and those that may account for General Food's behavior in the situation.

3. Analyze the two communications approaches tested in terms of their relative merits and explain why the "Presenter" commercial was more effective.

4. Evaluate the contributions made to the overall promotional strategy by the full-page newspaper ads and the store coupons.

18

Retailing Influences — Customer-Salesperson Interactions

EXAMPLES

1. Space-Age Packaging*

In the last few years Canadian food packagers and processors have made a number of pioneering efforts to bring space-age products to the supermarket shelf. The Europeans and Japanese have been quite successful with long-life milk, juice, and food. In Europe, 100 million packages of everything from ravioli to soya sauce — vacuum-sealed and sterilized in thin, foil retortable** pouches — are sold in a year. In Japan the figure is closer to half a billion.

Flash-sterilization is one of the techniques. In Western Europe, 40% of all fruit juice sales and approximately 50% of all milk sales are in UHTs — liquids that have been flash-sterilized at ultra-high temperatures and immediately sealed in brick-shaped, aseptic containers.

Another is the retort pouching, which produces quickie meals when heated in boiling water. Because the pouch is flat, it takes 30% to 50% less time to sterilize its contents. Whereas cans offer overcooked, sickly green peas, retorts offer firm, tasty peas, much like the frozen version. Magic Pantry of Hamilton is offering about ten entrées, from cabbage rolls to chili, as convenience foods for single people.

These innovations make consumers skeptical because they go against what people have been taught about food preservation — meat not refrigerated? Milk on the shelf for six months? Nevertheless, these developments offer many possibilities and advantages: energy-saving in processing, shipping, and storage; a reduction of refrigerator and freezer space needed by consumers. In addition, they open up a wealth

---

Adapted from Betsy Matthews, "Gourmet Treat: Vintage Steak Six Months Old," *Toronto Star* (11 October 1981), p. E3.

**Refers to the sterilization process. The retort pouch is made of a triple-laminate web that has an outer layer of polyester for strength and protection, a middle layer of aluminum, which is a barrier to moisture, light, and air, and an inner layer of polypropylene, which seals the heat from the sterilization process.

of export possibilities: long-life milk, for example, can be supplied to hot countries where refrigeration is scarce and where mixing powdered milk with local water may cause problems; the production of modified milk for the majority of the world's population that are lactose intolerant.

2. Beer Packaging in Ontario*

For a long time, the Ontario beer industry has been able to stay with standardized packaging for its product. Every manufacturer sold its brands in the same short, brown bottle. Recently, however, the introduction of US and European brands brewed in Canada has brought with it some deviations from the norm. Tall, slim bottles in green, brown, and white have been put on the market for the Lowenbrau, Amstel, and Miller High Life brands. Not only has the addition been expensive but it is also going to mean increased handling costs for the retail trade. For example, Labatt Breweries estimated that the new long-necked bottles with twist-off caps decreased profits for the year ending April 30, 1984 by about $20 million.

In the spring of 1984, another change was made in the industry when Molson introduced a 355-ml aluminum can following a ruling by the provincial government that made aluminum cans legal. Up to that time only steel cans were permitted. The other breweries quickly followed suit.

The industry feels that aluminum cans will significantly increase canned beer sales in the province. Until Molson introduced the new container, beer sold in cans had traditionally captured less than 1% of package beer sales in Ontario. A month after introduction of the aluminum can, the share had reached over 3%.

3. Fast-Food Retailing**

Fast-food retailing appears to be undergoing significant changes with the decline in its rate of growth. Industry predictions that fast foods would account for 50% of the food dollar spent outside the home by the mid 1980s failed to materialize. They currently stand at about 37%.

The hamburger market, in particular, appears to be facing a number of problems:

- consumer preferences appear to be shifting toward white meat: chicken and fish;

---

*Adapted from "New Beer Bottles Hurt Labatt Gains," *The Spectator* (16 June 1984), p. A12; John Partridge, "Carling Cuts Canned Beer Price," *The Globe and Mail* (9 June 1984), p. B4.

**Adapted from Lisa Stephens, "Fast Food Firms Vary Menus to Reflect Changing Tastes," *The Globe and Mail* (8 June 1984), p. R5; "Wendy Tries the Canadian Way," *Marketing* (30 March 1981), p. 5; Lawrence Moule, "Fierce Competition Has Restaurants Starving for Customers and Cash," *Toronto Star* (14 June 1981), p. E6.

- increased awareness of nutrition is broadening consumer palates toward fresh vegetables and whole grain; and
- the gourmet boom has caused shifts to a wider variety of foods.

In response to these trends, the hamburger companies have turned to clear segmentation strategies and to new product introduction. McDonald's, the largest hamburger chain in Canada with 450 outlets, aims at families with children, teenagers, and working mothers. Its sales of $693 million in 1983 made up more than half of the hamburger fast-food market in Canada. To appeal to children, McDonald's has Ronald McDonald and they arrange large group birthday parties on their premises. Changing consumer tastes have also led these retailers to introduce a number of new products in the last few years: Egg McMuffin, a breakfast entry; Sausage McMuffin; McRib, boneless pork on a bun (which failed); McChicken Sandwich (which failed in the US); and Chicken McNuggets, bite-size chicken pieces.

Wendy's aims at the young, urban professional ("Yuppies"), single or married with no children. It emphasizes custom grilling, salad bars, and smaller dining rooms with upscale decor. Children are totally absent from its advertising and public relations. Menu diversification has led to the introduction of an upgraded salad bar and a stuffed baked potato. Currently being tested are several upscale desserts and a breakfast omelette.

Harvey's also has its eyes on the Yuppies. Harvey's is moving away from its traditional eighteen-to-twenty-four young adult group to the expanding twenty-four-plus single or childless group with an appeal to the customized hamburger. They, too, are diversifying their menu. A recent addition was Fish Fingers, a tempura batter deep-fried fish. Before that, they had brought in the double burger, and steak-on-a-kaiser.

These are only a few of the ways in which retailers attempt to influence the consumer: variety in packaging, greater convenience, new products, and decor. They are triggers to the motivational process introduced by the retailer and most often based on changing consumer needs, tastes, and preferences. As the last link in the distribution chain that can influence the consumer decision, the retailer is of considerable importance to the marketer.

This chapter is devoted to a review of the main techniques developed by retailers to influence the choice of store, product, and brand.

FACTORS AFFECTING STORE CHOICE

Store choice may be as important as (or, in some areas, even more important than) product or brand choice. Store choice can be the result of external communications as well as of internal factors (i.e., within the store).

A store with a dominant consumer image may rely on just enough media advertising to reinforce its image. Another store may need heavy mass advertising in order to attract customers.

This is not to imply that that store's image is the product of only external communications. In fact, internal factors such as brands carried and "atmosphere" will also contribute significantly to consumers' perception of the store. In brief, *both the internal and external communications contribute in two areas*:

- store choice and store image; and
- product and brand choice.

The reasons for choosing particular stores can range from physical characteristics to emotional reactions, such as atmosphere or odor. Monroe and Guiltinan, using time-path analysis, have presented a model that they consider "a first step towards the specification of a directional model of store choice behavior" (that is, "the relative directions of influence among variables").[1] (See Figure 18.1.)

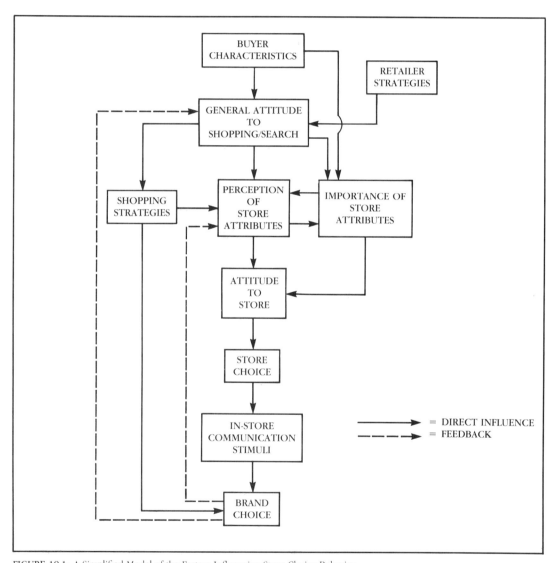

FIGURE 18.1: A Simplified Model of the Factors Influencing Store Choice Behavior

The model suggests that the characteristics of the household/buyer and retailer strategies together will determine how the consumer feels about shopping/search. How the consumer feels about shopping/search will influence the importance attached to different attributes and how the store's attributes are perceived. It will also determine the kinds of planning and budgeting the consumer employs. How the consumer perceives a store is dependent upon the importance of store attributes and the planning and budgeting considered necessary. It may even be that "store perceptions show an influence over attribute importance," suggesting a kind of satisficing by consumers in certain situations. Eventually, the attitude to the store is the result of the consumer's perceptions of the store attributes weighted against the importance of those attributes. A positive attitude will lead to the selection of the store, where proper communications can lead to brand choice. A positive experience will be fed back and stored as general opinion for subsequent perception of the store and the start of a repetitive process or store loyalty.

The two main groups of factors that influence store choice, therefore, are the buyer's characteristics and the retailer strategies (or store characteristics).

Buyer characteristics include demographics (age, income, family size), role or social relationships, life-style, personality, and economic status.

Demographic variables, by themselves, have not been found to be very helpful in understanding store choice.[2] Apart from geography, some correlation has been found between store choice and social-class indicators such as education and occupation of the household head, income, and family size.[3] Race has been found to be correlated with type of store shopped.[4]

The socio-psychological characteristics of the consumer (status, role, life-style, personality) have an important influence on shopping and search behavior. It has been found that this influence may be quite limited, since less than external information search in order to choose a store.[5] Nevertheless, search may be influenced by social relationships (status and role) in that they will determine the evaluative store attributes and their importance, by values and interests (life-style), and by level of aspiration and search propensity, which are related to the need for certainty and reactions to risk and ambiguity (personality).[6]

Consumer Typology

It appears that shoppers develop shopping orientations on the basis of their life-styles and personality; these orientations are expressed in their attitudes toward shopping. Stone's early work identified four types of shoppers[7] — economic, personalizing, ethical, and apathetic — and this has been found by later researchers to have high external validity.[8]

The **economic shopper** emphasizes price and quality and is inclined to shop around. He or she is not particularly interested in store personnel or other services, only in efficiency and price, quality, and product assortment.

The **personalizing shopper** looks to establish personal relationships with store personnel, so that the choice of store is strongly influenced by store personnel and much less by price, quality, or product assortment.

The **ethical shopper** is guided by considerations of duty and what is thought to be "right." He or she will choose a store because it is small (the shopper wants to "help the little guy") or patronize a store because it carries Canadian-made products.

The **apathetic shopper** does not care much for shopping, so that convenience is a very important criterion.

Although very general, these typologies go beyond physical and demographic attributes and introduce some psychological insights that can be helpful in understanding the consumer better.

A more recent attempt at a different typology has only expanded the number of types and remains essentially similar to Stone's.[9]

Store Attributes

Both the consumer's perception of a store's attributes and the perceived importance of these attributes, according to Monroe and Guiltinan, interact to determine the attitude toward the store and the resulting store choice.

The attributes are many, including the store's location, physical structure, product selection, price, personnel, advertising, services, and general characteristics.

Store Location

This involves mainly convenience in getting to and stopping at the store. Generally speaking, the greater the distance from the store, the less likely the consumer is to shop there. Such characteristics as actual distance, time required, the difficulty of the trip (e.g., if driving, the heaviness of traffic), and the proximity to other desirable retailers,[10] affect the likelihood that a shopper will go there.

One type of location choice decision involves the **choice between cities** in which to shop, and concerns consumers who live outside metropolitan areas. The reasons for the choice have not been clearly delineated. Early studies that suggested that the desirability of a location varies inversely with the distance and directly as the size of the population center in which the store is located have not been updated.[11] In addition, they ignore such factors as income level and consumer preferences.

On the other hand, studies have found that those who shop in outside towns or cities (outshoppers) differ in demographic and psychographic characteristics from those who do not.[12]

Intracity store choice can involve a choice between shopping centers and a choice between stores. One factor that has been investigated is driving time.[13] For some customers, the limit is fifteen minutes, unless the center is very attractive.[14] Consumers tend to overestimate both actual time and distance.[15]

It should also be noted that where store location has a strong impact on store image, it can be very influential in determining store choice. Thus a store located in an attractive area is more likely to be chosen than one that is in an unattractive area.

Physical Structure

Physical structure refers to the internal and external design of the store and consists of such aspects as architecture, decor, lighting, space allocation (layout), condition of maintenance, types of displays, arrangement of merchandise (easy to find), and checkouts. It is important to recognize that these physical attributes communicate (symbolize) certain ideas about the store (e.g., modern/old-fashioned, masculine/feminine, efficient/sloppy, clean/dirty, successful/unsuccessful) so that just what the final combination should be depends upon the image desired. This may be easier said than done but the point remains that physical design cannot be ignored and left to chance.[16]

Product Selection

The range of styles and brands of a product will clearly prove attractive to certain customers and will need to be adjusted to the expectations of the target market. Franchises and limited or exclusive distribution tend to bring certain customers looking for specific brands to those stores. Such variables as fully stocked/understocked, quality, and well-known/unknown brands can be important.

Price

Evidence on the role of price in influencing store choice is contradictory. Some studies, even for the same type of store, find that price is important, others that it is not.[17]

It seems that the importance of price varies by product, store, and customer.[18]

In the present context of inflation and spiralling prices, some of these relationships may be heightened and others may tend to change and give greater importance to price. Because price perception is a *subjective phenomenon*, actual price may often be less important than such attributes as low or high compared to other stores, value for money spent, and large versus small number of specially priced items, in influencing store choice.

Personnel

Customer reaction to store personnel, particularly for such attributes as courtesy, friendliness, helpfulness, and the adequacy of their number, can be quite crucial in store choice, even capable of negating the positive effects of other variables.

Advertising

Apart from the fact that advertising may be used to communicate information about the other determinants of store choice, the execution and format (and other cues) of the advertising itself may convey certain impressions of the sponsor and affect store choice. Shown advertisements of stores they have never heard of, consumers will attribute social class status to them or get impressions about them, such as untrustworthy or unreliable.

It appears, however, that advertising may not be as frequently noted as originally thought, particularly for the preponderance of low-involvement products on the market today. However, measures of the impact of advertising should also take into account that many individuals may be reluctant to identify advertising as the source of their information.

The effectiveness of store advertising may also be measured in terms of informativeness, helpfulness in planning purchases, its attractiveness, and its believability.

Sales promotion may also influence store choices. In recent years, there has been increased use of sweepstakes and contests.[19]

Services

Not much of a generalizable nature can be said about services except that they are additional benefits that could affect store choice. On the other hand, consumers are aware that services do affect product price and they are therefore inclined to compromise.

General attributes that appear to be related to store choice include store image characteristics such as:

- well-known;
- small/large number of stores;
- clientele;
- long-established;
- atmosphere;
- nationality; and
- appeal to friends.

The list of factors associated with store choice is large and no single factor can be expected to account for store preference. It is more likely that different combinations of the many variables will apply in different situations.

Using the semantic differential (see Chapter 6), it is possible to obtain a profile of store image by consumers on a number of attributes. The profiles of competitive stores provide useful insights as well. Perceptual mapping can also be developed from store attribute data.

The clientele and the store atmosphere are particularly to be noted. Consumers tend to patronize stores where they think people like themselves shop. They feel comfortable in surroundings and among others who share the same social class as themselves.[20]

The "surroundings" are created by both the elements attributable to the retailer (such as furniture, lighting, design, and shelf space) and the other shoppers in the store.[21] These all tend to "produce specific emotional effects in buyers."[22]

Retailer Strategies

Applying the model proposed by Monroe and Guiltinan brings us to the third source of influence on consumer store choice — retailer strategies. The first two were buyer characteristics and needs, and store attributes.

Since the strategies are initiated by the retailer, they are also perceived as store attributes. For example, advertising, sales promotions, personnel behavior, and services are often the result of carefully designed marketing strategy and reflect on the store image.

As stated in other contexts, such strategies are most effective when they are determined by carefully thought-out objectives *vis-à-vis* the target market, executed appropriately, and coordinated so that the impressions from each reinforce and support the impressions from the others and lead to a unified, consistent "message" about the store.

FACTORS AFFECTING IN-STORE BEHAVIOR

By in-store behavior I mean product and brand choice. Some of the same factors that influence store choice also affect product and brand choice. In this section, I examine each of the strategies applied by the retailer to influence product and/or brand choice. Other influences coming from the marketer (advertising, packaging), from the environment (social norms, friends, opinion leaders, reference group, family) or from the consumer (needs, values, attitudes, motives) have been the subject of most of the rest of the book so far.

The factors applied by the retailer and referred to in Figure 18.1 as "In-store communication stimuli" include:

- special displays;
- shelf-position;
- shelf space;
- pricing strategy;
- departmentalization;
- forced trial or out of stock; and
- sales personnel.

Special Displays

Special point-of-purchase displays take a variety of forms — end-of-aisle, "shelf talkers" (a strip of paper on the shelf front pointing out a particular offering), and "gondolas" (fancy displays set up separately). They draw the consumer's attention to particular products or brands with the result that they may:

- accelerate sales;
- attract new customers;
- introduce a new brand or package; and
- reinforce advertising strategies in other media.

Because they are variations from normal shelf stocking, special displays tend to give the impression of "a special price offer." A study by K-Mart found that sales had increased by 250% for sports products featured on audio-visual displays in the store.[23]

While special displays do tend to reduce normal shelf sales, total sales are generally higher. After the displays are removed, sales also tend to return rapidly to normal, indicating the effectiveness of the displays.

Shelf Position

Shelf positions at eye-level have traditionally been considered to be advantageous to the brand or brands located there. Usually the largest brand is awarded this position (turnover is fastest and profits highest) but recently a greater and greater proportion of the better shelf positions appear to be given to "private" or dealer brands, for obvious reasons.

Shelf Space

Once again, the biggest brands are likely to be allotted the most shelf space or shelf facings because they offer best profits. Both manufacturers and retailers appear to assume that sales are directly related to shelf space, although research on this point has been rather contradictory.[24] The effect may vary among products or across stores.[25]

It does stand to reason, however, that greater shelf space must confer an advantage if only because it results in greater visibility, particularly for new products or for fast-moving products.

Pricing

We were faced with the problem of what to do with six puppies. My husband drove all over town trying to give them away, with no success. Next we took advantage of free time offered by a local radio station to announce that we had six puppies to give away, but no one called. In a last attempt we again advertised them over the radio. This time we asked $20 each. They were all sold in two hours. We made $120 from something we couldn't give away.[26]

Retailers attempt any of a wide variety of pricing tactics to attract customers. Their primary interest is not to enhance sales of the particular brand but to bring customers in. Some of the practices employed are:

- **Price Leaders or Loss Leaders** — fast-moving brands are priced low and even possibly at a loss. Manufacturers have succeeded in getting the Canadian federal government to limit the extent to which this practice is applied to a particular brand, mainly to protect the brand from acquiring a "cheap" image.

  It is quite likely that the brand itself does not benefit, because the lower price may result in hoarding, causing sales to decline in subsequent periods.

- Another psychological pricing tactic frequently employed by retailers is **odd-even** pricing, where prices set are made up of odd numerals. For example an item will be listed at $134.99 instead of $135, based on the belief that consumers are influenced by the odd numerals, almost as if the odd price is perceived as significantly lower.

Although there does not appear to be any evidence to support this belief, retailers persist in the practice.

- **Multiple-Unit Pricing** is another frequent practice among retailers. With multiple pricing the retailer offers two or more items for what appears to be a lower unit price than the single item offering. For example, an item whose single price is ten cents may be offered at two for nineteen cents or three for twenty-eight cents.

The retailer may select a particular brand for this kind of treatment, or may cooperate with a manufacturer who provides the brand package in multiple units.

It is likely that multiple-pricing may generate temporary sales increases, which over the long run may be balanced out with declines. However, products such as soft drinks may actually enjoy real volume increases.

Some consumerists complain about multiple pricing on the ground that it causes some consumers to buy more than they had planned, almost as if they feel compelled to buy.

Other types of promotional pricing strategies are "cents off" specials and rebates.

It is not clear whether with these price promotions the marketer achieves the objective of brand switching. Switching may be only temporary.[27]

- **Dealer or Private Label Brands** are brands produced by or for the retailer. At times they carry a brand name that clearly identifies them with the retailer (e.g., Eatonia shirts by Eaton's, Domino brands by Dominion Food Stores). These "dealer brands" are in essence a pricing tactic to encourage use of the brand because the primary advantage they offer to the consumer is lower price.

At the same time, they offer higher profit margins to the retailer because of preferred shelf space and lower promotional costs.

The acceptance of such brands is strongly influenced by the retailer's corporate image, which may often lead to strong customer loyalty.

- **Generic Brands**, a variant of the dealer brand, carry no brand name. They have plain labels, carry only the product name (e.g., green beans) and are variously referred to as "white label," "no frills," "unbrand," "no-brand," or "no-name." It is noteworthy that generics are also, in essence, a *pricing tactic* because their chief claim is low price. Typically, they sell at up to 40% below national brands and up to 20% below dealer brands.[28]

Generics have been in Canada for only about seven years and about a year longer in the US. They appear to have had rather rapid acceptance in their early history but recently have levelled off. In 1980, it was estimated by leading grocers that by 1984, "generics" would account for 25% to 30% of total grocery sales in Canada, but that prediction does not appear to be likely to come true.

Most buyers seem to believe the lower price of generics is the result of packaging and promotion economies, although the stores admit privately that the real savings come from some amount of quality reduction through the use of standard grades. For example, cracked rather than whole peanuts are used to make no-name peanut butter, canned fruit has a lighter syrup or broken fruit slices, and detergents have a less pleasant odor.[29]

On the surface, current economic conditions seem to be ripe for generics, but all indications are that the appeal of "no-name" brands has been limited to a specific target group — the economic shopper. One source described the generic shopper in terms quite different from what might have been anticipated — slightly younger, better educated, and larger purchase customers.[30] In addition, they have larger families, are in the middle stages of the family lifecycle, and are mildly innovative.[31] The high-volume generic buyer appears to be closer to the general stereotype: relatively low income, less time for shopping, and rent rather than

own their own homes.[32] It appears that those with higher incomes and greater confidence are willing to take the risk of buying a product that may be inconsistent in quality. Those with less confidence prefer manufacturers' brands, since they are nationally accepted and promise consistent quality.

Departmentalization

Retailers attempt to facilitate the shopper's task and thus increase purchasing proclivities by displaying together products that go together. Thus there are shoe departments, cosmetics departments, and appliance departments. In the main, the arrangement of departments is intended to create certain traffic patterns. Within a department, products are arranged in proximity to other products with which they have a functional relationship.[33] Too much emphasis on forcing traffic patterns can lead to confusion and be counter-productive. There is some evidence that shoppers' perceptions of product locations in supermarkets can be quite inaccurate so that the task has to be carefully planned for the consumer, even perhaps providing cues or guides to a greater extent or of a different kind than are currently employed.[34]

The newest development in food retailing is the bulk food department, where consumers serve themselves from bins. One of its primary advantages is price.

Forced Trial or Out-of-Stock

Running out of stock of an item is to be avoided by the retailer because a customer may be *forced* to go to another retailer or to substitute another brand. In either case the forced trial could result in store or brand switching and the consequences can be very serious. Out-of-stock is, therefore, one kind of in-store circumstance that can influence store, product, or brand choice and, from the retailer's point of view (and the manufacturer's as well), is a very undesirable situation. This can become a problem when interest rates and inventory costs necessitate restrictions on inventory.

Sales Personnel (Customer-Salesperson Dyad)

Not very much of a conclusive nature is known about the so-called customer-salesperson dyad, so that the retailer is forced to rely on subjective opinions and on a few widely accepted notions. This is unfortunate because sales personnel are within the control of the marketer and have the potential to make valuable contributions to the sales and thus the success of the company.

Most of the research on sales influence has dealt with the characteristics of the sales staff.[35] Only recently has some attention been directed to the customer as well by studying the interaction between the customer and the salesperson.

A few factors have been identified as important in the customer-salesperson transaction.

Similarity

It seems that a sale is more likely to occur when customers perceive the salesperson as quite similar to themselves in physical, demographic, life-style, and background characteristics. Life insurance salespeople were found to be more successful with prospects who were similar to them in political affiliation, religion, and economic characteristics.[36] In another study it was found that paint sales personnel who were similar to the customers (e.g., similar painting problems) but were relatively inexperienced were more successful in making sales than those who were dissimilar but more experienced.[37]

When the influence derives from an identification with the salesperson, when he or she is perceived as a source of friendship or attraction, it is called **referent power** (see Chapter 15).

Expertise

It seems, too, that knowledgeability about the particular product (the influence of **expert power**) can be very influential since it contributes significantly to the credibility and trustworthiness of the salesperson.[38]

Woodside and Davenport found that the presence of both referent and expert power maximizes the chances of a successful transaction.[39]

Personality

The personalities of both customer and salesperson can influence the outcome of the interaction. One study found that dependent personalities prefer assertive salespeople and independent personalities are indifferent.[40]

There is a suggestion too that the dominant individual with high need-achievement is more likely to influence the outcome of the transaction through bargaining.[41]

Because customers perceive the salesperson as biased, it appears advisable that salespeople should pay close attention to the kinds of information and remarks they offer. A study done with appliance shoppers found that certain kinds of transaction behaviors were highly correlated with the decision to buy.[42] A sale was more likely to result when these types of behaviors occurred — frequent reference to bargaining limits; and reference to delivery, to styling, and to warranty. When the salesperson derogated a competitive product, attempted to change bargaining limits, or made frequent reference to quality or price, a sale was less likely to occur.

Sales staff should also attempt to "read" the customer and, to the best of their ability, adapt their "techniques" to the personality, needs, and motives of the prospect. In other words, the salespersons' empathy or "ability to put themselves in someone else's shoes" is extremely important. Aggressive selling may be acceptable to the independent individual,[43] but will evoke negative reactions from others.

Much of the customer-salesperson interaction is left to quick subjective decisions, because there are no guidelines for assessing the customer's personality, motives, and needs or for ensuring that the customer's true interests will be the decisive factor in the salesperson's behavior.

Impulse Purchasing

Also referred to as unplanned purchasing, impulse purchases are generally brought on by retailer strategies such as those we have been discussing: displays, price promotions, and sales personnel. A widely accepted classification of impulse buying identifies four types:

1. **pure impulse**, such as a novelty or escape purchase;

2. **reminder impulse**, such as when the person sees an item or an advertisement and is reminded that the stock at home needs to be replenished;

3. **suggestive impulse**, such as when the consumer sees the product for the first time and visualizes a need for it or when buying one product leads the consumer to try something not purchased before (e.g., buying lettuce and then selecting a salad dressing never considered or purchased before); and

4. **planned impulse**, such as when the shopper enters the store with the expectation of purchasing some products offered as specials.[44]

Strictly speaking, if the criterion of unplannedness, without the benefit of any prior thought, were applied, then only the pure impulse and the suggestive impulse purchase would be regarded as truly impulsive, spur-of-the-moment purchases. However, what all four types have in common is that all of the decisions occur at the point of purchase.[45]

What sort of decision process lies behind the impulse purchase? At first glance, it may appear that it is low-involvement, being of little importance to the consumer and low in risk. However, a closer look leads to the conclusion that an impulse purchase can be high- or low-involvement.

The shopper browsing in a food store who happens upon an exotic type of canned fruit and purchases it or the shopper standing in line at the check-out counter who reaches over and picks up a package of chewing gum is engaged in low-involvement decisions: there was no pre-planning or pre-evaluation. On the other hand, the man who, attracted by a window display, walks into a men's store and purchases an expensive suit on the spur of the moment is most likely engaged in a high-involvement decision. What appears to be an impulse purchase is most likely the result of search and evaluation that may have occurred long before the purchase; the evaluative criteria had also been decided; only the choice was left to be made. In the exceptional cases, where a high-involvement good may be purchased on impulse, triggered by in-store stimuli, dissonance is most likely to occur.

The research evidence on the frequency of impulse purchase is quite controversial, due mainly to definitional and methodological problems. As suggested earlier, the definitions used have tended to equate impulse purchases with unplanned purchases and to remain quite broad. Thus one study found that 39% of all department store shoppers and 62% of discount store shoppers purchased at least one item on an unplanned basis.[46]

The methodological problems involve the measurement procedures typically employed. Just before entering the store, consumers indicate what they intend to buy, either orally or from a list they may have and these items are checked against actual purchases when they leave the store. All items not on the first list are considered impulse purchases. There are several problems with this approach. Shoppers may forget to mention some items — the more items they plan to purchase the more they are likely to forget. Lists are not necessarily made of all the items they intend to purchase — for example, they could include only items they do not want to forget. Shoppers may also not take too kindly to being accosted on their way into the store and give abbreviated answers.

For these reasons, it appears that claims about the extent of impulse purchasing are exaggerated. Much of what appears to be true impulse may be the result of pre-purchase information search and evaluation.

SUMMARY

Consumer behavior is choice behavior involving store choice as well as product and brand choice. Strategies pursued by the retailer can influence these choices.

The reasons for store choice range from the psychological characteristics of the consumer to the physical attributes of the store. Demographic factors (age, income, family size), social relationships (friends, relatives), life-style, and personality can influence this decision. On the other hand, the store attributes, as perceived by the consumer, also exert some influence. Such attributes as location, physical structure (design, decor, lighting, and space allocation), product assortment and depth, price, personnel, advertising, and general image characteristics (reputation, nationality, reliability, atmosphere) are all important.

Particular retailer strategies such as advertising, sales promotions, and services also affect store choice.

In-store behavior is influenced by such retailer activities as special displays, shelf position, shelf space, pricing, and departmentalization. These can be effective in influencing both store choice and product or brand choice.

A final source of influence is the salesperson. It appears that the greater the perceived similarity between the salesperson and the customer, in terms of physical, demographic, life-style, and background characteristics, the greater the likelihood of a purchase. Other factors are expertise, personality, and particular transaction behaviors.

Unplanned (impulse) purchases are strongly influenced by in-store stimuli. It appears, however, that their frequency is exaggerated, mainly because of how impulse purchasing is defined and how it is measured.

QUESTIONS

1. Discuss the role of buyer characteristics in store choice.

2. Which would you say are the most important store attributes that influence store choice?

3. Stores have been described as having an "image," including a social-class image. Discuss this phenomenon in consumer behavior.

4. Describe the effects of special displays on in-store shopper behavior.

5. Basing your answer on past performance, what do you think will be the significance of generics five years from now? Why?

6. What are some of the important factors in the customer-salesperson dyad that affect the success of the interaction?

7. Discuss the adequacy of the concept of impulse purchases as it is currently defined and measured.

NOTES TO CHAPTER 18

[1]Kent B. Monroe and Joseph P. Guiltinan, "A Path-Analytic Exploration of Retail Patronage Influences," *Journal of Consumer Research*, 2 (June 1975), pp. 19-28.

[2]John U. Farley, "Dimensions of Supermarket Choice Patterns," *Journal of Marketing Research*, 5 (May 1968), pp. 206-9.

[3]Paul R. Winn and Terry L. Childers, "Demographics and Store Patronage Concentrations: Some Promising Results," in Kenneth L. Bernhardt (ed.), *Marketing: 1776 – 1976 and Beyond* (Chicago: American Marketing Association, 1976), pp. 82-6.

[4]Donald E. Sexton, Jr., "Differences in Food Shopping Habits by Area of Residence, Race, and Income," *Journal of Retailing*, 50 (Spring 1974), pp. 37-49.

[5]Elizabeth C. Hirschman and Michael K. Mills, "Sources Shoppers Use to Pick Stores," *Journal of Advertising Research*, 20 (February 1980), pp. 47-51.

[6]Francesco M. Nicosia, *Consumer Decision Processes* (Englewood Cliffs, New Jersey: Prentice-Hall, 1966); William R. Darden and Dub Ashton, "Psychographic Profiles of Patronage Preference Groups," *Journal of Retailing*, 50 (Winter 1974-75), pp. 99-111.

[7]G.R. Stone, "City Shoppers and Urban Identification: Observations on the Social Psychology of City Life," *American Journal of Sociology*, 60 (July 1954), pp. 36-45.

[8]William R. Darden and Fred D. Reynolds, "Shopping Orientations and Product Usage Rates," *Journal of Marketing Research*, 7 (November 1971), pp. 505-8.

[9]George P. Moschis, "Shopping Orientations and Consumer Uses of Information," *Journal of Retailing*, 52 (Summer 1976), pp. 61-70.

[10]Robert F. Kelly and Ronald Stephenson, "The Semantic Differential: An Information Source for Designing Retail Patronage Appeals," *Journal of Marketing*, 31 (October 1967), pp. 43-7.

[11]William J. Reilly, *The Law of Retail Gravitation* (New York: William J. Reilly Company, 1931); P.D. Converse, "New Laws of Retail Gravitation," *Journal of Marketing*, 14 (October 1949), pp. 379-84.

[12]John R. Thompson, "Characteristics and Behavior of Outshopping Consumers," *Journal of Retailing*, 47 (Spring 1971), pp. 70-80; Fred D. Reynolds and William R. Darden, "Intermarket Patronage: A Psychographic Study of Consumer Outshoppers," *Journal of Marketing*, 36 (October 1972), pp. 50-4.

[13]James A. Brunner and John L. Mason, "The Influence of Driving Time Upon Shopping Center Preference," *Journal of Marketing*, 32 (April 1968), pp. 57-61.

[14]William E. Cox, Jr., and Ernest F. Cooke, "Other Dimensions Involved in Shopping Center Preference," *Journal of Marketing*, 34 (October 1970), pp. 12-17; James W. Gentry and Alvin C. Burns, "How 'Important' are Evaluative Criteria in Shopping Center Patronage?" *Journal of Retailing*, 53 (Winter 1977-78), p. 77.

[15]Edward M. Mazze, "Determining Shopper Movement by Cognitive Maps," *Journal of Retailing*, 50 (Fall 1974), pp. 14-48.

[16]Jay D. Lindquist, "Meaning of Image," *Journal of Retailing*, 50 (Winter 1974-75), p. 31.

[17]"Consumer Behavior in the Supermarket," *Progressive Grocer* (October 1975), p. 37.

[18]Jo-Ann Zbytniewski, "Consumer Watch," *Progressive Grocer* (June 1980), p. 31.

[19]Franklynn Peterson and Judi Kesselman Turkel, "Catching Customers With Sweepstakes," *Fortune* (8 February 1982), pp. 84-8.

[20]Bruce L. Stern, Ronald F. Bush, and Joseph F. Hair, Jr., "The Self-Image/Store Image Matching Process: An Empirical Test," *Journal of Business*, 50 (January 1977), pp. 63-9.

[21]Robert J. Donovan and John R. Rossiter, "Store Atmosphere: An Environmental Psychology Approach," *Journal of Retailing*, 58 (Spring 1982), pp. 34-57.

[22]Philip Kotler, "Atmospherics as a Marketing Tool," *Journal of Retailing*, 49 (Winter 1973-74), pp. 48-64.

[23]"POP-AV Displays Boost Retail Sales," *Marketing News*, 2 (27 November 1981), p. 18.

[24]K.R. Cox, "The Responsiveness of Food Sales to Shelf Space Changes in Supermarkets," *Journal of Marketing Research*, 1 (May 1964), pp. 63-7; J.A. Kotzan and R.V. Evanson, "Responsiveness of Drug Store Sales to Shelf Space Allocations," *Journal of Marketing Research*, 6 (November 1969), pp. 465-9.

[25]Ronald C. Curhan, "Shelf Space Allocation and Profit Maximization in Mass Retailing," *Journal of Marketing*, 37 (July 1973), p. 56.

[26]Alex Vicaire, "Life's Like That," *Reader's Digest* (June 1981), p. 225.

[27]B.C. Cotton and Emerson M. Babb, "Consumer Response to Promotional Deals," *Journal of Marketing*, 42 (July 1978), pp. 109-13; J.A. Dodson, Alice M. Tybout, and Brian Sternthal, "Impact of Deals and Deal Retraction on Brand Switching," *Journal of Marketing Research*, 15 (February 1978), pp. 72-81; P.S. Raju and Manof Hastak, "Consumer Response to Deals: A Discussion of Theoretical Perspectives," in Jerry Olson (ed.), *Advances in Consumer Research*, 7 (Ann Arbor, Michigan: Association for Consumer Research, 1980), pp. 296-301; Robert C. Blattberg, Gary D. Eppen, and Joshua Lieberman, "A Theoretical and Empirical Evaluation of Price Deals for Consumer Nondurables," *Journal of Marketing*, 45 (Winter 1981), pp. 116-29.

[28]"A New Era in Marketing Has Emerged," *Marketing* (14 May 1979), pp. 23-8.

[29]"Generics Posing a Threat to National Brands," *Marketing* (12 March 1979), p. 23.

[30]"Newcomer Generics Get Growing Consumer Interest," *Advertising Age* (13 October 1978), p. 84.

[31]Joseph A. Bellizi, Harry F. Krueckeberg, John R. Hamilton, and Warren S. Martin, "Consumer Perceptions of National, Private, and Generic Brands," *Journal of Retailing*, 57 (Winter 1981), pp. 56-70.

[32]Kent L. Granzin, "An Investigation of the Market for Generic Products," *Journal of Retailing*, 57 (Winter 1981), pp. 39-55.

[33]"Consumer Behavior in the Supermarket — Part III," *Progressive Grocer* (January 1976), p. 68.

[34]Robert Sommer and Susan Aitkens, "Mental Mapping of Two Supermarkets," *Journal of Consumer Research*, 9 (September 1982), pp. 211-5.

[35]James C. Cotham III, "Selecting Salesmen: Approaches and Problems," *MSU Business Topics*, 18 (Winter 1970), pp. 64-72.

[36]Franklin B. Evans, "Selling as a Dyadic Relationship — A New Approach," *American Behavioral Scientist*, 6 (May 1963), pp. 76-9.

[37]T.C. Brock, "Communicator-Recipient Similarity and Decision Change," *Journal of Personality and Social Psychology*, 1 (June 1965), pp. 650-4.

[38]Paul Busch and D.T. Wilson, "An Experimental Analysis of a Salesman's Expert and Referent Basis of Social Power in the Buyer-Seller Dyad," *Journal of Marketing Research*, 13 (February 1976), pp. 3-11.

[39]Arch G. Woodside and J. William Davenport, Jr., "The Effect of Salesman Similarity and Expertise on Consumer Purchasing Behavior," *Journal of Marketing Research*, 11 (May 1974), pp. 198-202.

[40]James E. Stafford and Thomas V. Greer, "Consumer Preference for Types of Salesmen: A Study of Dependence-Independence Characteristics," *Journal of Retailing*, 41 (Summer 1965), pp. 27-33.

[41]G. David Hughes, Joseph B. Juhasz, and Bruno Contini, "The Influence of Personality on the Bargaining Process," *Journal of Business*, 46 (October 1973), pp. 593-603.

[42]Allan L. Pennington, "Customer-Salesman Bargaining Behavior in Retail Transactions," *Journal of Marketing Research*, 5 (August 1968), pp. 255-62.

[43]Stafford and Greer, op. cit.

[44]H. Stern, "The Significance of Impulse Buying Today," *Journal of Marketing*, 26 (April 1962), pp. 59-62.

[45]Danny N. Bellenger, Dan H. Robertson, and Elizabeth C. Hirschman, "Impulse Buying Varies by Product," *Journal of Advertising Research*, 18 (December 1978), p. 17.

[46]V. Kanti Prasad, "Unplanned Buying in Two Retail Settings," *Journal of Retailing*, 51 (Fall 1975), pp. 3-12.

TYLENOL*

Background

In September 1982, seven consumers in the Chicago area died after taking extra-strength Tylenol capsules that had been laced by unknown persons with cyanide. Apparently, the Tylenol packages had been opened and the killer or killers had presumably substituted cyanide for Tylenol in the capsules. This form of terrorism has created a bizarre situation for manufacturers and retailers because of the immensity of the potential threat to the consumer when one considers the number of foods and beverages, in addition to proprietary medicines, that could be vulnerable to such actions.

Tylenol, produced by McNeil Consumer Products Company, a subsidiary of Johnson and Johnson, accounted for $400 million in US sales and about $70 million in profits in 1982 and was the country's most popular over-the-counter pain reliever. With 37% of the market, Tylenol — which outsells Bayer aspirin, Bufferin, Excedrin, and Anacin combined — built its fortune on a reputation for safety. It faithfully courted doctors and pharmacists in pushing nonaspirin acetaminophen as a safe alternative to aspirin, which can cause stomach irritation. The recall of the Tylenol capsules that followed the poisonings, Johnson and Johnson announced, would result in a one-time charge against profit of $50 million!

Consumer Polls

From a number of public opinion polls commissioned by McNeil, it was learned that:

1. many consumers thought (wrongly!) that the Tylenol *tablets*, and not just the *capsules*, had been involved as well;

---

*Adapted from Michael Waldholz, "Tylenol Maker Mounting Campaign to Restore Trust of Doctors, Buyers," The Wall Street Journal (28 October 1982); Michael Waldholz, "Speedy Recovery," The Wall Street Journal (24 December 1982); "Johnson and Johnson Will Pay Dearly to Cure Tylenol," Business Week (29 November 1982).

2. many consumers did not realize that the company had been exonerated in the poisonings and that the deaths were confined to Chicago;

3. most significantly, *half* of Tylenol's previous users thought they would be unlikely to use the product again;

4. although many consumers were aware of the details of the poisoning incidents, there was a strong emotional element in their reactions. According to David Clare, Johnson and Johnson's president, "What we've got is a situation in which people intellectually know the product is safe and effective . . . but emotionally they just can't bear the trauma of going back to it";

5. 80% of all Tylenol users first began using the product at the suggestion of their doctor, dentist, or druggist; and

6. very significantly, most consumers wanted to hear something *from the company*.

Company Action

The reactions of the company took several forms, from silence, withdrawal of the product, to advertising and package change. At first, the company kept silent in order to minimize drawing attention to itself. It also voluntarily withdrew from the market the 93,000-bottle lot of Tylenol that contained the two bottles with cyanide. However, on the basis of the consumer surveys, the company decided to take more positive action. It started a drive to correct the misperceptions uncovered — that Tylenol tablets were also involved; that consumers seemed to be unaware that the authorities had freed Johnson and Johnson of all blame, and that the deaths were confined to the Chicago area.

First, in a 60-second television message, McNeil's medical director stressed that the poisonings occurred only in Chicago and involved only Tylenol *capsules* and said that the company was going to work hard to keep the consumers' trust it had earned over the years.

McNeil also sent about two million pieces of literature to doctors, dentists, nurses, and pharmacists spreading the word that the company's factories were not the source of the poisonings and asking them to keep reassuring patients and customers that Tylenol in tablet, liquid, or chewable forms had not been involved.

The company enlisted its sales force and that of other J&J products to promote this message.

The company quickly produced a tamper-resistant package for its capsule products: a new triple-seal package costing an additional 2.4 cents a bottle. The company also offered retailers higher-than-normal discounts, up to 25%, on orders.

Results

In the weeks following the poisoning news, Tylenol sales declined drastically, nearly 80%. However, about two months later, Tylenol's share of the $1.2 billion-a-year pain-reliever market came roaring back. One research company, which surveys grocery sales in four US towns, claimed that Tylenol had recaptured an astounding 95% of its original share, although much of that volume may represent free packages provided to win back consumers. By the end of 1983, Tylenol sales had regained their original levels.

The ability of Johnson & Johnson to pull off this *marketing miracle* can be attributed to a number of factors:

(a) the swift removal of the product from the market;
(b) the strong brand loyalty of Tylenol customers;
(c) the loyalty of its retailers (who held open the shelf store space used for Tylenol extra-strength capsules);
(d) the marketing blitz in which McNeil gave away 76 million coupons each worth $2.50, the price of a small bottle of Tylenol; and, of course,
(e) the package alteration that ensured against any recurrence of the problem.

QUESTIONS

1. Discuss the actions taken by the company in this major crisis. What other actions might have been taken?

2. What could retailers and producers do to avoid or prevent such acts of terrorism in the future?

3. More importantly, what emerged as crucial factors in the control of marketers that can significantly aid company recovery in such a crisis?

4. Comment on the role of marketing research in guiding the response of the company.

5. What other products can you think of that may be subject to a similar hazard or act of terrorism? Suggest how these products could be altered to frustrate any such attempts.

Synthesis, Postscript, and Prognosis

SYNTHESIS

From the discussion of consumer purchase (or consumer choice) decisions in the preceding chapters, it is clear that the eventual purchase behavior is the result of interactions among the various factors we have reviewed throughout this book. For example, problem recognition was described as being influenced by the motives, personality, life-style, cultural norms and values, and reference group (Chapter 3). Information processing is subjected to selective perception (which is influenced by both psychological and social factors) and the evaluative criteria used in information evaluation are the product of the same internal and external forces (Chapter 5).

Understanding how these factors interact to bring about a particular behavior is central to our entire study. Attempts to do this, to achieve such a synthesis — to delineate the relationships among variables — are referred to as *models*. There are many ways of describing such relationships, so that there are many types of models of varying degrees of complexity.

Types of Models

Over the years, many models have been developed to represent the different theories put forward to explain human behavior. (A theory seeks to explain a set of phenomena by identifying the important variables involved and indicating the interrelationships among them.) Three main classifications of models have been suggested:

- **conflict models**, which focus on the struggle between opposing forces that cannot be controlled (e.g., Freud's ego, id, and superego)

- **machine models**, which suggest that human behavior is the result of need stimuli that elicit responses reinforced by the satisfaction or pleasure that comes from the reduction of the need; and
- **open-system models**, which regard people as active participants who control, evaluate, and react to stimuli. Such models are transactional.[1]

The models we are going to discuss fall in the third category. They are systems models that attempt to clarify "relationships among inputs, motivational determinants, and goal-oriented behavior (and which can be) stated in graphic, symbolic, verbal, or mathematical forms. The final form is dependent upon the precision of the theories, facts, and assumptions upon which the model is built."[2]

In consumer behavior, there are models that deal with specific areas of interest (e.g., adoption, dissonance, media exposure)[3] and those that seek to explain all consumer behavior, referred to as **integrative - comprehensive models**. I will concentrate on the latter and include a section on what may be the most important specific models in consumer behavior — brand loyalty.

Functions of Models

Generally speaking, the function of theories or models is to provide an understanding of how a set of phenomena works, to provide "a coherent and systematic structure for a field of study."[4] For example, a theory of human behavior would hope to provide an explanation of all the forces and influences that affect human responses. The goal, perhaps idealistic in the case of human behavior, is to develop a comprehensive "grand theory" that would account for all relevant phenomena satisfactorily. Some feel that such an objective in consumer behavior would be quixotic.[5]

Models can have many functions. They can serve to describe, explain, predict, or control.

These functions, in that order, are a measure of the power of the model. The simplest models permit us to see more clearly what is going on; less simple ones help us understand; even less simple models allow us to predict what is likely to happen; and the most complex ones are able to describe, explain, and predict in such a way that control of circumstances and their outcomes becomes possible. The physical sciences provide many examples of models that permit control.

The models in consumer behavior are essentially descriptive, with some explanatory capabilities. Basically, they are elaborate flow charts that are far removed from the quantified, mathematical models of the physical sciences. Even so, the integrative models in consumer behavior are useful because:

- they identify the variables involved in behavior and the relationships among them, so that some explanation is possible;
- they may allow the possibility of a certain degree of prediction, particularly of group behavior; and
- they also hold out the possibility of integrating diverse research findings — indeed, of integrating or coordinating research efforts so that research has better direction and more relevant content. A good model *generates* researchable hypotheses and identifies gaps in our understanding and knowledge in the field.

A Brief History of Models in Consumer Behavior

A turning-point in the history of marketing came in 1960. Up to that time, there had been little more than armchair analysis of consumer behavior, undertaken by marketers and economists to answer specific problems. Explanations consisted largely of long lists of motives and no concentrated attempts had been made to develop a consistent, integrated body of knowledge about consumer behavior and motivation.

During the 1960s, the post-World War II shift of focus from production to marketing and the increasing emphasis on adapting to the needs of the consumer culminated in the emergence of consumer behavior as a legitimate field of study. Borrowing from the behavioral sciences, marketers and economists sought to explain consumer behavior with theories and hypotheses from disciplines such as psychoanalysis, perceptual psychology, social psychology, sociology, and anthropology.

The last twenty-five years have seen a burgeoning of consumer behavior research and numerous attempts at developing buyer behavior theory. These have been described as taking three basic approaches.[6]

The A Priori *Approach*

This uses theoretical conceptualizations that have made use of concepts and theories from other disciplines, such as the behavioral sciences. Examples are motivation research (Chapter 10), the attitude theories of Festinger and Fishbein (Chapters 11 and 12), the theory of perceived risk by Bauer[7] (Chapter 6), and even Howard's early model of buyer behavior.[8] Although this approach has been quite helpful, it has severe limitations. Not only are many of the concepts adopted still somewhat speculative, but they are not always relevant, having been developed for different purposes (see Chapters 2 and 13) and with more restricted applicability than marketing calls for.

The Empirical Approach

Some researchers adopted essentially the opposite approach and, focussing on consumer behavior itself, sought to formulate general laws about buyer behavior. The work of Ehrenberg typifies this approach.[9] The nature of the information no doubt brought about the evolution of quantitative models, such as brand loyalty predictive models and multidimensional scaling.[10] Unfortunately, this approach lacks ex-

planatory power, which may be the reason why interest in quantitative models has since waned.

The Eclectic Approach

This approach "attempts to incorporate the strengths of the *a priori* and empirical approaches but to avoid their weaknesses."[11] It combines relevant concepts and theories from other disciplines with the findings from empirical, research studies. Examples are the integrative-comprehensive models of Nicosia; Engel, Kollat, and Blackwell; and Howard and Sheth. While they have added greatly to our thinking in consumer behavior, these decision-process models are still essentially elaborate flow charts.

Integrative-Comprehensive Consumer Behavior Models

It does not seem likely that the phenomena of human behavior (including consumer behavior) will ever lend themselves to what appears to be the ultimate in models — mathematical precision, prediction, and control *à la* physical sciences. If we are to judge from psychology, which has investigated human behavior for well over a hundred years, reducing human behavioral phenomena to precise laws and to mathematical predictability and control may turn out to be an impossible task. Nevertheless, comprehensive models of consumer behavior have made valuable contributions to our understanding of the consumer and, indubitably, will grow in their efficacy and usefulness. I will trace the contributions that the three leading eclectic models have made.

The Nicosia Model

This was one of the earliest attempts at an integrative-comprehensive model.[12] Nicosia emphasized the idea of a purchasing *process* that consists of the purchase act as well as a number of steps that precede and follow it; and although he felt that quantification and mathematical formulation are important in a decision model, his attempts at adapting his model to computer simulation have not advanced the cause of consumer behavior by much.

Nicosia identified many of the variables and suggested a structure in his flow-chart model that set the pattern for later theorists (Figure 19.1). For him, the consumer seeks to satisfy certain goals and, through a rational process, reduces the choices down to a final selection. He recognized the influence on consumer decisions of both internal and external forces and the significance of feedback in what was not a one-way but a two-way process.

His was a great pioneering contribution, even though his model may now be seen as being over-reliant on rational considerations, more relevant to infrequently purchased products than to the low-cost, frequently purchased products that make up the bulk of consumer purchases, unclear in the definition of concepts such as attitude and motivation, too ambitious in attempting computer simulation, and confusing with respect to the interrelationships among variables.

The Engel (EKB) Model

Since its introduction in 1968, the eclectic model proposed by Engel, Kollat, and Blackwell has

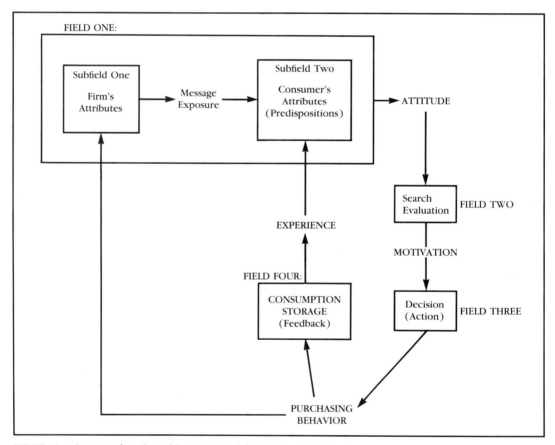

FIGURE 19.1: Summary Flow Chart of the Nicosia Model of Consumer Decision Processes

Based on Francesco M. Nicosia, *Consumer Decision Processes: Marketing and Advertising Implications* (Englewood Cliffs, New Jersey: Prentice-Hall, 1966), p. 156.

gone through a few revisions benefitting from other models and from research in the field. Figure 19.2 presents the fourth version.

It can be seen that the model is built around the stages in the decision process and is similar to Nicosia's model in many respects. The evaluation of products and brands is a long process that is influenced by personal goals. Personal goals themselves are the result of the interaction of a number of "endogenous and exogenous variables."[13] Other features of the model include:

- an elaborate information-processing mechanism that takes care of incoming stimuli from various sources;
- memory that affects and is affected by information processing;
- both of these early steps end up as information and experience that play a significant role in all of the stages of the decision process, and are themselves added to by the outcomes of the choice;
- a feedback mechanism that also, through dissatisfaction with the outcome, can initiate search anew and, in essence, re-start the process;
- an elaboration of the relationship between attitudes and behavior with the introduction of beliefs, intention, and normative compliance in recognition of the contributions of the Fishbein extended model;[14] and
- the roles of anticipated and unanticipated circumstances on intention and choice.

Formal Statement

The authors also included what they called "a formal statement of the model" in order "to permit comparison with the (other) models."[15]

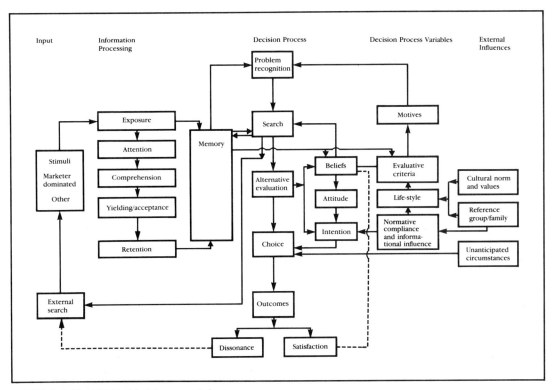

FIGURE 19.2: The EKB Model of Consumer Behavior

SOURCE: James F. Engel and Roger D. Blackwell, *Consumer Behavior*, 4th. ed. (New York: CBS College Publishing 1982), p. 687. Copyright © 1982 by CBS College Publishing. Reprinted with permission of Holt, Rinehart and Winston, CBS College Publishing.

It consists of a series of equations and definitions that indicate, in verbal form, the relationships among variables.

Evaluation

The primary merit of the EKB model is its *simplicity*. It is easy to follow and does not get overinvolved in the relationships among variables. With its new symbolic formulations, it may also become more testable than it has been.[16] The model displays a flexibility and adaptability that are to be admired. For example, earlier versions presented a rather vague relationship between the environmental influences and the central control unit.[17] This has been clarified. Similarly, the addition of such constructs as beliefs, intentions, normative compliance, anticipated and unanticipated circumstances, and the effects of different choice outcomes illustrates its adaptability.

Some have criticized the model for overemphasizing determinism in behavior.[18] Buyer behavior is made to look too mechanical and devoid of complexities. This kind of criticism is perhaps unfair because the objective of model-building is to simplify in order to increase comprehensibility.

The Howard Model

The first truly integrative model of buyer behavior proposed by Howard in 1963[19] was modified later in collaboration with Sheth to produce a more refined model intended mainly to explain brand choice behavior.[20] This model, like its predecessor, was based on learning theory, from which came perhaps Howard's greatest contribution to consumer behavior — the distinction between extensive problem solving, limited problem solving, and routinized response behavior. It came to be known as the *Howard-Sheth Model* and to be generally regarded as "the most thorough, comprehensive, and well-articulated model of the consumer. . . . It is distinguished by a richer specification of

variables and their interrelationships, and it attempts a much deeper and more detailed integration of theoretical positions from several behavioral sciences."[21]

Characteristics

Howard and his colleagues have actively engaged in testing and upgrading the model and a number of revisions have been made since 1969. The 1974 version is representative of the general adaptations and refinements that have been made and is presented in Figure 19.3.

The model suggests that information processing is a selective process. Of all the information available, that to which the individual is exposed is a function of the individual's media habits and/or specific search behavior. What is recalled is determined by subjective factors, such as receptivity and distortion effects. Where incoming information is unclear, the individual may be stimulated to undertake further search or it may result in distorted information. Retained information may stimulate a motive that generates initial or further search behavior and so on; motive stimulation may be sufficient to lead to evaluation wherein choice criteria (which result from retained information and the individual's motives) and what the individual knows about the brand interact with the incoming information and previous experience, resulting in brand attitude. Purchase is a direct result of intention, which is influenced by brand attitude, by retained information, by the reaction to the product from previous experience, and by how the individual feels about his or her competence to evaluate the brand. This confidence is a function of what one knows about the brand, incoming information, and previous experience with the brand.

Personality is one of many exogenous variables that influence the system but are viewed as external to the system because they are not influenced by it — culture, social class, reference groups, financial status, importance of purchase, and time pressure.

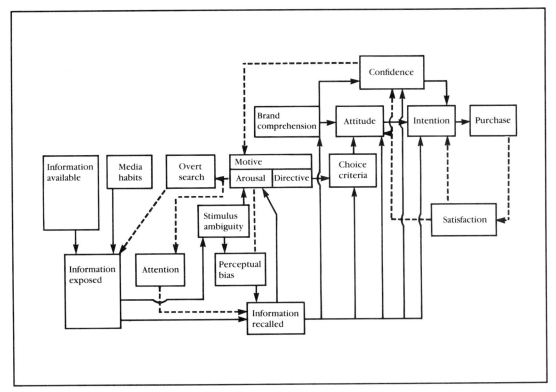

FIGURE 19.3: The Howard Model of Buyer Behavior, 1974 Version

SOURCE: Marketing Science Institute, *Consumer Behavior: Theory and Application.* Copyright© 1974 by Allyn and Bacon, Inc. Reprinted with permission.

Formal Statement

The relationships of these exogenous variables to the system are specified in a formal statement of the model in the form of twelve equations, which seek to indicate verbally the relationships among variables.[22] Since 1974, further revisions of the model have been made. The latest published version by Howard is presented in Figure 19.4.[23] This version introduces some interesting modifications to the earlier model:

(a) The concept of arousal is not related solely to motive. It has been separated out and defined as "a general effect, specific not to any particular brand but only to a product class.... Excessive arousal, however, can inhibit the effort to pay attention and to search, as it can any form of behavior."[24]

(b) Arousal is the result of not only motive stimulation, information (stimulus) ambiguity, and confidence in judging the quality of a brand but also level of aspiration (acceptable standards or ideal brand).

(c) In the attention and search that follow arousal, "the key element... is the construct 'level of aspiration,' which is defined as the standard of adequacy. For each of their choice criteria, consumers have a standard of adequacy. When all known brands are below that level, a consumer is stimulated to pay attention and search."[25]

(d) Attention, which is an "active selection" and "narrowing of the range of objects to which the consumer is responding,"[26] positively affects STM and LTM (two constructs that have replaced information recalled).

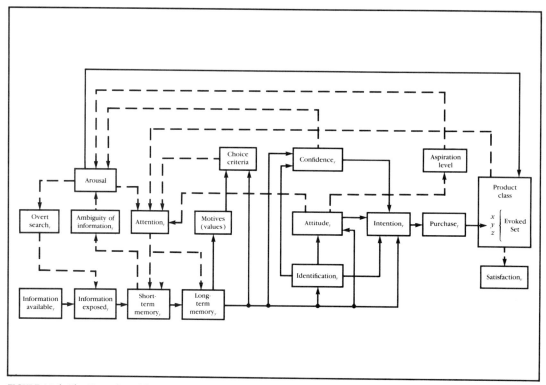

FIGURE 19.4: The Howard Model — 1977 Version

SOURCE: John A. Howard, *Consumer Behavior: Application of Theory* (1977), p. 138. Reprinted with permission of the McGraw-Hill Book Company, New York.

(e) Selectivity is provided by the feedback from long-term memory to short-term memory. "The consumer pays attention to and searches for that which is relevant and LTM tells STM what is relevant."[27]

(f) The construct of brand comprehension has been removed; its function now is seen as performed by LTM.

(g) Identification is introduced and appears to be the same as choice criteria.

It is important to recognize that most of the discussion about Howard's model applies implicitly to LPS rather than EPS, because the role of feedback from attitude, confidence, and product class would not exist in EPS. It implies, too, that "in EPS, attention and search activities would be much less sharply focused. They would be guided by feedback from motive intensity

to arousal, but they would lack the specific direction of feedback from stored meaning in LTM to STM . . . to make the information relevant."[28]

Quantification

Using a simplified version of the model, Howard developed a questionnaire for operationalizing five basic constructs, which yielded a number of quantified relationships on which predictions can be made.[29] A study with a panel of consumers regarding a new subcompact car produced useful response functions.[30] The variables measured were:

F = permanent memory
B = brand identification
A = attitude
C = confidence
I = intention

From the data, regression coefficients were derived for pairs of variables. Basically, the model suggests that "increasing the causal or independent variable by one scale point increases the caused or dependent variable by the amount of the coefficient shown."[31] For example, let us assume that the marketer knows that increasing advertising by $1 million will increase F by one point on a sixteen-point scale, then B would increase by 0.084 units. (See Figure 19.5.)

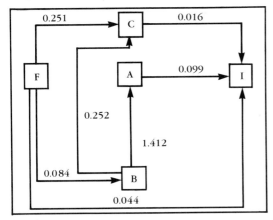

FIGURE 19.5: Simplified Model of LPS with Coefficients (subcompact cars)

SOURCE: John A. Howard, *Consumer Behavior: Application of Theory* (1977), p. 267. Reprinted with permission of the McGraw-Hill Book Company, New York.

This approach indicates the potential direction for consumer models, particularly for the purpose of prediction. But it seems purely suggestive. The problem of adequate measurement, for one, remains. There is the unavoidable reliance on subjective reporting and all its attendant deficiencies. Although tests have provided favorable support for the H model, "the necessity of continuing conceptual sophistication with methodological precision" remains a major issue.[32]

The EKB and Howard Models

Both models are quite similar, centered around the decision process and based on an elaborate information-processing mechanism. They both agree that the consumer is purposive and goal-oriented, and is active rather than passive. "He actively seeks information to satisfy his various motives, and he structures information coming from the environment as a guide to need satisfaction."[33] Individuals *develop* criteria for judging products and strategies for dealing with information (selectivity). The decision process is not necessarily conscious; feedback is an important factor, and both models allow for exogenous variables.

It seems fair to say that distinctions, except for a few, are more apparent than real. The H model, unlike the EKB model, does not allow for unanticipated circumstances, and may argue that these are exogenous.

"Confidence" is rejected by EKB and is heavily stressed by H. "Normative conpliance," as such, does not appear in the H model, although it could be argued that it is represented in the exogenous variables.

Among the less significant differences are:
(a) Unlike EKB, H does not specify "beliefs" as components of attitudes, as such. "Identification" (Figure 19.4) may be equivalent to beliefs;
(b) Normative compliance postulated by Fishbein is specifically included in EKB; it is only generally covered in the H model by exogenous factors;
(c) The 1977 version of the H model has introduced LTM, which is equivalent to "memory" in EKB;
(d) EKB suggests that attention is a function of exposure, active memory, and problem recognition. H suggests, and it seems more reasonable, that attention follows exposure and is a function of arousal, knowledge of the product class, choice criteria (values), and attitude;
(e) In EKB, search is a function of belief and attitude; in H, search follows arousal, which results from aspiration level, ambiguity of information, motives, and confidence. Search determines the information to which one is exposed;

(f) It has been said that H does not use dissonance as a variable. In fact, "satisfaction" implies degree of satisfaction or dissatisfaction and is equivalent to EKB's "outcomes";

(g) H's new "arousal" is equivalent to EKB's "problem recognition."

It should be noted, too, that while post-choice search as a function of dissonance seems at present to be unique to EKB, H could easily incorporate this relationship. The distinction between STM and LTM in the H model is a useful one. The construct of "confidence" also covers phenomena not included in EKB.

Specific Models — Brand Loyalty

It was indicated earlier that brand loyalty models fall into two categories: stochastic or probability and deterministic or non-probability (Chapter 9). They deal with repeat brand-choice behavior and can be described as routinized response behavior (RRB). Their purpose is to provide a method for predicting consumer performance at the next purchase.

Stochastic Models

Stochastic models assume that the behavior of consumers is the result of chance. Some believe that the behavior may be stochastic but the processes that lie behind it may not be; others that the choice process itself is random.[34]

One group of models — called the **Bernouilli** models — assume that the probability of purchase is independent of prior purchases or individual or environmental factors and is constant for the given brand.

The New Trier model was developed for those situations in which a brand purchased had never been tried before.[35] It too assumes no relationship to prior purchases.

Perhaps the best-known stochastic models are the *Markov* models, which are based on the assumption that the probability of purchase is influenced by earlier purchases. Versions of the model are referred to as "orders," which are related to how far back the influence is traced. Thus a first-order model takes into account only the last (most recent) purchase, a second-order model the last two purchases, and so on.

To illustrate with a first-order example: Suppose that of 100 consumers who had purchased a product, 60 had bought Brand A and 40 Brand B. Of the 60 A users, 48 had bought it the next time, and 12 bought another brand. Of the 40 B users, 20 switched to A and 20 bought some other brand. (See Figure 19.6.)

Time t	Time t + 1		
	A	B	Total
A	48	12	60
B	20	20	40

FIGURE 19.6: First-Order Markov Switching Matrix

Treating the numbers switching as probabilities (48/60, 20/40, etc.), the first-order Markov Model would develop the matrix of **transition probabilities** shown in Figure 19.7.

Time t	Time t + 1		
	A	B	Total
A	.8	.2	1.0
B	.5	.5	1.0

FIGURE 19.7: First-Order Markov Model: Transition Probability

Thus one can say that for a consumer who bought Brand A at time t there is a .8 probability that that consumer will buy A at the next purchase, t + 1.

This model makes two assumptions:

(a) that all individuals are similar (**homogeneity**), which may be fairly reasonable in routinized behavior,

(b) that the transition probabilities do not change for later purchases at times t + 2, t + 3, t + 4, etc. This assumption of **stationarity** is a

Time	Brand	
	A	**B**
t	60	40
t+1	$(60 \times .8) + (40 \times .5) = 48 + 20 = 68$	$(60 \times .2) + (60 \times .5) = 12 + 20 = 32$
t+2	$(68 \times .8) + (32 \times .5) = 54.4 + 16 = 70$	$(68 \times .2) + (32 \times .5) = 13.6 + 16 = 30$
t+3	$(70 \times .8) + (30 \times .5) = 56 + 15 = 71$	$(70 \times .2) + (30 \times .5) = 14 + 15 = 29$
t+4	$(71 \times .8) + (29 \times .5) = 56.8 + 14.5 = 71$	$(71 \times .2) + (29 \times .5) = 14.2 + 14.5 = 29$

FIGURE 19.8: Brand Shares At Later Purchases Using First-Order Markov Model

serious deficiency of the model since many things happen with time — changes in advertising, in price, and in availability of the brands.

Out of interest, if one accepted these assumptions, brand shares at later purchases would be as shown in Figure 19.8.

As can be seen, the market eventually reaches a state of equilibrium where the shares no longer change.

In addition to the two mentioned above, there are other problems such as:

- how does the model handle multiple-brand or multiple purchases?
- all consumers do not purchase at the same frequency.

Attempts have been made by a number of researchers to remove these deficiencies — for example, Lipstein and stationarity,[36] Morrison and homogeneity,[37] the development of second-order models, and the inclusion of multi-brand loyalty.[38] But not much in the way of empirical usefulness has resulted.

The Hendry Model is a zero-order, stochastic model (i.e., it assumes no influence of past purchase on current or later purchases). It is perhaps the most widely used stochastic model.

The Hendry model does not assume homogeneity and is based on groups rather than individual consumers. It very carefully defines the relevant product class (and the brands therein) before stochastic predictions are made. In other words, the brands competing against one another define the product class.

The model also assumes a bathtub-shaped purchase probability distribution — that is, for any brand, a large percentage of consumers will have a low probability and another large percentage will have a high probability of purchasing — and past purchases have no effect on later choices.

Both the zero-order and the first-order models, therefore, are quite limited in their usefulness to the marketing manager. They may lead to a clearer perception of the market, and point to possible brand-share directions, but stochastic models lack explanatory, diagnostic value. Deterministic models attempt to do this.

Deterministic Models

Deterministic models seek to relate causative factors (internal or external) to purchasing behavior. Some are rather superficial and attempt to estimate the relationship between a given factor (e.g., advertising) and behavior, without explaining why. Apart from these estimation models, there are the structural models, which aim to analyze the process behind the relationships and thus diagnose the causes.

The integrative-comprehensive models discussed in the previous section represent attempts in that direction. For brand loyalty purposes, their application to RRB (Routinized Response Behavior) situations would be the most relevant. A great deal is yet to be achieved before such models may permit behavioral prediction.

POSTSCRIPT

It has certainly become obvious by now that consumer behavior is a complex phenomenon. Not only are the forces underlying the behavior diverse and numerous but they exist at different levels and their interrelationships can make understanding difficult.

Disciplinary Problems

Above and beyond the conceptual content of the field are the many problems and obstacles deriving from the nature of these concepts and from the methods pursued in their identification, measurement, and analysis. It is to be hoped that alerting the student to the kinds of pitfalls to which the study of consumer behavior is susceptible will generate a tendency to make allowances and corrections (or, at the very least, generate a spirit of informed skepticism) that will result in better interpretations of consumer data.

Inferred Concepts

The basic model of human behavior involves three fundamental parts, as shown in Figure 19.9. The model states that every human action (response R — which may be physical or mental) is a reaction to an input (or stimulus — S) of some kind, from either an external or an internal source. The questions that are naturally asked relate to the processes that occurred within the organism to eventuate in the particular response. Some refer to this part as the **black**

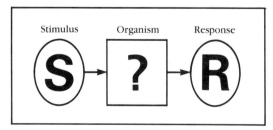

FIGURE 19.9: Basic Model of Human Behavior

box. As part of human behavior, consumer behavior seeks to explain what took place in the black box by making **inferences** about the operations and relationships of such inferred concepts as needs, attitudes, and motives and how they resulted in the particular response.

Because these constructs are inferred and not observable, they are the cause of considerable conflict and disagreement among analysts. Thus for any particular behavior, there can be many different interpretations, one as strongly held as another, such as the integrative-comprehensive models just reviewed.

Myopia

What makes the acceptance of such subjective interpretations yet more difficult is the confidence every individual has in his or her ability to understand and interpret another person's behavior (unless the person is "ill"). Most people seem to feel that they "know what makes another human tick." In some cases, this may be true (as, for example, in known situations with familiar individuals) but, in general, human behavior is the result of such varied and complex forces and influences that superficial analysis can be quite misleading.

A common phenomenon is **projection**,[39] in which one attributes one's own experiences and feelings to another individual in the same or a similar situation. For instance, one may be tempted to conclude that, because one found a certain play very entertaining, most others of the same age and social class would also find it entertaining. It is worth reminding ourselves that people are different and motivations are complex. We should not let ourselves be so myopic as to try to interpret another person's behavior by projecting our own feelings. More marketing managers than we would like to think are guilty of this kind of myopia. They are inclined to attribute their motivations to the consumers in their target market. And this may be compounded, as we saw in Chapter 15, by the fact that the target market may belong to a different social class, among other things, and may therefore have different needs, values, expectations, and attitudes.

Generalization or Stereotyping

Often one will attempt to explain another individual's behavior by generalizing about what that individual usually does or about what others who are similar (same race or color or religion or educational level) do. This kind of oversimplified generalization about the behavior of others can lead to erroneous conclusions.

The Consumer Is Not the Expert Even About Her/Himself

> Given the numerous biases in verbal reports and the all-too-often demonstrated discrepancy between what people *say* and what they actually *do*, it is nothing short of amazing that we persist in our slavish reliance on verbal reports as the mainstay of our research.[40]

A good part of the inaccuracy in consumer research is attributable to the assumption that individuals are aware of the reasons behind their actions. Too often the true reasons underlying consumer choice are completely unknown to the consumers. Recall the case described in Chapter 5, of the test conducted with two samples of ice cream to determine the influence of color on product choice. In a well-controlled experiment, consumers were found to express a taste preference for the cream-colored rather than the white product, even though the latter contained a higher proportion of butter-fat and was therefore richer in taste (objectively). Consumers were obviously reacting to the color cue and they did not know it.

It is worth quoting a bit more from the Jacoby article cited above:

> ... instruments for collecting verbal reports often contribute as much error variance as do interviewers or respondents, or even *more*. In general, a

large proportion of our questionnaires and interview schedules impair rather than enhance efforts to collect valid data. More often than not, we employ instruments which, from the respondent's perspective, are ambiguous, intimidating, confusing, and incomprehensible. Developing a self-administered questionnaire is one of the most difficult steps in the entire research process. Unfortunately, it is commonly the most neglected.[41]

Jacoby suggests that we should

> devote less time to studying what people *say they do* and spend more time examining what it is that they *do do*.... We also need to begin studying consumer behavior in terms of the dynamic process it is.... probably 99 + % of all consumer research conducted to date examines consumer behavior via static methods administered either before or after the fact. Instead of being captured and studied, the dynamic nature of consumer decision-making and behavior is squelched and the richness of the process ignored.... Examination reveals a surprising number of instances in which causation is implied or actually claimed on the basis of simple correlation. It bears repeating that no matter how highly correlated the rooster's crow is to the sun rising, the rooster does not cause the sun to rise.[42]

The consumer behavior analyst needs to keep in mind that, for a variety of reasons, the motives and opinions provided by consumers in response to questions can frequently be misleading and inaccurate. Even in those instances in which the reasons or motives are known and verbalizable, the respondent may very well choose (for example, for social reasons) to falsify or distort the answers. Such directly quoted responses often form the basis for disagreement with those who seek to interpret and explain in theoretical, objective terms. Unfortunately, marketers' acceptance of these explanations is not always forthcoming, because they are not based on responses stated by the consumer (who is, perhaps, the *least* qualified to analyze his or her own behavior — an observation that is indeed true of all human behavior!).

Thus, above and beyond the kinds of *methodological deficiencies* described earlier, there are a number of reasons the consumer may fail to provide the marketer with the "real" reason for behavior (choice, preference, opinion).

We have learned from psychoanalysis that there are some reasons that the individual has repressed and which, therefore, reside in the *unconscious*.

> It appeared to him [Freud] that the unconscious consisted essentially of motives.... The unconscious motives do not lie dormant.... When they threaten to emerge they awaken anxiety, shame, and a guilty feeling in the conscious self, which therefore resists and tries to hold them down.[43]

Such motives may never come to the surface without proper professional probing. While most consumer products may not involve such deep-seated motivations, it is conceivable that certain purchases involving high emotional as well as economic investment (cars, clothing, houses) are subject to the dictates or inhibitions of the unconscious.

Another kind of motivation, though not repressed, may remain unconscious since it is beyond the conscious awareness of the individual and is not accessible to conscious recollection, no matter how articulate or intelligent the individual. The influence of color in the ice cream test described earlier is an excellent example of this phenomenon. No amount of probing would yield the answer. It takes an imaginative, creative researcher to hit upon such a finding.

Another study was reported of a test between two new automobiles of identical make, model, year, and color. From a "hunch" the researcher had, the two cars were equipped with accelerators attached to springs of different strengths of resistance. It was found that the car with the lower resistance in the accelerator pedal was preferred because it was "faster," and "had greater pick-up." The unconscious input from the kinetic sense affected the overall preference of the respondent and this true insight, being beyond the pale of the individual's conscious experience, would never have been capable of conscious expression.

At another level, some motivations may lie, so to speak, in the **subconscious** or **preconscious**, just below the surface. In a regular interview, such motivations may not be verbalized in response to direct questions. On the other hand, certain other approaches may cause the individual to give expression, inadvertently and perhaps even without realizing its significance, to the idea. Instead of a direct question-and-answer approach, the opportunity for probing and wider discussion may elicit a response that would otherwise have remained unexpressed.

One should recognize too that *not all individuals are equally articulate* and it is possible that a consumer may be unable to verbalize feelings and reactions accurately or appropriately. The capable analyst can provide the kinds of avenues of expression that would make such responses come to light.[44]

Finally, as suggested earlier, an individual may deliberately distort or falsify a response to a question for one or more of several reasons — because it is a more proper answer, because it is the socially desirable answer, because it is less embarrassing, because it makes more sense, and so on.

The purpose of the preceding section has been to emphasize that in attempting to understand the consumer, the possibilities for invalid data are considerable. Too many consumer research studies rely almost completely on direct responses from the consumer. Their tables of findings may be neatly categorized and impressively drawn up — but how valid are the data? There is no guarantee, of course, that the other approaches alluded to are going to be any better, but at least a recognition of the pitfalls of the direct approach may induce the application of alternative questioning that would lead to a truer understanding of consumer behavior.

Socio-Cultural Problems

There are other problems of a socio-cultural nature that affect the study of consumer behavior and its relationship to the practice of marketing. These include the consumerism movement, consumer education, consumer deception, consumer choice regulation, and consumer complaints.

The Consumerism Movement has as its basic aim the protection of the consumer. It "encompasses the evolving set of activities of government, business, (and) independent organizations designed to protect the rights of consumers."[45] Kotler defines it as "a social movement seeking to augment the rights and powers of buyers in relation to sellers."[46]

Although the movement is not new, the current wave started in the 1960s with an enormous growth in products, services, and advertising that resulted in a virtual inability of the consumer to adjust adequately to the information boom. Consumer concern and anxiety were highlighted by the birth-control drug thalidomide, which was related to birth defects, and by such publications as Rachel Carson's *Silent Spring* (pesticides and the environment) and Ralph Nader's *Unsafe at Any Speed* (automobiles and safety).

The 1980s are beginning to evince a trend toward deregulation or decreased government intervention (something that consumers have been becoming very concerned about). The result is likely to be a consumer who seeks information, who has to be provided with relevant information, and who will be relied upon to make basic judgements. The trend in the 1980s may, therefore, be an emphasis on *consumer education*.

A basic question about the consumer movement is the extent to which consumer activists and organizations represent the attitudes, needs, and reactions of all consumers. Studies indicate that the two groups differ. One study found that the attitudes of consumerists were stronger than business executives or consumers on such issues as advertising, government protection, the environment, product information, and product safety.[47]

In the development of consumerism, the problem of health and safety has been a prominent issue — not just drugs and food but other defective and unsafe products such as toys, appliances, and automobiles as well as safety in highway and air travel. Consumer research may be most helpful in providing manufacturers with information about how consumers use products, about how different segments vary in their knowledge, in their inclinations to follow product-use instructions, and in their product maintenance habits, so that appropriate strategies may be developed. In some cases, consumer educational activities may be stepped up; in others, decisions may be made to introduce certain safety features. The latter course, for example, may be found appropriate more frequently with such products as bicycles, stairs, toys, ramps, swings, slides, and automobiles.

The consumer movement has clearly made an important contribution toward increasing the awareness of all levels of society (government, industry, and the public) with respect to product safety.

Consumer Education

If, in a deregulated economy, consumers need to rely more on their own knowledge of products, then companies will be forced to educate the public about such products. A fundamental question will be what is relevant information. Consumerists argue for product *performance* information, whereas in much of advertising the emphasis is on psychological association.[48]

Another fundamental question involves *how much* information should be provided. For example, how much information will be judged to be adequate to ensure a wise choice? Which evaluative criteria should be elaborated on and which not? And when does one reach the point of providing too much information? It will be recalled that this question was addressed in

Chapter 6, where the impact of information overload on the kind of decision made was discussed.

In a regulated economy, the consumer movement achieved greater disclosure of information — ingredients, packing dates, expiry dates, nutritional data, unit pricing, cautions, usage instructions, rates, charges, and credit. There is little reason to believe that this trend will decline if deregulation expands, so long as the consumer movement maintains its activism.

Studies suggest that use of such information is not widespread among those who need it most. Better educated and higher-income consumers tend to make greater use of such information.[49] However, it appears that its greater availability tends to increase consumer confidence.[50]

Day has also suggested a few other questions that need to be answered:

- can the information be comprehended?
- do information disclosures vary by segments (income, education)?
- what changes occur over time?[51]

Consumer Deception

Consumer deception has increased significantly in its share of consumer consciousness and in the awareness of government bodies and industry. A basic issue is the distinction between the objective and subjective aspects of this phenomenon. The objective may be described as focussing on the "act of deceiving by the advertiser" and the subjective on "the effect of the message on the consumer."[52] Both can occur together but a critical problem arises when a consumer is misled even though the source had no *intention* to deceive.

Thus Gardner suggests three categories of deception in advertising:

- the **unconscionable lie**: making a claim that is completely false;
- the **claim-fact discrepancy**: where the benefits claimed will be obtained only under certain conditions (not stated in the ad). For example, a dandruff shampoo may work as claimed only for people with a certain type of problem, but that problem is not the predominant dandruff-causing problem;
- the **claim-belief interaction**: in which an advertisement interacts with the accumulated attitudes and beliefs of the consumer in such a way as to leave a deceptive belief or attitude about the product. For example, the use of symbols, words, endorsements that lead the consumer to make certain inferences about the product that are not true — Hi-C and the assumption of high vitamin C content; "Brand X detergent contains blue crystals," which consumers interpret as greater cleaning power.[53]

A recent study reports on the effect of the measuring technique on responses. It found that recall is a more conservative measure than recognition.[54]

More and more frequently, companies are required, as a result of rulings on deceptive advertising, to undertake **corrective advertising**, as, for example, when Listerine was ordered to correct its claim that Listerine killed germs.

Consumer Choice Regulation

Many questions arise regarding the consumer's right to choose; that is, the right to have available an adequate number of brands from among which to choose. Governments have virtually controlled, at least in western economies, any tendency toward monopolies, and there cannot be said to be an absence of choice. However, consumerists themselves appear to be in favor of regulating choice when consumers are not doing what is "best" for them. They feel that too frequently consumers are "influenced by the sweet purrings of an attractive salesman (or woman) . . . beguiled by style at the expense of safety and stamina, by gleam instead of guts, by features and gimmicks in place of performance and economy."[55]

Some of this approach has been translated into laws requiring consumers to purchase certain products considered to be in their best interests — seat belts, helmets for bicyclists, or banning other items — such as cigarette advertising and children's advertising (Quebec).

Underlying all of this is the basic question of who, if not the consumer, should make the choice for the consumer? The government? Perhaps the guiding criterion should be the public interest. When individual consumer choices add up to a threat to the social good — environmental pollution, car emissions — then perhaps some regulation of consumer choice may be warranted.

Consumer Complaints

Much of the impetus for the consumer movement came from consumer dissatisfaction, not only with products but with services, promotion, pricing, and corporate response. There is no question that consumers have the right to express complaints and to receive proper redress.

The dissatisfactions of consumers involve product performance, packaging, repair services, pricing, advertising claims (deception), quality of advertising, amount of advertising, cost of advertising, salespersons, and interest rates. If these complaints are increasing (as they appear to be) then the crucial question becomes what channels of redress are open to consumers.

Cohen points out three ways for handling consumer complaints:

- first of all, by **preventing** them — through product quality, substantiation of claims, through proper conduct;
- through **restitution** or making good through refunds, replacements, corrective advertising; and/or
- by **punishing** the guilty party through fines, negative publicity and loss of profits, etc.[56]

If the most frequent response of consumers to an unsatisfactory product is to stop buying it, marketers would be well advised to pay particular care to quality controls and to avoid claim-benefit discrepancies. Where such approaches may not be foolproof it would be wise to establish mechanisms (warranties and twenty-four-hour hotlines, for example) for the prompt and equitable resolution of complaints.

It is worth noting that such claims for redress do not necessarily come from consumers. More and more, government bodies (the Federal Trade Commission in the US, the Department of Consumer and Corporate Affairs in Canada) are initiating such actions in the interests of all consumers.

PROGNOSIS

The most striking fact about the world in which we live is the *rapidity* of the rate at which change is taking place — change in technology, resources, environment, population size and composition, political relationships, and economic health.

This "accelerative thrust," as Toffler describes it, will engulf us all, in spite of ourselves, and bring about conditions that are likely to transform the consumer world in radical ways and in critical proportions.[57] The one thing that remains certain is that, no matter what the conditions, ways must be found to satisfy the needs and motives of an evolving society. And just as the society will survive, so will marketing.

Advances in production methods in the wake of computer technology, the development of new artificial materials and fabrics, the evolution of telecommunications, the microcomputer, and the phenomenal progress in transportation and travel will lead to drastic changes in consumer behavior:

- shopping by home computers;
- the decreasing need for shops and stores, only warehouses for storage and delivery;
- paying bills by computer; automatic deductions from bank accounts (cashless society);

- the role and nature of advertising;
- voluntary exposure to advertising;
- the advertising media used; and
- changes in the role of the package.

These are but a few of the effects and give some indication of the kind of society that will exist perhaps sooner than we think. By connecting the television to the telephone (the cables for both are to be found in most homes in the US and Canada), the world's information can be brought into our living rooms.

Through these interactive cables, through videodiscs, satellite communication, home terminals or receiving stations, cable TV, home teleprinters, an incredible diversity of information will be available to anyone who wants it. Adding a small keyboard to the telephone–television hookup, for example, will provide access to news, weather forecasts, stock quotations, movie listings, advertising, bank accounts, and any other data that can be transferred through a computer. A multitude of interconnected communication systems will envelope and enmesh the earth "in a sphere of channels for the immediate interchange of thought, information, and intellectual operations."[58]

The marriage of two phenomenal technologies — the microcomputer and telecommunications — will inevitably lead to profound changes in living, new social patterns, new life-styles, and new ways of generating and spending wealth. For example, if, as some estimate, the world's known supply of petroleum runs out in thirty-five years, telecommunications may become a substitute for petroleum.[59] With the increasing cost of energy, telecommunications could make working at the office obsolete. Most white-collar jobs could be done at home and working at home would be facilitated by the videophones that transmit pictures and documents as well as speech. Some homes will have machines that receive transmitted documents so that one can obtain business paper work, financial, or stock market reports, mail, bank statements, airline schedules and so on.

Consider for a moment the impact on consumer behavior and marketing:
- the clothing industry; no need for office dress; greater use of home casuals;
- downtown office areas will shrink;
- downtown restaurants, retail clothing and other stores will almost disappear;
- commuting will be virtually eliminated — its effects on the automobile industry;
- the rural to urban movement will become unnecessary, in many ways perhaps reversed;
- research, teaching, writing programs, and conferences could all be done at home;
- consumer research will be done at home through a central computer that collects and analyzes consumer data;
- everyone will have more leisure time because of increased automation and, with the average age of the population increasing, there will be more people in the more affluent stages of their lives; business will be responsible for satisfying the needs of a society with not only more free time but also more disposable income;
- changing life-styles will mean more time spent either at home or travelling;
- interactions with other families and groups will decrease so that group pressures to conform and even to compete will lessen;
- manufacturing will be increasingly run by process-control computers and production robots;
- tedious jobs like typing memos and mail delivery will disappear;
- bank tellers will no longer be necessary and electronic fund transfer will replace the enormous tedium of processing cheques and bills and credit-card paper work;
- computer networks will (indeed, already have) lace together corporate and government facilities. Quick answers (analysis, diagnosis) will revolutionize business decision making;
- telecommunications will form a substitute for certain types of travel, with telephone conference calls, picture phones, etc.; and

- work weeks will be shorter and could vary from three-day weeks, for example, to seven days of work followed by seven days off. What is significant is that life-styles and patterns will be drastically modified.

Some of these changes have already happened; others are occurring right now. It is not my intention to catalogue all of the effects of our galloping technology or to recite the very latest developments but simply to impress upon the reader's consciousness the rapidity, breadth, and depth of change that, more quickly than we think, will create a new world for marketers.

With the increasing cost of energy, technology will be forced to produce more durable goods making use of less packaging in order to save energy. Products will be geared to leisure in a society characterized by more travel and extensive hobbies (gourmet cooking, education, gardening, entertainment). To fulfill the new life-style, hosts of devices and gadgets will appear in the marketplace: home keyboards, terminals, viewdata screens, home teleprinters, interactive TV, and home computers for remote control of appliances (such as fire or burglar alarms, heating or air conditioning equipment). Homes could have automated greenhouses where the temperature and humidity would be closely monitored. A central home microcomputer could monitor heat levels in the home and distribute heat to rooms according to need; it could store the "family calendar" containing important events, planned trips, holidays, meetings, shopping lists, due dates for bills, and taxes.

By creating unique video channels for each home (comparable to the telephone), individuals will have access to enormous funds of information from around the world, reinforcing a tendency to isolation. And yet literal *international* cities will come into being — communities, campuses, laboratories, or corporate offices scattered across the earth but connected electronically and instantly accessible. Satellites will make possible instantaneous transmission and bring the world together. The "global village" will become a reality and the satellite will change the entire fabric of society.

Libraries could provide access to an incredible number of books and periodicals. Through home terminals viewers could view the same page of the same book simultaneously. The books and periodicals would be on microfilm accessed by computer using author, title, or subject.

Data and programs could come from anywhere — a central library, personal computer files next to the television set, or from across the continent. Governments, publishers, or private firms could distribute information without wasting tons of paper.

Educational systems will undergo fundamental changes. Telecommunications will make the knowledge of a few available to the masses. Educational packages will be marketed to the public through specialty stores.

The potential exists for all university campuses to be reduced to laboratories and libraries, perhaps even to become obsolete. Classes could be held from professors' homes with tests marked by computer. Students could be exposed to the experts in their field, no matter where they live. Learning languages, or mathematics, playing games, reading the paper, or a letter from across the continent (instant mail) could all be accessed with the press of a few buttons.

The role of the family and the interrelationships among its members will affect family decision making and family behavioral patterns. These new social patterns will mean new ways of generating and spending wealth, and the evolution of different needs, values, and motives that business will seek to satisfy with new types of consumer and industrial products through fundamentally changed strategies.

SUMMARY

This final chapter has attempted to tie three strings together. It has sought to synthesize the information presented in the book by discussing the key integrative models of consumer behavior, it has remarked on the kinds of obstacles and problems to which the study of consumer behavior is susceptible, and it has taken a look at the future of consumer behavior in our society.

It was pointed out that models are useful for identifying the variables involved in behavior and their interrelationships, for suggesting new interrelationships, for making predictions, and for integrating diverse research efforts. The two main models reviewed were the Engel, Kollat, and Blackwell (EKB) model and the Howard Model. Both models were assessed as being centered around the decision process and based on an elaborate information-processing mechanism. A brief discussion of the kinds of attempts made by Howard to offer quantitative prediction from his model was included. The

basic assumptions of the Markov Brand Loyalty model were also presented.

Some of the inherent problems of the discipline of consumer behavior were described — the inferred nature of behavioral concepts, the subjectivity of our interpretations, the tendency to generalize, and unconscious motives. A number of socio-cultural problems with which marketers have to contend include the consumerism movement, the evolving need for consumer education, the ethical question of consumer deception, consumer choice regulation, and consumer dissatisfaction and complaints.

The final section sought to emphasize the rapidity and depth of change in our society and to indicate the kinds of impact such changes may have on consumer values, attitudes, motives, and behavioral patterns for which marketers will need to develop radically different strategies.

QUESTIONS

1. Write an essay on the functions of models in the study of consumer behavior.

2. Describe the basic components of the EKB model and evaluate its contribution to the study of consumer behavior.

3. What are the primary differences between the EKB and the Howard and Sheth models?

4. Write an evaluation of specific models in consumer behavior, starting with the loyalty models discussed in the chapter.

5. Discuss how the very nature of the field of consumer behavior is its main limitation.

6. What are the main characteristics and trends of the consumerism movement in Canada and the US?

7. Review the main philosophical arguments surrounding the question of consumer choice regulation. State and justify your own position on this subject.

8. Write an essay, based on more recent evidence, on the kinds of changes that are likely to overtake the consumer and marketing worlds in the next ten to fifteen years.

NOTES TO CHAPTER 19

[1]J.D. Thompson and D.R. Van-Houten, *The Behavioral Sciences: An Interpretation* (Reading, Massachusetts: Addison-Wesley, 1970), pp. 4-13.

[2]James F. Engel, Roger D. Blackwell and David T. Kollat, *Consumer Behavior*, 3rd ed. (Hinsdale, Illinois: Dryden Press, 1978), p. 544.

[3]Flemming Hansen, *Consumer Choice Behavior: A Cognitive Theory* (Glencoe, Illinois: Free Press, 1972), pp. 436-38; Jagdish N. Sheth, *Models of Buyer Behavior* (New York: Harper and Row, 1974).

[4]J.A. Lunn, "Consumer Decision-Process Models," in Jagdish N. Sheth (ed.), *Models of Buyer Behavior* (New York: Harper and Row, 1974), p. 35.

[5]J. Paul Peter and Lawrence X. Tarpey, Sr., "A Comparative Analysis of Three Consumer Decision Strategies," *Journal of Consumer Research*, 2 (June 1975), p. 29.

[6]Adapted from Lunn, op. cit., pp. 38-41.

[7]Raymond A. Bauer, "Consumer Behavior as Risk Taking," in Robert S. Hancock (ed.), *Dynamic Marketing For a Changing World* (Chicago: American Marketing Association, 1960), pp. 389-98.

[8]John A. Howard, *Marketing Management Analysis and Planning*, rev. ed. (Homewood, Illinois: Richard D. Irwin, 1963).

[9]A.S.C. Ehrenberg, "Towards an Integrated Theory of Consumer Behavior," *Journal of the Marketing Research Society*, 11 (October 1969), pp. 305-37.

[10]Frank M. Bass, et al. (eds.), *Mathematical Models and Methods in Marketing* (Homewood, Illinois: Richard D. Irwin, 1961); Jagdish N. Sheth, *Models of Buyer Behavior* (New York: Harper and Row, 1974).

[11]Lunn, op. cit., p. 40.

[12]F.M. Nicosia, *Consumer Decision Processes: Marketing and Advertising Implications* (Englewood Cliffs, New Jersey: Prentice-Hall, 1966).

[13]James F. Engel and Roger D. Blackwell, *Consumer Behavior*, 4th ed. (New York: Dryden Press, 1982), p. 686.

[14]Martin Fishbein and Isek Ajzen, *Belief, Attitude, Intention, and Behavior: An Introduction to Theory and Research* (Reading, Massachusetts: Addison-Wesley, 1975).

[15]Engel and Blackwell, *Consumer Behavior*, 4th ed., pp. 686-8.

[16]Gerald Zaltman, Christian R.A. Pinson, and Reinhard Angelmar, *Metatheory and Consumer Research* (New York: Holt, Rinehart and Winston, 1973), pp. 118-21.

[17]See James F. Engel, David T. Kollat, and Roger D. Blackwell, *Consumer Behavior*, 2nd ed. (New York: Holt, Rinehart and Winston, 1968, 1973), p. 58.

[18]Frank M. Bass, "The Theory of Stochastic Preference and Brand Switching," *Journal of Marketing Research*, 11 (February 1974), pp. 1-20.

[19]Howard, op. cit.

[20]John A. Howard and Jagdish N. Sheth, *The Theory of Buyer Behavior* (New York: John Wiley & Sons, 1969).

[21]Lunn, op. cit., p. 44.

[22]Engel and Blackwell, *Consumer Behavior*, 4th ed., pp. 683-5.

[23]John A. Howard, *Consumer Behavior: Application of Theory* (New York: McGraw-Hill, 1977), p. 138.

[24]Ibid., p. 136.

[25]Ibid., p. 141.

[26]Ibid., p. 132.

[27]Ibid., p. 136.

[28]Ibid., p. 148.

[29]Ibid., p. 258.

[30]Ibid., p. 266-9.

[31]Ibid., p. 267.

[32]Lunn, op. cit., p. 47.

[33]Ibid., p. 50.

[34]W.F. Massy, D.B. Montgomery, and D.G. Morrison, *Stochastic Models of Buying Behavior* (Cambridge, Massachusetts: M.I.T. Press, 1970).

[35]David A. Aaker, "The New-Trier Stochastic Model of Brand Choice," *Management Science*, 17 (April 1971), pp. 435-50.

[36]B. Lipstein, "A Mathematical Model of Consumer Behavior," *Journal of Marketing Research*, 2 (August 1965), pp. 259-65.

[37]Donald G. Morrison, "Testing Brand-Switching Models," *Journal of Marketing Research*, 3 (November 1966), pp. 401-9.

[38]A.S.C. Ehrenberg and G.J. Goodhardt, "A Model of Multi-Brand Buying," *Journal of Marketing Research*, 7 (February 1970), pp. 77-84.

[39]Benjamin Kleinmuntz, *Personality Measurement* (Homewood, Illinois: Dorsey Press, 1967), pp. 259-260.

[40]Jacob Jacoby, "Consumer Research: State of the Art Review," *Journal of Marketing*, 42: 2 (April 1978), p. 89. Reprinted with permission of the American Marketing Association.

[41]Ibid., p. 90.

[42]Ibid.

[43]Robert S. Woodworth, *Contemporary Schools of Psychology* (New York: Ronald Press, 1948), pp. 170, 174.

[44]Harold H. Anderson and Gladys L. Anderson (eds.), *An Introduction to Projective Techniques* (Englewood Cliffs, New Jersey: Prentice-Hall, 1951); George H. Smith, *Motivation Research in Advertising and Marketing* (New York: McGraw-Hill, 1954); Pierre Martineau, *Motivation in Advertising* (New York: McGraw-Hill, 1957).

[45]David A. Aaker and George S. Day, *Consumerism: Search for the Consumer Interest*, 2nd ed. (New York: Free Press, 1974), p. 17.

[46]Philip Kotler, "What Consumerism Means for Marketers," *Harvard Business Review* (May-June 1972), pp. 48-57.

[47]Gregory M. Gazda and David R. Gourley, "Attitudes of Businessmen, Consumers, and Consumerists Toward Consumerism," *Journal of Consumer Affairs*, 9 (Winter 1975), pp. 176-83.

[48]George S. Day, "Full Disclosure of Comparative Performance Information to Consumers: Problems and Prospects," *Journal of Contemporary Business* (Winter 1975), pp. 53-68.

[49]Reed Moyer and Michael D. Hutt, *Macromarketing* (Santa Barbara, California: John Wiley & Sons, 1978), pp. 123-41.

[50]George S. Day, "Assessing the Effects of Information Disclosure Requirements," *Journal of Marketing*, 40 (April 1976), p. 43.

[51]*Ibid.*, pp. 42-52.

[52]David M. Gardner, "Deception in Advertising: A Conceptual Approach," *Journal of Marketing*, 39 (January 1975), pp. 40-6.

[53]*Ibid.*

[54]Richard W. Mizerski, "Viewer Miscomprehension Findings are Measurement Bound," *Journal of Marketing*, 46 (Fall 1982), pp. 32-4.

[55]Robert Moran, "Formulating Public Policy on Consumer Issues: Some Preliminary Findings," Working Paper P-57-A (Boston: Marketing Science Institute, September 1971), p. 35.

[56]Dorothy Cohen, "Remedies for Consumer Protection: Prevention, Restitution, or Punishment," *Journal of Marketing*, 39 (October 1975), pp. 24-31.

[57]Alvin Toffler, *Future Shock* (New York: Bantam, 1971).

[58]James Martin, *The Wired Society* (Englewood Cliffs, New Jersey: Prentice-Hall, 1978), p. 82.

[59]*Ibid.*, p. 182.

Indexes

Subject Index

Author Index